PAPER MONEY of the UNITED STATES

A COMPLETE ILLUSTRATED GUIDE WITH VALUATIONS

Eleventh Edition

Large Size Notes, Fractional Currency, Small Size Notes, Encased Postage Stamps from the First Year of Paper Money, 1861, to the Present

---

The standard reference work on paper money

by ROBERT FRIEDBERG

With additions and revisions by

IRA S. AND ARTHUR L. FRIEDBERG

THE COIN AND CURRENCY INSTITUTE, INC.

Book Publishers

P.O. Box 1057, Clifton, NJ 07014

PAPER MONEY OF THE UNITED STATES

A Complete Illustrated Guide With Valuations

Library of Congress Catalog Card No. 86-070306
ISBN 0-87184-511-3

SPECIAL NOTICE

Permission is hereby granted for the free use of the numbering system employed in this book by any newspaper, magazine or periodical; and also by any coin dealer, currency dealer or stamp dealer in any advertisement, circular, price list or auction catalogue issued for free distribution, and not offered for sale. This permission is granted only when proper acknowledgment is made by the user of this numbering system of its source. This proper acknowledgment shall consist of mention of the title of this book, or the name of the author, or both, and shall appear whenever and wherever this numbering system is used. However, written permission shall be required when this numbering system is used in any publication that is offered for sale.

OTHER BOOKS PUBLISHED BY
THE COIN AND CURRENCY INSTITUTE:

"GOLD COINS OF THE WORLD"
"COINS OF THE BRITISH WORLD"
"APPRAISING AND SELLING YOUR COINS"
"SO-CALLED DOLLARS"
"AMERICA'S FOREIGN COINS"
"MODERN WORLD COINS"

A PUBLICATION OF
THE COIN AND CURRENCY INSTITUTE, INC.

Printed in the United States of America

ELEVENTH EDITION

CONTENTS

Associate Editor
Arthur S. Goldenberg

ACKNOWLEDGEMENTS

Our thanks and gratitude are hereby acknowledged to the following who have helped to make possible the existence of "Paper Money Of The United States" in its various editions: —

The Honorable Secretary Of The Treasury
The Assistant Secretary Of The Treasury
The Chief, U.S. Secret Service
The Director, Bureau of Engraving and Printing
The Comptroller Of The Currency
U.S. Treasury Department, Fiscal Service
The National Archives, Fiscal Branch
The Federal Reserve Bank of Chicago
The American Numismatic Society of N.Y.
The Chase Manhattan Bank Museum of Moneys of the World

And to the following for their long continuing assistance, giving unselfishly of their time and numismatic experience, and who have contributed to the completeness or accuracy of this book by furnishing information on unpublished notes, by offering valuable suggestions or by rendering technical assistance: —

Mr. William T. Anton, Jr.
Mr. Mark S. Auerbach
Mr. Thomas C. Bain (dec'd)
Mr. R.J. Balbaton
Mr. Douglas B. Ball
Dr. Harry J. Barnett
Mr. Aubrey E. Bebee
Mr. Walter Breen
Mr. Vernon L. Brown
Mr. Robert Burgraff
Mr. Amon G. Carter, Jr. (dec'd)
Dr. Carlson R. Chambliss
Mr. Thomas Conklin
Mr. John F. Dahringer
Mr. Forrest W. Daniel
Mr. Charles Deibel
Mr. William H. Dillistin (dec'd)
Mr. William P. Donlon (dec'd)
Mr. William R. Fisher
Mr. Jack Friedberg
Mr. David L. Ganz
Mr. Louis A. Geller
Mr. Martin Gengerke
Mr. Len Glazer
Mr. Nate Gold (dec'd)
Mr. Gerald Goldenberg
Mr. Stephen L. Goldsmith
Mr. Robert W. Hearn
Mr. George H. Hubler
Mr. Curtis Iversen
Mr. Harry E. Jones
Mr. Arthur M. Kagin
Mr. Donald H. Kagin
Mr. Paul Kagin
Mr. Jules J. Karp
Mr. Theodore Kemm
Mr. David R. Koble
Mr. Arthur Leister
Mr. Dana Linett
Mr. Michael P. Marchioni
Mr. Lester Merkin
Mr. Steve Michaels
Mr. John H. Miller
Mr. Allen Mincho
Mr. John H. Morris, Jr.
Mr. Doug Murray
Mr. Charles H. Nehf
Mr. Frank Nowak
Mr. Dean Oakes
Mr. Chuck O'Donnell
Mr. V.H. Oswald, Sr.
Mr. J. Roy Pennell
Mr. Arnold Perl (dec'd)
Mr. M. Perlmutter
Mr. Jess Peters
Mr. W.A. Philpott, Jr. (dec'd)
Mr. K.B. Robertson
Mr. Thomas B. Ross
Mr. Matt H. Rothert
Mr. Stanley J. Roy
Mr. R.F. Schermerhorn (dec'd)
Mr. Neil Shafer
Mrs. Philip Sisselman
Mr. Norman Shultz
Mr. Leon L. Smith, Jr.
Mr. William A.E. Spies
Mr. Harvey Stack
Mr. James F. Stiff
Mr. James Thompson
Mr. M.O. Warns
Mr. Louis Werner (dec'd)
Mr. Thomas Werner
Mr. Herbert Weston
Mr. Louis Zara

PREFACE TO THE ELEVENTH EDITION

Market Prices Slip

Following the sharp decline in inflation in the early 1980's, the prices of all collectibles, including paper money, fell markedly from their highs. This followed the inflationary spiral of the late 1970's, when paper money values rose to record heights.

Although note prices today are lower than they were in the sky-is-the-limit 1979-80 period, they are still higher today than they were in the late 1970's. So, the overall cycle is still up. The result has been the return of the collector-based market rather than the investor and speculator market of 1980. While common notes are readily available, better notes in gem uncirculated condition as well as choice material in EF-AU condition are still hard to obtain for both collectors and dealers.

Star Notes

Two developments in the Star Note category are worthy of mention. Because of technological advances in printing, the Bureau has reduced the number of misprinted notes. This has resulted in less need for Star Notes, which are issued as replacements for damaged notes. Consequently, collectors will find it harder to obtain Star Notes from circulation in the future.

The other development involves the distribution system whereby Star Notes no longer have to be from the same district as the notes they replace. In the interest of efficiency, when misprinted notes need to be replaced, the Bureau will replace them with whatever Federal Reserve district happens to be on hand at the moment. This is instead of maintaining stocks of separately printed Star Notes for each district and issuing the same Star Note district as the note being replaced.

Distribution Change

In the past, Federal Reserve Notes were only distributed in their respective districts. For example, Richmond notes were distributed in the Richmond district, Dallas notes in the Dallas district, etc.

But, in a new development, the Treasury is now distributing Federal Reserve notes without regard to the districts imprinted on their face. From a bank in San Francisco you might possibly receive a note from Chicago, or Boston, or some other district. This should make it easier for collectors to obtain Federal Reserve notes from districts other than their own.

Uncut Sheets

As part of its Public Affairs program, the B.E.P. began selling uncut sheets of U.S. currency to the public on October 26, 1981. These sheets, which had been sold by the Bureau until 1953, when they were discontinued, have been resumed indefinitely. Just $1 and $2 sheets have been issued as of this writing.

The $1 sheets are offered in the 1981 series (Regan-Buchanan), 1981A (Regan-Ortega), and 1985 (Baker-Ortega) in sheets of 32 notes (full sheet), 16 notes (half sheet) and 4 notes (1/8 sheet).

The $2 sheets, all series of 1976 (Neff-Simon) are offered in sheets of 16 notes and 4 notes only. All of the $2 bills in the uncut sheets are Star Notes and are taken from stock, not printed separately for this purpose as the $1 bills are. The sheets of the $1 notes are numbered from 99,840,001-99,999,999. No other notes will be in circulation so numbered, and thus collectors and other purchasers can be assured of the authenticity of the sheets and are protected against fraudulent attempts to mutilate the sheets so as to produce bogus "miscuts."

Additions to the Eleventh Edition

The Appendix to this edition contains some new sections which will be of interest to all readers.

Appendix III, "Uncut Sheets of Small Size Notes," lists and prices those sheets which are known to have been officially issued and released to the public. Here, in a handy and brief format, the reader can determine at a glance for each sheet the catalog number, size, amount issued and present value.

Now that these sheets are once again being offered to the public, this section wil be a valuable additional reference.

The dramatic potential of United States paper money as an investment vehicle is nowhere better than in Appendix IV, "Price Survey of Uncirculated Large Size Type Notes."

The editors have compiled prices for selected uncirculated notes from the 1953, 1964, 1975 and present editions of this book, and the appreciation shown is nothing less than startling. The same notes which in 1953 had catalog value of $9,358.50 are listed in this edition for $289.580.00, and in only the last ten years, these prices have tripled.

Redesign of the Currency

As this edition was going to press, the Treasury Department confirmed its long-rumored plans to change the designs on United States Currency.

While not sweeping nor as drastic as previously speculated, and not requiring a recall of currency in circulation, this is noteworthy as the first redesign since the introduction of small size currency in 1928. Furthermore, it marks the Treasury's acknowledgement that extraordinary steps must be taken to combat the technological advances not only to counterfeiters, but with the perfection of color copying machines, to the general public.

The changes, siz years and 7.5 million in the making, are manifested in two areas — a polyester thread running vertically across the left side of each note, and the microprinting of the words "United States of America" around the portrait in letters smaller than the resolution threshold of present day copiers and scanners.

The new and old currencies will circulate side-by-side, with the latter remaining legal tender and being withdrawn only in the normal course of currency processing.

For further information on this development, please see page 256.

General Information on U. S. Currency

1. LEGAL TENDER STATUS

The first United States paper money under the Constitution dates from 1861 when the Demand Notes were issued. From then to now, all currency issued by the United States Government has remained valid.

All the old and obsolete notes described in this book are still legal tender at their face value and will be exchanged by banks or the Government, if the owner so desires, for current paper money.

In some cases, the actual redemption value is higher than the face value, and such notes will be redeemed by the Government at the higher value. These are the Compound Interest Notes, the Interest Bearing Notes and the Refunding Certificates. Please refer to Sections III, IV and V in the text for further information.

Only once in the past, has the Government ever recalled any of its paper money for any reason, or required its mandatory exchange for other types of paper money. This was in 1933, when the Gold Reserve Act required all holders of Gold Certificates to surrender them for ordinary currency. However, to this day, Gold Certificates will be exchanged like all other notes, even though they are no longer redeemable in actual gold coin.

The exalted position thus occupied by American Currency is unique in the annals of world finance. It is doubtful if any nation past or present, can point to such a long, unbroken series of currency issues, the integrity of which has so surely and confidently been maintained. The 3 Cent Fractional Currency Note of 1869 is still able to buy a 3 cent postage stamp, and the 1,000 Dollar Note of 1869 can still purchase its equivalent in the goods and services of today.

Americans can be quite proud of the basic soundness of this country's financial structure that has made all this possible. Collectors of old currency especially, can take a great deal of comfort in the knowledge that their valuable notes are so well fortified against loss of face value by the Government of the United States and its Treasury Department.

2. THE BEGINNINGS OF U.S. CURRENCY

Colonial Notes, Continental Currency, State Bank Notes

Paper money circulated in the United States long before 1861, when the Demand Notes were issued.

Various types of paper money, for example, were in use in all of the American Colonies while they were still under English rule. The issuance of this currency by the Colonies was a matter of urgent necessity since there was a shortage of coins in the growing nation.

Beginning in mid-1775, the Continental Congress authorized the issuance of currency to finance the Revolutionary War. This became known as Continental Currency. The notes were redeemable in Spanish Milled Dollars (a large silver coin of 8 Real denomination struck at any of the Spanish Colonial Mints in Mexico or South America). But the Continental Currency depreciated to a point where it cost more to print than it would buy. The depreciation of these notes is the source of the expression, "not worth a Continental."

After the Constitution was ratified, the coinage system of the United States was established. The first coins of the new country were struck in 1793 at the Philadelphia Mint, when copper cents and half cents were issued. From then on until 1861, the Government did not find it necessary to issue paper money as we know it.

However, during this interim, there were periods of war, financial stress and sometimes panic. To meet the drain on the Treasury caused by these events, and to overcome the deficits, the Government from time to time issued Treasury Notes. These notes were actually promissory notes which bore interest and which the Treasury redeemed as quickly as possible. They did not circulate as money, except for the small denomination notes of 1815. The 5, 10, 20 and 50 Dollar notes of 1815 were not interest bearing and did circulate as money for a brief period.

Some of the events which brought forth these Treasury Notes were the War of 1812, the Mexican War of 1846, the "Hard Times" of 1837-1843, the Panic of 1857 and the unsettling situation of 1860 just prior to the impending Civil War.

It was also during the latter part of this interim period (1793-1861) that the United States was virtually blanketed by issues of State Bank Notes. The country at this time was just beginning to prosper and grow, and it soon became apparent that there was insufficient money in actual circulation to meet the demands of trade and commerce.

Consequently, the various States granted charters to many private banks in their jurisdiction, and by the terms of these State Charters the banks were authorized to print and circulate their own currency.

Ostensibly, the backing for this currency was the amount of money on deposit in the Bank — there were none of the restraints that we know today. The tragic consequence of this banking system was that the banks failed with alarming ease. If bank borrowers defaulted on their loans because of poor business, or for other reasons, then the banks had no recourse but to close their doors, since they literally went "broke."

When that happened, the currency issued by the banks became worthless paper and a great deal of financial hardship was inflicted on the holders of these bank notes.

In the old days, the term "wildcat" was applied both to the banks and their currency. Today, these historical paper mementos are called "Broken Bank Notes." Some of them are of great beauty of design and color and they are widely collected by the present generation of currency collectors.

Soon after the Civil War began, the United States found itself in desperate need for money to finance the war. The only remedy that could be found was in an issue of paper money. Accordingly, Congress passed the Act of July 17, 1861 which permitted the Treasury Department to print and circulate paper money to the extent of 60 million dollars. In the meanwhile, the Government had suspended specie payments. The effect of this suspension was that this new paper money could not be converted into coin, either silver or gold. The public was thus forced to accept this money purely on faith and in a belief that the money would be good.

These first United States Notes are known as Demand Notes. They were followed in 1862 by the Legal Tender Notes and then by all the others as can be seen in the ensuing text.

3. THE TREASURY SEAL

Original Seal

New Seal

The Treasury Seal is a distinguishing feature of American Currency. In one form or another, it has appeared on every piece of paper money issued by the Treasury Department since 1862. (The Demand Notes of 1861 are without the seal, as are also the first three issues of Fractional Currency.)

The Treasury Seal, one might say, is the final stamp of approval that insures the legality of our currency. Combined with the expressed obligation of the government and the two signatures, it notarizes the contract, so to speak, made between the United States and the holders of its currency.

The Seal appears in several different forms and colors, as will be seen by referring to the illustrations and the text. It may be quite small, or large enough to fill up a substantial part of the note; it may be within a plain circle, or within a circle of rays, spikes or scallops; it may be red, brown, blue, green, gold or yellow. From the viewpoint of collecting, the kind of seal used makes a distinct variety out of a given note. Two notes may be otherwise similar in all respects, such as design, year and signatures and yet differ in the color, shape, or size of the seal.

The design of the Treasury Seal includes a shield on which appear a scale representing the emblem of Justice and a Key representing the emblem of official authority. These two symbols are separated by a chevron bearing 13 stars symbolic of the 13 original colonies or states. The legend around the seal is "THESAUR. AMER. SEPTENT. SIGIL.," the meaning of which is "The Seal of the Treasury of North America."

The Great Seal of the Treasury is older than the Constitution, having been used by the Board of Treasury under the Articles of Confederation. In 1778 the Continental Congress named John Witherspoon, Robert Morris and Richard Henry Lee to design seals for the Treasury and Navy. The committee reported on a design for the Navy the following year but there is no record of a report about one for the Treasury.

The Treasury considers that the actual creator of its seal probably was Francis Hopkinson, the Treasurer of Loans, who is known to have submitted bills to the Congress in 1780 authorizing the design of departmental seals, including the Board of Treasury. Although it is not certain that Hopkinson was the designer, the seal is similar to others by him.

After the Constitution was ratified in 1789, the Treasury adopted the same seal and it has been in use ever since, with only slight changes in design until 1968, when a major design change was made.

The new seal is simpler and less cluttered in appearance than the original one. The scale and key were both enlarged and five-pointed stars replace the more ornate six-pointed ones. The lover's knot and flowers were removed and the Latin legend has been replaced by an inscription in English, reading, "The Department of the Treasury." Below is the date of the founding of the Treasury Department, "1789."

The new seal made its first appearance on the $100 United States Note, Series of 1966. It is currently being used on all denominations of U.S. currency.

4. THE GREAT SEAL

Since 1935, the most familiar denomination of paper currency, the One Dollar note, has carried the Great Seal of the United States on its reverse. The Latin inscription, *E Pluribus Unum* — literally, "Out of Many (States), One (Nation)" — appears on the Seal's obverse on the right of the note.

The Seal's reverse on the left, bears two inscriptions: *Annuit Coeptis,* meaning "He" (God) Has Favored Our Undertakings," and *Novus Ordo Seclorum,* meaning "A New Order of the Ages." The eye in the triangle is a symbol of the all-seeing eye of God. The pyramid of 13 rows represents the 13 original colonies. The date *MDCCLXXVI* (1776) refers to the year of the signing of the Declaration of Independence. (The Great Seal appears on notes 1607-1621 and 1900-1909).

5. SIGNATURES

Except for the first two issues of Fractional Currency, all our notes bear the engraved facsimile signatures of two Treasury officials.

However, in the case of the Demand Notes of 1861, the names of these Treasury Officials do not appear on the notes, but the two signatures are those of Treasury employees signing for the officials. Please refer to Design Nos. 1, 2 and 3 in the text for the way in which these signatures appear.

From the series of 1862 through the series of 1923, the signatures appearing on our currency are of the Register of the Treasury and of the Treasurer of the United States.

However, on the large Federal Reserve Notes of 1914, and on all small size notes, the Register's name no longer appears but is replaced by the signature of the Secretary of the Treasury, the highest official of the Treasury Department. It is the Secretary's signature that now appears on our currency, alongside that of the Treasurer. There are several issues of currency which bear two other signatures in addition to those described above. These issues are the National Bank Notes, both large and small, and the Federal Reserve Bank Notes, both large and small. On the National Bank Notes, the two additional signatures are of the President and Cashier of the issuing bank; on the Federal Reserve Bank Notes, the two additional signatures are of the Governor and Cashier (or Deputy Governor) of the issuing bank.

There are also two issues that were countersigned by various assistant Treasurers. These are the Silver Certificates of 1878 and some of the Gold Certificates of 1882. All these notes are very rare.

The question is very often asked what the functions of the Register were during the period his signature appeared on our large notes and whether there is still today a Register of the Treasury. The Treasury Department advises that the office of the Register is still in existence and occupied, and that his functions during the issuance of large notes were as follows, "To receive from official agencies all bonds and other public debt securities, both bearer and registered, including collateral issue of interest coupons, representing principal and interest of the public debt when paid and canceled, or otherwise canceled and retired or voided, for any purpose whatever; to audit, hold in custody, and make disposition thereof; to record all bearer securities and other contiguous coupons prepared for issue and all such securities and coupons retired, and to record registered bonds issued and retired; to certify to the Comptroller General of the United States the clearance of the public debt disbursements of the Treasurer of the United States for all redeemed securities whether paid by the Treasurer direct or through the Federal Reserve Banks and charged against the Treasurer's account."

For a complete list of all the Registers and Treasurers, and their years in office concurrently, please refer to the table in the Appendix.

6. DATING U.S. PAPER MONEY

Every piece of United States paper money bears a date. It may be the date of an Act of Congress that authorized the issue or it may be the series year.

However, the year appearing on a given note is not necessarily the year in which it was printed and issued. This can be puzzling to a beginning currency collector, and it is certainly different from the minting of coins, which are usually struck only during the calendar year that appears on the coin.

Refer, for example, to a typical note in the text, let us say, number 234, which bears the date "Series of 1899" and the signatures of Elliott and Burke. This note could obviously not have been printed in 1899 since official public records indicate that the two signers were in office concurrently only from November 21, 1919 to January 5, 1921. Therefore, note number 234 could have been printed only during this period. The last issue of large notes is Series of 1923 with signatures of Woods and Tate, who were in office together for 7 months, 16 days during 1928 and 1929.

The table in the appendix gives a complete chronological listing of the various Treasury Officials who signed our currency. This table also indicates the exact periods of time during which they held office concurrently, so that by referring to this table, it will be quite simple to determine when any note was printed, with the exception of National Bank Notes. See under "The Dates of Issue" in the introduction to large size National Bank Notes on page 74.

7. SIZE

In accordance with Treasury Department regulations, the illustrations in this book are reduced to slightly less than three-fourths the size of the original notes.

With certain exceptions, the size of an average large note is 7-3/8 by 3-1/8 inches.

The Interest Bearing and Compound Interest Notes are slightly larger, especially in their width. The Refunding Certificates are slightly smaller but much wider and measure 6-3/4 by 3-5/8 inches.

As will be seen by the illustrations, Fractional Currency is of several sizes. However, these illustrations are uniformly somewhat less than three-fourths the size of the original notes. The actual size of the smallest piece of Fractional Currency is 2-1/2 by 1-5/8 inches and of the largest piece it is 4-3/8 by 2-1/8 inches.

NOTE: In the large size section, illustrated notes are indicated by a dot (•) after the description.

8. COLOR

The dominant colors of U.S. paper money are black and green. The obverses all bear portraits of famous Americans or allegorical scenes and are printed in black and white, considerably enlivened by colored seals, colored serial numbers and attractive colored embellishments.

The reverses are printed in varying shades of green except for the following classes of currency: The Refunding Certificates of 1879 are printed in black and white; the Silver Certificates of 1878 and 1880 are printed in a brownish black; the National Bank Notes of the First Charter Period are bi-colored, the central painting in black, the borders in green; the first issues of the National Bank Notes of 1882 are printed in brown; the National Gold Bank Notes are bi-colored, the central portion of gold coins in black, the borders in brown; the Gold Certificates are printed in a brilliant golden orange to simulate the color of gold.

The same coloration is typical of Fractional Currency except for certain issues, which are noted in the text. (See notes 1226-1383-a.)

9. ERROR AND FREAK NOTES; UNCUT SHEETS

From time to time, through human or mechanical failure, unusual notes have been printed and issued.

These accidents have taken different forms, and some of these notes are highly prized by collectors. All such notes are of greater or lesser rarity, since the Bureau of Engraving and Printing is most strict in the inspection and release of the finished currency, and will not issue any notes that are imperfect in any way.

Some of the errors that have occurred in the past are as follows: Without seal or seal only partly showing; serial numbers missing, incomplete or even different on the same note; a white unprinted portion showing on a note, where the paper had been accidentally folded; the seal or serial numbers upside down or printed on the reverse side of the note; the reverse inverted (a normal note is turned like the page of a book in order to read the reverse); two denominations on the same note.

By far, the most cherished and valuable error notes are those with two denominations, for example, a 5 Dollar obverse and a 10 Dollar reverse. Such notes are extremely rare, are in great demand and bring very high prices on the few occasions when they are offered for sale.

An extraordinary error like this is most likely caused during the process of printing, when a sheet which has already been printed on one side is inadvertently removed from its proper place and put with sheets of another denomination, which similarly have so far been printed on only one side.

Although not considered either errors or freaks, uncut sheets of notes are also collected for their unusual appeal. Uncut sheets will most frequently be found among the National Bank Notes, more rarely among the other series. The reason for this is that National Bank Notes were delivered to the banks by the Treasury Department in the form of complete sheets. Once at the banks, the notes had to be signed by the president and cashier, and the separation of the notes became a matter of convenience for the individual bank.

An uncut sheet of American paper money is a seldom seen oddity and is usually a conversation piece. Such an item makes a handsome and impressive addition to any collection of currency.

10. HIGH DENOMINATION NOTES

As will be seen in the text, the Government has issued some notes with a very high face value. These notes are of the denominations of 500, 1,000, 5,000 and 10,000 Dollars.

These high denomination notes are merely mentioned in the text as having once upon a time been issued, since the main concern of numismatists is with the small denomination notes from 1 to 100 Dollars. Although illustrated, the high denomination notes have not been priced, because they represent so much purchasing power and are of such great rarity as to make their collecting purely academic. They are quite beyond the reach of the ordinary collector because of their high face value, and just as much beyond the reach of the millionaire because of their extreme rarity, or because a few issues will be forever unobtainable, the last existing note having already been redeemed by the Treasury.

Although these high denomination notes were available to anyone who wanted them, they were not, as a matter of practice, to be found in ordinary circulation. They were held mainly by banks and clearing houses and were used to settle large cash balances.

Several examples of their rarity can be given, as taken from official Treasury records of Dec. 31, 1965.

500 Dollars. Silver Certificate. 14 pieces extant.
500 Dollars. National Bank Note. 6 pieces extant.
1,000 Dollars. Silver Certificate. 8 pieces extant.
1,000 Dollars. National Bank Note. 10 pieces extant.
1,000 Dollars. Treasury or Coin Note. 5 pieces extant.
5,000 Dollars. Legal Tender Note. None extant.
10,000 Dollars. Legal Tender Note. None extant.

The current small size notes were also issued in high denominations up to 10,000 Dollars. (See under Federal Reserve Notes.) The last 5,000 and 10,000 Dollar notes were issued during the tenure of Julian and Morgenthau. It is now the policy of the Treasury not to print any more high denomination notes from 500 to 10,000 Dollars, and these are now being slowly retired. The 100 Dollar note has thus become the largest note available.

11. RARITY

As collectors of currency quickly discover, many notes are quite difficult to obtain. Even after years of searching inquiry among all possible sources, some notes will remain elusive enough as to be almost unobtainable.

This rarity can be of two kinds, either of design or of condition. Great rarity is generally a combination of both.

The rarity of design is the more important since the notes involved exist in only one or two varieties, whereas notes of more common design may have numerous varieties of seals or signature combinations, making such designs far easier to acquire. Since most collectors are content with only one note of each distinctive design, the notes of rare design are in great demand and bring high prices.

The rarity of condition is concerned with those notes, irrespective of design, which are extremely difficult to acquire in new condition, although they may be fairly common in circulated state. This factor of condition is of the greatest importance to collectors who wish to build a complete collection of currency, since their aim is the acquisition of notes in the finest possible condition.

Several examples can be cited of notes of rare designs. They are here given in the order of their rarity: All Interest Bearing Notes, Compound Interest Notes and Refunding Certificates; all Demand Notes; all National Gold Bank Notes and all Silver Certificates of 1878 and 1880 (10 to 100 Dollars). Coincidentally, all the foregoing notes also represent the highest rarity of condition since they are practically unknown in new or uncirculated state. The average condition in which these notes appear is only fine.

The following specific notes can also be mentioned as of rare designs: Legal Tender 50 Dollars of 1869, Treasury or Coin 50 Dollars of 1891 and 100 Dollars of 1890 and 1891; Federal Reserve Bank Note 50 Dollars of 1918; all Legal Tender Notes of 1869; the 50 and 100 Dollar Notes of the Legal Tender issues of 1862-1863 and also of the First Charter National Bank Issues of 1863-1875; all notes of the Second Charter National Bank issues of 1882 with the denomination spelled out on the reverse, and all Treasury or Coin Notes of 1890.

Among notes which are of common design but very rare in new condition, note No. 49 is probably the most famous example. This design is quite common but only about five specimens are known of this particular variety.

In addition to the notes of rare condition mentioned in the third paragraph above, the following are also noteworthy as being most difficult to acquire in new condition: All Legal Tender Notes of 1869; all National Bank Notes of the First Charter Period, 1863-1875; and in general all 10, 20, 50, and 100 Dollar notes of all categories from 1862 to 1890 inclusive; also the following specific notes for which please refer to the text: Numbers 19, 21-25, 31, 32, 43, 45, 46, 53, 54, 55, 74-78, 220, 221, 243, 244, 265, 347-349, 353-355, 359-361.

A word would also be in order here regarding the so-called Educational Set of notes. Please see design numbers 61, 66 and 70. These notes are of extraordinary beauty and of great historical appeal and although not particularly rare, there has been such a persistent demand for them that they are expected to become very rare in time. Notes in a similar category are those of design number 68. These too have an unusual appeal and enjoy great popularity because of the numismatic reverse which shows a row of five silver Dollars.

12. GRADING AND CONDITION

The condition of a note is its state of preservation—its newness, its crispness, its color, its eye appeal.

The notes in this book have been priced in new, very fine and very good condition. In some cases, where the notes are very rare in new or very fine condition, they have been listed in only fine condition.

The following grading standards apply to paper money:

Gem Uncirculated: A note that is flawless, with the same freshness, crispness and bright color as when first printed. It must be perfectly centered, with full margins, and free of any marks, blemishes or traces of handling.

Choice Uncirculated: An uncirculated note which is fresher and brighter than the norm for its particular issue. Almost as nice as Gem Uncirculated, but not quite there. Must be reasonably well centered.

Uncirculated: A note which shows no trace of circulation. It may not have perfect centering and may have one or more pinholes, counting smudges, or other evidence of improper handling, while still retaining its original crispness.

Sometimes large size notes will be encountered which are obviously uncirculated, but which may have some tiny pin holes. It was customary in the old days to spindle or pin new notes together, and that is why so many uncirculated notes may show tiny pin holes. Such imperfections do not generally impair the choice appearance of a new note, and such notes are to be regarded as being in uncirculated condition, although they generally command slightly lower prices than notes in perfect condition.

About Uncirculated: A bright, crisp note that appears new but upon close examination shows a trace of very light use, such as a corner fold or faint crease. About Uncirculated is a borderline condition, applied to a note which may not be quite uncirculated, but yet is obviously better than an average Extra Fine note. Such notes command a price only slightly below a new note and are highly desirable.

Extra Fine: A note that shows some faint evidence of circulation, although it will still be bright and retain nearly full crispness. It may have two or three minor folds or creases but no tears or stains and no discolorations.

Very Fine: A note that has been in circulation, but not actively or for long. It still retains some crispness and is still choice enough in its condition to be altogether desirable. It may show folds or creases, or some light smudges from the hands of a past generation. Sometimes, Very Fine notes are the best available in certain rare issues, and they should accordingly be cherished just as much as uncirculated notes. See the section on rarity above.

Fine: A fine note shows evidence of much more circulation, has lost its crispness and very fine detail, and creases are more pronounced, although the note is still not seriously soiled or stained.

Very Good: A note that has had considerable wear or circulation and may be limp, soiled or dark in appearance and even have a small tear or two on an edge.

Good: A note that is badly worn, with margin or body tears, frayed margins and missing corners.

In general, discriminating collectors will not acquire Fine or worse notes because they have lost their aesthetic appeal, but this applies only to common notes. A really rare note has a ready market in even poor condition, because it may not otherwise exist, or if it is choice, will have an extremely high price commensurate with its great rarity.

13. VALUATIONS

No book of this nature would be either complete or desirable without an indication of the numismatic or collectors' value of the notes.

All large size notes and Fractional Currency are important collectors' items today, (small size notes are important also, but to a lesser degree) and the valuations given here are offered as a guide for collectors, or for students of the subject. These prices were most carefully prepared, and are based upon recent sales records, supply and demand, rarity, general activity and a thorough analytical study of the market. The prices thus represent an average at or about which the notes would be obtainable from a numismatic dealer when in stock.

The pricing of rare notes always poses a special problem since they come up for sale so seldom and the demand for them is so avid, that any price for a rare note can, at best, be only nominal. Some rare notes in the past have no doubt changed hands at much higher prices than here quoted, and it is conceivable that they will do so again, but as mentioned above, a fair average valuation has been attempted. It must also be borne in mind that many early notes, though not rare in themselves, are of the greatest rarity when in choice uncirculated condition. Such notes are practically priceless and command their own figure when offered.

14. "STAR" NOTES

When a note is found to be imperfect in the course of manufacture, it is replaced with a "star" note, that is a note bearing a star either before or after the serial number. In all other respects, the "star" note is indistinguishable from the regular notes, and, of course, worth the same face value.

On Federal Reserve Notes, the star appears after the serial number. On all other issues, the star precedes the serial number.

A "star" note is also used for the 100,000,000th note in a series, since the numbering machines cannot print over eight digits.

"Star" notes are indicated in the Small Size Notes section by an (*) appearing after the catalog number.

15. THE COLLECTING OF UNITED STATES CURRENCY

As will be seen by the illustrations in the text, large size notes offer the collector an abundance of colorful design, artistic subject matter and historical and educational data.

In the last 30 years or so, the collecting of this currency has increased to such an extent that notes which were once plentiful are now rare, and bring prices out of all proportion to what they brought in 1940. This difference can easily be seen by comparing price lists issued at different times since 1940. This trend is still continuing, and collectors throughout the country are competing with each other for the acquisition of choice notes. More and more, note collecting is becoming an adjunct of coin collecting, and now almost all numismatists collect both.

The designs of large notes, both obverse and reverse represent the best work of the best engravers of the nineteenth century. It is for good reason indeed that our old notes have so often been called masterpieces of the art of engraving, and beautiful enough to rank with other works of art.

So active has the collecting of large notes been, that there are now no major stocks in existence of choice and rare notes where one can select anything of his choice. Two of the greatest collections of paper money ever formed were broken up in recent years and the notes quickly absorbed by countless collectors. The collections referred to were those formed by the late Colonel Green (son of Hetty Green) and the late Albert A. Grinnell. The first collection was broken up in 1942 and the second was sold over a period from 1944 to 1946.

There are several ways of collecting large notes. One may collect just one note of each design or all the varieties of seal and signature of each design; or one may wish only the Legal Tender Notes or the Silver Certificates, or some other series; or one may collect the notes of a given denomination such as 1, 2 or 5 Dollar notes; etc.; or one may collect only notes of special artistic value, or of historical interest. In short, the collecting of currency, as in other collecting fields, is determined purely by personal preference and by purse.

The above paragraphs apply equally to Fractional Currency, which has also enjoyed great popularity in recent years.

By comparison with large notes, the small size currency of today is more standardized. Though it does not have the richness of color and design of the past, the collecting of small size currency nevertheless has its own charms, since the fewer basic designs have many interesting varieties that lend themselves to true numismatic study. Actually, the portraits that first appeared on these notes in 1929 have remained unchanged to the present day, but a glance at the illustrations will show many obvious differences in the overall appearance of these notes.

Despite their apparent paucity of design, the small size notes offer a rich paradise of variety and one who undertakes to acquire a complete set of small size notes has set himself upon a monumental task. It is believed that a complete set of uncirculated small size notes has not yet been formed, although it has been tried. Many of the notes just cannot be found in uncirculated condition.

A comparison will quickly show the difference. Large notes were issued from 1861 to 1929, a period of 68 years, which produced about 140 designs and about 1,200 varieties. The issue of small notes from 1929 to 1971 is a period of 42 years which has produced only 7 portrait types but about 1,184 varieties. The above comparisons are for notes up to the 100 Dollars and do not include either the large or small National Bank Notes which were issued by thousands of different banks.

A collection of currency can be kept in either of two standard ways, in bound albums especially made for currency or in individual heavy, transparent envelopes which can be filed upright in a box.

16. THE COUNTERFEIT CLAUSE

The counterfeiting of United States paper money is an extremely dangerous offense. Although the penalties on being convicted are very serious and heavy, nevertheless counterfeiters have indulged in this felony almost since our first notes were made.

In order to publicize the serious nature of counterfeiting and to acquaint the population with the penalties, many issues of our large notes bear an extract from the Criminal Code pertaining to the counterfeiting of United States paper money.

This counterfeit clause first appeared on the National Bank Notes of the First Charter period, and is last seen on the Legal Tender issues of the 1917 series. The punishment has become progressively worse since the 1860's when this clause first appeared.

On the National Bank Notes referred to above, the counterfeit clause reads as follows, "Every person making or engraving, or aiding to make or engrave, or passing or attempting to pass any imitation or alterations of this note, and every person having in possession a plate or impression made in imitation of it, or any paper made in imitation of that on which this note is printed, is by act of Congress approved June 3, 1864, guilty of felony, and subject to a fine not exceeding one thousand dollars, or imprisonment not exceeding fifteen years, or both."

On the Legal Tender issues of the 1917 series this clause appears as follows, "Counterfeiting or altering this note or passing any counterfeit or alteration of it, or having in possession any false or counterfeit plate or impression of it, or any paper made in imitation of the paper on which it is printed is felony and is punishable by $5,000 fine or 15 years' imprisonment at hard labor or both."

17. BIBLIOGRAPHY

The following publications have been consulted:

"United States Paper Money, Old Series, 1861-1923." By Limpert.

"Classified List of U.S. Postage and Fractional Currency." By Limpert.

"National and Federal Reserve Currency, 1928-1950." By Lloyd.

"The Standard Paper Money Catalogue, Part II." By Raymond.

"A Descriptive History of National Bank Notes." By Dillistin.

"National Banks of the Note Issuing Period 1863-1935." By Van Belkum.

"The Standard Handbook of Modern U.S. Paper Money." By O'Donnell.

"The Comprehensive Catalog of U.S. Paper Money." By Hessler.

PART ONE. LARGE SIZE NOTES

I. THE DEMAND NOTES OF 1861

The term "Greenback" for United States paper money originated with the issue of the Demand Notes of 1861. As mentioned earlier in this book, these Demand Notes are the first and earliest issue of United States currency as we know it.

They were issued in denominations of 5, 10 and 20 Dollars only, and were authorized by the Congressional Acts of July 17 and August 5, 1861. All notes bear the first date, "Act of July 17, 1861" and also the additional date of "Aug. 10th, 1861," which is probably the day the notes were first issued to the public.

Demand Notes are unique in United States Currency, in that they alone bear neither the Treasury Seal nor the actual names of the Treasurer and Register of the Treasury. They also have the serial number imprinted only once.

Sixty million dollars in currency was authorized to be issued by the above Acts. This was a very large sum for those days and involved the printing and signing of several million actual notes. At this time, a situation arose which was unprecedented.

The first plates made for the various denominations had blank spaces for two signatures, and below these spaces were engraved "Register of the Treasury" and "Treasurer of the United States."

These two busy and important Treasury officials obviously could not sit down and personally autograph several million notes. Therefore, a large staff of clerks from the Treasury Department was employed to sign their own names for the two officials. The way the plates were worded made it necessary for these clerks to write also the words "For the" in addition to their own names.

It quickly became apparent that this additional wording was both wasteful and inefficient and the plates were at once changed so that the finished printed note read as follows, "For the Register of the Treasury" and "For the Treasurer of the United States."

Compared to the total amount of notes issued, those released to the public before the plates were changed were small in number. Today, only a few survive and they are of the highest rarity and greatest historical interest.

The obligation on the Demand Notes is as follows. "The United States promised to pay to the bearer...... Dollars on demand.... Payable by the Assistant Treasurer of the United States at (New York, Philadelphia, Boston, Cincinnati or St. Louis). Receivable in payment of all public dues."

5 Dollar Notes

DESIGN NO. 1

(Notes 1-5)

Thomas Crawford's statue of Columbia on top of the U.S. Capitol in Washington. Head of Alexander Hamilton, the first Secretary of the Treasury, 1789-1795.

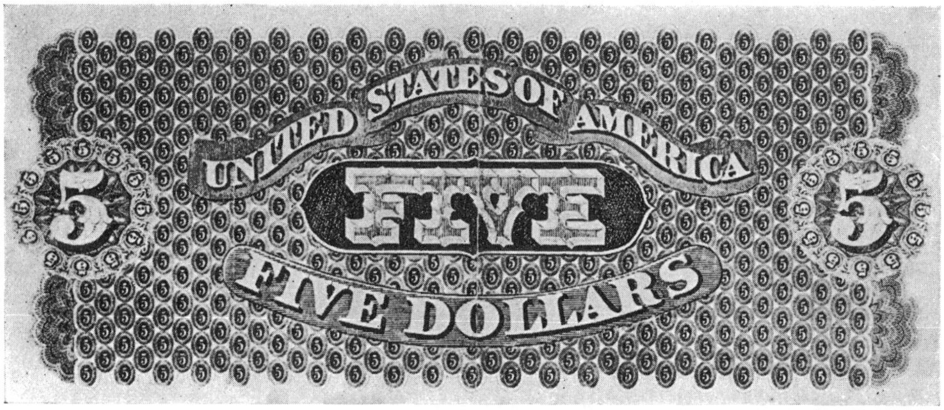

Reverse of Design No. 1.

Printed in green. The green reverses of the Demand Notes are the origin of the term "Greenback" as applied to U.S. paper money in general.

No.	Payable at	Very Good	Very Fine	No.	Payable at	Very Good	Very Fine
1.	New York	750.00	2,400.00	3a.	"For the" handwritten	2,200.00	6,500.00
1a.	"For the" handwritten	2,000.00	Rare	4.	Cincinnati		Very Rare
2.	Philadelphia	750.00	2,400.00	4a.	"For the" handwritten		Very Rare
2a.	"For the" handwritten	Rare	Rare	5.	St. Louis		Very Rare
3.	Boston	950.00	2,850.00	5a.	"For the" handwritten		Very Rare

10 Dollar Notes

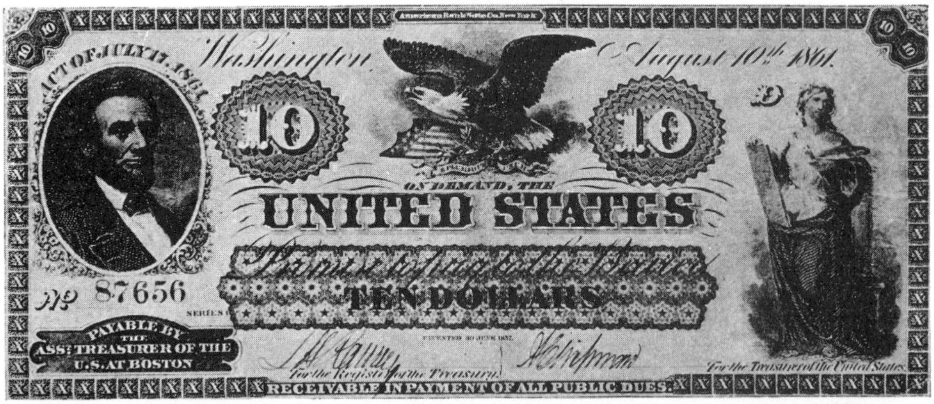

DESIGN NO. 2

(Notes 6-10a)

Head of Abraham Lincoln, 16th President of the United States, 1861-1865. At top center, an eagle with draped shield. At right, a female allegory representing Art.

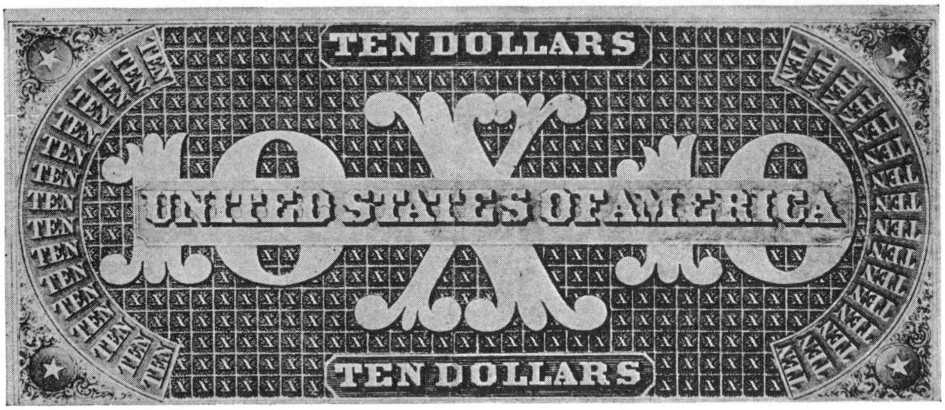

Reverse of Design No. 2

No.	Payable at	Very Good	Very Fine
6.	New York	1,400.00	4,250.00
6a.	"For the" handwritten	Rare	Rare
7.	Philadelphia	1,400.00	4,250.00
7a.	"For the" handwritten	Extremely Rare	
8.	Boston	1,600.00	4,400.00
8a.	"For the" handwritten	5,000.00	Rare
9.	Cincinnati	Extremely Rare	
9a.	"For the" handwritten	Extremely Rare	
10.	St. Louis	Extremely Rare	
10a.	"For the" handwritten	Unknown	

20 Dollar Notes

DESIGN NO. 3

(Notes 11-15)

Liberty holding sword and shield.

Reverse of Design No. 3.

This illustration by courtesy of Chase National Bank of New York.

No.	Payable at	Very Good
11.	New York	**9,500.00**
11a.	"For the" handwritten	**Unique**
12.	Philadelphia	**9,500.00**
12a.	"For the" handwritten	**Rare**
13.	Boston	**9,500.00**
13a.	"For the" handwritten	**Rare**
14.	Cincinnati	**Extremely Rare**
14a.	"For the" handwritten	**Extremely Rare**
15.	St. Louis	**No Specimen Known**

II. LEGAL TENDER ISSUES
(UNITED STATES NOTES)

There are five issues of Legal Tender Notes, which are also called United States Notes.

First Issue. These notes are dated March 10, 1862 and were issued in all denominations from 5 to 1,000 Dollars. The obligation on the obverse of all these notes is, "The United States promise to pay to the bearer...... Dollars.... Payable at the Treasury of the United States at New York." There are two separate obligations on the reverse side of these notes.

First Obligation. Earlier issues have the so-called First Obligation which reads as follows, "This note is a legal tender for all debts, public and private, except duties on imports and interest on the public debt, and is exchangeable for U.S. six per cent twenty year bonds, redeemable at the pleasure of the United States after five years."

Second Obligation. The later issues have so-called Second Obligation, which reads as follows, "This note is a legal tender for all debts, public and private, except duties on imports and interest on the public debt, and is receivable in payment of all loans made to the United States."

Notes of 1862 with the Second Obligation are much rarer than those with the First Obligation.

It will be observed that these notes are without the titles that appear on later issues which have the heading either "Treasury Note" or "United States Note."

Second Issue. These notes are dated August 1, 1862 and were issued in denominations 1 and 2 Dollars only. The obligation on these notes, both obverse and reverse, is the same as on the notes of the Second Obligation above.

Third Issue. These notes are dated March 10, 1863 and were issued in all denominations from 5 to 1,000 Dollars. The obligations, both obverse and reverse, are the same as on the notes of the Second Obligation of the First Issue.

Fourth Issue. All notes of this issue were printed under authority of the Congressional Act of March 3, 1863. The notes issued were from 1 to 10,000 Dollars and include the series of 1869, 1874, 1878, 1880, 1907, 1917 and 1923. The notes of 1869 are titled "Treasury Notes;" all later issues are titled "United States Notes." However, the obligation on all series is the same, "The United States will pay to bearer...... dollars.... This note is a legal tender at its face value for all debts public and private, except duties on imports and interest on the public debt.

Fifth Issue. This issue consisted only of 10 Dollar notes of the series of 1901. These notes were issued under authority of the Legal Tender Acts of 1862 and 1863. The obligation on these notes is as follows, "The United States of America will pay to the bearer ten dollars ... This note is a Legal Tender for ten dollars subject to the provisions of Section 3588 R.S.... This note is a Legal Tender at its face value for all debts public and private except duties on imports and interest on the public debt."

1 Dollar Notes

DESIGN NO. 4

(Notes 16-17)

Head of Salmon P. Chase, Secretary of the Treasury under Abraham Lincoln, 1861-1864, and Chief Justice of the U.S. Supreme Court, 1864-1873. He is probably best known to numismatists for his causing the motto "In God We Trust" to be adopted for our national coinage.

Reverse of Design No. 4.

All are Series of 1862, with signatures of Chittenden and Spinner and with small red seal.

No.		Very Good	Very Fine	Unc
16.	National Bank Note Co. printed twice above lower border	• 75.00	150.00	850.00
16a.	As above, with American Bank Note Co. monogram near center at right edge of obverse	75.00	175.00	950.00
17.	National Bank Note Co. and American Bank Note Co. printed above lower border	90.00	250.00	1,100.00
17a.	As above, with American Bank Note Co. monogram near center at right edge of obverse	80.00	175.00	950.00

DESIGN NO. 5

(Note 18)

Head of George Washington, first President of the United States, 1789-1797. At the left, Christopher Columbus in sight of land. This vignette was designed by Joseph P. Ourdan.

Reverse of Design No. 5.

No.	Series	Signatures		Seal	Very Good	Very Fine	Unc
18.	1869	Allison	Spinner	Large Red	**75.00**	**200.00**	**1,100.00**

DESIGN NO. 6

(Notes 19-39)

Vignettes similar to Design No. 5. Because of color, seal placement or embellishments, there are several distinct types of this design, as follows:

6a. Notes 19-27
6b. Notes 28-30
6c. Notes 31-33
6d. Notes 34-35
6e. Notes 36-39

Reverse of Design No. 6.

Because of its design, it is known as the "sawhorse reverse".

6a. Red floral ornament around "ONE DOLLAR" at right; seal at left.

No.	Series	Signatures		Seal	Very Good	Very Fine	Unc
19.	1874	Allison	Spinner	Small Red with rays	60.00	150.00	700.00
20.	1875	Allison	New	Small Red with rays	•50.00	90.00	400.00
21.			Same but Series A		150.00	450.00	1,500.00
22.			Same but Series B		150.00	450.00	1,500.00
23.			Same but Series C		175.00	475.00	1,500.00
24.			Same but Series D		200.00	550.00	1,800.00
25.			Same but Series E		225.00	600.00	2,250.00
26.	1875	Allison	Wyman	Small Red with rays	45.00	100.00	450.00
27.	1878	Allison	Gilfillan	Small Red with rays	45.00	150.00	650.00

6b. Large seal replaces floral ornament at right; red serial numbers.

28.	1880	Scofield	Gilfillan	Large Brown	40.00	80.00	400.00
29.	1880	Bruce	Gilfillan	Large Brown	40.00	80.00	400.00
30.	1880	Bruce	Wyman	Large Brown	40.00	80.00	400.00

6c. Same as above, except serial numbers are blue.

31.	1880	Rosecrans	Huston	Large Red	90.00	275.00	1,500.00
32.	1880	Rosecrans	Huston	Large Brown	100.00	300.00	1,750.00
33.	1880	Rosecrans	Nebeker	Large Brown	100.00	300.00	1,750.00

6d. Seal is now small and is moved to left side of note; blue serial numbers.

34.	1880	Rosecrans	Nebeker	Small Red, Scalloped	40.00	90.00	400.00
35.	1880	Tillman	Morgan	Small Red, Scalloped	40.00	90.00	400.00

6e. Serial numbers are red, and are no longer in ornamental frames.

36.	1917	Teehee	Burke	Small Red, Scalloped	18.00	45.00	160.00
37.	1917	Elliott	Burke	Small Red, Scalloped	18.00	45.00	160.00
37a.	1917	Burke	Elliott	(Signatures Reversed)	45.00	140.00	600.00
38.	1917	Elliott	White	Small Red, Scalloped	18.00	45.00	160.00
39.	1917	Speelman	White	Small Red, Scalloped	18.00	45.00	160.00

DESIGN NO. 7

(Note 40)

Head of George Washington. This was the last large size One Dollar note issued prior to the changeover to small size notes.

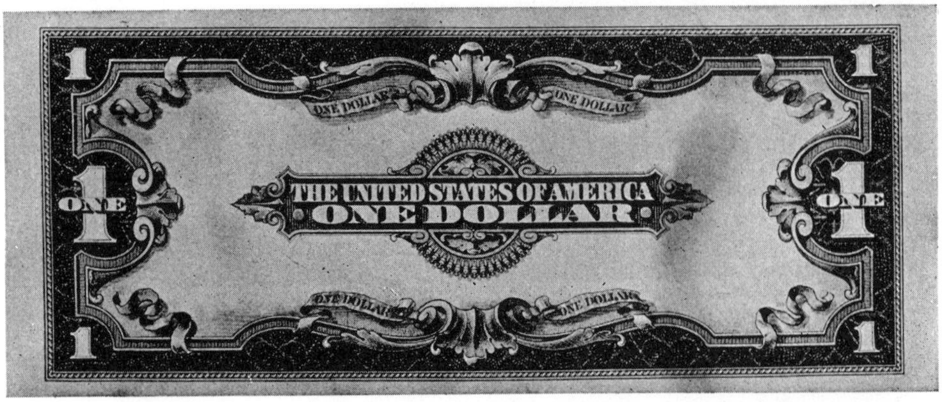

Reverse of Design No. 7.

The "cogwheel reverse."

No.	Series	Signatures		Seal	Very Good	Very Fine	Unc
40.	1923	Speelman	White	Small Red, Scalloped	25.00	65.00	225.00

2 Dollar Notes

DESIGN NO. 8

(Note 41)

Head of Alexander Hamilton.

Reverse of Design No. 8.

Series of 1862 with signatures of Chittenden and Spinner and with small red seal.

No.		Very Good	Very Fine	Unc
41.	National Bank Note Company printed vertically at left border	110.00	250.00	1,800.00
41a.	American Bank Note Company printed vertically at left border	110.00	275.00	2,000.00

DESIGN NO. 9

(Note 42)

Head of Thomas Jefferson, third President of the United States, 1801-1805. The portrait was engraved by James Smilie. At center, a view of the Capitol.

Reverse of Design No. 9.

42.	1869	Allison	Spinner	Large Red	125.00	400.00	2,000.00

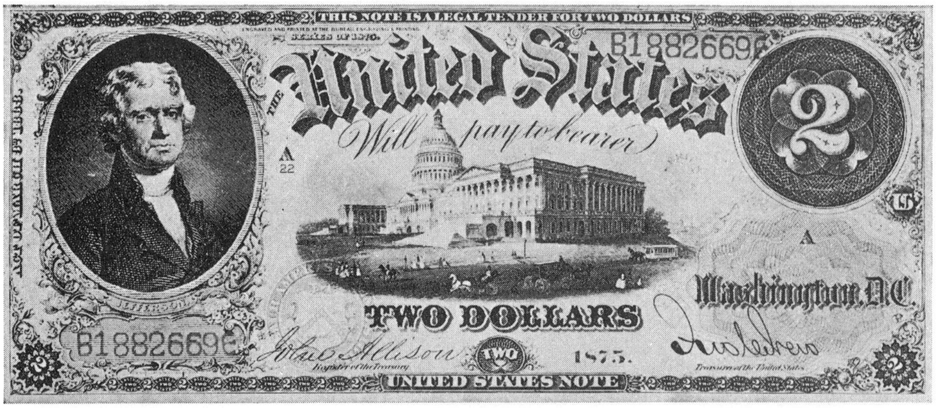

DESIGN NO. 10

(Notes 43-60)

Vignettes similar to Design No. 9. Because of color, seal placement or embellishments, there are several distinct types of the design, as follows:

10a. Notes 43-49
10b. Notes 50-52
10c. Notes 53-56
10d. Notes 57-60

Reverse of Design No. 10.

The "bracelet reverse."

10a. Red floral ornament around "Washington, D.C."; seal at left.

No.	Series	Signatures		Seal	Very Good	Very Fine	Unc
43.	1874	Allison	Spinner	Small Red with rays	100.00	250.00	1,000.00
44.	1875	Allison	New	Small Red with rays	•75.00	150.00	700.00
45.			Same but Series A		140.00	375.00	1,500.00
46.			Same but Series B		140.00	375.00	1,500.00
47.	1875	Allison	Wyman	Small Red with rays	75.00	150.00	675.00
48.	1878	Allison	Gilfillan	Small Red with rays	90.00	175.00	725.00
49.	1878	Scofield	Gilfillan	Small Red with rays	1,750.00	3,750.00	9,000.00

10b. Large seal replaces floral ornament at right; red serial numbers.

50.	1880	Scofield	Gilfillan	Large Brown	60.00	120.00	400.00
51.	1880	Bruce	Gilfillan	Large Brown	60.00	120.00	400.00
52.	1880	Bruce	Wyman	Large Brown	60.00	120.00	400.00

10c. Same as above, except serial numbers are blue.

53.	1880	Rosecrans	Huston	Large Red	125.00	350.00	1,400.00
54.	1880	Rosecrans	Huston	Large Brown	125.00	350.00	1,300.00
55.	1880	Rosecrans	Nebeker	Small Red, Scalloped	65.00	150.00	450.00
56.	1880	Tillman	Morgan	Small Red, Scalloped	60.00	125.00	375.00

10d. Same as above, except serial numbers are again red.

57.	1917	Teehee	Burke	Small Red, Scalloped	25.00	50.00	225.00
58.	1917	Elliott	Burke	Small Red, Scalloped	25.00	50.00	225.00
59.	1917	Elliott	White	Small Red, Scalloped	30.00	55.00	250.00
60.	1917	Speelman	White	Small Red, Scalloped	25.00	50.00	225.00

5 Dollar Notes

DESIGN NO. 11

(Notes 61-63a)

Obverse is similar to Design No. 1, but Treasury seal has been added and "On Demand" removed. The reverse shown is the Second Obligation. The wording of the First Obligation can be seen on Design No. 14.

No.	Act	Signatures		Seal	Very Good	Very Fine	Unc
61.	1862	Chittenden	Spinner	Small Red			
		American Bank Note Co. on upper border			**Extremely Rare**		
61a.	1862	Chittenden	Spinner	Small Red, "Series" on obverse			
		American Bank Note Co. on upper border			**100.00**	**275.00**	**1,500.00**

(The above notes with the First Obligation on reverse.)

No.	Act	Signatures		Seal	Very Good	Very Fine	Unc
62.	1862	Chittenden	Spinner	Small Red	**125.00**	**275.00**	**1,000.00**
63.	1863	Chittenden	Spinner	Small Red			
	American Bank Note Co. and National Bank Note Co. on lower border				**70.00**	**175.00**	**800.00**
63a.	1863	Chittenden	Spinner	Small Red, One Serial No.			
		American Bank Note Co. twice on lower border			**80.00**	**200.00**	**900.00**
63b.	1863	Chittenden	Spinner	Small Red, Two Serial Nos.			
	American Bank Note Co. twice on lower border				**70.00**	**175.00**	**800.00**

(The above three notes with the Second Obligation on reverse.)

DESIGN NO. 12

(Note 64)

Head of Andrew Jackson, seventh President of the United States, 1829-1833, from a painting by Thomas Sully, engraved by Alfred Sealey. At center, a Pioneer Family, engraved by Henry Gugler.

Reverse of Design No. 12.

No.	Series	Signatures		Seal	Very Good	Very Fine	Unc
64.	1869	Allison	Spinner	Large Red	**100.00**	**225.00**	**900.00**

DESIGN NO. 13

(Notes 65-92)

Vignettes similar to Design No. 12. Because of color, seal placement or embellishments, there are several distinct types of this design, as follows:

13a. Notes 65-69
13b. Notes 70-72
13c. Notes 73-82
13d. Notes 83-92

Reverse of Design No. 13.

No.	Series	Signatures		Seal	Very Good	Very Fine	Unc
		13a. Large red floral ornament around "Washington, D.C."; seal at left.					
65.	1875	Allison	New	Small Red with rays	•75.00	175.00	500.00
66.		As above but Series A			80.00	200.00	800.00
67.		As above but Series B			85.00	200.00	850.00
68.	1875	Allison	Wyman	Small Red with rays	70.00	175.00	500.00
69.	1878	Allison	Gilfillan	Small Red with rays	100.00	250.00	850.00
		13b. Large seal replaces floral ornament at right; red serial numbers.					
70.	1880	Scofield	Gilfillan	Large brown	300.00	800.00	Rare
71.	1880	Bruce	Gilfillan	Large Brown	70.00	140.00	475.00
72.	1880	Bruce	Wyman	Large Brown	70.00	140.00	475.00
		13c. Same as above but serial numbers are blue.					
73.	1880	Bruce	Wyman	Large Red, plain	70.00	150.00	600.00
74.	1880	Rosecrans	Jordan	Large Red, plain	70.00	175.00	625.00
75.	1880	Rosecrans	Hyatt	Large Red, plain	75.00	200.00	650.00
76.	1880	Rosecrans	Huston	Large Red with spikes	100.00	300.00	1,250.00
77.	1880	Rosecrans	Huston	Large Brown	70.00	175.00	625.00
78.	1880	Rosecrans	Nebeker	Large Brown	100.00	300.00	1,200.00
79.	1880	Rosecrans	Nebeker	Small Red, scalloped	55.00	140.00	400.00
80.	1880	Tillman	Morgan	Small Red, scalloped	55.00	140.00	400.00
81.	1880	Bruce	Roberts	Small Red, scalloped	55.00	140.00	400.00
82.	1880	Lyons	Roberts	Small Red, scalloped	55.00	140.00	400.00
		13d. Red "V" and "Dollars" added to design at left; Red Serial numbers.					
83.	1907	Vernon	Treat	Small Red, scalloped	35.00	60.00	275.00
84.	1907	Vernon	McClung	Small Red, scalloped	35.00	60.00	275.00
85.	1907	Napier	McClung	Small Red, scalloped	35.00	60.00	275.00
86.	1907	Napier	Thompson	Small Red, scalloped	125.00	350.00	1,000.00
87.	1907	Parker	Burke	Small Red, scalloped	35.00	60.00	275.00
88.	1907	Teehee	Burke	Small Red, scalloped	35.00	60.00	275.00
89.	1907	Elliott	Burke	Small Red, scalloped	40.00	70.00	300.00
90.	1907	Elliott	White	Small Red, scalloped	35.00	60.00	275.00
91.	1907	Speelman	White	Small Red, scalloped	32.50	60.00	250.00
92.	1907	Woods	White	Small Red, scalloped	35.00	65.00	300.00

10 Dollar Notes

DESIGN NO. 14

(Note 93)

Obverse is similar to Design No. 2, but Treasury Seal has been added and "On Demand" removed. The reverse shown is the First Obligation.

No.	Act	Signatures		Seal	Very Good	Very Fine	Unc
93.	1862	Chittenden	Spinner	Small Red	150.00	450.00	2,200.00

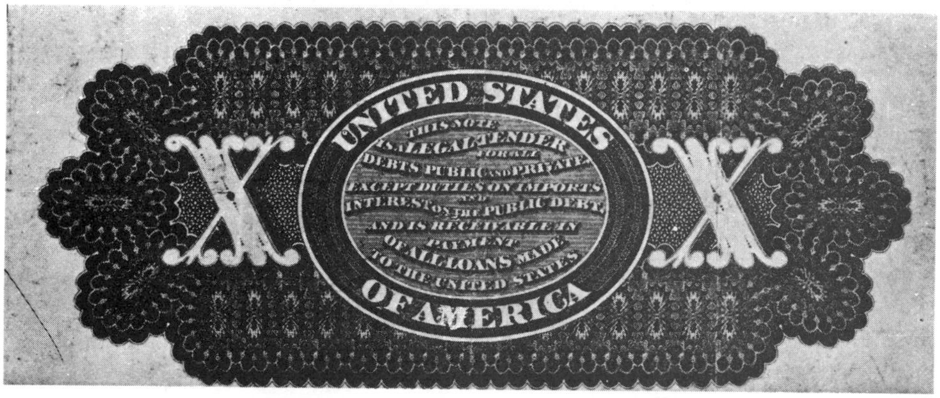

DESIGN NO. 14-a.

(Notes 94-95a)

Obverse is similar to Design No. 2, but Treasury Seal has been added and "On Demand" removed. The reverse shown is the Second Obligation.

This illustration by courtesy of Mr. Louis Werner.

No.	Act	Signatures		Seal	Very Good	Very Fine	Unc
94.	1862	Chittenden	Spinner	Small Red	175.00	425.00	1,600.00
95.	1863	Chittenden	Spinner	Small Red			
		National Bank Note Co. on lower border			125.00	400.00	1,400.00
95a.	1863	Chittenden	Spinner	Small Red, One Serial No.			
		American Bank Note Co. on lower border			150.00	425.00	1,750.00
95b.	1863	Chittenden	Spinner	Small Red, Two Serial Nos.			
		American Bank Note Co. on lower border			125.00	375.00	1,350.00

DESIGN NO. 15

(Note 96)

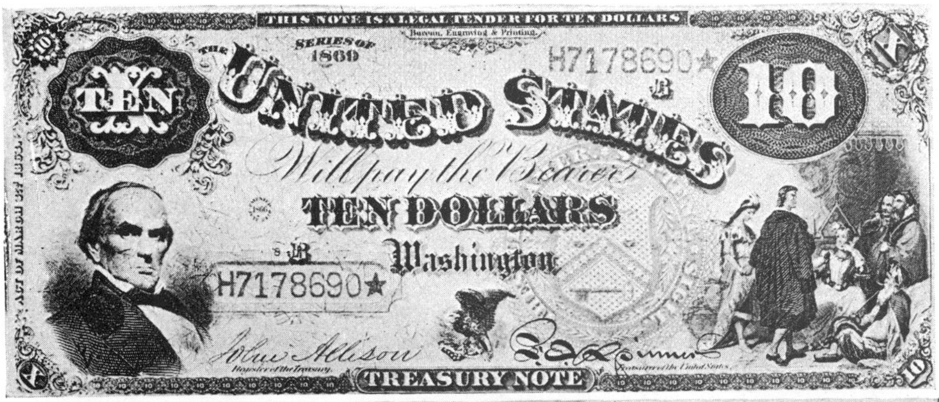

Head of Daniel Webster, U.S. Congressman and Senator; Secretary of State in 1841 and from 1850-1852. Engraved by Alfred Sealey. At the right, Indian Princess Pocahontas being presented to England's royal court. This is the first "Jackass" note, so called because the eagle on bottom of note looks like the head of a jackass when the note is held upside down. All notes from 96-113 are the so-called "Jackass" notes.

Reverse of Design No. 15.

No.	Act	Signatures		Seal	Very Good	Very Fine	Unc
96.	1869	Allison	Spinner	Large Red	160.00	450.00	1,900.00

DESIGN NO. 16

(Notes 97-113)

Vignettes similar to Design No. 15.
Because of color, seal placement or embellishments, there are several distinct types of this design, as follows:
16a. Notes 97-99
16b. Notes 100-102
16c. Notes 103-113

Reverse of Design No. 16.

16a. Red "TEN" in red ornamental design at right center; seal at left.

No.	Series	Signatures		Seal	Very Good	Very Fine	Unc
97.	1875	Allison	New	Small Red with rays	**135.00**	**350.00**	**2,000.00**
98.		Same as above but Series A			**150.00**	**350.00**	**2,100.00**
99.	1878	Allison	Gilfillan	Small Red with rays	**150.00**	**375.00**	**2,250.00**
		16b. Large seal replaces the red "TEN"; red serial numbers.					
100.	1880	Scofield	Gilfillan	Large Brown	**110.00**	**200.00**	**1,100.00**
101.	1880	Bruce	Gilfillan	Large Brown	**110.00**	**200.00**	**1,100.00**
102.	1880	Bruce	Wyman	Large Brown	**110.00**	**200.00**	**1,100.00**
		16c. Same as above but serial numbers are blue.					
103.	1880	Bruce	Wyman	Large Red, plain	**100.00**	**190.00**	**1,200.00**
104.	1880	Rosecrans	Jordan	Large Red, plain	**110.00**	**190.00**	**1,250.00**
105.	1880	Rosecrans	Hyatt	Large Red, plain	**110.00**	**190.00**	**1,250.00**
106.	1880	Rosecrans	Hyatt	Large Red with spikes	**115.00**	**240.00**	**1,350.00**
107.	1880	Rosecrans	Huston	Large Red with spikes	**120.00**	**270.00**	**1,400.00**
108.	1880	Rosecrans	Huston	Large Brown	**90.00**	**190.00**	**1,200.00**
109.	1880	Rosecrans	Nebeker	Large Brown	**Unique**		
110.	1880	Rosecrans	Nebeker	Small Red, scalloped	**80.00**	**175.00**	**1,000.00**
111.	1880	Tillman	Morgan	Small Red, scalloped	**80.00**	**175.00**	**1,000.00**
112.	1880	Bruce	Roberts	Small Red, scalloped	**80.00**	**175.00**	**1,000.00**
113.	1880	Lyons	Roberts	Small red, scalloped	**80.00**	**175.00**	**950.00**

DESIGN NO. 17

(Notes 114-122)

Bison between the explorers Meriwether Lewis and William Clark.
Black Diamond, the buffalo who appears on this note, also was the model used on the reverse of the Indian Head nickel in 1913.

Reverse of Design No. 17.

Female figure representing Columbia stands between two pillars and two scrolls.

No.	Series	Signatures		Seal	Very Good	Very Fine	Unc
114.	1901	Lyons	Roberts	Small Red, scalloped	100.00	275.00	1,500.00
115.	1901	Lyons	Treat	Small Red, scalloped	100.00	275.00	1,500.00
116.	1901	Vernon	Treat	Small Red, scalloped	100.00	275.00	1,500.00
117.	1901	Vernon	McClung	Small Red, scalloped	100.00	275.00	1,500.00
118.	1901	Napier	McClung	Small Red, scalloped	100.00	275.00	1,500.00
119.	1901	Parker	Burke	Small Red, scalloped	100.00	275.00	1,500.00
120.	1901	Teehee	Burke	Small Red, scalloped	100.00	275.00	1,500.00
121.	1901	Elliott	White	Small Red, scalloped	100.00	275.00	1,500.00
122.	1901	Speelman	White	Small Red, scalloped	100.00	275.00	1,500.00

DESIGN NO. 18

(Note 123)

Head of Andrew Jackson. This was the last large size Ten Dollar note issued prior to the advent of small size currency.

Reverse of Design No. 18.

No.	Series	Signatures		Seal	Very Good	Very Fine	Unc
123.	1923	Speelman	White	Small Red, scalloped	200.00	600.00	2,750.00

20 Dollar Notes

DESIGN NO. 19

(Notes 124-126)

Obverse is similar to Design No. 3, but Treasury Seal has been added and "On Demand" removed. The reverse shown is the Second Obligation.

No.	Act	Signatures		Seal	Very Good	Very Fine	Unc
124.	1862	Chittenden	Spinner	Red	175.00	650.00	3,500.00
		(The above note with the First Obligation on reverse.)					
125.	1862	Chittenden	Spinner	Red	300.00	700.00	3,000.00
126.	1863	Chittenden	Spinner	Red			
	National Bank Note Co. and American Bank Note Co. on lower border				175.00	500.00	2,500.00
126a.	1863	Chittenden	Spinner	Red, One Serial No.			
	American Bank Note Co. on lower border				200.00	550.00	2,750.00
126b.	1863	Chittenden	Spinner	Red, Two Serial Nos.			
	American Bank Note Co. on lower border				175.00	500.00	2,500.00
		(The above notes with the Second Obligation on reverse.)					

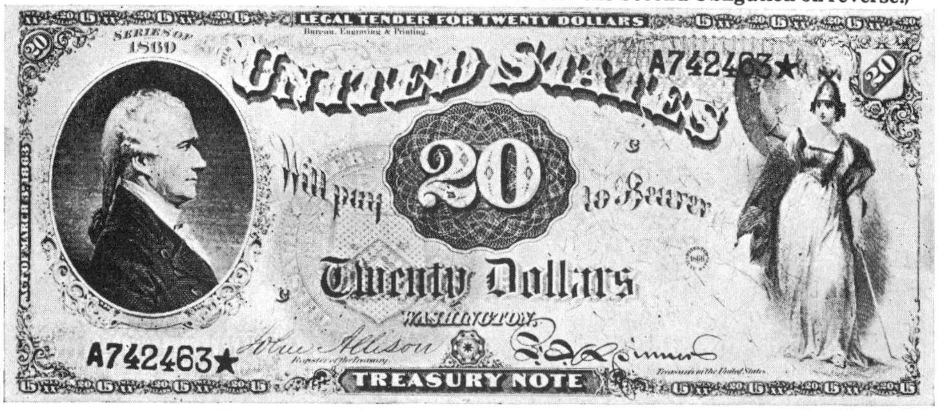

DESIGN NO. 20

(Note 127)

Head of Alexander Hamilton. Victory advancing holding shield and sword.

Reverse of Design No. 20.

The Arabic numeral 20 is repeated 105 times and the Roman Numeral XX appears 103 times in the reverse design.

No.	Act	Signatures		Seal	Very Good	Very Fine	Unc
127.	1869	Allison	Spinner	Large Red	375.00	1,250.00	5,000.00

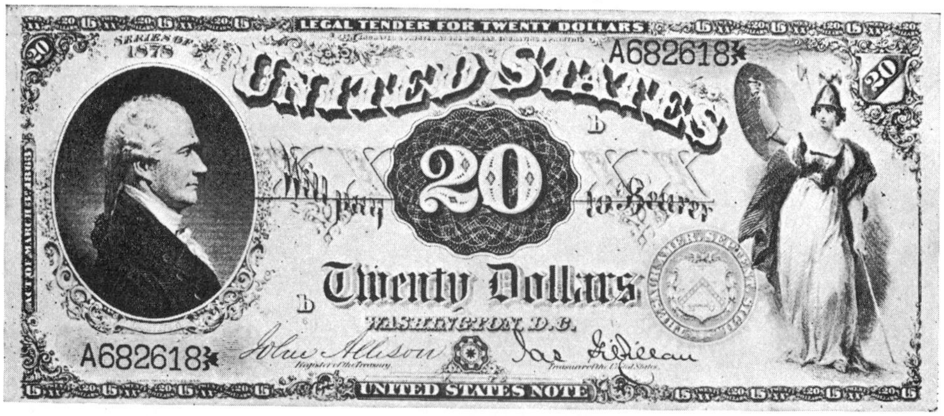

DESIGN NO. 21

(Notes 128-147)

Vignettes similar to Design No. 20. Because of color, seal placement or embellishments, there are several distinct types of this design, as follows:

21a. Notes 128-129
21b. Notes 130-145
21c. Notes 146-147

Reverse of Design No. 21.

No.	Series	Signatures		Seal	Very Good	Very Fine	Unc
		21a. A red "XX" at both right and left center of note.					
128.	1875	Allison	New	Small Red with rays	**175.00**	**425.00**	**2,000.00**
129.	1878	Allison	Gilfillan	Small Red with rays	**•175.00**	**475.00**	**2,200.00**
		21b. The pair of red "XX's" is removed; blue serial numbers.					
130.	1880	Scofield	Gilfillan	Large Brown	**125.00**	**325.00**	**1,700.00**
131.	1880	Bruce	Gilfillan	Large Brown	**125.00**	**325.00**	**1,700.00**
132.	1880	Bruce	Wyman	Large Brown	**110.00**	**275.00**	**1,650.00**
133.	1880	Bruce	Wyman	Large Red, plain	**130.00**	**325.00**	**1,650.00**
134.	1880	Rosecrans	Jordan	Large Red, plain	**135.00**	**325.00**	**1,650.00**
135.	1880	Rosecrans	Hyatt	Large Red, plain	**145.00**	**325.00**	**1,650.00**
136.	1880	Rosecrans	Hyatt	Large Red with spike	**150.00**	**350.00**	**1,750.00**
137.	1880	Rosecrans	Huston	Large Red with spike	**150.00**	**350.00**	**1,750.00**
138.	1880	Rosecrans	Huston	Large Brown	**135.00**	**350.00**	**1,750.00**
139.	1880	Rosecrans	Nebeker	Large Brown	**140.00**	**400.00**	**1,750.00**
140.	1880	Rosecrans	Nebeker	Small Red, scalloped	**90.00**	**240.00**	**1,300.00**
141.	1880	Tillman	Morgan	Small Red, scalloped	**90.00**	**235.00**	**1,300.00**
142.	1880	Bruce	Roberts	Small Red, scalloped	**100.00**	**250.00**	**1,300.00**
143.	1880	Lyons	Roberts	Small Red, scalloped	**90.00**	**240.00**	**1,300.00**
144.	1880	Vernon	Treat	Small Red, scalloped	**100.00**	**300.00**	**1,300.00**
145.	1880	Vernon	McClung	Small Red, scalloped	**100.00**	**300.00**	**1,300.00**
		21c. Same as above, but red serial numbers.					
146.	1880	Teehee	Burke	Small Red, scalloped	**100.00**	**225.00**	**1,000.00**
147.	1880	Elliott	White	Small Red, scalloped	**95.00**	**225.00**	**900.00**

50 Dollar Notes

DESIGN NO. 22

(Notes 148-150)

Head of Alexander Hamilton.

Reverse of Design No. 22.

The Second Obligation is shown.

No.	Act	Signatures		Seal	Very Good	Very Fine	Unc
148.	1862	Chittenden	Spinner	Red	1,250.00	3,500.00	12,000.00
		(The above note with the First Obligation on reverse.)					
149.	1862	Chittenden	Spinner	Red	Unknown		
150.	1863	Chittenden	Spinner	Red			
		National Bank Note Co. on top border			175.00	500.00	2,500.00
150a.	1863	Chittenden	Spinner	Red			
		National Bank Note Co. and American Bank Note Co. on top border			200.00	550.00	2,750.00
		(The above notes with the Second Obligation on reverse.)					

DESIGN NO. 23

(Note 151)

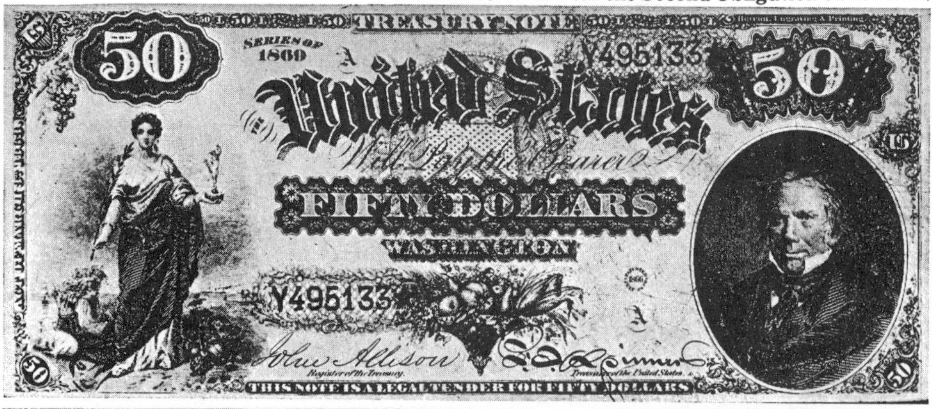

Head of Henry Clay, U.S. Congressman and Senator; Secretary of State from 1825-1829. At the left, a female figure representing Peace, holding a laurel branch and a statue of Mercury.

Reverse of Design No. 23.

This note is extremely rare, as only 24 notes are reported outstanding on U.S. Treasury Books.

No.	Act	Signatures		Seal	Very Good	Very Fine	Unc
151.	1869	Allison	Spinner	Large Red	3,000.00	7,500.00	20,000.00

DESIGN NO. 24

(Notes 152-164)

Head of Benjamin Franklin, 1706-1790, statesman, printer and scientist, and one of the drafters of the Declaration of Independence. Engraved by Charles Burt from the Duplessis portrait. At the right, Liberty dressed as Columbia. Because of color, seal placement or embellishments, there are several distinct types of this design, as follows:

24a. Notes 152-154
24b. Notes 155-164

Reverse of Design No. 24.

24a. A large red "L" is at both right and left center of note.

No.	Series	Signatures		Seal	Very Good	Very Fine	Unc
152.	1874	Spinner	Allison	Small Red with rays	**900.00**	**2,500.00**	**10,000.00**
153.	1875	Wyman	Allison	Small Red with rays	**Rare**		
154.	1878	Gilfillan	Allison	Small Red with rays	**•800.00**	**2,000.00**	**10,000.00**

24b. The two red "L's" are removed.

No.	Series	Signatures		Seal	Very Good	Very Fine	Unc
155.	1880	Gilfillan	Bruce	Large Brown	**500.00**	**1,000.00**	**4,000.00**
156.	1880	Wyman	Bruce	Large Brown	**475.00**	**1,000.00**	**4,000.00**
157.	1880	Jordan	Rosecrans	Large Red, plain	**500.00**	**1,000.00**	**4,000.00**
158.	1880	Hyatt	Rosecrans	Large Red, plain	**Rare**		
159.	1880	Hyatt	Rosecrans	Large Red, spiked	**350.00**	**900.00**	**4,000.00**
160.	1880	Huston	Rosecrans	Large Red, spiked	**350.00**	**900.00**	**4,000.00**
161.	1880	Huston	Rosecrans	Large Brown	**325.00**	**900.00**	**4,000.00**
162.	1880	Tillman	Morgan	Small Red, scalloped	**250.00**	**900.00**	**3,750.00**
163.	1880	Bruce	Roberts	Small Red, scalloped	**Rare**		
164.	1880	Lyons	Roberts	Small Red, scalloped	**250.00**	**750.00**	**3,250.00**

100 Dollar Notes

DESIGN NO. 25

(Notes 165-167)

Large American eagle. This was the first note to feature the American eagle.

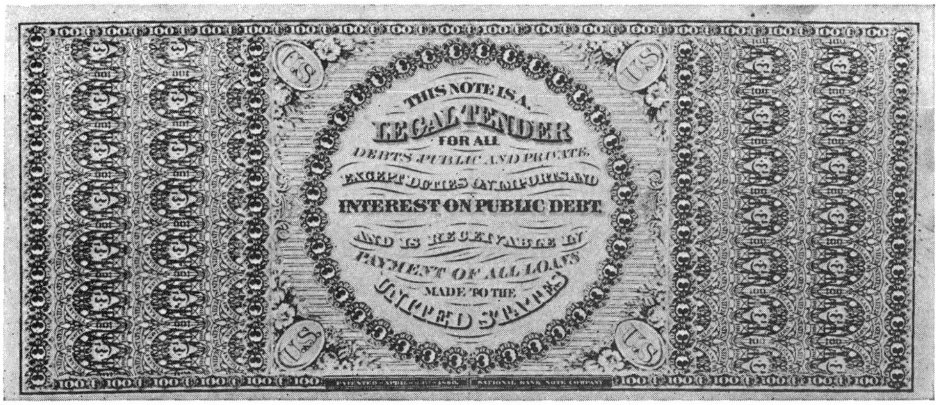

Reverse of Design No. 25.

The Second Obligation is shown.

Act of 1862, with signatures of Chittenden and Spinner and with red seal.

No.					Very Good	Very Fine	Unc
165.	American Bank Note Co. monogram in upper left				2,000.00	5,000.00	15,000.00
165a.	As above, No ABNCo monogram				2,250.00	5,500.00	17,500.00
	(The above notes with the First Obligation on reverse.)						
166.	1862	Chittenden	Spinner	Red	Unknown		
167.	1863	Chittenden	Spinner	Red, One Serial No.			
		National Bank Note Co. and American Bank Note Co. at top			2,000.00	5,000.00	15,000.00
167a.	1863	Chittenden	Spinner	Red, Two Serial Nos.			
		National Bank Note Co. only at top			2,000.00	5,000.00	15,000.00
	(The above notes with the Second Obligation on reverse.)						

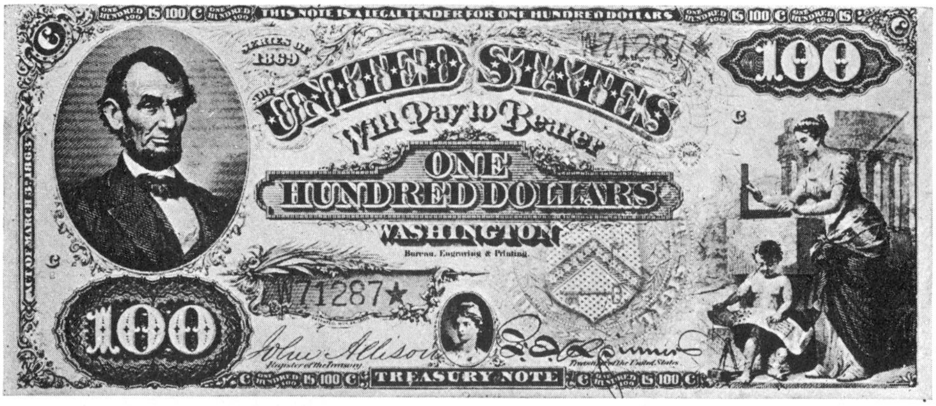

DESIGN NO. 26

(Note 168)

Head of Abraham Lincoln. At the right, an allegory representing Architecture.

Reverse of Design No. 26.

168.	1869	Allison	Spinner	Large Red	4,000.00	8,000.00	25,000.00

DESIGN NO. 27

(Notes 169-182)

Vignettes similar to Design No. 26. Because of color, seal placement or embellishments, there are several distinct types of this design, as follows:

27a. Notes 169-171
27b. Notes 172-182

Reverse of Design No. 27.

No.	Series	Signatures		Seal	Very Good	Very Fine	Unc
				27a. Top central floral design printed in red.			
169.	1875	Allison	New	Small Red with rays (Series A)	2,500.00	7,500.00	25,000.00
170.	1875	Allison	Wyman	Small Red with rays	• 2,500.00	7,000.00	25,000.00
171.	1878	Allison	Gilfillan	Small Red with rays	2,500.00	7,500.00	25,000.00
				27b. Top central floral design printed in black.			
172.	1880	Bruce	Gilfillan	Large Brown	1,200.00	2,500.00	8,000.00
173.	1880	Bruce	Wyman	Large Brown	1,200.00	2,500.00	8,000.00
174.	1880	Rosecrans	Jordan	Large Red, plain	1,200.00	2,500.00	8,000.00
175.	1880	Rosecrans	Hyatt	Large Red, plain	1,200.00	2,500.00	Rare
176.	1880	Rosecrans	Hyatt	Large Red, spiked	1,200.00	2,600.00	8,250.00
177.	1880	Rosecrans	Huston	Large Red, spiked	1,250.00	2,700.00	9,000.00
178.	1880	Rosecrans	Huston	Large Brown	1,200.00	2,600.00	8,250.00
179.	1880	Tillman	Morgan	Small Red, scalloped	1,200.00	2,500.00	8,000.00
180.	1880	Bruce	Roberts	Small Red, scalloped	1,200.00	2,500.00	8,000.00
181.	1880	Lyons	Roberts	Small Red, scalloped	1,200.00	2,500.00	8,000.00
182.	1880	Napier	McClung	Small Red, scalloped	Unknown		

500 Dollar Notes

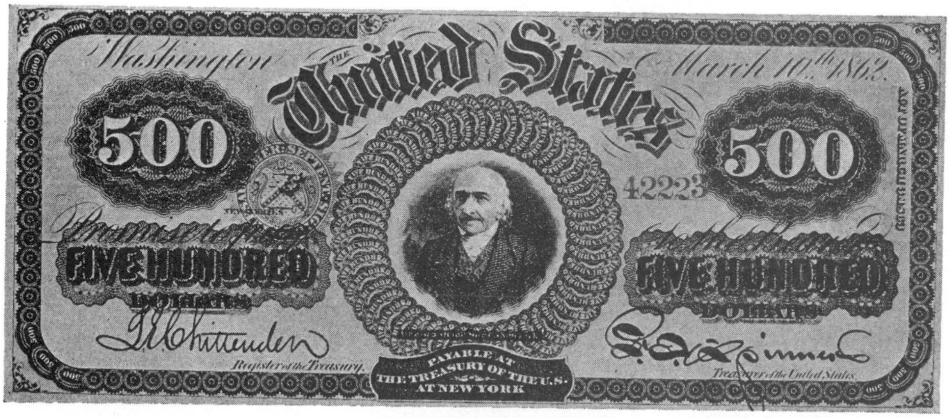

DESIGN NO. 28

(Notes 183a-183c)

Head of Albert Gallatin, Secretary of the Treasury under President Thomas Jefferson, 1801-1813.

Reverse of Design No. 28.

The Second Obligation is shown.

	Act					
183-a.	1862	Chittenden	Spinner	Red	First obligation	**Extremely Rare**
183-b.	1862	Chittenden	Spinner	Red	Second obligation	**Extremely Rare**
183-c.	1863	Chittenden	Spinner	Red	Second obligation, One Serial No.	**Extremely Rare**
183-d.	1863	Chittenden	Spinner	Red	Second obligation, Two Serial Nos.	**Extremely Rare**

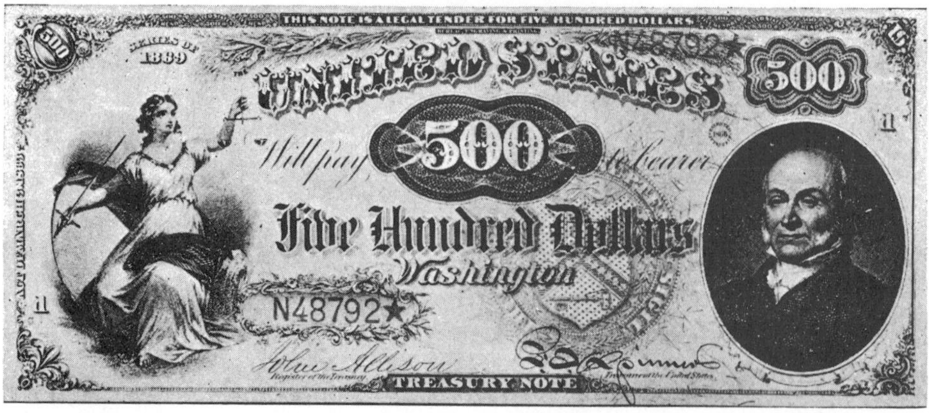

DESIGN NO. 29

(Note 184)

Head of John Quincy Adams, sixth President of the United States, 1825-1829. At the left is Justice seated.

Reverse of Design No. 29.

184.	1869	Allison	Spinner	Large Red	**Extremely Rare**

DESIGN NO. 30

(Notes 185a-185n)

Head of Major General Joseph King Mansfield, killed in action at the Battle of Antietam, 1862. At the left, a female allegory representing Victory.

The series of 1880 is without the two large red "D's" on the obverse, which appear the series of 1874, 1875 and 1878.

Reverse of Design No. 30.

No.	Series	Signatures		Seal	No.	Series	Signatures		Seal
185-a.	1874	Allison	Spinner	Small Red, rays	185-h.	1880	Rosecrans	Hyatt	Large Red, plain
185-b.	1875	Allison	New	Small Red, rays	185-i.	1880	Rosecrans	Huston	Large Red, spiked
185-c.	1875	Allison	Wyman	Small Red, rays	185-j.	1880	Rosecrans	Nebeker	Small Red, scalloped
185-d.	1878	Allison	Gilfillan	Small Red, rays	185-k.	1880	Tillman	Morgan	Small Red, scalloped
185-e.	1880	Scofield	Gilfillan	Large Brown	185-l.	1880	Bruce	Roberts	Small Red, scalloped
185-f.	1880	Bruce	Wyman	Large Brown	185-m.	1880	Lyons	Roberts	Small Red, scalloped
185-g.	1880	Rosecrans	Jordan	Large Red, plain	185-n.	1880	Napier	McClung	Small Red, scalloped

(The above notes are Extremely Rare.)

1,000 Dollar Notes

DESIGN NO. 31

(Notes 186a-186c)

Head of Robert Morris, Superintendent of Finance, 1781-1784. He was a signer of the Declaration of Independence.

Reverse of Design No. 31.

The Second Obligation is shown.

This illustration by courtesy of Mr. Amon G. Carter Jr.

No.	Act	Signatures		Seal		
186-a.	1862	Chittenden	Spinner	Red	First Obligation	**Unknown**
186-b.	1862	Chittenden	Spinner	Red	Second Obligation	**Unknown**
186-c.	1863	Chittenden	Spinner	Red	Second Obligation, One Serial No.	
	American Bank Note Co. at right, National Bank Note Co. at left.					**Extremely Rare**
186-d.	1863	Chittenden	Spinner	Red	Second Obligation, One Serial No.	
		American Bank Note Co. at right only.				**Extremely Rare**
186-e.	1863	Chittenden	Spinner	Red	Second Obligation, Two Serial Nos.	
		American Bank Note Co. at right only.				**Unique**

DESIGN NO. 31-a.

(Note 186d)

Head of De Witt Clinton, 1769-1828, Governor of New York, Mayor of New York City, U.S. Senator.

The seated figure is that of Christopher Columbus.

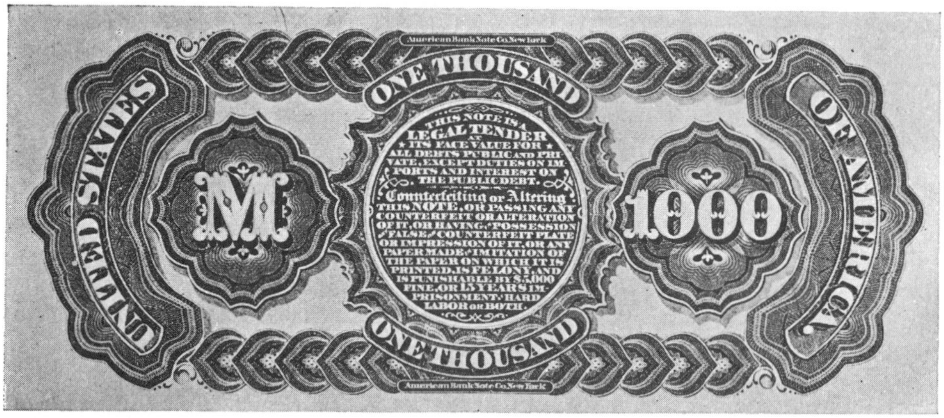

Reverse of Design No. 31-a.

186-d. 1869 Allison Spinner Large Red **Extremely Rare**

DESIGN NO. 32

(Notes 187a-187l)

Vignettes similar to Design No. 31-a.

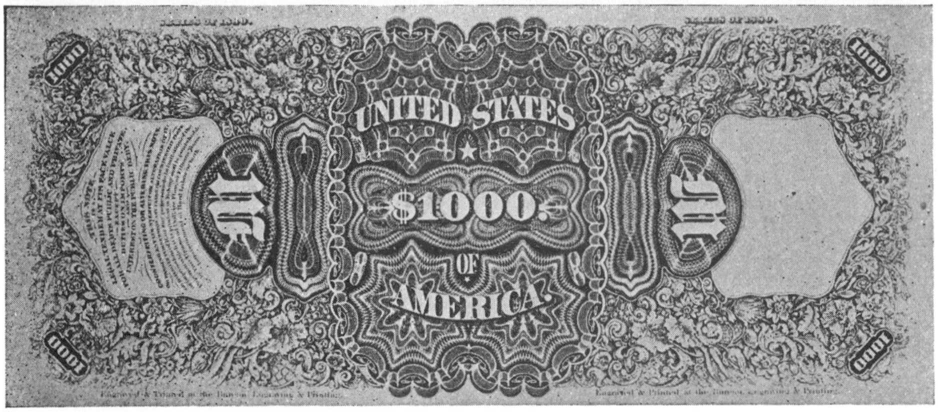

Reverse of Design No. 32.

No.	Series	Signatures		Seal	No.	Series	Signatures		Seal
187-a.	1878	Allison	Gilfillan	Small Red, rays	**187-g.**	1880	Tillman	Morgan	Small Red, scalloped
187-b.	1880	Bruce	Wyman	Large Brown	**187-h.**	1880	Tillman	Roberts	Small Red, scalloped
187-c.	1880	Rosecrans	Jordan	Large Red, plain	**187-i.**	1880	Bruce	Roberts	Small Red, scalloped
187-d.	1880	Rosecrans	Hyatt	Large Red, spiked	**187-j.**	1880	Lyons	Roberts	Small Red, scalloped
187-e.	1880	Rosecrans	Huston	Large Red, spiked	**187-k.**	1880	Vernon	Treat	Small Red, scalloped
187-f.	1880	Rosecrans	Nebeker	Large Brown	**187-l.**	1880	Napier	McClung	Small Red, scalloped

(The above notes are Extremely Rare.)

5,000 Dollar Notes

DESIGN NO. 33

(Note 188)

Head of James Madison, fourth President of the United States, 1809-1813.

Reverse of Design No. 33.

No.	Series	Signatures		Seal
188.	1878	Scofield	Gilfillan	Large Brown

(All specimens of this issue have been redeemed and none is outstanding. The illustration is of a non-negotiable note furnished the Chinese Government by the Treasury Department.)

10,000 Dollar Notes

DESIGN NO. 34

(Note 189)

Head of Andrew Jackson.

Reverse of Design No. 34.

189.	1878	Scofield	Gilfillan	Large Brown

(All specimens of this issue have been redeemed and none is outstanding. The illustration is of a sample note and was furnished by courtesy of the Bureau of Engraving and Printing.)

III. COMPOUND INTEREST TREASURY NOTES

These notes are really Legal Tender circulating notes, which for a period of three years, bore interest at six per cent, that was compounded twice a year. The Acts of Congress of March 3, 1863 and June 30, 1864 authorized the issue by the Treasury Department of these notes. It will be noted that the time of issue was late in the Civil War when the financial position of the Treasury was precarious and the country was almost bankrupt because of the cost of carrying on the war.

Money was very rare and the issue of these Compound Interest Treasury Notes was an attempt to alleviate this pressing problem.

They were issued in denominations of 10, 20, 50, 100, 500 and 1,000 Dollars, and were legal tender at their face value. The date of issue is printed in red on each note and the full interest was payable only at the end of the three year period after date of issue.

The reverse of each denomination shows in tabular form what the interest and redemption value was at the end of each six month period for the three years. For the redemption value of each denomination, please see the text.

The obverse of each note is surcharged in large gold letters with "Compound Interest Treasury Note" and the numerals of the denomination.

All notes of this issue are very rare today and are seldom seen. The 50 and 100 Dollar notes are of extraordinary rarity. Also, all denominations are extremely rare in really choice condition.

The obligation on these Compound Interest Treasury Notes is as follows, "Three years after date the United States will pay the bearer . . . . . . dollars with interest at the rate of six per cent compounded semi-annually . . . By Act of Congress, this note is a legal tender for . . . . . . dollars but bears interest at six per cent compounded every six months though payable only at maturity as follows . . . This sum $ . . . . . . will be paid the holder for principal and interest at maturity of note three years from date."

All of these notes have a small red treasury seal with spikes and the signatures of either Colby and Spinner or Chittenden and Spinner. The 50 and 100 Dollar notes are of great rarity and have been counterfeited extensively.

10 Dollar Notes

DESIGN NO. 35

(Note 190)

Head of Salmon P. Chase, Secretary of the Treasury under Abraham Lincoln, 1861-1864. At the center, an eagle. At the right, a female allegory representing Peace.

Reverse of Design No. 35.

Redemption value $11.94.

No.	Act of	Overprint Date	Signatures		Very Good	Fine
190.	1863	June 10, 1864	Chittenden	Spinner	**Extremely Rare**	
190-a.	1864	July 15, 1864	Chittenden	Spinner	**Extremely Rare**	
190-b.	1864	Aug. 15-Dec. 15, 1864	Colby	Spinner	**750.00**	**2,000.00**

20 Dollar Notes

DESIGN NO. 36

(Note 191)

Head of Abraham Lincoln. The female allegory at the left represents Victory. At the lower center is a mortar firing.

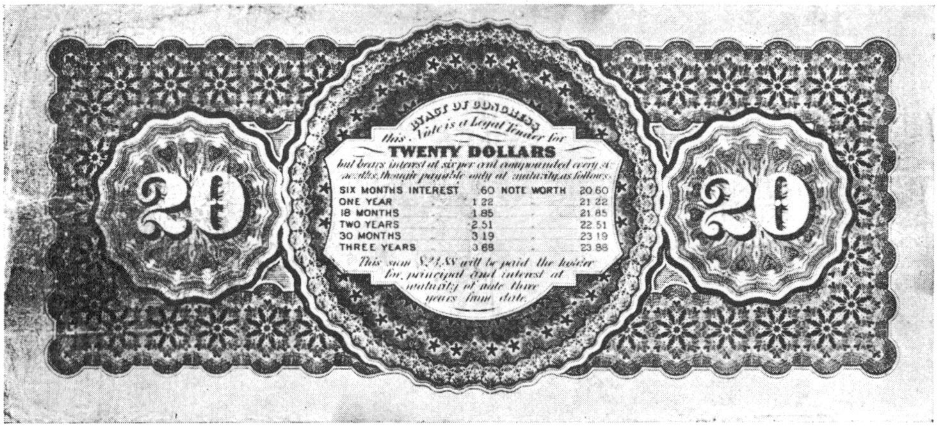

Reverse of Design No. 36.

Redemption value $23.88.

No.	Act of	Overprint Date	Signatures		Very Good	Fine
191.	1864	July 15, 1864	Chittenden	Spinner	**Extremely Rare**	
191-a.	1864	Aug. 15, 1864-Oct. 16, 1865	Colby	Spinner	**1,250.00**	**3,000.00**

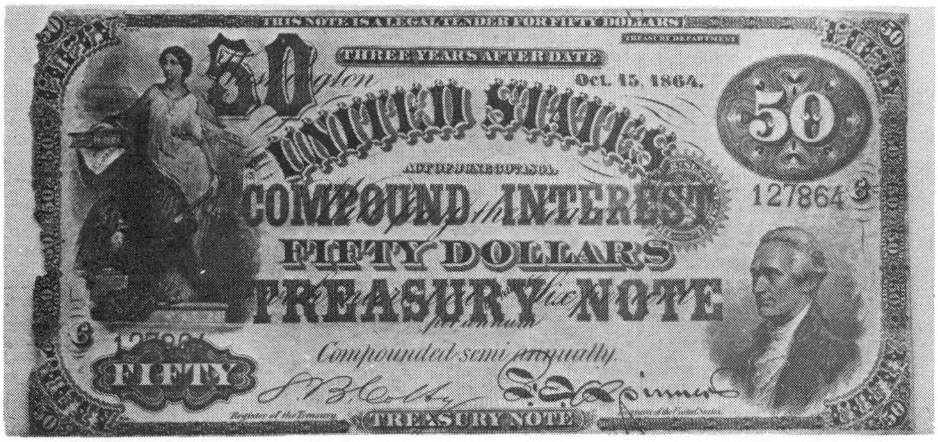

50 Dollar Notes

DESIGN NO. 37

(Note 192)

Head of Alexander Hamilton. At the left is a female allegory representing Loyalty.

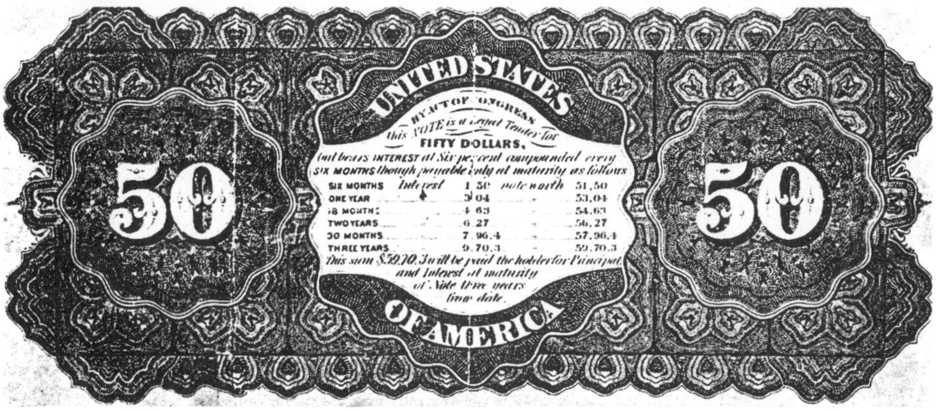

Reverse of Design No. 37.

Redemption value $59.70.

192.	1863	June 10, 1864	Chittenden	Spinner		**Unique**
192-a.	1864	July 15, 1864	Chittenden	Spinner		**Unknown**
192-b.	1864	Aug. 15, 1864-Sept. 1, 1865	Colby	Spinner	**4,000.00**	**Rare**

100 Dollar Notes

DESIGN NO. 38

(Note 193)

Standing figure of George Washington between female allegories representing The Guardian, at the left, and Justice.

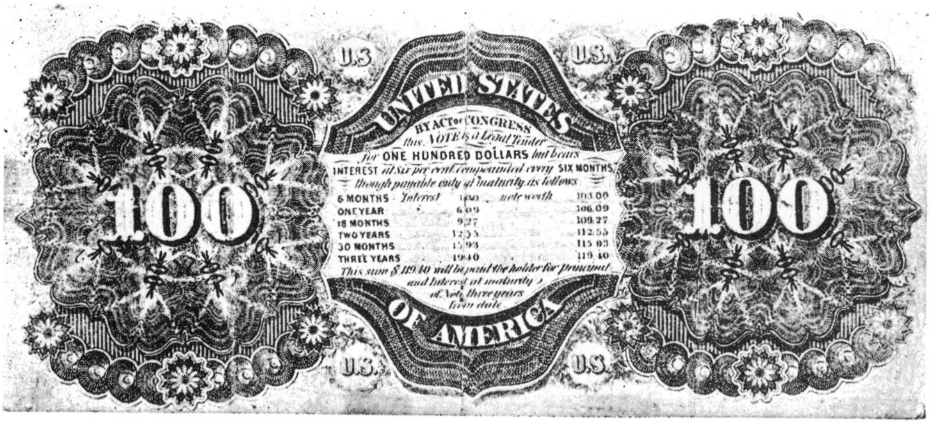

Reverse of Design No. 38.

Redemption value $119.40.

No.	Act of	Overprint Date	Signatures		Very Good	Fine
193.	1863	June 10, 1864	Chittenden	Spinner	**8,000.00**	**Rare**
193-a.	1864	July 15, 1864	Chittenden	Spinner		**Unknown**
193-b.	1864	Aug. 15, 1864-Sept. 1, 1865	Colby	Spinner		**Extremely Rare**

500 Dollar Notes

DESIGN NO. 39
(Notes 194-194-b)
Vignettes of the ship New Ironsides and The Standard Bearer.
Redemption value $597.03

No.	Act of	Overprint Date	Signatures		
194.	1863	June 10, 1864	Chittenden	Spinner	**Unknown**
194-a.	1864	July 15, 1864	Chittenden	Spinner	**Unknown**
194-b.	1864	Aug. 15, 1864-Oct. 1, 1865	Colby	Spinner	**Unknown**

1,000 Dollar Notes

DESIGN NO. 40
(Notes 195-195-a).
Vignettes of Liberty and Justice.
Redemption value $1,194.06

No.	Act of	Overprint Date	Signatures		
195.	1864	July 15, 1864	Chittenden	Spinner	**Unknown**
195-a.	1864	Aug. 15, 1864-Sept. 15, 1865	Colby	Spinner	**Unknown**

IV. INTEREST BEARING NOTES

The Interest Bearing Notes are the rarest of all issues of American currency. Even advanced collectors after many years of ardent search will not have had the pleasure of seeing one of these notes. Such rarity is only natural for these notes, and applies as well to all three types of American currency which bore interest, the Compound Interest Treasury Notes, the Refunding Certificates and these Interest Bearing Notes. When one considers the perilous state of the nation in those years, the scarcity of money and the general fear, it was a rare person indeed, one either supremely confident or sublimely ignorant, who did not turn in his interest bearing money the moment the interest became payable. That is why so few of these exist today and why so many of the higher values are completely unknown.

Like the Compound Interest Treasury Notes, the Interest Bearing issues were authorized by Congress because of the many financial emergencies during the Civil War years.

There are three separate issues of these notes, the One Year, Two Year and Three Year notes which indicate the length of time for which the interest was computed.

The One Year Notes bore interest at five per cent for one year. They were issued under the Act of Congress of March 3, 1863. The interest became payable to bearer at the end of the year upon presentation of the notes for redemption. They were issued in seven denominations from 10 to 5,000 Dollars. Please see the text for fuller descriptions.

The Two Year Notes bore interest at five per cent for two years. They were also issued under the Act of Congress of March 3, 1863. There were only four denominations of these notes from 50 to 1,000 Dollars. In this case, the interest became payable at the end of two years.

There are three known separate issues of the Three Year Notes. All of these bore interest at 7-3/10 per cent for a period of three years. The three Acts of Congress which authorized these issues are of July 17, 1861, June 30, 1864 and March 3, 1865. This interest of 7-3/10 per cent is the highest ever paid by the Government on its notes. The Three Year Notes were issued in five denominations from 50 to 5,000 Dollars.

The interest earned on these notes per day is actually stated on the notes. The 50 Dollar note has the clause "Interest one cent per day," the 100 Dollar note, "Two cents per day" and so on for the other denominations.

All Three Year Notes were made payable to order, and there is a line on the obverse for a name, and another line on the reverse for the endorsement of the payee. See Notes 207-212 in the text.

These notes are also distinguished by a feature unique in United States paper money. When first issued to the public, all Three Year Notes had five coupons attached, each coupon bearing the interest for a six month period. At the end of a six month period, one coupon could be detached and the interest on it collected. In this instance, the notes are like bonds. However, since they are Three Year Notes, there should have been six coupons, not five, and therefore the interest for the final six month period was payable only on presentation of the note itself. This method of payment is so stated on the notes.

For example, the full interest on a 100 Dollar Note was 21.90. Each of the five coupons, therefore, had a face value of 3.65 and the final 3.65 was paid when this 100 Dollar note was presented to the Treasury, at which time the holder received 103.65. (See Note 212 in the text.) This partly accounts for the extreme rarity of these notes, since all holders in the past were anxious to collect the interest. The obligations on these various types of Interest Bearing Notes are similar. On the One Year Notes, for example, it reads as follows, "Legal Tender for _____ Dollars. One year after date, the United States will pay to bearer _____ Dollars with interest at five per cent . . . This note is a legal tender at its face value, excluding interest, for all debts public and private except duties on imports and interest on the public debt."

On the Three Year Notes the obligation is "Three years after date, the United States promise to pay to the order of _____ dollars with 7-3/10 per cent interest payable semi-annually in lawful money." (See note 212 for the convertibility clause.)

A. ONE YEAR NOTES. Issued under the Act of March 3, 1863.

The notes of this issue bore interest at 5% for a period of one year.

DESIGN NO. 41

(Note 196)

Head of Salmon P. Chase. At the center is an eagle holding the flag. At the right is a female allegory representing Peace.

Reverse of Design No. 41.

This illustration by courtesy of the Chase National Bank of New York.

			Very Good	Fine
196.	10 Dollar Note. Very Rare (about 5 known).	ABN Co.	**Rare**	**Rare**
196a.	10 Dollar Note. Rare (about 25 known).	BEP	**900.00**	**1,500.00**

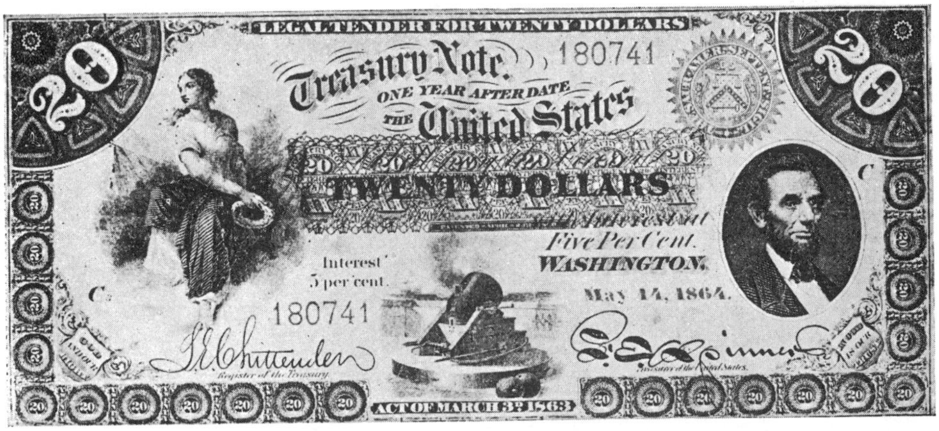

DESIGN NO. 42

(Note 197)

Head of Abraham Lincoln. The female allegory at the left represents Victory. At the lower center is a mortar firing.

Reverse of Design No. 42.

			Very Good	Fine
197.	20 Dollar Note. Very Rare (about 5 known).	ABN Co.	**Rare**	**Rare**
197a.	20 Dollar Note. Rare (about 20 known).	BEP	**1,300.00**	**2,500.00**

DESIGN NO. 43

(Note 198)

Head of Alexander Hamilton. At the left is a female allegory representing Loyalty.

Reverse of Design No. 43.

198. 50 Dollar Note (Three known). **Extremely Rare**

DESIGN NO. 44

(Note 199)

Washington standing between female allegories representing The Guardian, at the left, and Justice.

Reverse of Design No. 44.

This illustration by courtesy of Mr. Amon G. Carter Jr.

199.	100 Dollar Note.	**Extremely Rare**	
200.	500 Dollar Note. The Ship New Ironsides.	**Unknown**	**DESIGN NO. 45**
201.	1,000 Dollar Note. Liberty and Justice.	**Unknown**	**DESIGN NO. 46**
202.	5,000 Dollar Note. Female Allegory.	**Unknown**	**DESIGN NO. 47**

B. TWO YEAR NOTES. Issued under the Act of March 3, 1863.

The notes of this issue bore interest at 5% for a period of two years.

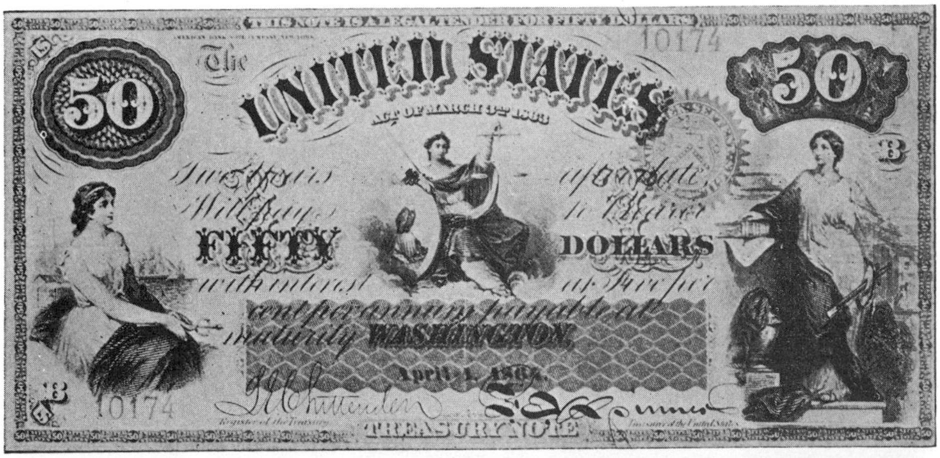

DESIGN NO. 48

(Note 203)

Allegory of three females representing Caduceus, at the left; Justice, center, and Loyalty.

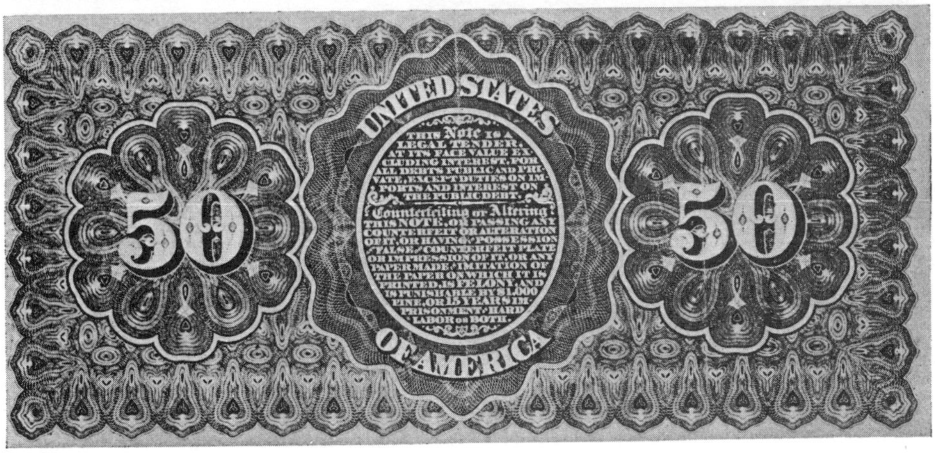

Reverse of Design No. 48.

203.	50 Dollar Note.	**Extremely Rare**

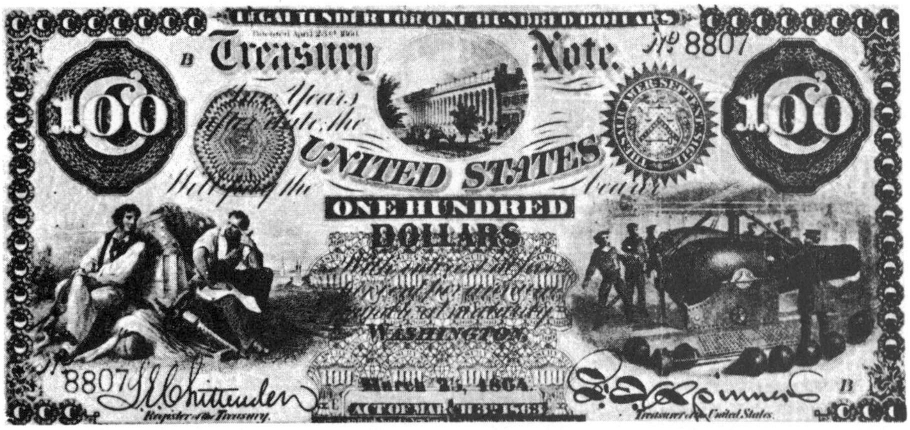

DESIGN NO. 49

(Note 204)

The vignettes show Science and Mechanics, left; the Treasury Building, top center, and Naval Ordnance, right.

Reverse of Design No. 49.

Illustration by courtesy of the Citizens National Bank, Lebanon, Ky.

The Two-Year Interest Bearing Note of 1864 shown above was discovered in 1961. It had previously been unknown in any collection and it was presumed that no specimens were extant.

204.	100 Dollar Note.	**Extremely Rare**	
205.	500 Dollar Note. Liberty and Eagle.	**Unknown**	**DESIGN NO. 50**
206.	1,000 Dollar Note. The Ships Guerriere and Constitution.	**Unknown**	**DESIGN NO. 51**

C. THREE YEAR NOTES. Issued with 5 coupons attached.

The notes of this issue bore interest at 7-3/10% for a period of three years. For an explanation of the coupons, please refer to the introduction of this section.

1. Notes issued under the Act of July 17, 1861.

DESIGN NO. 52

(Note 207)

With minor variations, the obverse is similar to Design No. 57. The reverse is as shown and is of a proof or specimen note. A unique specimen is known of this note with two of the coupons still attached.

207.	50 Dollar Note.	**Extremely Rare**	
208.	100 Dollar Note. Head of General Winfield Scott.	**Unknown**	**DESIGN NO. 53**
209.	500 Dollar Note. Head of George Washington.	**Unknown**	**DESIGN NO. 54**

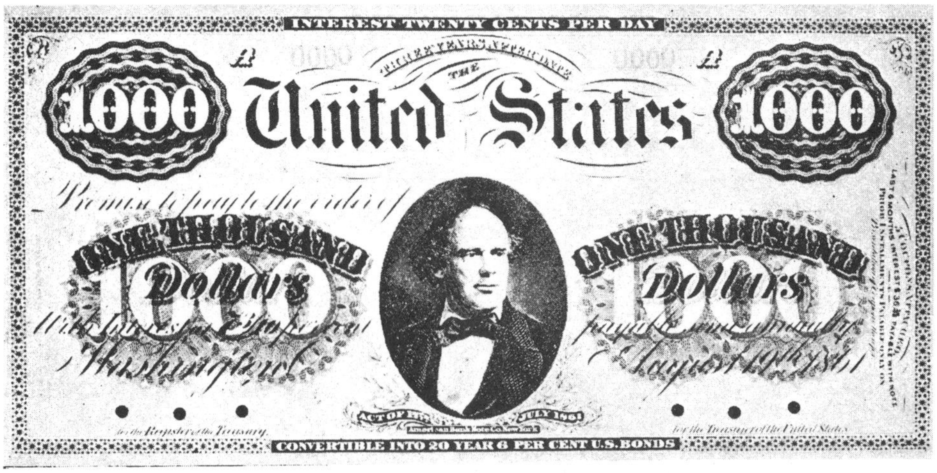

DESIGN NO. 55

(Note 210)

Head of Salmon P. Chase. This illustration is of a proof or specimen note.

Reverse of Design No. 55.

210. 1,000 Dollar Note. **Unknown**

DESIGN NO. 56

(Note 211)

The female allegory at the left represents Justice. At the top center is an Indian female. This illustration is of a proof or specimen note. A specimen to show the reverse of this note was not available.

211. 5,000 Dollar Note. **Unknown**

2. Notes issued under the Act of June 30, 1864.

DESIGN NO. 57

(Note 212)

Large eagle.

Reverse of Design No. 57.

212.	50 Dollar Note (Two known).	**Extremely Rare**
212-a.	100 Dollar Note. Probably issued.	**Unknown**

DESIGN NO. 57a.

DESIGN NO. 57-b.

(Note 212-b)

Head of Alexander Hamilton, top center, between a mortar firing, at the left, and the figure of George Washington.

Reverse of Design No. 57-b.

212-b.	500 Dollar Note.	**Extremely Rare**
212-c.	1,000 Dollar Note. Probably issued.	**Unknown**

DESIGN NO. 57-c.

3. Notes issued under the Act of March 3, 1865.

DESIGN NO. 57-d.
(Note 212-d)

With minor variations this obverse is similar to Design No. 57.

This reverse is similar to Design No. 57, except for the large "50" overprinted in gold ink.

This illustration and that of Design No. 57-e are of notes which are unique. They are the only ones which have survived in their original state of issue, with all 5 coupons still intact. A few other specimens are known of these notes, but some or all of the coupons have been removed.

212-d.	50 Dollar Note.	**Extremely Rare**

DESIGN NO. 57-e.

(Note 212-e.)

Head of General Winfield Scott, general-in-chief of the Army from 1841-1848 and 1855-1861.

Reverse of Design No. 57-e.

212-e.	100 Dollar Note.	**Extremely Rare**
212-f.	500 Dollar Note.	**Extremely Rare**

DESIGN NO. 57-f.

DESIGN NO. 57-g.

(Note 212-g.)

Justice seated. The illustration shows the last of the 5 coupons still attached.

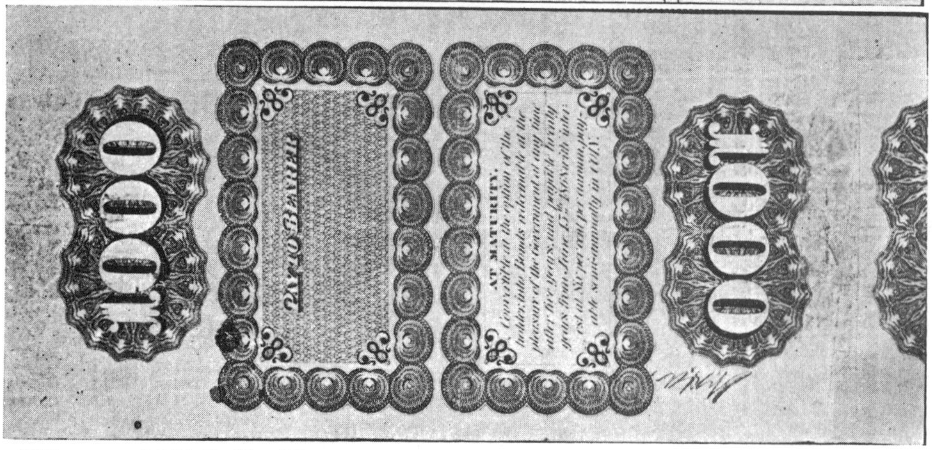

Reverse of Design No. 57-g.

212-g.	1000 Dollar Note.	**Unique**

V. REFUNDING CERTIFICATES

In order to make government securities more popular and more easily within the reach of the average citizen, Congress passed the Act of February 26, 1879.

This Act made it possible for the Treasury to issue to the public the refunding Certificates of 10 Dollar denomination. These certificates bore interest at the rate of four per cent per year and at the time of issue, it was meant for the interest to accrue indefinitely, as no time limit was set. This was the inducement for the public to keep on holding these notes.

However, in 1907, an Act of Congress stopped the interest on these notes as of July 1 of that year. By that time, the interest alone amounted to $11.30 and therefore the redemption value of these notes today is $21.30, more than double the original face value.

There were two types of these Refunding Certificates. On the first type, the name of the purchaser was written in on the obverse on a line provided for that purpose. The reverse of this type is completely different from the second type (see the illustrations in the text) as it consists of an assignment form for conversion of the note into a four per cent bond. This first type is of the highest rarity as only two specimens are reported extant.

The second type is the one usually seen, as is illustrated in the text. (See Design No. 58-b.)

The obligation on this note is as follows, "This certifies that the sum of Ten Dollars has been deposited with the Treasurer of the United States under Act of February 26th, 1879 convertible with accrued interest at 4 per cent per annum into 4 per cent bonds of the United States issued under the Acts of July 14, 1870 and January 20, 1871 upon presentation at the Office of the Treasurer of the U.S. in sums of $50. or multiples thereof."

Dated April 1, 1879 with signatures of Scofield and Gilfillan and bearing interest at 4 per cent.

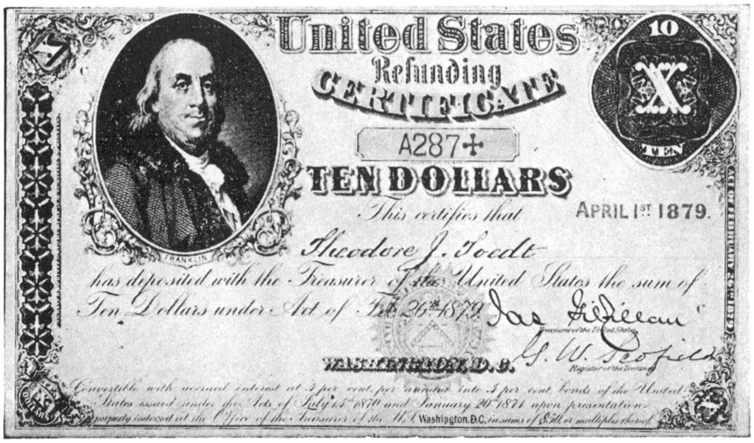

DESIGN NO. 58-a.

(Note 213)

Head of Benjamin Franklin.

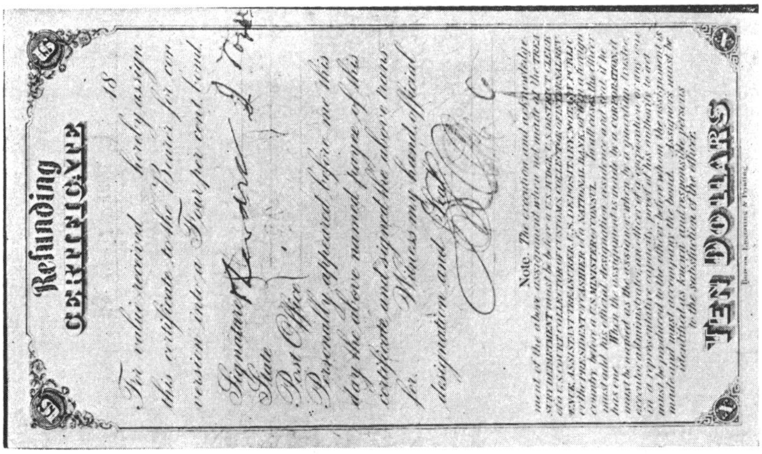

Reverse of Design No. 58-a.

213. 10 Dollar Note. Payable to order. **Extremely Rare**

DESIGN NO. 58-b.

(Note 214)

Head of Benjamin Franklin.

Reverse of Design No. 58-b.

214.	10 Dollar Note. Payable to bearer.	**Fine**	**950.00**

VI. SILVER CERTIFICATES

Like the Legal Tender Notes, the Silver Certificates are extensive and offer many varieties of design and subject matter.

Two Acts of Congress authorized all the Silver Certificates that were issued, the Acts of February 28, 1878 and August 4, 1886. Under these Acts, there were five different issues, as follows:

The first issue consisted of notes from 10 to 1,000 Dollars of the series of 1878 and 1880. These notes are particularly attractive because the reverses are black in color and do not look like conventional paper money. These notes are difficult to find in new condition. They are called on the obverse "Certificate of Deposit," which term does not appear on the later issues.

The obligation on this first issue is as follows, "This certifies that there have been deposited with the Treasurer of the U.S. at Washington, D.C. payable at his office to the bearer on demand ______ silver Dollars ... This certificate is receivable for customs, taxes and all public dues and when so received may be reissued."

All the notes of the 1878 series are countersigned by various Assistant Treasurers at New York, Washington and San Francisco in order to denote that silver had been deposited at their offices in these cities.

The second issue of Silver Certificates consisted of notes from 1 to 1,000 Dollars of the series of 1886, 1891 and 1908. The notes of the 1886 series are quite popular because of the attractive reverses which are entirely covered with fine, detailed lathe work. Please refer to the text for which denominations exist in any given series.

The third issue consisted only of 1, 2 and 5 Dollar notes of the series of 1896. These notes comprise the famous and ever popular Educational Set. These notes are both the most historical and most artistically designed of all issues of our currency.

The fourth issue consisted only of 1, 2 and 5 Dollar notes of the series of 1899. This issue is notable for the many signature combinations that appear on the notes.

The fifth issue consisted only of 1 and 5 Dollar notes of the series of 1923.

The obligation on the notes of the last four issues is as follows, "This certifies that there have been deposited in the Treasury of the United States (of America) ______ silver Dollars payable to the bearer on demand ... This certificate is receivable for customs, taxes and all public dues and when so received may be reissued."

1 Dollar Notes

DESIGN NO. 59

(Notes 215-221)

Head of Martha Washington, wife of George Washington. Engraved by Charles Burt from the Jalabert painting.

Reverse of Design No. 59.

Ornate floral design.

No.	Series	Signatures		Seal	Very Good	Very Fine	Unc
215.	1886	Rosecrans	Jordan	Small Red, plain	•65.00	175.00	1,000.00
216.	1886	Rosecrans	Hyatt	Small Red, plain	65.00	175.00	1,000.00
217.	1886	Rosecrans	Hyatt	Large Red	65.00	175.00	1,000.00
218.	1886	Rosecrans	Huston	Large Red	65.00	175.00	1,000.00
219.	1886	Rosecrans	Huston	Large Brown	70.00	195.00	1,000.00
220.	1886	Rosecrans	Nebeker	Large Brown	70.00	195.00	1,000.00
221.	1886	Rosecrans	Nebeker	Small red, scalloped	75.00	250.00	1,200.00

DESIGN NO. 60

(Notes 222-223)
The obverse is similar to Design No. 59.
The reverse is as shown.

No.	Series	Signatures		Seal	Very Good	Very Fine	Unc
222.	1891	Rosecrans	Nebeker	Small Red, scalloped	55.00	150.00	900.00
223.	1891	Tillman	Morgan	Small Red, scalloped	50.00	140.00	900.00

DESIGN NO. 61

(Notes 224-225)

This is the famous Educational Note, designed by Will H. Low and engraved by Charles Schlecht. History instructing youth: to right, the Constitution; in background, the Washington Monument and the Capitol; around the borders, the names of great Americans in wreaths.

Reverse of Design No. 61.

Heads of George and Martha Washington. Thomas F. Morris designed the reverse from a portrait of Martha Washington, engraved by Charles Burt in 1878, and a portrait of George Washington, engraved in 1867 by Alfred Sealey.

No.	Series	Signatures		Seal	Very Good	Very Fine	Unc
224.	1896	Tillman	Morgan	Small Red with rays	•75.00	225.00	1,000.00
225.	1896	Bruce	Roberts	Small Red with rays	75.00	225.00	1,000.00

DESIGN NO. 62

Notes 226-236)

Eagle over heads of Presidents Abraham Lincoln and Ulysses S. Grant. Engraved by G.F.C. Smillie.

Reverse of Design No. 62.

No.	Series	Signatures		Seal		Very Good	Very Fine	Unc
226.	1899	Lyons	Roberts	Blue	Date above Serial No.	35.00	55.00	200.00
226-a.	1899	Lyons	Roberts	Blue	Date below Serial No.	25.00	55.00	175.00
227.	1899	Lyons	Treat	Blue	Date below Serial No.	25.00	55.00	175.00
228.	1899	Vernon	Treat	Blue	Date below Serial No.	25.00	45.00	165.00
229.	1899	Vernon	McClung	Blue	Date below Serial No.	25.00	45.00	165.00
229-a.	1899	Vernon	McClung	Blue	Date to right of Seal	25.00	42.50	165.00
230.	1899	Napier	McClung	Blue	Date to right of Seal	25.00	45.00	165.00
231.	1899	Napier	Thompson	Blue	Date to right of Seal	100.00	250.00	700.00
232.	1899	Parker	Burke	Blue	Date to right of Seal	25.00	42.50	160.00
233.	1899	Teehee	Burke	Blue	Date to right of Seal	25.00	42.50	160.00
234.	1899	Elliott	Burke	Blue	Date to right of Seal	25.00	42.50	160.00
235.	1899	Elliott	White	Blue	Date to right of Seal	25.00	42.50	160.00
236.	1899	Speelman	White	Blue	Date to right of Seal	22.50	40.00	160.00

DESIGN NO. 63

(Notes 237-239)

Head of George Washington, from the painting by Gilbert C. Stuart. The reverse is similar to Design No. 7.

No.	Series	Signatures		Seal	Very Good	Very Fine	Unc
237.	1923	Speelman	White	Blue	•12.50	25.00	60.00
238.	1923	Woods	White	Blue	13.00	27.50	65.00
239.	1923	Woods	Tate	Blue	25.00	85.00	300.00

2 Dollar Notes

DESIGN NO. 64

(Notes 240-244)

Head of General Winfield Scott Hancock, Union general during the Civil War.

Reverse of Design No. 64.

No.	Series	Signatures		Seal	Very Good	Very Fine	Unc
240.	1886	Rosecrans	Jordan	Small Red	85.00	225.00	1,300.00
241.	1886	Rosecrans	Hyatt	Small Red	•85.00	225.00	1,300.00
242.	1886	Rosecrans	Hyatt	Large Red	95.00	250.00	1,300.00
243.	1886	Rosecrans	Huston	Large Red	100.00	275.00	1,450.00
244.	1886	Rosecrans	Huston	Large Brown	100.00	300.00	1,450.00

DESIGN NO. 65

(Notes 245-246)

Head of William Windom, Secretary of the Treasury 1881-1884 and 1889-1891.

Reverse of Design No. 65.

No.	Series	Signatures		Seal	Very Good	Very Fine	Unc
245.	1891	Rosecrans	Nebeker	Small Red	110.00	300.00	2,200.00
246.	1891	Tillman	Morgan	Small Red	•100.00	275.00	2,200.00

DESIGN NO. 66

(Notes 247-248)

The Second Note of the Educational Series, engraved by Charles Schlecht and G.F.C. Smillie after designs by Edwin H. Blashfield (figures) and Thomas F. Morris (frame, background). Science presenting steam and electricity to commerce and manufacture.

Reverse of Design No. 66.

Heads of inventors Robert Fulton and Samuel F.B. Morse. The portraits are attributed to engraver Lorenzo J. Hatch.

No.	Series	Signatures		Seal	Very Good	Very Fine	Unc
247.	1896	Tillman	Morgan	Small Red	•175.00	450.00	2,500.00
248.	1896	Bruce	Roberts	Small Red	175.00	450.00	2,500.00

DESIGN NO. 67

(Notes 249-258)

Head of George Washington between figures of Mechanics and Agriculture. The engraver was G.F.C. Smillie.

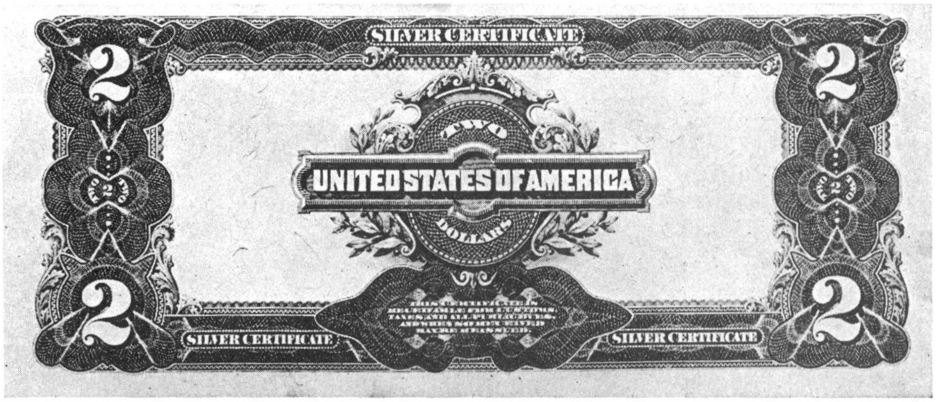

Reverse of Design No. 67.

No.	Series	Signatures		Seal	Very Good	Very Fine	Unc
249.	1899	Lyons	Roberts	Blue	**50.00**	**100.00**	**450.00**
250.	1899	Lyons	Treat	Blue	**50.00**	**100.00**	**450.00**
251.	1899	Vernon	Treat	Blue	**50.00**	**100.00**	**450.00**
252.	1899	Vernon	McClung	Blue	**50.00**	**100.00**	**450.00**
253.	1899	Napier	McClung	Blue	**50.00**	**100.00**	**450.00**
254.	1899	Napier	Thompson	Blue	**95.00**	**375.00**	**1,200.00**
255.	1899	Parker	Burke	Blue	**50.00**	**100.00**	**450.00**
256.	1899	Teehee	Burke	Blue	**50.00**	**100.00**	**450.00**
257.	1899	Elliott	Burke	Blue	**50.00**	**100.00**	**450.00**
258.	1899	Speelman	White	Blue	**50.00**	**100.00**	**450.00**

5 Dollar Notes

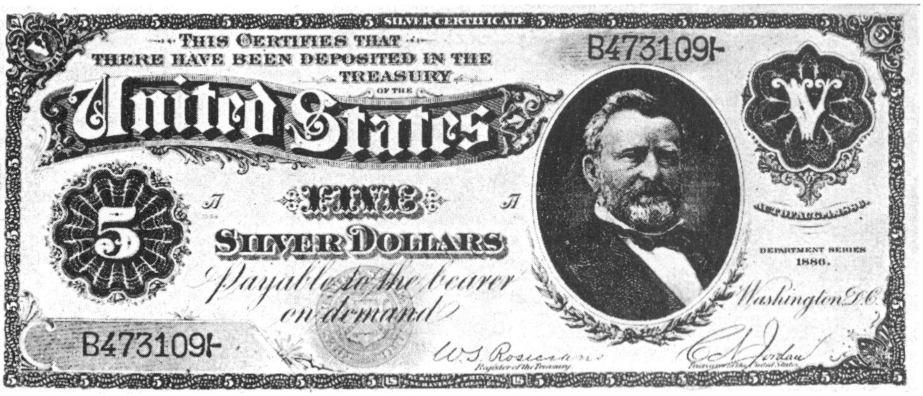

DESIGN NO. 68

(Notes 259-265)

Head of Ulysses S. Grant, 18th President of the United States, 1869-1873. The portrait was engraved by Lorenzo J. Hatch.

Reverse of Design No. 68.

5 Silver Dollars, the central one dated 1886, the same year as this series. Portions of the inscription "In God We Trust" are discernible on four of the coins.

No.	Series	Signatures		Seal	Very Good	Very Fine	Unc
259.	1886	Rosecrans	Jordan	Small Red, plain	•200.00	475.00	3,000.00
260.	1886	Rosecrans	Hyatt	Small Red, plain	200.00	475.00	3,000.00
261.	1886	Rosecrans	Hyatt	Large Red	200.00	475.00	3,000.00
262.	1886	Rosecrans	Huston	Large Red	200.00	475.00	3,000.00
263.	1886	Rosecrans	Huston	Large Brown	200.00	525.00	3,000.00
264.	1886	Rosecrans	Nebeker	Large Brown	200.00	525.00	3,000.00
265.	1886	Rosecrans	Nebeker	Small Red, scalloped	250.00	600.00	3,500.00

DESIGN NO. 69

(Notes 266-267)

The obverse is similar to Design No. 68. The reverse is as shown.

No.	Series	Signatures		Seal	Very Good	Very Fine	Unc
266.	1891	Rosecrans	Nebeker	Small Red, scalloped	100.00	275.00	2,300.00
267.	1891	Tillman	Morgan	Small Red	100.00	275.00	2,300.00

DESIGN NO. 70

(Notes 268-270)

The third and last of the Educational Series. Allegorical group showing electricity as the dominant force in the world. Engraved by G.F.C. Smillie from a painting by Walter Shirlaw, with border elements designed by Thomas F. Morris.

Reverse of Design No. 70.

Heads of Ulysses S. Grant and Philip Sheridan, Union Army generals during the Civil War. The portraits of the generals were engraved by Lorenzo J. Hatch, with the remainder engraved by G.F.C. Smillie; after Thomas F. Morris's design.

No.	Series	Signatures		Seal	Very Good	Very Fine	Unc
268.	1896	Tillman	Morgan	Small Red	250.00	650.00	4,500.00
269.	1896	Bruce	Roberts	Small Red	250.00	650.00	4,500.00
270.	1896	Lyons	Roberts	Small Red	•250.00	700.00	4,500.00

DESIGN NO. 71

(Notes 271-281)

Head of Ta-to-ka-in-yan-ka, also known as Running Antelope, a member of the Oncpapa tribe of Sioux Indians. George F.C. Smillie engraved the portrait. This is the only issue of U.S. paper money for which an Indian was selected as the central feature.

Reverse of Design No. 71.

No.	Series	Signatures		Seal	Very Good	Very Fine	Unc
271.	1899	Lyons	Roberts	Blue	95.00	215.00	1,000.00
272.	1899	Lyons	Treat	Blue	95.00	215.00	1,000.00
273.	1899	Vernon	Treat	Blue	95.00	195.00	1,000.00
274.	1899	Vernon	McClung	Blue	95.00	195.00	1,000.00
275.	1899	Napier	McClung	Blue	95.00	195.00	1,000.00
276.	1899	Napier	Thompson	Blue	120.00	450.00	2,000.00
277.	1899	Parker	Burke	Blue	95.00	195.00	1,000.00
278.	1899	Teehee	Burke	Blue	95.00	195.00	1,000.00
279.	1899	Elliott	Burke	Blue	95.00	195.00	1,000.00
280.	1899	Elliott	White	Blue	•95.00	195.00	1,000.00
281.	1899	Speelman	White	Blue	95.00	195.00	1,000.00

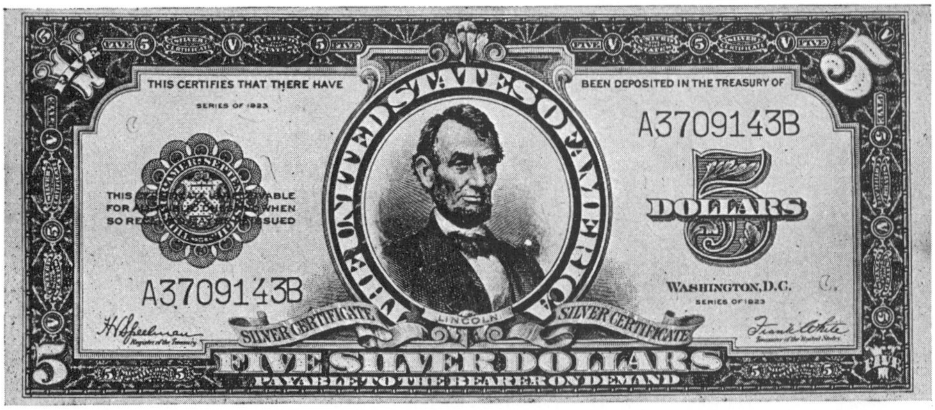

DESIGN NO. 72

(Note 282)

Head of Abraham Lincoln, after the Matthew Brady photograph of February 9, 1864. This note is known as the "porthole" note because of the circular design around Lincoln's head.

Reverse of Design No. 72.

No.	Series	Signatures		Seal	Very Good	Very Fine	Unc
282.	1923	Speelman	White	Blue	**125.00**	**300.00**	**1,400.00**

10 Dollar Notes

DESIGN NO. 73

(Notes 283-286)

Head of Robert Morris, a signer of the Declaration of Independence, and Superintendent of Finance, 1781-1784.

Reverse of Design No. 73.

Printed in brownish black ink.

This illustration by courtesy of Mr. Morris H. Loewenstern.

73. Seal at top of note; large "Ten" underneath.

Countersigned Notes; all with signatures of Scofield and Gilfillan and with large red seal and without the legend, "Series of 1878." All have engraved countersignatures except for the notes starred (*) which are autographed.

No.	Series	Countersigned By	Payable At	Deposited With	Fine
283.	1878	W.G. White	New York	Assistant Treasurer of the U.S.	**Unique**
284.	1878	J.C. Hopper	New York	Assistant Treasurer of the U.S.	**Extremely Rare**
284-a*.	1878	T. Hillhouse	New York	Assistant Treasurer of the U.S.	**Unknown**
284-b.	1878	T. Hillhouse	New York	Assistant Treasurer of the U.S.	**Rare**
284-c*.	1878	R.M. Anthony	San Francisco	Assistant Treasurer of the U.S.	**Unknown**
285*.	1878	A.U. Wyman	Washington, D.C.	Treasurer of the U.S.	**Rare**
285-a.	1878	A.U. Wyman	Washington, D.C.	Treasurer of the U.S.	**Rare**

73a. Seal at top of note; large "X" underneath.

Countersigned Notes; all with signatures of Scofield and Gilfillan and with large brown seal.

No.	Series	Countersigned By	Payable At	Deposited With	Fine
286.	1880	T. Hillhouse	New York	Assistant Treasurer of the U.S.	**5,000.00**
286-a.	1880	A.U. Wyman	Washington, D.C.	Treasurer of the U.S.	**Unknown**

DESIGN NO. 73-a

(Notes 287-290)

The obverse is as shown. With minor variations, the reverse is similar to Design No. 73. There are two distinct types of this design, as follows:
73a. Notes 287-289
73b. Note 290

73b. Seal at top of note; large "X" underneath.

Normal notes without a countersigned signature.

No.	Series	Signatures		Seal	Very Good	Very Fine	Unc
287.	1880	Scofield	Gilfillan	Large Brown	250.00	750.00	4,000.00
288.	1880	Bruce	Gilfillan	Large Brown	•250.00	750.00	4,000.00
289.	1880	Bruce	Wyman	Large Brown	250.00	750.00	4,000.00

73c. Seal in center of note; without the large brown "X".

No.	Series	Signatures		Seal	Very Good	Very Fine	Unc
290.	1880	Bruce	Wyman	Large Red	300.00	1,300.00	5,000.00

DESIGN NO. 74

(Notes 291-297)

Head of Thomas A. Hendricks, Vice President of the United States from March 4, 1885 to November 25, 1885. He died in office. The portrait was engraved by Charles Schlecht.

The So-called "Tombstone Note."

Reverse of Design No. 74.

No.	Series	Signatures		Seal	Very Good	Very Fine	Unc
291.	1886	Rosecrans	Jordan	Small Red, plain	225.00	550.00	3,500.00
292.	1886	Rosecrans	Hyatt	Small Red, plain	225.00	550.00	3,500.00
293.	1886	Rosecrans	Hyatt	Large Red	225.00	550.00	3,500.00
294.	1886	Rosecrans	Huston	Large Red	225.00	550.00	3,500.00
295.	1886	Rosecrans	Huston	Large Brown	225.00	550.00	3,500.00
296.	1886	Rosecrans	Nebeker	Large Brown	225.00	550.00	3,500.00
297.	1886	Rosecrans	Nebeker	Small Red, scalloped	290.00	900.00	4,500.00

DESIGN NO. 75

(Notes 298-304)

The obverse is similar to Design No. 74.
The reverse is as shown.
There are two distinct types of this design, as follows:
75a. Notes 298-301
75b. Notes 302-304

75a. With small plate letter only at left center of obverse.

No.	Series	Signatures		Seal	Very Good	Very Fine	Unc
298.	1891	Rosecrans	Nebeker	Small Red	110.00	275.00	1,000.00
299.	1891	Tillman	Morgan	Small Red	110.00	275.00	1,000.00
300.	1891	Bruce	Roberts	Small Red	110.00	275.00	1,000.00
301.	1891	Lyons	Roberts	Small Red	110.00	275.00	1,000.00

75b. Large blue "X" is added to left center of obverse.

No.	Series	Signatures		Seal	Very Good	Very Fine	Unc
302.	1908	Vernon	Treat	Blue	100.00	250.00	1,750.00
303.	1908	Vernon	McClung	Blue	100.00	250.00	1,750.00
304.	1908	Parker	Burke	Blue	100.00	250.00	1,750.00

20 Dollar Notes

DESIGN NO. 76

(Notes 305-308)

Head of Captain Stephen Decatur, naval hero of the War of 1812.
There are two distinct types of this design, as follows:
Notes 305-307
Note 308

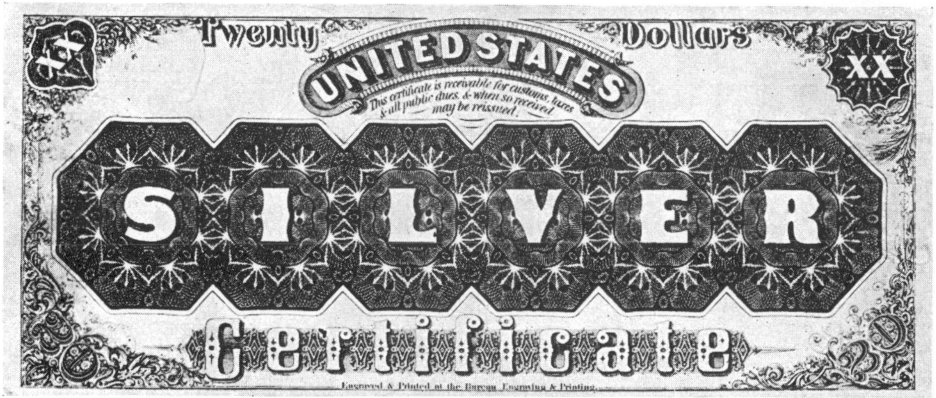

Reverse of Design No. 76.
Printed in brownish black ink.

76. Large seal at top of note, with large "Twenty" below on series of 1878; large "XX" below on Series of 1880.
Countersigned Notes; all with signatures of Scofield and Gilfillan and with large red seal except the 1880 series which has a large brown seal. The 1878 countersigned notes are without the legend, "Series of 1878." All have engraved countersignatures except No. 306-b, which is autographed.*

No.	Series	Countersigned By	Payable At	Deposited With	Fine
305.	1878	J.C. Hopper	New York	Assistant Treasurer of the U.S.	6,500.00
306.	1878	T. Hillhouse	New York	Assistant Treasurer of the U.S.	Extremely Rare
306-a.	1878	R.M. Anthony	San Francisco	Assistant Treasurer of the U.S.	Unknown
306-b*	1878	A.U. Wyman	Washington, D.C.	Treasurer of the U.S.	Extremely Rare
307.	1878	A.U. Wyman	Washington	Treasurer of the U.S.	6,500.00
308.	1880	T. Hillhouse	New York	Assistant Treasurer of the U.S.	• 10,000.00

DESIGN NO. 76-a

(Notes 309-312)

Head of Stephen Decatur. The reverse is similar to Design No. 76. There are two distinct types of this design, as follows:
76a. Notes 309-311
76b. Note 312

76a. Large seal at top of note with large "XX" below.
Normal notes without a countersigned signature.

No.	Series	Signatures		Seal	Very Good	Very Fine	Unc
309.	1880	Scofield	Gilfillan	Large Brown	**400.00**	**1,200.00**	**6,500.00**
310.	1880	Bruce	Gilfillan	Large Brown	**400.00**	**1,200.00**	**6,500.00**
311.	1880	Bruce	Wyman	Large Brown	**•400.00**	**1,200.00**	**6,500.00**

76b. Small seal at bottom of note and without the "XX".

No.	Series	Signatures		Seal	Very Good	Very Fine	Unc
312.	1880	Bruce	Wyman	Small Red	**1,200.00**	**3,500.00**	**12,500.00**

DESIGN NO. 77

(Notes 313-316)

Head of Daniel Manning, Secretary of the Treasury from 1885 to 1887. Lorenzo J. Hatch engraved the portrait. The allegorical figures represent Agriculture and Industry. There are two distinct types of this design, as follows:
77a. Notes 313-315
77b. Note 316

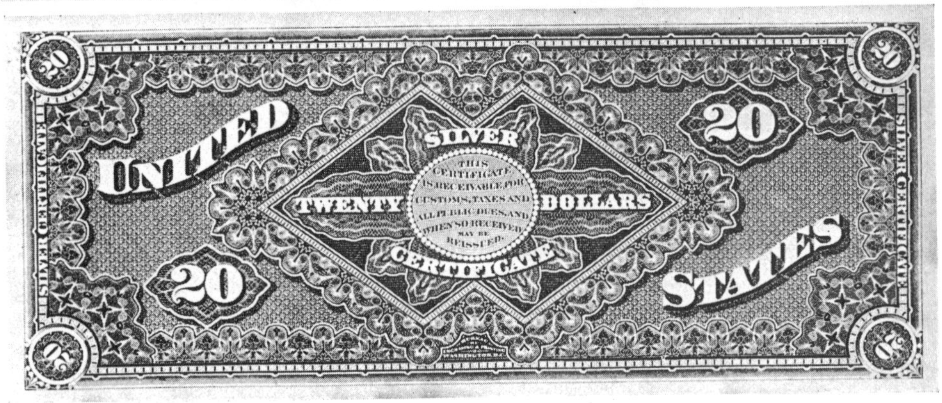

Reverse of Design No. 77.

77a. Large seal at upper left of note.

No.	Series	Signatures		Seal	Very Good	Very Fine	Unc
313.	1886	Rosecrans	Hyatt	Large Red	**•450.00**	**1,000.00**	**7,500.00**
314.	1886	Rosecrans	Huston	Large Brown	**450.00**	**1,000.00**	**7,500.00**
315.	1886	Rosecrans	Nebeker	Large Brown	**450.00**	**1,000.00**	**7,500.00**

77b. Small seal at lower right of note.

No.	Series	Signatures		Seal	Very Good	Very Fine	Unc
316.	1886	Rosecrans	Nebeker	Small Red	**750.00**	**2,500.00**	**11,000.00**

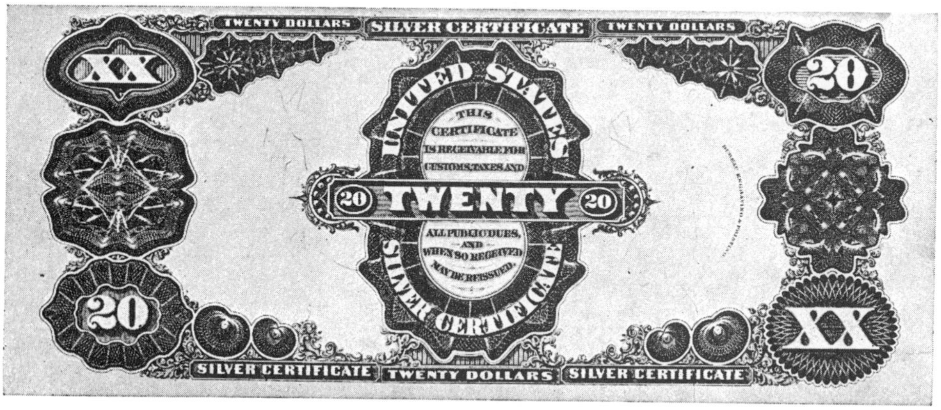

DESIGN NO. 78

(Notes 317-322)

The obverse is similar to Design No. 77. The reverse is as shown. There are two distinct types of this design, as follows:
78a. Notes 317-320
78b. Notes 321-322

No.	Series	Signatures		Seal	Very Good	Very Fine	Unc
	78a. The obverse is similar to Design No. 77b.						
317.	1891	Rosecrans	Nebeker	Small Red	150.00	400.00	3,000.00
318.	1891	Tillman	Morgan	Small Red	150.00	400.00	3,000.00
319.	1891	Bruce	Roberts	Small Red	150.00	400.00	3,000.00
320.	1891	Lyons	Roberts	Small Red	150.00	400.00	3,000.00
	78b. A large blue "XX" has been added to left center of note.						
321.	1891	Parker	Burke	Blue	135.00	375.00	2,750.00
322.	1891	Teehee	Burke	Blue	135.00	375.00	2,750.00

50 Dollar Notes

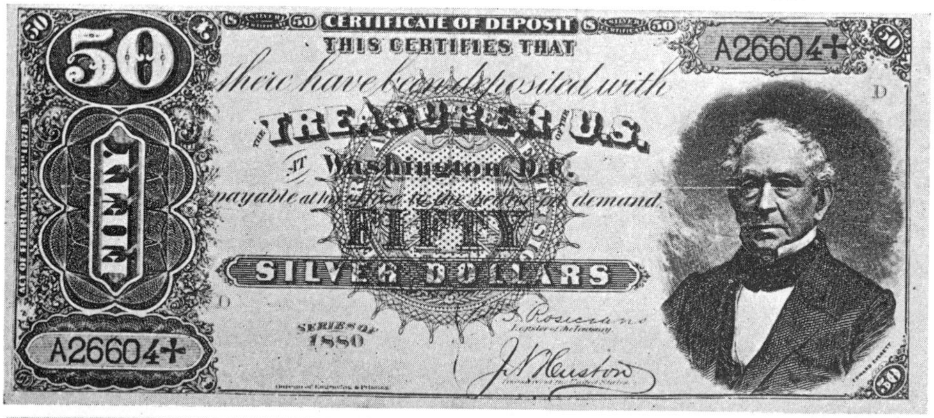

DESIGN NO. 79

(Notes 323-329)

Head of Edward Everett, Secretary of State under President Fillmore in 1852 and 1853. There are three distinct types of this design, as follows:
79a. Notes 323-327
79b. Note 328
79c. Note 329

Reverse of Design No. 79. Printed in brownish black ink.

79a. Large seal at top of note with large "Fifty" below on Series of 1878; large "L" below on Series of 1880.
Countersigned Notes; all three notes with signatures of Scofield and Gilfillan and with large red seal. The 1878 countersigned notes are without the legend, "Series of 1878." All have engraved countersignatures except the notes starred (*) which are autographed.

No.	Series	Countersigned By	Payable At	Fine
323*.	1878	W.G. White or J.C. Hopper	New York	Unknown
324.	1878	T. Hillhouse	New York	Extremely Rare
324-a.	1878	R.M. Anthony	San Francisco	Unique
324-b*.	1878	A.U. Wyman	Washington, D.C.	Unknown
324-c.	1878	A.U. Wyman	Washington, D.C.	Extremely Rare

Normal notes without a countersigned signature.

No.	Series	Signatures		Seal	Fine
325.	1880	Scofield	Gilfillan	Large Brown, rays	**Unique**
326.	1880	Bruce	Gilfillan	Large Brown, rays	**Extremely Rare**
327.	1880	Bruce	Wyman	Large Brown, rays	**Extremely Rare**
79b. Large seal in center of note and without the "L" or "Fifty".					
328.	1880	Rosecrans	Huston	Large Brown, spikes	**7,500.00**
79c. Small seal at right center of note.					
329.	1880	Rosecrans	Nebeker	Small Red	**9,500.00**

DESIGN NO. 80

(Notes 330-335)

Head of Edward Everett.

Reverse of Design No. 80.

No.	Series	Signatures		Seal	Very Good	Very Fine	Unc
330.	1891	Rosecrans	Nebeker	Small Red		**Extremely Rare**	
331.	1891	Tillman	Morgan	Small Red	**350.00**	**1,000.00**	**6,000.00**
332.	1891	Bruce	Roberts	Small Red	**350.00**	**1,000.00**	**6,000.00**
333.	1891	Lyons	Roberts	Small Red	**350.00**	**1,000.00**	**6,000.00**
334.	1891	Vernon	Treat	Small Red	**•350.00**	**1,000.00**	**6,000.00**
335.	1891	Parker	Burke	Blue	**350.00**	**1,000.00**	**6,000.00**

100 Dollar Notes

DESIGN NO. 81

(Notes 336-342)

Head of James Monroe, fifth President of the United States, 1817-1825. There are three distinct types of this design, as follows:

81a. Notes 336-340
81b. Note 341
81c. Note 342

Reverse of Design No. 81.

Printed in brownish black ink.

81a. Large seal at top of note, with large "100" below on Series of 1878; large "C" below on Series of 1880.
Countersigned Notes; all three notes with signatures of Scofield and Gilfillan and with a large red seal. The 1878 countersigned notes are without the legend, "Series of 1878." All have engraved countersignatures except the notes starred (*), which are autographed.

No.	Series	Countersigned By	Payable At	Fine
336.	1878	W.G. White	New York	Unique
336-a.	1878	J.C. Hopper or T. Hillhouse	New York	Unknown
337.*	1878	R.M. Anthony	San Francisco	Unique
337-a.*	1878	A.U. Wyman	Washington, D.C.	Unique
337-b.	1878	A.U. Wyman	Washington, D.C.	Extremely Rare

Normal notes without a countersigned signature.

No.	Series	Signatures		Seal	Fine
338.	1880	Scofield	Gilfillan	Large Brown, rays	Unknown
339.	1880	Bruce	Gilfillan	Large Brown, rays	Extremely Rare
340.	1880	Bruce	Wyman	Large Brown, rays	3,500.00
	81b. Large seal in center of note and without the "C" or "100".				
341.	1880	Rosecrans	Huston	Large Brown, spikes	3,250.00
	81c. Small seal at right bottom of note.				
342.	1880	Rosecrans	Nebeker	Small Red	4,000.00

DESIGN NO. 82

(Notes 343-344)

Head of James Monroe.

Reverse of Design No. 82.

No.	Series	Signatures		Seal	Very Good	Very Fine	Unc
343.	1891	Rosecrans	Nebeker	Small Red	1,800.00	4,500.00	Rare
344.	1891	Tillman	Morgan	Small Red	•1,600.00	4,250.00	Rare

500 Dollar Notes

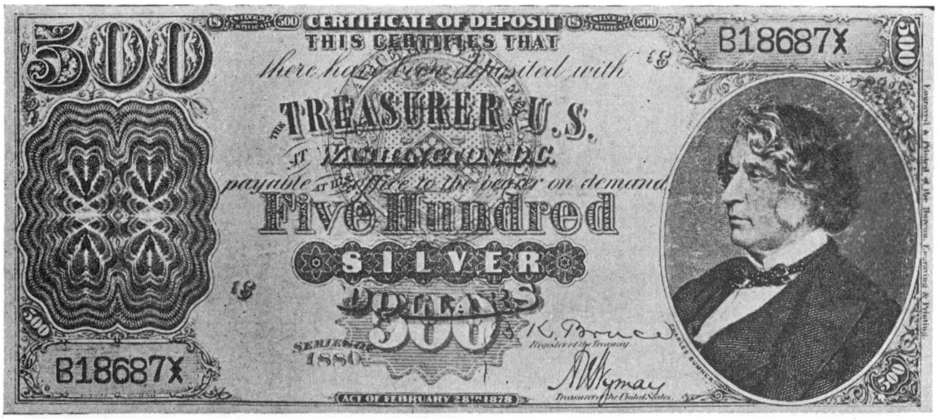

DESIGN NO. 83

(Notes 345-a — 345-d)

Head of Charles Sumner, 1811-1874, U.S. Senator and Statesman.

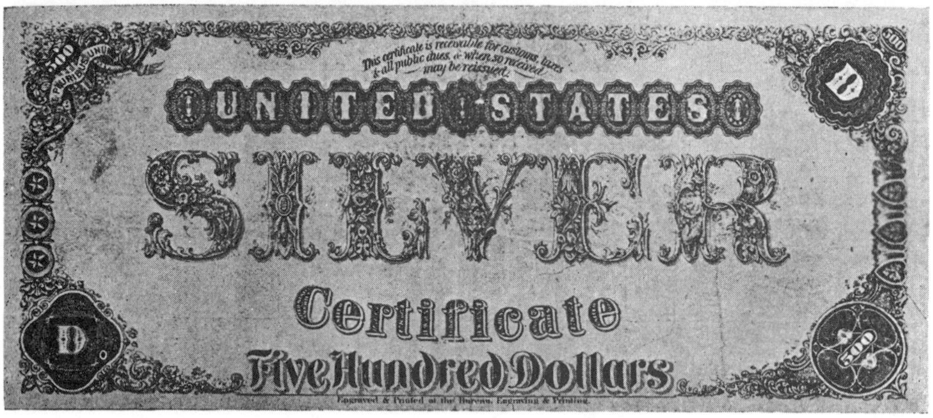

Reverse of Design No. 83.

Only 14 notes of this design are outstanding.

81d. The 1878 countersigned note is without the legend, "Series of 1878."

No.	Series	Signatures		Seal	
345-a.	1878	Scofield	Gilfillan	Large Red, rays (countersigned)	**Unique**
345-b.	1880	Scofield	Gilfillan	Large Brown	**Unknown**
345-c.	1880	Bruce	Gilfillan	Large Brown	**Rare**
345-d.	1880	Bruce	Wyman	Large Brown	**Extremely Rare**

1,000 Dollar Notes

DESIGN NO. 84

(Notes 346-a — 346-d)

Head of William L. Marcy, 1786-1857, Governor of New York, U.S. Senator, Secretary of War under President Polk and Secretary of State under President Pierce.

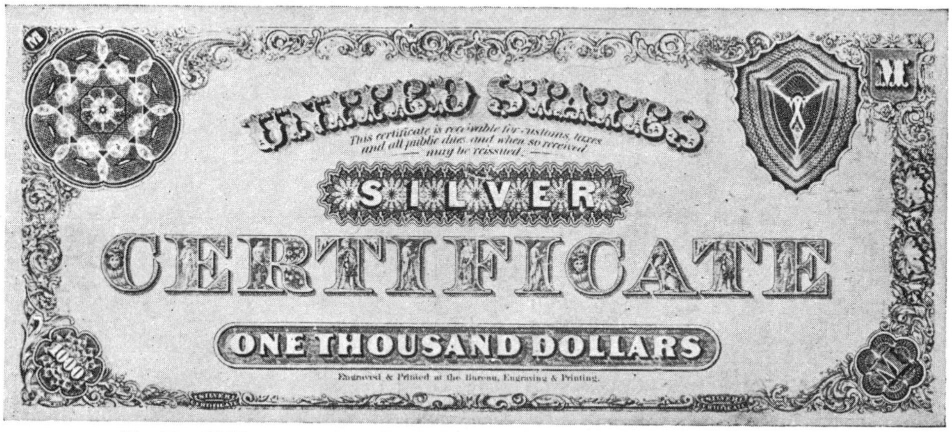

Reverse of Design No. 84.

Only 9 notes are outstanding of this design combined with Design No. 84-a.

81e. The 1878 countersigned note is without the legend, "Series of 1878."

No.	Series	Signatures		Seal	
346-a.	1878	Scofield	Gilfillan	Large Red, Rays (countersigned)	**Unknown**
346-b.	1880	Scofield	Gilfillan	Large Brown	**Unknown**
346-c.	1880	Bruce	Gilfillan	Large Brown	**Unknown**
346-d.	1880	Bruce	Wyman	Large Brown	**Extremely Rare**

DESIGN NO. 84-a

(Note 346-e)

Head of William L. Marcy.

Reverse of Design No. 84-a.

No	Series	Signatures		Seal	
346-e.	1891	Tillman	Morgan	Small Red	**Extremely Rare**

VII. TREASURY OR COIN NOTES

These notes were issued as a result of the Legal Tender Act of July 14, 1890. This Act authorized the Secretary of the Treasury to issue these notes in payment for silver bullion purchased by the Treasury Department. The entire issue of these notes thus became backed by metallic reserves. The notes were redeemable in actual coin, but whether silver or gold coin should be paid out, was left to the discretion of the Secretary of the Treasury.

The coin notes were issued in denominations of 1, 2, 5, 10, 20, 50, 100, and 1,000 Dollars of the series of 1890 and 1891. A 500 Dollar note with portrait of General Sherman was also authorized and a plate made, but only a proof impression of the note is known; it was not placed in circulation.

The notes of the 1890 Series are especially attractive because of the intricate designs on the reverse. The 1890 notes are all rare today, especially in new condition.

The obligation on the Treasury or Coin Notes is as follows, "The United States of America will pay to bearer _____ Dollars in coin . . . This note is a legal tender at its face value in payment of all debts public and private except when otherwise expressly stipulated in the contract."

1 Dollar Notes

DESIGN NO. 85

(Notes 347-349)

Head of Edwin M. Stanton, Secretary of War under Presidents Abraham Lincoln, 1862-1865, and Andrew Johnson, 1865-1868.

Reverse of Design No. 85.

No.	Series	Signatures		Seal	Very Good	Very Fine	Unc
347.	1890	Rosecrans	Huston	Large Brown	125.00	325.00	1,750.00
348.	1890	Rosecrans	Nebeker	Large Brown	•125.00	325.00	1,750.00
349.	1890	Rosecrans	Nebeker	Small Red	125.00	325.00	1,750.00

DESIGN NO. 86

(Notes 350-352)

The obverse is similar to Design No. 85. The reverse is as shown.

No.	Series	Signatures		Seal	Very Good	Very Fine	Unc
350.	1891	Rosecrans	Nebeker	Small Red	65.00	145.00	650.00
351.	1891	Tillman	Morgan	Small Red	65.00	145.00	650.00
352.	1891	Bruce	Roberts	Small Red	65.00	145.00	650.00

2 Dollar Notes

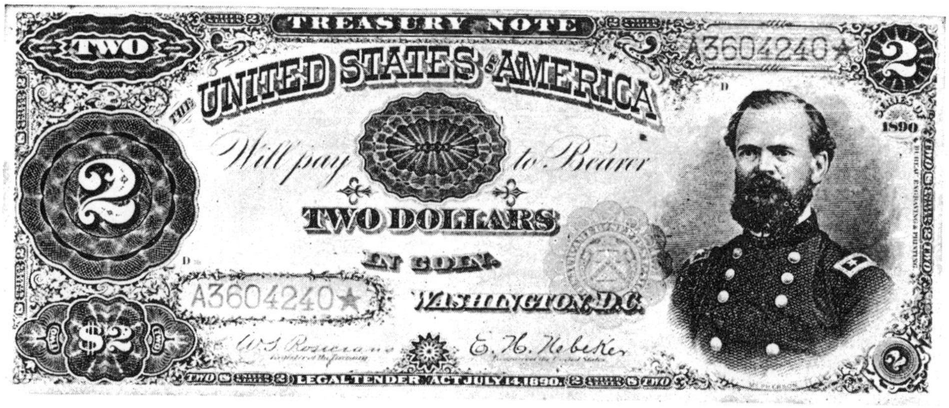

DESIGN NO. 87

(Notes 353-355)

Head of General James McPherson, Union Army general and a hero of the battle of Vicksburg. Engraved by Charles Burt.

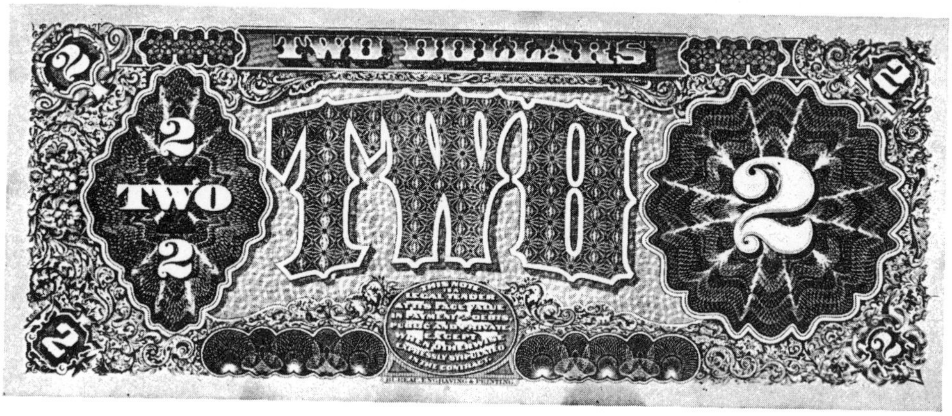

Reverse of Design No. 87.

No.	Series	Signatures		Seal	Very Good	Very Fine	Unc
353.	1890	Rosecrans	Huston	Large Brown	200.00	600.00	3,750.00
354.	1890	Rosecrans	Nebeker	Large Brown	•200.00	650.00	3,950.00
355.	1890	Rosecrans	Nebeker	Small Red	200.00	600.00	3,750.00

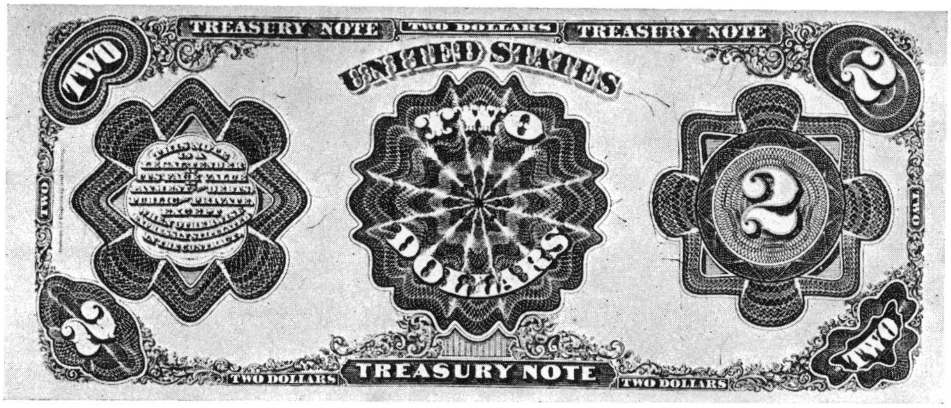

DESIGN NO. 88

(Notes 356-358)

The obverse is similar to Design No. 87. The reverse is as shown.

No.	Series	Signatures		Seal	Very Good	Very Fine	Unc
356.	1891	Rosecrans	Nebeker	Small Red	100.00	250.00	1,250.00
357.	1891	Tillman	Morgan	Small Red	100.00	250.00	1,250.00
358.	1891	Bruce	Roberts	Small Red	100.00	250.00	1,250.00

5 Dollar Notes

DESIGN NO. 89

(Notes 359-361)

Head of General George H. Thomas, Union Army general, famous as "the rock of Chicamauga." His portrait was engraved by Lorenzo J. Hatch.

Reverse of Design No. 89.

No.	Series	Signatures		Seal	Very Good	Very Fine	Unc
359.	1890	Rosecrans	Huston	Large Brown	•150.00	450.00	2,500.00
360.	1890	Rosecrans	Nebeker	Large Brown	150.00	500.00	4,000.00
361.	1890	Rosecrans	Nebeker	Small Red	150.00	450.00	2,500.00

DESIGN NO. 90

(Notes 362-365)

The obverse is similar to Design No. 89. The reverse is as shown.

No.	Series	Signatures		Seal	Very Good	Very Fine	Unc
362.	1891	Rosecrans	Nebeker	Small Red	125.00	275.00	1,250.00
363.	1891	Tillman	Morgan	Small Red	125.00	275.00	1,250.00
364.	1891	Bruce	Roberts	Small Red	125.00	275.00	1,250.00
365.	1891	Lyons	Roberts	Small Red	150.00	550.00	2,000.00

10 Dollar Notes

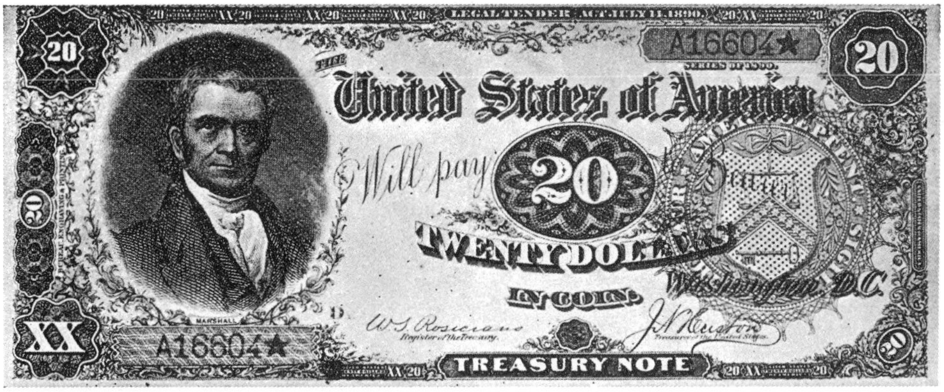

DESIGN NO. 91

(Notes 366-368)

Head of Philip H. Sheridan. He succeeded Sherman as Commander in Chief of the U.S. Army in 1884.

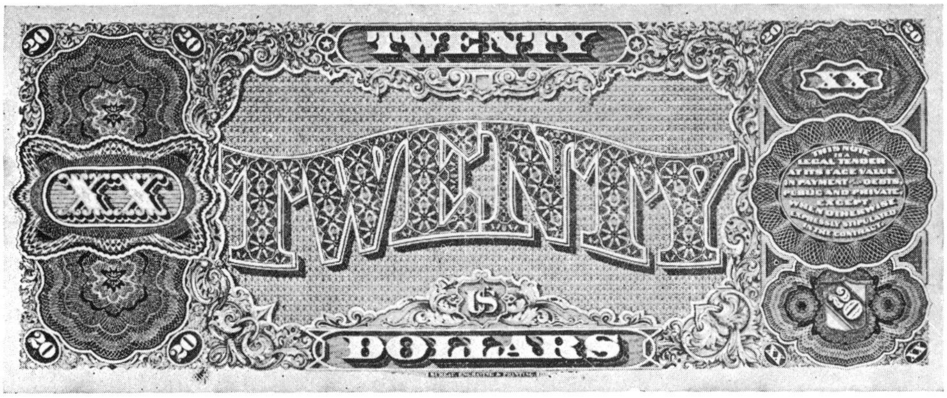

Reverse of Design No. 91.

No.	Series	Signatures		Seal	Very Good	Very Fine	Unc
366.	1890	Rosecrans	Huston	Large Brown	200.00	600.00	3,500.00
367.	1890	Rosecrans	Nebeker	Large Brown	200.00	600.00	4,000.00
368.	1890	Rosecrans	Nebeker	Small Red	•200.00	600.00	3,500.00

DESIGN NO. 92

(Notes 369-371)

The obverse is similar to Design No. 91. The reverse is as shown.

No.	Series	Signatures		Seal	Very Good	Very Fine	Unc
369.	1891	Rosecrans	Nebeker	Small Red	145.00	385.00	1,600.00
370.	1891	Tillman	Morgan	Small Red	145.00	385.00	1,600.00
371.	1891	Bruce	Roberts	Small Red	145.00	385.00	1,600.00

20 Dollar Notes

DESIGN NO. 93

(Notes 372-374)

Head of John Marshall, fourth Chief Justice of the United States, who served on the Supreme Court from 1801-1835. He was also Secretary of State from 1800-1801.

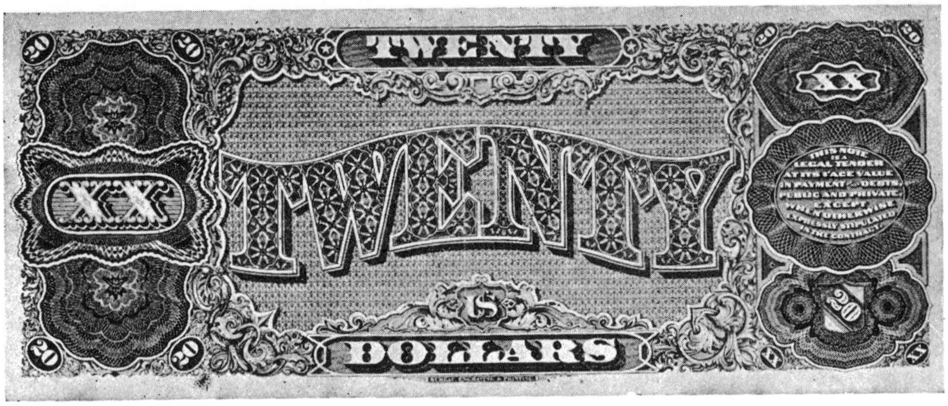

Reverse of Design No. 93.

No.	Series	Signatures		Seal	Very Good	Very Fine	Unc
372.	1890	Rosecrans	Huston	Large Brown	**•500.00**	**1,900.00**	**6,000.00**
373.	1890	Rosecrans	Nebeker	Large Brown	**Rare**	**Rare**	**Rare**
374.	1890	Rosecrans	Nebeker	Small Red	**500.00**	**1,900.00**	**6,000.00**

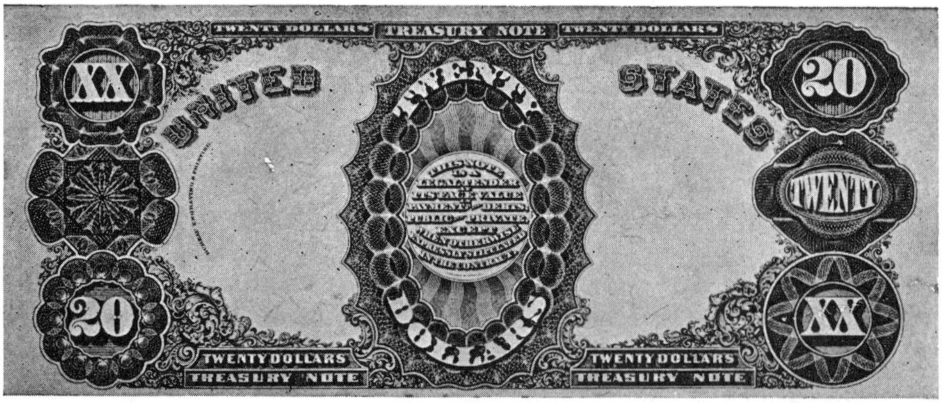

DESIGN NO. 94

(Notes 375 — 375-a)

The obverse is similar to Design No. 93. The reverse is as shown.

No.	Series	Signatures		Seal	Very Good	Very Fine	Unc
375.	1891	Tillman	Morgan	Small Red	**750.00**	**2,500.00**	**12,000.00**
375-a.	1891	Bruce	Roberts	Small Red	**—**	**Rare**	**—**

50 Dollar Note

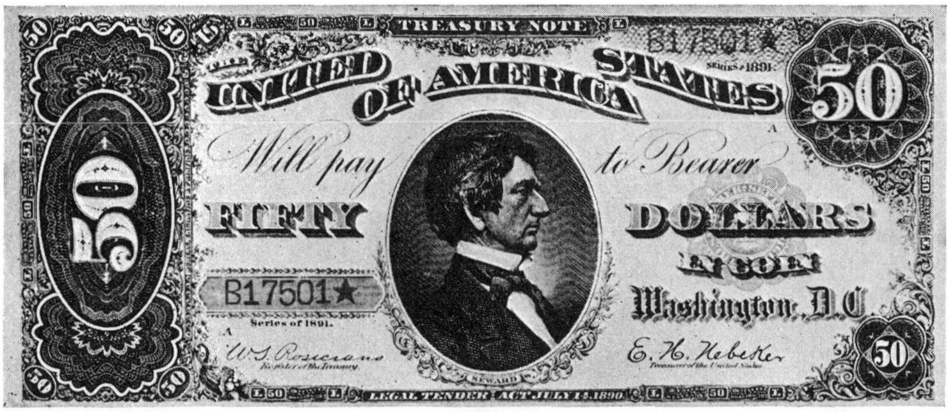

DESIGN NO. 95

(Note 376)

Head of William H. Seward, Secretary of State from 1860-1869. He negotiated the purchase of Alaska from Russia, a transaction which at the time was called "Seward's Folly." This note is extremely rare as only 25 pieces are still reported outstanding on U.S. Treasury books.

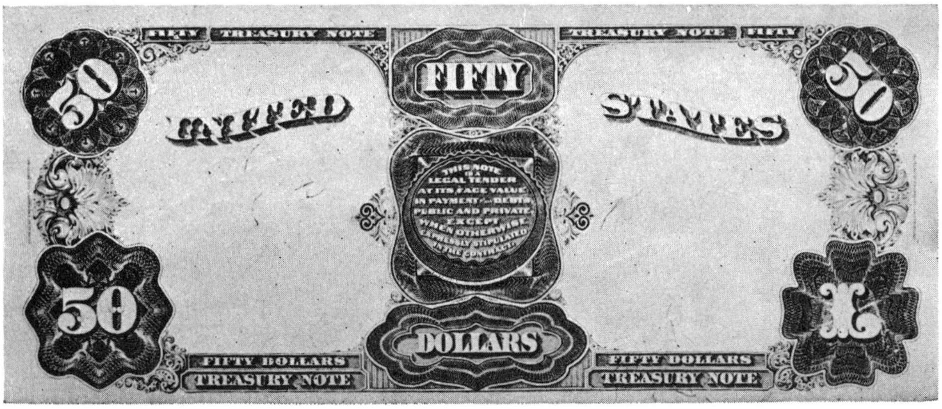

Reverse of Design No. 95.

No.	Series	Signatures		Seal	Very Good	Very Fine	Unc
376.	1891	Rosecrans	Nebeker	Small Red	9,000.00	17,500.00	Rare

100 Dollar Notes

DESIGN NO. 96

(Note 377)

Head of Admiral David Glasgow Farragut, 1801-1870, the first man to hold the rank of Admiral in the U.S. Navy.

Reverse of Design No. 96.

This is the famous "Watermelon" note, so called because of the shape of the large zeros.

No.	Series	Signatures		Seal	Very Good	Very Fine	Unc
377.	1890	Rosecrans	Huston	Large Brown	5,000.00	15,000.00	28,000.00

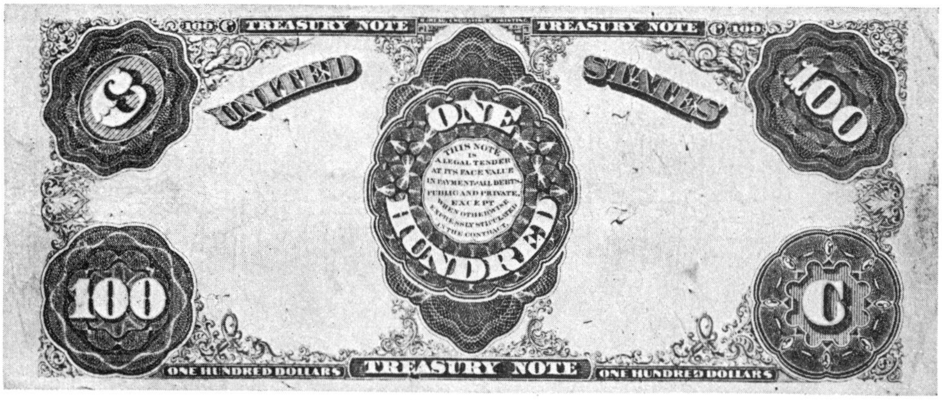

DESIGN NO. 97

(Note 378)

The obverse is similar to Design No. 96. The reverse is as shown.

No.	Series	Signatures		Seal	Very Good	Very Fine	Unc
378.	1891	Rosecrans	Nebeker	Small Red	10,000.00	19,000.00	Rare

500 Dollar Note

DESIGN NO. 97-a

(Note 379)

Head of General William Tecumseh Sherman, famous for his march to the sea during the Civil War.

Reverse of Design No. 97-a.

The illustration is of a sample note.

Copyrighted photograph courtesy of William T. Anton, Jr. and Morey Perlmutter.

No.	Series	Signatures		
379.	1891	Bruce	Roberts	Unknown

1,000 Dollar Notes

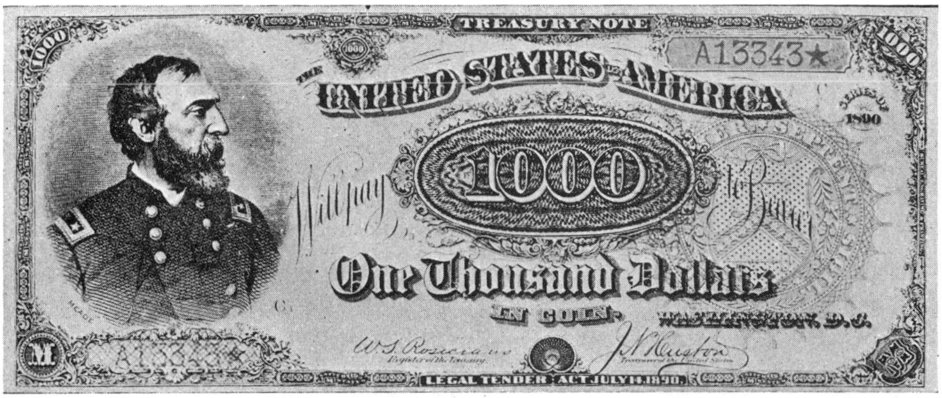

DESIGN NO. 98

(Notes 379-a — 379-b)

Head of General George Gordon Meade, commander of the Union troops at the battle of Gettysburg.

1000
THIS NOTE IS A LEGAL TENDER AT ITS FACE VALUE IN PAYMENT OF DEBTS PUBLIC AND PRIVATE EXCEPT WHEN OTHERWISE EXPRESSLY STIPULATED IN THE CONTRACT
One Thousand Dollars

Reverse of Design No. 98.

Only 25 notes are outstanding of this design combined with Design No. 98-a.

No.	Series	Signatures		Seal	
379-a.	1890	Rosecrans	Huston	Large Brown	**Extremely Rare**
379-b.	1890	Rosecrans	Nebeker	Small Red	**Unique**

DESIGN NO. 98-a

(Notes 379-c — 379-d)

The obverse is similar to Design No. 98. The reverse is as show. Only one specimen is known of each signature variety.

379-c.	1891	Tillman	Morgan	Small Red	**Extremely Rare**
379-d.	1891	Rosecrans	Nebeker	Small Red	**Unique**

VIII. NATIONAL BANK NOTES

The National Bank Notes form the most plentiful and extensive series of American paper money. These notes were issued from 1863 to 1929 by many thousands of banks throughout the country and in our territories, in many denominations and in three Charter Periods.

Indeed, so vast is the extent of the National Bank Notes that no collector can ever hope to complete them. Instead, they are collected either by Treasury signature combination or by locality, that is by state or city of issuing banks.

Origin. National Bank Notes came into being by passage of the National Banking Act of 1863, later supplemented by the Act of June 3, 1864. By the terms of these acts, the government was enabled to grant charters to banks which were then allowed to issue their own notes, but only up to 90% of the par value of the U.S. Government bonds which the banks had previously deposited with the government as security for the notes about to be issued. Each bank had its own charter number, which appeared on all notes issued after 1875. The charter for any bank was valid for a period of twenty years. After that period, a bank could renew the charter for an additional twenty years and continue to keep issuing notes — hence the relationship between the series of 1882 and 1902. A bank's charter began on the day when the Comptroller of Currency presented the bank with its "Certificate of Authority to Commence Business."

These National Bank Notes, although issued by individual banks, are nevertheless conventional United States paper money, fully negotiable, and were produced by the Bureau of Engraving and Printing under the same conditions as regular Treasury issues.

The basic designs on the National Bank Notes are the same for all banks. The only differences are in the name of the bank, the bank charter number, the bank signatures and the coat of arms of the state in which the bank was located.

The issues of National Bank Notes took place during three periods which have been called the First, Second and Third Charter Periods.

The Date on National Bank Notes. All National Bank Notes bear a full date (for example, November 7, 1912) on the face of the note, usually near the name of the city. This date is not necessarily the Charter date of the bank, but is generally somewhat later, and rarely, and surprisingly, even earlier; neither is it the date that the note was issued. The inconsistencies encountered and the many unknown contemporary factors involved in the production of these notes, have made it impossible to determine the exact significance of this date.

The Dates of Issue. Insofar as National Bank Notes are concerned, the dates when they were actually issued are not always consistent with the dates in office of those Treasury Officials whose signatures appear on the notes. (These officials are the Treasurer of the U.S. and the Register of the Treasury). Whereas the original plates bearing their facsimile signatures were no doubt prepared during the period of their combined tenure in the Treasury Department, it was actually the practice of the Bureau of Engraving and Printing to use such plates whenever needed at a later date. As a result, these plates were quite frequently used to print notes long after the particular officials had passed out of office, and perhaps even after their death. That is why it is possible to see notes issued as late as 1922 bearing signatures that could have been originally engraved only in the 1890's. The years when all types of National Bank Notes were actually issued to the public are shown in the following pages where these various types are listed by states.

Production. Until July 1875, National Bank Notes were wholly produced in New York City by the American, Continental or National Bank Note Companies. Their imprints appear on the notes. These three companies engraved and manufactured the plates and accomplished the main printing in their own premises on their own bank note paper. The Treasury Seal and Serial numbers, however, were printed later at the Treasury Department in Washington, D.C.

After March, 1875, the same distinctive paper was required to be used as was then being used for other U.S. currency, and after September of that year, the obverses, or face sides of the notes, began to be printed at the Bureau of Engraving and Printing. The reverses, or backs however, continued to be printed privately in New York by the bank note companies, except for the black portion of the 5 Dollar Note which was let out for printing to the Columbian Bank Note Company in Washington, D.C. (The green portion continued to be printed in New York.)

In January, 1877, all the reverse plates were transferred from New York to Washington, and thereafter the Bureau printed all the reverses as well, except for the black portion of the 5 Dollar Note, which still remained with the Columbian Bank Note Company.

Finally, about October 1877, the entire production of National Bank Notes was assigned permanently to the Bureau of Engraving and Printing.

Charter Numbers. As will be seen later, all National Bank Notes beginning with the series of 1875 bore the charter number of the bank. This charter number was printed prominently either once or twice on the face of each note. Since charter numbers were issued successively in time, it is possible to determine from this number in what year a given bank was chartered. The table at the end of this section gives this information in concise form and at the same time shows how many banks were chartered in each year. In consulting this table, it should be remembered that notes issued from 1929 to 1935 were of the small size, current type.

Serial Numbers. Two serial numbers, unlike each other, appear on the face of each National Bank Note. One is the Treasury Serial Number; the other is the Bank Serial Number. The Treasury Number indicates the running total of such sheets printed on a country-wide basis for all banks; the Bank Number indicates the running total of such sheets printed for the individual Bank. After August 22, 1925, the Treasury Serial Number was discontinued, and its place was taken by a duplicate impression of the Bank Serial Number.

Check or Plate Letters. National Bank Notes were most often printed in sheets of four notes, each note bearing identical serial numbers and differing from each other only by a check or plate letter (or by the denomination of the note). From this check letter it is possible to deduce the original position of the note on the sheet. This check letter appears twice on the face of each note and is usually a script capital letter from A to D. If all four notes on the sheet were of the same denomination, the letters appeared successively as A, B, C, D. If different denominations were printed on each sheet, which was customary, the first note of each denomination began with the check letter A. Some notes of later issues that were printed in large quantities have check letters beyond D. The short table below shows how each denomination was printed on the sheet of four in its most usual combination. The numerals used refer to the denomination: —

1-1-1-2
5-5-5-5
10-10-10-10
10-10-10-20
20-20-20-20
50-50-50-100
50-100

Other combinations exist but they were not as popular with the banks and in some cases sheets consisted of only two notes or of only one note. For example, the 50 and 100 Dollar brown backs of the 1882 series and of the red seal 1902 Series were printed one each on sheets of two notes. In this case, an equal number of each denomination was thus originally issued, unlike the usual combination in which the 50 Dollar note outnumbered the 100 Dollar note three to one. A more detailed listing of plate combinations may be found in "A Descriptive History of National Bank Notes" by William H. Dillistin.

Geographical Letters. In the later period of National Bank history, many thousands of notes were daily being presented to the Treasury Department for redemption. The sorting of these notes was complicated and time consuming and in order to increase sorting efficiency, a so-called geographical letter was printed on notes issued from about 1902 to 1924. These letters, which indicated the geographical region of the issuing bank, were printed in large capital type twice on the face of each note, in both cases near the charter number and in the same color ink as the charter number. The letters used and the various regions are as follows:

N for banks in New England
E for banks in the East
S for banks in the South
M for banks in the Mid-West
W for banks in the West
P for banks in the Pacific region

THE ALDRICH-VREELAND ACT

A knowledge of this Congressional Act is important for a fuller understanding of some of the notes issued during the Second and Third Charter Period. The Act was passed on May 30, 1908, and its provisions were to expire by statute on June 30, 1915. The purpose of the Aldrich-Vreeland Act was to create a supply of emergency money in case further panics occurred. The Panic of 1907 had shown that there was not enough currency in circulation to meet the demands of a financial emergency.

The purpose of the Act was accomplished by permitting National Banks to deposit with the Treasurer of the United States, not only United States bonds, but other securities as well, against the issue of additional circulating notes.

Until then (May 30, 1908) the security for National Bank Notes could consist only of U.S. bonds which the National Banks owned and had deposited as a pledge with the Treasurer of the U.S. in amounts up to 90% of the face value of currency actually issued by the banks. During this period, 1863-1908, all National Bank Notes bore the legend, "Secured by United States bonds deposited with the Treasurer of the United States."

After passage of the Act, the backs of the notes were changed and the security legend on the face of the notes was altered to read as follows, "Secured by United States bonds or other securities." These changes can best be seen by studying the illustrations of the notes of the Aldrich-Vreeland period, 1908-1915, as compared with notes of both earlier and later issues.

Immediately prior to May 30, 1908, two types of National Bank Notes were being issued concurrently; the Second Charter brown backs of the 1882 series and the Third Charter red seals of the 1902 series.

After May 30, 1908, those banks still under the Second Charter Period began to issue notes with the large "1882-1908" on back, replacing the brown backs, and being replaced in 1915 by the type with the denomination on back; those banks under the then existing Third Charter Period, began to issue notes with the small "1902-1908" on back and with a blue seal on face, replacing the red seals and being replaced in 1915 by notes without the "1902-1908" on back.

In accordance with the provisions of the Aldrich-Vreeland Act, National Banks were not permitted after 1915 to pledge "other securities" but once again could use only U.S. bonds to secure their currency. As noted directly above, new notes were issued to mark this legal reversion to type, and this was done so that a quick visual distinction could be made between those notes pledged with "other securities" and those pledged only with U.S. bonds.

Whereas in 1908, all face plates in use had religiously been altered by adding "other securities," the removal of this clause on notes issued after 1915 was only haphazard. Consequently, a certain volume of currency was issued from 1915 to 1929 bearing the anachronistic legend, "Secured by United States bonds or other securities." Such notes of this period are considered scarcer than those without the expression "other securities."

YEARS OF ISSUE OF CHARTER NUMBERS

As mentioned earlier, the Charter Number of the issuing bank was printed prominently on each note, beginning with the Series of 1875 (some notes of the Original Series, 1863-1875, are known with Charter Numbers). The table below shows which Charter Numbers were assigned during each calendar year from 1863 to 1935, (the note issuing period) as well as the number of banks chartered in each of these years. Thus if one knows the Charter Number of a given National Bank, a glance at the table will show in what year this bank was given its original charter. The first bank to be chartered was the First National Bank of Philadelphia, which received Charter No. 1 in June, 1863. The last bank to be chartered was the Roodhouse National Bank of Roodhouse, Illinois which received Charter No. 14,348 in December, 1935. National banks chartered after this date are not included in this list.

Charter Numbers	*Assigned During Year*	*Number of Banks Chartered*
1-179	1863	179
180-682	1864	503
683-1626	1865	944
1627-1665	1866	39
1666-1675	1867	10
1676-1688	1868	13
1689-1696	1869	8
1697-1759	1870	63
1760-1912	1871	153
1913-2073	1872	161
2074-2131	1873	58
2132-2214	1874	83
2215-2315	1875	101
2316-2344	1876	29
2345-2375	1877	31
2376-2405	1878	30
2406-2445	1879	40
2446-2498	1880	53
2499-2606	1881	108
2607-2849	1882	243
2850-3101	1883	252
3102-3281	1884	180
3282-3427	1885	146
3428-3612	1886	184
3613-3832	1887	220
3833-3954	1888	122
3955-4190	1889	236
4191-4494	1890	304
4495-4673	1891	179
4674-4832	1892	159
4833-4934	1893	102
4935-4983	1894	49
4984-5029	1895	46
5030-5054	1896	25
5055-5108	1897	54
5109-5165	1898	57
5166-5240	1899	75
5241-5662	1900	422
5663-6074	1901	412
6075-6566	1902	492
6567-7081	1903	514
7082-7541	1904	460
7542-8027	1905	486
8028-8489	1906	462
8490-8979	1907	490
8980-9302	1908	323
9303-9622	1909	320
9623-9913	1910	291
9914-10119	1911	206
10120-10305	1912	186
10306-10472	1913	167
10473-10672	1914	200
10673-10810	1915	138
10811-10932	1916	122
10933-11126	1917	194
11127-11282	1918	156
11283-11570	1919	288
11571-11903	1920	333
11904-12082	1921	179
12083-12287	1922	205
12288-12481	1923	194
12482-12615	1924	134
12616-12866	1925	251
12867-13022	1926	156
13023-13159	1927	137
13160-13269	1928	110
13270-13412	1929	143
13413-13516	1930	104
13517-13586	1931	70
13587-13654	1932	68
13655-13920	1933	266
13921-14317	1934	397
14318-14348	1935	31

(The highest Charter Number to appear on a National Bank Note is 14320, on the 10 Dollar Note of the Liberty National Bank & Trust Co. of Louisville, Ky. Chartered banks with later numbers did not issue any notes.)

The Issues of National Bank Notes By States

In the listings that follow, an attempt has been made for the first time in numismatic history to show categorically in what states or territories the various types of National Bank Notes were issued. At the same time the valuations indicate the relative rarity of a given note issued in one state as against the same note issued in another state. This valuation is based on the commonest signature variety of each type in the state of preservation indicated. These valuations are based on the relative quantities of notes known to be in existence, as brought to light by the author's research and experience. Notes issued by banks in small towns are usually scarcer than those of banks in large cities, since they probably issued fewer notes.

The term "rare" in this section indicates that the note in question was issued but that no specimen is as yet known. The term "not issued" indicates that the particular type of note was not issued by any of the banks in the state named, as is shown by the original Registers of the Treasury Department now in the National Archives.

It is the author's opinion that many notes now marked as "rare" will be discovered in time to come, and that, on the other hand, some notes will forever remain unknown.

It should be borne in mind that the Registers for the period 1913 to 1923 cannot be found, probably having been destroyed, and that therefore, the author's findings on four series of notes are partially incomplete and may be subject to some revision (1882 dates on back; 1882 value on back; 1902 dates on back; 1902 blue seal without dates on back).

A better understanding of the Territorial Issues can be gained by reviewing the years when the various note-issuing territories became states: — Arizona 1912 — Colorado 1876 — Idaho 1890 — Montana 1889 — Nebraska 1867 — New Mexico 1912 — Utah 1896 — Washington 1889 — Wyoming 1890 — Dakota Territory became the States of North and South Dakota in 1889 — Indian Territory existed from 1834 to 1907 and Oklahoma Territory from 1890 to 1907, both territories combining to form the State of Oklahoma in 1907 — Hawaii entered territorial status in 1900.

Notes of the First Charter Period

February 25, 1863 to July 11, 1882

(Notes of First Charter type were issued from 1863 to 1902)

Although the charter period was for 20 years, as prescribed by law, notes of First Charter types were actually issued for 40 years, that is until 1902.

This seeming irregularity is due to the fact that a charter was valid for 20 years from the date of a bank's organization and not for 20 years from the date of February 25, 1863. Once a bank was chartered during this period it kept issuing the same type notes for 20 years, notwithstanding that the Second Charter Period may have intervened in the meanwhile. A few examples will suffice to show how the system operated.

Charter No. 1 was given to the First National Bank of Philadelphia in June, 1863. It would have issued typical notes of the First Charter Period for 20 years or until June, 1882. If re-chartered, this bank would then in July, 1882 have begun to issue the brown back notes of the Second Charter Period.

Likewise, a bank chartered in 1873 issued First Charter notes until 1893, and if re-chartered, issued brown backs shortly thereafter.

An extreme example would be the case of any bank chartered in the year 1882 but before July 12th of that year, that is, in the last few months of the First Charter Period. Such a bank would have issued First Charter notes up to 1902. If this bank, however, were chartered in 1882 but before April 12th, its first re-charter notes in 1902 would have been brown backs; but if it had been chartered between April 12 and July 12, 1882, its first re-charter notes in 1902 would have been the red seals of the Third Charter Period, and such a bank would not have issued any notes at all of the Second Charter Period.

There were two series of notes issued under the First Charter Period, the so-called Original Series and the Series of 1875. The notes of the Original Series were issued from 1863 to 1875 and did not bear the charter number of the bank, except for some rare instances. The Series of 1875 came into being as a result of the Act of June 30, 1874, which henceforth required the charter number of the bank to be printed on all National Bank Notes.

The charter numbers were normally printed in red, but a few banks issued 5 Dollar notes with the charter number printed in black in script numerals rather than block numerals. These notes are very rare.

The serial numbers were printed in either red or blue, the records indicating that notes with blue serial numbers are somewhat scarcer.

National Bank Notes were first issued to the public on December 21, 1863, but notes are known dated in November 1863.

These notes were issued in denominations from 1 to 1,000 Dollars, there being two issues: the Original Series and the Series of 1875.

The obligation on notes of the First Charter Period is as follows, "This note is secured by bonds of the United States deposited with the U.S. Treasurer at Washington . . . The (name of bank and location) will pay the bearer on demand . . . . . . Dollars . . . This note is receivable at par in all parts of the United States, in payment of all taxes and excises and all other dues to the United States, except duties on imports, and also for all salaries and other debts and demands owing by the United States to individuals, corporations and associations within the United States, except interest on public debt."

Notes of this period rank among the most beautiful examples of our currency. The obverses bear vignettes pertaining to American history or tradition; the reverses, which are bicolored, show some of the famous paintings on Americana that hang in the Capitol at Washington. All notes of the First Charter Period are very rare in new condition, and when found so, they are of extraordinary beauty and appeal.

1 Dollar Notes

DESIGN NO. 99

(Notes 380-386)

The vignette, titled "Concordia," showing two maidens before an altar, was designed by T.A. Liebler and engraved by Charles Burt.

Reverse of Design No. 99.

"Landing of the Pilgrims" engraved by Charles Burt. Borders in green, the painting in black.

No.	Series	Signatures		Seal	Very Good	Very Fine	Extra Fine	Unc
380.	Original	Colby	Spinner	Red with rays	•125.00	350.00	450.00	1,200.00
381.	Original	Jeffries	Spinner	Red with rays	950.00	1,750.00	2,250.00	4,250.00
382.	Original	Allison	Spinner	Red with rays	125.00	350.00	450.00	1,200.00
383.	1875	Allison	New	Red with scallops	125.00	350.00	425.00	1,100.00
384.	1875	Allison	Wyman	Red with scallops	125.00	350.00	425.00	1,100.00
385.	1875	Allison	Gilfillan	Red with scallops	125.00	350.00	425.00	1,100.00
386.	1875	Scofield	Gilfillan	Red with scallops	125.00	350.00	450.00	1,200.00

These notes were issued from 1865 to 1878 in sheets of 1-1-1-2 and very rarely 1-1-2-2.

	State	Very Fine
S-1.	Alabama	800.00
S-2.	Arizona Terr.	Not Issued
S-3.	Arkansas	1,600.00
S-4.	California	Not Issued
S-5.	Colorado Territory	1,700.00
S-6.	Colorado State	1,800.00
S7.	Connecticut	375.00
S-8.	Dakota Territory	1,700.00
S-9.	Delaware	485.00
S-10.	District of Columbia	485.00
S-11.	Florida	Not Issued
S-12.	Georgia	975.00
S-13.	Idaho Territory	Rare
S-14.	Illinois	325.00
S-15.	Indian Terr.	Not Issued
S-16.	Indiana	350.00
S-17.	Iowa	350.00
S-18.	Kansas	485.00
S-19.	Kentucky	550.00
S-20.	Louisiana	600.00
S-21.	Maine	550.00
S-22.	Maryland	650.00
S-23.	Massachusetts	375.00
S-24.	Michigan	350.00
S-25.	Minnesota	550.00
S-26.	Mississippi	Not Issued
S-27.	Missouri	350.00
S-28.	Montana Territory	2,700.00
S-29.	Montana State	Not Issued
S-30.	Nebraska Territory	3,000.00
S-31.	Nebraska State	900.00
S-32.	Nevada	Not Issued
S-33.	New Hampshire	550.00
S-34.	New Jersey	350.00
S-35.	New Mexico Terr.	2,200.00
S-36.	New York	350.00
S-37.	North Carolina	650.00
S-38.	North Dakota	Not Issued
S-39.	Ohio	350.00
S-40.	Okla. Terr. & St.	Not Issued
S-41.	Oregon	Not Issued
S-42.	Pennsylvania	350.00
S-43.	Rhode Island	485.00
S-44.	South Carolina	700.00
S-45.	South Dakota	Not Issued
S-46.	Tennessee	750.00
S-47.	Texas	975.00
S-48.	Utah Territory	2,700.00
S-49.	Utah State	Not Issued
S-50.	Vermont	485.00
S-51.	Virginia	485.00
S-52.	Washington Terr.	Not Issued
S-53.	Washington State	Not Issued
S-54.	West Virginia	Rare
S-55.	Wisconsin	350.00
S-56.	Wyoming Territory	1,900.00
S-57.	Wyoming State	Not Issued

2 Dollar Notes

DESIGN NO. 100

(Notes 387-393)

Female holding flag. This is the well known "Lazy 2" note, so called because of the extreme horizontal shape of the 2.

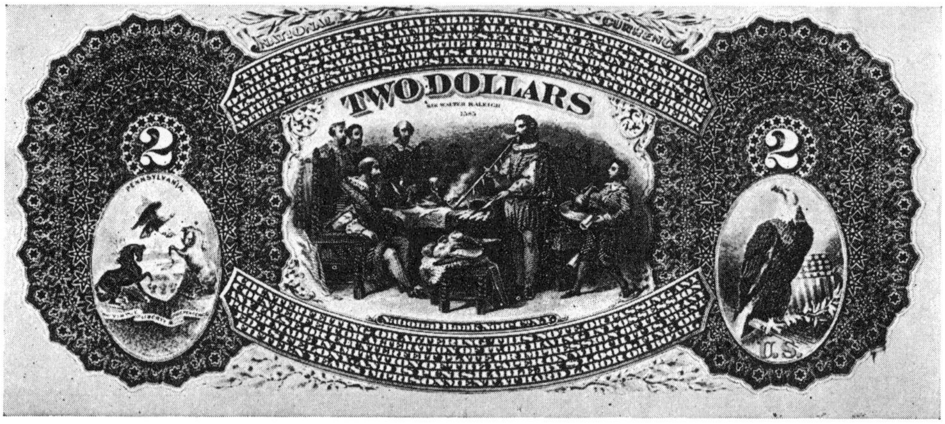

Reverse of Design No. 100.

Sir Walter Raleigh in England, 1585, exhibiting corn and smoking tobacco from America.

Borders in green, the painting in black.

No.	Series	Signatures		Seal	Very Good	Very Fine	Extra Fine	Unc
387.	Original	Colby	Spinner	Red with rays	400.00	750.00	1,000.00	2,750.00
388.	Original	Jeffries	Spinner	Red with rays	1,750.00	2,750.00	3,250.00	7,500.00
389.	Original	Allison	Spinner	Red with rays	400.00	750.00	1,000.00	2,750.00
390.	1875	Allison	New	Red with scallops	400.00	700.00	900.00	2,750.00
391.	1875	Allison	Wyman	Red with scallops	400.00	700.00	900.00	2,750.00
392.	1875	Allison	Gilfillan	Red with scallops	400.00	700.00	900.00	2,750.00
393.	1875	Scofield	Gilfillan	Red with scallops	425.00	750.00	1,000.00	2,800.00

These notes were issued from 1865 to 1878 in sheets of 1-1-1-2 and very rarely 1-1-2-2.

	State	Very Fine
S-58.	Alabama	Rare
S-59.	Arizona Territory	Not Issued
S-60.	Arkansas	Rare
S-61.	California	Not Issued
S-62.	Colorado Territory	2,600.00
S-63.	Colorado State	Rare
S-64.	Connecticut	1,050.00
S-65.	Dakota Territory	4,700.00
S-66.	Delaware	2,100.00
S-67.	District of Columbia	Rare
S-68.	Florida	Not Issued
S-69.	Georgia	Rare
S-70.	Idaho Territory	Rare
S-71.	Illinois	725.00
S-72.	Indian Territory	Not Issued
S-73.	Indiana	1,150.00
S-74.	Iowa	1,300.00
S-75.	Kansas	1,050.00
S-76.	Kentucky	1,050.00

	State	Very Fine
S-77.	Louisiana	Rare
S-78.	Maine	1,300.00
S-79.	Maryland	1,300.00
S-80.	Massachusetts	825.00
S-81.	Michigan	925.00
S-82.	Minnesota	1,150.00
S-83.	Mississippi	Not Issued
S-84.	Missouri	975.00
S-85.	Montana Territory	Rare
S-86.	Montana State	Not Issued
S-87.	Nebraska Territory	4,150.00
S-88.	Nebraska State	Rare
S-89.	Nevada	Not Issued
S-90.	New Hampshire	1,050.00
S-91.	New Jersey	775.00
S-92.	New Mexico Territor	Rare
S-93.	New York	725.00
S-94.	North Carolina	1,800.00
S-95.	North Dakota	Not Issued

	State	Very Fine
S-96.	Ohio	700.00
S-97.	Okla. Terr. & St.	Not Issued
S-98.	Oregon	Not Issued
S-99.	Pennsylvania	700.00
S-100.	Rhode Island	1,050.00
S-101.	South Carolina	Rare
S-102.	South Dakota	Not Issued
S-103.	Tennessee	2,100.00
S-104.	Texas	Rare
S-105.	Utah Territory	6,250.00
S-106.	Utah State	Not Issued
S-107.	Vermont	1,050.00
S-108.	Virginia	Rare
S-109.	Wash. Terr.	Not Issued
S-110.	Washington St.	Not Issued
S-111.	West Virginia	1,825.00
S-112.	Wisconsin	1,050.00
S-113.	Wyoming Territory	Rare
S-114.	Wyoming State	Not Issued

5 Dollar Notes

DESIGN NO. 101

(Notes 394-408)

At the left, Christopher Columbus in sight of land. At the right, presentation of an Indian Princess, representing America, to the Old World. Designed by Charles Fenton and engraved by Charles Burt.

Reverse of Design No. 101.

The Landing of Columbus, from a painting by John Vanderlyn. Borders in green, the painting in black.

No.	Series	Signatures		Seal	Very Good	Very Fine	Extra Fine	Unc
394.	Original	Chittenden	Spinner	Red with rays	125.00	325.00	600.00	1,500.00
397.	Original	Colby	Spinner	Red with rays	125.00	325.00	600.00	1,500.00
398.	Original	Jeffries	Spinner	Red with rays	1,100.00	2,500.00	4,000.00	Rare
399.	Original	Allison	Spinner	Red with rays	•125.00	325.00	600.00	1,350.00
401.	1875	Allison	New	Red with scallops	125.00	325.00	600.00	1,350.00
402.	1875	Allison	Wyman	Red with scallops	125.00	325.00	600.00	1,350.00
403.	1875	Allison	Gilfillan	Red with scallops	125.00	325.00	600.00	1,350.00
404.	1875	Scofield	Gilfillan	Red with scallops	175.00	400.00	700.00	1,500.00
405.	1875	Bruce	Gilfillan	Red with scallops	175.00	400.00	700.00	2,000.00
406.	1875	Bruce	Wyman	Red with scallops	200.00	450.00	750.00	2,750.00
406-a.	1875	Bruce	Jordan	Red with scallops	Rare	—	—	—
407.	1875	Rosecrans	Huston	Red with scallops	225.00	475.00	775.00	2,100.00
408.	1875	Rosecrans	Jordan	Red with scallops	200.00	450.00	750.00	3,500.00
408-a.	1875	Rosecrans	Nebeker	Red with scallops	Unique		-	-

These notes were issued from 1863 to 1902 in sheets of 5-5-5-5.

	State	Very Fine
S-115.	Alabama	650.00
S-116.	Arizona Territory	6,500.00
S-117.	Arkansas	3,500.00
S-118.	California	5,500.00
S-119.	Colorado Territory	3,500.00
S-120.	Colorado State	1,900.00
S-121.	Connecticut	475.00
S-122.	Dakota Territory	4,350.00
S-123.	Delaware	850.00
S-124.	Dist. of Columbia	700.00
S-125.	Florida	6,500.00
S-126.	Georgia	1,100.00
S-127.	Idaho Territory	Rare
S-128.	Illinois	325.00
S-129.	Indian Terr.	Not Issued
S-130.	Indiana	400.00
S-131.	Iowa	400.00
S-132.	Kansas	550.00
S-133.	Kentucky	550.00
S-134.	Louisiana	1,100.00
S-135.	Maine	650.00
S-136.	Maryland	450.00
S-137.	Massachusetts	450.00
S-138.	Michigan	475.00
S-139.	Minnesota	550.00
S-140.	Mississippi	Rare
S-141.	Missouri	550.00
S-142.	Montana Terr.	4,350.00
S-143.	Montana State	4,000.00
S-144.	Nebraska Terr.	Rare
S-145.	Nebraska State	975.00
S-146.	Nevada	Rare
S-147.	New Hampshire	550.00
S-148.	New Jersey	375.00
S-149.	New Mexico Terr.	3,250.00
S-150.	New York	325.00
S-151.	North Carolina	850.00
S-152.	North Dakota	1,900.00
S-153.	Ohio	350.00
S-154.	Okla. Terr. & St.	Not Issued
S-155.	Oregon	Rare
S-156.	Pennsylvania	325.00
S-157.	Rhode Island	550.00
S-158.	South Carolina	1,600.00
S-159.	South Dakota	Rare
S-160.	Tennessee	1,350.00
S-161.	Texas	1,900.00
S-162.	Utah Terr.	Rare
S-163.	Utah State	Rare
S-164.	Vermont	550.00
S-165.	Virginia	1,350.00
S-166.	Wash. Terr.	Not Issued
S-167.	Washington State	3,750.00
S-168.	West Virginia	1,600.00
S-169.	Wisconsin	750.00
S-170.	Wyoming Terr.	3,750.00
S-171.	Wyoming State	2,700.00

10 Dollar Notes

DESIGN NO. 102

(Notes 409-423-a)

At the left, Benjamin Franklin drawing electricity from the sky with a kite and a key. At right, Liberty soaring on an eagle, clutching lightning in her hand.

Reverse of Design No. 102.

DeSoto discovering the Mississippi in 1541, a painting by W.H. Powell, engraved by Frederick Girsch. Borders in green, the painting in black.

No.	Series	Signatures		Seal	Very Good	Very Fine	Extra Fine	Unc
409.	Original	Chittenden	Spinner	Red with rays	275.00	650.00	925.00	3,500.00
412.	Original	Colby	Spinner	Red with rays	200.00	600.00	850.00	2,500.00
413.	Original	Jeffries	Spinner	Red with rays	700.00	1,750.00	2,500.00	Rare
414.	Original	Allison	Spinner	Red with rays	200.00	600.00	850.00	2,500.00
416.	1875	Allison	New	Red with scallops	200.00	550.00	800.00	2,400.00
417.	1875	Allison	Wyman	Red with scallops	200.00	550.00	800.00	2,400.00
418.	1875	Allison	Gilfillan	Red with scallops	200.00	550.00	800.00	2,400.00
419.	1875	Scofield	Gilfillan	Red with scallops	•275.00	550.00	900.00	3,200.00
420.	1875	Bruce	Gilfillan	Red with scallops	275.00	550.00	900.00	3,200.00
421.	1875	Bruce	Wyman	Red with scallops	275.00	550.00	900.00	3,200.00
422.	1875	Rosecrans	Huston	Red with scallops	400.00	700.00	1,100.00	3,700.00
423.	1875	Rosecrans	Nebeker	Red with scallops	450.00	750.00	1,200.00	4,200.00
423-a.	1875	Tillman	Morgan	Red with scallops			Unknown	

These notes were issued from 1863 to 1902 in sheets of 10-10-10-20 and 10-10-10-10 and rarely in other combinations.

	State	Very Fine
S-172.	Alabama	2,000.00
S-173.	Arizona Territory	Not Issued
S-174.	Arkansas	5,000.00
S-175.	California	6,000.00
S-176.	Colorado Territory	4,000.00
S-177.	Colorado State	3,500.00
S-178.	Connecticut	750.00
S-179.	Dakota Territory	Rare
S-180.	Delaware	1,450.00
S-181.	District of Columbia	1,400.00
S-182.	Florida	Rare
S-183.	Georgia	2,250.00
S-184.	Idaho Territory	Rare
S-185.	Illinois	500.00
S-186.	Indian Terr.	Not Issued
S-187.	Indiana	675.00
S-188.	Iowa	650.00
S-189.	Kansas	1,250.00
S-190.	Kentucky	1,100.00
S-191.	Louisiana	1,950.00
S-192.	Maine	1,000.0
S-193.	Maryland	850.00
S-194.	Massachusetts	600.00
S-195.	Michigan	800.00
S-196.	Minnesota	900.00
S-197.	Mississippi	Rare
S-198.	Missouri	725.00
S-199.	Montana Territory	Rare
S-200.	Montana State	Rare
S-201.	Nebraska Territory	Rare
S-202.	Nebraska State	1,450.00
S-203.	Nevada	Rare
S-204.	New Hampshire	900.00
S-205.	New Jersey	625.00
S-206.	New Mexico Terr.	5,000.00
S-207.	New York	550.00
S-208.	North Carolina	1,750.00
S-209.	North Dakota	3,500.00
S-210.	Ohio	550.00
S-211.	Okla. Terr. & St.	Not Issued
S-212.	Oregon	4,500.00
S-213.	Pennsylvania	500.00
S-214.	Rhode Island	900.00
S-215.	South Carolina	4,000.00
S-216.	South Dakota	3,750.00
S-217.	Tennessee	2,000.00
S-218.	Texas	3,500.00
S-219.	Utah Territory	Rare
S-220.	Utah State	Rare
S-221.	Vermont	1,000.00
S-222.	Virginia	2,200.00
S-223.	Wash. Terr.	Not Issued
S-224.	Washington State	Rare
S-225.	West Virginia	3,000.00
S-226.	Wisconsin	900.00
S-227.	Wyoming Terr.	5,000.00
S-228.	Wyoming State	4,000.00

20 Dollar Notes

DESIGN NO. 103

(Notes 424-439)

At the left, the Battle of Lexington, April 19, 1775. At the right, Columbia leading procession.

Reverse of Design No. 103.

The Baptism of Pocahontas, painted by John G. Chapman. Borders in green, the painting in black.

This illustration by courtesy of the Chase National Bank of New York.

No.	Series	Signatures		Seal	Fine	Extremely Fine	Unc
424.	Original	Chittenden	Spinner	Red with rays	625.00	2,000.00	3,900.00
427.	Original	Colby	Spinner	Red with rays	575.00	1,750.00	3,750.00
428.	Original	Jeffries	Spinner	Red with rays	3,500.00	6,000.00	Rare
429.	Original	Allison	Spinner	Red with rays	625.00	1,750.00	3,750.00
431.	1875	Allison	New	Red with scallops	625.00	1,750.00	3,750.00
432.	1875	Allison	Wyman	Red with scallops	625.00	1,750.00	3,750.00
433.	1875	Allison	Gilfillan	Red with scallops	625.00	1,750.00	3,750.00
434.	1875	Scofield	Gilfillan	Red with scallops	625.00	1,750.00	3,750.00
435.	1875	Bruce	Gilfillan	Red with scallops	750.00	1,900.00	3,850.00
436.	1875	Bruce	Wyman	Red with scallops	850.00	2,000.00	4,000.00
437.	1875	Rosecrans	Huston	Red with scallops	1,000.00	2,200.00	4,100.00
438.	1875	Rosecrans	Nebeker	Red with scallops	1,350.00	2,750.00	4,400.00
439.	1875	Tillman	Morgan	Red with scallops	1,350.00	2,750.00	4,400.00

These notes were issued from 1863 to 1902 in sheets of 10-10-10-20 and rarely 10-10-20-20 and 20-20-20-20 as well as a few other rare combinations.

	State	*Fine*
S-229.	Alabama	2,350.00
S-230.	Arizona Territory	Not Issued
S-231.	Arkansas	Rare
S-232.	California	5,250.00
S-233.	Colorado Territory	4,250.00
S-234.	Colorado State	4,000.00
S-235.	Connecticut	925.00
S-236.	Dakota Territory	Rare
S-237.	Delaware	1,800.00
S-238.	Dist. of Columbia	1,550.00
S-239.	Florida	Not Issued
S-240.	Georgia	3,250.00
S-241.	Idaho Territory	Rare
S-242.	Illinois	625.00
S-243.	Indian Terr.	Not Issued
S-244.	Indiana	800.00
S-245.	Iowa	850.00
S-246.	Kansas	1,650.00
S-247.	Kentucky	1,500.00
S-248.	Louisiana	2,350.00
S-249.	Maine	1,300.00
S-250.	Maryland	900.00
S-251.	Massachusetts	800.00
S-252.	Michigan	900.00
S-253.	Minnesota	1,150.00
S-254.	Mississippi	Rare
S-255.	Missouri	900.00
S-256.	Montana Territory	Rare
S-257.	Montana State	5,250.00
S-258.	Nebraska Territory	Rare
S-259.	Nebraska State	1,550.00
S-260.	Nevada	Rare
S-261.	New Hampshire	1,150.00
S-262.	New Jersey	800.00
S-263.	New Mexico Terr.	4,250.00
S-264.	New York	625.00
S-265.	North Carolina	2,350.00
S-266.	North Dakota	3,250.00
S-267.	Ohio	700.00
S-268.	Okla. Terr. & St.	Not Issued
S-269.	Oregon	3,750.00
S-270.	Pennsylvania	650.00
S-271.	Rhode Island	1,300.00
S-272.	South Carolina	3,750.00
S-273.	South Dakota	3,250.00
S-274.	Tennessee	2,250.00
S-275.	Texas	3,750.00
S-276.	Utah Territory	Rare
S-277.	Utah State	8,000.00
S-278.	Vermont	1,300.00
S-279.	Virginia	2,750.00
S-280.	Wash. Terr.	Not Issued
S-281.	Washington State	Rare
S-282.	West Virginia	2,500.00
S-283.	Wisconsin	900.00
S-284.	Wyoming Terr.	4,750.00
S-285.	Wyoming State	Rare

50 Dollar Notes

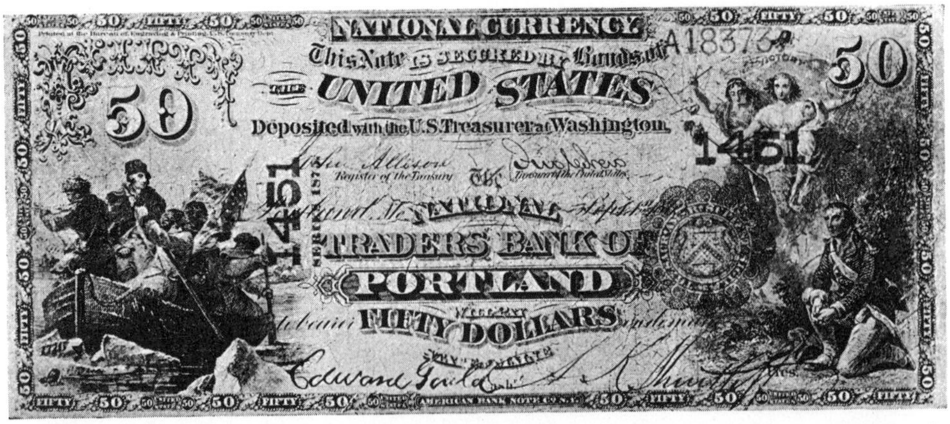

DESIGN NO. 104

(Notes 440-451)

At the left, Washington crossing the Delaware. At the right, Washington at prayer.

Reverse of Design No. 104.

"Embarkation of the Pilgrims," from a mural by Robert W. Weir. Borders in green, the painting in black.

No.	Series	Signatures		Seal	Very Good	Very Fine
440.	Original	Chittenden	Spinner	Red with rays	2,750.00	5,700.00
442.	Original	Colby	Spinner	Red with rays	2,500.00	5,500.00
443.	Original	Allison	Spinner	Red with rays	2,500.00	5,500.00
444.	1875	Allison	New	Red with scallops	• 2,500.00	5,500.00
444a.	1875	Allison	Wyman	Red with scallops	Rare	—
445.	1875	Allison	Gilfillan	Red with scallops	2,800.00	6,500.00
446.	1875	Scofield	Gilfillan	Red with scallops	2,800.00	6,300.00
447.	1875	Bruce	Gilfillan	Red with scallops	3,000.00	6,500.00
448.	1875	Bruce	Wyman	Red with scallops	3,000.00	6,500.00
449.	1875	Rosecrans	Huston	Red with scallops	3,100.00	6,700.00
450.	1875	Rosecrans	Nebeker	Red with scallops	3,100.00	6,700.00
451.	1875	Tillman	Morgan	Red with scallops	3,100.00	6,700.00

These notes were issued from 1863 to 1901 in sheets of 50-50-50-100 and rarely 50-100 and 100-100 as well as a few other rare combinations.

There are so few notes known of this type, that it is not possible to evaluate them by state. Accordingly, valuations have been omitted and all notes must be considered as rare except those marked "Not Issued."

	State	*Very Fine*
S-286.	Alabama	— —
S-287.	Arizona Terr.	Not Issued
S-288.	Arkansas	Not Issued
S-289.	California	— —
S-290.	Colorado Terr.	— —
S-291.	Colorado State	— —
S-292.	Connecticut	— —
S-293.	Dakota Terr.	Not Issued
S-294.	Delaware	— —
S-295.	Dist. of Columbia	— —
S-296.	Florida	Not Issued
S-297.	Georgia	— —
S-298.	Idaho Territory	Not Issued
S-299.	Illinois	— —
S-300.	Indian Terr.	Not Issued
S-301.	Indiana	— —
S-302.	Iowa	— —
S-303.	Kansas	— —
S-304.	Kentucky	— —
S-305.	Louisiana	— —
S-306.	Maine	— —
S-307.	Maryland	— —
S-308.	Massachusetts	— —
S-309.	Michigan	— —
S-301.	Minnestoa	— —
S-311.	Mississippi	— —
S-312.	Missouri	— —
S-313.	Montana Terr.	— —
S-314.	Montana State	— —
S-315.	Nebraska Terr.	Not Issued
S-316.	Nebraska State	— —
S-317.	Nevada	Not Issued
S-318.	New Hampshire	— —
S-319.	New Jersey	— —
S-320.	New Mex. Terr.	— —
S-321.	New York	— —
S-322.	North Carolina	— —
S-323.	North Dakota	Not Issued
S-324.	Ohio	— —
S-325.	Okla. Terr. & St.	Not Issued
S-326.	Oregon	Not Issued
S-327.	Pennsylvania	— —
S-328.	Rhode Island	— —
S-329.	South Carolina	— —
S-330.	South Dakota	Not Issued
S-331.	Tennessee	— —
S-332.	Texas	— —
S-333.	Utah Territory	— —
S-334.	Utah State	— —
S-335.	Vermont	— —
S-336.	Virginia	— —
S-337.	Wash. Terr.	Not Issued
S-338.	Washington St.	Not Issued
S-339.	West Virginia	Not Issued
S-340.	Wisconsin	— —
S-341.	Wyoming Terr.	Not Issued
S-342.	Wyoming State	Not Issued

100 Dollar Notes

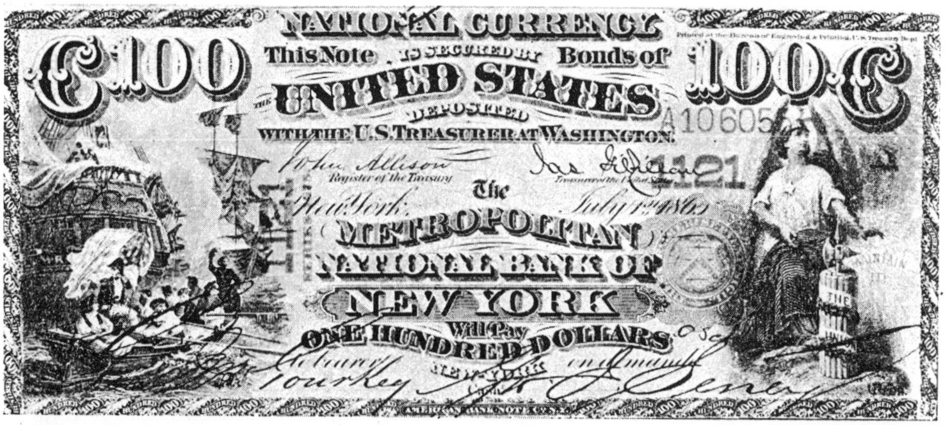

DESIGN NO. 105

(Notes 452-463)

At the left, Commodore Oliver H. Perry leaving the Lawrence, his flagship, during the battle of Lake Erie, September 10, 1813. At the right, Liberty seated by Fasces.

Reverse of Design No. 105.

The signing of the Declaration of Independence, from a painting by John Trumbull. Borders in green, the painting in black.

No.	Series	Signatures		Seal	Very Good	Very Fine
452.	Original	Chittenden	Spinner	Red with rays	3,250.00	6,500.00
454.	Original	Colby	Spinner	Red with rays	3,000.00	6,000.00
455.	Original	Allison	Spinner	Red with rays	3,000.00	6,000.00
456.	1875	Allison	New	Red with scallops	3,000.00	6,000.00
457.	1875	Allison	Wyman	Red with scallops	3,000.00	6,000.00
458.	1875	Allison	Gilfillan	Red with scallops	•3,000.00	6,000.00
459.	1875	Scofield	Gilfillan	Red with scallops	3,000.00	6,000.00
460.	1875	Bruce	Gilfillan	Red with scallops	3,500.00	7,000.00
461.	1875	Bruce	Wyman	Red with scallops	3,500.00	7,000.00
462.	1875	Rosecrans	Huston	Red with scallops	3,500.00	7,000.00
462-a.	1875	Rosecrans	Nebeker	Red with scallops	Rare	—
463.	1875	Tillman	Morgan	Red with scallops	Rare	—

These notes were issued from 1863 to 1901 in sheets of 50-50-50-100 and rarely 50-100 and 100-100 as well as a few other rare combinations.

There are so few notes known of this type, that it is not possible to evaluate them by state. Accordingly, valuations have been omitted and all notes must be considered as rare except those marked "Not Issued."

	State	*Very Fine*
S-343.	Alabama	— —
S-344.	Arizona Terr.	Not Issued
S-345.	Arkansas	Not Issued
S-346.	California	— —
S-347.	Colorado Terr.	— —
S-348.	Colorado State	— —
S-349.	Connecticut	— —
S-350.	Dakota Terr.	Not Issued
S-351.	Delaware	— —
S-352.	Dist. of Columbia	— —
S-353.	Florida	Not Issued
S-354.	Georgia	— —
S-355.	Idaho Territory	Not Issued
S-356.	Illinois	— —
S-357.	Indian Territory	Not Issued
S-358.	Indiana	— —
S-359.	Iowa	— —
S-360.	Kansas	— —
S-361.	Kentucky	— —
S-362.	Louisiana	— —
S-363.	Maine	— —
S-364.	Maryland	— —
S-365.	Massachusetts	— —
S-366.	Michigan	— —
S-367.	Minnesota	— —
S-368.	Mississippi	— —
S-369.	Missouri	— —
S-370.	Montana Terr.	— —
S-371.	Montana State	— —
S-372.	Nebraska Terr.	Not Issued
S-373.	Nebraska State	— —
S-374.	Nevada	Not Issued
S-375.	New Hampshire	— —
S-376.	New Jersey	— —
S-377.	New Mex. Terr.	— —
S-378.	New York	— —
S-379.	North Carolina	— —
S-380.	North Dakota	Not Issued
S-381.	Ohio	— —
S-382.	Okla. Terr. & St.	Not Issued
S-383.	Oregon	Not Issued
S-384.	Pennsylvania	— —
S-385.	Rhode Island	— —
S-386.	South Carolina	— —
S-387.	South Dakota	Not Issued
S-388.	Tennessee	— —
S-389.	Texas	— —
S-390.	Utah Territory	— —
S-391.	Utah State	— —
S-392.	Vermont	— —
S-393.	Virginia	— —
S-394.	Wash. Terr.	Not Issued
S-395.	Wash. State	Not Issued
S-396.	West Virginia	Not Issued
S-397.	Wisconsin	— —
S-398.	Wyoming Terr.	Not Issued
S-399.	Wyoming State	Not Issued

500 Dollar Notes

DESIGN NO. 106

(Note 464)

At the left, an allegory representing The Spirit of the Navy. At the right, the steamship Sirius arriving in New York harbor in 1838.

Reverse of Design No. 106.

The surrender of General John Burgoyne to General Horatio Gates at Saratoga on October 17, 1777. Engraved by Frederick Girsch, from a painting by John Trumbull. Borders in green, the painting in black. The note illustrated is the only specimen known to exist in a collection.

No.	Series	Signatures		Seal	
464.	Original	Colby	Spinner	Red with rays	**Extremely Rare**
464a.	1875	Allison	New	Red with scallops	**Extremely Rare**

(173 pieces are still outstanding.)

1,000 Dollar Notes

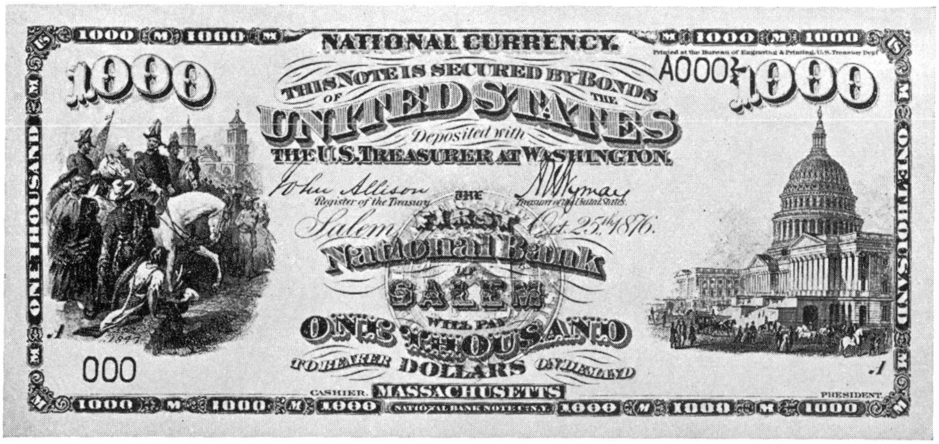

DESIGN NO. 107

(Note 465)

At the left, General Winfield Scott entering Mexico City in 1847 during the Mexican-American War, from a painting by John Trumbull. At the right, the United States Capitol.

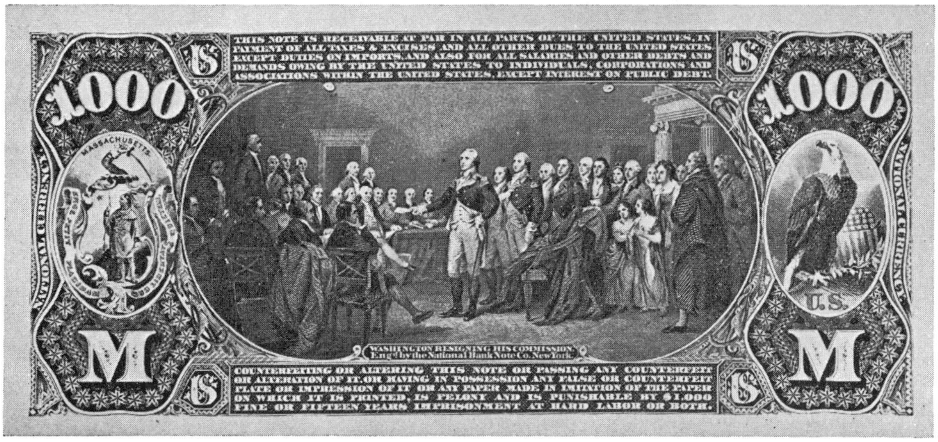

Reverse of Design No. 107.

Washington resigning his Commission, from a painting by John Trumbull. Borders in green, the painting in black.

465. 1,000 Dollar National Bank Note. (Unknown, although 21 pieces are still outstanding.)

(The illustration is of a sample note and was furnished by courtesy of the Bureau of Engraving and Printing.)

Notes of the Second Charter Period

July 12, 1882 to April 11, 1902

(Notes of Second Charter types were issued from 1882 to 1922.)

The Congressional Act of July 12, 1882 created the Second Charter Period, the notes of which bear the designation, "Series of 1882." The purpose of the Act was to make it possible for the banks chartered in 1863 and later to renew their charters at the end of their 20 year term, and also to enable newly organized banks to acquire an initial charter. New notes were designed to mark the transition and in all, three types of notes were issued during this period. As was typical of the First Charter Period, and for the same reasons, notes belonging to the Second Charter Period were issued for about 40 years or until 1922. The three types of notes are as follows:

Brown Backs. These were first placed in circulation in 1882 by two classes of banks; by old banks originally chartered in 1863 and then re-chartered in 1882, and by new banks organized and chartered between July 12, 1882 and April 11, 1902. Brown backs were issued from 1882 to 1908, and would no doubt have continued until 1922 had it not been for passage of the Aldrich-Vreeland Act (described on page 75) which resulted in the issuance of the second type. From 1902 to 1908 the brown backs, Series of 1882, were being issued concurrently with the red seals of the Third Charter Period, Series of 1902. The obligation on the notes of these two series is the same as on the First Charter Notes.

Dates on Back. All denominations of this type bear a large "1882-1908" in the central panel on the back which is green. Notes of this type are referred to as "Emergency Money" as they were issued under the provisions of the Aldrich-Vreeland Act already described. These notes were placed in circulation from June, 1908 to July, 1916, but quite inexplicably, 50 and 100 Dollar notes kept being issued until 1922. The notes of this second type were issued only by those banks that had been issuing brown backs and whose charters were still in force. As a bank's charter expired during this period (1908-1916) it would be re-chartered and would then issue notes of the Third Charter Period, Series of 1902 with "1902-1908" on back. Understandably, the number of such banks kept decreasing during this nine year period and the notes of this type are today quite scarce. When the Aldrich-Vreeland Act expired in 1915, the third type was issued.

Denomination on Back. All notes of this type bear the denomination of the note, spelled out in large letters in the same panel on the green back formerly occupied by "1882-1908." These notes were placed in circulation from 1916 to 1922 and were issued only by those banks that had been issuing the type with "1882-1908" on back, and whose charters were still in force. By this time (1916 to 1922) the number of such banks had dwindled considerably as charters kept expiring in the ensuing seven years, and the notes of this type were issued by fewer banks and over fewer years than any other types of National Bank Notes before or since. As a class, they are thus the rarest of all National Bank Notes. The 50 and 100 Dollar Notes of this type were issued only over a three year period in a ratio of three 50's to each 100 and at present only about two or three specimens of each note have been discovered. Unfortunately, the least is known about this most interesting series, since the Treasury registers pertaining to the issue and distribution of these notes cannot seem to be found.

As previously stated, the latter two types of green back notes, Dates on Back and Denomination on Back, were in the nature of emergency money. When the decision was made to increase the circulation of National Bank Notes, many of the banks did not own the required amounts of United States Bonds necessary to accomplish this. Therefore, Congress passed a bill enabling the banks to deposit with the Treasurer other types of securities. This addition is so stated on the notes; otherwise the obligation is the same as on previous issues.

First Issue. Series of 1882 with Brown Seal and Brown Back.

5 Dollar Notes

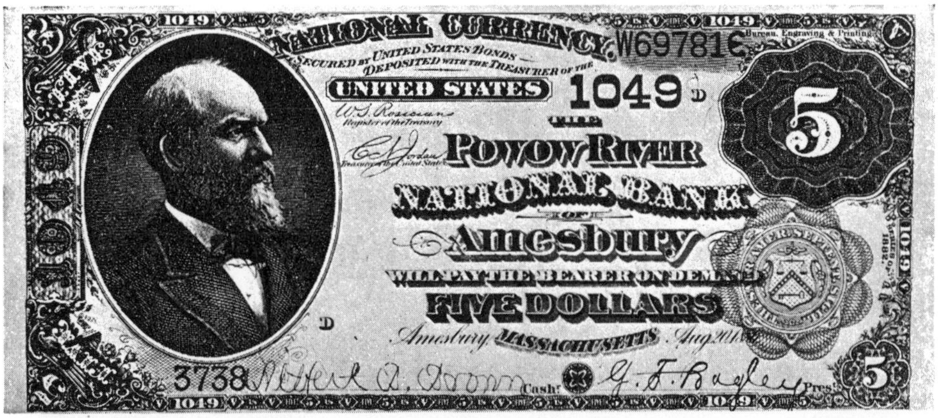

DESIGN NO. 108

(Notes 466-478)

Head of President James Garfield, assassinated seven months after he was elected to the Presidency in 1881.

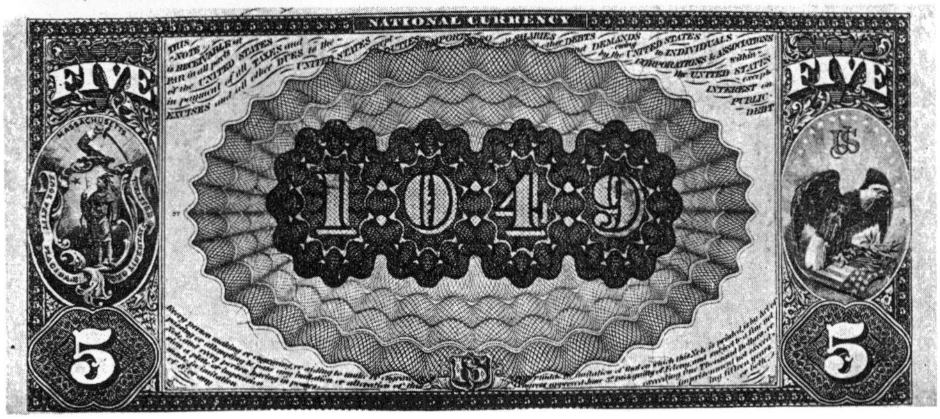

Reverse of Design No. 108.

The charter numbers and surrounding ornament are green, the rest of the reverse is brown. This brown back also appears on Design Nos. 109-112.

No.	Signatures		Very Good	Very Fine	Unc
466.	Bruce	Gilfillan	70.00	135.00	750.00
467.	Bruce	Wyman	70.00	135.00	750.00
468.	Bruce	Jordan	80.00	165.00	800.00
469.	Rosecrans	Jordan	70.00	135.00	750.00
470.	Rosecrans	Hyatt	70.00	135.00	750.00
471.	Rosecrans	Huston	70.00	135.00	750.00
472.	Rosecrans	Nebeker	70.00	135.00	750.00
473.	Rosecrans	Morgan	350.00	800.00	1,500.00
474.	Tillman	Morgan	70.00	135.00	850.00
475.	Tillman	Roberts	100.00	150.00	800.00
476.	Bruce	Roberts	70.00	135.00	800.00
477.	Lyons	Roberts	70.00	135.00	800.00
477-a.	Lyons	Treat		Unknown	
478.	Vernon	Treat	125.00	300.00	1,000.00

These notes were issued from 1882 to 1909 in sheets of 5-5-5-5.

	State	Very Fine
S-400.	Alabama	450.00
S-401.	Arizona Territory	Rare
S-402.	Arkansas	1,100.00
S-403.	California	155.00
S-404.	Colorado	1,000.00
S-405.	Connecticut	200.00
S-406.	Dakota Territory	3,500.00
S-407.	Delaware	650.00
S-408.	Dist. of Columbia	400.00
S-409.	Florida	1,600.00
S-410.	Georgia	450.00
S-411.	Hawaii Territory	1,100.00
S-412.	Idaho Territory	Rare
S-413.	Idaho State	Rare
S-414.	Illinois	120.00
S-415.	Indian Territory	1,600.00
S-416.	Indiana	155.00
S-417.	Iowa	225.00
S-418.	Kansas	300.00
S-419.	Kentucky	225.00
S-420.	Louisiana	375.00
S-421.	Maine	350.00
S-422.	Maryland	225.00
S-423.	Massachusetts	150.00
S-424.	Michigan	200.00
S-425.	Minnesota	275.00
S-426.	Mississippi	2,700.00
S-427.	Missouri	200.00
S-428.	Montana Terr.	2,500.00
S-429.	Montana State	1,850.00
S-430.	Nebraska	350.00
S-431.	Nevada	Rare
S-432.	New Hampshire	300.00
S-433.	New Jersey	200.00
S-434.	New Mexico Terr.	1,350.00
S-435.	New York	135.00
S-436.	North Carolina	575.00
S-437.	North Dakota	1,000.00
S-438.	Ohio	145.00
S-439.	Oklahoma Terr.	1,600.00
S-440.	Oklahoma State	1,600.00
S-441.	Oregon	750.00
S-442.	Pennsylvania	135.00
S-443.	Rhode Island	275.00
S-444.	South Carolina	1,100.00
S-445.	South Dakota	1,100.00
S-446.	Tennessee	675.00
S-447.	Texas	375.00
S-448.	Utah Territory	4,000.00
S-449.	Utah State	675.00
S-450.	Vermont	375.00
S-451.	Virginia	400.00
S-452.	Washington Terr.	5,250.00
S-453.	Washington State	1,350.00
S-454.	West Virginia	350.00
S-455.	Wisconsin	275.00
S-456.	Wyoming Territory	Rare
S-457.	Wyoming State	1,350.00

10 Dollar Notes

DESIGN NO. 109

(Notes 479-492)

At the left, Benjamin Franklin drawing electricity from the sky with a kite and a key. At the right, Liberty soaring on an eagle, clutching lightning in her hand.

Reverse of Design No. 109.

The charter numbers and surrounding ornament are green, the rest of the reverse is brown.

No.	Signatures		Very Good	Very Fine	Unc
479.	Bruce	Gilfillan	80.00	150.00	850.00
480.	Bruce	Wyman	80.00	150.00	850.00
481.	Bruce	Jordan	100.00	250.00	1,100.00
482.	Rosecrans	Jordan	80.00	150.00	850.00
483.	Rosecrans	Hyatt	80.00	150.00	850.00
484.	Rosecrans	Huston	80.00	150.00	850.00
485.	Rosecrans	Nebeker	80.00	150.00	850.00
486.	Rosecrans	Morgan	475.00	1,000.00	4,500.00
487.	Tillman	Morgan	80.00	150.00	850.00
488.	Tillman	Roberts	• 100.00	250.00	1,100.00
489.	Bruce	Roberts	80.00	150.00	850.00
490.	Lyons	Roberts	80.00	150.00	850.00
491.	Lyons	Treat	150.00	350.00	1,700.00
492.	Vernon	Treat	150.00	350.00	1,700.00

These notes were issued from 1882 to 1909 in sheets of 10-10-10-20 and rarely 10-10-10-10.

	State	*Very Fine*
S-458.	Alabama	450.00
S-459.	Arizona Terr.	Rare
S-460.	Arkansas	1,200.00
S-461.	California	225.00
S-462.	Colorado	950.00
S-463.	Connecticut	200.00
S-464.	Dakota Terr.	Rare
S-465.	Delaware	800.00
S-466.	District of Columbia	475.00
S-467.	Florida	1,600.00
S-468.	Georgia	450.00
S-469.	Hawaii Terr.	1,000.00
S-470.	Idaho Terr.	Rare
S-471.	Idaho State	4,250.00
S-472.	Illinois	150.00
S-473.	Indian Territory	2,000.00
S-474.	Indiana	185.00
S-475.	Iowa	250.00
S-476.	Kansas	325.00
S-477.	Kentucky	225.00
S-478.	Louisiana	400.00
S-479.	Maine	375.00
S-480.	Maryland	275.00
S-481.	Massachusetts	190.00
S-482.	Michigan	250.00
S-483.	Minnesota	275.00
S-484.	Mississippi	Rare
S-485.	Missouri	195.00
S-486.	Montana Terr.	2,750.00
S-487.	Montana State	1,850.00
S-488.	Nebraska	350.00
S-489.	Nevada	Rare
S-490.	New Hampshire	375.00
S-491.	New Jersey	225.00
S-492.	New Mexico Terr.	1,500.00
S-493.	New York	150.00
S-494.	North Carolina	700.00
S-495.	North Dakota	1,100.00
S-496.	Ohio	175.00
S-497.	Oklahoma Terr.	2,000.00
S-498.	Oklahoma State	1,750.00
S-499.	Oregon	800.00
S-500.	Pennsylvania	150.00
S-501.	Rhode Island	350.00
S-502.	South Carolina	1,350.00
S-503.	South Dakota	1,100.00
S-504.	Tennessee	700.00
S-505.	Texas	375.00
S-506.	Utah Territory	3,500.00
S-507.	Utah State	750.00
S-508.	Vermont	350.00
S-509.	Virginia	450.00
S-510.	Washington Terr.	5,000.00
S-511.	Washington State	1,350.00
S-512.	West Virginia	350.00
S-513.	Wisconsin	325.00
S-514.	Wyoming Territory	Rare
S-515.	Wyoming State	1,350.00

20 Dollar Notes

DESIGN NO. 110

(Notes 493-506)

At the left, the Battle of Lexington, April 19, 1775. At the right, Columbia leading procession.

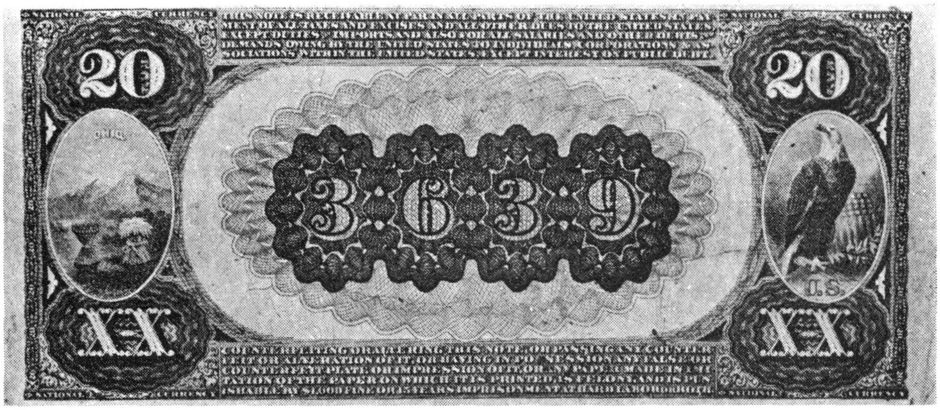

Reverse of Design No. 110.

The charter numbers and surrounding ornament are green, the rest of the reverse is brown.

No.	Signatures		Very Good	Very Fine	Unc
493.	Bruce	Gilfillan	100.00	225.00	950.00
494.	Bruce	Wyman	100.00	225.00	950.00
495.	Bruce	Jordan	135.00	300.00	1,300.00
496.	Rosecrans	Jordan	•100.00	225.00	950.00
497.	Rosecrans	Hyatt	100.00	225.00	950.00
498.	Rosecrans	Huston	100.00	225.00	950.00
499.	Rosecrans	Nebeker	100.00	225.00	950.00
500.	Rosecrans	Morgan	700.00	1,750.00	3,000.00
501.	Tillman	Morgan	100.00	225.00	950.00
502.	Tillman	Roberts	135.00	300.00	1,300.00
503.	Bruce	Roberts	100.00	225.00	950.00
504.	Lyons	Roberts	100.00	225.00	950,00
505.	Lyons	Treat	200.00	600.00	1,600.00
506.	Vernon	Treat	150.00	400.00	1,500.00

These notes were issued from 1882 to 1909 in sheets of 10-10-10-20.

	State	*Very Fine*
S-516.	Alabama	575.00
S-517.	Arizona Terr.	2,500.00
S-518.	Arkansas	1,750.00
S-519.	California	300.00
S-520.	Colorado	1,100.00
S-521.	Connecticut	300.00
S-522.	Dakota Territory	Rare
S-523.	Delaware	800.00
S-524.	Dist. of Columbia	500.00
S-525.	Florida	2,250.00
S-526.	Georgia	575.00
S-527.	Hawaii Territory	1,100.00
S-528.	Idaho Territory	Rare
S-529.	Idaho State	Rare
S-530.	Illinois	225.00
S-531.	Indian Territory	1,850.00
S-532.	Indiana	225.00
S-533.	Iowa	325.00
S-534.	Kansas	400.00
S-535.	Kentucky	325.00
S-536.	Louisiana	500.00
S-537.	Maine	525.00
S-538.	Maryland	375.00
S-539.	Massachusetts	225.00
S-540.	Michigan	300.00
S-541.	Minnesota	375.00
S-542.	Mississippi	Rare
S-543.	Missouri	275.00
S-544.	Montana Territory	3,250.00
S-545.	Montana State	1,850.00
S-546.	Nebraska	475.00
S-547.	Nevada	Rare
S-548.	New Hampshire	450.00
S-549.	New Jersey	300.00
S-550.	New Mexico Terr.	1,800.00
S-551.	New York	225.00
S-552.	North Carolina	750.00
S-553.	North Dakota	1,350.00
S-554.	Ohio	225.00
S-555.	Oklahoma Terr.	1,950.00
S-556.	Oklahoma State	2,000.00
S-557.	Oregon	1,350.00
S-558.	Pennsylvania	225.00
S-559.	Rhode Island	525.00
S-560.	South Carolina	1,350.00
S-561.	South Dakota	1,350.00
S-562.	Tennessee	800.00
S-563.	Texas	525.00
S-564.	Utah Territory	Rare
S-565.	Utah State	1,100.00
S-566.	Vermont	500.00
S-567.	Virginia	500.00
S-568.	Washington Terr.	4,250.00
S-569.	Washington State	1,350.00
S-570.	West Virginia	500.00
S-571.	Wisconsin	400.00
S-572.	Wyoming Territory	Rare
S-573.	Wyoming State	1,350.00

50 Dollar Notes

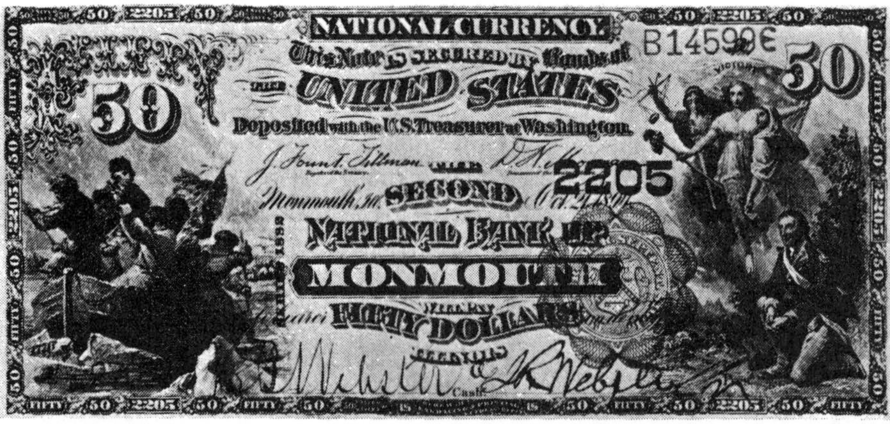

DESIGN NO. 111

(Notes 507-518-a)

At the left, Washington crossing the Delaware. At right, Washington at prayer.

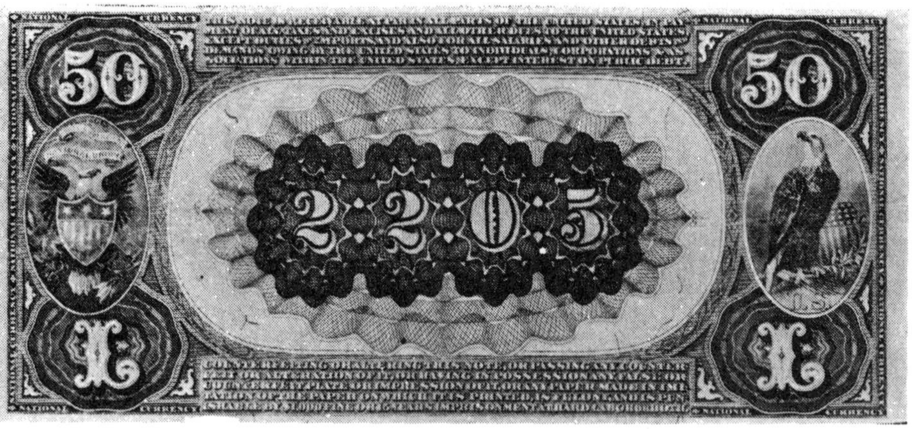

Reverse of Design No. 111.

The charter numbers and surrounding ornament are green, the rest of the reverse is brown.

No.	Signatures		Very Good	Very Fine	Unc
507.	Bruce	Gilfillan	350.00	750.00	3,000.00
508.	Bruce	Wyman	350.00	750.00	3,000.00
509.	Bruce	Jordan	400.00	800.00	3,250.00
510.	Rosecrans	Jordan	350.00	750.00	3,000.00
511.	Rosecrans	Hyatt	350.00	750.00	3,000.00
512.	Rosecrans	Huston	350.00	750.00	3,000.00
513.	Rosecrans	Nebeker	350.00	750.00	3,000.00

No.	Signatures		Very Good	Very Fine	Unc
514.	Rosecrans	Morgan	950.00	2,000.00	3,500.00
515.	Tillman	Morgan	• 350.00	750.00	3,000.00
516.	Tillman	Roberts	400.00	800.00	3,200.00
517.	Bruce	Roberts	350.00	750.00	3,000.00
518.	Lyons	Roberts	350.00	750.00	3,000.00
518-a.	Vernon	Treat	950.00	2,000.00	4,000.00

These notes were issued from 1882 to 1909 in sheets of 50-100.

Only relatively few of these notes are in existence and it is not possible to evaluate them by state. Accordingly, the valuations have been omitted. The known specimens of these notes are generally from the largest and most populous states. The same relative rarity would apply as exists within the 5 Dollar notes.

	State	*Very Fine*
S-574.	Alabama	— —
S-575.	Arizona Terr.	— —
S-576.	Arkansas	— —
S-577.	California	— —
S-578.	Colorado	— —
S-579.	Connecticut	— —
S-580.	Dakota Territory	— —
S-581.	Delaware	— —
S-582.	District of Col.	— —
S-583.	Florida	— —
S-584.	Georgia	— —
S-585.	Hawaii Territory	— —
S-586.	Idaho Terr.	Not Issued
S-587.	Idaho State	— —
S-588.	Illinois	— —
S-589.	Indian Territory	— —
S-590.	Indiana	— —
S-591.	Iowa	— —
S-592.	Kansas	— —
S-593.	Kentucky	— —
S-594.	Louisiana	— —
S-595.	Maine	— —
S-596.	Maryland	— —
S-597.	Massachusetts	— —
S-598.	Michigan	— —
S-599.	Minnesota	— —
S-600.	Mississippi	— —
S-601.	Missouri	— —
S-602.	Montana Terr.	— —
S-603.	Montana State	— —
S-604.	Nebraska	— —
S-605.	Nevada	Not Issued
S-606.	New Hampshire	— —
S-607.	New Jersey	— —
S-608.	New Mex. Terr.	— —
S-609.	New York	— —
S-610.	North Carolina	— —
S-611.	North Dakota	— —
S-612.	Ohio	— —
S-613.	Oklahoma Terr.	— —
S-614.	Oklahoma State	— —
S-615.	Oregon	— —
S-616.	Pennsylvania	— —
S-617.	Rhode Island	— —
S-618.	South Carolina	— —
S-619.	South Dakota	— —
S-620.	Tennessee	— —
S-621.	Texas	— —
S-622.	Utah Territory	— —
S-623.	Utah State	— —
S-624.	Vermont	— —
S-625.	Virginia	— —
S-626.	Wash. Terr.	Not Issued
S-267.	Wash. State	— —
S-628.	West Virginia	— —
S-629.	Wisconsin	— —
S-630.	Wyoming Terr.	Not Issued
S-631.	Wyoming State	Not Issued

100 Dollar Notes

DESIGN NO. 112

(Notes 519-531)

At the left, Commodore Oliver H. Perry leaving the Lawrence, his flagship, during the battle of Lake Erie, September 10, 1813. At the right, Liberty seated by Fasces.

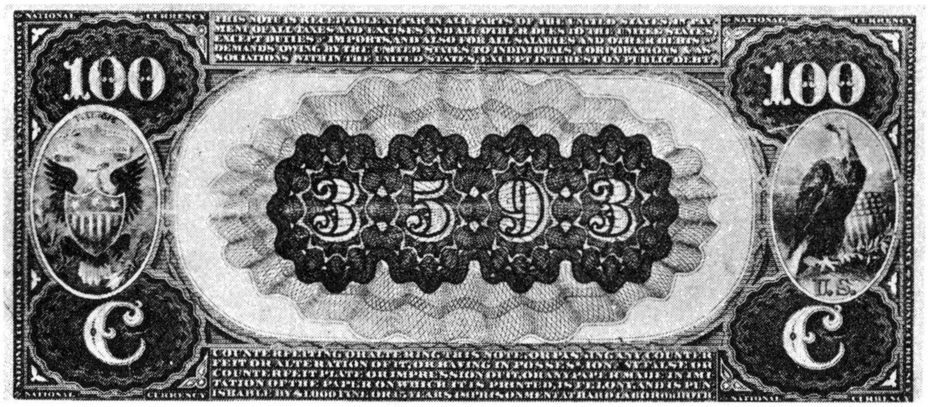

Reverse of Design No. 112.

The charter numbers and surrounding ornament are green, the rest of the reverse is brown.

No.	Signatures		Very Good	Very Fine	Unc
519.	Bruce	Gilfillan	500.00	1,100.00	4,750.00
520.	Bruce	Wyman	500.00	1,100.00	4,750.00
521.	Bruce	Jordan	500.00	1,100.00	4,750.00
522.	Rosecrans	Jordan	•500.00	1,100.00	4,750.00
523.	Rosecrans	Hyatt	500.00	1,100.00	4,750.00
524.	Rosecrans	Huston	500.00	1,100.00	4,750.00
525.	Rosecrans	Nebeker	500.00	1,100.00	4,750.00
526.	Rosecrans	Morgan	1,000.00	2,500.00	5,000.00
527.	Tillman	Morgan	500.00	1,100.00	4,750.00
528.	Tillman	Roberts	500.00	1,100.00	4,750.00
529.	Bruce	Roberts	500.00	1,100.00	4,750.00
530.	Lyons	Roberts	500.00	1,100.00	4,750.00
531.	Vernon	Treat	1,000.00	2,750.00	5,250.00

These notes were issued from 1882 to 1909 in sheets of 50-100.

Only relatively few of these notes are in existence and it is not possible to evaluate them by state. Accordingly, the valuations have been omitted. The known specimens of these notes are generally from the largest and most populous states. The same relative rarity would apply as exists within the 5 Dollar notes.

	State	*Very Fine*
S-632.	Alabama	— —
S-633.	Arizona Terr.	— —
S-634.	Arkansas	— —
S-635.	California	— —
S-636.	Colorado	— —
S-637.	Connecticut	— —
S-638.	Dakota Territory	— —
S-639.	Delaware	— —
S-640.	Dist. of Col.	— —
S-641.	Florida	— —
S-642.	Georgia	— —
S-643.	Hawaii Territory	— —
S-644.	Idaho Territory	Not Issued
S-645.	Idaho State	— —
S-646.	Illinois	— —
S-647.	Indian Terr.	— —
S-648.	Indiana	— —
S-649.	Iowa	— —
S-650.	Kansas	— —
S-651.	Kentucky	— —
S-652.	Louisiana	— —
S-653.	Maine	— —
S-654.	Maryland	— —
S-655.	Massachusetts	— —
S-656.	Michigan	— —
S-657.	Minnesota	— —
S-658.	Mississippi	— —
S-659.	Missouri	— —
S-660.	Montana Terr.	— —
S-661.	Montana State	— —
S-662.	Nebraska	— —
S-663.	Nevada	Not Issued
S-664.	New Hampshire	— —
S-665.	New Jersey	— —
S-666.	New Mex. Terr.	— —
S-667.	New York	— —
S-668.	North Carolina	— —
S-669.	North Dakota	— —
S-670.	Ohio	— —
S-671.	Oklahoma Terr.	— —
S-672.	Oklahoma State	— —
S-673.	Oregon	— —
S-674.	Pennsylvania	— —
S-675.	Rhode Island	— —
S-676.	South Carolina	— —
S-677.	South Dakota	— —
S-678.	Tennessee	— —
S-679.	Texas	— —
S-680.	Utah Territory	— —
S-681.	Utah State	— —
S-682.	Vermont	— —
S-683.	Virginia	— —
S-684.	Wash. Terr.	Not Issued
S-685.	Wash. State	— —
S-686.	West Virginia	— —
S-687.	Wisconsin	— —
S-688.	Wyoming Terr.	Not Issued
S-689.	Wyoming State	Not Issued

Second Issue. Series of 1882 with Blue Seal and with "1882-1908" on Green Back.

5 Dollar Notes

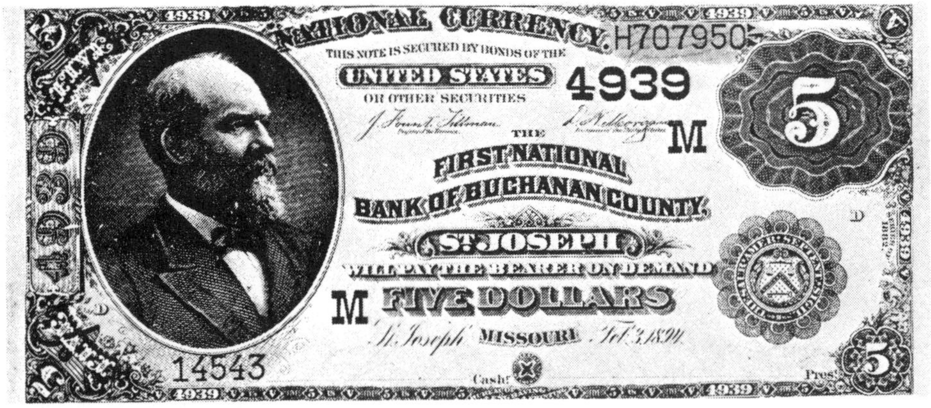

DESIGN NO. 113

(Notes 532-538-b)

Head of President James Garfield, assassinated seven months after he was elected to the Presidency in 1881.

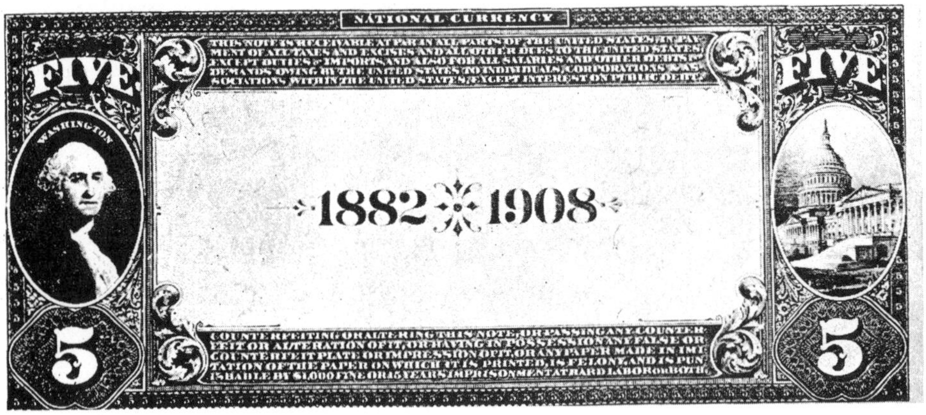

Reverse of Design No. 113.

At the left, head of George Washington. At the right, the U.S. Capitol.

No.	Signatures		Very Good	Very Fine	Unc
532.	Rosecrans	Huston	85.00	175.00	850.00
533.	Rosecrans	Nebeker	85.00	175.00	850.00
533-a.	Rosecrans	Morgan	450.00	900.00	1,500.00
534.	Tillman	Morgan	· 85.00	175.00	850.00
535.	Tillman	Roberts	95.00	175.00	850.00
536.	Bruce	Roberts	95.00	175.00	950.00
537.	Lyons	Roberts	85.00	160.00	850.00
538.	Vernon	Treat	95.00	195.00	950.00
538-a.	Vernon	McClung		Unknown	
538-b.	Napier	McClung	450.00	900.00	1,800.00

These notes were issued from 1908 to 1916 in sheets of 5-5-5-5.

	State	*Very Fine*
S-690.	*Alabama*	400.00
S-691.	Arizona Territory	3,000.00
S-692.	Arizona State	1,750.00
S-693.	Arkansas	850.00
S-694.	California	250.00
S-695.	Colorado	600.00
S-696.	Connecticut	475.00
S-697.	Delaware	800.00
S-698.	District of Columbia	475.00
S-699.	Florida	1,000.00
S-700.	Georgia	400.00
S-701.	Hawaii Territory	900.00
S-702.	Idaho	2,250.00
S-703.	Illinois	175.00
S-704.	Indiana	185.00
S-705.	Iowa	210.00
S-706.	Kansas	275.00
S-707.	Kentucky	225.00
S-708.	Louisiana	550.00
S-709.	Maine	1,000.00
S-710.	Maryland	375.00
S-711.	Massachusetts	250.00
S-712.	Michigan	225.00
S-713.	Minnesota	250.00
S-714.	Mississippi	1,000.00
S-715.	Missouri	225.00
S-716.	Montana	850.00
S-717.	Nebraska	325.00
S-718.	Nevada	Not Issued
S719.	New Hampshire	450.00
S-720.	New Jersey	200.00
S-721.	New Mexico Terr.	1,750.00
S-722.	New Mexico State	850.00
S-723.	New York	175.00
S-724.	North Carolina	500.00
S-725.	North Dakota	750.00
S-726.	Ohio	175.00
S-727.	Oklahoma	450.00
S-728.	Oregon	500.00
S-729.	Pennsylvania	175.00
S-730.	Rhode Island	400.00
S-731.	South Carolina	650.00
S-732.	South Dakota	675.00
S-733.	Tennessee	600.00
S-734.	Texas	550.00
S-735.	Utah	700.00
S-736.	Vermont	500.00
S-737.	Virginia	300.00
S-738.	Washington	800.00
S-739.	West Virginia	500.00
S-740.	Wisconsin	250.00
S-741.	Wyoming	800.00

10 Dollar Notes

DESIGN NO. 114

(Notes 539-548)

At the left, Benjamin Franklin drawing electricity from the sky with a kite and a key. At the right, Liberty soaring on an eagle, clutching lightning in her hand.

Reverse of Design No. 114.

At the left, head of William P. Fessenden, Secretary of the Treasury in 1864. At the right, seated figure representing Mechanics.

No.	Signatures		Very Good	Very Fine	Unc
539.	Rosecrans	Huston	100.00	250.00	1,100.00
540.	Rosecrans	Nebeker	100.00	250.00	1,100.00
541.	Rosecrans	Morgan	550.00	1,100.00	2,000.00
542.	Tillman	Morgan	100.00	250.00	1,100.00
543.	Tillman	Roberts	125.00	275.00	1,100.00
544.	Bruce	Roberts	125.00	275.00	1,100.00
545.	Lyons	Roberts	100.00	250.00	1,100.00
546.	Vernon	Treat	125.00	275.00	1,250.00
547.	Vernon	McClung	150.00	350.00	1,300.00
548.	Napier	McClung	140.00	30.00	1,250.00

These notes were issued from 1908 to 1922 in sheets of 10-10-10-10 and 10-10-10-20.

	State	*Very Fine*
S-742.	Alabama	500.00
S-743.	Arizona Territory	3,000.00
S-744.	Arizona State	1,500.00
S-745.	Arkansas	850.00
S-746.	California	275.00
S-747.	Colorado	700.00
S-748.	Connecticut	475.00
S-749.	Delaware	750.00
S-750.	District of Columbia	500.00
S-751.	Florida	1,000.00
S-752.	Georgia	450.00
S-753.	Hawaii Territory	850.00
S-754.	Idaho	Rare
S-755.	Illinois	250.00
S-756.	Indiana	250.00
S-757.	Iowa	275.00
S-758.	Kansas	300.00
S-759.	Kentucky	275.00
S-760.	Louisiana	625.00
S-761.	Maine	1,000.00
S-762.	Maryland	425.00
S-763.	Massachusetts	325.00
S-764.	Michigan	275.00
S-765.	Minnesota	300.00
S-766.	Mississippi	1,000.00
S-767.	Missouri	275.00
S-768.	Montana	725.00
S-769.	Nebraska	325.00
S-770.	Nevada	Not Issued
S-771.	New Hampshire	500.00
S-772.	New Jersey	250.00
S-773.	New Mexico Terr.	1,500.00
S-774.	New Mexico State	850.00
S-775.	New York	250.00
S-776.	North Carolina	550.00
S-777.	North Dakota	750.00
S-778.	Ohio	225.00
S-779.	Oklahoma	500.00
S-780.	Oregon	625.00
S-781.	Pennsylvania	250.00
S-782.	Rhode Island	600.00
S-783.	South Carolina	750.00
S-784.	South Dakota	750.00
S-785.	Tennessee	600.00
S-786.	Texas	400.00
S-787.	Utah	900.00
S-788.	Vermont	500.00
S-789.	Virginia	350.00
S-790.	Washington	750.00
S-791.	West Virginia	500.00
S-792.	Wisconsin	275.00
S-793.	Wyoming	850.00

20 Dollar Notes

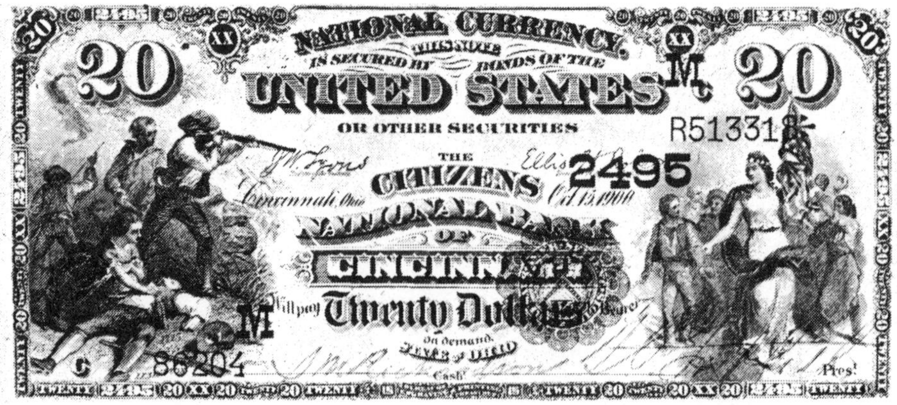

DESIGN NO. 115

(Notes 549-557)

At the left, the Battle of Lexington, April 19, 1775. At the right, Columbia leading procession.

Reverse of Design No. 115.

No.	Signatures		Very Good	Very Fine	Unc
549.	Rosecrans	Huston	135.00	325.00	1,300.00
550.	Rosecrans	Nebeker	135.00	325.00	1,300.00
551.	Rosecrans	Morgan	600.00	1,400.00	2,350.00
552.	Tillman	Morgan	135.00	325.00	1,300.00
553.	Tillman	Roberts	135.00	325.00	1,300.00
554.	Bruce	Roberts	160.00	350.00	1,350.00
555.	Lyons	Roberts	• 135.00	325.00	1,300.00
556.	Vernon	Treat	160.00	350.00	1,350.00
556-a.	Vernon	McClung		Unknown	
557.	Napier	McClung	190.00	400.00	2,500.00

These notes were issued from 1908 to 1916 in sheets of 10-10-10-20.

	State	*Very Fine*
S-794.	Alabama	650.00
S-794a.	Alaska Territory	Rare
S-795.	Arizona Territory	3,750.00
S-796.	Arizona State	1,700.00
S-797.	Arkansas	1,100.00
S-798.	California	375.00
S-799.	Colorado	800.00
S-800.	Connecticut	575.00
S-801.	Delaware	1,100.00
S-802.	District of Columbia	600.00
S-803.	Florida	1,600.00
S-804.	Georgia	500.00
S-805.	Hawaii Territory	1,300.00
S-806.	Idaho	2,750.00
S-807.	Illinois	325.00
S-808.	Indiana	325.00
S-809.	Iowa	350.00
S-810.	Kansas	425.00
S-811.	Kentucky	400.00
S-812.	Louisiana	750.00
S-813.	Maine	1,000.00
S-814.	Maryland	475.00
S-815.	Massachusetts	375.00
S-816.	Michigan	400.00
S-817.	Minnesota	375.00
S-818.	Mississippi	1,350.00
S-819.	Missouri	375.00
S-820.	Montana	950.00
S-821.	Nebraska	450.00
S-822.	Nevada	Not Issued
S-823.	New Hampshire	800.00
S-824.	New Jersey	350.00
S-825.	New Mexico Terr.	1,850.00
S-826.	New Mexico State	1,100.00
S-827.	New York	325.00
S-828.	North Carolina	650.00
S-829.	North Dakota	850.00
S-830.	Ohio	325.00
S-831.	Oklahoma	600.00
S-832.	Oregon	675.00
S-833.	Pennsylvania	325.00
S-834.	Rhode Island	800.00
S-835.	South Carolina	900.00
S-836.	South Dakota	1,000.00
S-837.	Tennessee	800.00
S-838.	Texas	475.00
S-839.	Utah	Rare
S-840.	Vermont	850.00
S-841.	Virginia	425.00
S-842.	Washington	1,000.00
S-843.	West Virginia	600.00
S-844.	Wisconsin	400.00
S-845.	Wyoming	1,100.00

50 Dollar Notes

DESIGN NO. 116

(Notes 558-565)

At the left, Washington crossing the Delaware. At the right, Wcshington at prayer.

Reverse of Design No. 116.

This illustration by courtesy of Mr. W.A. Philpott, Jr.

No.	Signatures		Very Good	Very Fine	Unc
558.	Rosecrans	Huston	450.00	850.00	4,000.00
559.	Rosecrans	Nebeker	450.00	850.00	4,000.00
560.	Tillman	Morgan	450.00	850.00	4,000.00
561.	Tillman	Roberts	500.00	900.00	4,100.00
562.	Bruce	Roberts	500.00	875.00	4,100.00
563.	Lyons	Roberts	• 450.00	850.00	4,000.00
564.	Vernon	Treat	525.00	925.00	4,250.00
565.	Napier	McClung	550.00	950.00	4,500.00

These notes were issued from 1910 to 1922 in sheets of 50-50-50-100.

Only relatively few of these notes are in existence and it is not possible to evaluate them by state. Accordingly, the valuations have been omitted. The known specimens of these notes are generally from the largest and most populous states. The same relative rarity would apply as exists within the 10 Dollar notes.

	State	*Very Fine*
S-846.	Alabama	– –
S-847.	Arizona Terr.	– –
S-848.	Arizona State	– –
S-849.	Arkansas	– –
S-850.	California	– –
S-851.	Colorado	– –
S-852.	Connecticut	– –
S-853.	Delaware	– –
S-854.	District of Col.	– –
S-855.	Florida	– –
S-856.	Georgia	– –
S-857.	Hawaii Territory	**Not Issued**
S-858.	Idaho	– –
S-859.	Illinois	– –
S-860	Indiana	– –
S-861.	Iowa	– –
S-862.	Kansas	– –
S-863.	Kentucky	– –
S-864.	Louisiana	– –
S-865.	Maine	**Not Issued**
S-866.	Maryland	– –
S-867.	Massachusetts	– –
S-868.	Michigan	– –
S-869.	Minnestoa	– –
S-870.	Mississippi	**Not Issued**
S-871.	Missouri	– –
S-872.	Montana	– –
S-873.	Nebraska	– –
S-874.	Nevada	**Not Issued**
S-875.	New Hampshire	– –
S-876.	New Jersey	– –
S-877.	New Mex. Terr.	– –
S-878.	New Mex. State	– –
S-879.	New York	– –
S-880.	North Carolina	– –
S-881.	North Dakota	– –
S-882.	Ohio	– –
S-883.	Oklahoma	– –
S-884.	Oregon	**Not Issued**
S-885.	Pennsylvania	– –
S-886.	Rhode Island	**Not Issued**
S-887.	South Carolina	– –
S-888.	South Dakota	– –
S-889.	Tennessee	– –
S-890.	Texas	– –
S-891.	Utah	– –
S-892.	Vermont	– –
S-893.	Virginia	– –
S-894.	Washington	– –
S-895.	West Virginia	– –
S-896.	Wisconsin	**Not Issued**
S-897.	Wyoming	**Not Issued**

100 Dollar Notes

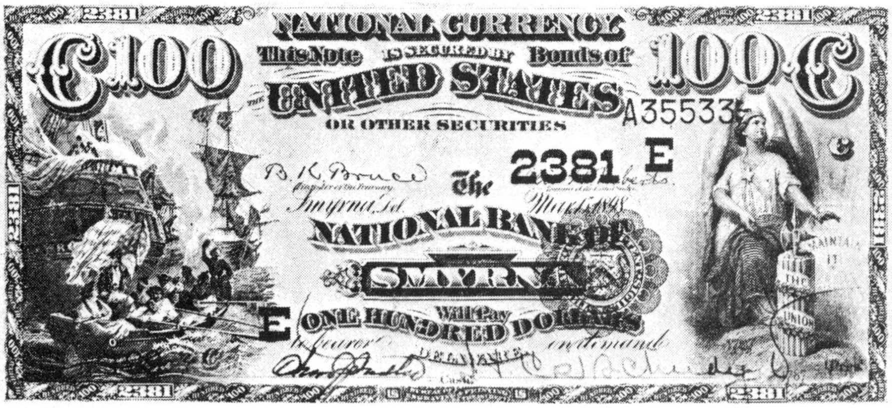

DESIGN NO. 117

(Notes 566-572-a)

At the left, Commodore Oliver H. Perry leaving the Lawrence, his flagship, during the battle of Lake Erie, September 10, 1813. At the right, Liberty seated by Fasces.

Reverse of Design No. 117.

No.	Signatures		Very Good	Very Fine	Unc	No.	Signatures		Very Good	Very Fine	Unc
566.	Rosecrans	Huston	550.00	1,200.00	6,000.00	570.	Bruce	Roberts	• 575.00	1,250.00	6,250.00
567.	Rosecrans	Nebeker	575.00	1,250.00	6,250.00	571.	Lyons	Roberts	550.00	1,200.00	6,000.00
568.	Tillman	Morgan	575.00	1,250.00	6,250.00	572.	Vernon	Treat	650.00	1,350.00	6,500.00
569.	Tillman	Roberts	575.00	1,250.00	6,250.00	572-a.	Napier	McClung	800.00	1,500.00	6,750.00

These notes were issued from 1910 to 1922 in sheets of 50-50-50-100.

Only relatively few of these notes are in existence and it is not possible to evaluate them by state. Accordingly, the valuations have been omitted. The known specimens of these notes are generally from the largest and most populous states. The same relative rarity would apply as exists within the 20 Dollar notes.

	State	*Very Fine*
S-898.	Alabama	— —
S-899.	Arizona Terr.	— —
S-900.	Arizona State	— —
S-901.	Arkansas	— —
S-902.	California	— —
S-903.	Colorado	— —
S-904.	Connecticut	— —
S-905.	Delaware	— —
S-906.	District of Col.	— —
S-907.	Florida	— —
S-908.	Georgia	— —
S-909.	Hawaii Territory	**Not Issued**
S-910.	Idaho	— —
S-911.	Illinois	— —
S-912.	Indiana	— —
S-913.	Iowa	— —
S-914.	Kansas	— —
S-915.	Kentucky	— —

	State	*Very Fine*
S-916.	Louisiana	— —
S-917.	Maine	**Not Issued**
S-918.	Maryland	— —
S-919.	Massachusetts	— —
S-920.	Michigan	— —
S-921.	Minnesota	— —
S-922.	Mississippi	**Not Issued**
S-923.	Missouri	— —
S-924.	Montana	— —
S-925.	Nebraska	— —
S-926.	Nevada	**Not Issued**
S-927.	New Hampshire	— —
S-928.	New Jersey	— —
S-929.	New Mex. Terr.	— —
S-930.	New Mex. State	— —
S-931.	New York	— —
S-932.	North Carolina	— —

	State	*Very Fine*
S-933.	North Dakota	— —
S-934.	Ohio	— —
S-935.	Oklahoma	— —
S-936.	Oregon	**Not Issued**
S-937.	Pennsylvania	— —
S-938.	Rhode Island	**Not Issued**
S-939.	South Carolina	— —
S-940.	South Dakota	— —
S-941.	Tennessee	— —
S-942.	Texas	— —
S-943.	Utah	— —
S-944.	Vermont	— —
S-945.	Virginia	— —
S-946.	Washington	— —
S-947.	West Virginia	— —
S-948.	Wisconsin	**Not Issued**
S-949.	Wyoming	**Not Issued**

Third Issue. Series of 1882 with Blue Seal and with denomination spelled out across Green Back.

5 Dollar Notes

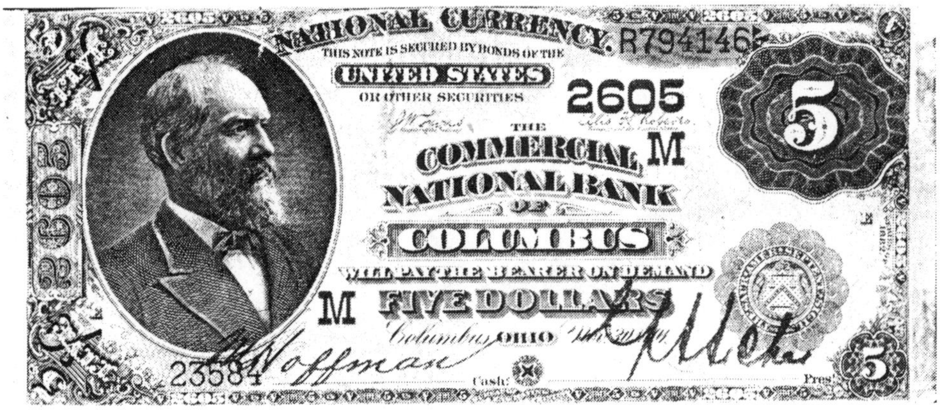

DESIGN NO. 118

(Notes 573-575-b)

Head of President James Garfield, assassinated seven months after he was elected to the Presidency in 1881.

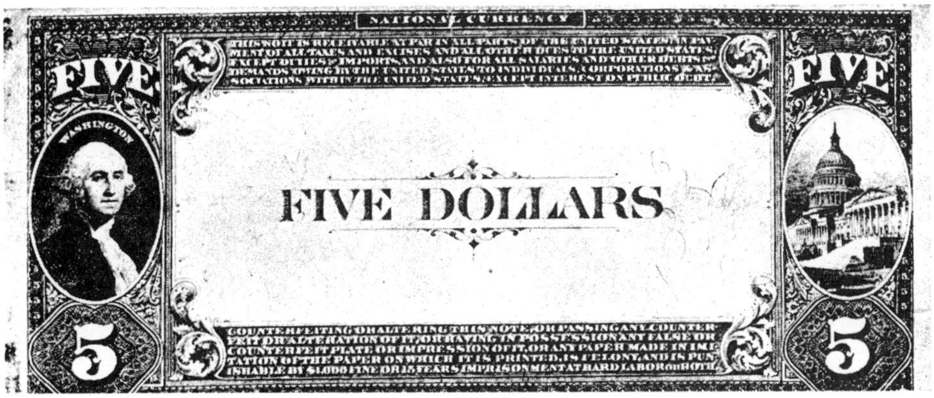

Reverse of Design No. 113.

At the left, head of George Washington. At the right, the U.S. Capitol.

No.	Signatures		Very Good	Very Fine	Unc
573.	Tillman	Morgan	125.00	400.00	1,250.00
573-a.	Tillman	Roberts	200.00	750.00	2,000.00
574.	Lyons	Roberts	•125.00	400.00	1,250.00
574-a.	Bruce	Roberts	200.00	750.00	2,000.00
574-b.	Lyons	Treat		**Unknown**	
575.	Vernon	Treat	175.00	600.00	1,500.00
575-a.	Napier	McClung	275.00	700.00	1,750.00
575-b.	Teehee	Burke		**Rare**	

These notes were issued from 1916 to 1922 in sheets of 5-5-5-5.

	State	*Very Fine*
S-950.	Alabama	— —
S-951.	Arizona	**Not Issued**
S-952.	Arkansas	— —
S-953.	California	— —
S-954.	Colorado	— —
S-955.	Connecticut	— —
S-956.	Delaware	— —
S-957.	District of Col.	— —
S-958.	Florida	— —
S-959.	Georgia	— —
S-960.	Hawaii Territory	— —
S-961.	Idaho	— —
S-962.	Illinois	— —
S-963.	Indiana	— —
S-964.	Iowa	— —
S-965.	Kansas	— —
S-966.	Kentucky	— —
S-967.	Louisiana	— —
S-968.	Maine	— —
S-969.	Maryland	— —
S-970.	Massachusetts	— —
S-971.	Michigan	— —
S-972.	Minnesota	— —
S-973.	Mississippi	— —
S-974.	Missouri	— —
S-975.	Montana	— —
S-976.	Nebraska	— —
S-977.	Nevada	— —
S-978.	New Hampshire	— —
S-979.	New Jersey	— —
S-980.	New Mexico	— —
S-981.	New York	— —
S-982.	North Carolina	— —
S-983.	North Dakota	— —
S-984.	Ohio	— —
S-985.	Oklahoma	— —
S-986.	Oregon	— —
S-987.	Pennsylvania	— —
S-988.	Rhode Island	— —
S-989.	South Carolina	— —
S-900.	South Dakota	— —
S-991.	Tennessee	— —
S-992.	Texas	— —
S-993.	Utah	— —
S-994.	Vermont	— —
S-995.	Virginia	— —
S-996.	Washington	— —
S-997.	West Virginia	— —
S-998.	Wisconsin	— —
S-999.	Wyoming	— —

10 Dollar Notes

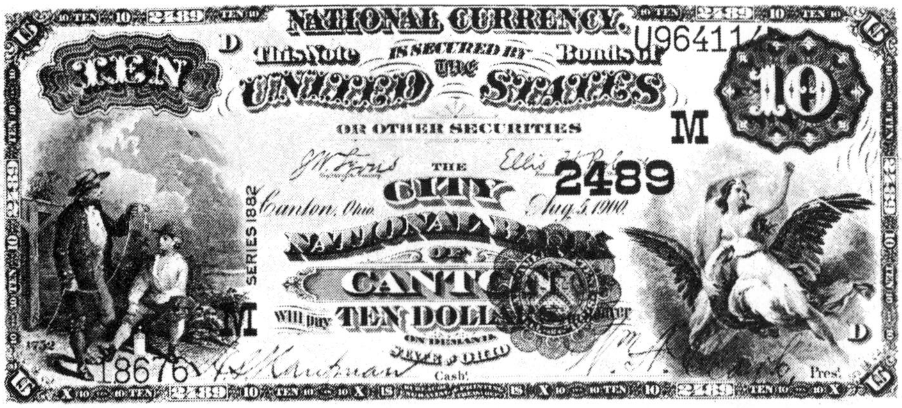

DESIGN NO. 119

(Notes 576-579-b)

At the left, Benjamin Franklin drawing electricity from the sky with a kite and a key. At the right, Liberty soaring on an eagle, clutching lightning in her hand.

Reverse of Design No. 119.

At the left, head of William P. Fessenden, Secretary of the Treasury in 1864. At the right, seated figure representing Mechanics.

No.	Signatures		Very Good	Very Fine	Unc
576.	Tillman	Morgan	150.00	750.00	1,500.00
576-a.	Tillman	Roberts	150.00	700.00	1,500.00
576-b.	Bruce	Roberts	150.00	750.00	1,500.00
577.	Lyons	Roberts	• 140.00	500.00	1,400.00
577-a.	Lyons	Treat		**Unknown**	
578.	Vernon	Treat	275.00	800.00	1,600.00
579.	Napier	McClung	200.00	775.00	1,600.00
579-a.	Parker	Burke		**Unknown**	
579-b.	Teehee	Burke		**Rare**	

These notes were issued from 1916 to 1922 in sheets of 10-10-10-10 and 10-10-10-20.

	State	*Very Fine*
S-1000.	Alabama	— —
S-1001.	Arizona	— —
S-1002.	Arkansas	— —
S-1003.	California	— —
S-1004.	Colorado	— —
S-1005.	Connecticut	— —
S-1006.	Delaware	— —
S-1007.	District of Col.	— —
S-1008.	Florida	— —
S-1009.	Georgia	— —
S-1010.	Hawaii Terr.	— —
S-1011.	Idaho	— —
S-1012.	Illinois	— —
S-1013.	Indiana	— —
S-1014.	Iowa	— —
S-1015.	Kansas	— —
S-1016.	Kentucky	— —
S-1017.	Louisiana	— —
S-1018.	Maine	— —
S-1019.	Maryland	— —
S-1020.	Massachusetts	— —
S-1021.	Michigan	— —
S-1022.	Minnesota	— —
S-1023.	Mississippi	— —
S-1024.	Missouri	— —
S-1025.	Montana	— —
S-1026.	Nebraska	— —
S-1027.	Nevada	— —
S-1028.	New Hampshire	— —
S-1029.	New Jersey	— —
S-1030.	New Mexico	— —
S-1031.	New York	— —
S-1032.	North Carolina	— —
S-1033.	North Dakota	— —
S-1034.	Ohio	— —
S-1035.	Oklahoma	— —
S-1036.	Oregon	— —
S-1037.	Pennsylvania	— —
S-1038.	Rhode Island	— —
S-1039.	South Carolina	— —
S-1040.	South Dakota	— —
S-1041.	Tennessee	— —
S-1042.	Texas	— —
S-1043.	Utah	— —
S-1044.	Vermont	— —
S-1045.	Virginia	— —
S-1046.	Washington	— —
S-1047.	West Virginia	— —
S-1048.	Wisconsin	— —
S-1049.	Wyoming	— —

20 Dollar Notes

DESIGN NO. 120

(Notes 580-585)

At the left, the Battle of Lexington, April 19, 1775. At the right, Columbia leading procession.

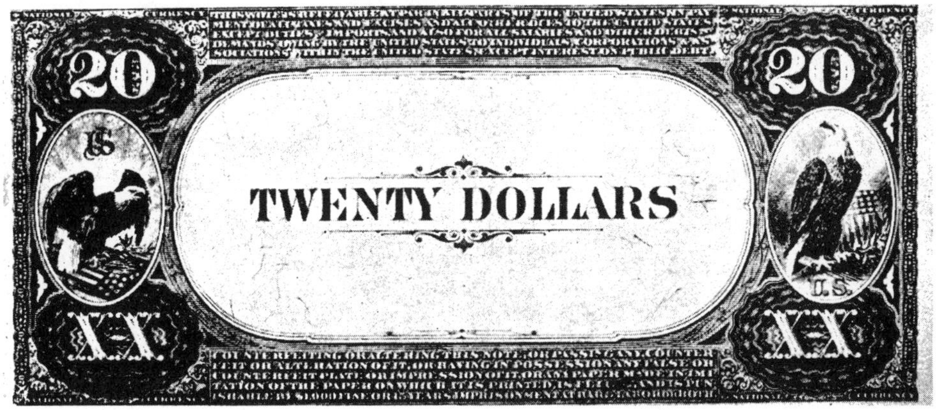

Reverse of Design No. 120.

No.	Signatures		Very Good	Very Fine	Unc
580.	Tillman	Morgan	325.00	900.00	2,800.00
580-a.	Tillman	Roberts		Rare	
580-b.	Bruce	Roberts		Rare	
581.	Lyons	Roberts	• 175.00	750.00	2,800.00
582.	Lyons	Treat	275.00	1,100.00	2,800.00
583.	Vernon	Treat	275.00	1,100.00	2,800.00
584.	Napier	McClung	225.00	900.00	2,800.00
584-a.	Parker	Burke		Rare	
585.	Teehee	Burke	275.00	1,100.00	3,600.00

These notes were issued from 1916 to 1922 in sheets of 10-10-10-20.

	State	*Very Fine*
S-1050.	Alabama	— —
S-1051.	Arizona	— —
S-1052.	Arkansas	— —
S-1053.	California	— —
S-1054.	Colorado	— —
S-1055.	Connecticut	— —
S-1056.	Delaware	— —
S-1057.	District of Col.	— —
S-1058.	Florida	— —
S-1059.	Georgia	— —
S-1060.	Hawaii Terr.	— —
S-1061.	Idaho	— —
S-1062.	Illinois	— —
S-1063.	Indiana	— —
S-1064.	Iowa	— —
S-1065.	Kansas	— —
S-1066.	Kentucky	— —
S-1067.	Louisiana	— —
S-1068.	Maine	— —
S-1069.	Maryland	— —
S-1070.	Massachusetts	— —
S-1071.	Michigan	— —
S-1072.	Minnesota	— —
S-1073.	Mississippi	— —
S-1074.	Missouri	— —
S-1075.	Montana	— —
S-1076.	Nebraska	— —
S-1077.	Nevada	— —
S-1078.	New Hampshire	— —
S-1079.	New Jersey	— —
S-1080.	New Mexico	— —
S-1081.	New York	— —
S-1082.	North Carolina	— —
S-1083.	North Dakota	— —
S-1084.	Ohio	— —
S-1085.	Oklahoma	— —
S-1086.	Oregon	— —
S-1087.	Pennsylvania	— —
S-1088.	Rhode Island	— —
S-1089.	South Carolina	— —
S-1090.	South Dakota	— —
S-1091.	Tennessee	— —
S-1092.	Texas	— —
S-1093.	Utah	— —
S-1094.	Vermont	— —
S-1095.	Virginia	— —
S-1096.	Washington	— —
S-1097.	West Virginia	— —
S-1098.	Wisconsin	— —
S-1099.	Wyoming	— —

50 Dollar Notes

DESIGN NO. 121

(Note 586)

At the left, Washington crossing the Delaware. At the right, Washington at prayer.

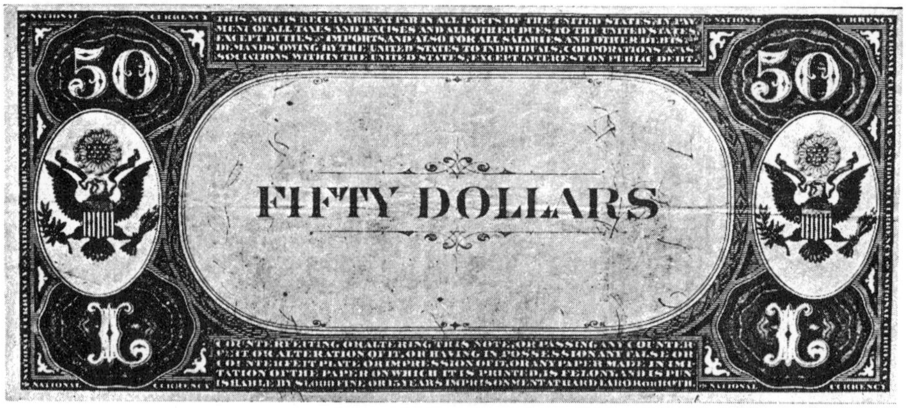

Reverse of Design No. 121.

This illustration by courtesy of the Federal Reserve Bank of Chicago.

No.	Signatures			
586.	Lyons	Roberts	Very Rare	(4 known)

These notes were issued from 1919 to 1921 in sheets of 50-50-50-100.
(These notes were only issued in Louisiana and Ohio.)

	State	Very Fine
S-1117.	Louisiana	— —
S-1134.	Ohio	— —

100 Dollar Notes

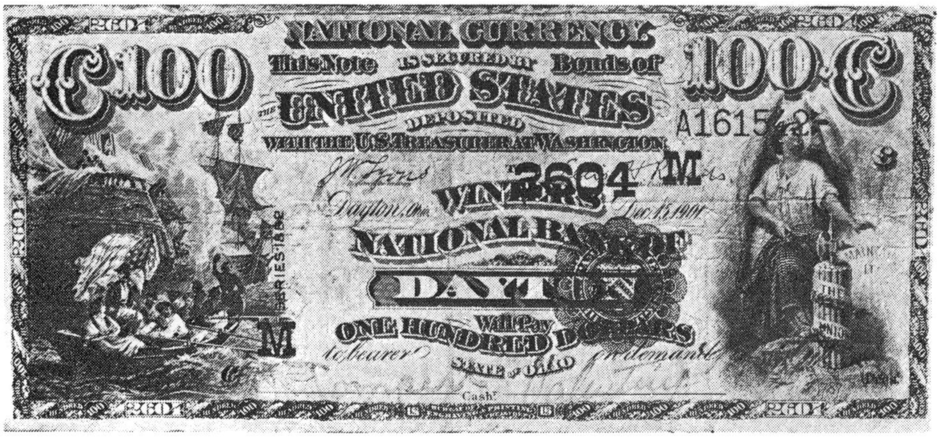

DESIGN NO. 121-a.

(Note 586-a)

At the left, Commodore Oliver H. Perry leaving the Lawrence, his flagship, during the battle of Lake Erie, September 10, 1813. At the right, Liberty seated by Fasces.

Reverse of Design No. 121-a.

This illustration by courtesy of the Federal Reserve Bank of Chicago.

No.	Signatures			
586-a.	Lyons	Roberts	**Very Rare**	(1 known)

These notes were issued from 1919 to 1921 in sheets of 50-50-50-100.

(These notes were only issued in Louisiana and Ohio. At present, only one note from the Canal-Commercial National Bank of New Orleans and one note from the Winters National Bank of Dayton, Ohio (pictured above) are known, and it has been reported that the latter note has been redeemed.)

	State	*Very Fine*
S-1167.	Louisiana	— —
S-1184.	Ohio	— —

Notes of the Third Charter Period

April 12, 1902 to April 11, 1922

(Notes of Third Charter types were issued from 1902 to 1929)

Charter periods came to an official end in 1922. After that date congressional legislation gave all National Banks, both those in existence and those yet to be formed a permanent corporate status, so that it no longer became necessary for a bank to renew its charter.

The Congressional Act of April 12, 1902 created the Third Charter Period, the notes of which bear the designation, "Series of 1902."

The Act was passed to prolong the corporate life of these banks whose 20 year charters were due to expire beginning with the year 1902. The charters of such banks could thus be legally renewed and at the same time charters could be granted to National Banks organizing for the first time.

Large size notes of Third Charter types were issued from 1902 to 1929. In July, 1929, they were discontinued and were replaced by small size National Bank Notes of completely new designs.

When the Third Charter Period became law, new notes were issued to mark the transition, as had also been done at the commencement of the Second Charter Period. Three types of notes were likewise issued under the Third Charter Period and they are briefly described below.

Red Seals. These notes, which bear a red seal, were issued from 1902 to 1908, and like the brown backs would no doubt have continued until 1922 were it not for the changes made as a result of the Aldrich-Vreeland Act of 1908.

Of the three types of notes issued during the Third Charter Period, the red seals are by far the scarcest. They were issued by fewer banks and over fewer years than the other two types and are quite rare in comparison.

Blue Seals with Dates on Back. This type is analogous to the "Dates on back" issue of the Second Charter Period, but the changes made here were not as extreme, since the basic designs of the notes remained untouched. On the face, the color of the seal was now blue, rather than red; on the back, the dates "1902-1908" were added at the top in available white space. Notes of this type were issued from 1908 to 1915 and like the Second Charter Notes of these years, they are referred to as "Emergency Money." Likewise paralleling the Second Charter Notes, the 50 and 100 Dollar notes of this type kept being issued as late as 1926 for no explainable reason.

Blue Seals Only. These were issued from 1915 to 1929 and first appeared in 1915 upon expiration of the Aldrich-Vreeland Act. They differ from the type above mainly by the absence of the dates "1902-1908" from the back. The color of the seal remained blue. Notes of this type are the commonest and most plentiful of all National Bank Notes, more of these being in existence than of any other type. They are the last of the large size National Bank Notes and were discontinued in 1929 not because of any change in National Bank policy, but because of the introduction of the small size National Bank Notes.

The obligation on the Red Seal notes is the same as on the brown backs of the Second Charter Period, namely that the notes are secured by United States Bonds.

The obligation on the Blue Seal notes is the same as on the green backs of the Second Charter Period, wherein the notes are secured by United States Bonds "or other securities."

5 Dollar Notes

First Issue. Series of 1902 with Red Seal

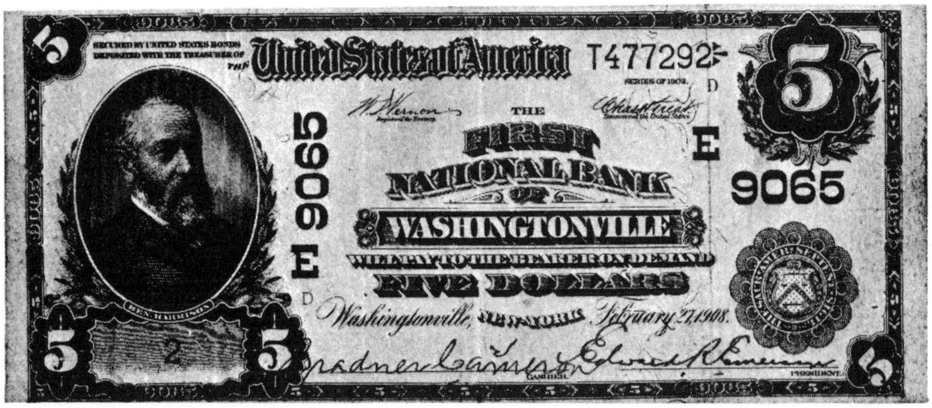

DESIGN NO. 122

(Notes 587-589)

Head of President Benjamin Harrison, 23rd President of the United States, 1889-1893.

Reverse of Design No. 122.

The Landing of the Pilgrims.

No.	Signatures		Very Good	Very Fine	Unc
587.	Lyons	Roberts	75.00	175.00	600.00
588.	Lyons	Treat	85.00	225.00	700.00
589.	Vernon	Treat	•90.00	250.00	750.00

These notes were issued from 1902 to 1908 in sheets of 5-5-5-5.

	State	*Very Fine*		*State*	*Very Fine*		*State*	*Very Fine*
S-1200.	Alabama	700.00	S-1217.	Kentucky	300.00	S-1235.	Ohio	190.00
S-1200a.	Alaska	2,000.00	S-1218.	Louisiana	550.00	S-1236.	Oklahoma Terr.	2,250.00
S-1201.	Arizona Territory	6,000.00	S-1219.	Maine	850.00	S-1237.	Oklahoma State	4,500.00
S-1202.	Arkansas	1,500.00	S-1220.	Maryland	275.00	S-1238.	Oregon	1,000.00
S-1203.	California	350.00	S-1221.	Massachusetts	200.00	S-1239.	Pennsylvania	175.00
S-1204.	Colorado	800.00	S-1222.	Michigan	350.00	S-1240.	Puerto Rico	**Rare**
S-1205.	Connecticut	200.00	S-1223.	Minnesota	400.00	S-1241.	Rhode Island	2,000.00
S-1206.	Delaware	3,000.00	S-1224.	Mississippi	1,750.00	S-1242.	South Carolina	3,000.00
S-1207.	District of Columbia	750.00	S-1225.	Missouri	250.00	S-1243	South Dakota	2,000.00
S-1208.	Florida	2,250.00	S-1226.	Montana	5,000.00	S-1244.	Tennessee	750.00
S-1209.	Georgia	750.00	S-1227.	Nebraska	425.00	S-1245.	Texas	500.00
S-1210.	Hawaii Terr.	**Not Issued**	S-1228.	Nevada	3,500.00	S-1246.	Utah	5,000.00
S-1211.	Idaho	2,250.00	S-1229.	New Hampshire	800.00	S-1247.	Vermont	750.00
S-1212.	Illinois	150.00	S-1230.	New Jersey	300.00	S-1248.	Virginia	500.00
S-1213.	Indian Territory	2,250.00	S-1231.	New Mexico Terr.	2,250.00	S-1249.	Washington	1,500.00
S-1214.	Indiana	200.00	S-1232.	New York	175.00	S-1250.	West Virginia	400.00
S-1215.	Iowa	425.00	S-1233.	North Carolina	1,000.00	S-1251.	Wisconsin	300.00
S-1216.	Kansas	400.00	S-1234.	North Dakota	1,750.00	S-1252.	Wyoming	2,750.00

5 Dollar Notes

Second Issue. Series of 1902 with Blue Seal and with "1902-1908" on back.

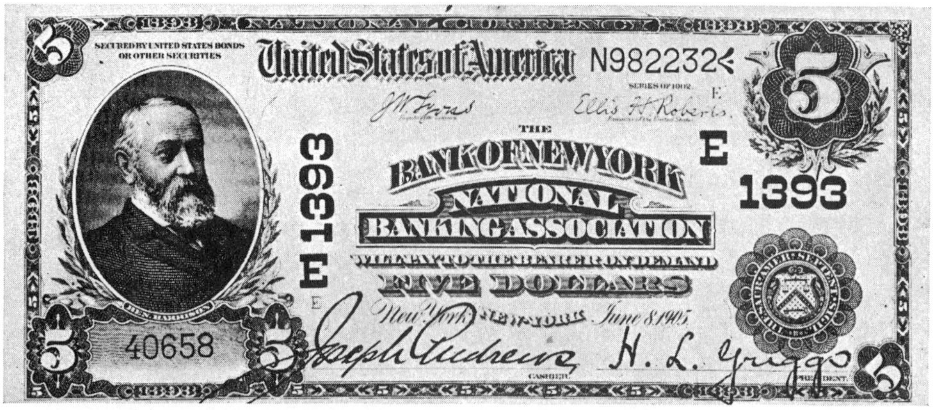

DESIGN NO. 122-a

(Notes 590-597-a)

Head of President Benjamin Harrison.

Reverse of Design No. 122-a.

The Landing of the Pilgrims.

No.	Signatures		Very Good	Very Fine	Unc
590.	Lyons	Roberts	•30.00	60.00	350.00
591.	Lyons	Treat	30.00	60.00	350.00
592.	Vernon	Treat	30.00	60.00	350.00
593.	Vernon	McClung	30.00	60.00	350.00
594.	Napier	McClung	35.00	65.00	375.00
595.	Napier	Thompson	45.00	125.00	450.00
596.	Napier	Burke	35.00	65.00	375.00
597.	Parker	Burke	35.00	65.00	375.00
597-a.	Teehee	Burke	60.00	175.00	475.00

These notes were issued from 1908 to 1916 in sheets of 5-5-5-5.

	State	Very Fine
S-1253.	Alabama	175.00
S-1254.	Alaska	Rare
S-1255.	Arizona Territory	1,250.00
S-1256.	Arizona State	1,000.00
S-1257.	Arkansas	200.00
S-1258.	California	60.00
S-1259.	Colorado	150.00
S-1260.	Connecticut	75.00
S-1261.	Delaware	200.00
S-1262.	District of Columbia	150.00
S-1263.	Florida	175.00
S-1264.	Georgia	150.00
S-1265.	Hawaii Terr.	Rare
S-1266.	Idaho	200.00
S-1267.	Illinois	60.00
S-1268.	Indiana	60.00
S-1269.	Iowa	65.00
S-1270.	Kansas	85.00
S-1271.	Kentucky	65.00
S-1272.	Louisiana	140.00
S-1273.	Maine	150.00
S-1274.	Maryland	75.00
S-1275.	Massachusetts	65.00
S-1276.	Michigan	70.00
S-1277.	Minnesota	75.00
S-1278.	Mississippi	200.00
S-1279.	Missouri	65.00
S-1280.	Montana	200.00
S-1281.	Nebraska	100.00
S-1282.	Nevada	750.00
S-1283.	New Hampshire	100.00
S-1284.	New Jersey	60.00
S-1285.	New Mexico Terr.	1,000.00
S-1286.	New Mexico State	350.00
S-1287.	New York	60.00
S-1288.	North Carolina	125.00
S-1289.	North Dakota	150.00
S-1290.	Ohio	60.00
S-1291.	Oklahoma	125.00
S-1292.	Oregon	150.00
S-1293.	Pennsylvania	60.00
S-1294.	Porto Rico	Rare
S-1295.	Rhode Island	130.00
S-1296.	South Carolina	100.00
S-1297.	South Dakota	150.00
S-1298.	Tennessee	150.00
S-1259.	Texas	75.00
S-1300.	Utah	275.00
S-1301.	Vermont	100.00
S-1302.	Virginia	90.00
S-1303.	Washington	150.00
S-1304.	West Virginia	100.00
S-1305.	Wisconsin	65.00
S-1306.	Wyoming	300.00

5 Dollar Notes

Third Issue. Series of 1902 with Blue Seal and without "1902-1908" on back.

DESIGN NO. 122-b

(Notes 598-612)

Head of President Benjamin Harrison.

Reverse of Design No. 122-b.

The Landing of the Pilgrims.

No.	Signatures		Very Good	Very Fine	Unc
598.	Lyons	Roberts	•25.00	50.00	300.00
599.	Lyons	Treat	25.00	50.00	300.00
600.	Vernon	Treat	25.00	50.00	300.00
601.	Vernon	McClung	25.00	50.00	300.00
602.	Napier	McClung	25.00	50.00	300.00
603.	Napier	Thompson	40.00	125.00	400.00
604.	Napier	Burke	25.00	50.00	300.00
605.	Parker	Burke	25.00	50.00	300.00
606.	Teehee	Burke	25.00	50.00	300.00
607.	Elliott	Burke	25.00	50.00	300.00
608.	Elliott	White	25.00	50.00	300.00
609.	Speelman	White	25.00	50.00	325.00
610.	Woods	White	27.50	75.00	350.00
611.	Woods	Tate	30.00	85.00	400.00
612.	Jones	Woods	150.00	500.00	1,350.00

These notes were issued from 1916 to 1929 in sheets of 5-5-5-5.

	State	*Very Fine*
S-1307.	Alabama	90.00
S-1308.	Alaska	1,750.00
S-1309.	Arizona	500.00
S-1310.	Arkansas	100.00
S-1311.	California	60.00
S-1312.	Colorado	90.00
S-1313.	Connecticut	60.00
S-1314.	Delaware	150.00
S-1315.	District of Columbia	100.00
S-1316.	Florida	120.00
S-1317.	Georgia	100.00
S-1318.	Hawaii Territory	750.00
S-1319.	Idaho	200.00
S-1320.	Illinois	50.00
S-1321.	Indiana	50.00
S-1322.	Iowa	60.00
S-1323.	Kansas	65.00
S-1324.	Kentucky	50.00
S-1325.	Louisiana	90.00
S-1326.	Maine	90.00
S-1327.	Maryland	55.00
S-1328.	Massachusetts	50.00
S-1329.	Michigan	60.00
S-1330.	Minnesota	60.00
S-1331.	Mississippi	125.00
S-1332.	Missouri	50.00
S-1333.	Montana	200.00
S-1334.	Nebraska	70.00
S-1335.	Nevada	600.00
S-1336.	New Hampshire	90.00
S-1337.	New Jersey	50.00
S-1338.	New Mexico	300.00
S-1339.	New York	50.00
S-1340.	North Carolina	60.00
S-1341.	North Dakota	75.00
S-1342.	Ohio	50.00
S-1343.	Oklahoma	90.00
S-1344.	Oregon	160.00
S-1345.	Pennsylvania	50.00
S-1346.	Rhode Island	120.00
S-1347.	South Carolina	125.00
S-1348.	South Dakota	135.00
S-1349.	Tennessee	100.00
S-1350.	Texas	65.00
S-1351.	Utah	200.00
S-1352.	Vermont	90.00
S-1353.	Virginia	60.00
S-1354.	Washington	125.00
S-1355.	West Virginia	60.00
S-1356.	Wisconsin	65.00
S-1357.	Wyoming	775.00

10 Dollar Notes

First Issue. Series of 1902 with Red Seal.

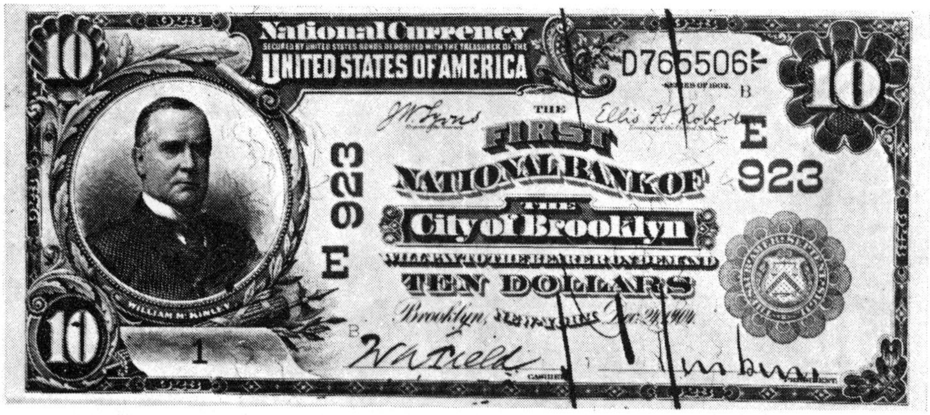

DESIGN NO. 123

(Notes 613-615)

Head of President William McKinley, 25th President of the United States, who was shot at the Pan American Exposition in Buffalo and died September 14, 1901.

Reverse of Design No. 123.

No.	Signatures		Very Good	Very Fine	Unc
613.	Lyons	Roberts	•85.00	200.00	750.00
614.	Lyons	Treat	95.00	250.00	850.00
615.	Vernon	Treat	100.00	275.00	900.00

These notes were issued from 1902 to 1908 in sheets of 10-10-10-20 and rarely 10-10-10-10.

	State	*Very Fine*
S-1358.	Alabama	750.00
S-1358a.	Alaska	5,000.00
S-1359.	Arizona Territory	6,000.00
S-1360.	Arkansas	1,800.00
S-1361.	California	300.00
S-1362.	Colorado	800.00
S-1363.	Connecticut	300.00
S-1364.	Delaware	3,250.00
S-1365.	District of Columbia	850.00
S-1366.	Florida	2,250.00
S-1367.	Georgia	800.00
S-1368.	Hawaii Terr.	Not Issued
S-1369.	Idaho	2,500.00
S-1370.	Illinois	200.00
S-1371.	Indian Territory	2,250.00
S-1372.	Indiana	250.00
S-1373.	Iowa	450.00
S-1374.	Kansas	450.00
S-1375.	Kentucky	350.00
S-1376.	Louisiana	600.00
S-1377.	Maine	950.00
S-1378.	Maryland	275.00
S-1379.	Massachusetts	250.00
S-1380.	Michigan	350.00
S-1381.	Minnesota	325.00
S-1382.	Mississippi	1,800.00
S-1383.	Missouri	275.00
S-1384.	Montana	5,000.00
S-1385.	Nebraska	400.00
S-1386.	Nevada	5,000.00
S-1387.	New Hampshire	850.00
S-1388.	New Jersey	325.00
S-1389.	New Mexico Terr.	2,250.00
S-1390.	New York	200.00
S-1391.	North Carolina	1,000.00
S-1392.	North Dakota	2,250.00
S-1393.	Ohio	200.00
S-1394.	Oklahoma Territory	2,250.00
S-1395.	Oklahoma State	5,000.00
S-1396.	Oregon	1,250.00
S-1397.	Pennsylvania	200.00
S-1398.	Porto Rico	10,000.00
S-1399.	Rhode Island	2,000.00
S-1400.	South Carolina	3,000.00
S-1401.	South Dakota	2,500.00
S-1402.	Tennessee	1,000.00
S-1403.	Texas	500.00
S-1404.	Utah	5,000.00
S-1405.	Vermont	850.00
S-1406.	Virginia	500.00
S-1407.	Washington	1,250.00
S-1408.	West Virginia	450.00
S-1409.	Wisconsin	300.00
S-1410.	Wyoming	3,500.00

10 Dollar Notes

Second Issue. Series of 1902 with Blue Seal and with "1902-1908" on back.

DESIGN NO. 123-a

(Notes 616-623-a)

Head of President William McKinley.

Reverse of Design No. 123-a.

No.	Signatures		Very Good	Very Fine	Unc
616.	Lyons	Roberts	35.00	75.00	400.00
617.	Lyons	Treat	35.00	75.00	400.00
618.	Vernon	Treat	•35.00	75.00	400.00
619.	Vernon	McClung	35.00	75.00	400.00
620.	Napier	McClung	35.00	85.00	400.00
621.	Napier	Thompson	40.00	125.00	500.00
622.	Napier	Burke	35.00	85.00	400.00
623.	Parker	Burke	35.00	85.00	400.00
623-a.	Teehee	Burke	45.00	150.00	550.00

These notes were issued from 1908 to 1916 in sheets of 10-10-10-10 and 10-10-10-20.

	State	Very Fine
S-1411.	Alabama	150.00
S-1412.	Alaska	**Rare**
S-1413.	Arizona Territory	1,250.00
S-1414.	Arizona State	750.00
S-1415.	Arkansas	250.00
S-1416.	California	90.00
S-1417.	Colorado	200.00
S-1418.	Connecticut	90.00
S-1419.	Delaware	225.00
S-1420.	District of Columbia	200.00
S-1421.	Florida	200.00
S-1422.	Georgia	200.00
S-1423.	Hawaii Terr.	**Rare**
S-1424.	Idaho	250.00
S-1425.	Illinois	75.00
S-1426.	Indiana	75.00
S-1427.	Iowa	100.00
S-1428.	Kansas	100.00

	State	Very Fine
S-1429.	Kentucky	75.00
S-1430.	Louisiana	150.00
S-1431.	Maine	150.00
S-1432.	Maryland	90.00
S-1433.	Massachusetts	75.00
S-1434.	Michigan	90.00
S-1435.	Minnestoa	90.00
S-1436.	Mississippi	200.00
S-1437.	Missouri	90.00
S-1348.	Montana	225.00
S-1439.	Nebraska	125.00
S-1440.	Nevada	500.00
S-1441.	New Hampshire	100.00
S-1442.	New Jersey	75.00
S-1443.	New Mexico Terr.	1,750.00
S-1444.	New Mexico State	600.00
S-1445.	New York	75.00
S-1446.	North Carolina	125.00

	State	Very Fine
S-1447.	North Dakota	150.00
S-1448.	Ohio	75.00
S-1449.	Oklahoma	135.00
S-1450.	Oregon	200.00
S-1451.	Pennsylvania	75.00
S-1452.	Porto Rico	**Rare**
S-1453.	Rhode Island	140.00
S-1454.	South Carolina	130.00
S-1455.	South Dakota	150.00
S-1456.	Tennessee	125.00
S-1457.	Texas	125.00
S-1458.	Utah	225.00
S-1459.	Vermont	100.00
S-1460.	Virginia	100.00
S-1461.	Washington	130.00
S-1462.	West Virginia	90.00
S-1463.	Wisconsin	90.00
S-1464.	Wyoming	300.00

10 Dollar Notes

Third Issue. Series of 1902 with Blue Seal and without "1902-1908" on back.

DESIGN NO. 123-b

(Notes 624-638)

Head of President William McKinley.

Reverse of Design No. 123-b.

No.	Signatures		Very Good	Very Fine	Unc
624.	Lyons	Roberts	•30.00	65.00	350.00
625.	Lyons	Treat	30.00	65.00	350.00
626.	Vernon	Treat	30.00	65.00	350.00
627.	Vernon	McClung	30.00	65.00	350.00
628.	Napier	McClung	30.00	65.00	350.00
629.	Napier	Thompson	75.00	150.00	500.00
630.	Napier	Burke	30.00	65.00	350.00
631.	Parker	Burke	30.00	65.00	350.00
632.	Teehee	Burke	30.00	65.00	350.00
633.	Elliott	Burke	30.00	65.00	350.00
634.	Elliott	White	30.00	65.00	350.00
635.	Speelman	White	30.00	65.00	350.00
636.	Woods	White	35.00	80.00	375.00
637.	Woods	Tate	45.00	125.00	425.00
638.	Jones	Woods	150.00	550.00	1,400.00

These notes were issued from 1916 to 1929 in sheets of 10-10-10-10 and 10-10-10-20.

	State	*Very Fine*
S-1465.	Alabama	100.00
S-1466.	Alaska	2,000.00
S-1467.	Arizona	500.00
S-1468.	Arkansas	150.00
S-1469.	California	85.00
S-1470.	Colorado	110.00
S-1471.	Connecticut	90.00
S-1472.	Delaware	175.00
S-1473.	District of Columbia	130.00
S-1474.	Florida	165.00
S-1475.	Georgia	110.00
S-1476.	Hawaii Territory	650.00
S-1477.	Idaho	250.00
S-1478.	Illinois	65.00
S-1479.	Indiana	65.00
S-1480.	Iowa	85.00
S-1481.	Kansas	85.00
S-1482.	Kentucky	80.00
S-1483.	Louisiana	135.00
S-1484.	Maine	95.00
S-1485.	Maryland	90.00
S-1486.	Massachusetts	70.00
S-1487.	Michigan	75.00
S-1488.	Minnesota	80.00
S-1489.	Mississippi	175.00
S-1490.	Missouri	80.00
S-1491.	Montana	200.00
S-1492.	Nebraska	100.00
S-1493.	Nevada	700.00
S-1494.	New Hampshire	100.00
S-1495.	New Jersey	75.00
S-1496.	New Mexico	250.00
S-1497.	New York	65.00
S-1498.	North Carolina	125.00
S-1499.	North Dakota	140.00
S-1500.	Ohio	65.00
S-1501.	Oklahoma	120.00
S-1502.	Oregon	200.00
S-1503.	Pennsylvania	65.00
S-1504.	Rhode Island	130.00
S-1505.	South Carolina	140.00
S-1506.	South Dakota	150.00
S-1507.	Tennessee	130.00
S-1508.	Texas	130.00
S-1509.	Utah	200.00
S-1510.	Vermont	110.00
S-1511.	Virginia	90.00
S-1512.	Washington	150.00
S-1513.	West Virginia	100.00
S-1514.	Wisconsin	100.00
S-1515.	Wyoming	300.00

20 Dollar Notes

First Issue. Series of 1902 with Red Seal.

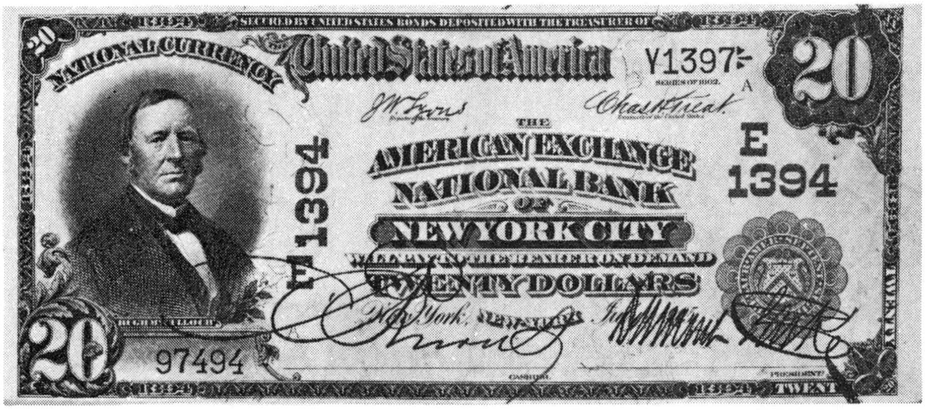

DESIGN NO. 124

(Notes 639-641)

Head of Hugh McCulloch, Comptroller of the Currency from 1863-1865; Secretary of the Treasury from 1865-1869 and from 1884-1885.

Reverse of Design No. 124.

No.	Signatures		Very Good	Very Fine	Unc
639.	Lyons	Roberts	90.00	250.00	1,000.00
640.	Lyons	Treat	110.00	300.00	1,100.00
641.	Vernon	Treat	140.00	350.00	1,100.00

These notes were issued from 1902 to 1908 in sheets of 10-10-10-20.

	State	Very Fine
S-1516.	Alabama	800.00
S-1517.	Arizona Territory	7,000.00
S-1518.	Arkansas	2,000.00
S-1519.	California	350.00
S-1520.	Colorado	800.00
S-1521.	Connecticut	300.00
S-1522.	Delaware	4,500.00
S-1523.	District of Columbia	900.00
S-1524.	Florida	2,500.00
S-1525.	Georgia	850.00
S-1526.	Hawaii Terr.	Not Issued
S-1527.	Idaho	3,000.00
S-1528.	Illinois	250.00
S-1529.	Indian Territory	2,500.00
S-1530.	Indiana	275.00
S-1531.	Iowa	450.00
S-1532.	Kansas	450.00
S-1533.	Kentucky	400.00
S-1534.	Louisiana	700.00
S-1535.	Maine	1,100.00
S-1536.	Maryland	375.00
S-1537.	Massachusetts	275.00
S-1538.	Michigan	425.00
S-1539.	Minnesota	425.00
S-1540.	Mississippi	2,250.00
S-1541.	Missouri	325.00
S-1542.	Montana	5,500.00
S-1543.	Nebraska	500.00
S-1544.	Nevada	5,500.00
S-1545.	New Hampshire	1,000.00
S-1546.	New Jersey	375.00
S-1547.	New Mexico Terr.	2,500.00
S-1548.	New York	250.00
S-1549.	North Carolina	1,250.00
S-1550.	North Dakota	1,250.00
S-1551.	Ohio	275.00
S-1552.	Oklahoma Territory	2,500.00
S-1553.	Oklahoma State	5,000.00
S-1554.	Oregon	1,500.00
S-1555.	Pennsylvania	250.00
S-1556.	Porto Rico	Rare
S-1557.	Rhode Island	2,250.00
S-1558.	South Carolina	3,250.00
S-1559.	South Dakota	2,500.00
S-1560.	Tennessee	1,000.00
S-1561.	Texas	625.00
S-1562.	Utah	5,250.00
S-1563.	Vermont	1,250.00
S-1564.	Virginia	550.00
S-1565.	Washington	2000.00
S-1566.	West Virginia	475.00
S-1567.	Wisconsin	375.00
S-1568.	Wyoming	5,000.00

20 Dollar Notes

Second Issue. Series of 1902 with Blue Seal and with "1902-1908" on back.

DESIGN NO. 124-a

(Notes 642-649-a)

Head of Hugh McCulloch.

Reverse of Design No. 124-a.

No.	Signatures		Very Good	Very Fine	Unc
642.	Lyons	Roberts	• 55.00	100.00	450.00
643.	Lyons	Treat	55.00	100.00	450.00
644.	Vernon	Treat	55.00	100.00	450.00
645.	Vernon	McClung	55.00	100.00	450.00
646.	Napier	McClung	55.00	100.00	475.00
647.	Napier	Thompson	75.00	140.00	600.00
648.	Napier	Burke	55.00	110.00	500.00
649.	Parker	Burke	55.00	110.00	500.00
649-a.	Teehee	Burke	80.00	250.00	675.00

These notes were issued from 1908 to 1916 in sheets of 10-10-10-20.

	State	*Very Fine*
S-1569.	Alabama	200.00
S-1570.	Alaska	Rare
S-1571.	Arizona Territory	1,250.00
S-1572.	Arizona State	850.00
S-1573.	Arkansas	250.00
S-1574.	California	110.00
S-1575.	Colorado	240.00
S-1576.	Connecticut	135.00
S-1577.	Delaware	275.00
S-1578.	District of Columbia	150.00
S-1579.	Florida	300.00
S-1580.	Georgia	200.00
S-1581.	Hawaii Terr.	1,000.00
S-1582.	Idaho	300.00
S-1583.	Illinois	100.00
S-1584.	Indiana	100.00
S-1585.	Iowa	100.00
S-1586.	Kansas	150.00
S-1587.	Kentucky	125.00
S-1588.	Louisiana	175.00
S-1589.	Maine	190.00
S-1590.	Maryland	125.00
S-1591.	Massachusetts	125.00
S-1592.	Michigan	135.00
S-1593.	Minnesota	140.00
S-1594.	Mississippi	200.00
S-1595.	Missouri	100.00
S-1596.	Montana	300.00
S-1597.	Nebraska	160.00
S-1598.	Nevada	750.00
S-1599.	New Hampshire	165.00
S-1600.	New Jersey	110.00
S-1601.	New Mexico Terr.	1,750.00
S-1602.	New Mexico State	650.00
S-1603.	New York	100.00
S-1604.	North Carolina	160.00
S-1605.	North Dakota	200.00
S-1606.	Ohio	100.00
S-1607.	Oklahoma	200.00
S-1608.	Oregon	250.00
S-1609.	Pennsylvania	100.00
S-1610.	Porto Rico	Rare
S-1611.	Rhode Island	175.00
S-1612.	South Carolina	160.00
S-1613.	South Dakota	225.00
S-1614.	Tennessee	160.00
S-1615.	Texas	160.00
S-1616.	Utah	250.00
S-1617.	Vermont	200.00
S-1618.	Virginia	160.00
S-1619.	Washington	180.00
S-1620.	West Virginia	150.00
S-1621.	Wisconsin	120.00
S-1622.	Wyoming	400.00

20 Dollar Notes

Third Issue. Series of 1902 with Blue Seal and without "1902-1908" on back.

DESIGN NO. 124-b

(Notes 650-663-a)

Head of Hugh McCulloch.

Reverse of Design No. 124-b.

No.	Signatures		Very Good	Very Fine	Unc
650.	Lyons	Roberts	50.00	95.00	400.00
651.	Lyons	Treat	50.00	95.00	400.00
652.	Vernon	Treat	50.00	95.00	400.00
653.	Vernon	McClung	50.00	95.00	400.00
654.	Napier	McClung	50.00	95.00	400.00
655.	Napier	Thompson	80.00	150.00	500.00
656.	Napier	Burke	60.00	100.00	425.00
657.	Parker	Burke	60.00	100.00	425.00
658.	Teehee	Burke	50.00	95.00	400.00
659.	Elliott	Burke	50.00	95.00	400.00
660.	Elliott	White	50.00	95.00	400.00
661.	Speelman	White	50.00	95.00	400.00
662.	Woods	White	125.00	250.00	600.00
663.	Woods	Tate	150.00	350.00	750.00
663-a.	Jones	Woods	Rare	—	—

These notes were issued from 1916 to 1929 in sheets of 10-10-10-20.

	State	*Very Fine*
S-1623.	Alabama	125.00
S-1624.	Alaska	300.00
S-1625.	Arizona	500.00
S-1626.	Arkansas	175.00
S-1627.	California	100.00
S-1628.	Colorado	150.00
S-1629.	Connecticut	95.00
S-1630.	Delaware	200.00
S-1631.	District of Columbia	135.00
S-1632.	Florida	200.00
S-1633.	Georgia	150.00
S-1634.	Hawaii Territory	850.00
S-1635.	Idaho	225.00
S-1636.	Illinois	95.00
S-1637.	Indiana	95.00
S-1638.	Iowa	115.00
S-1639.	Kansas	110.00
S-1640.	Kentucky	95.00
S-1641.	Louisiana	150.00
S-1642.	Maine	125.00
S-1643.	Maryland	95.00
S-1644.	Massachusetts	95.00
S-1645.	Michigan	100.00
S-1646.	Minnesota	110.00
S-1647.	Mississippi	165.00
S-1648.	Missouri	125.00
S-1649.	Montana	200.00
S-1650.	Nebraska	125.00
S-1651.	Nevada	800.00
S-1652.	New Hampshire	125.00
S-1653.	New Jersey	115.00
S-1654.	New Mexico	225.00
S-1655.	New York	95.00
S-1656.	North Carolina	150.00
S-1657.	North Dakota	175.00
S-1658.	Ohio	95.00
S-1659.	Oklahoma	150.00
S-1660.	Oregon	200.00
S-1661.	Pennsylvania	95.00
S-1662.	Rhode Island	150.00
S-1663.	South Carolina	160.00
S-1664.	South Dakota	175.00
S-1665.	Tennessee	150.00
S-1666.	Texas	150.00
S-1667.	Utah	225.00
S-1668.	Vermont	125.00
S-1669.	Virginia	120.00
S-1670.	Washington	150.00
S-1671.	West Virginia	125.00
S-1672.	Wisconsin	115.00
S-1673.	Wyoming	300.00

50 Dollar Notes

First Issue. Series of 1902 with Red Seal.

DESIGN NO. 125

(Notes 664-666)

Head of John Sherman, Secretary of the Treasury from 1877-1881 and Secretary of State from 1897-1898.

Reverse of Design No. 125.

"Mechanics and Navigation" engraved by G.F.C. Smillie after Ostrander Smith's design.

No.	Signatures		Very Good	Very Fine	Unc
664.	Lyons	Roberts	•450.00	925.00	3,750.00
665.	Lyons	Treat	500.00	950.00	4,000.00
666.	Vernon	Treat	550.00	1,000.00	4,200.00

These notes were issued from 1902 to 1908 in sheets of 50-100.

Only relatively few of these notes are in existence and it is not possible to evaluate them by state. Accordingly, the valuations have been omitted. The known specimens of these notes are generally from the largest and most populous states. The same relative rarity would apply as exists within the 5 Dollar notes.

	State	*Very Fine*
S-1674.	Alabama	— —
S-1675.	Arizona Terr.	Not Issued
S-1676.	Arkansas	— —
S-1677.	California	— —
S-1678.	Colorado	— —
S-1679.	Connecticut	— —
S-1680.	Delaware	— —
S-1681.	Dist. of Col.	Not Issued
S-1682.	Florida	— —
S-1683.	Georgia	Not Issued
S-1684.	Hawaii Terr.	Not Issued
S-1685.	Idaho	— —
S-1686.	Illinois	— —
S-1687.	Indian Terr.	— —
S-1688.	Indiana	— —
S-1689.	Iowa	— —
S-1690.	Kansas	— —
S-1691.	Kentucky	— —
S-1692.	Louisiana	— —
S-1693.	Maine	— —
S-1694.	Maryland	— —
S-1695.	Massachusetts	— —
S-1696.	Michigan	— —
S-1697.	Minnesota	— —
S-1698.	Mississippi	— —
S-1699.	Missouri	— —
S-1700.	Montana	— —
S-1701.	Nebraska	— —
S-1702.	Nevada	— —
S-1703.	New Hampshire	— —
S-1704.	New Jersey	— —
S-1705.	New Mexico Terr.	Not Issued
S-1706.	New York	— —
S-1707.	North Carolina	— —
S-1708.	North Dakota	— —
S-1709.	Ohio	— —
S-1710.	Oklahoma Terr.	— —
S-1711.	Oklahoma State	— —
S-1712.	Oregon	— —
S-1713.	Pennsylvania	— —
S-1714.	Porto Rico	— —
S-1715.	Rhode Island	— —
S-1716.	South Carolina	Not Issued
S-1717.	South Dakota	— —
S-1718.	Tennessee	— —
S-1719.	Texas	— —
S-1720.	Utah	Not Issued
S-1721.	Vermont	— —
S-1722.	Virginia	— —
S-1723.	Washington	— —
S-1724.	West Virginia	— —
S-1725.	Wisconsin	— —
S-1726.	Wyoming	Not Issued

50 Dollar Notes

Second Issue. Series of 1902 with Blue Seal and with "1902-1908" on back.

DESIGN NO. 125-a

(Notes 667-674-a)

Head of John Sherman.

Reverse of Design No. 125-a.

No.	Signatures		Very Good	Very Fine	Unc
667.	Lyons	Roberts	150.00	275.00	1,200.00
668.	Lyons	Treat	150.00	275.00	1,200.00
669.	Vernon	Treat	•150.00	275.00	1,200.00
670.	Vernon	McClung	150.00	275.00	1,200.00
671.	Napier	McClung	150.00	275.00	1,300.00
672.	Napier	Thompson	160.00	325.00	1,350.00
673.	Napier	Burke	150.00	275.00	1,200.00
674.	Parker	Burke	150.00	275.00	1,200.00
674-a.	Teehee	Burke	200.00	500.00	1,500.00

These notes were issued from 1908 to 1926 in sheets of 50-50-50-100 and rarely 50-100.

Only relatively few of these notes are in existence, and it is not possible to evaluate them by state. Accordingly, the valuations have been omitted. The known specimens of these notes are generally from the largest and most populous states. The same relative rarity would apply as exists within the 10 Dollar notes.

	State	*Very Fine*
S-1727.	Alabama	— —
S-1728.	Alaska	**Not Issued**
S-1729.	Arizona Terr.	— —
S-1730.	Arizona State	**Not Issued**
S-1731.	Arkansas	— —
S-1732.	California	— —
S-1733.	Colorado	— —
S-1734.	Connecticut	— —
S-1735.	Delaware	— —
S-1736.	Dist. of Col.	**Not Issued**
S-1737.	Florida	— —
S-1738.	Georgia	— —
S-1739.	Hawaii Terr.	**Not Issued**
S-1740.	Idaho	— —
S-1741.	Illinois	— —
S-1742.	Indiana	— —
S-1743.	Iowa	— —
S-1744.	Kansas	— —
S-1745.	Kentucky	— —
S-1746.	Louisiana	— —
S-1747.	Maine	**Not Issued**
S-1748.	Maryland	— —
S-1749.	Massachusetts	— —
S-1750.	Michigan	— —
S-1751.	Minnesota	— —
S-1752.	Mississippi	— —
S-1753.	Missouri	— —
S-1754.	Montana	— —
S-1755.	Nebraska	— —
S-1756.	Nevada	— —
S-1757.	New Hampshire	— —
S-1758.	New Jersey	— —
S-1759.	New Mexico Terr.	**Not Issued**
S-1760.	New Mexico State	**Not Issued**
S-1761.	New York	— —
S-1762.	North Carolina	— —
S-1763.	North Dakota	— —
S-1764.	Ohio	— —
S-1765.	Oklahoma	— —
S-1766.	Oregon	— —
S-1767.	Pennsylvania	— —
S-1768.	Porto Rico	— —
S-1769.	Rhode Island	— —
S-1770.	South Carolina	**Not Issued**
S-1771.	South Dakota	— —
S-1772.	Tennessee	— —
S-1773.	Texas	— —
S-1774.	Utah	— —
S-1775.	Vermont	— —
S-1776.	Virginia	— —
S-1777.	Washington	— —
S-1778.	West Virginia	— —
S-1779.	Wisconsin	— —
S-1780.	Wyoming	**Not Issued**

50 Dollar Notes

Third Issue. Series of 1902 with Blue Seal and without "1902-1908" on back.

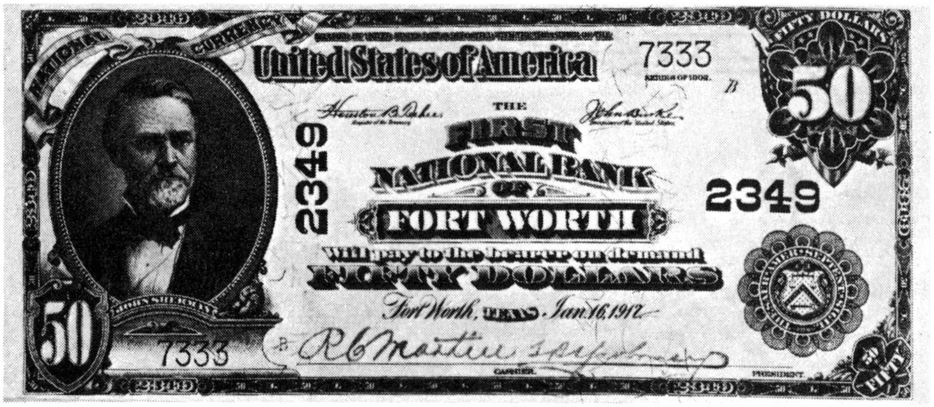

DESIGN NO. 125-b

(Notes 675-685-a)

Head of John Sherman.

Reverse of Design No. 125-b.

No.	Signatures		Very Good	Very Fine	Unc
675.	Lyons	Roberts	125.00	240.00	1,200.00
676.	Lyons	Treat	125.00	240.00	1,200.00
677.	Vernon	Treat	125.00	240.00	1,200.00
678.	Vernon	McClung	125.00	240.00	1,200.00
679.	Napier	McClung	125.00	240.00	1,200.00
679-a.	Napier	Thompson	150.00	325.00	1,200.00
680.	Napier	Burke	125.00	250.00	1,200.00
681.	Parker	Burke	125.00	250.00	1,200.00
682.	Teehee	Burke	•125.00	240.00	1,200.00
683.	Elliott	Burke	125.00	240.00	1,200.00
684.	Elliott	White	125.00	240.00	1,200.00
685.	Speelman	White	125.00	240.00	1,200.00
685-a.	Woods	White	200.00	500.00	1,600.00

These notes were issued from 1916 to 1929 in sheets of 50-50-50-100.

Only relatively few of these notes are in existence, and it is not possible to evaluate them by state. Accordingly, the valuations have been omitted. The known specimens of these notes are generally from the largest and most populous states. The same relative rarity would apply as exists within the 10 Dollar notes.

	State	*Very Fine*
S-1781.	Alabama	Not Issued
S-1782.	Alaska	Not Issued
S-1783.	Arizona	Not Issued
S-1784.	Arkansas	Not Issued
S-1785.	California	— —
S-1786.	Colorado	— —
S-1787.	Connecticut	— —
S-1788.	Delaware	— —
S-1789.	Dist. of Col.	— —
S-1790.	Florida	— —
S-1791.	Georgia	Not Issued
S-1792.	Hawaii Terr.	Not Issued
S-1793.	Idaho	— —
S-1794.	Illinois	— —
S-1795.	Indiana	— —
S-1796.	Iowa	— —
S-1797.	Kansas	— —
S-1798.	Kentucky	— —
S-1799.	Louisiana	— —
S-1800.	Maine	Not Issued
S-1801.	Maryland	— —
S-1802.	Massachusetts	— —
S-1803.	Michigan	— —
S-1804.	Minnesota	— —
S-1805.	Mississippi	— —
S-1806.	Missouri	— —
S-1807.	Montana	— —
S-1808.	Nebraska	— —
S-1809.	Nevada	— —
S-1810.	New Hampshire	— —
S-1811.	New Jersey	— —
S-1812.	New Mexico	Not Issued
S-1813.	New York	— —
S-1814.	North Carolina	— —
S-1815.	North Dakota	— —
S-1816.	Ohio	— —
S-1817.	Oklahoma	— —
S-1818.	Oregon	— —
S-1819.	Pennsylvania	— —
S-1820.	Rhode Island	— —
S-1821.	South Carolina	Not Issued
S-1822.	South Dakota	— —
S-1823.	Tennessee	— —
S-1824.	Texas	— —
S-1825.	Utah	— —
S-1826.	Vermont	— —
S-1827.	Viriginia	Not Issued
S-1828.	Washington	— —
S-1829.	West Virginia	— —
S-1830.	Wisconsin	— —
S-1831.	Wyoming	Not Issued

100 Dollar Notes

First Issue. Series of 1902 with Red Seal.

DESIGN NO. 126

(Notes 686-688)

Head of John J. Knox, Comptroller of Currency from 1872-1884.

Reverse of Design No. 126.

No.	Signatures		Very Good	Very Fine	Unc
686.	Lyons	Roberts	•600.00	1,100.00	4,750.00
687.	Lyons	Treat	600.00	1,100.00	4,750.00
688.	Vernon	Treat	675.00	1,200.00	5,000.00

These notes were issued from 1902 to 1908 in sheets of 50-100.

Only relatively few of these notes are in existence and it is not possible to evaluate them by state. Accordingly, the valuations have been omitted. The known specimens of these notes are generally from the largest and most populous states. The same relative rarity would apply as exists within the 5 Dollar notes.

	State	Very Fine
S-1832.	Alabama	— —
S-1833.	Arizona Terr.	Not Issued
S-1834.	Arkansas	— —
S-1835.	California	— —
S-1836.	Colorado	— —
S-1837.	Connecticut	— —
S-1838.	Delaware	— —
S-1839.	Dist. of Col.	Not Issued
S-1840.	Florida	— —
S-1841.	Georgia	Not Issued
S-1842.	Hawaii Terr.	Not Issued
S-1843.	Idaho	— —
S-1844.	Illinois	— —
S-1845.	Indian Terr.	— —
S-1846.	Indiana	— —
S-1847.	Iowa	— —
S-1848.	Kansas	— —
S-1849.	Kentucky	— —
S-1850.	Louisiana	— —
S-1851.	Maine	— —
S-1852.	Maryland	— —
S-1853.	Massachusetts	— —
S-1854.	Michigan	— —
S-1855.	Minnesota	— —
S-1856.	Mississippi	— —
S-1857.	Missouri	— —
S-1858.	Montana	— —
S-1859.	Nebraska	— —
S-1860.	Nevada	— —
S-1861.	New Hampshire	— —
S-1862.	New Jersey	— —
S-1863.	New Mexico Terr.	Not Issued
S-1864.	New York	— —
S-1865.	North Carolina	— —
S-1866.	North Dakota	— —
S-1867.	Ohio	— —
S-1868.	Oklahoma Terr.	— —
S-1869.	Oklahoma State	— —
S-1870.	Oregon	— —
S-1871.	Pennsylvania	— —
S-1872.	Porto Rico	— —
S-1873.	Rhode Island	— —
S-1874.	South Carolina	Not Issued
S-1875.	South Dakota	— —
S-1876.	Tennessee	— —
S-1877.	Texas	— —
S-1878.	Utah	Not Issued
S-1879.	Vermont	— —
S-1880.	Virginia	— —
S-1881.	Washington	— —
S-1882.	West Virginia	— —
S-1883.	Wisconsin	— —
S-1884.	Wyoming	Not Issued

100 Dollar Notes

Second Issue. Series of 1902 with Blue Seal and with "1902-1908" on back.

DESIGN NO. 126-a

(Notes 689-697)

Head of John J. Knox.

Reverse of Design No. 126-a.

No.	Signatures		Very Good	Very Fine	Unc
689.	Lyons	Roberts	•225.00	375.00	1,800.00
690.	Lyons	Treat	225.00	375.00	1,800.00
691.	Vernon	Treat	225.00	375.00	1,800.00
692.	Vernon	McClung	225.00	375.00	1,800.00
693.	Napier	McClung	225.00	375.00	1,800.00
694.	Napier	Thompson	250.00	450.00	1,850.00
695.	Napier	Burke	225.00	425.00	1,800.00
696.	Parker	Burke	225.00	425.00	1,800.00
697.	Teehee	Burke	250.00	475.00	1,900.00

These notes were issued from 1908 to 1926 in sheets of 50-50-50-100 and rarely 50-100.

Only relatively few of these notes are in existence, and it is not possible to evaluate them by state. Accordingly, the valuations have been omitted. The known specimens of these notes are generally from the largest and most populous states. The same relative rarity would apply as exists within the 20 Dollar notes.

	State	*Very Fine*
S-1885.	Alabama	——
S-1886.	Alaska	**Not Issued**
S-1887.	Arizona Terr.	——
S-1888.	Arizona State	**Not Issued**
S-1889.	Arkansas	——
S-1890.	California	——
S-1891.	Colorado	——
S-1892.	Connecticut	——
S-1893.	Delaware	——
S-1894.	Dist. of Col.	**Not Issued**
S-1895.	Florida	——
S-1896.	Georgia	——
S-1897.	Hawaii Terr.	**Not Issued**
S-1898.	Idaho	——
S-1899.	Illinois	——
S-1900.	Indiana	——
S-1901.	Iowa	——
S-1902.	Kansas	——
S-1903.	Kentucky	——
S-1904.	Louisiana	——
S-1905.	Maine	**Not Issued**
S-1906.	Maryland	——
S-1907.	Massachusetts	——
S-1908.	Michigan	——
S-1909.	Minnesota	——
S-1910.	Mississippi	——
S-1911.	Missouri	——
S-1912.	Montana	——
S-1913.	Nebraska	——
S-1914.	Nevada	——
S-1915.	New Hampshire	——
S-1916.	New Jersey	——
S-1917.	New Mexico Terr.	**Not Issued**
S-1918.	New Mexico State	**Not Issued**
S-1919.	New York	——
S-1920.	North Carolina	——
S-1921.	North Dakota	——
S-1922.	Ohio	——
S-1923.	Oklahoma	——
S-1924.	Oregon	——
S-1925.	Pennsylvania	——
S-1926.	Porto Rico	——
S-1927.	Rhode Island	——
S-1928.	South Carolina	**Not Issued**
S-1929.	South Dakota	——
S-1930.	Tennessee	——
S-1931.	Texas	——
S-1932.	Utah	——
S-1933.	Vermont	——
S-1934.	Virginia	——
S-1935.	Washington	——
S-1936.	West Virginia	——
S-1937.	Wisconsin	——
S-1938.	Wyoming	**Not Issued**

100 Dollar Notes

Third Issue. Series of 1902 with Blue Seal and without "1902-1908" on back.

DESIGN NO. 126-b

(Notes 698-707-a)

Head of John J. Knox.

Reverse of Design No. 126-b.

No.	Signatures		Very Good	Very Fine	Unc
698.	Lyons	Roberts	225.00	350.00	1,750.00
699.	Lyons	Treat	225.00	350.00	1,750.00
700.	Vernon	Treat	225.00	350.00	1,750.00
701.	Vernon	McClung	225.00	350.00	1,750.00
702.	Napier	McClung	225.00	350.00	1,750.00
702-a.	Napier	Thompson	250.00	400.00	2,000.00
702-b.	Napier	Burke		Unknown	
703.	Parker	Burke	225.00	375.00	1,850.00
704.	Teehee	Burke	225.00	350.00	1,750.00
705.	Elliott	Burke	•225.00	350.00	1,750.00
706.	Elliott	White	225.00	350.00	1,750.00
707.	Speelman	White	225.00	350.00	1,750.00
707-a.	Woods	White		Rare	

These notes were issued from 1916 to 1929 in sheets of 50-50-50-100.

Only relatively few of these notes are in existence, and it is not possible to evaluate them by state. Accordingly, the valuations have been omitted. The known specimens of these notes are generally from the largest and most populous states. The same relative rarity would apply as exists within the 20 Dollar notes.

	State	Very Fine
S-1939.	Alabama	Not Issued
S-1940.	Alaska	Not Issued
S-1941.	Arizona	Not Issued
S-1942.	Arkansas	Not Issued
S-1943.	California	— —
S-1944.	Colorado	— —
S-1945.	Connecticut	— —
S-1946.	Delaware	— —
S-1947.	Dist. of Col.	Not Issued
S-1948.	Florida	— —
S-1949.	Georgia	Not Issued
S-1950.	Hawaii Terr.	Not Issued
S-1951.	Idaho	— —
S-1952.	Illinois	— —
S-1953.	Indiana	— —
S-1954.	Iowa	— —
S-1955.	Kansas	— —
S-1956.	Kentucky	— —
S-1957.	Louisiana	— —
S-1958.	Maine	Not Issued
S-1959.	Maryland	— —
S-1960.	Massachusetts	— —
S-1961.	Michigan	— —
S-1962.	Minnesota	— —
S-1963.	Mississippi	— —
S-1964.	Missouri	— —
S-1965.	Montana	— —
S-1966.	Nebraska	— —
S-1967.	Nevada	— —
S-1968.	New Hampshire	— —
S-1969.	New Jersey	— —
S-1970.	New Mexico	Not Issued
S-1971.	New York	— —
S-1972.	North Carolina	— —
S-1973.	North Dakota	— —
S-1974.	Ohio	— —
S-1975.	Oklahoma	— —
S-1976.	Oregon	— —
S-1977.	Pennsylvania	— —
S-1978.	Rhode Island	— —
S-1979.	South Carolina	Not Issued
S-1980.	South Dakota	— —
S-1981.	Tennessee	— —
S-1982.	Texas	— —
S-1983.	Utah	— —
S-1984.	Vermont	— —
S-1985.	Virginia	Not Issued
S-1986.	Washington	— —
S-1987.	West Virginia	Not Issued
S-1988.	Wisconsin	— —
S-1989.	Wyoming	Not Issued

IX. FEDERAL RESERVE BANK NOTES

With the establishment of the Federal Reserve System, a new type of currency came into existence. The notes issued under this system are the Federal Reserve Bank Notes and the Federal Reserve Notes.

The Federal Reserve Bank Notes were also inscribed "National Currency"; the Federal Reserve Notes are not so inscribed and are currency of the system proper, and not of the individual banks in the system.

The obverse designs of these two issues are markedly different; the reverses are similar. See the illustrations.

There were two separate issues of the Federal Reserve Bank Notes, the series of 1915 and the series of 1918.

The first issue was authorized by the Federal Reserve Act of December 23, 1913 and consisted only of 5, 10 and 20 Dollar notes. These were not issued by all twelve banks in the system but only by the banks at Atlanta, Chicago, Kansas City, Dallas and San Francisco. The last named bank issued 5 Dollar notes only.

As mentioned above, these notes are inscribed "National Currency" and are similar in general to National Bank Notes. The obligation to pay the bearer on demand is made by the specific Federal Reserve Bank and not by the United States.

The obligation on the first issue of Federal Reserve Bank Notes is similar to that on the National Bank Notes of the First Charter Period, which see. There is a slight variance in the wording but not in the meaning.

The second issue of Federal Reserve Bank Notes were authorized by the Act of April 23, 1918 and all notes of this issue are series of 1918. The denominations consisted of 1, 2, 5, 10, 20 and 50 Dollar Notes and these notes were issued by all twelve banks. Each bank did not necessarily issue all the denominations. For example, the 50 Dollar Notes emanated only from the St. Louis Bank, the 20 Dollar Notes only from the Atlanta and St. Louis banks, etc. Please see the text for the full list.

Part of the obligation on this issue differs from that on the first issue, as follows, "Secured by United States bonds or United States Certificates of indebtedness or United States one-year gold notes, deposited with the Treasurer of the United States of America . . ." The rest of the obligation is the same.

Although modern, the Federal Reserve Bank Notes are all quite scarce and are avidly collected. Most of the issue has long since been redeemed and according to Treasury Department records only a little more than 2 million dollars is still outstanding out of a total issue of nearly 762 million dollars.

1 Dollar Notes

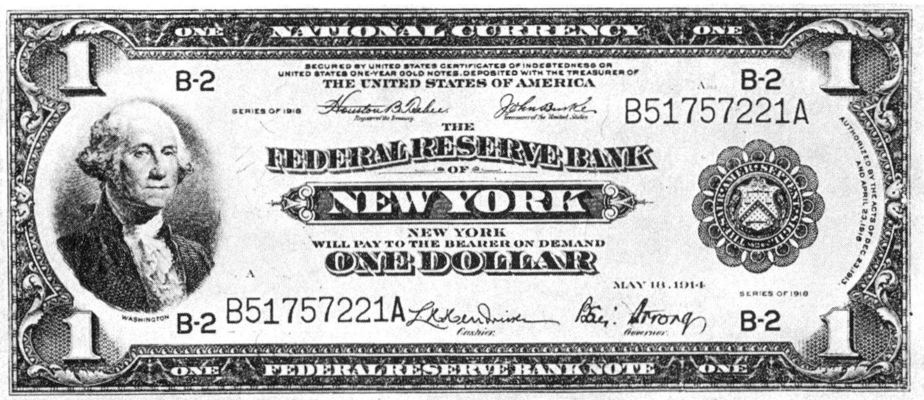

DESIGN NO. 127

(Notes 708-746)

Head of George Washington.

Reverse of Design No. 127.

Eagle holding American flag.

No.	Issuing Bank	Series	Government Signatures		Bank Signatures		Very Good	Very Fine	Unc
708.	Boston	1918	Teehee	Burke	Bullen	Morss	22.50	47.50	140.00
709.	Boston	1918	Teehee	Burke	Willett	Morss	32.50	115.00	475.00
710.	Boston	1918	Elliott	Burke	Willett	Morss	22.50	45.00	140.00
711.	New York	1918	Teehee	Burke	Sailer	Strong	22.50	45.00	140.00
712.	New York	1918	Teehee	Burke	Hendricks	Strong	•22.50	45.00	140.00
713.	New York	1918	Elliott	Burke	Hendricks	Strong	22.50	45.00	140.00
714.	Philadelphia	1918	Teehee	Burke	Hardt	Passmore	22.50	45.00	140.00
715.	Philadelphia	1918	Teehee	Burke	Dyer	Passmore	24.00	55.00	150.00

No.	Issuing Bank	Series	Government Signatures		Bank Signatures		Very Good	Very Fine	Unc
716.	Philadelphia	1918	Elliott	Burke	Dyer	Passmore	24.00	75.00	175.00
717.	Philadelphia	1918	Elliott	Burke	Dyer	Norris	22.50	42.50	140.00
718.	Cleveland	1918	Teehee	Burke	Baxter	Fancher	22.50	42.50	140.00
719.	Cleveland	1918	Teehee	Burke	Davis	Fancher	22.50	42.50	140.00
720.	Cleveland	1918	Elliott	Burke	Davis	Fancher	22.50	42.50	140.00
721.	Richmond	1918	Teehee	Burke	Keesee	Seay	24.00	70.00	175.00
722.	Richmond	1918	Elliott	Burke	Keesee	Seay	24.00	70.00	175.00
723.	Atlanta	1918	Teehee	Burke	Pike	McCord	23.00	60.00	150.00
724.	Atlanta	1918	Teehee	Burke	Bell	McCord	24.00	80.00	175.00
725.	Atlanta	1918	Teehee	Burke	Bell	Wellborn	23.00	60.00	150.00
726.	Atlanta	1918	Elliott	Burke	Bell	Wellborn	24.00	65.00	160.00
727.	Chicago	1918	Teehee	Burke	McCloud	McDougal	22.50	42.50	140.00
728.	Chicago	1918	Teehee	Burke	Cramer	McDougal	22.50	45.00	140.00
729.	Chicago	1918	Elliott	Burke	Cramer	McDougal	22.50	42.50	140.00
730.	St. Louis	1918	Teehee	Burke	Attebery	Wells	24.00	75.00	175.00
731.	St. Louis	1918	Teehee	Burke	Attebery	Biggs	23.00	60.00	175.00
732.	St. Louis	1918	Elliott	Burke	Attebery	Biggs	24.00	65.00	175.00
733.	St. Louis	1918	Elliott	Burke	White	Biggs	24.00	70.00	175.00
734.	Minneapolis	1918	Teehee	Burke	Cook	Wold	32.50	115.00	225.00
735.	Minneapolis	1918	Teehee	Burke	Cook	Young	125.00	800.00	2,800.00
736.	Minneapolis	1918	Elliott	Burke	Cook	Young	32.50	120.00	475.00
737.	Kansas City	1918	Teehee	Burke	Anderson	Miller	23.00	60.00	160.00
738.	Kansas City	1918	Elliott	Burke	Anderson	Miller	23.00	60.00	160.00
739.	Kansas City	1918	Elliott	Burke	Helm	Miller	23.00	60.00	160.00
740.	Dallas	1918	Teehee	Burke	Talley	Van Zandt	24.00	70.00	175.00
741.	Dallas	1918	Elliott	Burke	Talley	Van Zandt	36.00	185.00	900.00
742.	Dallas	1918	Elliott	Burke	Lawder	Van Zandt	24.00	65.00	175.00
743.	San Francisco	1918	Teehee	Burke	Clerk	Lynch	23.00	60.00	150.00
744.	San Francisco	1918	Teehee	Burke	Clerk	Calkins	23.00	60.00	150.00
745.	San Francisco	1918	Elliott	Burke	Clerk	Calkins	23.00	60.00	150.00
746.	San Francisco	1918	Elliott	Burke	Ambrose	Calkins	23.00	60.00	150.00

2 Dollar Notes

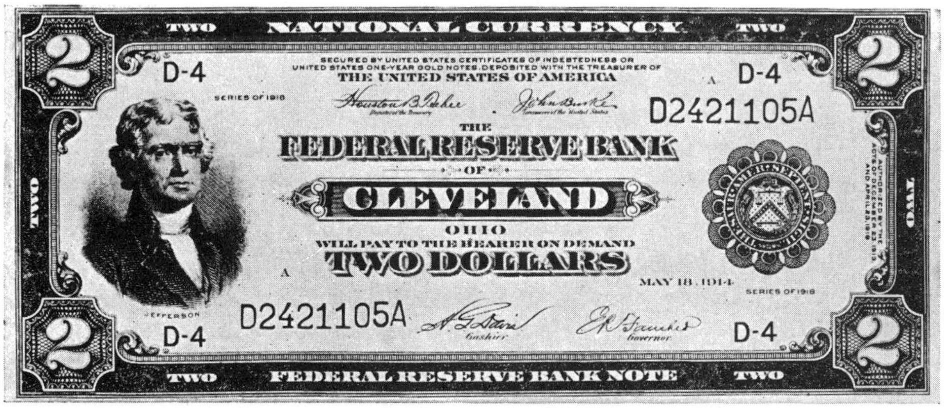

DESIGN NO. 128

(Notes) 747-780)

Head of Thomas Jefferson, the third President of the United States, 1801-1805.

Reverse of Design No. 128.

A battleship of the period of 1914.

No.	Issuing Bank	Series	Government Signatures		Bank Signatures		Very Good	Very Fine	Unc
747.	Boston	1918	Teehee	Burke	Bullen	Morss	60.00	155.00	550.00
748.	Boston	1918	Teehee	Burke	Willett	Morss	70.00	175.00	600.00
749.	Boston	1918	Elliott	Burke	Willett	Morss	60.00	155.00	550.00
750.	New York	1918	Teehee	Burke	Sailer	Strong	60.00	150.00	550.00
751.	New York	1918	Teehee	Burke	Hendricks	Strong	60.00	150.00	550.00
752.	New York	1918	Elliott	Burke	Hendricks	Strong	60.00	155.00	550.00
753.	Philadelphia	1918	Teehee	Burke	Hardt	Passmore	60.00	155.00	550.00
754.	Philadelphia	1918	Teehee	Burke	Dyer	Passmore	60.00	155.00	550.00
755.	Philadelphia	1918	Elliott	Burke	Dyer	Passmore	70.00	225.00	900.00
756.	Philadelphia	1918	Elliott	Burke	Dyer	Norris	60.00	155.00	550.00
757.	Cleveland	1918	Teehee	Burke	Baxter	Fancher	65.00	170.00	600.00
758.	Cleveland	1918	Teehee	Burke	Davis	Fancher	• 65.00	170.00	600.00
759.	Cleveland	1918	Elliott	Burke	Davis	Fancher	65.00	170.00	600.00
760.	Richmond	1918	Teehee	Burke	Keesee	Seay	70.00	200.00	750.00
761.	Richmond	1918	Elliott	Burke	Keesee	Seay	70.00	175.00	600.00
762.	Atlanta	1918	Teehee	Burke	Pike	McCord	70.00	175.00	600.00
763.	Atlanta	1918	Teehee	Burke	Bell	McCord	85.00	225.00	900.00
764.	Atlanta	1918	Elliott	Burke	Bell	Wellborn	70.00	200.00	800.00
765.	Chicago	1918	Teehee	Burke	McCloud	McDougal	60.00	155.00	550.00
766.	Chicago	1918	Teehee	Burke	Cramer	McDougal	60.00	155.00	550.00
767.	Chicago	1918	Elliott	Burke	Cramer	McDougal	60.00	155.00	550.00
768.	St. Louis	1918	Teehee	Burke	Attebery	Wells	75.00	200.00	700.00
769.	St. Louis	1918	Teehee	Burke	Attebery	Biggs	75.00	200.00	750.00
770.	St. Louis	1918	Elliott	Burke	Attebery	Biggs	75.00	225.00	800.00
771.	St. Louis	1918	Elliott	Burke	White	Biggs	75.00	200.00	700.00
772.	Minneapolis	1918	Teehee	Burke	Cook	Wold	75.00	200.00	750.00
773.	Minneapolis	1918	Elliott	Burke	Cook	Young	75.00	200.00	800.00
774.	Kansas City	1918	Teehee	Burke	Anderson	Miller	75.00	200.00	700.00
775.	Kansas City	1918	Elliott	Burke	Helm	Miller	75.00	200.00	750.00
776.	Dallas	1918	Teehee	Burke	Talley	Van Zandt	75.00	200.00	750.00
777.	Dallas	1918	Elliott	Burke	Talley	Van Zandt	75.00	200.00	750.00
778.	San Francisco	1918	Teehee	Burke	Clerk	Lynch	75.00	200.00	700.00
779.	San Francisco	1918	Elliott	Burke	Clerk	Calkins	75.00	200.00	700.00
780.	San Francisco	1918	Elliott	Burke	Ambrose	Calkins	75.00	200.00	700.00

5 Dollar Notes

DESIGN NO. 129

(Notes 781-809a)

Head of Abraham Lincoln.

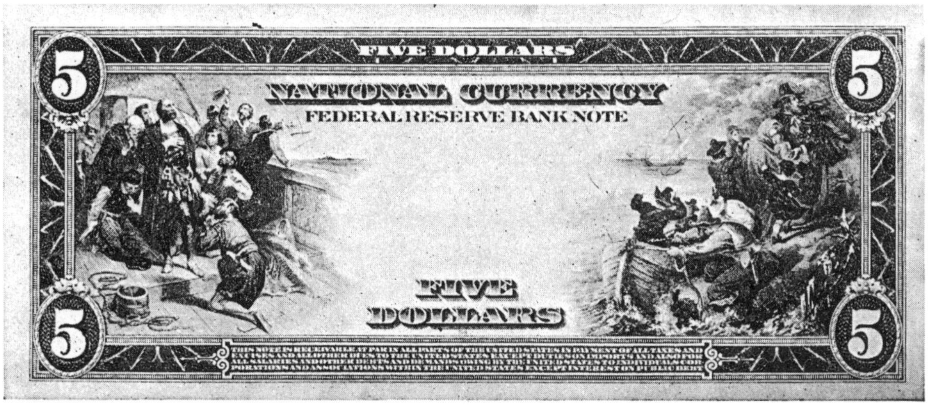

Reverse of Design No. 129.

At the left, Columbus in sight of land. At the right, the landing of the Pilgrims.

No.	Issuing Bank	Series	Government Signatures		Bank Signatures		Very Good	Very Fine	Unc
781.	Boston	1918	Teehee	Burke	Bullen	Morss	350.00	900.00	3,250.00
782.	New York	1918	Teehee	Burke	Hendricks	Strong	•40.00	85.00	400.00
783.	Philadelphia	1918	Teehee	Burke	Hardt	Passmore	40.00	85.00	400.00
784.	Philadelphia	1918	Teehee	Burke	Dyer	Passmore	40.00	90.00	425.00
785.	Cleveland	1918	Teehee	Burke	Baxter	Fancher	40.00	85.00	400.00
786.	Cleveland	1918	Teehee	Burke	Davis	Fancher	42.50	90.00	425.00
787.	Cleveland	1918	Elliott	Burke	Davis	Fancher	40.00	85.00	425.00
788.	Atlanta	1915	Teehee	Burke	Bell	Wellborn	55.00	375.00	950.00
789.	Atlanta	1915	Teehee	Burke	Pike	McCord	50.00	200.00	600.00
790.	Atlanta	1918	Teehee	Burke	Pike	McCord	40.00	85.00	400.00
791.	Atlanta	1918	Teehee	Burke	Bell	Wellborn	40.00	90.00	425.00
792.	Atlanta	1918	Elliott	Burke	Bell	Wellborn	42.50	95.00	450.00
793.	Chicago	1915	Teehee	Burke	McLallen	McDougal	40.00	80.00	400.00
794.	Chicago	1918	Teehee	Burke	McCloud	McDougal	40.00	80.00	400.00
795.	Chicago	1918	Teehee	Burke	Cramer	McDougal	45.00	110.00	400.00
796.	St. Louis	1918	Teehee	Burke	Attebery	Wells	45.00	125.00	500.00
797.	St. Louis	1918	Teehee	Burke	Attebery	Biggs	45.00	125.00	500.00
798.	St. Louis	1918	Elliott	Burke	White	Biggs	45.00	125.00	500.00
799.	Minneapolis	1918	Teehee	Burke	Cook	Wold	55.00	225.00	650.00
800.	Kansas City	1915	Teehee	Burke	Anderson	Miller	45.00	125.00	500.00
800a.	Kansas City	Same but with Anderson-Miller large signatures handsigned.					50.00	180.00	575.00
801.	Kansas City	1915	Teehee	Burke	Cross	Miller	47.50	145.00	525.00
801a.	Kansas City	Same but with Cross-Miller large signatures handsigned and with Cross as Acting Secretary.					50.00	180.00	575.00
802.	Kansas City	1915	Teehee	Burke	Helm	Miller	50.00	195.00	600.00
802a.	Kansas City	Same but with Helm as Acting Cashier.					50.00	185.00	575.00
803.	Kansas City	1918	Teehee	Burke	Anderson	Miller	47.50	130.00	500.00
804.	Kansas City	1918	Elliott	Burke	Helm	Miller	45.00	120.00	500.00
805.	Dallas	1915	Teehee	Burke	Hoopes	Van Zandt	50.00	195.00	600.00
806.	Dallas	1915	Teehee	Burke	Talley	Van Zandt	65.00	275.00	650.00
807.	Dallas	1918	Teehee	Burke	Talley	Van Zandt	47.50	130.00	500.00
808.	San Francisco	1915	Teehee	Burke	Clerk	Lynch	50.00	195.00	600.00
809.	San Francisco	1918	Teehee	Burke	Clerk	Lynch	50.00	195.00	600.00
809a.	San Francisco	Similar, but with date May 18, 1914. (All other San Francisco notes are with date May 20, 1914.)					500.00	1,000.00	3,500.00

No 5 Dollar Federal Reserve Bank notes were issued by the Richmond Bank.

10 Dollar Notes

DESIGN NO. 130

(Notes 810-821)

Head of Andrew Jackson.

Reverse of Design No. 130.

Farm and Factory scenes.

No.	Issuing Bank	Series	Government Signatures		Bank Signatures		Very Good	Very Fine	Unc
810.	New York	1918	Teehee	Burke	Hendricks	Strong	150.00	425.00	1,600.00
811.	Atlanta	1915	Teehee	Burke	Bell	Wellborn	160.00	450.00	1,600.00
812.	Atlanta	1918	Elliott	Burke	Bell	Wellborn	150.00	425.00	1,600.00
813.	Chicago	1915	Teehee	Burke	McLallen	McDougal	• 125.00	400.00	1,500.00
814.	Chicago	1918	Teehee	Burke	McCloud	McDougal	150.00	425.00	1,600.00
815.	St. Louis	1918	Teehee	Burke	Attebery	Wells	175.00	500.00	1,750.00
816.	Kansas City	1915	Teehee	Burke	Anderson	Miller	125.00	400.00	1,500.00
817.	Kansas City	1915	Teehee	Burke	Cross	Miller	125.00	400.00	1,500.00
817a.	Kansas City	Same but with Cross-Miller large signatures handsigned, and with Cross as Acting Secretary.					175.00	600.00	2,000.00
818.	Kansas City	1915	Teehee	Burke	Helm	Miller	125.00	400.00	1,500.00
819.	Dallas	1915	Teehee	Burke	Hoopes	Van Zandt	125.00	425.00	1,500.00
820.	Dallas	1915	Teehee	Burke	Gilbert	Van Zandt	175.00	525.00	1,800.00
821.	Dallas	1915	Teehee	Burke	Talley	Van Zandt	125.00	400.00	1,500.00

No 10 Dollar Federal Reserve Bank Notes were issued by the banks at Boston, Philadelphia, Cleveland, Richmond, Minneapolis and San Francisco.

20 Dollar Notes

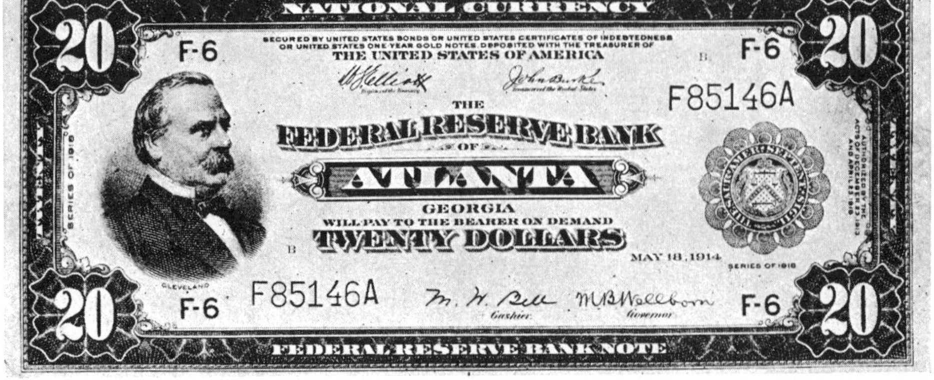

DESIGN NO. 131

(Notes 822-830)

Head of Grover Cleveland, 21st President of the United States, 1885-1889, and 1893-1897.

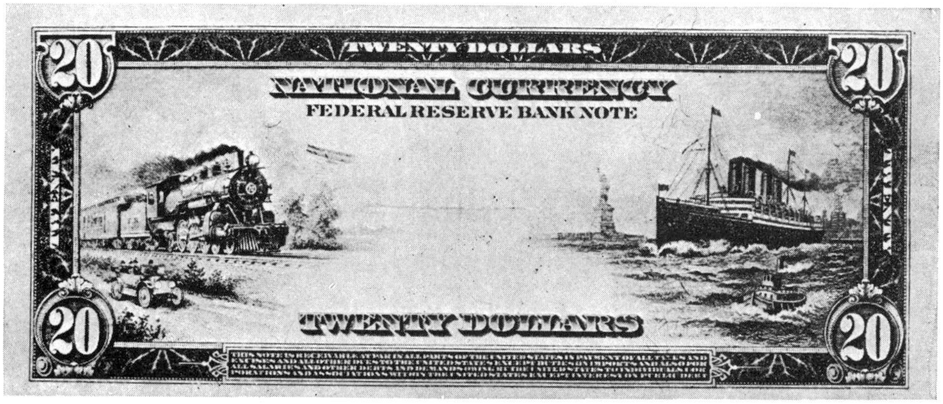

Reverse of Design No. 131.

The vignettes represent land, sea and air transportation.

No.	Issuing Bank	Series	Government Signatures		Bank Signatures		Very Good	Very Fine	Unc
822.	Atlanta	1915	Teehee	Burke	Bell-Cashier	Wellborn	250.00	575.00	2,600.00
822-1.	Atlanta	Same but with Bell-Secretary.					275.00	625.00	2,800.00
822a.	Atlanta	1915	Teehee	Burke	Pike	McCord	350.00	1,500.00	6,000.00
823.	Atlanta	1918	Elliott	Burke	Bell	Wellborn	250.00	575.00	2,600.00
824.	Chicago	1915	Teehee	Burke	McLallen	McDougal	275.00	625.00	2,750.00
825.	St. Louis	1918	Teehee	Burke	Attebery	Wells	300.00	1,000.00	4,000.00
826.	Kansas City	1915	Teehee	Burke	Anderson	Miller	225.00	525.00	2,600.00
827.	Kansas City	1915	Teehee	Burke	Cross	Miller	225.00	525.00	2,600.00
827a.	Kansas City	Same but with Cross-Miller large signatures handsigned, and with Cross as Acting Secretary.					225.00	525.00	2,600.00
828.	Dallas	1915	Teehee	Burke	Hoopes	Van Zandt	300.00	800.00	4,000.00
829.	Dallas	1915	Teehee	Burke	Gilbert	Van Zandt	350.00	1,500.00	6,000.00
830.	Dallas	1915	Teehee	Burke	Talley	Van Zandt	300.00	800.00	4,000.00

No 20 Dollar Federal Reserve Bank Notes were issued bv the banks at Boston, New York, Philadelphia, Cleveland, Richmond, Minneapolis and San Francisco.

50 Dollar Note

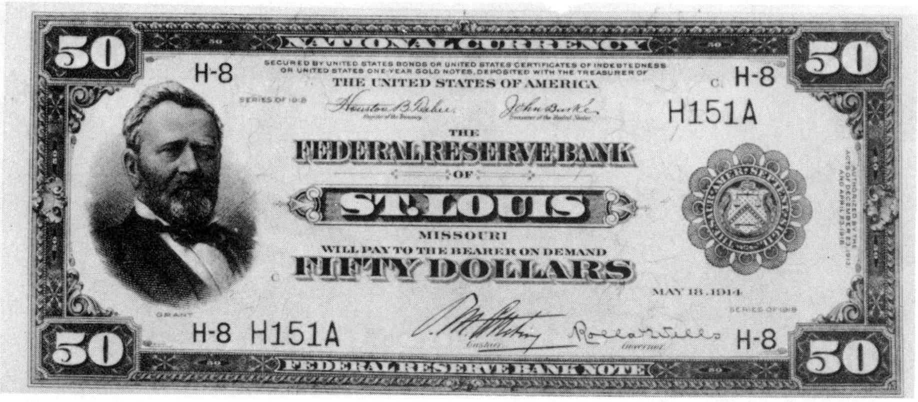

DESIGN NO. 132

(Note 831)

Head of Ulysses S. Grant. This note is very rare as only 33 pieces are reported outstanding on U.S. Treasury books.

Reverse of Design No. 132.

Figure of Panama between two ships.

No.	Issuing Bank	Series	Government Signatures		Bank Signatures		Very Good	Very Fine	Unc
831.	St. Louis	1918	Teehee	Burke	Attebery	Wells	1,500.00	3,750.00	9,500.00

This is the only bank that issued a 50 Dollar Federal Reserve Bank Note.

X. FEDERAL RESERVE NOTES

These were issued under the same Act which authorized the first issue of Federal Reserve Bank Notes, namely the Federal Reserve Act of December 23, 1913.

All denominations were issued from 5 to 10,000 Dollars. The notes from 5 to 100 Dollars are series of 1914, those from 500 to 10,000 Dollars are series of 1918.

The Federal Reserve Notes were issued by the United States to all twelve Federal Reserve Banks and through them to the member banks and the public. The notes were not issued by the banks themselves (as were the Federal Reserve Bank Notes) and the obligations to pay the bearer is borne by the government, and not by the banks. Hence, these notes were not secured by United States bonds or other securities. (In practice, they were secured, but the nature of the security is not certified on the notes).

The obligation on the Federal Reserve Notes is completely unlike that on the Federal Reserve Bank Notes, and is as follows, "The United States of America will pay to the bearer on demand ...... Dollars ... This note is receivable by all national and member banks and Federal Reserve Banks and for all taxes, customs and other public dues. It is redeemable in gold on demand at the Treasury Department of the United States in the city of Washington, District of Columbia or in gold or lawful money at any Federal Reserve Bank."

The reverses of all the following notes are similar to the reverses of the Federal Reserve Bank Notes, except that the words "National Currency" and "Bank" have been removed.

IMPORTANT NOTE: There were three separate issues of notes bearing the White-Mellon signatures and two issues bearing the Burke-McAdoo names. The first issue has a large letter and a numeral in the left bottom of the obverse (see Design No. 133 and 134). The second issue has a small letter and numeral in the same place (see Design No. 135). The third issue has again a large letter and numeral, but slightly higher and more to the left and in addition the seal on each side of the note has been moved closer to the center.

These issues are designated as a-b-c, or a-b, next to the city, depending on whether the note in question exists in all three issues. The lack of a letter alongside the city of White-Mellon or Burke-McAdoo signatures indicates that only the first or "a" issue exists.

The valuations for notes with the White-Mellon or Burke-McAdoo signatures are for the commonest, or first of the three issues of these signatures. The second issue would be valued about 25% more than the first issue and the third about 50% more than the first issue.

5 Dollar Notes

DESIGN NO. 133

(Notes 832-891)

Head of Abraham Lincoln.

The reverse is similar to Design No. 129.

A. Series of 1914 With Red Seal and Signatures of Burke and McAdoo

No.	Issuing Bank	Very Good	Very Fine	Unc
832.	Boston a-b	50.00	90.00	400.00
833.	New York a-b	40.00	80.00	375.00
834.	Philadelphia a-b	40.00	80.00	375.00
835.	Cleveland a-b	40.00	80.00	375.00
836.	Richmond	45.00	85.00	400.00
837.	Atlanta a-b	45.00	85.00	400.00
838.	Chicago a-b	40.00	80.00	375.00
839.	St. Louis a-b	40.00	80.00	375.00
840.	Minneapolis	45.00	85.00	400.00
841.	Kansas City a-b	45.00	85.00	400.00
842.	Dallas a-b	50.00	90.00	400.00
843.	San Francisco a-b	55.00	100.00	500.00

B. Series of 1914 With Blue Seal

No.	Issuing Bank	Signatures		Very Fine	Unc
844.	Boston	Burke	McAdoo	25.00	90.00
845.	Boston	Burke	Glass	30.00	100.00
846.	Boston	Burke	Houston	25.00	90.00
847.	Boston a-b	White	Mellon	25.00	90.00
848.	New York	Burke	McAdoo	25.00	90.00
849.	New York	Burke	Glass	30.00	100.00
850.	New York	Burke	Houston	25.00	90.00
851.	New York a-b-c	White	Mellon	25.00	90.00
852.	Philadelphia	Burke	McAdoo	25.00	90.00
853.	Philadelphia	Burke	Glass	30.00	100.00
854.	Philadelphia	Burke	Houston	25.00	90.00
855.	Philadelphia a-b-c	White	Mellon	25.00	90.00
856.	Cleveland	Burke	McAdoo	30.00	100.00
857.	Cleveland	Burke	Glass	32.50	100.00
858.	Cleveland	Burke	Houston	25.00	90.00
859.	Cleveland a-b-c	White	Mellon	25.00	90.00
860.	Richmond	Burke	McAdoo	32.50	100.00
861.	Richmond	Burke	Glass	35.00	110.00
862.	Richmond	Burke	Houston	32.50	100.00
863.	Richmond a-b	White	Mellon	30.00	100.00
864.	Atlanta	Burke	McAdoo	30.00	100.00
865.	Atlanta	Burke	Glass	45.00	150.00
866.	Atlanta	Burke	Houston	30.00	100.00
867.	Atlanta	White	Mellon	27.50	90.00
868.	Chicago	Burke	McAdoo	27.50	95.00
869.	Chicago	Burke	Glass	30.00	100.00
870.	Chicago	Burke	Houston	27.50	95.00
871.	Chicago a-b-c	White	Mellon	27.50	95.00
872.	St. Louis	Burke	McAdoo	27.50	95.00
873.	St. Louis	Burke	Glass	30.00	100.00
874.	St. Louis	Burke	Houston	27.50	95.00
875.	St. Louis a-b	White	Mellon	27.50	95.00
876.	Minneapolis	Burke	McAdoo	27.50	95.00
877.	Minneapolis	Burke	Glass	45.00	150.00
878.	Minneapolis	Burke	Houston	32.50	110.00
879.	Minneapolis	White	Mellon	30.00	100.00
880.	Kansas City	Burke	McAdoo	27.50	95.00
881.	Kansas City	Burke	Glass	37.50	110.00
882.	Kansas City	Burke	Houston	27.50	95.00
883.	Kansas City a-b	White	Mellon	27.50	95.00
884.	Dallas	Burke	McAdoo	45.00	150.00
885.	Dallas	Burke	Glass	45.00	150.00
886.	Dallas	Burke	Houston	27.50	95.00
887.	Dallas a-b	White	Mellon	27.50	95.00
888.	San Francisco	Burke	McAdoo	30.00	100.00
889.	San Francisco	Burke	Glass	40.00	110.00
890.	San Francisco	Burke	Houston	32.50	110.00
891.	San Francisco a-b-c	White	Mellon	30.00	100.00

10 Dollar Notes

DESIGN NO. 134

(Notes 892-951)

Head of Andrew Jackson. The reverse is similar to Design No. 130.

A. Series of 1914 With Red Seal and Signatures of Burke and McAdoo

No.	Issuing Bank	Very Good	Very Fine	Unc
892.	Boston a-b	55.00	110.00	600.00
893.	New York a-b	50.00	85.00	575.00
894.	Philadelphia a-b	50.00	85.00	575.00
895.	Cleveland a-b	45.00	85.00	575.00
896.	Richmond	50.00	95.00	575.00
897.	Atlanta a-b	50.00	95.00	575.00
898.	Chicago a-b	45.00	85.00	550.00
899.	St. Louis a-b	50.00	95.00	575.00
900.	Minneapolis	50.00	95.00	575.00
901.	Kansas City a-b	50.00	95.00	575.00
902.	Dallas a-b	55.00	110.00	600.00
903.	San Francisco a-b	55.00	110.00	600.00

B. Series of 1914 With Blue Seal

No.	Issuing Bank	Signatures		Very Fine	Unc
904.	Boston	Burke	McAdoo	25.00	110.00
905.	Boston	Burke	Glass	32.50	110.00
906.	Boston	Burke	Houston	25.00	100.00
907.	Boston a-b	White	Mellon	25.00	100.00
908.	New York	Burke	McAdoo	27.50	100.00
909.	New York	Burke	Glass	35.00	110.00
910.	New York	Burke	Houston	•25.00	100.00
911.	New York a-b-c	White	Mellon	25.00	100.00
912.	Philadelphia	Burke	McAdoo	25.00	100.00
913.	Philadelphia	Burke	Glass	35.00	110.00
914.	Philadelphia	Burke	Houston	25.00	100.00
915.	Philadelphia a-c	White	Mellon	25.00	100.00
916.	Cleveland	Burke	McAdoo	25.00	100.00
917.	Cleveland	Burke	Glass	35.00	110.00
918.	Cleveland	Burke	Houston	25.00	100.00
919.	Cleveland a-b-c	White	Mellon	25.00	100.00
920.	Richmond	Burke	McAdoo	27.50	100.00
921.	Richmond	Burke	Glass	35.00	110.00
922.	Richmond	Burke	Houston	27.50	100.00
923.	Richmond	White	Mellon	27.50	100.00
924.	Atlanta	Burke	McAdoo	27.50	100.00
925.	Atlanta	Burke	Glass	35.00	110.00
926.	Atlanta	Burke	Houston	27.50	100.00
927.	Atlanta a-b	White	Mellon	27.50	100.00
928.	Chicago	Burke	McAdoo	25.00	100.00
929.	Chicago	Burke	Glass	32.50	110.00
930.	Chicago	Burke	Houston	25.00	100.00
931.	Chicago a-b-c	White	Mellon	25.00	100.00
932.	St. Louis	Burke	McAdoo	27.50	100.00
933.	St. Louis	Burke	Glass	35.00	110.00
934.	St. Louis	Burke	Houston	27.50	100.00
935.	St. Louis	White	Mellon	27.50	100.00
936.	Minneapolis	Burke	McAdoo	27.50	100.00
937.	Minneapolis	Burke	Glass	35.00	110.00
938.	Minneapolis	Burke	Houston	25.00	100.00
939.	Minneapolis	White	Mellon	25.00	100.00
940.	Kansas City	Burke	McAdoo	27.50	100.00
941.	Kansas City	Burke	Glass	40.00	125.00
942.	Kansas City	Burke	Houston	27.50	100.00
943.	Kansas City	White	Mellon	27.50	100.00
944.	Dallas	Burke	McAdoo	27.50	100.00
945.	Dallas	Burke	Glass	35.00	110.00
946.	Dallas	Burke	Houston	27.50	100.00
947.	Dallas	White	Mellon	27.50	100.00
948.	San Francisco	Burke	McAdoo	27.50	100.00
949.	San Francisco	Burke	Glass	40.00	125.00
950.	San Francisco	Burke	Houston	35.00	110.00
951.	San Francisco a-b-c	White	Mellon	27.50	100.00

20 Dollar Notes

DESIGN NO. 135

(Notes 952-1011)

Head of Grover Cleveland.

The reverse is similar to Design No. 131.

A. Series of 1914 With Red Seal and Signatures of Burke and McAdoo

No.	Issuing Bank	Very Good	Very Fine	Unc
952.	Boston	75.00	160.00	750.00
953.	New York a-b	50.00	125.00	700.00
954.	Philadelphia a-b	50.00	125.00	700.00
955.	Cleveland a-b	50.00	125.00	700.00
956.	Richmond	50.00	125.00	700.00
957.	Atlanta a-b	50.00	125.00	700.00
958.	Chicago a-b	50.00	125.00	700.00
959.	St. Louis a-b	50.00	125.00	700.00
960.	Minneapolis	50.00	125.00	700.00
961.	Kansas City a-b	50.00	125.00	700.00
962.	Dallas	50.00	125.00	700.00
963.	San Francisco	50.00	150.00	725.00

B. Series of 1914 With Blue Seal

No.	Issuing Bank	Signatures		Very Fine	Unc
964.	Boston	Burke	McAdoo	40.00	175.00
965.	Boston	Burke	Glass	42.50	200.00
966.	Boston	Burke	Houston	40.00	175.00
967.	Boston	White	Mellon	40.00	175.00
968.	New York	Burke	McAdoo	40.00	175.00
969.	New York	Burke	Glass	42.50	200.00
970.	New York	Burke	Houston	40.00	175.00
971.	New York a-b-c	White	Mellon	40.00	175.00
972.	Philadelphia	Burke	McAdoo	40.00	175.00
973.	Philadelphia	Burke	Glass	42.50	200.00
974.	Philadelphia	Burke	Houston	40.00	175.00
975.	Philadelphia a-b-c	White	Mellon	40.00	175.00
976.	Cleveland	Burke	McAdoo	40.00	175.00
977.	Cleveland	Burke	Glass	42.50	200.00
978.	Cleveland	Burke	Houston	40.00	175.00
979.	Cleveland a-b	White	Mellon	40.00	175.00
980.	Richmond	Burke	McAdoo	42.50	200.00
981.	Richmond	Burke	Glass	42.50	200.00
982.	Richmond	Burke	Houston	40.00	175.00
983.	Richmond	White	Mellon	40.00	175.00
984.	Atlanta	Burke	McAdoo	40.00	175.00
985.	Atlanta	Burke	Glass	45.00	225.00
986.	Atlanta	Burke	Houston	40.00	175.00
987.	Atlanta	White	Mellon	40.00	175.00
988.	Chicago	Burke	McAdoo	40.00	175.00
989.	Chicago	Burke	Glass	42.50	200.00
990.	Chicago	Burke	Houston	40.00	175.00
991.	Chicago a-b-c	White	Mellon	40.00	175.00
992.	St. Louis	Burke	McAdoo	42.50	200.00
993.	St. Louis	Burke	Glass	42.50	200.00
994.	St. Louis	Burke	Houston	40.00	185.00
995.	St. Louis	White	Mellon	40.00	185.00
996.	Minneapolis	Burke	McAdoo	40.00	175.00
997.	Minneapolis	Burke	Glass	42.50	200.00
998.	Minneapolis	Burke	Houston	40.00	175.00
999.	Minneapolis	White	Mellon	40.00	175.00
1000.	Kansas City	Burke	McAdoo	40.00	175.00
1001.	Kansas City	Burke	Glass	45.00	225.00
1002.	Kansas City	Burke	Houston	40.00	175.00
1003.	Kansas City a-b	White	Mellon	40.00	175.00
1004.	Dallas	Burke	McAdoo	40.00	175.00
1005.	Dallas	Burke	Glass	42.50	200.00
1006.	Dallas	Burke	Houston	40.00	175.00
1007.	Dallas a-b	White	Mellon	40.00	175.00
1008.	San Francisco	Burke	McAdoo	42.50	200.00
1009.	San Francisco	Burke	Glass	45.00	225.00
1010.	San Francisco	Burke	Houston	40.00	175.00
1011.	San Francisco a-b-c	White	Mellon	40.00	175.00

50 Dollar Notes

DESIGN NO. 136

(Notes 1012-1071)

Head of Ulysses S. Grant.

The reverse is similar to Design No. 132.

A. Series of 1914 With Red Seal and Signatures of Burke and McAdoo

No.	Issuing Bank	Very Good	Very Fine	Unc
1012.	Boston a-b	140.00	350.00	2,000.00
1013.	New York a-b	125.00	325.00	2,000.00
1014.	Philadelphia a-b	125.00	325.00	2,000.00
1015.	Cleveland a-b	125.00	325.00	2,000.00
1016.	Richmond	140.00	350.00	2,000.00
1017.	Atlanta a-b	140.00	350.00	2,000.00
1018.	Chicago a-b	125.00	325.00	2,000.00
1019.	St. Louis a-b	140.00	350.00	2,000.00
1020.	Minneapolis	140.00	350.00	2,000.00
1021.	Kansas City a-b	140.00	350.00	2,000.00
1022.	Dallas	140.00	350.00	2,000.00
1023.	San Francisco	140.00	350.00	2,000.00

B. Series of 1914 With Blue Seal

No.	Issuing Bank	Signatures		Very Fine	Unc
1024.	Boston	Burke	McAdoo	110.00	850.00
1025.	Boston	Burke	Glass	125.00	900.00
1026.	Boston	Burke	Houston	110.00	850.00
1027.	Boston	White	Mellon	110.00	850.00
1028.	New York	Burke	McAdoo	110.00	850.00
1029.	New York	Burke	Glass	125.00	850.00
1030.	New York	Burke	Houston	110.00	850.00
1031.	New York a-b	White	Mellon	110.00	850.00
1032.	Philadelphia	Burke	McAdoo	110.00	850.00
1033.	Philadelphia	Burke	Glass	125.00	850.00
1034.	Philadelphia	Burke	Houston	110.00	850.00
1035.	Philadelphia	White	Mellon	110.00	850.00

No.	Issuing Bank	Signatures		Very Fine	Unc
1036.	Cleveland	Burke	McAdoo	110.00	850.00
1037.	Cleveland	Burke	Glass	125.00	850.00
1038.	Cleveland	Burke	Houston	110.00	850.00
1039.	Cleveland a-b	White	Mellon	110.00	850.00
1040.	Richmond	Burke	McAdoo	125.00	850.00
1041.	Richmond	Burke	Glass	150.00	900.00
1042.	Richmond	Burke	Houston	110.00	850.00
1043.	Richmond	White	Mellon	110.00	850.00
1044.	Atlanta	Burke	McAdoo	110.00	850.00
1045.	Atlanta	Burke	Glass	125.00	850.00
1046.	Atlanta	Burke	Houston	110.00	850.00
1047.	Atlanta	White	Mellon	110.00	850.00
1048.	Chicago	Burke	McAdoo	110.00	850.00
1049.	Chicago	Burke	Glass	125.00	850.00
1050.	Chicago	Burke	Houston	110.00	850.00
1051.	Chicago	White	Mellon	110.00	850.00
1052.	St. Louis	Burke	McAdoo	125.00	850.00
1053.	St. Louis	Burke	Glass	150.00	900.00

No.	Issuing Bank	Signatures		Very Fine	Unc
1054.	St. Louis	Burke	Houston	125.00	850.00
1055.	St. Louis	White	Mellon	125.00	850.00
1056.	Minneapolis	Burke	McAdoo	120.00	850.00
1057.	Minneapolis	Burke	Glass	150.00	900.00
1058.	Minneapolis	Burke	Houston	120.00	850.00
1059.	Minneapolis	White	Mellon	120.00	850.00
1060.	Kansas City	Burke	McAdoo	110.00	850.00
1061.	Kansas City	Burke	Glass	125.00	850.00
1062.	Kansas City	Burke	Houston	110.00	850.00
1063.	Kansas City	White	Mellon	110.00	850.00
1064.	Dallas	Burke	McAdoo	125.00	850.00
1065.	Dallas	Burke	Glass	150.00	900.00
1066.	Dallas	Burke	Houston	125.00	850.00
1067.	Dallas	White	Mellon	125.00	850.00
1068.	San Francisco	Burke	McAdoo	125.00	850.00
1069.	San Francisco	Burke	Glass	150.00	900.00
1070.	San Francisco	Burke	Houston	125.00	850.00
1071.	San Francisco	White	Mellon	125.00	850.00

100 Dollar Notes

DESIGN NO. 137

(Notes 1072-1131)

Head of Benjamin Franklin.

Reverse of Design No. 137.

Allegorical group of five figures.

A. Series of 1914 With Red Seal and Signatures of Burke and McAdoo

No.	Issuing Bank	Very Good	Very Fine	Unc
1072.	Boston a-b	225.00	500.00	2,000.00
1073.	New York a-b	225.00	500.00	2,000.00
1074.	Philadelphia a-b	225.00	500.00	2,000.00
1075.	Cleveland a-b	225.00	500.00	2,000.00
1076.	Richmond	225.00	500.00	2,000.00
1077.	Atlanta a-b	225.00	500.00	2,000.00
1078.	Chicago a-b	225.00	500.00	2,000.00
1079.	St. Louis a-b	225.00	500.00	2,000.00
1080.	Minneapolis	225.00	500.00	2,000.00
1081.	Kansas City a-b	225.00	500.00	2,000.00
1082.	Dallas	225.00	500.00	2,000.00
1083.	San Francisco a-b	225.00	500.00	2,000.00

B. Series of 1914 With Blue Seal

No.	Issuing Bank	Signatures		Very Fine	Unc
1084.	Boston	Burke	McAdoo	175.00	850.00
1085.	Boston	Burke	Glass	200.00	950.00
1086.	Boston	Burke	Houston	175.00	850.00
1087.	Boston	White	Mellon	175.00	850.00
1088.	New York	Burke	McAdoo	175.00	850.00
1089.	New York	Burke	Glass	200.00	900.00
1090.	New York	Burke	Houston	175.00	850.00
1091.	New York	White	Mellon	175.00	850.00
1092.	Philadelphia	Burke	McAdoo	175.00	850.00
1093.	Philadelphia	Burke	Glass	200.00	900.00
1094.	Philadelphia	Burke	Houston	175.00	850.00
1095.	Philadelphia	White	Mellon	175.00	850.00
1096.	Cleveland	Burke	McAdoo	175.00	850.00
1097.	Cleveland	Burke	Glass	200.00	900.00
1098.	Cleveland	Burke	Houston	175.00	850.00
1099.	Cleveland	White	Mellon	175.00	850.00
1100.	Richmond	Burke	McAdoo	200.00	900.00
1101.	Richmond	Burke	Glass	200.00	900.00
1102.	Richmond	Burke	Houston	175.00	850.00
1103.	Richmond	White	Mellon	175.00	850.00
1104.	Atlanta	Burke	McAdoo	175.00	850.00
1105.	Atlanta	Burke	Glass	200.00	900.00
1106.	Atlanta	Burke	Houston	175.00	850.00
1107.	Atlanta	White	Mellon	175.00	850.00
1108.	Chicago	Burke	McAdoo	175.00	850.00
1109.	Chicago	Burke	Glass	200.00	900.00
1110.	Chicago	Burke	Houston	175.00	850.00
1111.	Chicago	White	Mellon	175.00	850.00
1112.	St. Louis	Burke	McAdoo	175.00	850.00
1113.	St. Louis	Burke	Glass	200.00	900.00
1114.	St. Louis	Burke	Houston	175.00	850.00
1115.	St. Louis	White	Mellon	175.00	850.00
1116.	Minneapolis	Burke	McAdoo	175.00	850.00
1117.	Minneapolis	Burke	Glass	200.00	900.00
1118.	Minneapolis	Burke	Houston	175.00	850.00
1119.	Minneapolis	White	Mellon	175.00	850.00
1120.	Kansas City	Burke	McAdoo	175.00	850.00
1121.	Kansas City	Burke	Glass	200.00	900.00
1122.	Kansas City	Burke	Houston	175.00	850.00
1123.	Kansas City	White	Mellon	175.00	850.00
1124.	Dallas	Burke	McAdoo	175.00	850.00
1125.	Dallas	Burke	Glass	220.00	950.00
1126.	Dallas	Burke	Houston	175.00	850.00
1127.	Dallas	White	Mellon	175.00	850.00
1128.	San Francisco	Burke	McAdoo	220.00	950.00
1129.	San Francisco	Burke	Glass	220.00	950.00
1130.	San Francisco	Burke	Houston	210.00	875.00
1131.	San Francisco	White	Mellon	210.00	875.00

500 Dollar Notes

DESIGN NO. 138

(Note 1132)

Head of John Marshall. His portrait also appears on Design No. 93.

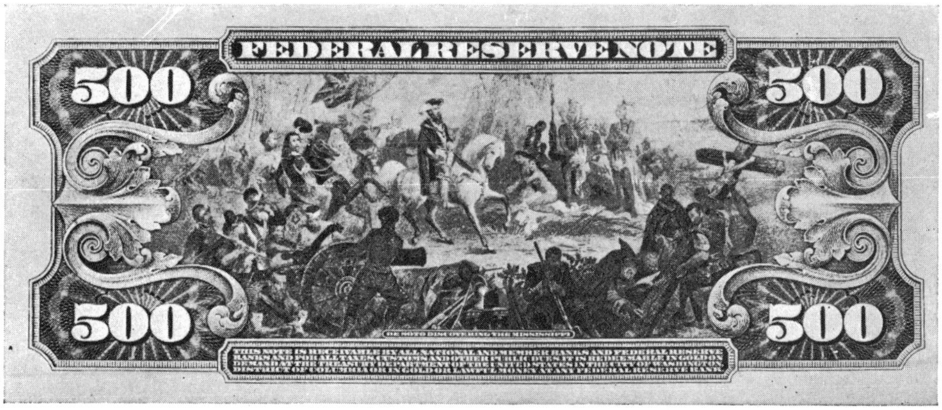

Reverse of Design No. 138.

De Soto discovering the Mississippi.

1132. 500 Dollar Note. Series of 1918. Different bank varieties are known.

1,000 Dollar Notes

DESIGN NO. 139

(Note 1133)

Head of Alexander Hamilton.

Reverse of Design No. 139.

American eagle with flag.

1133. 1000 Dollar Note. Series of 1918. Different bank varieties are known.

5,000 Dollar Notes

DESIGN NO. 140

(Note 1134)

Head of James Madison, fourth President of the United States, 1809-1817.

Reverse of Design No. 140.

George Washington resigning his Commission.

This illustration by courtesy of the Federal Reserve Bank of Chicago.

1134. 5000 Dollar Note. Series of 1918. Different bank varieties were issued.

10,000 Dollar Notes

DESIGN NO. 141

(Note 1135)

Head of Salmon P. Chase.

Reverse of Design No. 141.

The Embarkation of the Pilgrims.

1135. 10,000 Dollar Note. Series of 1918. Different bank varieties were issued.

XI. THE NATIONAL GOLD BANK NOTES OF CALIFORNIA

These notes are the most romantic of all our currency issues. Their existence is directly traceable to the California Gold Rush of 1848 and they remain today as tangible mementos of the Winning of the West.

These notes are instinctively associated with gold. First, the paper on which they are printed is yellowish in imitation of gold and secondly, the reverses show a group of American gold coins of all denominations from 1 to 20 Dollars. See the illustration in the text.

As the population of California continued to grow, trade and commerce increased to such an extent that the California banks were soon handling enormous quantities of gold coin in their daily transactions. In those days in California, gold was the universal medium of exchange. The counting and handling of so much coin was burdensome and time consuming and was a barrier to the efficient operation of the banks.

Therefore, in order to facilitate these numerous gold transactions, Congress passed the Act of July 12, 1870, which authorized nine Gold Banks in California and one in Boston to issue and circulate currency redeemable in gold coin. This was indeed remarkable, since the Treasury Department had not yet resumed specie payments (which were not to come until 1879.) The denominations issued were 5, 10, 20, 50, 100 and 500 Dollars, but not all banks issued all denominations.

The vignettes on the obverse of these notes are the same as on the National Bank Notes of the First Charter Period.

The name of the Boston bank that was authorized to issue National Gold Bank Notes was the Kidder National Gold Bank of Boston, Mass. It is believed that its entire issue of gold notes was recalled and destroyed before they were released to the public. Only two Specimen notes are known to exist, one of 50 Dollars and the other of 100 Dollars.

These banks were Gold Banks in addition to being National Banks, and so their operation came under the general provisions of the National Banking Act of 1863 and they were required to deposit the legal amount of United States Bonds with the Treasurer of the United States.

It must be remembered that the obligation of redeeming these notes in gold coin rested with the bank and not with the government.

These notes were readily accepted in California at par with gold, and they went through a long life of active and useful circulation. Indeed, so active was this circulation that very few notes have survived in their original new condition.

Any National Gold Bank Note in crisp new condition is practically unheard of and is an outstanding rarity. The general condition in which these notes are found is one of advanced circulation and notes in very fine or better condition are extremely rare. In addition, it may be stated that all these notes, regardless of their preservation, are very rare today and are greatly in demand by collectors.

The obligation on these National Gold Bank Notes is as follows. "This note is secured by bonds of the United States deposited with the U.S. Treasurer at Washington.... The (name of bank and city) will pay ...... Dollars to bearer in gold coin on demand.... This note is receivable at par in all parts of the United States in payment of all taxes and excises and all other dues to the United States, except duties on imports, and also for all salaries and other debts and demands owing by the United States to individuals, corporations, and associations within the United States, except interest on public debt."

All the notes in this section have a red Treasury Seal and the signatures of Allison and Spinner except the following:

1153 and 1163 have the signatures of Bruce and Gilfillan

1147, 1150 and 1157 have the signatures of Scofield and Gilfillan

ALL NOTES IN THIS SECTION ARE VERY RARE IN A STATE OF PRESERVATION BETTER THAN VERY GOOD

5 Dollar Notes

DESIGN NO. 142

(Notes 1136-1141)

Vignettes similar to Design No. 101, but the wording pertains to gold coin.

Reverse of Design No. 142.

A group of gold coins, showing the 1, 2½, 3, 5, 10 and 20 Dollar pieces.

No.	Date	Name of Bank	City	Fair	Very Good
1136.	1870	First National Gold Bank	San Francisco	•450.00	1,000.00
1137.	1872	National Gold Bank and Trust Company	San Francisco	550.00	1,100.00
1138.	1872	National Gold Bank of D.O. Mills and Co.	Sacramento	550.00	1,050.00
1139.	1873	First National Gold Bank	Santa Barbara	650.00	1,450.00
1140.	1873	First National Gold Bank	Stockton	550.00	1,100.00
1141.	1874	Farmer's National Gold Bank	San Jose	550.00	1,050.00

10 Dollar Notes

DESIGN NO. 143
(Notes 1142-1151-a)
Obverse: Vignettes similar to Design No. 102.
Reverse: Similar to Design No. 142.

No.	Date	Name of Bank	City	Fair	Very Good
1142.	1870	First National Gold Bank	San Francisco	550.00	1,100.00
1143.	1872	National Gold Bank and Trust Company	San Francisco	600.00	1,250.00
1144.	1872	National Gold Bank of D.O. Mills and Co.	Sacramento	575.00	1,100.00
1145.	1873	First National Gold Bank	Santa Barbara	700.00	1,350.00
1146.	1873	First National Gold Bank	Stockton	600.00	1,250.00
1147.	1875	Series. First National Gold Bank	Stockton	600.00	1,275.00
1148.	1874	Farmer's National Gold Bank	San Jose	600.00	1,250.00
1149.	1874	First National Gold Bank	Petaluma	600.00	1,275.00
1150.	1875	Series. First National Gold Bank	Petaluma	600.00	1,275.00
1151.	1875	First National Gold Bank	Oakland	600.00	1,275.00
1151-a.	1875	Union National Gold Bank	Oakland	800.00	1,700.00

20 Dollar Notes

DESIGN NO. 144
(Notes 1152-1159-b)
Obverse: Vignettes similar to Design No. 103.
Reverse: Similar to Design No. 142.

No.	Date	Name of Bank	City	Fair	Very Good
1152.	1870	First National Gold Bank	San Francisco	725.00	1,700.00
1153.	1875	Series. First National Gold Bank	San Francisco	750.00	1,800.00
1154.	1872	National Gold Bank of D.O. Mills and Co.	Sacramento	725.00	1,700.00
1155.	1873	First National Gold Bank	Stockton	725.00	1,700.00
1156.	1874	Farmer's National Gold Bank	San Jose	725.00	1,700.00
1157.	1875	Series. First National Gold Bank	Petaluma	800.00	1,900.00
1158.	1875	First National Gold Bank	Oakland	900.00	2,000.00
1159.	1875	Union National Gold Bank	Oakland	900.00	2,000.00
1159-a.	1873	First National Gold Bank	Santa Barbara	1,050.00	2,300.00
1159-b.	1872	National Gold Bank and Trust Company	San Francisco	Unknown	

50 Dollar Notes

DESIGN NO. 145
(Notes 1160-1161-f)
Obverse: Vignettes similar to Design No. 104.
Reverse: Similar to Design No. 142.

No.	Date	Name of Bank	City	Fair	Very Good
1160.	1870	First National Gold Bank	San Francisco	3,250.00	5,500.00
1161.	1874	Farmer's National Gold Bank	San Jose	3,500.00	6,000.00
1161-a.	1872	National Gold Bank and Trust Company	San Francisco	Unknown	
1161-b.	1872	National Gold Bank of D.O. Mills and Co.	Sacramento	Unknown	
1161-c.	1873	First National Gold Bank	Stockton	Unknown	
1161-d.	1873	First National Gold Bank	Santa Barbara	Unknown	
1161-e.	1875	Series. First National Gold Bank	San Francisco	Unknown	
1161-f.	1875	Union National Gold Bank	Oakland	Unknown	

100 Dollar Notes

DESIGN NO. 146

(Notes 1162-1166-IV)

Obverse: Vignettes similar to Design No. 105.
Reverse: Similar to Design No. 142.

No.	Date	Name of Bank	City	Fair	Very Good
1162.	1870	First National Gold Bank	San Francisco	**4,250.00**	**8,500.00**
1163.	1875	Series. First National Gold Bank	San Francisco	**4,250.00**	**8,500.00**
1164.	1873	First National Gold Bank	Santa Barbara	**4,250.00**	**8,500.00**
1165.	1874	First National Gold Bank	Petaluma	**4,250.00**	**8,500.00**
1166.	1875	Union National Gold Bank	Oakland	**4,250.00**	**8,500.00**
1166-I	1872	National Gold Bank and Trust Company	San Francisco	**Unknown**	
1166-II.	1872	National Gold Bank of D.O. Mills and Co.	Sacramento	**Unknown**	
1166-III.	1873	First National Gold Bank	Stockton	**Rare**	
1166-IV.	1874	Farmer's National Gold Bank	San Jose	**Unknown**	

500 Dollar Notes

DESIGN NO. 146-a

(Note 1166-a)

Obverse: Vignettes similar to Design No. 106.
Reverse: Similar to Design No. 142.

1166-a. This denomination was issued by three banks — the two in San Francisco, and the one in Sacramento. No specimen of these notes is now known to exist, although 4 notes are still outstanding.

A Countersigned Gold Certificate, Series of 1882

Illustrated to show the minor differences between the countersigned and normal issues of Series of 1882. Notes 1175, 1189 and 1202 are countersigned.

This illustration by courtesy of Mr. Arthur M. Kagin.

XII. GOLD CERTIFICATES

Gold Certificates are colorful and vivid and are among the most attractive of all currency issues. Their reverses are a brilliant golden orange, symbolic of the gold coin they represent.

Although there were nine emissions of gold certificates, only four of the issues were circulated to any extent, namely the fourth, seventh, eighth and ninth issues.

The first three issues appeared between 1865 and 1875. Some of the notes were printed on only one side. They remained in general within the confines of banks and clearing houses and were used in settling gold balances.

The fifth and sixth issues were series of 1888 and 1900 and consisted of 5,000 and 10,000 Dollar notes only.

The fourth issue was the earliest for general circulation. The notes of this issue are series of 1882 and consist of all denominations from 20 to 10,000 Dollars. The 20, 50 and 100 Dollar notes are still occasionally seen.

The seventh issue consisted only of 10 and 20 Dollar notes of the series of 1905, 1906 and 1907. The 20 Dollar notes of 1905 are considered the most beautiful of all gold certificates because of their color. Their basic design is similar to that of other 20 Dollar notes, but the obverse center portion of the paper is gold tinted and part of the legends are printed in gold ink, and not the black and white of other issues. These notes also have a red seal and red serial numbers. Thus, the color combination formed by black and white and gold and red, makes a very pleasing impression.

The eighth issue consisted only of 1,000 Dollar Notes of the series of 1907.

The ninth and last issue of Gold Certificates forms the notes that are most frequently seen today. These notes are series of 1913 and 1922 and the issue consisted of all denominations from 10 to 1,000 Dollars. The series of 1913 appears only on 50 Dollar notes. See the text for a complete tabulation.

The obligation on gold certificates is as follows, "This certifies that there have been deposited in the Treasury of the United States of America ...... Dollars in gold coin payable (or repayable, series 1882) to the bearer on demand."

In addition to the preceding, the notes of series 1922 bear the following, "This certificate is a legal tender in the amount thereof in payment of all debts and dues public and private. Acts of March 14, 1900, as amended and December 24, 1919."

THE REVERSES OF ALL GOLD CERTIFICATES ARE A BRILLIANT GOLDEN ORANGE COLOR.

Gold Certificates of the First Issue. Act of March 3, 1863.

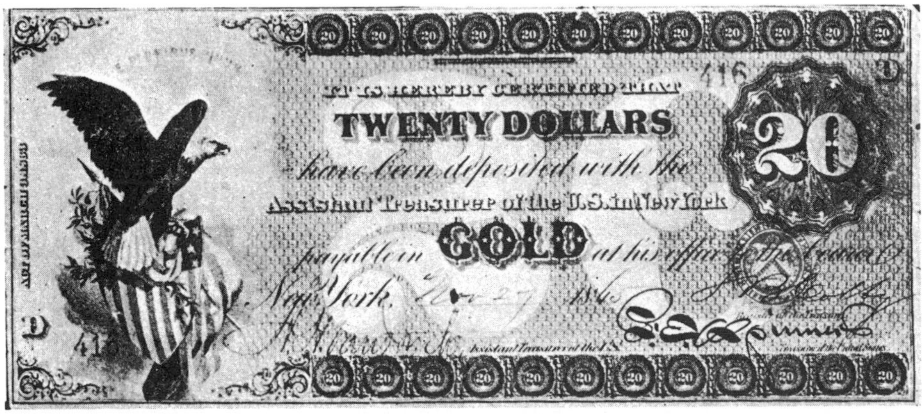

DESIGN NO. 146-b

(Note 1166-b)

Eagle on draped shield. Countersigned and dated by hand. These notes have one or more handwritten signatures.

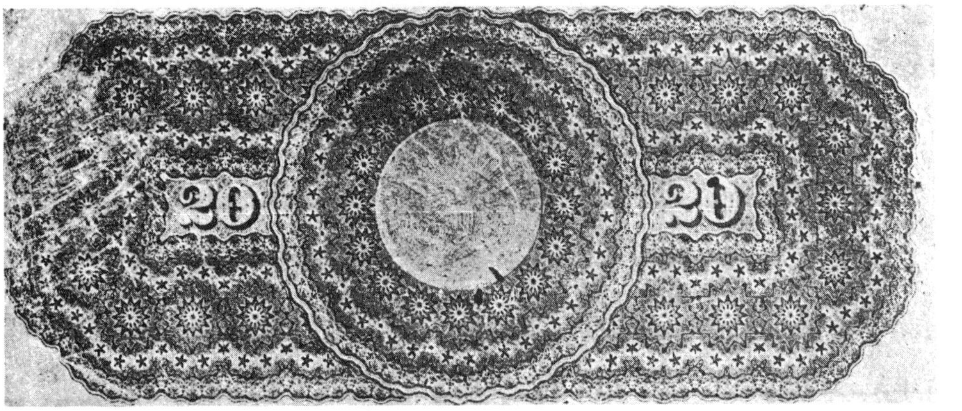

Reverse of Design No. 146-b

This illustration by courtesy of Mr. Arthur M. Kagin.

1166-b. 20 Dollar Note. Extremely Rare.

DESIGN NO. 146-c

(Note 1166-c)

Eagle on draped shield. Countersigned and dated by hand.

Reverse of Design No. 146-c.

1166-c.	100 Dollar Note.	Extremely Rare	
1166-d.	500 Dollar Note.	Unknown	**DESIGN NO. 146-d**
1166-e.	1,000 Dollar Note.	Unique	**DESIGN NO. 146-e**
1166-f.	5,000 Dollar Note.	Unique	**DESIGN NO. 146-f**
1166-g.	10,000 Dollar Note.	Unknown	**DESIGN NO. 146-g**

Gold Certificates of the Second Issue. Act of March 3, 1863.

Countersigned and dated in 1870 or 1871 by hand.

1166-h.	100 Dollar Note.	Head of Benton.	Unknown	**DESIGN NO. 146-h**
1166-i.	500 Dollar Note.	Head of Lincoln.	Unique	**DESIGN NO. 146-i**
1166-j.	1,000 Dollar Note.	Head of Hamilton.	Unknown	**DESIGN NO. 146-j**
1166-k.	5,000 Dollar Note.	Head of Madison.	Unknown	**DESIGN NO. 146-k**
1166-l.	10,000 Dollar Note.	Head of Jackson.	Unknown	**DESIGN NO. 146-l**

Gold Certificates of the Third Issue. Act of March 3, 1863.

Countersigned and dated by hand.

This illustration by courtesy of Mr. R.F. Schermerhorn.

DESIGN NO. 146-m

(Note 1166-m)

Head of Thomas Hart Benton (1782-1858), who served in the United States Senate and House of Representatives for over 30 years.

This note is printed on only one side, and the reverse is blank.

1166-m.	100 Dollar Note. Series of 1875.		Extremely Rare	
1166-n.	500 Dollar Note. Series of 1875.	Head of Lincoln	Unknown	**DESIGN NO. 146-n**
1166-o.	1,000 Dollar Note. Series of 1875.	Head of Hamilton.	Unknown	**DESIGN NO. 146-o**

Gold Certificates of the Fourth and Later Issues.

10 Dollar Notes

DESIGN NO. 147

(Notes 1167-1173)

Head of Michael Hillegas, the first Treasurer of the United States, 1775-1789. (The obverse of the 1907 issues differs slightly from the 1922 issue. The reverses are similar.)

Reverse of Design No. 147.

No.	Series	Signatures		Seal		Very Good	Very Fine	Unc
1167.	1907	Vernon	Treat	Gold		40.00	80.00	425.00
1168.	1907	Vernon	McClung	Gold		40.00	80.00	425.00
1169.	1907	Napier	McClung	Gold	Act of 1882	40.00	80.00	425.00
1169a.	1907	Napier	McClung	Gold	Act of 1907	40.00	80.00	425.00
1170.	1907	Napier	Thompson	Gold	Act of 1882	60.00	140.00	550.00
1170a.	1907	Napier	Thompson	Gold	Act of 1907	60.00	140.00	550.00
1171.	1907	Parker	Burke	Gold		40.00	80.00	425.00
1172.	1907	Teehee	Burke	Gold		40.00	80.00	425.00
1173.	1922	Speelman	White	Gold		35.00	70.00	350.00

20 Dollar Notes

DESIGN NO. 148

(Notes 1174-1178)

Head of President James A. Garfield, engraved by Charles Burt.

Reverse of Design No. 148.

Large eagle carrying a lightning bolt. This vignette, named "Ocean Telegraph," commemorated the completion of the Atlantic cable in 1858.

No.	Series	Signatures		Seal	Very Good	Very Fine	Unc
1174.	1882	Bruce	Gilfillan	Brown	1,400.00	3,000.00	Rare
1175.	1882	Bruce	Gilfillan	Brown	2,500.00	6,000.00	Rare
(The above note is countersigned by Thomas C. Acton, Ass't. Treasurer, and payable at New York.)							
1176.	1882	Bruce	Wyman	Brown	1,250.00	2,400.00	Rare
1177.	1882	Rosecrans	Huston	Large Brown	1,250.00	2,400.00	Rare
1178.	1882	Lyons	Roberts	Small Red	90.00	275.00	2,250.00

DESIGN NO. 149

(Notes 1179-1187)

Head of George Washington. (The obverses of the 1905, 1906 and 1922 issues all differ slightly in some respects. The reverses of all issues are similar.) Numbers 1179 and 1180 are the famous "Technicolor" notes, so called because of their coloring.

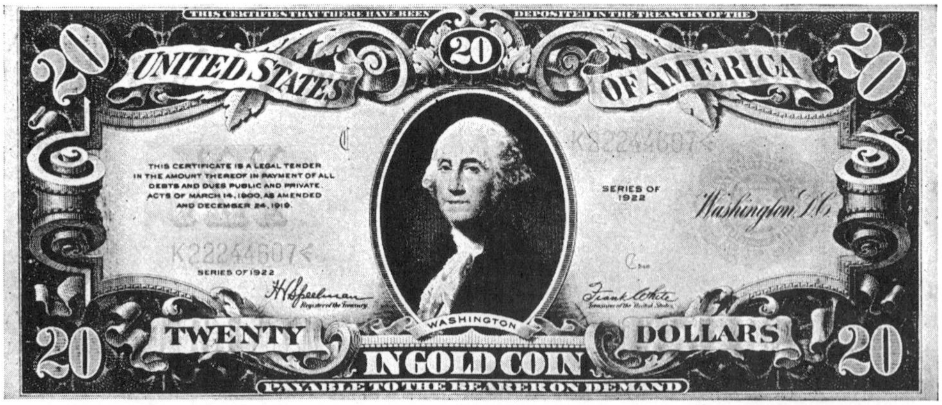

Reverse of Design No. 149.

No.	Series	Signatures		Seal	Very Good	Very Fine	Unc
1179.	1905	Lyons	Roberts	Small Red	250.00	750.00	6,000.00
1180.	1905	Lyons	Treat	Small Red	250.00	850.00	6,000.00
1181.	1906	Vernon	Treat	Gold	55.00	150.00	600.00
1182.	1906	Vernon	McClung	Gold	55.00	150.00	600.00
1183.	1906	Napier	McClung	Gold	55.00	150.00	600.00
1184.	1906	Napier	Thompson	Gold	75.00	200.00	850.00
1185.	1906	Parker	Burke	Gold	55.00	150.00	600.00
1186.	1906	Teehee	Burke	Gold	55.00	150.00	600.00
1187.	1922	Speelman	White	Gold	50.00	100.00	450.00

50 Dollar Notes

DESIGN NO. 150

(Notes 1188-1197)

Head of Silas Wright, 1795-1847, famous contemporary figure in government. He was both a U.S. Senator (1833-1844) and Governor of New York (1845-1847). Wright's portrait was engraved by Charles Burt from a painting by Alonzo Chappell.

Reverse of Design No. 150. Eagle on Draped Shield.

No.	Series	Signatures		Seal	Very Good	Very Fine	Unc
1188.	1882	Bruce	Gilfillan	Brown		**Extremely Rare**	
1189.	1882	Bruce	Gilfillan	Brown		**Rare**	

(The above note is countersigned by Thomas C. Acton, Ass't. Treasurer, and payable at New York.)

No.	Series	Signatures		Seal	Very Good	Very Fine	Unc
1190.	1882	Bruce	Wyman	Brown		**Extremely Rare**	
1191.	1882	Rosecrans	Hyatt	Large Red		**Extremely Rare**	
1192.	1882	Rosecrans	Huston	Large Brown		**Rare**	
1193.	1882	Lyons	Roberts	Small Red	200.00	450.00	2,500.00
1194.	1882	Lyons	Treat	Small Red	200.00	450.00	2,500.00
1195.	1882	Vernon	Treat	Small Red	200.00	450.00	2,500.00
1196.	1882	Vernon	McClung	Small Red	200.00	450.00	2,500.00
1197.	1882	Napier	McClung	Small Red	200.00	450.00	2,500.00

DESIGN NO. 151

(Notes 1198-1200)

Head of Ulysses S. Grant.

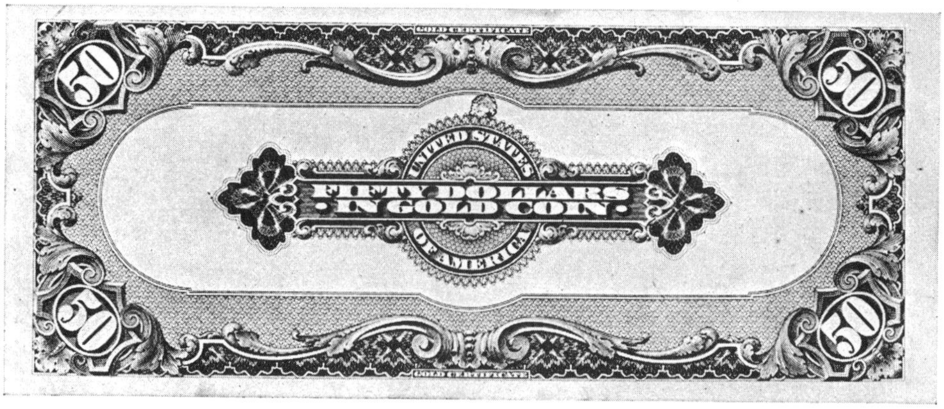

Reverse of Design No. 151.

No.	Series	Signatures		Seal	Very Good	Very Fine	Unc
1198.	1913	Parker	Burke	Gold	**150.00**	**400.00**	**2,000.00**
1199.	1913	Teehee	Burke	Gold	**150.00**	**400.00**	**2,000.00**
1200.	1922	Speelman	White	Gold	**125.00**	**275.00**	**4,250.00**

100 Dollar Notes

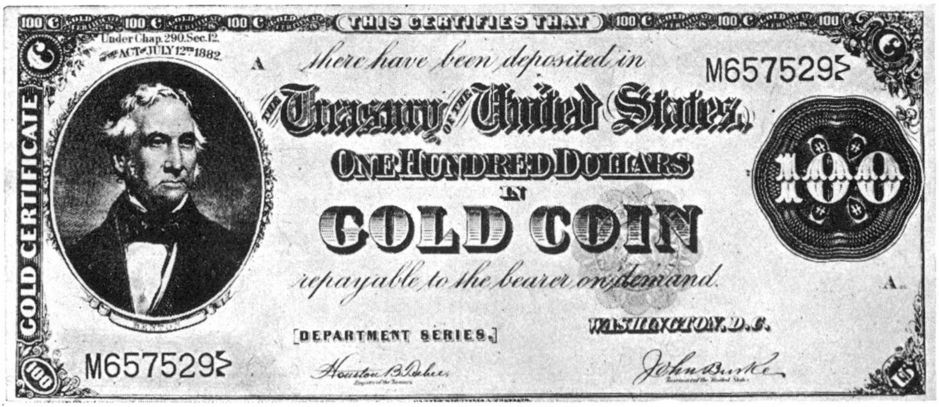

DESIGN NO. 152

(Notes 1201-1215)

Head of Thomas Hart Benton, who served in both the U.S. Senate, 1821-1851, and in the U.S. House of Representatives, 1853-1855. (The obverse of the 1882 issues differs in several minor respects from the 1922 issue. The reverses are similar.)

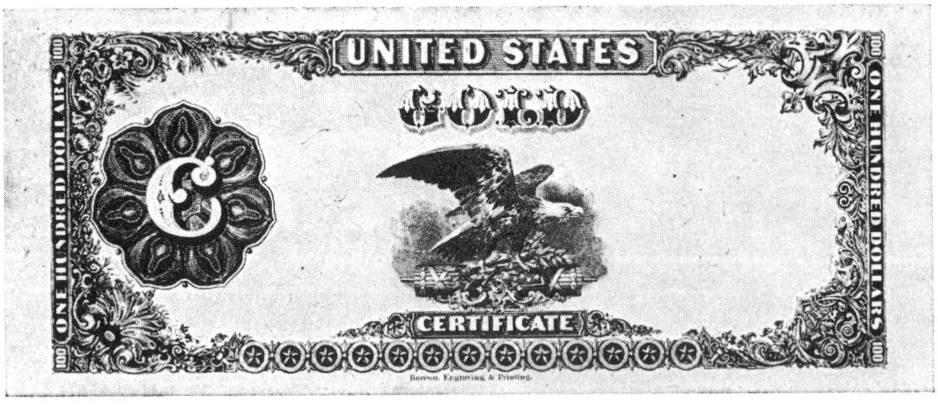

Reverse of Design No. 152. Eagle on fasces.

No.	Series	Signatures		Seal	Very Good	Very Fine	Unc
1201.	1882	Bruce	Gilfillan	Brown		**Extremely Rare**	
1202.	1882	Bruce	Gilfillan	Brown		**Extremely Rare**	

(The above note is countersigned by Thomas C. Acton, Ass't. Treasurer, and payable at New York.)

No.	Series	Signatures		Seal	Very Good	Very Fine	Unc
1203.	1882	Bruce	Wyman	Brown			**Unknown**
1204.	1882	Rosecrans	Hyatt	Large Red		**Extremely Rare**	
1205.	1882	Rosecrans	Huston	Large Brown		**Extremely Rare**	
1206.	1882	Lyons	Roberts	Small Red	**250.00**	**500.00**	**3,000.00**
1207.	1882	Lyons	Treat	Small Red	**250.00**	**500.00**	**3,000.00**
1208.	1882	Vernon	Treat	Small Red	**250.00**	**500.00**	**3,000.00**

No.	Series	Signatures		Seal	Very Good	Very Fine	Unc
1209.	1882	Vernon	McClung	Small Red	250.00	500.00	3,000.00
1210.	1882	Napier	McClung	Small Red	250.00	500.00	3,000.00
1211.	1882	Napier	Thompson	Small Red	360.00	750.00	3,750.00
1212.	1882	Napier	Burke	Small Red	250.00	500.00	3,000.00
1213.	1882	Parker	Burke	Small Red	250.00	500.00	3,000.00
1214.	1882	Teehee	Burke	Small Red	•250.00	500.00	3,000.00
1215.	1922	Speelman	White	Small Red	200.00	350.00	1,800.00

500 Dollar Notes

DESIGN NO. 153

(Notes 1216-1217)

Head of Abraham Lincoln.

Reverse of Design No. 153.

No.	Series	Signatures		Seal	Very Good	Very Fine	Unc
1215-a.		Bruce	Gilfillan	Brown			Unknown
1215-b.		Bruce	Gilfillan	Brown			Unknown

(The above note is countersigned by Thomas C. Acton, Ass't. Treasurer, and payable at New York.)

No.	Series	Signatures		Seal	Very Good	Very Fine	Unc
1215-c.		Bruce	Wyman	Brown			Unknown
1215-d.		Rosecrans	Hyatt	Large Red			Unknown
1216.	1882	Lyons	Roberts	Small Red	900.00	1,600.00	Rare
1216-a.	1882	Parker	Burke	Small Red	900.00	1,600.00	Rare
1216-b.	1882	Teehee	Burke	Small Red	900.00	1,600.00	Rare
1217.	1922	Speelman	White	Small Red	750.00	1,400.00	Rare

1,000 Dollar Notes

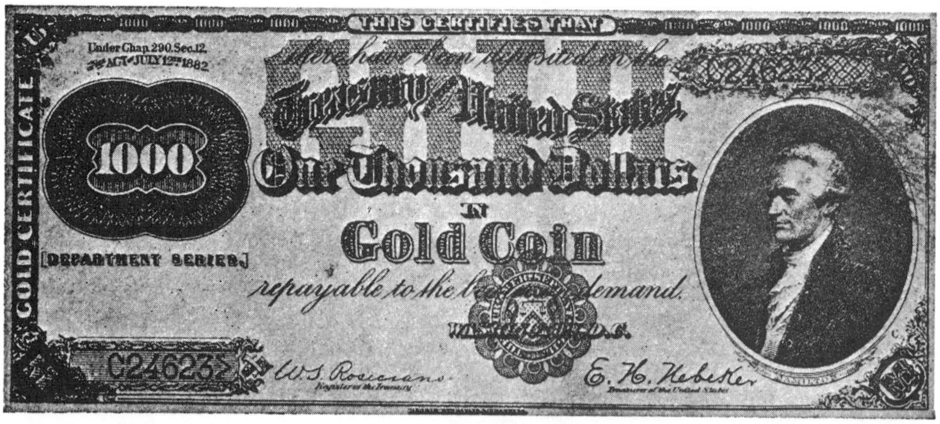

DESIGN NO. 154

(Notes 1218-1218-g)

Head of Alexander Hamilton.

Reverse of Design No. 154.

No.	Series	Signatures		Seal	
1218.	1882	Bruce	Gilfillan	Brown	**Unknown**
1218-a.	1882	Bruce	Gilfillan	Brown	**Unique**

(The above note is countersigned by Thomas C. Acton, Ass't. Treasurer, and payable at New York.)

1218-b.	1882	Bruce	Wyman	Brown	**Extremely Rare**
1218-c.	1882	Rosecrans	Hyatt	Large Red	**Unique**
1218-d.	1882	Rosecrans	Huston	Large Brown	**Unique**
1218-e.	1882	Rosecrans	Nebeker	Small Red	**Extremely Rare**
1218-f.	1882	Lyons	Roberts	Small Red	**Unique**
1218-g.	1882	Lyons	Treat	Small Red	**Rare**

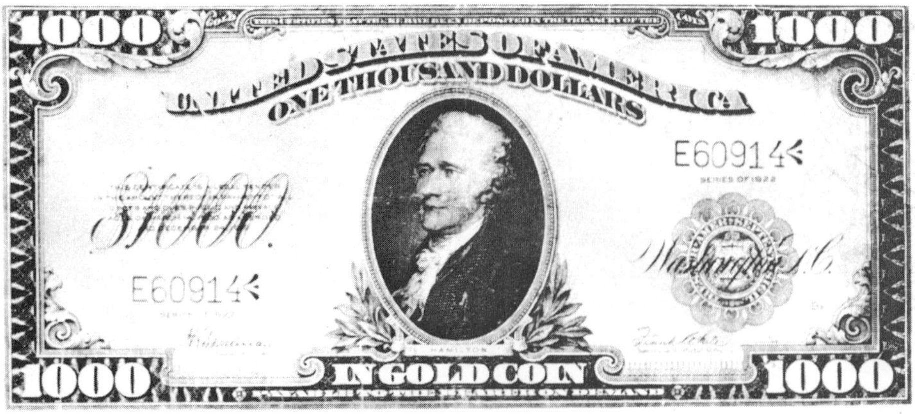

DESIGN NO. 154-a

(Notes 1219-1220)

Head of Alexander Hamilton.

Reverse of Design No. 154-a.

No.	Series	Signatures		Seal	Very Good	Fine	Unc
1219.	1907	Vernon	Treat	Gold			**Rare**
1219a.	1907	Vernon	McClung	Gold			**Unknown**
1219b.	1907	Napier	McClung	Gold			**Rare**
1219c.	1907	Napier	Burke	Gold			**Rare**
1219d.	1907	Parker	Burke	Gold			**Very Rare**
1219e.	1907	Teehee	Burke	Gold	1,500	2,000	**Rare**
1220.	1922	Speelman	White	Gold	1,500	2,000	**Rare**

5,000 Dollar Notes

DESIGN NO. 155

(Notes 1221-1222)

Head of James Madison.

Reverse of Design No. 155.

No.	Series	Signatures		Seal	
1221.	1882	Bruce	Gilfillan	Brown	**Extremely Rare**
1221-a.	1882	Bruce	Gilfillan	Brown	**Extremely Rare**

(The above note is countersigned by Thomas C. Acton, Ass't. Treasurer, and payable at New York.)

No.	Series	Signatures		Seal	
1221-b.	1882	Bruce	Wyman	Brown	Unknown
1221-c.	1882	Rosecrans	Hyatt	Large Red	Unknown
1221-d.	1882	Rosecrans	Nebeker	Small Red	Unknown
1221-e.	1882	Lyons	Roberts	Small Red	Unknown
1221-f.	1882	Vernon	Treat	Small Red	Unknown
1221-g.	1882	Vernon	McClung	Small Red	Unknown
1221-h.	1882	Napier	McClung	Small Red	Unknown
1221-i.	1882	Parker	Burke	Small Red	Unknown
1221-j.	1882	Teehee	Burke	Small Red	Extremely Rare
1222.	1888	Rosecrans	Hyatt	Large Red	All Redeemed, None Outstanding
1222-a.	1888	Rosecrans	Nebeker	Small Red	All Redeemed, None Outstanding
1222-b.	1888	Lyons	Roberts	Small Red	All Redeemed, None Outstanding

10,000 Dollar Notes

DESIGN NO. 156

(Notes 1223-1225)

Head of Andrew Jackson.

Reverse of Design No. 156.

No.	Series	Signatures		Seal	
1223.	1882	Bruce	Gilfillan	Brown	Unknown
1223-a.	1882	Bruce	Gilfillan	Brown	Unknown

(The above note is countersigned by Thomas C. Acton, Ass't. Treasurer, and payable at New York.)

1223-b.	1882	Bruce	Wyman	Brown	Unknown
1223-c.	1882	Rosecrans	Hyatt	Large Red	Unknown
1223-d.	1882	Rosecrans	Nebeker	Small Red	Unknown
1223-e.	1882	Lyons	Roberts	Small Red	Unknown
1223-f.	1882	Vernon	Treat	Small Red	Unknown
1223-g.	1882	Teehee	Burke	Small Red	Extremely Rare
1224.	1888	Rosecrans	Hyatt	Large Red	All Redeemed, None Outstanding
1224-a.	1888	Rosecrans	Nebeker	Small Red	All Redeemed, None Outstanding
1224-b.	1888	Lyons	Roberts	Small Red	All Redeemed, None Outstanding
1225.	1900				Extremely Rare

PART TWO
XIII. FRACTIONAL CURRENCY

The average person is surprised and somewhat incredulous when informed that there is such a thing as a genuine American 50 cent bill, or even a 3 cent bill. With the great profusion of change in the pockets and purses of the last few generations, it does indeed seem strange to learn of valid United States paper money of 3, 5, 10, 15, 25 and 50 Cent denominations.

Yet it was not always so. During the early years of the Civil War, the banks suspended specie payments, which act had the effect of putting a premium on all coins. Under such conditions, coins of all denominations were jealously guarded and hoarded and soon had all but disappeared from circulation.

This was an intolerable situation since it became impossible for merchants to give small change to their customers. For a time, we reverted somewhat to the ancient barter system and one had to accept his change in the form of goods or produce which he did not necessarily want at that time.

The lives of millions of people were thus intimately affected and importunate demands were made on the Treasury Department to remedy this chaotic state of affairs.

Accordingly, on the recommendation of General Spinner who at that time was the Treasurer, Congress passed the Act of July 17, 1862 which authorized an issue of 5, 10, 25 and 50 Cent notes. These became known as Postage Currency, because they bore facsimiles of the then current 5 and 10 cent postage stamps. This was the first of five issues produced by the government from 1862 to 1876. The later issues were called Fractional Currency, and were authorized by another act of Congress, that of March 3, 1863. In general, all issues of Postage and Fractional Currency were receivable for all United States Postage Stamps.

In the fourteen years that Fractional Currency was produced, nearly 369 million dollars of it was issued. Finally, Congress passed the Acts of January 14, 1875 and April 17, 1876 which authorized the redemption of Fractional Currency in actual silver coins. It is now estimated by the government that not quite 2 million dollars in all types of Fractional Currency is still outstanding.

First Issue. August 21, 1862 to May 27, 1863

This is the so-called Postage Currency. The issue consisted of 5, 10, 25 and 50 Cent notes which were produced at first with perforations and later with straight edges. The obverse of this issue was printed by the National Bank Note Co., the reverse by the American Bank Note Co., both of New York. The monogram of this latter company appears on the reverse of these notes, but was removed when the company no longer printed the reverses.

The four notes of this issue are widely collected by stamp collectors in addition to being collected by numismatists.

The obligation on these is as follows, "Exchangeable for United States Notes by any Assistant Treasurer or designated U.S. Depositary in sums not less than five dollars. Receivable in payment of all dues to the U. States less than five Dollars."

Second Issue. October 10, 1863 to February 23, 1867

This issue consisted of 5, 10, 25 and 50 Cent Notes. The obverses of all denominations have the bust of Washington in a bronze oval frame but each reverse is distinguished by a different color.

The obligation on this issue differs slightly, and is as follows, "Exchangeable for United States Notes by the Assistant Treasurers and designated depositaries of the U.S. in sums not less than three dollars. Receivable in payment of all dues to the United States less than five dollars except customs."

Third Issue. December 5, 1864 to August 16, 1869

This issue consisted of 3, 5, 10, 25 and 50 Cent Notes. Each denomination is of a different design, as will be seen in the text.

The obligation on the Third Issue Notes is similar to that on the Second Issue.

Fourth Issue. July 14, 1869 to February 16, 1875

The notes of this issue consist of the 10, 15, 25 and 50 Cent denominations, each of a different design. With this issue, the Treasury Seal appears for the first time on Fractional Currency.

The 15 Cent notes appeared only in this issue and they are much scarcer than the other denominations.

The obligation on the fourth issue is similar to that on the Second Issue.

Fifth Issue. February 26, 1874 to February 15, 1876

The notes of this issue consist only of 10, 25 and 50 Cent denominations, each of a different design.

The obligation is similar to that of the Second Issue.

3 Cent Notes

The 3 Cent Notes are of the Third Issue of Fractional Currency.

DESIGN NO. 163

(Notes 1226-1227)

Head of George Washington.

No.	Variety	Very Good	Very Fine	Unc
1226.	With light background to portrait.	10.00	22.50	70.00
1227.	With dark background to portrait.	12.00	25.00	100.00

5 Cent Notes

First Issue

DESIGN NO. 164

(Notes 1228-1231)

Copy of a contemporary 5 cent postage stamp with head of Thomas Jefferson. Brown obverse, black reverse.

No.	Variety	Very Good	Very Fine	Unc
1228.	Perforated edges; with monogram of American Bank Note Co. (ABCO) on reverse.	12.50	30.00	135.00
1229.	Perforated edges; without monogram.	15.00	32.50	185.00
1230.	Straight edges; with monogram.	7.50	15.00	70.00
1231.	Straight edges; without monogram.	15.00	40.00	175.00

Second Issue

DESIGN NO. 165

(Notes 1232-1235)

Head of George Washington in bronze oval frame. Brown reverse.

No.	Variety	Very Good	Very Fine	Unc
1232.	Without small surcharged figures on corners of reverse.	9.00	20.00	60.00
1233.	With surcharge "18-63" on corners of reverse.	9.00	20.00	65.00
1234.	With surcharge "18-63" and "S".	12.50	27.50	110.00
1235.	With surcharge "18-63" and "R-1". Fiber paper.	15.00	40.00	275.00

Third Issue

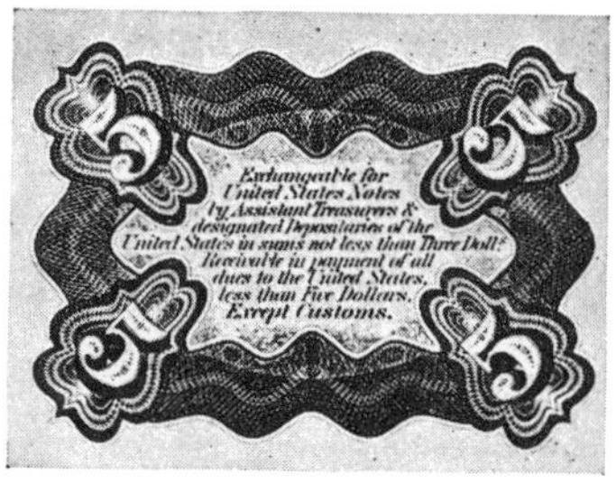

DESIGN NO. 166

(Notes 1236-1239)

Head of Spencer M. Clark, First Superintendent of the National Currency Bureau (now the Bureau of Engraving and Printing) under Abraham Lincoln.

No.	Variety	Very Good	Very Fine	Unc
1236.	Red reverse.	12.50	30.00	100.00
1237.	Red reverse; with design letter "a" on obverse.	15.00	35.00	150.00
1238.	Green reverse.	7.00	12.00	70.00
1239.	Green reverse; with design letter "a" on obverse.	10.00	17.50	85.00

10 Cent Notes

First Issue

DESIGN NO. 167

(Notes 1240-1243)

Copy of a contemporary 10 cent stamp with head of George Washington. Green obverse, black reverse.

No.	Variety	Very Good	Very Fine	Unc
1240.	Perforated edges; with monogram of American Bank Note Co. (ABCO) on reverse.	12.50	35.00	140.00
1241.	Perforated edges; without monogram.	12.50	35.00	185.00
1242.	Straight edges; with monogram.	8.00	22.50	70.00
1243.	Straight edges; without monogram.	17.50	50.00	225.00

Second Issue

DESIGN NO. 168

(Notes 1244-1249)

Head of George Washington in bronze oval frame. Green reverse.

No.	Variety	Very Good	Very Fine	Unc
1244.	Without small surcharged figures on corners of reverse.	9.00	18.00	60.00
1245.	With surcharge "18-63".	9.00	20.00	65.00
1246.	With surcharge "18-63" and "S".	10.00	25.00	80.00
1247.	With surcharge "18-63" and "1".	10.00	25.00	225.00
1248.	With surcharge "0-63".	375.00	900.00	2,250.00
1249.	With surcharge "18-63" and "T-1"; fiber paper.	15.00	50.00	200.00

Third Issue

DESIGN NO. 169

(Notes 1251-1256)

Head of George Washington.

No.	Variety	Very Good	Very Fine	Unc
1251.	Red reverse.	12.50	25.00	125.00
1252.	Red reverse with design numeral "1" on obverse.	15.00	30.00	150.00
1253.	Red reverse with autographed signatures of Colby and Spinner.	17.50	45.00	175.00
1254.	Red reverse with autographed signatures of Jeffries and Spinner.	22.50	65.00	250.00
1255.	Green reverse.	7.50	17.50	60.00
1255a.	Green reverse with autographed signatures of Colby and Spinner.		Extremely Rare	
1256.	Green reverse with design numeral "1" on obverse.	8.00	22.50	75.00

Fourth Issue

DESIGN NO. 170

(Notes 1257-1261)

Bust of Liberty.

No.	Variety	Very Good	Very Fine	Unc
1257.	Large red seal; watermarked paper with pink silk fibers.	7.50	15.00	65.00
1258.	Large red seal; unwatermarked paper with pink silk fibers.	7.50	17.50	75.00
1259.	Large red seal; paper with violet silk fibers and blue right end on obverse.	7.50	17.50	80.00
1260.	The note previously listed does not exist.			
1261.	Smaller red seal; paper with violet silk fibers and blue right end on obverse.	7.50	20.00	70.00

Fifth Issue

DESIGN NO. 171

(Notes 1264-1266-a)

Head of William M. Meredith, Secretary of the Treasury, 1849-1850.

No.	Variety	Very Good	Very Fine	Unc
1264.	Green seal.	9.00	17.50	75.00
1265.	Red seal with long, thin key.	6.00	10.00	40.00
1266.	Red seal with short, thick key.	6.00	10.00	40.00
1266-a.	The note previously listed does not exist.			

15 Cent Notes

Fourth Issue

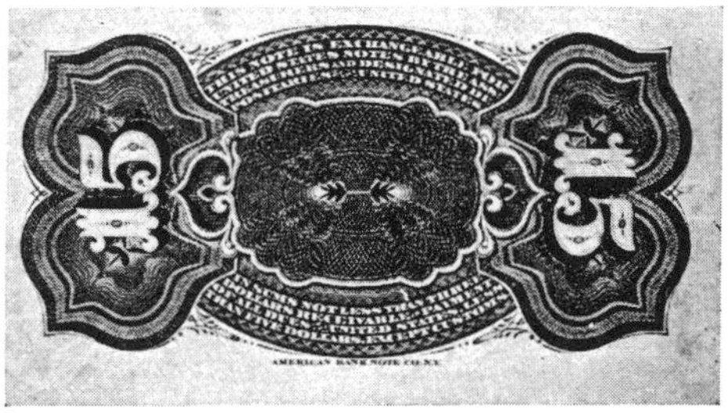

DESIGN NO. 172

(Notes 1267-1271)

Bust of Columbia.

No.	Variety	Very Good	Very Fine	Unc
1267.	Large red seal; watermarked paper with pink silk fibers.	15.00	35.00	135.00
1268.	Large red seal; unwatermarked paper with pink silk fibers.	15.00	37.50	150.00
1269.	Large red seal; paper with violet fibers and blue right end on obverse.	17.50	40.00	195.00
1270.	The note previously listed does not exist.			
1271.	Smaller red seal; paper with violet fibers and blue right end on obverse.	15.00	37.50	175.00

25 Cent Notes

First Issue

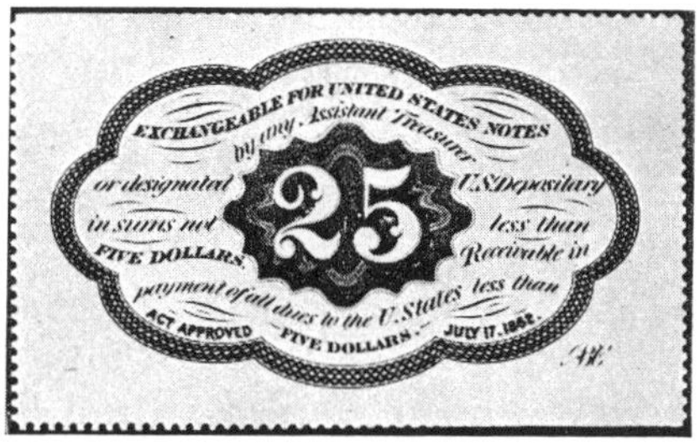

DESIGN NO. 174

(Notes 1279-1282)

Five 5 cent stamps of the type of Design No. 164. Brown obverse, black reverse.

No.	Variety	Very Good	Very Fine	Unc
1279.	Perforated edges; with monogram of American Bank Note Co. (ABCO) on reverse.	20.00	40.00	225.00
1280.	Perforated edges; without monogram.	20.00	45.00	300.00
1281.	Straight edges; with monogram.	10.00	22.50	125.00
1282.	Straight edges; without monogram.	22.50	65.00	360.00

Second Issue

DESIGN NO. 175

(Notes 1283-1290-a)

Head of George Washington in bronze oval frame Purple reverse.

No.	Variety	Very Good	Very Fine	Unc
1283.	Without small surcharged figures on corners of reverse.	9.00	22.50	100.00
1284.	With surcharge "18-63".	12.50	30.00	125.00
1285.	With surcharge "18-63" and "A".	12.50	30.00	135.00
1286.	With surcharge "18-63" and "S".	12.50	30.00	125.00
1288.	With surcharge "18-63" and "2".	15.00	35.00	135.00
1289.	With surcharge "18-63" and "T-1"; fiber paper.	20.00	40.00	250.00
1290.	With surcharge "18-63" and "T-2"; fiber paper.	20.00	45.00	250.00

Third Issue

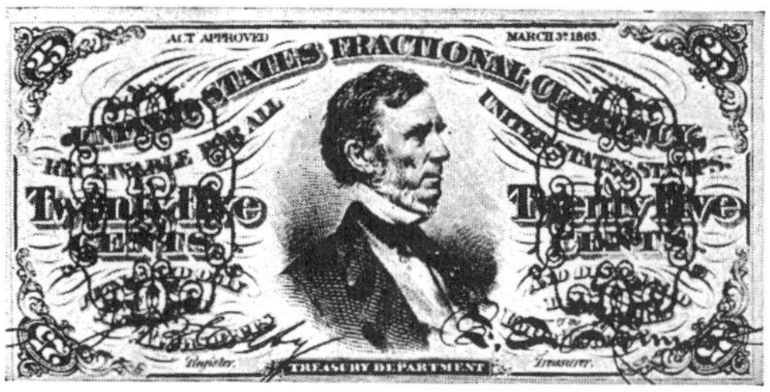

DESIGN NO. 176

(Notes 1291-1300)

Bust of William P. Fessenden, Secretary of the Treasury in 1864 under President Lincoln.

No.	Variety	Very Good	Very Fine	Unc
1291.	Red reverse.	12.50	32.50	125.00
1292.	Red reverse with small design letter "a" on obverse.	15.00	37.50	150.00
1293.	Red reverse with large design letter "a" on obverse.	15.00	37.50	170.00
1294.	Green reverse.	9.00	20.00	60.00
1295.	Green reverse with small design letter "a" on obverse.	10.00	22.50	80.00
1296.	Green reverse with large design letter "a" on obverse.	750.00	1,500.00	3,500.00
1297.	Green reverse with surcharge "M-2-6-5"; fiber paper.	17.50	50.00	175.00
1298.	Same as above but with design letter "a" on obverse.	25.00	75.00	250.00
1299.	Green reverse with surcharge "M-2-6-5"; the two ornamental designs on obverse surcharged in heavy solid bronze, and not merely outlined as on previous issues; fiber paper.	175.00	350.00	1,000.00
1300.	Same as above but with design letter "a" on obverse.	325.00	800.00	2,750.00

Fourth Issue

DESIGN NO. 177

(Notes 1301-1307)

Bust of George Washington.

No.	Variety	Very Good	Very Fine	Unc
1301.	Large red seal; watermarked paper with pink silk fibers.	8.50	17.50	75.00
1302.	Large red seal; unwatermarked paper with pink silk fibers.	8.50	17.50	80.00
1303.	Large red seal; paper with violet fibers and blue right end on obverse.	8.50	17.50	100.00
1307.	Smaller red seal; paper with violet fibers and blue right end on obverse.	8.00	17.50	80.00

Fifth Issue

DESIGN NO. 178

(Notes 1308-1309-a)

Bust of Robert J. Walker, Secretary of the Treasury 1845-1849.

No.	Variety	Very Good	Very Fine	Unc
1308.	With long, thin key in Treasury Seal (5 millimeters).	6.00	12.50	35.00
1309.	With short, thick key in Treasury Seal (4 millimeters).	6.00	12.50	35.00

50 Cent Notes

First Issue

DESIGN NO. 179

(Notes 1310-1313)

Five 10 cent stamps of the type of Design No. 167. Green obverse, black reverse.

No.	Variety	Very Good	Very Fine	Unc
1310.	Perforated edges; with monogram of American Bank Note Co. (ABCO) on reverse.	20.00	45.00	250.00
1310a.	As above, except 14 perforations per 20mm instead of 12 perforations.		Rare	
1311.	Perforated edges; without monogram.	30.00	60.00	400.00
1312.	Plain edges; with monogram.	15.00	25.00	130.00
1313.	Plain edges; without monogram.	35.00	95.00	425.00

Second Issue

DESIGN NO. 180

(Notes 1314-1323)

Head of George Washington in bronze oval frame. Red reverse.

No.	Variety	Very Good	Very Fine	Unc
1314.	Without small surcharged figures on corners of reverse.		Unknown	
1316.	With surcharge "18-63".	15.00	42.50	225.00
1317.	With surcharge "18-63" and "A".	12.50	27.50	175.00
1318.	With surcharge "18-63" and "1".	12.50	27.50	175.00
1320.	With surcharge "18-63" and "O-1"; fiber paper.	20.00	50.00	300.00
1321.	With surcharge "18-63" and "R-2"; fiber paper.	22.50	70.00	350.00
1322.	With surcharge "18-63" and "T-1"; fiber paper.	25.00	40.00	200.00

Third Issue

DESIGN NO. 181 (Notes 1324-1338). *Head of General F.E. Spinner, Treasurer of the United States, 1861-1875.*

181a. Red Reverse With Surcharge "A-2-6-5".

No.	Variety	Very Good	Very Fine	Unc
1324.	Without design figures on obverse.	19.00	45.00	250.00
1325.	Design figures "1" and "a" on obverse.	32.50	125.00	450.00
1326.	Design figure "1" only on obverse.	22.50	55.00	275.00
1327.	Design figure "a" only on obverse.	22.50	55.00	300.00
1328.	With autographed signatures of Colby and Spinner.	22.50	65.00	250.00
1329.	With autographed signatures of Allison and Spinner.	27.50	90.00	375.00
1330.	With autographed signatures of Allison and New.	800.00	1,500.00	3,500.00

181b. Green Reverse Without Surcharge.

No.	Variety	Very Good	Very Fine	Unc
1331.	Without design figures on obverse.	12.50	25.00	125.00
1332.	Design figures "1" and "a" on obverse.	20.00	60.00	300.00
1333.	Design figure "1" only on obverse.	12.50	30.00	175.00
1334.	Design figure "a" only on obverse.	15.00	35.00	185.00

181c. Green Reverse With Surcharge "A-2-6-5".

No.	Variety	Very Good	Very Fine	Unc
1335.	Without design figures on obverse.	17.50	50.00	250.00
1336.	Design figures "1" and "a" on obverse.	60.00	250.00	1,200.00
1337.	Design figure "1" only on obverse.	17.50	80.00	400.00
1338.	Design figure "a" only on obverse.	20.00	100.00	450.00

DESIGN NO. 182

(Notes 1339-1342)

The obverse is similar to Design No. 181. The reverse is as shown.

No.	Variety	Very Good	Very Fine	Unc
1339.	Green reverse; without surcharges and design figures.	15.00	35.00	175.00
1340.	Green reverse; design figures "1" and "a" on obverse.	25.00	70.00	450.00
1341.	Green reverse; design figure "1" only on obverse.	17.50	40.00	210.00
1342.	Green reverse; design figure "a" only on obverse.	17.50	45.00	250.00

DESIGN NO. 183 (Notes 1343-1373-a) *Seated figure of Justice holding Scales.*

183a. Red Reverse Without Surcharge.

No.	Variety	Very Good	Very Fine	Unc
1343.	Without design figures on obverse.	25.00	55.00	325.00
1344.	With design figures "1" and "a" on obverse.	80.00	275.00	1,250.00
1345.	With design figure "1" only on obverse.	25.00	70.00	420.00
1346.	With design figure "a" only on obverse.	30.00	75.00	440.00

183b. Red Reverse With Surcharge "A-2-6-5".

No.	Variety	Very Good	Very Fine	Unc
1347.	Without design figures on obverse.	25.00	70.00	300.00
1348.	With design figures "1" and "a" on obverse.	80.00	275.00	1,250.00
1349.	With design figure "1" only on obverse.	25.00	75.00	425.00
1350.	With design figure "a" only on obverse.	30.00	80.00	450.00

183c. Red Reverse With Surcharge "S-2-6-4"; Printed Signatures.

No.	Variety	Very Good	Very Fine	Unc
1351.	Without design figures on obverse; fiber paper.	1,250.00	2,500.00	7,000.00
1352.	With design figures "1" and "a" on obverse; fiber paper.		Rare	
1353.	With design figure "1" only on obverse; fiber paper.	2,200.00	3,500.00	8,500.00
1354.	With design figure "a" only on obverse; fiber paper.	2,400.00	3,500.00	8,000.00

183d. Red Reverse; Autographed Signatures of Colby and Spinner.

No.	Variety	Very Good	Very Fine	Unc
1355.	Without surcharges and design figures.	27.50	60.00	250.00
1356.	With surcharge "A-2-6-5" on reverse.	30.00	75.00	350.00
1357.	With surcharge "S-2-6-4"; fiber paper.	55.00	175.00	700.00

183e. Green Reverse Without Surcharge.

No.	Variety	Very Good	Very Fine	Unc
1358.	Without design figures on obverse.	20.00	45.00	225.00
1359.	With design figures "1" and "a" on obverse.	70.00	250.00	900.00
1360.	With design figure "1" only on obverse.	20.00	45.00	275.00
1361.	With design figure "a" only on obverse.	22.50	50.00	300.00

183f. Green Reverse With Surcharge "A-2-6-5" Compactly Spaced.

No.	Variety	Very Good	Very Fine	Unc
1362.	Without design figures on obverse.	22.50	45.00	225.00
1363.	With design figures "1" and "a" on obverse.	55.00	200.00	700.00
1364.	With design figure "1" only on obverse.	22.50	45.00	275.00
1365.	With design figure "a" only on obverse.	27.50	60.00	300.00

183g. Green Reverse With Surcharge "A-2-6-5" Widely Spaced.

No.	Variety	Very Good	Very Fine	Unc
1366.	Without design figures on obverse.	30.00	70.00	325.00
1367.	With design figures "1" and "a" on obverse.	115.00	400.00	1,600.00
1368.	With design figure "1" only on obverse.	32.50	80.00	450.00
1369.	With design figure "a" only on obverse.	32.50	80.00	500.00

183h. Green Reverse With Surcharge "A-2-6-5"; Fiber Paper.

No.	Variety	Very Good	Very Fine	Unc
1370.	Without design figures on obverse.	40.00	100.00	425.00
1371.	With design figures "1" and "a" on obverse.	175.00	800.00	1,850.00
1372.	With design figure "1" only on obverse.	45.00	110.00	525.00
1373.	With design figure "a" only on obverse.	50.00	140.00	600.00
1373-a.	Green reverse with surcharge "S-2-6-4"; fiber paper; printed signatures; without design figure or letter.	1,000.00	4,500.00	Rare

Fourth Issue

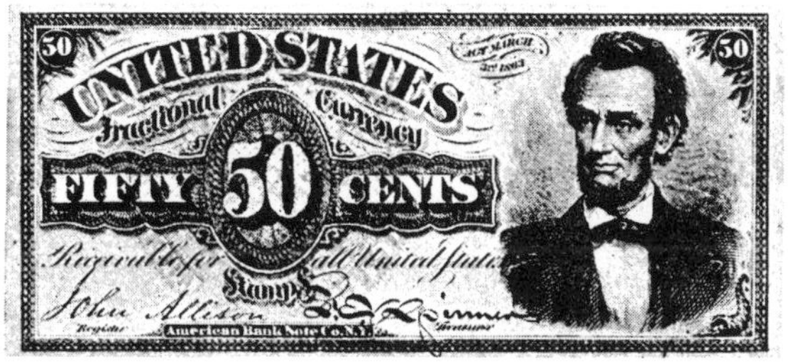

DESIGN NO. 184 (Notes 1374-1375) *Head of Abraham Lincoln.*

No.	Variety	Very Good	Very Fine	Unc
1374.	Large seal; watermarked paper with pink silk fibers.	25.00	60.00	250.00
1375.	Large seal; unwatermarked paper with pink silk fibers.	25.00	60.00	250.00

DESIGN NO. 185 (Notes 1376-1377) *Bust of Edwin M. Stanton, Secretary of War under President Lincoln.*

No.	Variety	Very Good	Very Fine	Unc
1376.	Small red seal; paper with violet fibers and blue right end on obverse.	20.00	40.00	175.00

DESIGN NO. 186

(Note 1379)

Bust of Samuel Dexter, Secretary of both the War and Treasury Departments, 1800-1801.

No.	Variety	Very Good	Very Fine	Unc
1379.	Green seal; paper with light violet fibers and blue right end on obverse.	17.50	30.00	125.00

Fifth Issue

DESIGN NO. 187 (Notes 1380-1381) *Bust of William H. Crawford, Secretary of both the War and Treasury Departments, 1815-1825.*

No.	Variety	Very Good	Very Fine	Unc
1380.	Red seal; paper on obverse a light pink color with silk fibers.	12.50	22.50	60.00
1381.	Red seal; white paper with silk fibers and blue right end on obverse.	12.50	22.50	60.00

FRACTIONAL CURRENCY SHIELDS

Fractional Currency Shields were made by the Treasury Department in Washington in 1866 and 1867. The outside dimensions of the shield are 20x25" and on the shield are mounted 39 specimens of fractional currency. Each note was printed on one side only, so that obverse and reverse appear as separate notes. As made, the shields are covered with glass and framed. The Treasury Department produced these shields for sale to banks so that they might detect counterfeit notes by comparison with the genuine notes on the shield. Complete and intact shields are now much in demand and are available only occasionally.

This illustration by courtesy of Mr. Theodore Kemm.

1382.	FRACTIONAL CURRENCY SHIELD. With gray background.	2,600.00
1383.	FRACTIONAL CURRENCY SHIELD. With pink background.	Very Rare
1383-a.	FRACTIONAL CURRENCY SHIELD. With green background.	Very Rare

INVERTED REVERSES. Some notes of the first three issues are known with inverted reverses, or inverted surcharges. Notes of the Second and Third Issues are known with surcharges partially or entirely missing. All such notes are very rare.

XIV. PROOFS AND SPECIMENS

These issues were not placed in circulation and all specimens are Proofs or Essays. The obverses and reverses of these notes were printed separately, with the back of each piece either being blank or having the word "SPECIMEN" printed in bronze, so that a complete note actually consists of two pieces. There are two varieties of each note and these are distinguished by a wide or narrow margin on all four sides.

Sometimes two or three reverses will share a common obverse, or vice versa. In these cases, one may collect one obverse note with its various reverses to form a type collection, or assemble a complete set of matching obverses and reverses. In the latter case, some obverses or reverses will be duplicated. While most collectors prefer to assemble complete sets of Specimen notes, as a guide to type collectors we have indicated in the listing below those cases where notes share a common obverse or reverse.

The illustrations of the notes listed below appear in the preceding pages of the book. For ease in referring to the illustrations, the Specimens below bear the same numbers as the regular issue notes, with the addition of the suffix letters "SP" to signify that the note is a Specimen.

Proofs and Specimens of Fourth and Fifth Issue notes are very rare.

The prices quoted are for Specimens in new condition.

Proofs of the Following Notes Are Known:

3 Cent Notes

No.	Description	Narrow Margin	Wide Margin
1226-SP.	Obverse with light background to portrait.	90.00	Rare
1227-SP.	Obverse with dark background to portrait.	60.00	175.00
	Reverse of above 2 notes.	52.50	150.00

5 Cent Notes

No.	Description	Narrow Margin	Wide Margin
1231-SP.	Obverse with straight edges.	60.00	150.00
	Reverse of above note without monogram.	60.00	140.00
1232-SP.	Obverse.	55.00	150.00
	Reverse of above note without surcharge.	55.00	150.00
1236-SP.	Red Reverse.	55.00	150.00
1238-SP.	Green Reverse.	55.00	150.00
	Obverse of above 2 notes.	55.00	175.00

10 Cent Notes

No.	Description	Narrow Margin	Wide Margin
1243-SP.	Obverse with straight edges.	55.00	200.00
	Reverse of above note without monogram.	55.00	200.00
1244-SP.	Obverse.	50.00	175.00
	Reverse of above note without surcharge.	50.00	175.00
1251-SP.	Obverse with printed signatures of Colby and Spinner.	60.00	180.00
1253-SP.	Obverse with autographed signatures of Colby and Spinner.	70.00	225.00
1254-SP.	Obverse with autographed signatures of Jeffries and Spinner.	160.00	2,000.00
	Red Reverse of above 3 notes.	55.00	180.00
1255-SP.	Green Reverse.	55.00	180.00
	Obverse of above note (same obverse as 1251-SP).	55.00	180.00

15 Cent Notes

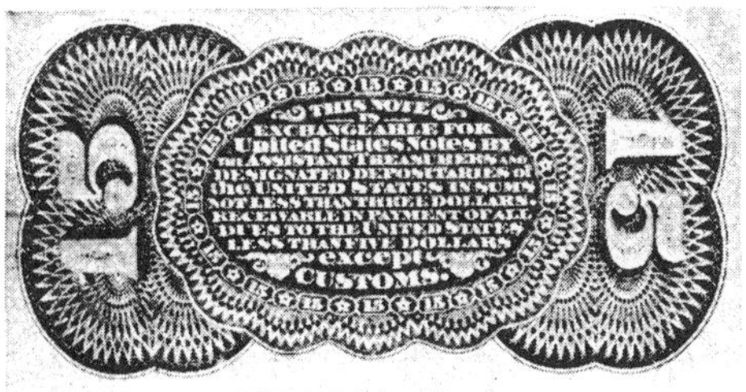

DESIGN NO. 173

(Notes 1272-SP — 1276-SP)

Heads of Union generals William T. Sherman and Ulysses S. Grant.

These notes exist only as specimens.

No.	Description	Narrow Margin	Wide Margin
1272-SP.	Obverse with printed signatures of Colby and Spinner.	165.00	350.00
	Green Reverse of above note.	110.00	250.00
1273-SP.	Obverse with autographed signatures of Colby and Spinner.	850.00	Rare
1274-SP.	Obverse with autographed signatures of Jeffries and Spinner.	200.00	475.00
1275-SP.	Obverse with autographed signatures of Allison and Spinner.	225.00	500.00
1276-SP.	Obverse without any signatures.	Rare	Rare
	Red Reverse of above 4 notes.	110.00	225.00

25 Cent Notes

No.	Description	Narrow Margin	Wide Margin
1282-SP.	Obverse with straight edges.	70.00	200.00
	Reverse of above note without monogram.	70.00	150.00
1283-SP.	Obverse.	55.00	185.00
	Reverse of above note without surcharge.	55.00	145.00
1291-SP.	Red Reverse without surcharge.	55.00	160.00
1294-SP.	Green Reverse without surcharge.	55.00	140.00
	Obverse of above 2 notes.	60.00	185.00

50 Cent Notes

No.	Description	Narrow Margin	Wide Margin
1313-SP.	Obverse with plain edges.	80.00	200.00
	Reverse of above note without monogram.	80.00	185.00
1314-SP.	Obverse.	60.00	240.00
	Reverse of above note without surcharge.	60.00	200.00
1324-SP.	Obverse with printed signatures of Colby and Spinner.	75.00	250.00
1328-SP.	Obverse with autographed signatures of Colby and Spinner.	80.00	275.00
1329-SP.	Obverse with autographed signatures of Allison and Spinner.	Rare	Rare
1330-a-SP.	Obverse. Same as Obverse of Design No. 181 but with autographed signatures of Jeffries and Spinner. THIS NOTE EXISTS ONLY AS A SPECIMEN.	100.00	3,750.00
	Red Reverse of above 4 notes without surcharge.	60.00	225.00
1331-SP.	Green Reverse without surcharge.	65.00	200.00
	Obverse of above note (same obverse as 1324-SP).	75.00	225.00
1339-SP.	Green Reverse without surcharge.	1,500.00	7,500.00
	Obverse of above note (same obverse as 1324-SP).	75.00	225.00
1343-SP.	Obverse with printed signatures of Colby and Spinner.	75.00	250.00
1355-SP.	Obverse with autographed signatures of Colby and Spinner.	80.00	275.00
1357-a-SP.	Obverse, Same as Obverse of Design No. 183 but with autographed signatures of Jeffries and Spinner. THIS NOTE EXISTS ONLY AS A SPECIMEN.	160.00	3,750.00
	Red Reverse of above 3 notes without surcharge.	60.00	200.00
1358-SP.	Green Reverse without surcharge.	60.00	200.00
	Obverse of above note (same obverse as 1343-SP).	75.00	250.00

PART THREE. SMALL SIZE NOTES

After sixty-eight years of existence, our large size currency felt the impact of modern times and was discontinued to be replaced with the smaller size notes we are now using. To the present generation, doubtless, our present currency must seem the only kind we have ever had, since outside of numismatic circles, large notes are rarely seen or heard of today. In this instance, they are just as unfamiliar to the growing generation as are gold coins.

In the interim sixty-eight years, our country had reached the peak of its expansion. The rapid growth of industry, agriculture and population had brought with it an ever increasing demand for the currency to accommodate this expansion.

By the 1920's, the Treasury Department was purchasing many tons of the high grade, especially prepared paper that was needed to print our currency. Since the number of notes produced annually had now reached astronomical figures compared to the past, it was soon realized that many millions of dollars could be saved if our currency were reduced in size.

This was ultimately decided upon, and on July 10, 1929, the first of our current, reduced size notes were placed in circulation.

In the section following, "star" notes are indicated by an asterisk (*) appearing after the catalog number.

(Our special thanks to Mr. Chuck O'Donnell for making available the results of his extensive research into the records at the Bureau of Engraving and Printing, enabling us to present accurate totals for the number of small size notes printed.)

XV. LEGAL TENDER NOTES

Only 1, 2, 5 and 100 Dollar notes have been issued. Of these, the 1, 2 and 5 Dollar notes are now obsolete and only the 100 Dollar notes are still current. The Act of May 3, 1878 decreed that the amount of United States Notes outstanding must be maintained at $346,681,016, and the requirement is being satisfied through circulation of the 100 Dollar note.

Until the series of 1963, the obligation is as follows, "The United States of America will pay to the bearer on demand ...... Dollars ... This note is a legal tender at its face value for all debts public and private."

With the 1963 series, the "will pay to the bearer on demand" clause was dropped from the obligation and the legal tender clause was changed to read, "This note is legal tender for all debts, public and private."

(Additional information on this series will be found in the introduction to large size Legal Tender Notes on page 14.)

All the following have a Red Seal.

1 Dollar Notes

All issues are with the head of George Washington.

DESIGN NO. 188.
(Note 1500)

Reverse of Design No. 188.

No.	Series	Signatures		No. Printed	Very Fine	Unc
1500.	1928	Woods	Woodin	1,872,012	25.00	70.00

No.	Series	Signatures		No. Printed	Very Fine	Unc
1500*.	1928	Woods	Woodin		1,200.00	2,500.00

2 Dollar Notes

All issues are with the head of Thomas Jefferson.

DESIGN NO. 189.
(Notes 1501-1508 Incl.)

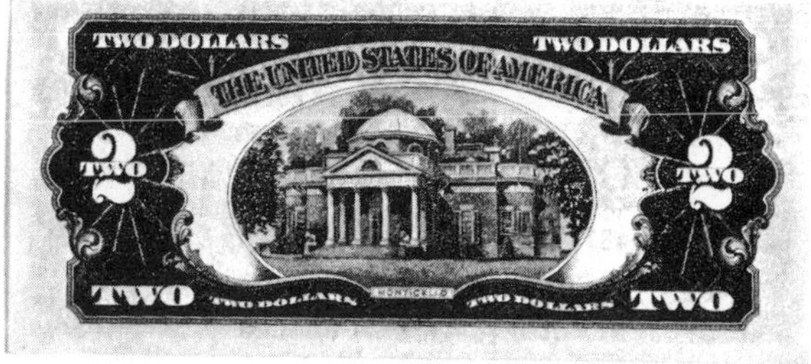

Reverse of Design No. 189.
View of Monticello.

No.	Series	Signatures		No. Printed	Very Fine	Unc.
1501.	1928	Tate	Mellon	55,889,424	6.00	25.00
1501*.	1928	Tate	Mellon		40.00	150.00
1502.	1928-A	Woods	Mellon	46,859,136	25.00	135.00
1502*.	1928-A	Woods	Mellon		650.00	1,500.00
1503.	1928-B	Woods	Mills	9,001,632	85.00	400.00
1503*.	1928-B	Woods	Mills		2,500.00	Rare
1504.	1928-C	Julian	Morgenthau	86,584,008	6.00	45.00
1504*.	1928-C	Julian	Morgenthau		225.00	675.00

No.	Series	Signatures		No. Printed	Very Fine	Unc
1505.	1928-D	Julian	Morgenthau	146,381,364	3.50	12.50
1505*.	1928-D	Julian	Morgenthau		15.00	125.00
1506.	1928-E	Julian	Vinson	5,261,016	12.50	35.00
1506*.	1928-E	Julian	Vinson		2,000.00	Rare
1507.	1928-F	Julian	Snyder	43,349,292	5.00	15.00
1507*.	1928-F	Julian	Snyder		17.50	150.00
1508.	1928-G	Clark	Snyder	52,208,000	3.00	10.00
1508*.	1928-G	Clark	Snyder		20.00	100.00

DESIGN NO. 190 (Notes 1509-1512 Incl.)

Reverse of Design No. 190.

No.	Series	Signatures		No. Printed	Very Fine	Unc
1509.	1953	Priest	Humphrey	45,360,000	-	8.00
1509*.	1953	Priest	Humphrey	2,160,000	3.00	10.00
1510.	1953-A	Priest	Anderson	18,000,000	-	5.00
1510*.	1953-A	Priest	Anderson	720,000	3.50	20.00

No.	Series	Signatures		No. Printed	Very Fine	Unc
1511.	1953-B	Smith	Dillon	10,800,000	-	5.00
1511*.	1953-B	Smith	Dillon	720,000	3.00	9.00
1512.	1953-C	Granahan	Dillon	5,760,000	-	5.00
1512*.	1953-C	Granahan	Dillon	360,000	3.00	10.00

DESIGN NO. 191 (Notes 1513-1514)

Reverse of Design No. 191. *With motto "In God We Trust."*

No.	Series	Signatures		No.Printed	Very Fine	Unc
1513.	1963	Granahan	Dillon	15,360,000	-	4.00
1513*.	1963	Granahan	Dillon	640,000	-	6.00

No.	Series	Signatures		No. Printed	Very Fine	Unc
1514.	1963-A	Granahan	Fowler	3,200,000	-	7.50
1514*.	1963-A	Granahan	Fowler	640,000	-	12.50

5 Dollar Notes

All issues are with the head of Abraham Lincoln

DESIGN NO. 192 (Notes 1525-1531 Incl.)

Reverse of Design No. 192. *View of the Lincoln Memorial*

No.	Series	Signatures		No. Printed	Very Fine	Unc
1525.	1928	Woods	Mellon	267,209,616	7.00	25.00
1525*.	1928	Woods	Mellon		65.00	325.00
1526.	1928-A	Woods	Mills	58,194,600	10.00	35.00
1526*.	1928-A	Woods	Mills		750.00	1,750.00
1527.	1928-B	Julian	Morgenthau	147,827,340	6.00	20.00
1527*.	1928-B	Julian	Morgenthau		30.00	125.00
1528.	1928-C	Julian	Morgenthau	214,735,765	6.00	17.50

No.	Series	Signatures		No. Printed	Very Fine	Unc
1528*.	1928-C	Julian	Morgenthau		25.00	165.00
1529.	1928-D	Julian	Vinson	9,297,120	30.00	125.00
1529*.	1928-D	Julian	Vinson		500.00	1,500.00
1530.	1928-E	Julian	Snyder	109,952,760	6.00	20.00
1530*.	1928-E	Julian	Snyder		50.00	200.00
1531.	1928-F	Clark	Snyder	104,194,704	6.00	20.00
1531*.	1928-F	Clark	Snyder		17.50	95.00

DESIGN NO. 193 (Notes 1532-1535 Incl.)

Reverse of Design No. 193.

No.	Series	Signatures		No. Printed	Unc
1532.	1953	Priest	Humphrey	120,880,000	17.50
1532*.	1953	Priest	Humphrey	5,760,000	75.00
1533.	1953-A	Priest	Anderson	90,280,000	20.00
1533*.	1953-A	Priest	Anderson	5,400,000	35.00

No.	Series	Signatures		No. Printed	Unc
1534.	1953-B	Smith	Dillon	44,640,000	10.00
1534*.	1953-B	Smith	Dillon	2,160,000	20.00
1535.	1953-C	Granahan	Dillon	8,640,000	15.00
1535*.	1953-C	Granahan	Dillon	320,000	30.00

DESIGN NO. 194 (Note 1536)

Reverse of Design No. 194.

With motto "In God We Trust."

No.	Series	Signatures		No. Printed	Unc
1536.	1963	Granahan	Dillon	63,360,000	10.00

No.	Series	Signatures		No. Printed	Unc
1536*.	1963	Granahan	Dillon	3,840,000	15.00

100 Dollar Notes

All issues are with the head of Benjamin Franklin.

DESIGN NO. 194-a

(Notes 1550-1551 Incl.)

Reverse of Design No. 194-a.

No.	Series	Signatures		No. Printed	Unc
1550.	1966	Granahan	Fowler	768,000	175.00
1550*.	1966	Granahan	Fowler	128,000	300.00

No.	Series	Signatures		No. Printed	Unc
1551.	1966-A	Elston	Kennedy	512,000	425.00

XVI. SILVER CERTIFICATES

Only 1, 5 and 10 Dollar notes were issued and all are now obsolete, abolished by the Act of June 4, 1963. During the tenure of Julian and Morgenthau, a different type of paper was used for part of the 1 Dollar notes series of 1935-A. An "R" and an "S" were used as control letters and were surcharged in red on the obverses of the notes. The obligation is as follows, "This certifies that there is on deposit in the Treasury of the United States of America ...... Dollars in silver payable to the bearer on demand ... This certificate is a legal tender for all debts public and private." The foregoing obligation varies somewhat among each series. The differences can be seen by referring to the illustrations. On June 24, 1968, by Congressional Act, the Treasury halted the practice of redeeming silver certificates with silver bullion.

The motto "In God We Trust" appears on the reverse of 1 Dollar Notes beginning with the series 1935-G. The 1935-G series, however, appears both with and without the motto.

(Additional information on this series will be found in the introduction to large size Silver Certificates on page 49.)

All the following have a Blue Seal.

1 Dollar Notes

All issues are with the head of George Washington.

DESIGN NO. 195.
(Notes 1600-1605 Incl.)

Reverse of Design No. 195.

No.	Series	Signatures		No. Printed	Very Fine	Unc
1600.	1928	Tate	Mellon	638,296,908	5.00	12.50
1600*.	1928	Tate	Mellon		20.00	85.00
1601.	1928-A	Woods	Mellon	2,267,809,500	5.00	10.00
1601*.	1928-A	Woods	Mellon		15.00	50.00
1602.	1928-B	Woods	Mills	674,597,808	5.00	12.50
1602*.	1928-B	Woods	Mills		25.00	200.00
1603.	1928-C	Woods	Woodin	5,364,348	100.00	350.00
1603*.	1928-C	Woods	Woodin		2,000.00	Rare
1604.	1928-D	Julian	Woodin	14,451,372	65.00	250.00
1604*.	1928-D	Julian	Woodin		750.00	Rare
1605.	1928-E	Julian	Morgenthau	3,519,324	250.00	1,200.00
1605*.	1928-E	Julian	Morgenthau		3,000.00	Rare

DESIGN NO. 196

(Note 1606)

The obverse is as shown.
The reverse is similar to Design No. 188.

No.	Series	Signatures		No. Printed	Very Fine	Unc
1606.	1934	Julian	Morgenthau	682,176,000	6.00	19.50
1606*.	1934	Julian	Morgenthau	7,680,000	25.00	325.00

DESIGN NO. 197
(Notes 1607-1616 Incl.)
(Also Note 2306)

Reverse of Design No. 197.

Obverse of No. 197 showing location of R & S Surcharge in red ink, as appears only on notes 1609 and 1610.

No.	Series	Signatures		No. Printed	Very Fine	Unc
1607.	1935	Julian	Morgenthau	1,681,552,000	-	10.00
1607*.	1935	Julian	Morgenthau		25.00	125.00
1608.	1935-A	Julian	Morgenthau	6,111,832,000	-	3.00
1608*.	1935-A	Julian	Morgenthau		5.00	15.00
1609.	1935-A	Julian	Morgenthau (R)	1,184,000	25.00	150.00
1609*.	1935-A	Julian	Morgenthau (R)	12,000	850.00	2,000.00
1610.	1935-A	Julian	Morgenthau (S)	1,184,000	20.00	125.00
1610*.	1935-A	Julian	Morgenthau (S)	12,000	750.00	1,750.00

No.	Series	Signatures		No. Printed		Unc
1611.	1935-B	Julian	Vinson	806,612,000	5.50	7.00
1611*.	1935-B	Julian	Vinson		17.50	45.00
1612.	1935-C	Julian	Snyder	3,088,108,000	3.00	5.00
1612*.	1935-C	Julian	Snyder		6.00	20.00
1613W.	1935-D	Clark	Snyder	4,656,968,000		6.00
1613W*.	1935-D	Clark	Snyder			10.00
1613N.	1935-D	Clark	Snyder			6.00
1613N*.	1935-D	Clark	Snyder			9.00

No.	Series	Signatures		No. Printed	Unc
1614.	1935-E	Priest	Humphrey	5,134,056,000	5.00
1614*.	1935-E	Priest	Humphrey		9.50
1615.	1935-F	Priest	Anderson	1,173,360,000	4.00
1615*.	1935-F	Priest	Anderson	53,200,000	8.00
1616.	1935-G	Smith	Dillon	194,600,000	4.00
1616*.	1935-G	Smith	Dillon	8,640,000	8.00

DESIGN NO. 198

(Notes 1617-1621 Incl.)

The obverse is similar to Design No. 197. The reverse is as shown, with motto "In God We Trust."

No.	Series	Signatures		No. Printed	Unc
1617.	1935-G	Smith	Dillon	31,320,000	5.00
1617*.	1935-G	Smith	Dillon	1,080,000	25.00
1618.	1935-H	Granahan	Dillon	30,520,000	3.50
1618*.	1935-H	Granahan	Dillon	1,436,000	10.50
1619.	1957	Priest	Anderson	2,609,600,000	3.50
1619*.	1957	Priest	Anderson	307,640,000	4.75
1620.	1957-A	Smith	Dillon	1,594,080,000	3.50
1620*.	1957-A	Smith	Dillon	94,720,000	4.75
1621.	1957-B	Granahan	Dillon	718,400,000	3.50
1621*.	1957-B	Granahan	Dillon	49,280,000	4.75

5 Dollar Notes

All issues are with the head of Abraham Lincoln

DESIGN NO. 199
(Notes 1650-1654 Incl.)
(Also Note 2307)

Reverse of Design No. 199. View of the Lincoln Memorial.

No.	Series	Signatures		No. Printed	Very Fine	Unc
1650.	1934	Julian	Morgenthau	393,088,368	10.00	30.00
1650*.	1934	Julian	Morgenthau		22.50	165.00
1651.	1934-A	Julian	Morgenthau	656,265,948	8.50	20.00
1651*.	1934-A	Julian	Morgenthau		12.50	45.00
1652.	1934-B	Julian	Vinson	59,128,500	10.00	40.00
1652*.	1934-B	Julian	Vinson		55.00	250.00
1653.	1934-C	Julian	Snyder	403,146,148	8.50	20.00
1653*.	1934-C	Julian	Snyder		10.00	50.00
1654.	1934-D	Clark	Snyder	486,146,148	8.50	20.00
1654*.	1934-D	Clark	Snyder		10.00	40.00

DESIGN NO. 200
(Notes 1655-1658)

Reverse of Design No. 200.

No.	Series	Signatures		No. Printed	Unc
1655.	1953	Priest	Humphrey	339,600,000	15.00
1655*.	1953	Priest	Humphrey	15,120,000	35.00
1656.	1953-A	Priest	Anderson	232,400,000	15.00
1656*.	1953-A	Priest	Anderson	12,960,000	25.00

No.	Series	Signatures		No. Printed	Unc
1657.	1953-B	Smith	Dillon	73,000,000†	15.00
1657*.	1953-B	Smith	Dillon	3,240,000	750.00
1658.	1953-C	Granahan	Dillon	Not released	

†Only 14,196,000 notes were released.

10 Dollar Notes

All issues are with the head of Alexander Hamilton.

DESIGN NO. 201
(Note 1700)

Reverse of Design No. 201. View of the U.S. Treasury Building.

No.	Series	Signatures		Delivered	Very Fine	Unc
1700.	1933	Julian	Woodin	216,000	1,250.00	4,000.00
1700-a.	1933-A	Julian	Morgenthau	28,000	Unknown	

DESIGN NO. 202
(Notes 1701-1705 Incl.)
(Also Notes 2308-2309)

Reverse of Design No. 202.

No.	Series	Signatures		No. Printed	Very Fine	Unc
1701.	1934	Julian	Morgenthau	88,692,864	20.00	40.00
1701*.	1934	Julian	Morgenthau		35.00	350.00
1702.	1934-A	Julian	Morgenthau	42,346,428	20.00	40.00
1702*.	1934-A	Julian	Morgenthau		35.00	275.00
1703.	1934-B	Julian	Vinson	337,740	125.00	700.00
1703*.	1934-B	Julian	Vinson		500.00	2,000.00
1704.	1934-C	Julian	Snyder	20,032,632	17.50	30.00
1704*.	1934-C	Julian	Snyder		22.50	75.00
1705.	1934-D	Clark	Snyder	11,801,112	15.00	30.00
1705*.	1934-D	Clark	Snyder		45.000	325.00

DESIGN NO. 203
(Notes 1706-1708 Incl.)

Reverse of Design No. 203.

No.	Series	Signatures		No. Printed	Unc
1706.	1953	Priest	Humphrey	10,440,000	35.00
1706*.	1953	Priest	Humphrey	576,000	85.00
1707.	1953-A	Priest	Anderson	1,080,000	90.00
1707*.	1953-A	Priest	Anderson	144,000	85.00
1708.	1953-B	Smith	Dillon	720,000	35.00

XVII. NATIONAL BANK NOTES

These were issued from July, 1929 to May, 1935, after which date National Bank Notes ceased to be issued. This discontinuance was brought about by the Treasury recall of certain United States bonds, thus making them unavailable as security for further issues of National Bank Notes.

Only 5, 10, 20, 50 and 100 Dollar notes were issued and all are now obsolete. The obligation is as follows, "National Currency secured by United States bonds deposited with the Treasurer of the United States of America ... The (name of bank and city) will pay to the bearer on demand ...... Dollars ... Redeemable in lawful money of the United States at United States Treasury or at the bank of issue."

Charter Numbers. A complete list of the years of issue of the Charter Numbers of the National Banks will be found on page 75.

The Valuations. The listings that follow show in what states or territories the various types of National Bank Notes were issued. At the same time the valuations indicate the relative rarity of a given note issued in one state as against the same note issued in another state. The values given are for the most common specimens of each type. Notes issued by banks in small towns are usually scarcer than those of banks in large cities, since they probably issued fewer notes.

(More detailed information on this series will be found in the introduction to large size National Bank Notes on page 74.)

There are two distinct types for each denomination of National Bank Notes. On Type One, which was issued from July, 1929 to May, 1933, the charter number appears twice in heavy black numerals on the face of each note. On Type Two, which was issued from May, 1933 to 1935, the charter number appears four times, the two additional appearances being printed in brown ink alongside of the twice appearing serial number. The illustrations for Design Nos. 204 and 208 are Type One; Design Nos. 205, 206 and 207 are Type Two.

All are series 1929 with the signatures of Jones and Woods and with a small brown seal. In addition, the notes bear two signatures of the issuing National Bank, those of its president and cashier, along with the signatures of the Register of the Treasury and the Treasurer of the United States.

5 Dollar Notes

All issues are with the head of Abraham Lincoln.

TYPE 1

DESIGN NO. 204

(Notes 1800-1 — 1800-2)

The obverse is as shown.
The reverse is similar to Design No. 192.

No.	Type	Very Fine	Unc
1800-1.	Type 1	25.00	42.50
1800-2.	Type 2	30.00	60.00

The valuations listed below are for Type I notes. Type II notes generally command higher prices.

These notes were issued from 1929 to 1935 in sheets of six notes.

No.	*State*	*Very Fine*
S-1990.	Alabama	30.00
S-1991.	Alaska	1,500.00
S-1992.	Arizona	150.00
S-1993.	Arkansas	50.00
S-1994.	California	35.00
S-1995.	Colorado	45.00
S-1996.	Connecticut	35.00
S-1997.	Delaware	50.00
S-1998.	District of Columbia	35.00
S-1999.	Florida	60.00
S-2000.	Georgia	50.00
S-2001.	Hawaii	100.00
S-2002.	Idaho	90.00
S-2003.	Illinois	25.00
S-2004.	Indian	25.00
S-2005.	Iowa	30.00
S-2006.	Kansas	35.00
S-2007.	Kentucky	30.00
S-2008.	Louisiana	40.00
S-2009.	Maine	35.00
S-2010.	Maryland	40.00
S-2011.	Massachusetts	30.00
S-2012.	Michigan	35.00
S-2013.	Minnesota	35.00
S-2014.	Mississippi	50.00
S-2015.	Missouri	30.00
S-2016.	Montana	100.00
S-2017.	Nebraska	35.00
S-2018.	Nevada	300.00
S-2019.	New Hamsphire	45.00
S-2020.	New Jersey	30.00
S-2021.	New Mexico	90.00
S-2022.	New York	25.00
S-2023.	North Carolina	45.00
S-2024.	North Dakota	60.00
S-2025.	Ohio	25.00
S-2026.	Oklahoma	37.50
S-2027.	Oregon	60.00
S-2028.	Pennsylvania	25.00
S-2029.	Rhode Island	60.00
S-2030.	South Carolina	50.00
S-2031.	South Dakota	60.00
S-2032.	Tennessee	50.00
S-2033.	Texas	45.00
S-2034.	Utah	75.00
S-2035.	Vermont	40.00
S-2036.	Virginia	45.00
S-2037.	Washington	60.00
S-2038.	West Virginia	45.00
S-2039.	Wisconsin	35.00
S-2040.	Wyoming	120.00

10 Dollar Notes

All issues are with the head of Alexander Hamilton.

DESIGN NO. 205

(Notes 1801-1 — 1801-2)

The obverse is as shown. The reverse is similar to Design No. 201.

No.	Type	Very Fine	Unc
1801-1.	Type 1	32.50	65.00
1801-2.	Type 2	40.00	80.00

These notes were issued from 1929 to 1935 in sheets of six notes.

The valuations below are for Type I notes. Type II notes generally command higher prices.

	State	Very Fine
S-2041.	Alabama	45.00
S-2042.	Alaska	1,700.00
S-2043.	Arizona	160.00
S-2044.	Arkansas	60.00
S-2045.	California	40.00
S-2046.	Colorado	60.00
S-2047.	Connecticut	40.00
S-2048.	Delaware	75.00
S-2049.	District of Columbia	55.00
S-2050.	Florida	65.00
S-2051.	Georgia	50.00
S-2052.	Hawaii	150.00
S-2053.	Idaho	75.00
S-2054.	Illinois	32.50
S-2055.	Indiana	32.50
S-2056.	Iowa	45.00
S-2057.	Kansas	40.00
S-2058.	Kentucky	35.00
S-2059.	Louisiana	50.00
S-2060.	Maine	60.00
S-2061.	Maryland	45.00
S-2062.	Massachusetts	32.50
S-2063.	Michigan	45.00
S-2064.	Minnesota	45.00
S-2065.	Mississippi	65.00
S-2066.	Missouri	32.50
S-2067.	Montana	125.00
S-2068.	Nebraska	45.00
S-2069.	Nevada	400.00
S-2070.	New Hampshire	55.00
S-2071.	New Jersey	40.00
S-2072.	New Mexico	90.00
S-2073.	New York	32.50
S-2074.	North Carolina	65.00
S-2075.	North Dakota	75.00
S-2076.	Ohio	32.50
S-2077.	Oklahoma	50.00
S-2078.	Oregon	65.00
S-2079.	Pennsylvania	32.50
S-2080.	Rhode Island	50.00
S-2081.	South Carolina	65.00
S-2082.	South Dakota	70.00
S-2083.	Tennessee	60.00
S-2084.	Texas	50.00
S-2085.	Utah	90.00
S-2086.	Vermont	90.00
S-2087.	Virginia	45.00
S-2088.	Washington	75.00
S-2089.	West Virginia	55.00
S-2090.	Wisconsin	50.00
S-2091.	Wyoming	125.00

20 Dollar Notes

All issues are with the head of Andrew Jackson.

TYPE 2

DESIGN NO. 206 (Notes 1802-1 — 1802-2)

Reverse of Design No. 206. View of the White House.

No.	Type	Very Fine	Unc
1802-1.	Type 1	45.00	75.00
1802-2.	Type 2	52.50	85.00

These notes were issued from 1929 to 1935 in sheets of six notes.

The valuations below are for Type I notes. Type II notes generally command higher prices.

	State	Very Fine
S-2092.	Alabama	65.00
S-2093.	Alaska	1,900.00
S-2094.	Arizona	180.00
S-2095.	Arkansas	75.00
S-2096.	California	55.00
S-2097.	Colorado	75.00
S-2098.	Connecticut	55.00
S-2099.	Delaware	75.00
S-2100.	District of Columbia	65.00
S-2101.	Florida	80.00
S-2102.	Georgia	65.00
S-2103.	Hawaii	175.00
S-2104.	Idaho	125.00
S-2105.	Illinois	45.00
S-2106.	Indiana	45.00
S-2107.	Iowa	60.00
S-2108.	Kansas	60.00
S-2109.	Kentucky	50.00
S-2110.	Louisiana	60.00
S-2111.	Maine	75.00
S-2112.	Maryland	55.00
S-2113.	Massachusetts	50.00
S-2114.	Michigan	55.00
S-2115.	Minnesota	55.00
S-2116.	Mississippi	80.00
S-2117.	Missouri	50.00
S-2118.	Montana	140.00
S-2119.	Nebraska	55.00
S-2120.	Nevada	500.00
S-2121.	New Hampshire	75.00
S-2122.	New Jersey	50.00
S-2123.	New Mexico	125.00
S-2124.	New York	45.00
S-2125.	North Carolina	70.00
S-2126.	North Dakota	100.00
S-2127.	Ohio	45.00
S-2128.	Oklahoma	75.00
S-2129.	Oregon	75.00
S-2130.	Pennsylvania	45.00
S-2131.	Rhode Island	95.00
S-2132.	South Carolina	70.00
S-2133.	South Dakota	125.00
S-2134.	Tennessee	70.00
S-2135.	Texas	65.00
S-2136.	Utah	110.00
S-2137.	Vermont	125.00
S-2138.	Virginia	60.00
S-2139.	Washington	80.00
S-2140.	West Virginia	75.00
S-2141.	Wisconsin	60.00
S-2142.	Wyoming	135.00

50 Dollar Notes

All issues are with the head of Ulysses S. Grant.

TYPE 2

DESIGN NO. 207 (Notes 1803-1 — 1803-2)

Reverse of Design No. 207. View of the U.S. Capitol.

No.	Type	Very Fine	Unc
1803-1.	Type 1	125.00	225.00
1803-2.	Type 2	200.00	325.00

These notes were issued from 1929 to 1935 in sheets of six notes.

Although issued in recent times, so many of these notes have been redeemed that there are now relatively few of them in existence. It is thus not possible to evaluate them by state and the valuations have been omitted. The same relative rarity would apply as exists within the 20 Dollar notes.

No.	*State*	
S-2143.	Alabama	Not Issued
S-2144.	Alaska	Not Issued
S-2145.	Arizona	Not Issued
S-2146.	Arkansas	Not Issued
S-2147.	California	— —
S-2148.	Colorado	— —
S-2149.	Connecticut	— —
S-2150.	Delaware	— —
S-2151.	Dist. of Col.	— —
S-2152.	Florida	— —
S-2153.	Georgia	Not Issued
S-2154.	Hawaii	— —
S-2155.	Idaho	— —
S-2156.	Illinois	— —
S-2157.	Indiana	— —
S-2158.	Iowa	— —
S-2159.	Kansas	— —
S-2160.	Kentucky	— —
S-2161.	Louisiana	— —
S-2162.	Maine	Not Issued
S-2163.	Maryland	— —
S-2164.	Massachusetts	— —
S-2165.	Michigan	— —
S-2166.	Minnesota	— —
S-2167.	Mississippi	— —
S-2168.	Missouri	— —
S-2169.	Montana	— —
S-2170.	Nebraska	— —
S-2171.	Nevada	— —
S-2172.	New Hampshire	— —
S-2173.	New Jersey	— —
S-2174.	New Mexico	Not Issued
S-2175.	New York	— —
S-2176.	North Carolina	— —
S-2177.	North Dakota	— —
S-2178.	Ohio	— —
S-2179.	Oklahoma	— —
S-2180.	Oregon	— —
S-2181.	Pennsylvania	— —
S-2182.	Rhode Island	— —
S-2183.	South Carolina	Not Issued
S-2184.	South Dakota	— —
S-2185.	Tennessee	— —
S-2186.	Texas	— —
S-2187.	Utah	— —
S-2188.	Vermont	— —
S-2189.	Virginia	— —
S-2190.	Washington	— —
S-2191.	West Virginia	— —
S-2192.	Wisconsin	— —
S-2193.	Wyoming	— —

100 Dollar Notes

All issues are with the head of Benjamin Franklin.

TYPE 1

DESIGN NO. 208 (Notes 1804-1 — 1804-2)

Reverse of Design No. 208. View of Independence Hall.

No.	Type	Very Fine	Unc
1804-1.	Type 1	175.00	250.00
1804-2.	Type 2	225.00	375.00

These notes were issued from 1929 to 1935 in sheets of six notes.

Although issued in recent times, so many of these notes have been redeemed that there are now relatively few of them in existence. It is thus not possible to evaluate them by state and the valuations have been omitted. The same relative rarity would apply as exists within the 20 Dollar notes.

No.	*State*	
S-2194.	Alabama	Not Issued
S-2195.	Alaska	Not Issued
S-2196.	Arizona	Not Issued
S-2197.	Arkansas	Not Issued
S-2198.	California	— —
S-2199.	Colorado	— —
S-2200.	Connecticut	— —
S-2201.	Delaware	— —
S-2202.	Dist. of Col.	— —
S-2203.	Florida	— —
S-2204.	Georgia	Not Issued
S-2205.	Hawaii	— —
S-2206.	Idaho	— —
S-2207.	Illinois	— —
S-2208.	Indiana	— —
S-2209.	Iowa	— —
S-2210.	Kansas	— —
S-2211.	Kentucky	— —
S-2212.	Louisiana	— —
S-2213.	Maine	Not Issued
S-2214.	Maryland	— —
S-2215.	Massachusetts	— —
S-2216.	Michigan	— —
S-2217.	Minnesota	— —
S-2218.	Mississippi	— —
S-2219.	Missouri	— —
S-2220.	Montana	— —
S-2221.	Nebraska	— —
S-2222.	Nevada	— —
S-2223.	New Hampshire	— —
S-2224.	New Jersey	— —
S-2225.	New Mexico	Not Issued
S-2226.	New York	— —
S-2227.	North Carolina	— —
S-2228.	North Dakota	— —
S-2229.	Ohio	— —
S-2230.	Oklahoma	— —
S-2231.	Oregon	— —
S-2232.	Pennsylvania	— —
S-2233.	Rhode Island	— —
S-2234.	South Carolina	Not Issued
S-2235.	South Dakota	— —
S-2236.	Tennessee	— —
S-2237.	Texas	— —
S-2238.	Utah	Not Issued
S-2239.	Vermont	— —
S-2240.	Virginia	— —
S-2241.	Washington	— —
S-2242.	West Virginia	— —
S-2243.	Wisconsin	— —
S-2244.	Wyoming	— —

XVIII. FEDERAL RESERVE BANK NOTES

Only 5, 10, 20, 50 and 100 Dollar notes were issued and all are now obsolete. The obligation is as follows, "National Currency secured by United States bonds deposited with the Treasurer of the United States of America or by like deposit of other securities . . . The (name of bank and city) will pay to the bearer on demand . . . . . . Dollars . . . Redeemable in lawful money of the United States at United States Treasury or at the bank of issue."

(Additional information on this series will be found in the introduction to large size Federal Reserve Bank Notes on page 118.)

All are series of 1929 with signatures of Jones and Woods and with a brown seal that is larger than on the National Bank Notes preceding. In addition, the notes bear two signatures of the issuing Federal Reserve Bank, those of its Governor and Cashier, or of its Governor and Deputy Governor (N.Y.) or of its Governor and Ass't. Deputy Governor (Chicago) or of its Governor and Controller (St. Louis).

5 Dollar Notes

All issues are with the head of Abraham Lincoln

DESIGN NO. 209

(Notes 1850-A - 1850-L Incl.)

The obverse is as shown.
The reverse is similar to Design No. 192.

No.	Issuing Bank	No. Printed	Very Fine	Unc
1850-A.	Boston	3,180,000	20.00	65.00
1850-B.	New York	2,100,000	15.00	70.00
1850-C.	Philadelphia	3,096,000	20.00	50.00
1850-D.	Cleveland	4,236,000	15.00	45.00
1850-F	Atlanta	1,884,000	22.50	150.00
1850-G.	Chicago	5,988,000	12.50	45.00
1850-H.	St. Louis	276,000	150.00	900.00
1850-I.	Minneapolis	684,000	25.00	250.00
1850-J.	Kansas City	2,460,000	20.00	85.00
1850-K.	Dallas	996,000	20.00	45.00
1850-L.	San Francisco	360,000	1,500.00	4,500.00

10 Dollar Notes

All issues are with the head of Alexander Hamilton

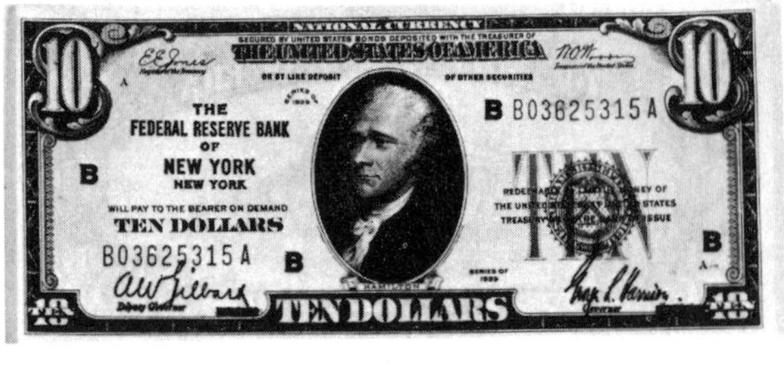

DESIGN NO. 210

(Notes 1860-A - 1860-L Incl.)

The obverse is as shown.
The reverse is similar to Design No. 201.

No.	Issuing Bank	No. Printed	Very Fine	Unc
1860-A.	Boston	1,680,000	22.50	95.00
1860-B.	New York	5,556,000	20.00	60.00
1860-C.	Philadelphia	1,416,000	22.50	65.00
1860-D	Cleveland	2,412,000	22.50	70.00
1860-E	Richmond	1,356,000	25.00	120.00
1860-F.	Atlanta	1,056,000	25.00	100.00
1860-G.	Chicago	3,156,000	20.00	40.00
1860-H.	St. Louis	1,584,000	25.00	40.00
1860-I.	Minneapolis	558,000	27.50	90.00
1860-J.	Kansas City	1,284,000	25.00	75.00
1860-K.	Dallas	504,000	30.00	750.00
1860-L	San Francisco	1,080,000	25.00	125.00

20 Dollar Notes

All issues are with the head of Andrew Jackson

DESIGN NO. 211

Notes 1870-A - 1870-L Incl.)

The obverse is as shown.
The reverse is similar to
Design No. 206.

No.	Issuing Bank	No. Printed	Unc
1870-A.	Boston	972,000	90.00
1870-B.	New York	2,568,000	65.00
1870-C.	Philadelphia	1,008,000	80.00
1870-D.	Cleveland	1,020,000	80.00
1870-E.	Richmond	1,632,000	125.00
1870-F.	Atlanta	960,000	150.00
1870-G.	Chicago	2,028,000	45.00
1870-H.	St. Louis	444,000	55.00
1870-I.	Minneapolis	864,000	60.00
1870-J.	Kansas City	612,000	55.00
1870-K.	Dallas	468,000	200.00
1870-L.	San Francisco	888,000	125.00

50 Dollar Notes

All issues are with the head of Ulysses S. Grant

DESIGN NO. 212

(Notes 1880-B - 1880-L Incl.)

The obverse is as shown.
The reverse is similar to
Design No. 207.

No.	Issuing Bank	No. Printed	Unc
1880-B.	New York	636,000	125.00
1880-D.	Cleveland	684,000	125.00
1880-G.	Chicago	300,000	100.00
1880-I.	Minneapolis	132,000	125.00
1880-J.	Kansas City	276,000	100.00
1880-K.	Dallas	168,000	275.00
1880-L.	San Francisco	576,000	200.00

100 Dollar Notes

All issues are with the head of Benjamin Franklin

DESIGN NO. 213

(Notes 1890-B - 1890-K Incl.)

The obverse is as shown.
The reverse is similar to
Design No. 208.

No.	Issuing Bank	No. Printed	Unc
1890-B.	New York	480,000	140.00
1890-D.	Cleveland	276,000	140.00
1890-E.	Richmond	142,000	200.00
1890-G.	Chicago	384,000	140.00
1890-I.	Minneapolis	144,000	140.00
1890-J.	Kansas City	96,000	165.00
1890-K.	Dallas	36,000	300.00

XIX. FEDERAL RESERVE NOTES

Federal Reserve Notes form the largest issues of our contemporary currency and are the mainstay of our present currency system. All denominations from 1 to 10,000 Dollars have been issued but only the 1, 5, 10, 20, 50 and 100 Dollar notes are still current. Notes of 500 Dollars and higher are no longer being printed. The notes of all issues of the 1928 series were redeemable in gold and the obligation on these notes is as follows, "The United States of America will pay to the bearer on demand . . . . . . Dollars . . . Redeemable in gold on demand at the United States Treasury, or in gold or lawful money at any Federal Reserve Bank."

After passage of the Gold Reserve Act of 1933, paper money no longer became redeemable in gold. The obligation on succeeding issues of Federal Reserve Notes was therefore altered, and beginning with the series of 1934, that portion pertaining to gold convertibility was amended to read as follows, "This note is legal tender for all debts, public and private, and is redeemable in lawful money at the United States Treasury, or at any Federal Reserve Bank."

Beginning with the series of 1963, the inscriptions — "Will pay to the bearer on demand" and "Is redeemable in lawful money at the United States Treasury, or at any Federal Reserve Bank" — were dropped. The obligation now reads as follows, "This note is legal tender for all debts, public and private."

(Additional information on this series will be found in the introduction to large size Federal Reserve Notes on page 124.)

All the following have a Green Seal.

1 Dollar Notes

All issues are with the head of George Washington

DESIGN NO. 214
(Notes 1900-A - 1909-L Incl.)

Reverse of Design No. 214.

1. Series of 1963.

Signatures of Granahan and Dillon.

No.	Issuing Bank	No. Printed	Unc	No.	Issuing Bank	No. Printed	Unc
1900-A.	Boston	87,680,000	4.00	1900-G.	Chicago	279,360,000	4.00
1900-A*.	Boston	6,400,000	4.75	1900-G*.	Chicago	19,840,000	4.50
1900-B.	New York	219,200,000	4.00	1900-H.	St. Louis	99,840,000	4.00
1900-B*.	New York	15,360,000	4.50	1900-H*.	St. Louis	9,600,000	4.75
1900-C.	Philadelphia	123,680,000	4.00	1900-I.	Minneapolis	44,800,000	4.00
1900-C*.	Philadelphia	10,880,000	4.75	1900-I*.	Minneapolis	5,120,000	4.75
1900-D.	Cleveland	108,320,000	4.00	1900-J.	Kansas City	88,960,000	4.00
1900-D*.	Cleveland	8,320,000	4.50	1900-J*.	Kansas City	8,960,000	4.75
1900-E.	Richmond	159,520,000	4.00	1900-K.	Dallas	85,760,000	4.00
1900-E*.	Richmond	12,160,000	4.75	1900-K*.	Dallas	8,960,000	4.75
1900-F.	Atlanta	221,120,000	4.00	1900-L.	San Francisco	199,999,999	4.00
1900-F*.	Atlanta	19,200,000	4.50	1900-L*.	San Francisco	14,720,000	4.50

2. Series of 1963-A.

Signatures of Granahan and Fowler.

No.	Issuing Bank	No. Printed	Unc	No.	Issuing Bank	No. Printed	Unc
1901-A.	Boston	319,840,000	3.50	1901-G.	Chicago	784,480,000	3.25
1901-A*.	Boston	19,840,000	3.75	1901-G*.	Chicago	52,640,000	3.50
1901-B.	New York	657,600,000	3.25	1901-H.	St. Louis	264,000,000	3.50
1901-B*.	New York	47,680,000	3.50	1901-H*.	St. Louis	17,920,000	3.75
1901-C.	Philadelphia	375,520,000	3.25	1901-I.	Minneapolis	112,160,000	3.50
1901-C*.	Philadelphia	26,240,000	3.50	1901-I*.	Minneapolis	7,040,000	4.00
1901-D.	Cleveland	337,120,000	3.25	1901-J.	Kansas City	219,200,000	3.50
1901-D*.	Cleveland	21,120,000	3.75	1901-J*.	Kansas City	14,720,000	3.75
1901-E.	Richmond	532,000,000	3.25	1901-K.	Dallas	288,960,000	3.50
1901-E*.	Richmond	41,600,000	3.50	1901-K*.	Dallas	19,184,000	3.75
1901-F.	Atlanta	636,480,000	3.25	1901-L.	San Francisco	576,800,000	3.25
1901-F*.	Atlanta	40,960,000	3.50	1901-L*.	San Francisco	43,040,000	3.50

3. Series of 1963-B.

Signatures of Granahan and Barr.

No.	Issuing Bank	No. Printed	Unc	No.	Issuing Bank	No. Printed	Unc
1902-B.	New York	123,040,000	4.00	1902-G*.	Chicago	2,400,000	4.50
1902-B*.	New York	3,680,000	4.50	1902-J.	Kansas City	44,800,000	4.00
1902-E.	Richmond	93,600,000	4.00	1902-J*.	Kansas City	None printed	—
1902-E*.	Richmond	3,200,000	8.00	1902-L.	San Francisco	106,400,000	4.00
1902-G.	Chicago	91,040,000	4.00	1902-L*.	San Francisco	3,040,000	4.50

4. Series of 1969.

Signatures of Elston and Kennedy. With new Treasury seal.

No.	Issuing Bank	No. Printed	Unc	No.	Issuing Bank	No. Printed	Unc
1903-A.	Boston	99,200,000	3.00	1903-G.	Chicago	359,520,000	3.00
1903-A*.	Boston	5,120,000	3.50	1903-G*.	Chicago	12,160,000	3.50
1903-B.	New York	269,120,000	3.00	1903-H.	St. Louis	74,880,000	3.00
1903-B*.	New York	14,080,000	3.50	1903-H*.	St. Louis	3,840,000	3.50
1903-C.	Philadelphia	68,480,000	3.00	1903-I.	Minneapolis	48,000,000	3.00
1903-C*.	Philadelphia	3,776,000	3.50	1903-I*.	Minneapolis	1,920,000	3.50
1903-D.	Cleveland	120,480,000	3.00	1903-J.	Kansas City	95,360,000	3.00
1903-D*.	Cleveland	5,760,000	3.50	1903-J*.	Kansas City	5,760,000	3.50
1903-E.	Richmond	250,560,000	3.00	1903-K.	Dallas	113,440,000	3.00
1903-E*.	Richmond	10,880,000	3.50	1903-K*.	Dallas	5,120,000	3.50
1903-F.	Atlanta	185,120,000	3.00	1903-L.	San Francisco	226,240,000	3.00
1903-F*.	Atlanta	7,680,000	3.50	1903-L*.	San Francisco	9,600,000	3.50

5. Series of 1969-A.

Signatures of Kabis and Kennedy.

No.	Issuing Bank	No. Printed	Unc	No.	Issuing Bank	No. Printed	Unc
1904-A.	Boston	40,480,000	3.00	1904-G.	Chicago	75,680,000	3.00
1904-A*.	Boston	1,120,000	3.50	1904-G*.	Chicago	4,480,000	3.50
1904-B.	New York	122,400,000	3.00	1904-H.	St. Louis	41,420,000	3.00
1904-B*.	New York	6,240,000	3.50	1904-H*.	St. Louis	1,280,000	3.50
1904-C.	Philadelphia	44,960,000	3.00	1904-I.	Minneapolis	21,760,000	3.00
1904-C*.	Philadelphia	1,760,000	3.50	1904-I*.	Minneapolis	640,000	7.00
1904-D.	Cleveland	30,080,000	3.00	1904-J.	Kansas City	40,480,000	3.00
1904-D*.	Cleveland	1,280,000	3.50	1904-J*.	Kansas City	1,120,000	3.50
1904-E.	Richmond	66,080,000	3.00	1904-K.	Dallas	27,520,000	3.00
1904-E*.	Richmond	3,200,000	3.50	1904-K*.	Dallas	None Printed	—
1904-F.	Atlanta	70,560,000	3.00	1904-L.	San Francisco	51,840,000	3.00
1904-F*.	Atlanta	2,400,000	3.50	1904-L*.	San Francisco	3,840,000	3.50

6. Series of 1969-B.

Signatures of Kabis and Connally.

No.	Issuing Bank	No. Printed	Unc	No.	Issuing Bank	No. Printed	Unc
1905-A.	Boston	94,720,000	3.00	1905-G.	Chicago	204,480,000	3.00
1905-A*.	Boston	1,920,000	3.25	1905-G*.	Chicago	4,480,000	3.25
1905-B.	New York	329,440,000	3.00	1905-H.	St. Louis	59,520,000	3.00
1905-B*.	New York	7,040,000	3.25	1905-H*.	St. Louis	1,920,000	3.25
1905-C.	Philadelphia	133,280,000	3.00	1905-I.	Minneapolis	33,920,000	3.00
1905-C*.	Philadelphia	3,200,000	4.00	1905-I*.	Minneapolis	640,000	10.00
1905-D.	Cleveland	91,520,000	3.00	1905-J.	Kansas City	67,200,000	3.00
1905-D*.	Cleveland	4,480,000	3.25	1905-J*.	Kansas City	2,560,000	3.25
1905-E.	Richmond	180,000,000	3.00	1905-K.	Dallas	116,640,000	3.00
1905-E*.	Richmond	3,840,000	3.25	1905-K*.	Dallas	5,120,000	3.25
1905-F.	Atlanta	200,000,000	3.00	1905-L.	San Francisco	208,960,000	3.00
1905-F*.	Atlanta	3,840,000	3.25	1905-L*.	San Francisco	5,760,000	3.25

7. Series of 1969-C.

Signatures of Banuelos and Connally.

No.	Issuing Bank	No. Printed	Unc	No.	Issuing Bank	No. Printed	Unc
1906-B.	New York	49,920,000	2.75	1906-H.	St. Louis	23,680,000	2.75
1906-B*.	New York	None Printed	—	1906-H*.	St. Louis	640,000	5.00
1906-D.	Cleveland	15,520,000	3.00	1906-I.	Minneapolis	25,600,000	2.75
1906-D*.	Cleveland	480,000	5.00	1906-I*.	Minneapolis	640,000	5.00
1906-E.	Richmond	61,600,000	2.75	1906-J.	Kansas City	38,560,000	2.75
1906-E*.	Richmond	480,000	5.00	1906-J*.	Kansas City	1,120,000	4.50
1906-F.	Atlanta	60,960,000	2.75	1906-K.	Dallas	29,440,000	2.75
1906-F*.	Atlanta	3,680,000	4.00	1906-K*.	Dallas	640,000	5.00
1906-G.	Chicago	137,120,000	2.75	1906-L.	San Francisco	101,280,000	2.75
1906-G*.	Chicago	1,748,000	4.00	1906-L*.	San Francisco	2,400,000	4.00

8. Series of 1969-D.

Signatures of Banuelos and Shultz.

No.	Issuing Bank	No. Printed	Unc	No.	Issuing Bank	No. Printed	Unc	No.	Issuing Bank	No. Printed	Unc
1907-A.	Boston	187,040,000	2.50	1907-E.	Richmond	374,240,000	2.50	1907-I.	Minneapolis	83,200,000	2.50
1907-A*.	Boston	1,120,000	2.75	1907-E*.	Richmond	8,480,000	2.75	1907-I*.	Minneapolis	None Printed	—
1907-B.	New York	468,480,000	2.50	1907-F.	Atlanta	377,440,000	2.50	1907-J.	Kansas City	185,760,000	2.50
1907-B*.	New York	4,480,000	2.75	1907-F*.	Atlanta	5,280,000	2.75	1907-J*.	Kansas City	3,040,000	2.75
1907-C.	Philadelphia	218,560,000	2.50	1907-G.	Chicago	378,080,000	2.50	1907-K.	Dallas	158,240,000	2.50
1907-C*.	Philadelphia	4,320,000	2.75	1907-G*.	Chicago	5,270,000	2.75	1907-K*.	Dallas	6,240,000	2.75
1907-D.	Cleveland	161,440,000	2.50	1907-H.	St. Louis	168,480,000	2.50	1907-L.	San Francisco	400,640,000	2.50
1907-D*.	Cleveland	2,400,000	2.75	1907-H*.	St. Louis	1,760,000	2.75	1907-L*.	San Francisco	6,400,000	2.75

9. Series of 1974.

Signatures of Neff and Simon.

No.	Issuing Bank	No. Printed	Unc	No.	Issuing Bank	No. Printed	Unc	No.	Issuing Bank	No. Printed	Unc
1908-A.	Boston	269,760,000	Current	1908-E.	Richmond	644,000,000	Current	1908-I.	Minneapolis	144,160,000	Current
1908-A*.	Boston	2,400,000	Current	1908-E*.	Richmond	4,960,000	Current	1908-I*.	Minneapolis	480,000	Current
1908-B.	New York	740,320,000	Current	1908-F.	Atlanta	599,680,000	Current	1908-J.	Kansas City	223,520,000	Current
1908-B*.	New York	8,800,000	Current	1908-F*.	Atlanta	5,632,000	Current	1908-J*.	Kansas City	2,144,000	Current
1908-C.	Philadelphia	308,800,000	Current	1908-G.	Chicago	473,600,000	Current	1908-K.	Dallas	330,560,000	Current
1908-C*.	Philadelphia	1,600,000	Current	1908-G*.	Chicago	4,992,000	Current	1908-K*.	Dallas	1,216,000	Current
1908-D.	Cleveland	240,960,000	Current	1908-H.	St. Louis	291,520,000	Current	1908-L.	San Francisco	736,960,000	Current
1908-D*.	Cleveland	960,000	Current	1908-H*.	St. Louis	2,880,000	Current	1908-L*.	San Francisco	3,520,000	Current

10. Series of 1977.

Signatures of Morton and Blumenthal.

No.	Issuing Bank	No. Printed	Unc	No.	Issuing Bank	No. Printed	Unc	No.	Issuing Bank	No. Printed	Unc
1909-A.	Boston	188,160,000	Current	1909-E.	Richmond	418,560,000	Current	1909-I.	Minneapolis	115,200,000	Current
1909-A*.	Boston	3,072,000	Current	1909-E*.	Richmond	6,400,000	Current	1909-I*.	Minneapolis	2,944,000	Current
1909-B.	New York	635,520,000	Current	1909-F.	Atlanta	565,120,000	Current	1909-J.	Kansas City	223,360,000	Current
1909-B*.	New York	10,112,000	Current	1909-F*.	Atlanta	8,960,000	Current	1909-J*.	Kansas City	3,840,000	Current
1909-C.	Philadelphia	216,960,000	Current	1909-G.	Chicago	615,680,000	Current	1909-K.	Dallas	289,280,000	Current
1909-C*.	Philadelphia	4,480,000	Current	1909-G*.	Chicago	9,472,000	Current	1909-K*.	Dallas	4,608,000	Current
1909-D.	Cleveland	213,120,000	Current	1909-H.	St. Louis	199,680,000	Current	1909-L.	San Francisco	516,480,000	Current
1909-D*.	Cleveland	3,328,000	Current	1909-H*.	St. Louis	2,048,000	Current	1909-L*.	San Francisco	8,320,000	Current

11. Series of 1977-A.

Signatures of Morton and Miller.

No.	Issuing Bank	No. Printed	Unc	No.	Issuing Bank	No. Printed	Unc	No.	Issuing Bank	No. Printed	Unc
1910-A.	Boston		Current	1910-E.	Richmond		Current	1910-I.	Minneapolis		Current
1910-A*.	Boston		Current	1910-E*.	Richmond		Current	1910-I*.	Minneapolis		Current
1910-B.	New York		Current	1910-F.	Atlanta		Current	1910-J.	Kansas City		Current
1910-B*.	New York		Current	1910-F*.	Atlanta		Current	1910-J*.	Kansas City		Current
1910-C.	Philadelphia		Current	1910-G.	Chicago		Current	1910-K.	Dallas		Current
1910-C*.	Philadelphia		Current	1910-G*.	Chicago		Current	1910-K*.	Dallas		Current
1910-D.	Cleveland		Current	1910-H.	St. Louis		Current	1910-L.	San Francisco		Current
1910-D*.	Cleveland		Current	1910-H*.	St. Louis		Current	1910-L*.	San Francisco		Current

12. Series of 1981.

Signatures of Buchanan and Regan.

No.	Issuing Bank	No. Printed	Unc	No.	Issuing Bank	No. Printed	Unc	No.	Issuing Bank	No. Printed	Unc
1911-A.	Boston		Current	1911-E.	Richmond		Current	1911-I.	Minneapolis		Current
1911-A*.	Boston		Current	1911-E*.	Richmond		Current	1911-I*.	Minneapolis		Current
1911-B.	New York		Current	1911-F.	Atlanta		Current	1911-J.	Kansas City		Current
1911-B*.	New York		Current	1911-F*.	Atlanta		Current	1911-J*.	Kansas City		Current
1911-C.	Philadelphia		Current	1911-G.	Chicago		Current	1911-K.	Dallas		Current
1911-C*.	Philadelphia		Current	1911-G*.	Chicago		Current	1911-K*.	Dallas		Current
1911-D.	Cleveland		Current	1911-H.	St. Louis		Current	1911-L.	San Francisco		Current
1911-D*.	Cleveland		Current	1911-H*.	St. Louis		Current	1911-L*.	San Francisco		Current

13. Series of 1981-A.

Signatures of Ortega and Regan.

No.	Issuing Bank	No. Printed	Unc	No.	Issuing Bank	No. Printed	Unc	No.	Issuing Bank	No. Printed	Unc
1912-A.	Boston		Current	1912-E.	Richmond		Current	1912-I.	Minneapolis		Current
1912-A*.	Boston		Current	1912-E*.	Richmond		Current	1912-I*.	Minneapolis		Current
1912-B.	New York		Current	1912-F.	Atlanta		Current	1912-J.	Kansas City		Current
1912-B*.	New York		Current	1912-F*.	Atlanta		Current	1912-J*.	Kansas City		Current
1912-C.	Philadelphia		Current	1912-G.	Chicago		Current	1912-K.	Dallas		Current
1912-C*.	Philadelphia		Current	1912-G*.	Chicago		Current	1912-K*.	Dallas		Current
1912-D.	Cleveland		Current	1912-H.	St. Louis		Current	1912-L.	San Francisco		Current
1912-D*.	Cleveland		Current	1912-H*.	St. Louis		Current	1912-L*.	San Francisco		Current

14. Series of 1985.

Signatures of Ortega and Baker.

No.	Issuing Bank	No. Printed	Unc	No.	Issuing Bank	No. Printed	Unc	No.	Issuing Bank	No. Printed	Unc
1913-A.	Boston		Current	1913-E.	Richmond		Current	1913-I.	Minneapolis		Current
1913-A*.	Boston		Current	1913-E*.	Richmond		Current	1913-I*.	Minneapolis		Current
1913-B.	New York		Current	1913-F.	Atlanta		Current	1913-J.	Kansas City		Current
1913-B*.	New York		Current	1913-F*.	Atlanta		Current	1913-J*.	Kansas City		Current
1913-C.	Philadelphia		Current	1913-G.	Chicago		Current	1913-K.	Dallas		Current
1913-C*.	Philadelphia		Current	1913-G*.	Chicago		Current	1913-K*.	Dallas		Current
1913-D.	Cleveland		Current	1913-H.	St. Louis		Current	1913-L.	San Francisco		Current
1913-D*.	Cleveland		Current	1913-H*.	St. Louis		Current	1913-L*.	San Francisco		Current

2 Dollar Notes

All issues are with the head of Thomas Jefferson

DESIGN NO. 214-a.
(Notes 1935-A - 1935-L Incl.)

Reverse of Design No. 214-a. Shortened version of John Trumbull's famous painting, "The Signing of the Declaration of Independence."

1. Series of 1976.
Signatures of Neff and Simon.

No.	Issuing Bank	No. Printed	Unc	No.	Issuing Bank	No. Printed	Unc
1935-A.	Boston	29,440,000	Current	1935-G.	Chicago	84,480,000	Current
1935-A*.	Boston	1,280,000	Current	1935-G*.	Chicago	1,280,000	Current
1935-B.	New York	67,200,000	Current	1935-H.	St. Louis	39,040,000	Current
1935-B*.	New York	2,560,000	Current	1935-H*.	St. Louis	1,280,000	Current
1935-C.	Philadelphia	33,280,000	Current	1935-I.	Minneapolis	23,680,000	Current
1935-C*.	Philadelphia	1,280,000	Current	1935-I*.	Minneapolis	640,000	Current
1935-D.	Cleveland	31,360,000	Current	1935-J.	Kansas City	24,960,000	Current
1935-D*.	Cleveland	1,280,000	Current	1935-J*.	Kansas City	640,000	Current
1935-E.	Richmond	56,960,000	Current	1935-K.	Dallas	41,600,000	Current
1935-E*.	Richmond	640,000	Current	1935-K*.	Dallas	1,280,000	Current
1935-F.	Atlanta	60,800,000	Current	1935-L.	San Francisco	82,560,000	Current
1935-F*.	Atlanta	1,280,000	Current	1935-L*.	San Francisco	1,920,000	Current

5 Dollar Notes

All issues are with the head of Abraham Lincoln

DESIGN NO. 215 (Notes 1950-A - 1951-L Incl.)

Reverse of Design No. 215. View of the Lincoln Memorial.

1. Series of 1928.
Signatures of Tate and Mellon.

No.	Issuing Bank	No. Printed	Unc	No.	Issuing Bank	No. Printed	Unc
1950-A.	Boston	8,025,300	45.00	1950-G.	Chicago	12,320,052	45.00
1950-B.	New York	14,701,884	40.00	1950-H.	St. Louis	4,675,200	50.00
1950-C.	Philadelphia	11,819,712	40.00	1950-I.	Minneapolis	4,284,300	65.00
1950-D.	Cleveland	9,049,500	42.50	1950-J.	Kansas City	4,480,800	55.00
1950-E.	Richmond	6,027,600	47.50	1950-K.	Dallas	8,137,824	40.00
1950-F.	Atlanta	10,964,400	42.50	1950-L.	San Francisco	9,792,000	47.50

2. Series of 1928-A.
Signatures of Woods and Mellon.

1951-A.	Boston	9,404,352	42.50	1951-G.	Chicago	37,882,176	40.00
1951-B.	New York	42,878,196	40.00	1951-H.	St. Louis	2,731,824	47.50
1951-C.	Philadelphia	10,806,012	40.00	1951-I.	Minneapolis	652,800	55.00
1951-D.	Cleveland	6,822,000	40.00	1951-J.	Kansas City	3,572,400	45.00
1951-E.	Richmond	2,409,900	40.00	1951-K	Dallas	2,564,400	52.50
1951-F.	Atlanta	3,537,600	45.00	1951-L	San Francisco	6,565,500	40.00

DESIGN NO. 216

(Notes 1952-A - 1960-L Incl.)

The obverse is as shown.
The reverse is similar to
Design No. 215.

3. Series of 1928-B.
Signatures of Woods and Mellon.

No.	Issuing Bank	No. Printed	Unc	No.	Issuing Bank	No. Printed	Unc
1952-A.	Boston	28,430,724	**40.00**	1952-G.	Chicago	17,157,036	**40.00**
1952-B.	New York	51,157,536	**37.50**	1952-H.	St. Louis	20,251,716	**42.50**
1952-C.	Philadelphia	25,698,396	**40.00**	1952-I.	Minneapolis	6,954,060	**55.00**
1952-D.	Cleveland	24,874,272	**40.00**	1952-J.	Kansas City	10,677,636	**45.00**
1952-E.	Richmond	15,151,932	**45.00**	1952-K.	Dallas	4,334,400	**45.00**
1952-F.	Atlanta	13,386,420	**45.00**	1952-L.	San Francisco	28,840,000	**40.00**

4. Series of 1928-C.
Signatures of Woods and Mills.

1953-D.	Cleveland	3,293,640	**Rare**	1953-L.	San Francisco	266,304	**Rare**
1953-F.	Atlanta	2,056,200	550.00				

5. Series of 1928-D.
Signatures of Woods and Woodin.

1954-F. Atlanta. This note is very rare. 1,281,600 1,100.00

6. Series of 1934.
Signatures of Julian and Morgenthau.

	A. Notes with a vivid, light green seal.				*B. Notes with a darker and duller blue green seal.*	
1955-A.	Boston	30,510,036	**40.00**	1956-A.	Boston	**37.50**
1955-B.	New York	47,888,760	**37.50**	1956-B.	New York	**35.00**
1955-C.	Philadelphia	47,327,760	**37.50**	1956-C.	Philadelphia	**35.00**
1955-D.	Cleveland	62,273,508	**34.50**	1956-D.	Cleveland	**32.00**
1955-E.	Richmond	62,128,452	**34.50**	1956-E.	Richmond	**32.00**
1955-F.	Atlanta	50,548,608	**37.50**	1956-F.	Atlanta	**35.00**
1955-G.	Chicago	31,299,156	**40.00**	1956-G.	Chicago	**37.50**
1955-H.	St. Louis	48,737,280	**37.50**	1956-H.	St. Louis	**35.00**
1955-I.	Minneapolis	16,795,392	**45.00**	1956-I.	Minneapolis	**42.50**
1955-J.	Kansas City	31,854,432	**42.50**	1956-J.	Kansas City	**40.00**
1955-K.	Dallas	33,332,208	**42.50**	1956-K.	Dallas	**40.00**
1955-L.	San Francisco	39,324,168	**40.00**	1956-L.	San Francisco	**37.50**

(The number of notes printed is the combined total for both light and dark seal notes.)

7. Series of 1934-A.
Signatures of Julian and Morgenthau.

1957-A.	Boston	23,231,568	**30.00**	1957-F.	Atlanta	22,811,916	**30.00**
1957-B.	New York	143,199,336	**30.00**	1957-G.	Chicago	88,376,376	**30.00**
1957-C.	Philadelphia	30,691,632	**30.00**	1957-H.	St. Louis	7,843,452	**32.50**
1957-D.	Cleveland	1,610,676	**35.00**	1957-L.	San Francisco	72,118,452	**30.00**
1957-E.	Richmond	6,555,168	**32.50**				

8. Series of 1934-B.
Signatures of Julian and Vinson.

1958-A.	Boston	3,457,800	**37.50**	1958-G.	Chicago	9,070,932	**32.50**
1958-B.	New York	14,099,580	**32.50**	1958-H.	St. Louis	4,307,712	**42.50**
1958-C.	Philadelphia	8,306,820	**32.50**	1958-I.	Minneapolis	2,482,500	**45.00**
1958-D.	Cleveland	11,348,184	**32.50**	1958-J.	Kansas City	73,800	**65.00**
1958-E.	Richmond	5,902,848	**32.50**	1958-L.	San Francisco	9,910,296	**42.50**
1958-F.	Atlanta	4,314,048	**37.50**				

9. Series of 1934-C.
Signatures of Julian and Snyder.

1959-A.	Boston	14,463,600	**25.00**	1959-G.	Chicago	60,598,812	**20.00**
1959-B.	New York	74,383,248	**20.00**	1959-H.	St. Louis	20,393,340	**30.00**
1959-C.	Philadelphia	22,879,212	**20.00**	1959-I.	Minneapolis	5,089,200	**32.50**
1959-D.	Cleveland	19,898,256	**20.00**	1959-J.	Kansas City	8,313,504	**30.00**
1959-E.	Richmond	23,800,524	**20.00**	1959-K.	Dallas	5,107,800	**35.00**
1959-F.	Atlanta	23,572,968	**20.00**	1959-L.	San Francisco	9,451,944	**20.00**

10. Series of 1934-D.
Signatures of Clark and Snyder.

No.	Issuing Bank	No. Printed	Unc	No.	Issuing Bank	No. Printed	Unc
1960-A	Boston	12,660,552	25.00	1960-G.	Chicago	36,601,680	25.00
1960-B.	New York	50,976,576	22.50	1960-H.	St. Louis	8,093,412	27.50
1960-C.	Philadelphia	12,106,740	25.00	1960-I.	Minneapolis	3,594,900	30.00
1960-D.	Cleveland	8,969,052	25.00	1960-J.	Kansas City	6,538,740	27.50
1960-E.	Richmond	13,333,032	25.00	1960-K.	Dallas	4,139,016	30.00
1960-F.	Atlanta	9,599,352	25.00	1960-L.	San Francisco	11,704,200	25.00

DESIGN NO. 217

(Notes 1961-A - 1966-L Incl.)

The obverse is as shown.
The reverse is similar to
Design No. 215.

11. Series of 1950.
Signatures of Clark and Snyder.

1961-A.	Boston	30,672,000	17.50	1961-G.	Chicago	85,104,000	17.50
1961-A*.	Boston	408,000	50.00	1961-G*.	Chicago	1,176,000	40.00
1961-B.	New York	106,768,000	17.50	1961-H.	St. Louis	36,864,000	22.50
1961-B*.	New York	1,464,000	35.00	1961-H*.	St. Louis	552,000	50.00
1961-C.	Philadelphia	44,784,000	17.50	1961-I.	Minneapolis	11,796,000	17.50
1961-C*.	Philadelphia	600,000	40.00	1961-I*.	Minneapolis	144,000	50.00
1961-D.	Cleveland	54,000,000	17.50	1961-J.	Kansas City	25,428,000	17.50
1961-D*.	Cleveland	744,000	40.00	1961-J*.	Kansas City	360,000	50.00
1961-E.	Richmond	47,088,000	17.50	1961-K.	Dallas	22,848,000	17.50
1961-E*.	Richmond	684,000	40.00	1961-K*.	Dallas	372,000	50.00
1961-F.	Atlanta	52,416,000	17.50	1961-L.	San Francisco	55,008,000	17.50
1961-F*.	Atlanta	696,000	40.00	1961-L*.	San Francisco	744,000	40.00

12. Series of 1950-A.
Signatures of Priest and Humphrey.

1962-A.	Boston	53,568,000	15.00	1962-G.	Chicago	129,296,000	15.00
1962-A*.	Boston	2,808,000	20.00	1962-G*.	Chicago	6,264,000	20.00
1962-B.	New York	186,472,000	15.00	1962-H.	St. Louis	54,936,000	15.00
1962-B*.	New York	9,216,000	20.00	1962-H*.	St. Louis	3,384,000	24.00
1962-C.	Philadelphia	69,616,000	15.00	1962-I.	Minneapolis	11,232,000	20.00
1962-C*.	Philadelphia	4,320,000	20.00	1962-I*.	Minneapolis	864,000	30.00
1962-D.	Cleveland	45,360,000	15.00	1962-J.	Kansas City	29,952,000	17.50
1962-D*.	Cleveland	2,376,000	20.00	1962-J*.	Kansas City	1,088,000	24.00
1962-E.	Richmond	76,672,000	15.00	1962-K.	Dallas	24,984,000	17.50
1962-E*.	Richmond	5,400,000	20.00	1962-K*.	Dallas	1,368,000	24.00
1962-F.	Atlanta	86,464,000	15.00	1962-L.	San Francisco	90,712,000	15.00
1962-F*.	Atlanta	5,040,000	20.00	1962-L*.	San Francisco	----	

13. Series of 1950-B.
Signatures of Priest and Anderson.

1963-A.	Boston	30,880,000	14.50	1963-G.	Chicago	104,320,000	13.50
1963-A*.	Boston	2,520,000	17.50	1963-G*.	Chicago	6,120,000	17.50
1963-B.	New York	85,960,000	13.50	1963-H.	St. Louis	25,840,000	17.50
1963-B*.	New York	4,680,000	17.50	1963-H*.	St. Louis	1,440,000	20.00
1963-C.	Philadelphia	43,560,000	13.50	1963-I.	Minneapolis	20,880,000	20.00
1963-C*.	Philadelphia	2,880,000	17.50	1963-I*.	Minneapolis	792,000	25.00
1963-D.	Cleveland	38,800,000	13.50	1963-J.	Kansas City	32,400,000	14.50
1963-D*.	Cleveland	2,880,000	17.50	1963-J*.	Kansas City	2,520,000	17.50
1963-E.	Richmond	52,920,000	13.50	1963-K.	Dallas	52,120,000	13.50
1963-E*.	Richmond	2,080,000	17.50	1963-K*.	Dallas	3,240,000	17.50
1963-F.	Atlanta	80,560,000	13.50	1963-L.	San Francisco	56,080,000	13.50
1963-F*.	Atlanta	3,960,000	17.50	1963-L*.	San Francisco	3,600,000	17.50

14. Series of 1950-C.
Signatures of Smith and Dillon.

No.	Issuing Bank	No. Printed	Unc	No.	Issuing Bank	No. Printed	Unc
1964-A.	Boston	20,880,000	13.50	1964-G.	Chicago	56,880,000	12.50
1964-A*.	Boston	720,000	20.00	1964-G*.	Chicago	3,240,000	17.50
1964-B.	New York	47,440,000	12.50	1964-H.	St. Louis	22,680,000	13.50
1964-B*.	New York	2,880,000	17.50	1964-H*.	St. Louis	720,000	20.00
1964-C.	Philadelphia	29,520,000	13.50	1964-I.	Minneapolis	12,960,000	17.50
1964-C*.	Philadelphia	1,800,000	17.50	1964-I*.	Minneapolis	720,000	20.00
1964-D.	Cleveland	33,840,000	13.50	1964-J.	Kansas City	24,760,000	13.50
1964-D*.	Cleveland	1,800,000	17.50	1964-J*.	Kansas City	1,800,000	17.50
1964-E.	Richmond	33,480,000	13.50	1964-K.	Dallas	3,960,000	22.50
1964-E*.	Richmond	2,160,000	17.50	1964-K*.	Dallas	360,000	30.00
1964-F.	Atlanta	54,360,000	12.50	1964-L.	San Francisco	25,920,000	13.50
1964-F*.	Atlanta	3,240,000	17.50	1964-L*.	San Francisco	1,440,000	17.50

15. Series of 1950-D.
Signatures of Granahan and Dillon.

1965-A.	Boston	25,200,000	12.50	1965-G.	Chicago	67,240,000	12.50
1965-A*.	Boston	1,080,000	17.50	1965-G*.	Chicago	3,600,000	17.50
1965-B.	New York	102,160,000	12.50	1965-H.	St. Louis	20,160,000	12.50
1965-B*.	New York	5,040,000	17.50	1965-H*.	St. Louis	720,000	20.00
1965-C.	Philadelphia	21,520,000	12.50	1965-I.	Minneapolis	7,920,000	17.50
1965-C*.	Philadelphia	1,080,000	17.50	1965-I*.	Minneapolis	360,000	30.00
1965-D.	Cleveland	23,400,000	12.50	1965-J.	Kansas City	11,160,000	15.00
1965-D*.	Cleveland	1,080,000	17.50	1965-J*.	Kansas City	720,000	20.00
1965-E.	Richmond	42,490,000	12.50	1965-K.	Dallas	7,200,000	17.50
1965-E*.	Richmond	1,080,000	17.50	1965-K*.	Dallas	360,000	30.00
1965-F.	Atlanta	35,200,000	12.50	1965-L.	San Francisco	53,280,000	12.50
1965-F*.	Atlanta	1,800,000	17.50	1965-L*.	San Francisco	3,600,000	17.50

16. Series of 1950-E.
Signatures of Granahan and Fowler.

1966-B.	New York	82,000,000	15.00	1966-G*.	Chicago	1,080,000	27.50
1966-B*.	New York	6,678,000	17.50	1966-L.	San Francisco	24,400,000	20.00
1966-G.	Chicago	14,760,000	25.00	1966-L*.	San Francisco	1,800,000	27.50

DESIGN NO. 217-A (Notes 1967-A - 1974-L Incl.)

Reverse of Design No. 217-A. *With motto "In God We Trust."*

17. Series of 1963.
Signatures of Granahan and Dillon.

1967-A.	Boston	4,480,000	16.00	1967-G.	Chicago	22,400,000	11.00
1967-A*.	Boston	640,000	20.00	1967-G*.	Chicago	3,200,000	17.50
1967-B.	New York	12,160,000	13.50	1967-H.	St. Louis	14,080,000	13.50
1967-B*.	New York	1,280,000	17.50	1967-H*.	St. Louis	1,920,000	17.50
1967-C.	Philadelphia	8,320,000	14.50	1967-J.	Kansas City	1,920,000	18.50
1967-C*.	Philadelphia	1,920,000	17.50	1967-J*.	Kansas City	640,000	20.00
1967-D.	Cleveland	10,240,000	11.00	1967-K.	Dallas	5,760,000	14.50
1967-D*.	Cleveland	1,920,000	17.50	1967-K*.	Dallas	1,920,000	17.50
1967-F.	Atlanta	17,920,000	11.00	1967-L.	San Francisco	18,560,000	11.00
1967-F*.	Atlanta	2,560,000	17.50	1967-L*.	San Francisco	1,920,000	17.50

18. Series of 1963-A.

Signatures of Granahan and Fowler.

No.	Issuing Bank	No. Printed	Unc	No.	Issuing Bank	No. Printed	Unc
1968-A.	Boston	77,440,000	10.00	1968-G.	Chicago	213,440,000	10.00
1968-A*.	Boston	5,760,000	12.50	1968-G*.	Chicago	16,640,000	12.50
1968-B.	New York	98,080,000	10.00	1968-H.	St. Louis	56,960,000	10.00
1968-B*.	New York	7,680,000	12.50	1968-H*.	St. Louis	5,120,000	12.50
1968-C.	Philadelphia	106,400,000	10.00	1968-I.	Minneapolis	32,640,000	12.50
1968-C*.	Philadelphia	10,240,000	12.50	1968-I*.	Minneapolis	3,200,000	15.00
1968-D.	Cleveland	83,840,000	10.00	1968-J.	Kansas City	55,040,000	10.00
1968-D*.	Cleveland	7,040,000	12.50	1968-J*.	Kansas City	5,760,000	12.50
1968-E.	Richmond	118,560,000	10.00	1968-K.	Dallas	64,000,000	10.00
1968-E*.	Richmond	10,880,000	12.50	1968-K*.	Dallas	3,840,000	15.00
1968-F.	Atlanta	117,920,000	10.00	1968-L.	San Francisco	128,900,000	10.00
1968-F*.	Atlanta	9,600,000	12.50	1968-L*.	San Francisco	12,153,000	12.50

19. Series of 1969.

Signatures of Elston and Kennedy. With new Treasury seal.

No.	Issuing Bank	No. Printed	Unc	No.	Issuing Bank	No. Printed	Unc
1969-A.	Boston	51,200,000	10.00	1969-G.	Chicago	125,600,000	10.00
1969-A*.	Boston	1,920,000	12.00	1969-G*.	Chicago	5,120,000	12.00
1969-B.	New York	198,560,000	10.00	1969-H.	St. Louis	27,520,000	10.00
1969-B*.	New York	8,960,000	12.00	1969-H*.	St. Louis	1,280,000	12.00
1969-C.	Philadelphia	69,120,000	10.00	1969-I.	Minneapolis	16,640,000	10.00
1969-C*.	Philadelphia	2,560,000	12.00	1969-I*.	Minneapolis	640,000	12.00
1969-D.	Cleveland	56,320,000	10.00	1969-J.	Kansas City	48,640,000	10.00
1969-D*.	Cleveland	2,560,000	12.00	1969-J*.	Kansas City	3,192,000	12.00
1969-E.	Richmond	84,480,000	10.00	1969-K.	Dallas	39,680,000	10.00
1969-E*.	Richmond	3,200,000	12.00	1969-K*.	Dallas	1,920,000	12.00
1969-F.	Atlanta	84,480,000	10.00	1969-L.	San Francisco	103,840,000	10.00
1969-F*.	Atlanta	3,840,000	12.00	1969-L*.	San Francisco	4,480,000	12.00

20. Series of 1969-A.

Signatures of Kabis and Connally.

No.	Issuing Bank	No. Printed	Unc	No.	Issuing Bank	No. Printed	Unc
1970-A.	Boston	23,040,000	10.00	1970-G.	Chicago	60,800,000	10.00
1970-A*.	Boston	1,280,000	12.00	1970-G*.	Chicago	1,920,000	12.00
1970-B.	New York	62,240,000	10.00	1970-H.	St. Louis	15,360,000	10.00
1970-B*.	New York	1,760,000	12.00	1970-H*.	St. Louis	640,000	13.00
1970-C.	Philadelphia	41,160,000	10.00	1970-I.	Minneapolis	8,960,000	10.00
1970-C*.	Philadelphia	1,920,000	12.00	1970-I*.	Minneapolis	----	
1970-D.	Cleveland	21,120,000	10.00	1970-J.	Kansas City	17,920,000	10.00
1970-D*.	Cleveland	640,000	13.00	1970-J*.	Kansas City	640,000	13.00
1970-E.	Richmond	37,920,000	10.00	1970-K.	Dallas	21,120,000	10.00
1970-E*.	Richmond	1,120,000	12.00	1970-K*.	Dallas	640,000	13.00
1970-F.	Atlanta	25,120,000	10.00	1970-L.	San Francisco	44,800,000	10.00
1970-F*.	Atlanta	480,000	15.00	1970-L*.	San Francisco	1,920,000	12.00

21. Series of 1969-B.

Signatures of Banuelos and Connally.

No.	Issuing Bank	No. Printed	Unc	No.	Issuing Bank	No. Printed	Unc
1971-A.	Boston	5,760,000	10.00	1971-G.	Chicago	27,040,000	10.00
1971-A*.	Boston	None printed		1971-G*.	Chicago	480,000	15.00
1971-B.	New York	34,560,000	10.00	1971-H.	St. Louis	5,120,000	10.00
1971-B*.	New York	634,000	13.00	1971-H*.	St. Louis	None Printed	
1971-C.	Philadelphia	5,120,000	10.00	1971-I.	Minneapolis	8,320,000	10.00
1971-C*.	Philadelphia	None printed		1971-I*.	Minneapolis	None Printed	
1971-D.	Cleveland	12,160,000	10.00	1971-J.	Kansas City	8,320,000	10.00
1971-D*.	Cleveland	None printed		1971-J*.	Kansas City	640,000	13.00
1971-E.	Richmond	15,360,000	10.00	1971-K.	Dallas	12,160,000	10.00
1971-E*.	Richmond	640,000	13.00	1971-K*.	Dallas	None Printed	
1971-F.	Atlanta	18,560,000	10.00	1971-L.	San Francisco	23,160,000	10.00
1971-F*.	Atlanta	640,000	13.00	1971-L*.	San Francisco	640,000	13.00

22. Series of 1969-C.

Signatures of Banuelos and Shultz.

No.	Issuing Bank	No. Printed	Unc	No.	Issuing Bank	No. Printed	Unc
1972-A.	Boston	50,720,000	10.00	1972-G.	Chicago	54,400,000	10.00
1972-A*.	Boston	1,920,000	12.00	1972-G*.	Chicago	None printed	
1972-B.	New York	120,000,000	10.00	1972-H.	St. Louis	37,760,000	10.00
1972-B*.	New York	2,400,000	12.00	1972-H*.	St. Louis	1,280,000	12.00
1972-C.	Philadelphia	53,760,000	10.00	1972-I.	Minneapolis	14,080,000	10.00
1972-C*.	Philadelphia	1,280,000	12.00	1972-I*.	Minneapolis	None printed	
1972-D.	Cleveland	43,680,000	10.00	1972-J.	Kansas City	41,120,000	10.00
1972-D*.	Cleveland	1,120,000	12.00	1972-J*.	Kansas City	1,920,000	12.00
1972-E.	Richmond	73,760,000	10.00	1972-K.	Dallas	41,120,000	10.00
1972-E*.	Richmond	640,000	13.00	1972-K*.	Dallas	1,920,000	12.00
1972-F.	Atlanta	81,440,000	10.00	1972-L.	San Francisco	80,800,000	10.00
1972-F*.	Atlanta	3,200,000	12.00	1972-L*.	San Francisco	3,680,000	12.00

23. Series of 1974.

Signatures of Neff and Simon.

No.	Issuing Bank	No. Printed	Unc	No.	Issuing Bank	No. Printed	Unc
1973-A.	Boston	58,240,000	Current	1973-G.	Chicago	95,520,000	Current
1973-A*.	Boston	1,408,000	Current	1973-G*.	Chicago	1,760,000	Current
1973-B.	New York	153,120,000	Current	1973-H.	St. Louis	64,800,000	Current
1973-B*.	New York	2,656,000	Current	1973-H*.	St. Louis	1,760,000	Current
1973-C.	Philadelphia	53,920,000	Current	1973-I.	Minneapolis	41,600,000	Current
1973-C*.	Philadelphia	3,040,000	Current	1973-I*.	Minneapolis	2,560,000	Current
1973-D.	Cleveland	78,080,000	Current	1973-J.	Kansas City	42,240,000	Current
1973-D*.	Cleveland	1,920,000	Current	1973-J*.	Kansas City	2,176,000	Current
1973-E.	Richmond	135,200,000	Current	1973-K.	Dallas	57,600,000	Current
1973-E*.	Richmond	1,760,000	Current	1973-K*.	Dallas	1,408,000	Current
1973-F.	Atlanta	127,520,000	Current	1973-L.	San Francisco	139,680,000	Current
1973-F*.	Atlanta	3,040,000	Current	1973-L*.	San Francisco	5,088,000	Current

24. Series of 1977.

Signatures of Morton and Blumenthal.

No.	Issuing Bank	No. Printed	Unc	No.	Issuing Bank	No. Printed	Unc
1974-A.	Boston	60,800,000	Current	1974-G.	Chicago	177,920,000	Current
1974-A*.	Boston	1,664,000	Current	1974-G*.	Chicago	2,816,000	Current
1974-B.	New York	183,040,000	Current	1974-H.	St. Louis	46,080,000	Current
1974-B*.	New York	3,072,000	Current	1974-H*.	St. Louis	128,000	Current
1974-C.	Philadelphia	78,720,000	Current	1974-I.	Minneapolis	21,760,000	Current
1974-C*.	Philadelphia	1,280,000	Current	1974-I*.	Minneapolis	None printed	Current
1974-D.	Cleveland	72,960,000	Current	1974-J.	Kansas City	78,080,000	Current
1974-D*.	Cleveland	1,152,000	Current	1974-J*.	Kansas City	1,408,000	Current
1974-E.	Richmond	110,720,000	Current	1974-K.	Dallas	60,800,000	Current
1974-E*.	Richmond	2,816,000	Current	1974-K*.	Dallas	2,408,000	Current
1974-F.	Atlanta	127,360,000	Current	1974-L.	San Francisco	135,040,000	Current
1974-F*.	Atlanta	1,920,000	Current	1974-L*.	San Francisco	2,432,000	Current

25. Series of 1977-A.

Signatures of Morton and Miller.

No.	Issuing Bank	Unc	No.	Issuing Bank	Unc
1975-A.	Boston	Current	1975-G.	Chicago	Current
1975-A*.	Boston	Current	1975-G*.	Chicago	Current
1975-B.	New York	Current	1975-H.	St. Louis	Current
1975-B*.	New York	Current	1975-H*.	St. Louis	Current
1975-C.	Philadelphia	Current	1975-I.	Minneapolis	Current
1975-C*.	Philadelphia	Current	1975-I*.	Minneapolis	Current
1975-D.	Cleveland	Current	1975-J.	Kansas City	Current
1975-D*.	Cleveland	Current	1975-J*.	Kansas City	Current
1975-E.	Richmond	Current	1975-K.	Dallas	Current
1975-E*.	Richmond	Current	1975-K*.	Dallas	Current
1975-F.	Atlanta	Current	1975-L.	San Francisco	Current
1975-F*.	Atlanta	Current	1975-L*.	San Francisco	Current

26. Series of 1981.

Signatures of Buchanan and Regan.

No.	Issuing Bank	Unc	No.	Issuing Bank	Unc
1976-A.	Boston	Current	1976-G.	Chicago	Current
1976-A*.	Boston	Current	1976-G*.	Chicago	Current
1976-B.	New York	Current	1976-H.	St. Louis	Current
1976-B*.	New York	Current	1976-H*.	St. Louis	Current
1976-C.	Philadelphia	Current	1976-I.	Minneapolis	Current
1976-C*.	Philadelphia	Current	1976-I*.	Minneapolis	Current
1976-D.	Cleveland	Current	1976-J.	Kansas City	Current
1976-D*.	Cleveland	Current	1976-J*.	Kansas City	Current
1976-E.	Richmond	Current	1976-K.	Dallas	Current
1976-E*.	Richmond	Current	1976-K*.	Dallas	Current
1976-F.	Atlanta	Current	1976-L.	San Francisco	Current
1976-F*.	Atlanta	Current	1976-L*.	San Francisco	Current

27. Series of 1981-A.

Signatures of Ortega and Regan.

No.	Issuing Bank	Unc	No.	Issuing Bank	Unc
1977-A.	Boston	Current	1977-G.	Chicago	Current
1977-A*.	Boston	Current	1977-G*.	Chicago	Current
1977-B.	New York	Current	1977-H.	St. Louis	Current
1977-B*.	New York	Current	1977-H*.	St. Louis	Current
1977-C.	Philadelphia	Current	1977-I.	Minneapolis	Current
1977-C*.	Philadelphia	Current	1977-I*.	Minneapolis	Current
1977-D.	Cleveland	Current	1977-J.	Kansas City	Current
1977-D*.	Cleveland	Current	1977-J*.	Kansas City	Current
1977-E.	Richmond	Current	1977-K.	Dallas	Current
1977-E*.	Richmond	Current	1977-K*.	Dallas	Current
1977-F.	Atlanta	Current	1977-L.	San Francisco	Current
1977-F*.	Atlanta	Current	1977-L*.	San Francisco	Current

28. Series of 1985.

Signatures of Ortega and Baker.

No.	Issuing Bank	Unc	No.	Issuing Bank	Unc
1978-A.	Boston	Current	1978-G.	Chicago	Current
1978-A*.	Boston	Current	1978-G*.	Chicago	Current
1978-B.	New York	Current	1978-H.	St. Louis	Current
1978-B*.	New York	Current	1978-H*.	St. Louis	Current
1978-C.	Philadelphia	Current	1978-I.	Minneapolis	Current
1978-C*.	Philadelphia	Current	1978-I*.	Minneapolis	Current
1978-D.	Cleveland	Current	1978-J.	Kansas City	Current
1978-D*.	Cleveland	Current	1978-J*.	Kansas City	Current
1978-E.	Richmond	Current	1978-K.	Dallas	Current
1978-E*.	Richmond	Current	1978-K*.	Dallas	Current
1978-F.	Atlanta	Current	1978-L.	San Francisco	Current
1978-F*.	Atlanta	Current	1978-L*.	San Francisco	Current

10 Dollar Notes

All issues are with the head of Alexander Hamilton

DESIGN NO. 218
(Notes 2000-A — 2001-L Incl.)

Reverse of Design No. 218.
View of the U.S. Treasury Building.

1. Series of 1928.

Signatures of Tate and Mellon.

No.	Issuing Bank	No. Printed	Unc	No.	Issuing Bank	No. Printed	Unc
2000-A.	Boston	9,804,552	50.00	2000-G.	Chicago	8,130,000	50.00
2000-B.	New York	11,295,796	50.00	2000-H.	St. Louis	4,124,100	60.00
2000-C.	Philadelphia	8,114,412	50.00	2000-I.	Minneapolis	3,874,440	65.00
2000-D.	Cleveland	7,570,680	50.00	2000-J.	Kansas City	3,620,400	60.00
2000-E.	Richmond	4,534,800	55.00	2000-K.	Dallas	4,855,500	60.00
2000-F.	Atlanta	6,807,720	55.00	2000-L.	San Francisco	7,086,900	50.00

2. Series of 1928-A.

Signatures of Woods and Mellon.

2001-A.	Boston	2,893,440	42.50	2001-G.	Chicago	8,715,000	40.00
2001-B.	New York	18,631,056	40.00	2001-H.	St. Louis	531,600	55.00
2001-C.	Philadelphia	2,710,680	42.50	2001-I.	Minneapolis	102,600	80.00
2001-D.	Cleveland	5,610,000	42.50	2001-J.	Kansas City	410,400	55.00
2001-E.	Richmond	552,300	55.00	2001-K.	Dallas	961,800	52.50
2001-F.	Atlanta	3,033,480	42.50	2001-L.	San Francisco	2,547,900	45.00

DESIGN NO. 219

(Notes 2002-A — 2009-L Incl.)

The obverse is as shown.
The reverse is similar to
Design No. 218.

3. Series of 1928-B.

Signatures of Woods and Mellon.

2002-A.	Boston	33,218,088	37.50	2002-G.	Chicago	38,035,000	35.00
2002-B.	New York	44,458,308	35.00	2002-H.	St. Louis	10,814,664	37.50
2002-C.	Philadelphia	22,689,216	37.50	2002-I.	Minneapolis	5,294,460	42.50
2002-D.	Cleveland	17,418,024	37.50	2002-J.	Kansas City	7,748,040	42.50
2002-E.	Richmond	12,714,504	37.50	2002-K.	Dallas	3,396,096	45.00
2002-F.	Atlanta	5,246,700	37.50	2002-L.	San Francisco	22,695,300	37.50

4. Series of 1928-C.

Signatures of Woods and Mills.

2003-B.	New York	2,902,678	175.00	2003-F.	Atlanta	688,380	Rare
2003-D.	Cleveland	4,230,428	400.00	2003-G.	Chicago	2,423,400	85.00
2003-E.	Richmond	304,800	Rare				

5. Series of 1934.

Signatures of Julian and Morgenthau.

A. Notes with a vivid, light green seal.

2004-A.	Boston	46,276,152	32.50	2004-G.	Chicago	69,962,064	30.00
2004-B.	New York	117,298,008	32.50	2004-H.	St. Louis	22,593,204	42.50
2004-C.	Philadelphia	34,770,768	35.00	2004-I.	Minneapolis	16,840,980	45.00
2004-D.	Cleveland	28,764,108	40.00	2004-J.	Kansas City	22,627,824	45.00
2004-E.	Richmond	16,437,252	40.00	2004-K.	Dallas	21,403,488	40.00
2004-F.	Atlanta	20,656,872	42.50	2004-L.	San Francisco	37,402,308	32.50

The number of notes printed is the combined total for both light and dark seal notes.
B. Notes with a darker and duller blue green seal.

No.	Issuing Bank	Unc	No.	Issuing Bank	Unc
2005-A.	Boston	30.00	2005-G.	Chicago	30.00
2005-B.	New York	30.00	2005-H.	St. Louis	30.00
2005-C.	Philadelphia	32.50	2005-I.	Minneapolis	40.00
2005-D.	Cleveland	32.50	2005-J.	Kansas City	35.00
2005-E.	Richmond	32.50	2005-K.	Dallas	35.00
2005-F.	Atlanta	40.00	2005-L.	San Francisco	30.00

6. Series of 1934-A.
Signatures of Julian and Morgenthau.

2006-A.	Boston	104,540,088	25.00	2006-G.	Chicago	177,285,960	25.00
2006-B.	New York	281,940,996	25.00	2006-H.	St. Louis	50,694,312	45.00
2006-C.	Philadelphia	95,338,032	25.00	2006-I.	Minneapolis	16,340,016	40.00
2006-D.	Cleveland	93,332,004	30.00	2006-J.	Kansas City	31,069,978	30.00
2006-E.	Richmond	101,037,912	32.50	2006-K.	Dallas	28,263,156	32.50
2006-F.	Atlanta	85,478,160	32.50	2006-L.	San Francisco	125,537,592	30.00

7. Series of 1934-B.
Signatures of Julian and Vinson.

2007-A.	Boston	3,999,600	35.00	2007-G.	Chicago	18,130,836	30.00
2007-B.	New York	34,815,948	27.50	2007-H.	St. Louis	6,849,348	37.50
2007-C.	Philadelphia	10,339,020	30.00	2007-I.	Minneapolis	2,254,800	40.00
2007-D.	Cleveland	1,394,700	35.00	2007-J.	Kansas City	3,835,764	40.00
2007-E.	Richmond	4,018,272	35.00	2007-K.	Dallas	3,085,200	37.50
2007-F.	Atlanta	6,746,076	35.00	2007-L.	San Francisco	9,076,800	30.00

8. Series of 1934-C.
Signatures of Julian and Snyder.

2008-A.	Boston	42,431,404	25.00	2008-G.	Chicago	105,875,412	22.50
2008-B.	New York	115,675,644	22.50	2008-H.	St. Louis	36,541,404	30.00
2008-C.	Philadelphia	46,874,760	25.00	2008-I.	Minneapolis	11,944,848	40.00
2008-D	Cleveland	332,400	22.50	2008-J.	Kansas City	20,874,072	30.00
2008-E.	Richmond	37,422,600	27.50	2008-K.	Dallas	25,642,620	30.00
2008-F.	Atlanta	44,838,264	27.50	2008-L.	San Francisco	49,164,480	25.00

9. Series of 1934-D.
Signatures of Clark and Snyder.

2009-A.	Boston	19,917,900	27.50	2009-G.	Chicago	55,943,844	22.50
2009-B.	New York	64,067,904	22.50	2009-H.	St. Louis	15,828,048	30.00
2009-C.	Philadelphia	18,432,000	25.00	2009-I.	Minneapolis	5,237,220	40.00
2009-D.	Cleveland	20.291,316	25.00	2009-J.	Kansas City	7,992,000	35.00
2009-E.	Richmond	18,090,312	27.50	2009-K.	Dallas	7,178,196	35.00
2009-F.	Atlanta	17,064,816	27.50	2009-L.	San Francisco	23,956,584	22.50

DESIGN NO. 220.

(Notes 2010-A — 2015-L Incl.)

The obverse is as shown. The reverse is similar to Design No. 218.

10. Series of 1950.
Signatures of Clark and Snyder.

No.	Issuing Bank	No. Printed	Unc	No.	Issuing Bank	No. Printed	Unc
2010-A.	Boston	70,992,000	22.50	2010-G.	Chicago	161,056,000	21.00
2010-A*.	Boston	1,008,000	27.50	2010-G*.	Chicago	2,088,000	26.50
2010-B.	New York	218,576,000	21.00	2010-H.	St. Louis	47,808,000	27.50
2010-B*.	New York	2,568,000	26.50	2010-H*.	St. Louis	648,000	30.00
2010-C.	Philadelphia	76,320,000	22.50	2010-I.	Minneapolis	18,864,000	30.00
2010-C*.	Philadelphia	1,008,000	27.50	2010-I*.	Minneapolis	252,000	35.00
2010-D.	Cleveland	76,032,000	22.50	2010-J.	Kansas City	36,332,000	27.50
2010-D*.	Cleveland	1,008,000	27.50	2010-J*.	Kansas City	456,000	32.50
2010-E.	Richmond	61,776,000	25.00	2010-K.	Dallas	33,264,000	27.50
2010-E*.	Richmond	876,000	30.00	2010-K*.	Dallas	480,000	32.50
2010-F.	Atlanta	63,792,000	22.50	2010-L.	San Francisco	76,896,000	21.00
2010-F*.	Atlanta	864,000	30.00	2010-L*.	San Francisco	1,152,000	27.50

11. Series of 1950-A.
Signatures of Priest and Humphrey.

2011-A.	Boston	104,248,000	18.00	2011-G.	Chicago	235,064,000	18.00
2011-A*.	Boston	5,112,000	25.00	2011-G*.	Chicago	11,160,000	25.00
2011-B.	New York	356,664,000	18.00	2011-H.	St. Louis	46,512,000	27.50
2011-B*.	New York	16,992,000	25.00	2011-H*.	St. Louis	2,880,000	32.50
2011-C.	Philadelphia	71,920,000	21.00	2011-I.	Minneapolis	8,136,000	27.50
2011-C*.	Philadelphia	3,672,000	25.00	2011-I*.	Minneapolis	432,000	35.00
2011-D.	Cleveland	75,088,000	21.00	2011-J.	Kansas City	25,488,000	25.00
2011-D*.	Cleveland	3,672,000	25.00	2011-J*.	Kansas City	2,304,000	32.50
2011-E.	Richmond	82,144,000	21.00	2011-K.	Dallas	21,816,000	25.00
2011-E*.	Richmond	4,392,000	25.00	2011-K*.	Dallas	1,584,000	30.00
2011-F.	Atlanta	73,288,000	21.00	2011-L.	San Francisco	101,584,000	18.00
2011-F*.	Atlanta	3,816,000	25.00	2011-L*.	San Francisco	6,408,000	25.00

12. Series of 1950-B.
Signatures of Priest and Anderson.

2012-A.	Boston	49,240,000	17.50	2012-G.	Chicago	165,080,000	17.50
2012-A*.	Boston	2,880,000	22.50	2012-G*.	Chicago	6,480,000	22.50
2012-B.	New York	170,840,000	17.50	2012-H.	St. Louis	33,040,000	17.50
2012-B*.	New York	8,280,000	22.50	2012-H*.	St. Louis	1,800,000	22.50
2012-C.	Philadelphia	66,880,000	17.50	2012-I.	Minneapolis	13,320,000	22.50
2012-C*.	Philadelphia	3,240,000	22.50	2012-I*.	Minneapolis	720,000	27.50
2012-D.	Cleveland	55,360,000	17.50	2012-J.	Kansas City	33,480,000	17.50
2012-D*.	Cleveland	2,880,000	22.50	2012-J*.	Kansas City	2,520,000	22.50
2012-E.	Richmond	51,120,000	17.50	2012-K.	Dallas	26,280,000	18.50
2012-E*.	Richmond	2,880,000	22.50	2012-K*.	Dallas	1,440,000	22.50
2012-F.	Atlanta	66,520,000	17.50	2012-L.	San Francisco	55,000,000	17.50
2012-F*.	Atlanta	2,880,000	22.50	2012-L*.	San Francisco	2,880,000	22.50

13. Series of 1950-C.
Signatures of Smith and Dillon.

2013-A.	Boston	51,120,000	17.50	2013-G.	Chicago	69,400,000	17.50
2013-A*.	Boston	2,160,000	22.50	2013-G*.	Chicago	3,600,000	22.50
2013-B.	New York	126,520,000	17.50	2013-H.	St. Louis	23,040,000	18.50
2013-B*.	New York	6,840,000	22.50	2013-H*.	St. Louis	1,080,000	22.50
2013-C.	Philadelphia	25,200,000	18.50	2013-I.	Minneapolis	9,000,000	22.50
2013-C*.	Philadelphia	720,000	27.50	2013-I*.	Minneapolis	720,000	27.50
2013-D.	Cleveland	33,120,000	18.50	2013-J.	Kansas City	23,320,000	18.50
2013-D*.	Cleveland	1,800,000	22.50	2013-J*.	Kansas City	800,000	27.50
2013-E.	Richmond	45,640,000	17.50	2013-K.	Dallas	17,640,000	18.50
2013-E*.	Richmond	1,800,000	22.50	2013-K*.	Dallas	720,000	27.50
2013-F.	Atlanta	38,880,000	17.50	2013-L.	San Francisco	35,640,000	17.50
2013-F*.	Atlanta	1,800,000	22.50	2013-L*.	San Francisco	1,800,000	22.50

14. Series of 1950-D.
Signatures of Granahan and Dillon.

No.	Issuing Bank	No. Printed	Unc
2014-A.	Boston	38,800,000	17.50
2014-A*.	Boston	1,800,000	22.50
2014-B.	New York	150,320,000	17.50
2014-B*.	New York	6,840,000	22.50
2014-C.	Philadelphia	19,080,000	17.50
2014-C*.	Philadelphia	1,080,000	22.50
2014-D.	Cleveland	24,120,000	17.50
2014-D*.	Cleveland	360,000	30.00
2014-E.	Richmond	33,840,000	17.50
2014-E*.	Richmond	720,000	27.50
2014-F.	Atlanta	36,000,000	17.50
2014-F*.	Atlanta	1,440,000	22.50
2014-G.	Chicago	115,480,000	17.50
2014-G*.	Chicago	5,040,000	22.50
2014-H.	St. Louis	10,440,000	18.50
2014-H*.	St. Louis	720,000	27.50
2014-J.	Kansas City	15,480,000	17.50
2014-J*.	Kansas City	1,080,000	22.50
2014-K.	Dallas	18,280,000	17.50
2014-K*.	Dallas	800,000	27.50
2014-L.	San Francisco	62,560,000	17.50
2014-L*.	San Francisco	3,600,000	22.50

15. Series of 1950-E.
Signatures of Granahan and Fowler.

2015-B.	New York	12,600,000	20.00
2015-B*.	New York	2,621,000	22.50
2015-G.	Chicago	65,080,000	20.00
2015-G*.	Chicago	4,320,000	22.50
2015-L.	San Francisco	17,280,000	22.50
2015-L*.	San Francisco	720,000	27.50

DESIGN NO. 221
(Notes 2016-A — 2023-L Incl.)

Reverse of Design No. 221.
With motto "In God We Trust."

16. Series of 1963.
Signatures of Granahan and Dillon.

2016-A.	Boston	5,760,000	22.50
2016-B.	New York	24,960,000	20.00
2016-C.	Philadelphia	6,400,000	20.00
2016-D.	Cleveland	7,040,000	20.00
2016-E.	Richmond	4,480,000	22.50
2016-F.	Atlanta	10,880,000	20.00
2016-G.	Chicago	35,200,000	20.00
2016-H.	St. Louis	13,440,000	22.50
2016-J.	Kansas City	3,840,000	25.00
2016-K.	Dallas	5,120,000	20.00
2016-L.	San Francisco	14,080,000	20.00

17. Series of 1963-A.
Signatures of Granahan and Fowler.

2017-A.	Boston	131,360,000	17.50
2017-A*.	Boston	6,400,000	18.50
2017-B.	New York	199,360,000	17.50
2017-B*.	New York	9,600,000	18.50
2017-C.	Philadelphia	100,000,000	17.50
2017-C*.	Philadelphia	4,480,000	18.50
2017-D.	Cleveland	72,960,000	17.50
2017-D*.	Cleveland	3,840,000	18.50
2017-E.	Richmond	114,720,000	17.50
2017-E*.	Richmond	5,120,000	18.50
2017-F.	Atlanta	80,000,000	17.50
2017-F*.	Atlanta	3,840,000	18.50
2017-G.	Chicago	195,520,000	17.50
2017-G*.	Chicago	9,600,000	18.50
2017-H.	St. Louis	43,520,000	17.50
2017-H*.	St. Louis	1,920,000	18.50
2017-I.	Minneapolis	16,640,000	20.00
2017-I*.	Minneapolis	640,000	23.50
2017-J.	Kansas City	31,360,000	17.50
2017-J*.	Kansas City	1,920,000	18.50
2017-K.	Dallas	51,200,000	17.50
2017-K*.	Dallas	1,920,000	18.50
2017-L.	San Francisco	87,200,000	17.50
2017-L*.	San Francisco	5,120,000	18.50

18. Series of 1969.

Signatures of Elston and Kennedy. With new Treasury seal.

No.	Issuing Bank	No. Printed	Unc	No.	Issuing Bank	No. Printed	Unc
2018-A.	Boston	74,880,000	**17.50**	**2018-G.**	Chicago	142,240,000	**17.50**
2018-A*.	Boston	2,560,000	**18.50**	**2018-G*.**	Chicago	6,400,000	**18.50**
2018-B.	New York	247,360,000	**17.50**	**2018-H.**	St. Louis	22,400,000	**17.50**
2018-B*.	New York	10,240,000	**18.50**	**2018-H*.**	St. Louis	640,000	**20.00**
2018-C.	Philadelphia	56,960,000	**17.50**	**2018-I.**	Minneapolis	12,800,000	**17.50**
2018-C*.	Philadelphia	2,560,000	**18.50**	**2018-I*.**	Minneapolis	1,280,000	**18.50**
2018-D.	Cleveland	57,600,000	**17.50**	**2018-J.**	Kansas City	31,360,000	**17.50**
2018-D*.	Cleveland	2,560,000	**18.50**	**2018-J*.**	Kansas City	1,280,000	**18.50**
2018-E.	Richmond	56,960,000	**17.50**	**2018-K.**	Dallas	30,080,000	**17.50**
2018-E*.	Richmond	2,560,000	**18.50**	**2018-K*.**	Dallas	1,280,000	**18.50**
2018-F.	Atlanta	53,760,000	**17.50**	**2018-L.**	San Francisco	56,320,000	**17.50**
2018-F*.	Atlanta	2,560,000	**18.50**	**2018-L*.**	San Francisco	3,185,000	**18.50**

19. Series of 1969-A.

Signatures of Kabis and Connally.

2019-A.	Boston	41,120,000	**17.00**	**2019-G.**	Chicago	80,160,000	**17.00**
2019-A*.	Boston	1,920,000	**18.50**	**2019-G*.**	Chicago	3,560,000	**18.50**
2019-B.	New York	111,840,000	**17.00**	**2019-H.**	St. Louis	15,360,000	**17.00**
2019-B*.	New York	3,840,000	**18.50**	**2019-H*.**	St. Louis	640,000	**20.00**
2019-C.	Philadelphia	24,320,000	**17.00**	**2019-I.**	Minneapolis	8,320,000	**17.00**
2019-C*.	Philadelphia	1,920,000	**18.50**	**2019-I*.**	Minneapolis	None printed	
2019-D.	Cleveland	23,680,000	**17.00**	**2019-J.**	Kansas City	10,880,000	**17.00**
2019-D*.	Cleveland	1,276,000	**18.50**	**2019-J*.**	Kansas City	None printed	
2019-E.	Richmond	25,600,000	**17.00**	**2019-K.**	Dallas	20,480,000	**17.00**
2019-E*.	Richmond	640,000	**20.00**	**2019-K*.**	Dallas	640,000	**20.00**
2019-F.	Atlanta	20,480,000	**17.00**	**2019-L.**	San Francisco	27,520,000	**17.00**
2019-F*.	Atlanta	640,000	**20.00**	**2019-L*.**	San Francisco	1,280,000	**18.50**

20. Series of 1969-B.

Signatures of Banuelos and Connally.

2020-A.	Boston	16,640,000	**17.00**	**2020-G.**	Chicago	32,640,000	**17.00**
2020-A*.	Boston	None printed		**2020-G*.**	Chicago	1,268,000	**18.50**
2020-B.	New York	60,320,000	**17.00**	**2020-H.**	St. Louis	8,960,000	**17.00**
2020-B*.	New York	1,920,000	**18.50**	**2020-H*.**	St. Louis	1,280,000	**18.50**
2020-C.	Philadelphia	16,000,000	**17.00**	**2020-I.**	Minneapolis	3,200,000	**17.00**
2020-C*.	Philadelphia	None printed		**2020-I*.**	Minneapolis	None printed	
2020-D.	Cleveland	12,800,000	**17.00**	**2020-J.**	Kansas City	5,120,000	**17.00**
2020-D*.	Cleveland	None printed		**2020-J*.**	Kansas City	640,000	**20.00**
2020-E.	Richmond	12,160,000	**17.00**	**2020-K.**	Dallas	5,760,000	**17.00**
2020-E*.	Richmond	640,000	**20.00**	**2020-K*.**	Dallas	None printed	
2020-F.	Atlanta	13,440,000	**17.00**	**2020-L.**	San Francisco	23,840,000	**17.00**
2020-F*.	Atlanta	640,000	**20.00**	**2020-L*.**	San Francisco	640,000	**20.00**

21. Series of 1969-C.

Signatures of Banuelos and Shultz.

2021-A.	Boston	44,800,000	**Current**	**2021-G.**	Chicago	55,200,000	**Current**
2021-A*.	Boston	640,000	**Current**	**2021-G*.**	Chicago	880,000	**Current**
2021-B.	New York	203,200,000	**Current**	**2021-H.**	St. Louis	29,800,000	**Current**
2021-B*.	New York	7,040,000	**Current**	**2021-H*.**	St. Louis	1,280,000	**Current**
2021-C.	Philadelphia	69,920,000	**Current**	**2021-I.**	Minneapolis	11,520,000	**Current**
2021-C*.	Philadelphia	1,280,000	**Current**	**2021-I*.**	Minneapolis	640,000	**Current**
2021-D.	Cleveland	46,880,000	**Current**	**2021-J.**	Kansas City	23,040,000	**Current**
2021-D*.	Cleveland	2,400,000	**Current**	**2021-J*.**	Kansas City	640,000	**Current**
2021-E.	Richmond	45,600,000	**Current**	**2021-K.**	Dallas	24,960,000	**Current**
2021-E*.	Richmond	1,120,000	**Current**	**2021-K*.**	Dallas	640,000	**Current**
2021-F.	Atlanta	46,240,000	**Current**	**2021-L.**	San Francisco	56,960,000	**Current**
2021-F*.	Atlanta	1,920,000	**Current**	**2021-L*.**	San Francisco	640,000	**Current**

22. Series of 1974.

Signatures of Neff and Simon.

2022-A.	Boston	104,480,000	**Current**	**2022-G.**	Chicago	104,320,000	**Current**
2022-A*.	Boston	1,888,000	**Current**	**2022-G*.**	Chicago	4,352,000	**Current**
2022-B.	New York	239,040,000	**Current**	**2022-H.**	St. Louis	46,240,000	**Current**
2022-B*.	New York	4,192,000	**Current**	**2022-H*.**	St. Louis	1,120,000	**Current**
2022-C.	Philadelphia	69,280,000	**Current**	**2022-I.**	Minneapolis	27,520,000	**Current**
2022-C*.	Philadelphia	2,400,000	**Current**	**2022-I*.**	Minneapolis	1,024,000	**Current**
2022-D.	Cleveland	82,080,000	**Current**	**2022-J.**	Kansas City	24,320,000	**Current**
2022-D*.	Cleveland	1,760,000	**Current**	**2022-J*.**	Kansas City	640,000	**Current**
2022-E.	Richmond	105,760,000	**Current**	**2022-K.**	Dallas	39,840,000	**Current**
2022-E*.	Richmond	3,040,000	**Current**	**2022-K*.**	Dallas	1,760,000	**Current**
2022-F.	Atlanta	75,520,000	**Current**	**2022-L.**	San Francisco	70,560,000	**Current**
2022-F*.	Atlanta	3,200,000	**Current**	**2022-L*.**	San Francisco	1,760,000	**Current**

23. Series of 1977.
Signatures of Morton and Blumenthal.

No.	Issuing Bank	No. Printed	Unc	No.	Issuing Bank	No. Printed	Unc
2023-A.	Boston	96,640,000	Current	2023-G.	Chicago	174,720,000	Current
2023-A*.	Boston	2,688,000	Current	2023-G*.	Chicago	3,968,000	Current
2023-B.	New York	277,120,000	Current	2023-H.	St. Louis	46,720,000	Current
2023-B*.	New York	7,296,000	Current	2023-H*.	St. Louis	896,000	Current
2023-C.	Philadelphia	83,200,000	Current	2023-I.	Minneapolis	10,240,000	Current
2023-C*.	Philadelphia	896,000	Current	2023-I*.	Minneapolis	256,000	Current
2023-D.	Cleveland	83,200,000	Current	2023-J.	Kansas City	50,560,000	Current
2023-D*.	Cleveland	768,000	Current	2023-J*.	Kansas City	1,024,000	Current
2023-E.	Richmond	71,040,000	Current	2023-K.	Dallas	53,760,000	Current
2023-E*.	Richmond	1,920,000	Current	2023-K*.	Dallas	640,000	Current
2023-F.	Atlanta	88,960,000	Current	2023-L.	San Francisco	73,600,000	Current
2023-F*.	Atlanta	1,536,000	Current	2023-L*.	San Francisco	1,792,000	Current

24. Series of 1977-A.
Signatures of Morton and Miller.

2024-A.	Boston		Current	2024-G.	Chicago		Current
2024-A*.	Boston		Current	2024-G*.	Chicago		Current
2024-B.	New York		Current	2024-H.	St. Louis		Current
2024-B*.	New York		Current	2024-H*.	St. Louis		Current
2024-C.	Philadelphia		Current	2024-I.	Minneapolis		Current
2024-C*.	Philadelphia		Current	2024-I*.	Minneapolis		Current
2024-D.	Cleveland		Current	2024-J.	Kansas City		Current
2024-D*.	Cleveland		Current	2024-J*.	Kansas City		Current
2024-E.	Richmond		Current	2024-K.	Dallas		Current
2024-E*.	Richmond		Current	2024-K*.	Dallas		Current
2024-F.	Atlanta		Current	2024-L.	San Francisco		Current
2024-F*.	Atlanta		Current	2024-L*.	San Francisco		Current

25. Series of 1981.
Signatures of Buchanan and Regan.

2025-A.	Boston		Current	2025-G.	Chicago		Current
2025-A*.	Boston		Current	2025-G*.	Chicago		Current
2025-B.	New York		Current	2025-H.	St. Louis		Current
2025-B*.	New York		Current	2025-H*.	St. Louis		Current
2025-C.	Philadelphia		Current	2025-I.	Minneapolis		Current
2025-C*.	Philadelphia		Current	2025-I*.	Minneapolis		Current
2025-D.	Cleveland		Current	2025-J.	Kansas City		Current
2025-D*.	Cleveland		Current	2025-J*.	Kansas City		Current
2025-E.	Richmond		Current	2025-K.	Dallas		Current
2025-E*.	Richmond		Current	2025-K*.	Dallas		Current
2025-F.	Atlanta		Current	2025-L.	San Francisco		Current
2025-F*.	Atlanta		Current	2025-L*.	San Francisco		Current

26. Series of 1981-A.
Signatures of Ortega and Regan.

2026-A.	Boston		Current	2026-G.	Chicago		Current
2026-A*.	Boston		Current	2026-G*.	Chicago		Current
2026-B.	New York		Current	2026-H.	St. Louis		Current
2026-B*.	New York		Current	2026-H*.	St. Louis		Current
2026-C.	Philadelphia		Current	2026-I.	Minneapolis		Current
2026-C*.	Philadelphia		Current	2026-I*.	Minneapolis		Current
2026-D	Cleveland		Current	2026-J.	Kansas City		Current
2026-D*.	Cleveland		Current	2026-J*.	Kansas City		Current
2026-E.	Richmond		Current	2026-K.	Dallas		Current
2026-E*.	Richmond		Current	2026-K*.	Dallas		Current
2026-F.	Atlanta		Current	2026-L.	San Francisco		Current
2026-F*.	Atlanta		Current	2026-L*.	San Francisco		Current

27. Series of 1985.
Signatures of Ortega and Baker.

2027-A.	Boston		Current	2027-G.	Chicago		Current
2027-A*.	Boston		Current	2027-G*.	Chicago		Current
2027-B.	New York		Current	2027-H.	St. Louis		Current
2027-B*.	New York		Current	2027-H*.	St. Louis		Current
2027-C.	Philadelphia		Current	2027-I.	Minneapolis		Current
2027-C*.	Philadelphia		Current	2027-I*.	Minneapolis		Current
2027-D.	Cleveland		Current	2027-J.	Kansas City		Current
2027-D*.	Cleveland		Current	2027-J*.	Kansas City		Current
2027-E.	Richmond		Current	2027-K.	Dallas		Current
2027-E*.	Richmond		Current	2027-K*.	Dallas		Current
2027-F.	Atlanta		Current	2027-L.	San Francisco		Current
2027-F*.	Atlanta		Current	2027-L*.	San Francisco		Current

20 Dollar Notes

All issues are with the head of Andrew Jackson

DESIGN NO. 222
(Notes 2050-A — 2051-K Incl.)

Reverse of Design No. 222. View of the White House.

1. Series of 1928.

Signatures of Tate and Mellon.

No.	Issuing Bank	No. Printed	Unc	No.	Issuing Bank	No. Printed	Unc
2050-A.	Boston	3,790,880	**60.00**	**2050-G.**	Chicago	10,891,740	**55.00**
2050-B.	New York	12,797,200	**55.00**	**2050-H.**	St. Louis	2,523,300	**70.00**
2050-C.	Philadelphia	3,797,200	**60.00**	**2050-I.**	Minneapolis	2,633,100	**80.00**
2050-D.	Cleveland	10,626,900	**65.00**	**2050-J.**	Kansas City	2,584,500	**70.00**
2050-E.	Richmond	4,119,600	**80.00**	**2050-K.**	Dallas	1,568,500	**65.00**
2050-F.	Atlanta	3,842,388	**70.00**	**2050-L.**	San Francisco	8,404,800	**55.00**

2. Series of 1928-A.

Signatures of Woods and Mellon.

2051-A.	Boston	1,293,900	**65.00**	**2051-F.**	Atlanta	1,442,400	**70.00**
2051-B.	New York	1,055,800	**60.00**	**2051-G.**	Chicago	822,000	**55.00**
2051-C.	Philadelphia	1,717,200	**55.00**	**2051-H.**	St. Louis	573,300	**65.00**
2051-D.	Cleveland	625,200	**60.00**	**2051-J.**	Kansas City	113,900	**65.00**
2051-E.	Richmond	1,534,500	**70.00**	**2051-K.**	Dallas	1,032,000	**70.00**

DESIGN NO. 223

(Notes 2052-A — 2056-L Incl.)

The obverse is as shown. The reverse is similar to Design No. 222.

3. Series of 1928-B.

Signatures of Woods and Mellon.

2052-A.	Boston	7,749,636	**55.00**	**2052-G.**	Chicago	17,220,276	**52.50**
2052-B.	New York	19,448,436	**52.50**	**2052-H.**	St. Louis	3,834,600	**65.00**
2052-C.	Philadelphia	8,095,548	**52.50**	**2052-I.**	Minneapolis	3,298,920	**65.00**
2052-D.	Cleveland	11,684,196	**52.50**	**2952-J.**	Kansas City	4,941,252	**65.00**
2052-E.	Richmond	4,413,900	**60.00**	**2052-K.**	Dallas	2,406,060	**65.00**
2052-F.	Atlanta	2,390,240	**65.00**	**2052-L.**	San Francisco	9,689,124	**55.00**

4. Series of 1928-C.

Signatures of Woods and Mills.

2053-G.	Chicago	3,363,300	225.00	**2053-L.**	San Francisco	1,420,200	300.00

5. Series of 1934.

Signatures of Julian and Morgenthau.

As on the 5 and 10 Dollar notes, there are two distinct shades of green seals in this series, the light, vivid green and the darker, duller blue green. The values, however, are about the same for the 20 Dollar notes.

2054-A.	Boston	37,673,068	**47.50**	**2054-G.**	Chicago	20,777,832	**45.00**
2054-B.	New York	27,573,264	**45.00**	**2054-H.**	St. Louis	27,174,552	**55.00**
2054-C.	Philadelphia	53,209,968	**45.00**	**2054-I.**	Minneapolis	16,795,116	**55.00**
2054-D.	Cleveland	48,301,416	**45.00**	**2054-J.**	Kansas City	28,865,304	**50.00**
2054-E.	Richmond	36,259,224	**45.00**	**2054-K.**	Dallas	20,852,160	**50.00**
2054-F.	Atlanta	41,547,660	**45.00**	**2054-L.**	San Francisco	32,203,956	**45.00**

6. Series of 1934-A.

Signatures of Julian and Morgenthau.

2055-A.	Boston	3,302,416	**55.00**	**2055-G.**	Chicago	91,141,452	**50.00**
2055-B.	New York	102,555,538	**52.50**	**2055-H.**	St. Louis	3,701,568	**60.00**
2055-C.	Philadelphia	3,371,316	**50.00**	**2055-I.**	Minneapolis	1,162,500	**65.00**
2055-D.	Cleveland	23,475,108	**52.50**	**2055-J.**	Kansas City	3,221,184	**55.00**
2055-E.	Richmond	46,816,224	**52.50**	**2055-K.**	Dallas	2,531,700	**52.50**
2055-F.	Atlanta	6,756,816	**52.50**	**2055-L.**	San Francisco	94,454,112	**50.00**

7. Series of 1934-B.

Signatures of Julian and Vinson.

No.	Issuing Bank	No. Printed	Unc	No.	Issuing Bank	No. Printed	Unc
2056-A.	Boston	3,904,800	50.00	2056-G.	Chicago	9,084,600	47.50
2056-B.	New York	14,876,436	47.50	2056-H.	St. Louis	5,817,300	50.00
2056-C.	Philadelphia	3,271,452	50.00	2056-I.	Minneapolis	2,304,800	55.00
2056-D.	Cleveland	2,814,600	50.00	2056-J.	Kansas City	3,524,244	55.00
2056-E.	Richmond	9,451,632	50.00	2056-K.	Dallas	2,807,388	55.00
2056-F.	Atlanta	6,887,640	47.50	2056-L.	San Francisco	5,289,540	47.50

DESIGN NO. 224

(Notes 2057-A — 2058-L Incl.)

The obverse is similar to Design No. 223. The reverse is as shown, with view of remodeled White House.

8. Series of 1934-C.

Signatures of Julian and Snyder.

This series exists with two different reverses: Design No. 206 and Design No. 224.

2057-A.	Boston	7,397,352	42.50	2057-G.	Chicago	26,031,660	40.00
2057-B.	New York	18,668,148	40.00	2057-H.	St. Louis	13,276,984	40.00
2057-C.	Philadelphia	11,590,752	40.00	2057-I.	Minneapolis	3,490,200	50.00
2057-D.	Cleveland	17,912,424	40.00	2057-J.	Kansas City	9,675,468	42.50
2057-E.	Richmond	22,526,568	40.00	2057-K.	Dallas	10,205,364	42.50
2057-F.	Atlanta	18,858,876	40.00	2057-L.	San Francisco	20,580,000	40.00

9. Series of 1934-D.

Signatures of Clark and Snyder.

2058-A.	Boston	4,520,000	40.00	2058-G.	Chicago	15,187,596	40.00
2058-B.	New York	27,894,260	40.00	2058-H.	St. Louis	5,923,248	42.50
2058-C.	Philadelphia	6,022,428	42.50	2058-I.	Minneapolis	2,422,416	47.50
2058-D.	Cleveland	8,981,688	40.00	2058-J.	Kansas City	4,211,904	42.50
2058-E.	Richmond	14,055,984	42.50	2058-K.	Dallas	3,707,364	42.50
2058-F.	Atlanta	7,495,440	42.50	2058-L.	San Francisco	12,015,228	40.00

DESIGN NO. 225

(Notes 2059-A — 2064-L Incl.)

The obverse is as shown. The reverse is similar to Design No. 224.

10. Series of 1950.

Signatures of Clark and Snyder.

2059-A.	Boston	23,184,000	37.50	2059-G.	Chicago	70,464,000	37.50
2059-B.	New York	80,064,000	35.00	2059-H.	St. Louis	27,352,000	37.50
2059-C.	Philadelphia	29,520,000	37.50	2059-I.	Minneapolis	9,216,000	42.50
2059-D.	Cleveland	51,120,000	35.00	2059-J.	Kansas City	22,752,000	37.50
2059-E.	Richmond	67,536,000	37.50	2059-K.	Dallas	22,656,000	37.50
2059-F.	Atlanta	39,312,000	37.50	2059-L.	San Francisco	70,272,000	35.00

11. Series of 1950-A.

Signatures of Priest and Humphrey.

2060-A.	Boston	19,656,000	32.50	2060-G.	Chicago	73,720,000	32.50
2060-B.	New York	82,568,000	32.50	2060-H.	St. Louis	22,680,000	35.00
2060-C.	Philadelphia	16,560,000	35.00	2060-I.	Minneapolis	5,544,000	40.00
2060-D.	Cleveland	50,320,000	35.00	2060-J.	Kansas City	22,968,000	35.00
2060-E.	Richmond	69,544,000	35.00	2060-K.	Dallas	10,728,000	37.50
2060-F.	Atlanta	27,648,000	35.00	2060-L.	San Francisco	85,528,000	32.50

12. Series of 1950-B.
Signatures of Priest and Anderson.

No.	Issuing Bank	No. Printed	Unc	No.	Issuing Bank	No. Printed	Unc
2061-A.	Boston	5,040,000	37.50	2061-G.	Chicago	80,560,000	30.00
2061-B.	New York	49,960,000	30.00	2061-H.	St. Louis	19,440,000	32.50
2061-C.	Philadelphia	7,920,000	37.50	2061-I.	Minneapolis	12,240,000	37.50
2061-D.	Cleveland	38,160,000	30.00	2061-J.	Kansas City	28,440,000	32.50
2061-E.	Richmond	42,120,000	30.00	2061-K.	Dallas	11,880,000	37.50
2061-F.	Atlanta	40,240,000	30.00	2061-L.	San Francisco	51,040,000	30.00

13. Series of 1950-C.
Signatures of Smith and Dillon.

2062-A.	Boston	7,200,000	32.50	2062-G.	Chicago	29,160,000	30.00
2062-B.	New York	43,200,000	30.00	2062-H.	St. Louis	12,960,000	32.50
2062-C.	Philadelphia	7,560,000	32.50	2062-I.	Minneapolis	6,480,000	37.50
2062-D.	Cleveland	28,440,000	30.00	2062-J.	Kansas City	18,360,000	35.00
2062-E.	Richmond	37,000,000	30.00	2062-K.	Dallas	9,000,000	37.50
2062-F.	Atlanta	19,080,000	32.50	2062-L.	San Francisco	45,360,000	30.00

14. Series of 1950-D.
Signatures of Granahan and Dillon.

2063-A.	Boston	9,320,000	32.50	2063-G.	Chicago	67,960,000	30.00
2063-B.	New York	64,280,000	30.00	2063-H.	St. Louis	6,120,000	35.00
2063-C.	Philadelphia	5,400,000	35.00	2063-I.	Minneapolis	3,240,000	37.50
2063-D.	Cleveland	23,760,000	30.00	2063-J.	Kansas City	8,200,000	32.50
2063-E.	Richmond	30,240,000	30.00	2063-K.	Dallas	6,480,000	32.50
2063-F.	Atlanta	22,680,000	30.00	2063-L.	San Francisco	69,400,000	30.00

15. Series of 1950-E.
Signatures of Granahan and Fowler.

2064-B.	New York	8,640,000	35.00	2064-L.	San Francisco	8,640,000	35.00
2064-G.	Chicago	9,360,000	35.00				

DESIGN NO. 225-a.
(Notes 2065-A — 2072-L Incl.)

Reverse of Design No. 225-a.
With motto "In God We Trust."

16. Series of 1963.
Signatures of Granahan and Dillon.

2065-A.	Boston	2,560,000	32.50	2065-G.	Chicago	2,560,000	32.50
2065-B.	New York	16,640,000	30.00	2065-H.	St. Louis	3,200,000	32.50
2065-D.	Cleveland	7,680,000	30.00	2065-J.	Kansas City	3,840,000	32.50
2065-E.	Richmond	4,480,000	32.50	2065-K.	Dallas	2,560,000	33.50
2065-F.	Atlanta	10,240,000	30.00	2065-L.	San Francisco	7,040,000	30.00

17. Series of 1963-A.
Signatures of Granahan and Fowler.

2066-A.	Boston	23,680,000	30.00	2066-G.	Chicago	156,320,000	30.00
2066-A*.	Boston	1,280,000	40.00	2066-G*.	Chicago	7,040,000	37.50
2066-B.	New York	93,600,000	30.00	2066-H.	St. Louis	34,560,000	30.00
2066-B*.	New York	3,840,000	37.50	2066-H*.	St. Louis	1,920,000	37.50
2066-C.	Philadelphia	17,920,000	30.00	2066-I.	Minneapolis	10,240,000	30.00
2066-C*.	Philadelphia	640,000	40.00	2066-I*.	Minneapolis	640,000	40.00
2066-D.	Cleveland	68,480,000	30.00	2066-J.	Kansas City	37,120,000	30.00
2066-D*.	Cleveland	2,560,000	37.50	2066-J*.	Kansas City	1,920,000	37.50
2066-E.	Richmond	128,800,000	30.00	2066-K.	Dallas	38,400,000	30.00
2066-E*.	Richmond	5,760,000	37.50	2066-K*.	Dallas	1,280,000	37.50
2066-F.	Atlanta	42,880,000	30.00	2066-L.	San Francisco	169,120,000	30.00
2066-F*.	Atlanta	1,920,000	37.50	2066-L*.	San Francisco	8,320,000	35.00

18. Series of 1969.

Signatures of Elston and Kennedy. With new Treasury seal.

No.	Issuing Bank	No. Printed	Unc	No.	Issuing Bank	No. Printed	Unc
2067-A.	Boston	19,200,000	25.00	2067-G.	Chicago	107,680,000	25.00
2067-A*.	Boston	1,280,000	30.00	2067-G*.	Chicago	3,200,000	30.00
2067-B.	New York	106,400,000	25.00	2067-H.	St. Louis	19,200,000	25.00
2067-B*.	New York	5,106,000	30.00	2067-H*.	St. Louis	640,000	35.00
2067-C.	Philadelphia	10,880,000	25.00	2067-I.	Minneapolis	12,160,000	25.00
2067-C*.	Philadelphia	1,280,000	30.00	2067-I*.	Minneapolis	640,000	35.00
2067-D.	Cleveland	60,160,000	25.00	2067-J.	Kansas City	39,040,000	25.00
2067-D*.	Cleveland	2,560,000	30.00	2067-J*.	Kansas City	1,280,000	30.00
2067-E.	Richmond	66,560,000	25.00	2067-K.	Dallas	25,600,000	25.00
2067-E*.	Richmond	2,560,000	30.00	2067-K*.	Dallas	640,000	35.00
2067-F.	Atlanta	36,480,000	25.00	2067-L.	San Francisco	103,840,000	25.00
2067-F*.	Atlanta	1,280,000	30.00	2067-L*.	San Francisco	5,120,000	30.00

19. Series of 1969-A.

Signatures of Kabis and Connally.

2068-A.	Boston	13,440,000	25.00	2068-G.	Chicago	81,640,000	25.00
2068-A*.	Boston	None Printed		2068-G*.	Chicago	1,920,000	30.00
2068-B.	New York	69,760,000	25.00	2068-H.	St. Louis	14,080,000	25.00
2068-B*.	New York	2,460,000	30.00	2068-H*.	St. Louis	640,000	35.00
2068-C.	Philadelphia	13,440,000	25.00	2068-I.	Minneapolis	7,040,000	25.00
2068-C*.	Philadelphia	None Printed		2068-I*.	Minneapolis	None Printed	
2068-D.	Cleveland	29,440,000	25.00	2068-J.	Kansas City	16,040,000	25.00
2068-D*.	Cleveland	640,000	35.00	2069-J*.	Kansas City	None Printed	
2068-E.	Richmond	42,400,000	25.00	2068-K.	Dallas	14,720,000	25.00
2068-E*.	Richmond	1,920,000	30.00	2068-K*.	Dallas	640,000	35.00
2068-F.	Atlanta	13,440,000	25.00	2068-L.	San Francisco	50,560,000	25.00
2068-F*.	Atlanta	None Printed		2068-L*.	San Francisco	1,280,000	30.00

20. Series of 1969-B.

Signatures of Banuelos and Connally.

2069-B.	New York	39,200,000	Current	2069-H.	St. Louis	5,120,000	Current
2069-B*.	New York	———		2069-H*.	St. Louis	None Printed	
2069-D.	Cleveland	6,400,000	Current	2069-I.	Minneapolis	2,560,000	Current
2069-D*.	Cleveland	None Printed		2069-I*.	Minneapolis	None Printed	
2069-E.	Richmond	27,520,000	Current	2069-J.	Kansas City	3,840,000	Current
2069-E*.	Richmond	None Printed		2069-J*.	Kansas City	640,000	Current
2069-F.	Atlanta	14,080,000	Current	2069-K.	Dallas	12,160,000	Current
2069-F*.	Atlanta	640,000	Current	2069-K*.	Dallas	None Printed	
2069-G.	Chicago	14,240,000	Current	2069-L.	San Francisco	26,000,000	Current
2069-G*.	Chicago	1,112,000	Current	2069-L*.	San Francisco	640,000	Current

21. Series of 1969-C.

Signatures of Banuelos and Shultz.

2070-A.	Boston	17,280,000	Current	2070-G.	Chicago	78,720,000	Current
2070-A*.	Boston	640,000	Current	2070-G*.	Chicago	640,000	Current
2070-B.	New York	135,200,000	Current	2070-H.	St. Louis	33,920,000	Current
2070-B*.	New York	1,640,000	Current	2070-H*.	St. Louis	640,000	Current
2070-C.	Philadelphia	40,960,000	Current	2070-I.	Minneapolis	14,080,000	Current
2070-C*.	Philadelphia	640,000	Current	2070-I*.	Minneapolis	640,000	Current
2070-D.	Cleveland	57,760,000	Current	2070-J.	Kansas City	32,000,000	Current
2070-D*.	Cleveland	480,000	Current	2070-J*.	Kansas City	640,000	Current
2070-E.	Richmond	80,160,000	Current	2070-K.	Dallas	31,360,000	Current
2070-E*.	Richmond	1,920,000	Current	2070-K*.	Dallas	1,920,000	Current
2070-F.	Atlanta	35,840,000	Current	2070-L.	San Francisco	82,080,000	Current
2070-F*.	Atlanta	640,000	Current	2070-L*.	San Francisco	1,120,000	Current

22. Series of 1974.

Signatures of Neff and Simon.

2071-A.	Boston	56,960,000	Current	2071-G.	Chicago	249,920,000	Current
2071-A*.	Boston	768,000	Current	2071-G*.	Chicago	4,608,000	Current
2071-B.	New York	296,640,000	Current	2071-H.	St. Louis	73,120,000	Current
2071-B*.	New York	7,616,000	Current	2071-H*.	St. Louis	1,120,000	Current
2071-C.	Philadelphia	59,680,000	Current	2071-I.	Minneapolis	39,040,000	Current
2071-C*.	Philadelphia	1,760,000	Current	2071-I*.	Minneapolis	1,280,000	Current
2071-D.	Cleveland	148,000,000	Current	2071-J.	Kansas City	74,400,000	Current
2071-D*.	Cleveland	3,296,000	Current	2071-J*.	Kansas City	736,000	Current
2071-E.	Richmond	149,920,000	Current	2071-K.	Dallas	68,640,000	Current
2071-E*.	Richmond	3,040,000	Current	2071-K*.	Dallas	608,000	Current
2071-F.	Atlanta	53,280,000	Current	2071-L.	San Francisco	128,800,000	Current
2071-F*.	Atlanta	480,000	Current	2071-L*.	San Francisco	4,320,000	Current

23. Series of 1977.

Signatures of Morton and Blumenthal.

2072-A.	Boston		Current	2072-G.	Chicago		Current
2072-A*.	Boston		Current	2072-G*.	Chicago		Current
2072-B.	New York		Current	2072-H.	St. Louis		Current
2072-B*.	New York		Current	2072-H*.	St. Louis		Current
2072-C.	Philadelphia		Current	2072-I.	Minneapolis		Current
2072-C*.	Philadelphia		Current	2072-I*.	Minneapolis		Current
2072-D.	Cleveland		Current	2072-J.	Kansas City		Current
2072-D*.	Cleveland		Current	2072-J*.	Kansas City		Current
2072-E.	Richmond		Current	2072-K.	Dallas		Current
2072-E*.	Richmond		Current	2072-K*.	Dallas		Current
2072-F.	Atlanta		Current	2072-L.	San Francisco		Current
2072-F*.	Atlanta		Current	2072-L*.	San Francisco		Current

24. Series of 1981.

Signatures of Buchanan and Regan.

No.	Issuing Bank	No. Printed	Unc	No.	Issuing Bank	No. Printed	Unc
2073-A.	Boston	56,960,000	Current	2073-G.	Chicago	249,920,000	Current
2073-A*.	Boston	768,000	Current	2073-G*.	Chicago	4,608,000	Current
2073-B.	New York	296,640,000	Current	2073-H.	St. Louis	73,120,000	Current
2073-B*.	New York	7,616,000	Current	2073-H*.	St. Louis	1,120,000	Current
2073-C.	Philadelphia	59,680,000	Current	2073-I.	Minneapolis	39,040,000	Current
2073-C*.	Philadelphia	1,760,000	Current	2073-I*.	Minneapolis	1,280,000	Current
2073-D.	Cleveland	148,000,000	Current	2073-J.	Kansas City	74,400,000	Current
2073-D*.	Cleveland	3,296,000	Current	2073-J*.	Kansas City	736,000	Current
2073-E.	Richmond	149,920,000	Current	2073-K.	Dallas	68,640,000	Current
2073-E*.	Richmond	3,040,000	Current	2073-K*.	Dallas	608,000	Current
2073-F.	Atlanta	53,280,000	Current	2073-L.	San Francisco	128,800,000	Current
2073-F*.	Atlanta	480,000	Current	2073-L*.	San Francisco	4,320,000	Current

25. Series of 1981-A.

Signatures of Ortega and Regan.

2074-A.	Boston		Current	2074-G.	Chicago		Current
2074-A*.	Boston		Current	2074-G*.	Chicago		Current
2074-B.	New York		Current	2074-H.	St. Louis		Current
2074-B*.	New York		Current	2074-H*.	St. Louis		Current
2074-C.	Philadelphia		Current	2074-I.	Minneapolis		Current
2074-C*.	Philadelphia		Current	2074-I*.	Minneapolis		Current
2074-D.	Cleveland		Current	2074-J.	Kansas City		Current
2074-D*.	Cleveland		Current	2074-J*.	Kansas City		Current
2074-E.	Richmond		Current	2074-K.	Dallas		Current
2074-E*.	Richmond		Current	2074-K*.	Dallas		Current
2074-F.	Atlanta		Current	2074-L.	San Francisco		Current
2074-F*	Atlanta		Current	2074-L*.	San Francisco		Current

26. Series of 1985.

Signatures of Ortega and Baker.

2075-A.	Boston		Current	2075-G.	Chicago		Current
2075-A*.	Boston		Current	2075-G*.	Chicago		Current
2075-B.	New York		Current	2075-H.	St. Louis		Current
2075-B*.	New York		Current	2075-H*.	St. Louis		Current
2075-C.	Philadelphia		Current	2075-I.	Minneapolis		Current
2075-C*.	Philadelphia		Current	2075-I*.	Minneapolis		Current
2075-D.	Cleveland		Current	2075-J.	Kansas City		Current
2075-D*.	Cleveland		Current	2075-J*.	Kansas City		Current
2075-E.	Richmond		Current	2075-K.	Dallas		Current
2075-E*.	Richmond		Current	2075-K*.	Dallas		Current
2075-F.	Atlanta		Current	2075-L.	San Francisco		Current
2075-F*.	Atlanta		Current	2075-L*.	San Francisco		Current

50 Dollar Notes

All issues are with the head of Ulysses S. Grant

DESIGN NO. 226

(Notes 2100-A - 2101-L Incl.)

Reverse of Design No. 226.

View of the U.S. Capitol.

1. Series of 1928.

Signatures of Woods and Mellon.

No.	Issuing Bank	No. Printed	Unc	No.	Issuing Bank	No. Printed	Unc
2100-A.	Boston	265,200	135.00	2100-G.	Chicago	1,348,620	120.00
2100-B.	New York	1,351,800	120.00	2100-H.	St. Louis	627,300	150.00
2100-C.	Philadelphia	997,056	120.00	2100-I.	Minneapolis	106,200	190.00
2100-D.	Cleveland	1,161,900	130.00	2100-J.	Kansas City	252,600	150.00
2100-E.	Richmond	539,400	135.00	2100-K.	Dallas	109,920	190.00
2100-F.	Atlanta	538,800	140.00	2100-L.	San Francisco	447,600	140.00

2. Series of 1928-A.

Signatures of Woods and Mellon.

2101-A.	Boston	1,834,989	115.00	2101-G.	Chicago	5,263,956	110.00
2101-B.	New York	3,392,328	115.00	2101-H.	St. Louis	880,500	150.00
2101-C.	Philadelphia	3,078,944	115.00	2101-I.	Minneapolis	780,240	160.00
2101-D.	Cleveland	2,453,364	120.00	2101-J.	Kansas City	791,604	145.00
2101-E.	Richmond	1,516,500	125.00	2101-K.	Dallas	701,496	145.00
2101-F.	Atlanta	338,400	160.00	2101-L.	San Francisco	1,522,620	130.00

DESIGN NO. 227

(Notes 2102-A - 2106-K Incl.)

The obverse is as shown. The reverse is similar to Design No. 226.

3. Series of 1934.

Signatures of Julian and Morgenthau.

The two shades of green seals also exist in this series.

No.	Issuing Bank	No. Printed	Unc	No.	Issuing Bank	No. Printed	Unc
2102-A.	Boston	2,729,400	100.00	2102-G.	Chicago	8,675,940	95.00
2102-B.	New York	17,894,676	90.00	2102-H.	St. Louis	1,497,144	110.00
2102-C.	Philadelphia	5,833,200	95.00	2102-I.	Minneapolis	539,700	115.00
2102-D.	Cleveland	8,817,720	90.00	2102-J.	Kansas City	1,133,520	110.00
2102-E.	Richmond	4,826,628	90.00	2102-K.	Dallas	1,194,876	110.00
2102-F.	Atlanta	3,069,348	110.00	2102-L.	San Francisco	8,101,200	100.00

4. Series of 1934-A.

Signatures of Julian and Morgenthau.

2103-A.	Boston	406,200	95.00	2103-H.	St. Louis	361,944	120.00
2103-B.	New York	4,710,648	90.00	2103-I.	Minneapolis	93,300	160.00
2103-D.	Cleveland	864,168	90.00	2103-J.	Kansas City	189,300	115.00
2103-E.	Richmond	2,235,372	90.00	2103-K.	Dallas	266,700	110.00
2103-F.	Atlanta	416,100	120.00	2103-L.	San Francisco	162,000	115.00
2103-G.	Chicago	1,014,600	90.00				

5. Series of 1934-B.

Signatures of Julian and Vinson.

2104-C.	Philadelphia	509,100	115.00	2104-H.	St. Louis	306,000	125.00
2104-D.	Cleveland	359,100	125.00	2104-I.	Minneapolis	120,000	135.00
2104-E.	Richmond	596,700	120.00	2104-J.	Kansas City	221,340	130.00
2104-F.	Atlanta	416,720	120.00	2104-K.	Dallas	120,108	140.00
2104-G.	Chicago	306,000	150.00	2104-L.	San Francisco	441,000	115.00

6. Series of 1934-C.

Signatures of Julian and Snyder.

2105-A.	Boston	117,600	115.00	2105-G.	Chicago	294,432	110.00
2105-B.	New York	1,556,400	85.00	2105-H.	St. Louis	535,200	95.00
2105-C.	Philadelphia	107,283	115.00	2105-I.	Minneapolis	118,800	115.00
2105-D.	Cleveland	374,400	85.00	2105-J.	Kansas City	303,600	110.00
2105-E.	Richmond	1,821,960	85.00	2105-K.	Dallas	429,900	105.00
2105-F.	Atlanta	107,640	115.00				

7. Series of 1934-D.

Signatures of Clark and Snyder.

2106-A.	Boston	279,600	125.00	2106-F.	Atlanta	216,000	130.00
2106-B.	New York	898,776	100.00	2106-G.	Chicago	494,016	120.00
2106-C.	Philadelphia	699,000	110.00	2106-K.	Dallas	103,200	150.00
2106-E.	Richmond	156,000	140.00				

DESIGN NO. 228

(Notes 2107-A - 2112-L Incl.)

The obverse is as shown. The reverse is similar to Design No. 226.

8. Series of 1950.
Signatures of Clark and Snyder.

No.	Issuing Bank	No. Printed	Unc	No.	Issuing Bank	No. Printed	Unc
2107-A.	Boston	1,248,000	82.50	2107-G.	Chicago	4,212,000	75.00
2107-B.	New York	10,236,000	75.00	2107-H.	St. Louis	892,000	87.50
2107-C.	Philadelphia	2,352,000	77.50	2107-I.	Minneapolis	384,000	95.00
2107-D.	Cleveland	6,180,000	75.00	2107-J.	Kansas City	696,000	87.50
2107-E.	Richmond	5,064,000	75.00	2107-K.	Dallas	1,100,000	82.50
2107-F.	Atlanta	1,812,000	82.50	2107-L.	San Francisco	3,996,000	77.50

9. Series of 1950-A.
Signatures of Priest and Humphrey.

2108-A.	Boston	720,000	77.50	2108-G.	Chicago	2,016,000	72.50
2108-B.	New York	6,480,000	72.50	2108-H.	St. Louis	576,000	75.00
2108-C.	Philadelphia	1,728,000	75.00	2108-J.	Kansas City	144,000	90.00
2108-D.	Cleveland	1,872,000	75.00	2108-K.	Dallas	864,000	72.50
2108-E.	Richmond	2,016,000	75.00	2108-L.	San Francisco	576,000	75.00
2108-F.	Atlanta	288,000	82.50				

10. Series of 1950-B.
Signatures of Priest and Anderson.

2109-A.	Boston	864,000	80.00	2109-G.	Chicago	4,320,000	75.00
2109-B.	New York	8,352,000	75.00	2109-H.	St. Louis	576,000	82.50
2109-C.	Philadelphia	2,592,000	75.00	2109-J.	Kansas City	1,008,000	77.50
2109-D.	Cleveland	1,728,000	75.00	2109-K.	Dallas	1,008,000	77.50
2109-E.	Richmond	1,584,000	75.00	2109-L.	San Francisco	1,872,000	75.00

11. Series of 1950-C.
Signatures of Smith and Dillon.

2110-A.	Boston	720,000	72.50	2110-H.	St. Louis	576,000	72.50
2110-B.	New York	5,328,000	72.50	2110-I.	Minneapolis	144,000	85.00
2110-C.	Philadelphia	1,296,000	72.50	2110-J.	Kansas City	432,000	75.00
2110-D.	Cleveland	1,296,000	72.50	2110-K.	Dallas	720,000	75.00
2110-E.	Richmond	1,296,000	72.50	2110-L.	San Francisco	1,152,000	75.00
2110-G.	Chicago	1,728,000	72.50				

12. Series of 1950-D.
Signatures of Granahan and Dillon.

2111-A.	Boston	1,728,000	72.50	2111-G.	Chicago	4,176,000	72.50
2111-B.	New York	7,200,000	72.50	2111-H.	St. Louis	1,440,000	72.50
2111-C.	Philadelphia	2,736,000	72.50	2111-I.	Minneapolis	288,000	85.00
2111-D.	Cleveland	2,880,000	72.50	2111-J.	Kansas City	720,000	72.50
2111-E.	Richmond	2,616,000	72.50	2111-K.	Dallas	1,296,000	72.50
2111-F.	Atlanta	576,000	72.50	2111-L.	San Francisco	2,160,000	72.50

13. Series of 1950-E.
Signatures of Granahan and Fowler.

2112-B.	New York	3,024,000	75.00	2112-L.	San Francisco	1,296,000	75.00
2112-G.	Chicago	1,008,000	75.00				

DESIGN NO. 228-a.
(Notes 2113-A - 2119-L Incl.)

Reverse of Design No. 228-a.
With motto "In God We Trust."

14. Series of 1963-A.

Signatures of Granahan and Fowler.

No.	Issuing Bank	No. Printed	Unc	No.	Issuing Bank	No. Printed	Unc
2113-A.	Boston	1,536,000	72.50	2113-G.	Chicago	6,912,000	72.50
2113-A*.	Boston	320,000	85.00	2113-G*.	Chicago	768,000	85.00
2113-B.	New York	11,008,000	72.50	2113-H.	St. Louis	512,000	75.00
2113-B*.	New York	1,408,000	85.00	2113-H*.	St. Louis	128,000	90.00
2113-C.	Philadelphia	3,328,000	72.50	2113-I.	Minneapolis	512,000	75.00
2113-C*.	Philadelphia	704,000	85.00	2113-I*.	Minneapolis	128,000	90.00
2113-D.	Cleveland	3,584,000	72.50	2113-J.	Kansas City	512,000	75.00
2113-D*.	Cleveland	256,000	87.50	2113-J*.	Kansas City	64,000	95.00
2113-E.	Richmond	3,072,000	72.50	2113-K.	Dallas	1,536,000	72.50
2113-E*.	Richmond	704,000	85.00	2113-K*.	Dallas	128,000	90.00
2113-F.	Atlanta	768,000	75.00	2113-L.	San Francisco	4,352,000	72.50
2113-F*.	Atlanta	384,000	87.50	2113-L*.	San Francisco	704,000	85.00

15. Series of 1969.

Signatures of Elston and Kennedy. With new Treasury seal.

2114-A.	Boston	2,048,000	65.00	2114-G.	Chicago	9,728,000	65.00
2114-A*.	Boston	None Printed		2114-G*.	Chicago	256,000	75.00
2114-B.	New York	12,032,000	65.00	2114-H.	St. Louis	256,000	70.00
2114-B*.	New York	384,000	75.00	2114-H*.	St. Louis	None Printed	
2114-C.	Philadelphia	3,584,000	65.00	2114-I.	Minneapolis	512,000	65.00
2114-C*.	Philadelphia	128,000	80.00	2114-I*.	Minneapolis	None Printed	
2114-D.	Cleveland	3,584,000	65.00	2114-J.	Kansas City	1,280,000	65.00
2114-D*.	Cleveland	192,000	80.00	2114-J*.	Kansas City	64,000	85.00
2114-E.	Richmond	2,560,000	65.00	2114-K.	Dallas	1,536,000	65.00
2114-E*.	Richmond	64,000	85.00	2114-K*.	Dallas	64,000	85.00
2114-F.	Atlanta	256,000	70.00	2114-L.	San Francisco	6,912,000	65.00
2114-F*.	Atlanta	None Printed		2114-L*.	San Francisco	256,000	75.00

16. Series of 1969-A.

Signatures of Kabis and Connally.

2115-A.	Boston	1,536,000	60.00	2115-G.	Chicago	3,584,000	60.00
2115-A*.	Boston	128,000	65.00	2115-G*.	Chicago	192,000	65.00
2115-B.	New York	9,728,000	60.00	2115-H.	St. Louis	256,000	60.00
2115-B*.	New York	704,000	65.00	2115-H*.	St. Louis	None Printed	
2115-C.	Philadelphia	2,560,000	60.00	2115-I.	Minneapolis	512,000	60.00
2115-C*.	Philadelphia	None Printed		2115-I*.	Minneapolis	None Printed	
2115-D.	Cleveland	2,816,000	60.00	2115-J.	Kansas City	256,000	60.00
2115-D*.	Cleveland	None Printed		2115-J*.	Kansas City	None Printed	
2115-E.	Richmond	2,304,000	60.00	2115-K.	Dallas	1,024,000	60.00
2115-E*.	Richmond	64,000	65.00	2115-K*.	Dallas	64,000	65.00
2115-F.	Atlanta	256,000	60.00	2115-L.	San Francisco	5,120,000	60.00
2115-F*.	Atlanta	64,000	65.00	2115-L*.	San Francisco	256,000	65.00

17. Series of 1969-B.

Signatures of Banuelos and Connally.

2116-A.	Boston	1,024,000	Current	2116-G.	Chicago	1,024,000	Current
2116-B.	New York	2,560,000	Current	2116-K.	Dallas	1,024,000	Current
2116-E.	Richmond	1,536,000	Current	2116-K*.	Dallas	128,000	Current
2116-F.	Atlanta	512,000	Current				

18. Series of 1969-C.

Signatures of Banuelos and Shultz.

2117-A.	Boston	1,792,000	Current	2117-G.	Chicago	6,784,000	Current
2117-A*.	Boston	64,000	Current	2117-G*.	Chicago	576,000	Current
2117-B.	New York	7,040,000	Current	2117-H.	St. Louis	2,688,000	Current
2117-B*.	New York	192,000	Current	2117-H*.	St. Louis	64,000	Current
2117-C.	Philadelphia	3,584,000	Current	2117-I.	Minneapolis	256,000	Current
2117-C*.	Philadelphia	256,000	Current	2117-I*.	Minneapolis	64,000	Current
2117-D.	Cleveland	5,120,000	Current	2117-J.	Kansas City	1,280,000	Current
2117-D*.	Cleveland	192,000	Current	2117-J*.	Kansas City	128,000	Current
2117-E.	Richmond	2,304,000	Current	2117-K.	Dallas	3,456,000	Current
2117-E*.	Richmond	64,000	Current	2117-K*.	Dallas	64,000	Current
2117-F.	Atlanta	256,000	Current	2117-L.	San Francisco	4,608,000	Current
2117-F*.	Atlanta	64,000	Current	2117-L*.	San Francisco	256,000	Current

19. Series of 1974.

Signatures of Neff and Simon.

2118-A.	Boston	3,840,000	Current	2118-G.	Chicago	30,720,000	Current
2118-A*.	Boston	256,000	Current	2118-G*.	Chicago	2,688,000	Current
2118-B.	New York	38,400,000	Current	2118-H.	St. Louis	2,560,000	Current
2118-B*.	New York	768,000	Current	2118-H*.	St. Louis	128,000	Current
2118-C.	Philadelphia	7,040,000	Current	2118-I.	Minneapolis	3,200,000	Current
2118-C*.	Philadelphia	384,000	Current	2118-I*.	Minneapolis	192,000	Current
2118-D.	Cleveland	22,400,000	Current	2118-J.	Kansas City	4,480,000	Current
2118-D*.	Cleveland	640,000	Current	2118-J*.	Kansas City	192,000	Current
2118-E.	Richmond	14,080,000	Current	2118-K.	Dallas	8,320,000	Current
2118-E*.	Richmond	576,000	Current	2118-K*.	Dallas	128,000	Current
2118-F.	Atlanta	1,280,000	Current	2118-L.	San Francisco	7,680,000	Current
2118-F*.	Atlanta	64,000	Current	2118-L*.	San Francisco	64,000	Current

20. Series of 1977.

Signatures of Morton and Blumenthal.

No.	Issuing Bank	Unc	No.	Issuing Bank	Unc	No.	Issuing Bank	Unc
2119-A.	Boston	Current	2119-E.	Richmond	Current	2119-I.	Minneapolis	Current
2119-A*.	Boston	Current	2119-E*.	Richmond	Current	2119-I*.	Minneapolis	Current
2119-B.	New York	Current	2119-F.	Atlanta	Current	2119-J.	Kansas City	Current
2119-B*.	New York	Current	2119-F*.	Atlanta	Current	2119-J*.	Kansas City	Current
2119-C.	Philadelphia	Current	2119-G.	Chicago	Current	2119-K.	Dallas	Current
2119-C*.	Philadelphia	Current	2119-G*.	Chicago	Current	2119-K*.	Dallas	Current
2119-D.	Cleveland	Current	2119-H.	St. Louis	Current	2119-L.	San Francisco	Current
2119-D*.	Cleveland	Current	2119-H*.	St. Louis	Current	2119-L*.	San Francisco	Current

21. Series of 1981.

Signatures of Buchanan and Regan.

No.	Issuing Bank	Unc	No.	Issuing Bank	Unc	No.	Issuing Bank	Unc
2120-A.	Boston	Current	2120-E.	Richmond	Current	2120-I.	Minneapolis	Current
2120-A*.	Boston	Current	2120-E*.	Richmond	Current	2120-I*.	Minneapolis	Current
2120-B.	New York	Current	2120-F.	Atlanta	Current	2120-J.	Kansas City	Current
2120-B*.	New York	Current	2120-F*.	Atlanta	Current	2120-J*.	Kansas City	Current
2120-C.	Philadelphia	Current	2120-G.	Chicago	Current	2120-K.	Dallas	Current
2120-C*.	Philadelphia	Current	2120-G*.	Chicago	Current	2120-K*.	Dallas	Current
2120-D.	Cleveland	Current	2120-H.	St. Louis	Current	2120-L.	San Francisco	Current
2120-D*.	Cleveland	Current	2120-H*.	St. Louis	Current	2120-L*.	San Francisco	Current

22. Series of 1981-A.

Signatures of Ortega and Regan.

2121-A.	Boston	Current	2121-E.	Richmond	Current	2121-I.	Minneapolis	Current
2121-A*.	Boston	Current	2121-E*.	Richmond	Current	2121-I*.	Minneapolis	Current
2121-B.	New York	Current	2121-F.	Atlanta	Current	2121-J.	Kansas City	Current
2121-B*.	New York	Current	2121-F*.	Atlanta	Current	2121-J*.	Kansas City	Current
2121-C.	Philadelphia	Current	2121-G.	Chicago	Current	2121-K.	Dallas	Current
2121-C*.	Philadelphia	Current	2121-G*.	Chicago	Current	2121-K*.	Dallas	Current
2121-D.	Cleveland	Current	2121-H.	St. Louis	Current	2121-L.	San Francisco	Current
2121-D*.	Cleveland	Current	2121-H*.	St. Louis	Current	2121-L*.	San Francisco	Current

23. Series of 1985.

Signatures of Ortega and Baker.

2122-A.	Boston	Current	2122-E.	Richmond	Current	2122-I.	Minneapolis	Current
2122-A*.	Boston	Current	2122-E*.	Richmond	Current	2122-I*.	Minneapolis	Current
2122-B.	New York	Current	2122-F.	Atlanta	Current	2122-J.	Kansas City	Current
2122-B*.	New York	Current	2122-F*.	Atlanta	Current	2122-J*.	Kansas City	Current
2122-C.	Philadelphia	Current	2122-G.	Chicago	Current	2122-K.	Dallas	Current
2122-C*.	Philadelphia	Current	2122-G*.	Chicago	Current	2122-K*.	Dallas	Current
2122-D.	Cleveland	Current	2122-H.	St. Louis	Current	2122-L.	San Francisco	Current
2122-D*.	Cleveland	Current	2122-H*.	St. Louis	Current	2122-L*.	San Francisco	Current

100 Dollar Notes

All issues are with the head of Benjamin Franklin

DESIGN NO. 229
(Notes 2150-A — 2150-L Incl.)

1. Series of 1928.

Signatures of Woods and Mellon.

Reverse of Design No. 229. View of Independence Hall.

No.	Issuing Bank	No. Printed	Unc	No.	Issuing Bank	No. Printed	Unc
2150-A.	Boston	376,000	210.00	2150-G.	Chicago	783,300	200.00
2150-B.	New York	755,400	200.00	2150-H.	St. Louis	187,200	210.00
2150-C.	Philadelphia	389,100	200.00	2150-I.	Minneapolis	102,000	235.00
2150-D.	Cleveland	542,400	205.00	2150-J.	Kansas City	234,612	210.00
2150-E.	Richmond	364,416	220.00	2150-K.	Dallas	80,140	235.00
2150-F.	Atlanta	357,000	210.00	2150-L.	San Francisco	486,000	200.00

DESIGN NO. 230

(Notes 2151-A — 2156-K Incl.)

The obverse is as shown. The reverse is similar to Design No. 229.

2. Series of 1928-A.

Signatures of Woods and Mellon.

2151-A.	Boston	980,400	200.00	2151-G.	Chicago	4,010,424	200.00
2151-B.	New York	2,938,176	200.00	2151-H.	St. Louis	749,544	210.00
2151-C.	Philadelphia	1,496,844	200.00	2151-I.	Minneapolis	503,040	215.00
2151-D.	Cleveland	992,436	200.00	2151-J.	Kansas City	681,804	200.00
2151-E.	Richmond	621,364	210.00	2151-K.	Dallas	594,456	215.00
2151-F.	Atlanta	371,400	210.00	2151-L.	San Francisco	1,228,032	200.00

3. Series of 1934.

Signatures of Julian and Morgenthau.

The two shades of green seals also exist in this series.

No.	Issuing Bank	No. Printed	Unc	No.	Issuing Bank	No. Printed	Unc
2152-A.	Boston	3,710,000	185.00	2152-G.	Chicago	7,075,000	185.00
2152-B.	New York	3,086,000	185.00	2152-H.	St. Louis	2,106,192	185.00
2152-C.	Philadelphia	2,776,800	185.00	2152-I.	Minneapolis	852,600	200.00
2152-D.	Cleveland	3,447,108	185.00	2152-J.	Kansas City	1,932,900	200.00
2152-E.	Richmond	4,317,600	185.00	2152-K.	Dallas	1,506,516	200.00
2152-F.	Atlanta	3,264,420	185.00	2152-L.	San Francisco	6,521,940	185.00

4. Series of 1934-A.

Signatures of Julian and Morgenthau.

2153-A.	Boston	102,000	180.00	2153-G.	Chicago	3,328,800	190.00
2153-B.	New York	15,278,892	180.00	2153-H.	St. Louis	434,208	190.00
2153-C.	Philadelphia	588,000	180.00	2153-I.	Minneapolis	153,000	195.00
2153-D.	Cleveland	645,300	180.00	2153-J.	Kansas City	455,000	190.00
2153-E.	Richmond	770,000	200.00	2153-K.	Dallas	226,164	190.00
2153-F.	Atlanta	589,886	200.00	2153-L.	San Francisco	1,130,400	180.00

5. Series of 1934-B.

Signatures of Julian and Vinson.

2154-A.	Boston	41,400	240.00	2154-G.	Chicago	396,000	185.00
2154-C.	Philadelphia	39,600	240.00	2154-H.	St. Louis	676,200	190.00
2154-D.	Cleveland	61,200	240.00	2154-I.	Minneapolis	377,000	190.00
2154-E.	Richmond	977,400	185.00	2154-J.	Kansas City	364,500	220.00
2154-F.	Atlanta	645,000	185.00	2154-K.	Dallas	392,700	200.00

6. Series of 1934-C.

Signatures of Julian and Snyder.

2155-A.	Boston	13,800	250.00	2155-H.	St. Louis	957,000	165.00
2155-B.	New York	1,556,400	175.00	2155-I.	Minneapolis	392,904	170.00
2155-C.	Philadelphia	13,200	250.00	2155-J.	Kansas City	401,100	170.00
2155-D.	Cleveland	1,473,200	175.00	2155-K.	Dallas	280,700	170.00
2155-F.	Atlanta	493,900	170.00	2155-L.	San Francisco	432,600	170.00
2155-G.	Chicago	612,000	170.00				

7. Series of 1934-D.

Signatures of Clark and Snyder.

2156-B.	New York	156	RARE	2156-G.	Chicago	78,000	225.00
2156-C.	Philadelphia	308,400	200.00	2156-H.	St. Louis	166,800	200.00
2156-F.	Atlanta	260,400	200.00	2156-K.	Dallas	66,000	225.00

DESIGN NO. 231.

(Notes 2157-A — 2162-L Incl.)

The obverse is as shown. The reverse is similar to Design No. 229.

8. Series of 1950.

Signatures of Clark and Snyder.

2157-A.	Boston	768,000	165.00	2157-G.	Chicago	4,428,000	135.00
2157-B.	New York	3,908,000	140.00	2157-H.	St. Louis	1,284,000	145.00
2157-C.	Philadelphia	1,332,000	145.00	2157-I.	Minneapolis	564,000	165.00
2157-D.	Cleveland	1,632,000	145.00	2157-J.	Kansas City	864,000	155.00
2157-E.	Richmond	4,076,000	140.00	2157-K.	Dallas	1,216,000	145.00
2157-F.	Atlanta	1,824,000	145.00	2157-L.	San Francisco	2,524,000	140.00

9. Series of 1950-A.

Signatures of Priest and Humphrey.

No.	Issuing Bank	No. Printed	Unc	No.	Issuing Bank	No. Printed	Unc.
2158-A.	Boston	1,008,000	140.00	2158-G.	Chicago	864,000	140.00
2158-B.	New York	2,880,000	135.00	2158-H.	St. Louis	432,000	145.00
2158-C.	Philadelphia	576,000	145.00	2158-I.	Minneapolis	144,000	165.00
2158-D.	Cleveland	288,000	155.00	2158-J.	Kansas City	288,000	155.00
2158-E.	Richmond	2,160,000	135.00	2158-K.	Dallas	432,000	145.00
2158-F.	Atlanta	288,000	155.00	2158-L.	San Francisco	720,000	140.00

10. Series of 1950-B.

Signatures of Priest and Anderson.

2159-A.	Boston	720,000	140.00	2159-G.	Chicago	2,592,000	130.00
2159-B.	New York	6,636,000	130.00	2159-H.	St. Louis	1,152,000	130.00
2159-C.	Philadelphia	720,000	140.00	2159-I.	Minneapolis	288,000	150.00
2159-D.	Cleveland	432,000	140.00	2159-J.	Kansas City	720,000	140.00
2159-E.	Richmond	1,008,000	130.00	2159-K.	Dallas	1,728,000	130.00
2159-F.	Atlanta	576,000	140.00	2159-L.	San Francisco	2,880,000	130.00

11. Series of 1950-C.

Signatures of Smith and Dillon.

2160-A.	Boston	864,000	130.00	2160-G.	Chicago	1,584,000	130.00
2160-B.	New York	2,448,000	130.00	2160-H.	St. Louis	720,000	135.00
2160-C.	Philadelphia	576,000	135.00	2160-I.	Minneapolis	288,000	155.00
2160-D.	Cleveland	576,000	135.00	2160-J.	Kansas City	432,000	140.00
2160-E.	Richmond	1,440,000	130.00	2160-K.	Dallas	720,000	135.00
2160-F.	Atlanta	1,296,000	130.00	2160-L.	San Francisco	2,160,000	130.00

12. Series of 1950-D.

Signatures of Granahan and Dillon.

2161-A.	Boston	1,872,000	130.00	2161-G.	Chicago	4,608,000	130.00
2161-B.	New York	7,632,000	130.00	2161-H.	St. Louis	1,440,000	130.00
2161-C.	Philadelphia	1,872,000	130.00	2161-I.	Minneapolis	432,000	135.00
2161-D.	Cleveland	1,584,000	130.00	2161-J.	Kansas City	864,000	135.00
2161-E.	Richmond	2,880,000	130.00	2161-K.	Dallas	1,728,000	130.00
2161-F.	Atlanta	1,872,000	130.00	2161-L.	San Francisco	3,312,000	130.00

13. Series of 1950-E.

Signatures of Granahan and Fowler.

2162-B.	New York	3,024,000	135.00	2162-L.	San Francisco	2,736,000	135.00
2162-G.	Chicago	576,000	135.00				

DESIGN NO. 231-a
(Notes 2163-A — 2167-L Incl.)

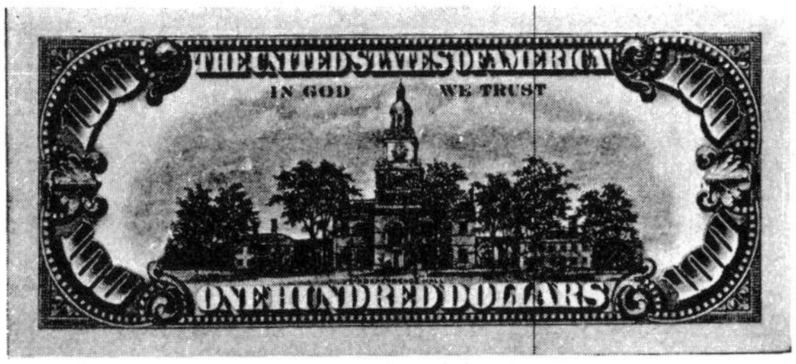

Reverse of Design No. 231-a.
With motto "In God We Trust."

14. Series of 1963-A.

Signatures of Granahan and Fowler.

No.	Issuing Bank	No. Printed	Unc	No.	Issuing Bank	No. Printed	Unc
2163-A.	Boston	1,536,000	120.00	2163-G.	Chicago	4,352,000	120.00
2163-A*.	Boston	128,000	130.00	2163-G*.	Chicago	512,000	130.00
2163-B.	New York	12,544,000	120.00	2163-H.	St. Louis	1,536,000	120.00
2163-B*.	New York	1,536,000	130.00	2163-H*.	St. Louis	256,000	130.00
2163-C.	Philadelphia	1,792,000	120.00	2163-I.	Minneapolis	512,000	125.00
2163-C*.	Philadelphia	192,000	130.00	2163-I*.	Minneapolis	128,000	130.00
2163-D.	Cleveland	2,304,000	120.00	2163-J.	Kansas City	1,024,000	120.00
2163-D*.	Cleveland	192,000	130.00	2163-J*.	Kansas City	128,000	130.00
2163-E.	Richmond	2,816,000	120.00	2163-K.	Dallas	1,536,000	120.00
2163-E*.	Richmond	192,000	130.00	2163-K*.	Dallas	192,000	130.00
2163-F.	Atlanta	1,280,000	120.00	2163-L.	San Francisco	6,400,000	120.00
2163-F*.	Atlanta	128,000	130.00	2163-L*.	San Francisco	832,000	130.00

15. Series of 1969.

Signatures of Elston and Kennedy. With new Treasury seal.

2164-A.	Boston	2,048,000	120.00	2164-G.	Chicago	5,888,000	120.00
2164-A*.	Boston	128,000	130.00	2164-G*.	Chicago	256,000	130.00
2164-B.	New York	11,520,000	120.00	2164-H.	St. Louis	1,280,000	120.00
2164-B*.	New York	128,000	130.00	2164-H*.	St. Louis	64,000	130.00
2164-C.	Philadelphia	2,560,000	120.00	2164-I.	Minneapolis	512,000	125.00
2164-C*.	Philadelphia	128,000	130.00	2164-I*.	Minneapolis	64,000	130.00
2164-D.	Cleveland	768,000	120.00	2164-J.	Kansas City	1,792,000	120.00
2164-D*.	Cleveland	64,000	130.00	2164-J*.	Kansas City	384,000	130.00
2164-E.	Richmond	2,560,000	120.00	2164-K.	Dallas	2,048,000	120.00
2164-E*.	Richmond	192,000	130.00	2164-K*.	Dallas	128,000	130.00
2164-F.	Atlanta	2,304,000	120.00	2164-L.	San Francisco	7,168,000	120.00
2164-F*.	Atlanta	128,000	130.00	2164-L*.	San Francisco	320,000	130.00

16. Series of 1969-A.

Signatures of Kabis and Connally.

2165-A.	Boston	1,280,000	115.00	2165-G.	Chicago	5,376,000	115.00
2165-A*.	Boston	320,000	125.00	2165-G*.	Chicago	320,000	125.00
2165-B.	New York	11,264,000	115.00	2165-H.	St. Louis	1,024,000	115.00
2165-B*.	New York	640,000	125.00	2165-H*.	St. Louis	664,000	125.00
2165-C.	Philadelphia	2,048,000	115.00	2165-I.	Minneapolis	1,024,000	115.00
2165-C*.	Philadelphia	448,000	125.00	2165-I*.	Minneapolis	None Printed	
2165-D.	Cleveland	1,280,000	115.00	2165-J.	Kansas City	512,000	115.00
2165-D*.	Cleveland	192,000	125,00	2165-J*.	Kansas City	None Printed	
2165-E.	Richmond	2,304,000	115.00	2165-K.	Dallas	3,328,000	115.00
2165-E*.	Richmond	192,000	125,00	2165-K*.	Dallas	128,000	125.00
2165-F.	Atlanta	2,304,000	115.00	2165-L.	San Francisco	4,352,000	115.00
2165-F*.	Atlanta	640,000	125.00	2165-L*.	San Francisco	576,000	125.00

17. Series of 1969-B.

None printed.

18. Series of 1969-C.

Signatures of Banuelos and Shultz.

2166-A.	Boston	2,048,000	Current	2166-G.	Chicago	6,016,000	Current
2166-A*.	Boston	64,000	Current	2166-G*.	Chicago	320,000	Current
2166-B.	New York	15,616,000	Current	2166-H.	St. Louis	5,376,000	Current
2166-B*.	New York	256,000	Current	2166-H*.	St. Louis	64,000	Current
2166-C.	Philadelphia	2,816,000	Current	2166-I.	Minneapolis	512,000	Current
2166-C*.	Philadelphia	64,000	Current	2166-I*.	Minneapolis	64,000	Current
2166-D.	Cleveland	3,456,000	Current	2166-J.	Kansas City	4,736,000	Current
2166-D*.	Cleveland	64,000	Current	2166-J*.	Kansas City	192,000	Current
2166-E.	Richmond	7,296,000	Current	2166-K.	Dallas	2,944,000	Current
2166-E*.	Richmond	128,000	Current	2166-K*.	Dallas	64,000	Current
2166-F.	Atlanta	2,432,000	Current	2166-L.	San Francisco	10,240,000	Current
2166-F*.	Atlanta	64,000	Current	2166-L*.	San Francisco	512,000	Current

19. Series of 1974.

Signatures of Neff and Simon.

2167-A.	Boston	11,520,000	Current	2167-G.	Chicago	26,880,000	Current
2167-A*.	Boston	320,000	Current	2167-G*.	Chicago	1,216,000	Current
2167-B.	New York	62,720,000	Current	2167-H.	St. Louis	5,760,000	Current
2167-B*.	New York	1,728,000	Current	2167-H*.	St. Louis	192,000	Current
2167-C.	Philadelphia	7,680,000	Current	2167-I.	Minneapolis	4,480,000	Current
2167-C*.	Philadelphia	192,000	Current	2167-I*.	Minneapolis	256,000	Current
2167-D.	Cleveland	8,320,000	Current	2167-J.	Kansas City	5,760,000	Current
2167-D*.	Cleveland	256,000	Current	2167-J*.	Kansas City	448,000	Current
2167-E.	Richmond	11,520,000	Current	2167-K.	Dallas	10,240,000	Current
2167-E*.	Richmond	256,000	Current	2167-K*.	Dallas	192,000	Current
2167-F.	Atlanta	4,480,000	Current	2167-L.	San Francisco	29,440,000	Current
2167-F*.	Atlanta	128,000	Current	2167-L*.	San Francisco	896,000	Current

20. Series of 1977.

Signatures of Morton and Blumenthal

No.	Issuing Bank	Unc.	No.	Issuing Bank	Unc	No.	Issuing Bank	Unc
2168-A.	Boston	Current	2168-E.	Richmond	Current	2168-I.	Minneapolis	Current
2168-A*.	Boston	Current	2168-E*.	Richmond	Current	2168-I*.	Minneapolis	Current
2168-B.	New York	Current	2168-F.	Atlanta	Current	2168-J.	Kansas City	Current
2168-B*.	New York	Current	2168-F*.	Atlanta	Current	2168-J*.	Kansas City	Current
2168-C.	Philadelphia	Current	2168-G.	Chicago	Current	2168-K.	Dallas	Current
2168-C*.	Philadelphia	Current	2168-G*.	Chicago	Current	2168-K*.	Dallas	Current
2168-D.	Cleveland	Current	2168-H.	St. Louis	Current	2168-L.	San Francisco	Current
2168-D*.	Cleveland	Current	2168-H*.	St. Louis	Current	2168-L*.	San Francisco	Current

21. Series of 1981.

Signatures of Buchanan and Regan.

No.	Issuing Bank	Unc.	No.	Issuing Bank	Unc	No.	Issuing Bank	Unc
2169-A.	Boston	Current	2169-E.	Richmond	Current	2169-I.	Minneapolis	Current
2169-A*.	Boston	Current	2169-E*.	Richmond	Current	2169-I*.	Minneapolis	Current
2169-B.	New York	Current	2169-F.	Atlanta	Current	2169-J.	Kansas City	Current
2169-B*.	New York	Current	2169-F*.	Atlanta	Current	2169-J*.	Kansas City	Current
2169-C.	Philadelphia	Current	2169-G.	Chicago	Current	2169-K.	Dallas	Current
2169-C*.	Philadelphia	Current	2169-G*.	Chicago	Current	2169-K*.	Dallas	Current
2169-D.	Cleveland	Current	2169-H.	St. Louis	Current	2169-L.	San Francisco	Current
2169-D*.	Cleveland	Current	2169-H*.	St. Louis	Current	2169-L*.	San Francisco	Current

22. Series of 1981-A.

Signatures of Ortega and Regan.

2170-A.	Boston	Current	2170-E.	Richmond	Current	2170-I.	Minneapolis	Current
2170-A*.	Boston	Current	2170-E*.	Richmond	Current	2170-I*.	Minneapolis	Current
2170-B.	New York	Current	2170-F.	Atlanta	Current	2170-J.	Kansas City	Current
2170-B*.	New York	Current	2170-F*.	Atlanta	Current	2170-J*.	Kansas City	Current
2170-C.	Philadelphia	Current	2170-G.	Chicago	Current	2170-K.	Dallas	Current
2170-C*.	Philadelphia	Current	2170-G*.	Chicago	Current	2170-K*.	Dallas	Current
2170-D.	Cleveland	Current	2170-H.	St. Louis	Current	2170-L.	San Francisco	Current
2170-D*.	Cleveland	Current	2170-H*.	St. Louis	Current	2170-L*.	San Francisco	Current

23. Series of 1985.

Signatures of Ortega and Baker.

2171-A.	Boston	Current	2171-E.	Richmond	Current	2171-I.	Minneapolis	Current
2171-A*.	Boston	Current	2171-E*.	Richmond	Current	2171-I*.	Minneapolis	Current
2171-B.	New York	Current	2171-F.	Atlanta	Current	2171-J.	Kansas City	Current
2171-B*.	New York	Current	2171-F*.	Atlanta	Current	2171-J*.	Kansas City	Current
2171-C.	Philadelphia	Current	2171-G.	Chicago	Current	2171-K.	Dallas	Current
2171-C*.	Philadelphia	Current	2171-G*.	Chicago	Current	2171-K*.	Dallas	Current
2171-D.	Cleveland	Current	2171-H.	St. Louis	Current	2171-L.	San Francisco	Current
2171-D*.	Cleveland	Current	2171-H*.	St. Louis	Current	2171-L*.	San Francisco	Current

HIGH DENOMINATION NOTES

Valuations have not been placed on any of the following 500, 1,000, 5,000 and 10,000 Dollar notes. Because of their high face value, they are beyond the reach of the ordinary collector and the market for them is limited. (See under "High Denomination Notes," page 8.)

500 Dollar Notes

All issues are with the head of William McKinley

DESIGN NO. 232. (a and b)

Reverse of Design No. 232.

Federal Reserve Note and Gold Certificate. (Notes 2200-2204) (Also Note 2406)

1. Series of 1928.

Signatures of Woods and Mellon.

No.	Issuing Bank	No. Printed	No.	Issuing Bank	No. Printed
2200-A.	Boston	69,120	2200-G.	Chicago	573,600
2200-B.	New York	299,400	2200-H.	St. Louis	66,180
2200-C.	Philadephia	135,120	2200-I.	Minneapolis	34,680
2200-D.	Cleveland	166,440	2200-J.	Kansas City	510,720
2200-E.	Richmond	84,720	2200-K.	Dallas	70,560
2200-F.	Atlanta	69,360	2200-L.	San Francisco	64,080

2. Series of 1934.
Signatures of Julian and Morgenthau.

No.	Issuing Bank	No. Printed	No.	Issuing Bank	No. Printed
2201-A.	Boston	56,628	2201-G.	Chicago	212,400
2201-B.	New York	288,000	2201-H.	St. Louis	24,000
2201-C.	Philadelphia	31,200	2201-I.	Minneapolis	24,000
2201-D.	Cleveland	39,000	2201-J.	Kansas City	40,800
2201-E.	Richmond	40,800	2201-K.	Dallas	31,200
2201-F.	Atlanta	46,200	2201-L.	San Francisco	83,400

3. Series of 1934-A.
Signatures of Julian and Morgenthau.

2202-B.	New York	276,000	2202-H.	St. Louis	57,600
2202-C.	Philadelphia	45,300	2202-I.	Minneapolis	14,400
2202-D.	Cleveland	28,800	2202-J.	Kansas City	55,200
2202-E.	Richmond	36,000	2202-K.	Dallas	34,800
2202-G.	Chicago	214,800	2202-L.	San Francisco	93,000

4. Series of 1934-B.
Signatures of Julian and Vinson.

2203-F.	Atlanta	2,472

5. Series of 1934-C.
Signatures of Julian and Snyder.

2204-A.	Boston	1,440	2204-B.	New York	204

1,000 Dollar Notes
All issues are with the head of Grover Cleveland

DESIGN NO. 233. **(a and b)**

Reverse of Design No. 233.

Federal Reserve Note and Gold Certificate. (Notes 2210-2213 Incl.) (Also Note 2407)

1. Series of 1928.
Signatures of Woods and Mellon.

No.	Issuing Bank	No. Printed	No.	Issuing Bank	No. Printed
2210-A.	Boston	58,320	2210-G.	Chicago	355,800
2210-B.	New York	139,200	2210-H.	St. Louis	60,000
2210-C.	Philadelphia	96,708	2210-I.	Minneapolis	26,640
2210-D.	Cleveland	79,680	2210-J.	Kansas City	62,172
2210-E.	Richmond	66,840	2210-K.	Dallas	42,960
2210-F.	Atlanta	47,400	2210-L.	San Francisco	67,920

2. Series of 1934.
Signatures of Julian and Morgenthau.

2211-A.	Boston	46,200	2211-G.	Chicago	167,040
2211-B.	New York	332,784	2211-H.	St. Louis	22,440
2211-C.	Philadelphia	33,000	2211-I.	Minneapolis	12,000
2211-D.	Cleveland	35,400	2211-J.	Kansas City	51,840
2211-E.	Richmond	19,560	2211-K.	Dallas	46,800
2211-F.	Atlanta	67,800	2211-L.	San Francisco	90,600

3. Series of 1934-A.
Signatures of Julian and Morgenthau.

No.	Issuing Bank	No. Printed	No.	Issuing Bank	No. Printed
2212-A.	Boston	30,000	2212-G.	Chicago	134,400
2212-B.	New York	174,348	2212-H.	St. Louis	39,600
2212-C.	Philadelphia	78,000	2212-I.	Minneapolis	4,800
2212-D.	Cleveland	28,800	2212-J.	Kansas City	21,600
2212-E.	Richmond	16,800	2212-L.	San Francisco	36,600
2212-F.	Atlanta	80,964			

4. Series of 1934-C.
Signatures of Julian and Snyder.

2213-A.	Boston	1,200	2213-B.	New York	168

5,000 Dollar Notes
All issues are with the head of James Madison

DESIGN NO. 234. (a and b)

Reverse of Design No. 234.

Federal Reserve Note and Gold Certificate. (Notes 2220-2223) (Also Note 2408)

1. Series of 1928.
Signatures of Woods and Mellon.

No.	Issuing Bank	No. Printed	No.	Issuing Bank	No. Printed
2220-A.	Boston	1,320	2220-G.	Chicago	3,480
2220-B.	New York	2,640	2220-J.	Kansas City	720
2220-D.	Cleveland	3,000	2220-K.	Dallas	360
2220-E.	Richmond	3,984	2220-L.	San Francisco	51,300
2220-F.	Atlanta	1,440			

2. Series of 1934.
Signatures of Julian and Morgenthau.

2221-A.	Boston	9,480	2221-G.	Chicago	6,600
2221-B.	New York	11,520	2221-H.	St. Louis	2,400
2221-C.	Philadelphia	3,000	2221-J.	Kansas City	2,400
2221-D.	Cleveland	1,680	2221-K.	Dallas	2,400
2221-E.	Richmond	2,400	2221-L.	San Francisco	6,000
2221-F.	Atlanta	3,600			

3. Series of 1934-A.
Signatures of Julian and Morgenthau.

2222-H.	St. Louis	1,440

4. Series of 1934-B.
Signatures of Julian and Vinson.

2223-A.	Boston	1,200	2223-B.	New York	12

10,000 Dollar Notes

All issues are with the head of Salmon P. Chase

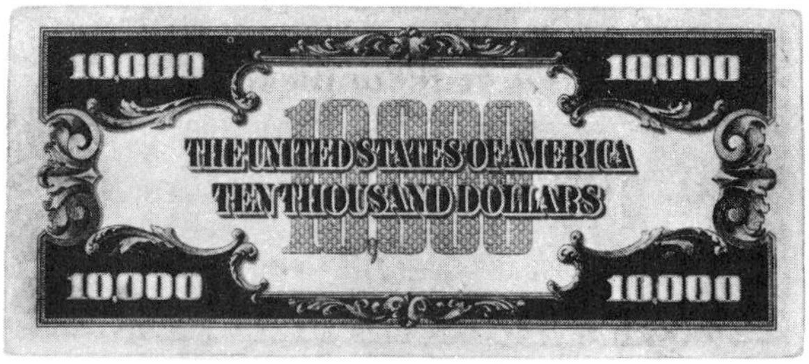

DESIGN NO. 235. **(a and b)**

Reverse of Design No. 235.

Federal Reserve Note and Gold Certificate. (Notes 2230-2233) (Also Note 2409)

1. Series of 1928.

Signatures of Woods and Mellon.

No.	Issuing Bank	No. Printed
2230-A.	Boston	1,320
2230-B.	New York	4,680
2230-D.	Cleveland	960
2230-E.	Richmond	3,024
2230-F.	Atlanta	1,440
2230-G.	Chicago	1,800
2230-H.	St. Louis	480
2230-I.	Minneapolis	480
2230-J.	Kansas City	480
2230-K.	Dallas	360
2230-L.	San Francisco	1,824

2. Series of 1934.

Signatures of Julian and Morgenthau.

2231-A.	Boston	9,720
2231-B.	New York	11,520
2231-C.	Philadelphia	6,000
2231-D.	Cleveland	1,480
2231-E.	Richmond	1,200
2231-F.	Atlanta	2,400
2231-G.	Chicago	3,840
2231-H.	St. Louis	2,040
2231-J.	Kansas City	1,200
2231-K.	Dallas	1,200
2231-L.	San Francisco	3,600

3. Series of 1934-A.

Signatures of Julian and Morgenthau.

2232-G.	Chicago	1,560

4. Series of 1934-B.

Signatures of Julian and Vinson.

2233-B.	New York	24

XX. EMERGENCY NOTES
ISSUED DURING WORLD WAR II

1. Notes Issued for Hawaii After the Attack on Pearl Harbor.

1 Dollar Notes

Silver Certificate Surcharged "Hawaii" on both sides; with Signatures of Julian and Morgenthau and with a Brown Seal (not Blue).

DESIGN NO. 236
(Note 2300)

Reverse of Design No. 236

No.	Denomination	Series	No. Printed	Very Fine	Unc
2300.	1 Dollar	1935-A	35,052,000	10.00	35.00

No.	Denomination	Series	No. Printed	Very Fine	Unc
2300*.	1 Dollar	1935-A		100.00	750.00

5 Dollar Notes

Federal Reserve Notes of San Francisco with Same Surcharge, Seal and Signatures.

DESIGN NO. 237.
(Notes 2301, 2302)

Reverse of Design No. 237.

No.	Denomination	Series	No. Printed	Very Fine	Unc
2301.	5 Dollars	1934	9,416,000	40.00	175.00
2301*.	5 Dollars	1934		165.00	750.00

No.	Denomination	Series	No. Printed	Very Fine	Unc
2302.	5 Dollars	1934-A	inc. above	20.00	150.00
2302*.	5 Dollars	1934-A		125.00	950.00

10 Dollar Notes

Federal Reserve Notes of San Francisco with Same Surcharge, Seal and Signatures.

DESIGN NO. 238.
(Note 2303)

Reverse of Design No. 238.

No.	Denomination	Series	No. Printed	Very Fine	Unc
2303.	10 Dollars	1934-A	10,424,000	30.00	225.00

No.	Denomination	Series	No. Printed	Very Fine	Unc
2303*.	10 Dollars	1934-A		125.00	1,100.00

20 Dollar Notes

Federal Reserve Notes of San Francisco with Same Surcharge, Seal and Signatures.

DESIGN NO. 239. (Notes 2304, 2305)

Reverse of Design No. 239.

No.	Denomination	Series	No. Printed	Very Fine	Unc
2304.	20 Dollars	1934	11,246,000	100.00	1,250.00
2304*.	20 Dollars	1934		375.00	2,000.00
2305.	20 Dollars	1934-A	inc. above	30.00	850.00
2305*.	20 Dollars	1934-A		300.00	1,400.00

2. Notes Issued for Use With the Armed Forces in Europe and North Africa.

These Notes are Silver Certificates with Signatures of Julian and Morgenthau and with a Yellow Seal (not Blue).

No.	Denomination	Series	Design No.	No. Printed	Very Fine	Unc
2306.	1 Dollar	1935-A	197	26,916,000	15.00	50.00
2306*.	1 Dollar	1935-A	197		85.00	750.00
2307.	5 Dollars	1934-A	199	16,710,000	17.50	95.00
2307*.	5 Dollars	1934-A	199		50.00	200.00
2308.	10 Dollars	1934	202	21,860,000	1,000.00	4,000.00
2308*.	10 Dollars	1934	202		Rare	
2309.	10 Dollars	1934-A	202		20.00	125.00
2309*.	10 Dollars	1934-A	202		50.00	350.00

XXI. GOLD CERTIFICATES

All are now obsolete. The issue was short lived as the Gold Reserve Act of 1933 required the surrender of all gold certificates, of both the large and small size. On April 24, 1964, Secretary of the Treasury C. Douglas Dillon removed all restrictions on the acquisition or holding of gold certificates and it is now legal to collect them. Unlike the large notes, the reverses of these gold certificates were printed in green. Small size gold certificates are considered much scarcer than the old large size notes. The obligation is as follows, "This certifies that there have been deposited in the Treasury of the United States of America . . . . . . Dollars in gold coin payable to the bearer on demand . . . This certificate is a legal tender in the amount thereof in payment of all debts and dues public and private."

(Additional information on this series will be found in the introduction to large size Gold Certificates on page 135.)

All the following have a Gold Seal.

10 Dollar Notes

DESIGN NO. 240
(Notes 2400, 2401)

Reverse of Design No. 240.

No.	Denomination	Series	Signatures		No. Printed	Very Fine	Unc
2400.	10 Dollars	1928	Woods	Mellon	130,812,000	35.00	200.00
2400*.	10 Dollars	1928	Woods	Mellon		125.00	550.00
2401.	10 Dollars	1928-A	Woods	Mills	2,544,000	Not Issued	

20 Dollar Notes

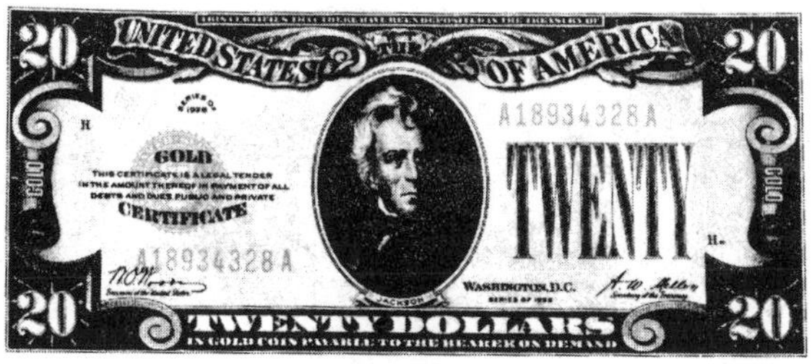

DESIGN NO. 241
(Notes 2402, 2403)

Reverse of Design No. 241.

No.	Denomination	Series	Signatures		No. Printed	Very Fine	Unc
2402.	20 Dollars	1928	Woods	Mellon	66,204,000	35.00	175.00
2402*.	20 Dollars	1928	Woods	Mellon		250.00	900.00
2403.	20 Dollars	1928-A	Woods	Mills	1,500,000	Not Issued	

50 Dollar Notes

DESIGN NO. 242.
(Note 2404)

Reverse of Design No. 242.

No.	Denomination	Series	Signatures		No. Printed	Very Fine	Unc
2404.	50 Dollars	1928	Woods	Mellon	5,520,000	**100.00**	**500.00**
2404*.	50 Dollars	1928	Woods	Mellon		**175.00**	**600.00**

100 Dollar Notes

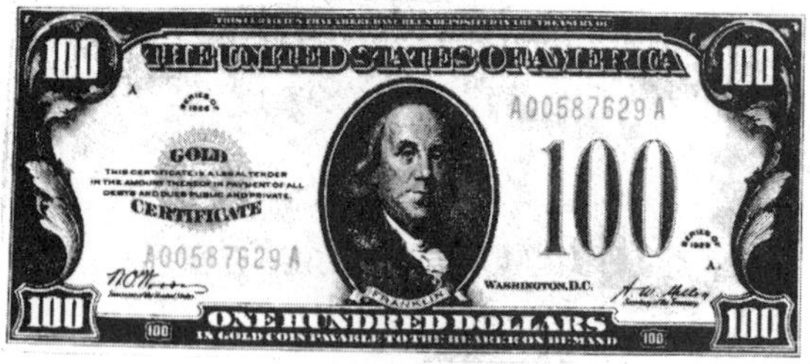

DESIGN NO. 243.
(Notes 2405, 2406)

Reverse of Design No. 243.

No.	Denomination	Series	Signatures		No. Printed	Very Fine	Unc
2405.	100 Dollars	1928	Woods	Mellon	3,240,000	**175.00**	**1,000.00**
2405*.	100 Dollars	1928	Woods	Mellon		**350.00**	**2,000.00**
2406.	100 Dollars	1934	Julian	Morgenthau	120,000	**Not Issued**	

The Following High Denominations Were Also Issued.
The designs are the same as the Federal Reserve Notes indicated except that the obligation and seal are different.

No.	Denomination	Series	Signatures		Design No.	No. Printed	Unc
2407.	500 Dollars	1928	Woods	Mellon	232	420,000	**Rare**
2408.	1,000 Dollars	1928	Woods	Mellon	233	288,000	**Rare**
2409.	1,000 Dollars	1934	Julian	Morgenthau	233	84,000	**Rare**
2410.	5,000 Dollars	1928	Woods	Mellon	234	24,000	**Rare**
2411.	10,000 Dollars	1928	Woods	Mellon	235	48,000	**Rare**
2412.	10,000 Dollars	1934	Julian	Morgenthau	235	36,000	**Rare**
2413.	100,000 Dollars	1934	Julian	Morgenthau		42,000	—

PART FOUR.

XXII. ENCASED POSTAGE STAMPS

Although not strictly paper money, Encased Postage Stamps have been included in this volume because they are essentially government printed paper that was actually used as money.

Encased Postage Stamps had their beginnings under the same circumstances that produced Fractional Currency — namely, the absence of circulating coin during the years of the Civil War.

A Mr. J. Gault was responsible for the issuance of Encased Postage Stamps, which were his own invention for alleviating the shortage of coins. He patented his Encased Postage Stamp in 1862, and subsequently issued them in denominations of 1, 2, 3, 5, 10, 12, 24, 30 and 90 Cents. They were at once popular and welcome, as anything would have been in those years that enabled one to make small change.

Since postage stamps were already being widely used in lieu of coins, a way had to be found to prolong their life. After only a very short time of going from hand to hand, stamps quickly became worthless as postage and unacceptable as money. Accordingly, Mr. Gault devised a round, brassy metal frame in which a stamp could be encased, so that it would not be subject to dirt, wear or tear. A layer of clear transparent mica covered the face of the frame, so that the stamp could be seen without being touched. The back of the frame was solid metal. Many merchants used the back of Encased Postage Stamps as an advertising medium and embossed messages on them. The illustration in the text will show the general appearance of an Encased Postage Stamp. The text proper lists all of the merchants whose names and products appear on the backs.

The denominations of Encased Postage Stamps were necessarily limited by the then current issues of the Post Office. The stamp issues of 1861 were used for this purpose, and this accounts for such unusual denominations as 12, 24, 30 and 90 Cents, which are completely foreign to our coinage system. At least, Encased Postage Stamps gave the public the familiar roundness of coins.

Like the first issues of Fractional Currency (Postage Currency) Encased Postage Stamps are collected by both coin and stamp collectors. As will be seen in the text, there are many rare and valuable items in existence, and the search for these is no less intense than for rare large notes.

At present, there is no current numismatic book that catalogues the entire series of Encased Postage Stamps. It is hoped that their inclusion in this volume will therefore be welcome and will help to further the science of numismatics.

The illustration above is typical of all examples. They are all of the same size and differ only in the denomination on the obverse and in the advertisement on the reverse. **The prices quoted are for specimens in Very Fine condition, light circulation wear on the case, and with all the mica clear and unbroken. All encased postage is very rare in new condition.**

1 CENT STAMPS

No.	Issued By	Value
EP-1.	Aerated Bread Co., New York	1,250.00
EP-2.	Ayer's Cathartic Pills	175.00
EP-3.	"Take Ayer's Pills"	175.00
EP-4.	Ayer's Sarsaparilla Small "Ayer's"	500.00
EP-4a.	As above but medium "Ayer's"	150.00
EP-5.	Bailey & Co., Philadelphia	600.00
EP-6.	Bates, Joseph L., Boston "Fancy Goods"	325.00
EP-6a.	As above but "Fancygoods" in one word	300.00
EP-7.	Brown's Bronchial Troches	700.00
EP-8.	Buhl, F. & Co., Detroit	250.00
EP-9.	Burnett's Cocoaine Kalliston	275.00
EP-10.	Burnett's Cooking Extracts	400.00
EP-11.	Claflin, A.M., Hopkinton, R.I.	4,000.00
EP-12.	Dougan, New York	1,750.00
EP-13.	Drake's Plantation Bitters	250.00
EP-13a.	Ellis, McAlpin & Co., Cincinnati	1,500.00
EP-14.	Evans, C.G.	650.00
EP-15.	Gage Brothers & Drake, Chicago	325.00
EP-16.	Gault, J., Plain frame	250.00
EP-17.	Gault, J., Ribbed Frame	600.00
EP-17a.	Hopkins, L.C. & Co., Cincinnati	950.00
EP-18.	Hunt & Nash, Irving House, N.Y	400.00
EP-19.	Kirkpatrick & Gault, N.Y.	375.00
EP-20.	Lord and Taylor, N.Y.	625.00
EP-21.	Mendum's Family Wine Emporium, N.Y.	400.00
EP-22.	Miles, B.F. John W., Chicago	2,500.00
EP-23.	Norris, John W., Chicago	1,600.00
EP-24.	North American Life Insurance Co., N.Y. Straight Inscr	375.00
EP-24a.	As above but curved inscr	350.00
EP-24b.	Pearce, Tolle & Holton, Cincinnati	2,100.00
EP-25.	Schapker & Bussing, Evansville, Ind.	550.00
EP-26.	Shillito, John & Co., Cincinnati	575.00
EP-27.	Steinfeld, S., N.Y.	850.00
EP-28.	Taylor N.G. & Co., Philadelphia	900.00
EP-29.	Weir & Larminie, Montreal, Canada	1,500.00
EP-30.	White the Hatter, N.Y.	1,200.00

2 CENT STAMPS

EP-31.	Gault, J., Very Rare, not a regular issue	**Extremely Rare**

3 CENT STAMPS

EP-32.	Ayer's Cathartic Pills	165.00
EP-32a.	As above but with longer arrows	175.00
EP-33.	"Take Ayer's Pills"	165.00
EP-34.	Ayer's Sarsaparilla, Plain frame	525.00
EP-34a.	As above but medium "Ayer's". (EP-34 is small)	165.00
EP-34b.	As above but large "Ayer's"	325.00
EP-35.	Ayer's Sarsaparilla, Ribbed frame	650.00
EP-36.	Bailey & Co., Philadelphia	625.00
EP-37.	Bates, Joseph L., Boston "Fancy Goods"	450.00
EP-37a.	Same, "Fancygoods" in one word	475.00
EP-38.	Brown's Bronchial Troches	275.00
EP-38a.	Buhl, F. & Co., Detroit	750.00
EP-39.	Burnett's Cocoaine Kalliston	225.00
EP-40.	Burnett's Cooking Extracts	225.00
EP-40a.	Claflin, A.M. Hopkinton, R.I.	4,250.00
EP-41.	Dougan, N.Y.	1,200.00
EP-42.	Drake's Plantation Bitters	200.00
EP-43.	Ellis, McAlpin & Co., Cincinnati	1,000.00
EP-44.	Evans, C.G.	600.00

3 CENT STAMPS

No.	Issued By	Value
EP-45.	Gage Brothers & Drake, Chicago	400.00
EP-46.	Gault, J., Plain frame	200.00
EP-47.	Gault, J., Ribbed frame	450.00
EP-48.	Hopkins, L.C. & Co., Cincinnati	1,250.00
EP-49.	Hunt & Nash, Irving House, N.Y.	450.00
EP-49a.	Same, but with ribbed frame	900.00
EP-50.	Kirkpatrick & Gault, N.Y.	475.00
EP-51.	Lord & Taylor, N.Y.	750.00
EP-52.	Mendum's Family Wine Emporium, N.Y.	700.00
EP-52a.	Norris, John W., Chicago	1,000.00
EP-53.	North American Life Insurance Co., N.Y.	450.00
EP-53a.	As above, but curved inscr	550.00
EP-54.	Pearce, Tolle & Holton, Cincinnati	1,350.00
EP-55.	Schapker & Bussing, Evansville, Ind.	650.00
EP-56.	Shillito, John & Co., Cincinnati	475.00
EP-57.	Taylor, N.G. & Co., Philadelphia	800.00
EP-58.	Weir & Larminie, Montreal, Canada	1,600.00
EP-59.	White the Hatter, N.Y.	1,000.00

5 CENT STAMPS

No.	Issued By	Value
EP-60.	Ayer's Cathartic Pills	250.00
EP-60a.	As above but with longer arrows	275.00
EP-61.	"Take Ayer's Pills", Plain frame	200.00
EP-62.	"Take Ayer's Pills", Ribbed frame	850.00
EP-63.	Ayer's Sarsaparilla, Medium "Ayer's"	200.00
EP-63a.	Ayer's Sarsaparilla, Large "Ayer's"	525.00
EP-64.	Bailey & Co., Philadelphia	750.00
EP-65.	Bates, Joseph L., Boston, Plain frame	600.00
EP-66.	Bates, Joseph L., Boston, Ribbed frame	850.00
EP-66a.	Same, "Fancygoods" in one word, Plain	750.00
EP-67.	Brown's Bronchial Troches	225.00
EP-68.	Buhl, F. & Co., Detroit	750.00
EP-69.	Burnett's Cocoaine Kalliston	325.00
EP-70.	Burnett's Cooking Extracts	300.00
EP-71.	Claflin, A.M., Hopkinton, R.I.	4,500.00
EP-72.	Cook, H.A., Evansville, Ind.	850.00
EP-73.	Dougan, N.Y.	1,250.00
EP-74.	Drake's Plantation Bitters, Plain frame	275.00
EP-75.	Drake's Plantation Bitters, Ribbed frame	700.00
EP-76.	Ellis, McAlpin & Co., Cincinnati	1,250.00
EP-76a.	Evans, C.G.	900.00
EP-77.	Gage Brothers & Drake, Chicago	350.00
EP-78.	Gault, J., Plain frame	225.00
EP-79.	Gault, J., Ribbed frame	600.00
EP-80.	Hopkins, L.C. & Co., Cincinnati	1,500.00
EP-81.	Hunt & Nash, Irving House, N.Y., Plain frame	600.00
EP-82.	Hunt & Nash, Irving House, N.Y., Ribbed frame	600.00
EP-83.	Kirkpatrick & Gault, N.Y.	225.00
EP-84.	Lord & Taylor, N.Y.	850.00
EP-85.	Mendum's Family Wine Emporium, N.Y.	550.00
EP-86.	Miles, B.F., Peoria	2,750.00
EP-87.	Norris, John W., Chicago	1,200.00
EP-88.	North American Life Insurance Co., N.Y., Plain frame, straight inscr.	550.00
EP-88a.	North American Life Ins. Co., N.Y., Ribbed frame	1,000.00
EP-89.	Pearce, Tolle & Holton, Cincinnati	1,750.00
EP-90.	Sands Ale	1,400.00
EP-91.	Schapker & Bussing, Evansville, Ind.	500.00
EP-92.	Shillito, John & Co., Cincinnati	450.00
EP-93.	Steinfeld, S., N.Y.	850.00
EP-93a.	Taylor, N.G. & Co., Philadelphia	950.00
EP-94.	Weir & Larminie, Montreal, Canada	1,300.00
EP-95.	White the Hatter, N.Y.	1,100.00

9 CENT STRIPS

No.	Issued By	Value
EP-95a.	Three 3¢ stamps in a brass, rectangular frame, sometimes referred to as having a Feuchtwanger back. Of doubtful origin	350.00

10 CENT STAMPS

No.	Issued By	Value
EP-96.	Ayer's Cathartic Pills Short arrows	400.00
EP-96a.	As above but long arrows	425.00
EP-97.	"Take Ayer's Pills"	400.00
EP-98.	Ayer's Sarsaparilla, Plain frame	500.00
EP-98a.	As above but medium "Ayer's." (EP-98 is small)	350.00
EP-98b.	As above, but large "Ayer's"	575.00
EP-99.	Ayer's Sarsaparilla, Ribbed frame	850.00
EP-100.	Bailey & Co., Philadelphia	750.00
EP-101.	Bates, Joseph L., Boston, Plain frame	450.00
EP-102.	Bates, Joseph L., Boston, Ribbed frame	800.00
EP-102a.	Same, "Fancygoods" in one word. Plain	400.00
EP-103.	Brown's Bronchial Troches	425.00
EP-104.	Buhl, F. & Co., Detroit	1,000.00
EP-105.	Burnett's Cocoaine Kalliston	350.00
EP-106.	Burnett's Cooking Extracts, Plain frame	350.00
EP-107.	Burnett's Cooking Extracts, Ribbed frame	750.00
EP-108.	Cook, H.A., Evansville, Ind.	750.00
EP-108a.	Claflin, A.M., Hopkinton, R.I.	5,500.00
EP-109.	Dougan, N.Y.	2,000.00
EP-110.	Drake's Plantation Bitters, Plain frame	350.00
EP-111.	Drake's Plantation Bitters, Ribbed frame	850.00
EP-112.	Ellis, McAlpin & Co., Cincinnati	1,400.00
EP-113.	Evans, C.G.	1,000.00
EP-114.	Gage Brothers & Drake, Chicago, Plain frame	425.00
EP-115.	Gage Brother & Drake, Chicago, Ribbed frame	900.00
EP-116.	Gault, J., Plain frame	350.00
EP-117.	Gault, J., Ribbed frame	700.00
EP-117a.	Hopkins, L.C. & Co., Cincinnati	1,400.00
EP-118.	Hunt & Nash, Irving House, N.Y., Plain frame	475.00
EP-119.	Hunt & Nash, Irving House, N.Y., Ribbed frame	650.00
EP-120.	Kirkpatrick & Gault, N.Y.	325.00
EP-121.	Lord & Taylor, N.Y.	1,000.00
EP-122.	Mendum's Family Wine Emporium, N.Y., Plain frame	500.00
EP-123.	Mendum's Family Wine Emporium, N.Y., Ribbed frame	900.00
EP-124.	Norris, John W., Chicago	1,650.00
EP-125.	North American Life Insurance Co., N.Y., Plain frame, straight inscr.	550.00
EP-125a.	As above, but curved inscr.	750.00
EP-126.	North American Life Insurance Co., N.Y., Ribbed frame, curved inscr.	1,300.00
EP-127.	Pearce, Tolle & Holton, Cincinnati	2,000.00
EP-128.	Sands Ale	1,750.00
EP-129.	Schapker & Bussing, Evansville, Ind.	700.00
EP-130.	Shillito, John & Co., Cincinnati	675.00
EP-131.	Steinfeld, S., N.Y.	1,400.00
EP-132.	Taylor, N. & Co., Philadelphia	1,500.00
EP-133.	Weir & Larminie, Montreal, Canada	1,400.00
AE-134.	White the Hatter, N.Y.	1,200.00

12 CENT STAMPS

No.	Issued By	Value
EP-135.	Ayer's Cathartic Pills	500.00
EP-136.	"Take Ayer's Pills"	750.00
EP-137.	Ayer's Sarsaparilla, Medium "Ayer's"	750.00
EP-137a.	As above, but small "Ayer's"	1,250.00
EP-138.	Bailey & Co., Philadelphia	1,400.00
EP-139.	Bates, Joseph L., Boston	800.00
EP-140.	Brown's Bronchial Troches	800.00
EP-141.	Buhl, F. & Co., Detroit	1,250.00
EP-142.	Burnett's Cocoaine Kalliston	800.00
EP-143.	Burnett's Cooking Extracts	800.00

12 CENT STAMPS

No.	Issued By	Value
EP-144.	Claflin, A.M., Hopkinton, R.I.	6,000.00
EP-145.	Drake's Plantation Bitters	800.00
EP-146.	Ellis, McAlpin & Co., Cincinnati	1,250.00
EP-147.	Gage Brothers & Drake, Chicago	800.00
EP-148.	Gault, J., Plain frame	700.00
EP-149.	Gault, J., Ribbed frame	1,100.00
EP-150.	Hunt & Nash, Irving House, N.Y., Plain frame	850.00
EP-151.	Hunt & Nash, Irving House, N.Y., Ribbed frame	1,200.00
EP-152.	Kirkpatrick & Gault, N.Y.	650.00
EP-153.	Lord & Taylor, N.Y.	1,800.00
EP-154.	Mendum's Family Wine Emporium, N.Y.	1,100.00
EP-155.	North American Life Insurance Co., N.Y.	950.00
EP-156.	Pearce, Tolle & Holton, Cincinnati	2,000.00
EP-156a.	Sands Ale	2,000.00
EP-157.	Schapker & Bussing, Evansville, Ind.	1,200.00
EP-158.	Shillito, John & Co., Cincinnati	1,600.00
EP-159.	Steinfeld, S., N.Y.	2,000.00
EP-159a.	Taylor, N.G. & Co., Philadelphia	2,000.00

24 CENT STAMPS

No.	Issued By	Value
EP-159b.	Ayer's Cathartic Pills	1,600.00
EP-160.	Ayer's Sarsaparilla	1,600.00
EP-161.	Brown's Bronchial Troches	Unique
EP-162.	Buhl, F. & Co., Detroit	1,600.00
EP-163.	Burnett's Cocoaine Kalliston	1,950.00
EP-164.	Burnett's Cooking Extracts	1,750.00
EP-165.	Drake's Plantation Bitters	1,600.00
EP-166.	Ellis, McAlpin & Co., Cincinnati	1,600.00
EP-167.	Gault, J., Plain frame	1,600.00
		1,500.00
EP-168.	Gault, J., Ribbed frame	2,000.00
EP-169.	Hunt & Nash, Irving House, N.Y., Plain frame	1,750.00
EP-170.	Hunt & Nash, Irving House, N.Y., Ribbed frame	2,250.00
EP-171.	Kirkpatrick & Gault, N.Y.	1,750.00
EP-172.	Lord & Taylor, N.Y.	2,100.00
EP-172a.	Pearce, Tolle & Holton, Cincinnati	2,250.00

30 CENT STAMPS

No.	Issued By	Value
EP-172b.	Ayer's Cathartic Pills	2,250.00
EP-173.	Ayer's Sarsaparilla	2,000.00
EP-174.	Brown's Bronchial Troches	2,500.00
EP-175.	Burnett's Cocoaine Kalliston	2,250.00
EP-176.	Burnett's Cooking Extracts	2,250.00
EP-177.	Drake's Plantation Bitters	2,250.00
EP-178.	Gault, J., Plain frame	1,950.00
EP-179.	Gault, J., Ribbed frame	2,600.00
EP-180.	Hunt & Nash, Irving House, N.Y.	2,350.00
EP-181.	Kirkpatrick & Gault, N.Y.	2,000.00
EP-182.	Lord & Taylor, N.Y.	2,750.00
EP-183.	Sands Ale	2,850.00

90 CENT STAMPS

No.	Issued By	Value
EP-183a.	"Take Ayer's Pills"	6,250.00
EP-183b.	Ayer's Sarsaparilla	5,900.00
EP-184.	Burnett's Cocoaine Kalliston	5,900.00
EP-184a.	Burnett's Cooking Extracts	Unique
EP-185.	Drake's Plantation Bitters	6,000.00
EP-186.	Gault, J.	5,500.00
EP-187.	Kirkpatrick & Gault, N.Y.	5,900.00
EP-188.	Lord & Taylor, N.Y.	6,500.00

According to Arnold Perl, well-known authority on encased postage, a number of other, unlisted specimens have been seen bearing stamps other than the conventional ones. Several bear the 1851 1¢ stamp, envelope stamps, etc. Research indicates these to be trial pieces or specimens — never released for general issuance by Gault. They are unquestionably authentic and a part, at least, of the history of encased U.S. postage stamps.

PART FIVE. SUPPLEMENT

XXIII. LIST OF NATIONAL BANKS

The following list was compiled from official records of the Treasury Department, mainly from the National Bank Redemption Agency and the Comptroller of the Currency.

The banks are arranged by state, and numerically by charter numbers within the state. Numismatically, this arrangement was deemed best since it forms a chronological history of banking in each state, from which it is possible to deduce important numismatic information, such as the types of notes possible to have been issued in each state, the relative frequency of such notes, etc.

A further breakdown of the banks could have been made by listing them under their cities alphabetically arranged within their states, such as exists in most government records for purely fiscal purposes. Such a listing would have destroyed the chronology of bank formation in each state and would have served no useful numismatic purpose. Those who wish to make their own city-list of banks can easily extract the information required from the state-list below.

In consulting or using this list of banks, the following points might be helpful:-

1. The name of the bank as listed here was its name at the time it was given its charter. Subsequent mergers, liquidations or other events caused many banks to change or alter their names. That is why certain bank notes exist bearing the same charter numbers but differently named banks.

2. Not all banks issued circulating notes. Many did not; others had notes printed but did not issue them and these were later cancelled and destroyed at the Treasury Department; in some cases, banks failed shortly after organization; in other cases, the entire issue of a bank's notes may subsequently have been redeemed. In the interest of completeness, all 14,348 banks have been listed that were chartered during the note issuing period, 1863-1935. New national banks continued to be chartered after this period, but they are not listed here.

3. It will be both practical and instructive to use this list in conjunction with the list entitled "Years of issue of charter numbers."

4. An analysis of the charter numbers will reveal more graphically than any words can, the pattern of expansion, growth and prosperity of this country. It will be noted that the earlier charter numbers are concentrated in the populous, long-established eastern part of the country; later charter numbers in the southern and western areas. The establishment of new frontiers, new cities and towns, and new industrial, mining and agricultural centers brought with it the formation of thousands of new national banks.

5. It goes without saying that a note from a bank situated in a city or town of small population would be of greater numismatic and historical interest than a similar type note issued by a large bank in a metropolis. Many of these small banks had a capital of only $25,000.00 and their note issues were correspondingly small. There is no doubt that there are many unique national bank notes presently in the hands of collectors — unique in the sense that the specific note is the only surviving example of the notes of that type issued by the specific national bank named thereon. Only time, further research and the exchange of information will reveal which notes are truly unique.

6. Almost every aspect of American life is touched upon in the varied names of the national banks. These names are interesting enough to be read almost as literature. Similarly, a perusal of the list of the cities themselves is a revelation of local geography.

ALABAMA

Charter #	City	Name of Bank
1537.	Selma	First N.B.
1560.	Huntsville	N.B. of Huntsville
1595.	Mobile	First N.B.
1736.	Selma	City N.B.
1814.	Montgomery	First N.B.
1817.	Mobile	Alabama N.B.
1822.	Gainesville	Gainesville N.B.
1853.	Tuskaloosa	First N.B.
2029.	Montgomery	Merchants and Planters' N.B.
2065.	Birmingham	N.B. of Birmingham
2309.	Eufaula	Eufaula N.B.
3041.	Anniston	First N.B.
3185.	Birmingham	First N.B.
3442.	Birmingham	Berney N.B.
3452.	Opelika	First N.B.
3587.	Birmingham	Alabama N.B.
3617.	Sheffield	First N.B.
3622.	Eufaula	East Alabama N.B.
3663.	Gadsden	First N.B.
3678.	Tuscaloosa	Merchants' N.B.
3679.	Birmingham	Birmingham N.B.
3699.	Decatur	First N.B.
3734.	Birmingham	American N.B.
3899.	Talladega	First N.B.
3931.	Eutaw	First N.B.
3981.	Florence	First N.B.
3993.	Birmingham	City N.B.
4064.	Fort Payne	First N.B.
4067.	Huntsville	First N.B.
4135.	Florence	Florence N.B.
4180.	Montgomery	Merchants and Planters' — Farley N.B.
4220.	Bessemer	First N.B.
4250.	Anniston	Anniston N.B.
4319.	Jacksonville	First N.B.
4394.	Demopolis	First N.B.
4591.	Bridgeport	First N.B.
4689.	Huntsville	Farmers and Merchants' N.B.
4838.	Talladega	Isbell N.B.
5024.	Eufaula	Commercial N.B.
5219.	Mobile	City N.B.
5249.	Dothan	First N.B.
5572.	Greenville	First N.B.
5593.	Troy	First N.B.
5664.	Thomasville	First N.B.
5693.	Greensboro	First N.B.
5714.	Geneva	First N.B.
5877.	Montgomery	Fourth N.B.
5909.	Dothan	Dothan N.B.
5962.	Ensley	First N.B.
5970.	Andalusia	First N.B.
5983.	Jackson	First N.B.
5987.	Abbeville	First N.B.
6021.	Anniston	City N.B.
6146.	Athens	First N.B.
6173.	Tuscaloosa	City N.B.
6319.	Enterprise	First N.B.
6380.	Albany	Morgan County N.B.
6759.	Sheffield	Sheffield N.B.
6835.	Citronelle	First N.B.
6897.	Elba	First N.B.
6961.	Bessemer	First N.B.
7020.	Birmingham	Traders' N.B.
7044.	Troy	Farmers and Merchants' N.B.
7062.	Mobile	Bank of Mobile N.B. Assn.
7073.	Oxford	First N.B.
7084.	Selma	Selma N.B.
7097.	Cullman	First N.B.
7141.	Montgomery	American N.B.
7148.	Linden	First N.B.
7371.	Thomasville	Citizens' N.B.
7417.	Alexander City	First N.B.
7424.	Headland	First N.B.
7429.	Brundidge	First N.B.
7451.	Sylacauga	First N.B.
7464.	Piedmont	First N.B.
7467.	Union Springs	First N.B.
7484.	Sylacauga	Merchants and Planters' N.B.
7516.	Lineville	First N.B.
7551.	Lineville	Lineville N.B.
7558.	Talladega	Talladega N.B.
7568.	Wetumpka	First N.B.
7592.	Hartford	First N.B.
7629.	Ozark	First N.B.
7687.	Evergreen	First N.B.
7746.	Jasper	First N.B.
7871.	Slocomb	First N.B.
7932.	Dothan	Houston N.B.
7938.	Dothan	Third N.B.
7940.	Slocomb	Slocomb N.B.
7951.	Attalla	First N.B.
7975.	Hayneville	First N.B.
7985.	Opp	First N.B.
7991.	Brantley	First N.B.
7992.	Luverne	First N.B.
8028.	Samson	First N.B.
8067.	Hartsville	First N.B.
8095.	Columbia	First N.B.
8217.	Camden	Camden N.B.
8284.	Montgomery	Exchange N.B.
8458.	Midland City	First N.B.
8460.	Montgomery	Capital N.B.
8560.	Gadsden	Gadsden N.B.
8765.	Huntsville	Henderson N.B.
8856.	Lineville	Citizens' N.B.
8910.	Florala	First N.B.
8963.	Scottsboro	First N.B.
9055.	Prattville	First N.B.
9506.	Pell City	First N.B.
9550.	Opelika	Farmers' N.B.
9580.	Ashland	First N.B.
9614.	Cullman	Leeth N.B.
9681.	Dozier	First N.B.
9855.	Stevenson	First N.B.
9925.	Oxford	Oxford N.B.
9927.	Newville	First N.B.
10035.	Demopolis	Commercial N.B.
10066.	Childersburg	First N.B.
10102.	Ashford	First N.B.
10131.	Lincoln	First N.B.
10307.	Geneva	Farmers' N.B.
10336.	Decatur	City N.B.
10377.	Fayette	First N.B.
10421.	Enterprise	Farmers and Merchants' N.B.
10423.	Albany	Central N.B.
10441.	Boaz	First N.B.
10457.	New Brockton	First N.B.
10654.	Seale	First N.B.
10697.	Atmore	First N.B.
10732.	Mobile	Nat. City Bank
10766.	Tallassee	First N.B.
10799.	La Pine	First N.B.
10879.	Sylacauga	City N.B.
10959.	Abbeville	Henry N.B.
10990.	Guntersville	First N.B.
11168.	Bridgeport	American N.B.
11233.	Reform	First N.B.
11259.	Coffee Springs	First N.B.
11281.	Tuscumbia	First N.B.
11337.	Collinsville	First N.B.
11445.	Headland	Farmers and Merchants' N.B.
11451.	Fort Payne	First N.B.
11515.	Clanton	First N.B.
11613.	Haleyville	First N.B.
11635.	Opelika	N.B. of Opelika
11753.	Anniston	Commercial N.B.
11766.	Fairfield	First N.B.
11819.	Albertville	First N.B.
11820.	Albertville	Albertville N.B.
11846.	Russellville	First N.B.
11870.	Boaz	N.B. of Boaz
11905.	Bessemer	City N.B.
11955.	Andalusia	Andalusia N.B.
12006.	Oneonta	First N.B.
12455.	Auburn	First N.B.
12642.	Monroeville	First N.B.
12906.	Birmingham, Ensley	Ensley N.B.
12960.	Goodwater	First N.B.
12962.	Union Springs	American N.B.
12993.	Montgomery	Alabama N.B.
13097.	Mobile	Merchants N.B.
13128.	Hartford	Hartford N.B.
13195.	Mobile	Mobile N.B.
13358.	Birmingham	Woodlawn-American N.B
13359.	Leeds	Leeds-American N.B.
13412.	Gadsden	American N.B.
13414.	Mobile	American N.B. and Trust Co.
13728.	Gadsden	First N.B.
13752.	Headland	Headland N.B.
13789.	Bessemer	First N.B.
14160.	Tuscumbia	First N.B.

ALASKA

Charter #	City	Name of Bank
5117.	Juneau	First N.B.
7718.	Fairbanks	First N.B.
10705.	Seward	Harriman N.B.
12072.	Anchorage	First N.B.
12578.	Ketchikan	First N.B.

ARIZONA

Charter #	City	Name of Bank
2639.	Tucson	First N.B.
3054.	Phoenix	First N.B.
3122.	Prescott	First N.B.
3728.	Phoenix	N.B. of Arizona
4287.	Tucson	Consolidated N.B.
4440.	Tucson	Arizona N.B.
4729.	Phoenix	Phoenix N.B.
4851.	Prescott	Prescott N.B.
5720.	Tempe	Tempe N.B.
5821.	Clifton	First N.B.
6439.	Tombstone	First N.B.

Charter #	City	Name of Bank
6579.	Globe	First N.B.
6591.	Nogales	First N.B.
6633.	Douglas	First N.B.
7182.	Bisbee	First N.B.
7591.	Yuma	First N.B.
8193.	Globe	Globe N.B.
9608.	Yuma	Yuma N.B.
10998.	Florence	First N.B.
11012.	Nogales	Nogales N.B.
11120.	Flagstaff	First N.B.
11130.	Mesa	First N.B.
11139.	Glendale	First N.B.
11159.	Tucson	Tucson N.B.
11395.	Chandler	First N.B.
11559.	Phoenix	Commercial N.B.
11663.	Casa Grande	First N.B.
12198.	Holbrook	First N.B.
12581.	Winslow	First N.B.
13262.	Prescott	First N.B.
14324.	Phoenix	Valley N.B.

ARKANSAS

Charter #	City	Name of Bank
1631.	Fort Smith	First N.B.
1648.	Little Rock	First N.B.
1950.	Fort Smith	First N.B.
2776.	Pine Bluff	First N.B.
2832.	Hot Springs	Arkansas N.B.
2887.	Hot Springs	Hot Springs N.B.
3300.	Little Rock	Exchange N.B.
3318.	Little Rock	American N.B.
3634.	Fort Smith	American N.B.
3662.	Helena	First N.B.
4066.	Camden	Camden N.B.
4401.	Texarkana	Gate City N.B.
4582.	Russellville	First N.B.
4995.	Fort Smith	Fort Smith N.B.
5849.	Waldron	First N.B.
5890.	Harrison	First N.B.
5929.	De Queen	First N.B.
6680.	Pine Bluff	Simmons N.B.
6706.	Perry	First N.B.
6758.	Newport	First N.B.
6786.	Greenwood	First N.B.
6846.	Paragould	First N.B.
6902.	Little Rock	State N.B.
7046.	El Dorado	First N.B.
7138.	Texarkana	State N.B.
7163.	Mena	First N.B.
7240.	Fort Smith	Merchants' N.B.
7311.	Corning	First N.B.
7323.	El Dorado	Citizens' N.B.
7346.	Fayetteville	First N.B.
7361.	Van Buren	First N.B.
7523.	Bentonville	First N.B.
7531.	Hot Springs	Citizens' N.B.
7556.	Batesville	First N.B.
7634.	Malvern	First N.B.
7789.	Rogers	First N.B.
7829.	Mena	N.B. of Mena
7952.	Fayetteville	N.B. of Fayetteville
8030.	Prairie Grove	First N.B.
8086.	Jonesboro	First N.B.
8135.	Bentonville	Benton County N.B.
8237.	Gravette	First N.B.
8495.	Eureka Springs	First N.B.
8594.	Hope	Hope N.B.
8763.	Springdale	First N.B.
8786.	Fayetteville	Arkansas N.B.
8864.	Batesville	N.B. of Batesville
8952.	Huntsville	First N.B.
9022.	Newark	First N.B.
9037.	Little Rock	England N.B.
9324.	Earle	First N.B.
9332.	Walnut Ridge	First N.B.
9354.	Lewisville	First N.B.
9494.	Benton	First N.B.
9501.	Fordyce	First N.B.
9633.	Clarksville	First N.B.
9871.	Siloam Springs	First N.B.
10004.	Paragould	N.B. of Commerce
10060.	Huttig	First N.B.
10087.	Arkdelphia	Citizens' N.B.
10138.	Leslie	First N.B.
10178.	De Witt	First N.B.
10406.	Berryville	First N.B.
10422.	Green Forest	First N.B.
10434.	Morrilton	First N.B.
10439.	Judsonia	First N.B.
10447.	Horatio	First N.B.
10459.	Stuttgart	First N.B.
10484.	Tuckerman	First N.B.
10486.	Ashdown	First N.B.
10550.	Forrest City	First N.B.
10579.	Hope	Citizens' N.B.
10609.	Fort Smith	City N.B.
10723.	Cotton Plant	First N.B.
10750.	Rogers	American N.B.
10768.	Pine Bluff	N.B. of Arkansas
10794.	Marshall	First N.B.
10795.	Marshall	Arkansas N.B.
10801.	Harrison	People's N.B.
10807.	Wynne	First N.B.
10853.	Rector	First N.B.
10854.	Marianna	Lee County N.B.
10867.	Newport	Farmers' N.B.
10983.	Greenwood	First N.B.
11046.	Junction City	First N.B.
11113.	Mineral Springs	First N.B.
11116.	Monette	First N.B.
11122.	Marked Tree	First N.B.
11180.	Heber Springs	First N.B.
11195.	Mansfield	First N.B.
11196.	Mansfield	N.B. of Mansfield
11214.	Belmont	Army N.B.
11221.	Des Arc	First N.B.
11225.	Benton	Farmers and Merchants' N.B.
11234.	Helena	Interstate N.B.
11262.	Lake Village	First N.B.
11276.	Dardanelle	First N.B.
11312.	Black Rock	First N.B.
11322.	Lepanto	First N.B.
11367.	Heber Springs	Arkansas N.B.
11542.	Hughes	Planters' N.B.
11580.	Clarksville	Farmers' N.B.
11592.	Paris	First N.B.
11645.	Pocahontas	First N.B.
11651.	Blytheville	First N.B.
11748.	Hartford	First N.B.
11825.	Lincoln	First N.B.
11830.	Hartford	Farmers and Miners' N.B.
12083.	Walnut Ridge	Planter's N.B.
12156.	Stuttgart	People's N.B.
12219.	Cotton Plant	Farmers' N.B.
12238.	Lamar	First N.B.
12291.	Harrison	Citizens' N.B.
12296.	Holly Grove	First N.B.
12340.	Gentry	First N.B.
12429.	El Dorado	N.B. of Commerce
12447.	North Little Rock	First N.B.
12533.	Hope	First N.B.
12813.	Eudora	First N.B.
12914.	Tuckerman	First N.B.
12985.	Ozark	First N.B.
13155.	Paragould	New First N.B.
13210.	Gurdon	First N.B.
13274.	Siloam Springs	First N.B.
13280.	McGehee	First N.B.
13506.	Siloam Springs	Hutchings First N.B.
13520.	Helena	Phillips N.B.
13534.	Ashdown	First N.B.
13543.	Green Forest	First N.B.
13632.	Lake Village	First N.B.
13637.	Forrest City	N.B. of Eastern Arkansas
13693.	Mena	Planters N.B.
13719.	Conway	First N.B.
13949.	Little Rock	Peoples N.B.
13958.	Little Rock	Union N.B.
14000.	Little Rock	Commercial N.B.
14056.	Pine Bluff	N.B. of Commerce
14096.	Camden	Citizens N.B.
14097.	Marianna	First N.B.
14209.	Paris	First N.B.
14238.	Malvern	Malvern N.B.

CALIFORNIA

Charter #	City	Name of Bank
1741.	San Francisco	First Nat. Gold Bank
1994.	San Francisco	Nat. Gold Bank and Trust Co.
2014.	Sacramento	Nat. Gold Bank of D.O. Mills and Co.
2077.	Stockton	First Nat. Gold Bank.
2104.	Santa Barbara	First Nat. Gold Bank
2158.	San Jose	Farmers' Nat. Gold Bank
2193.	Petaluma	First Nat. Gold Bank
2248.	Oakland	First Nat. Gold Bank
2266.	Oakland	Union Nat. Gold Bank
2412.	Stockton	First N.B.
2431.	Alameda	First N.B.
2456.	Santa Barbara	County N.B. and Trust Co.
2491.	Los Angeles	First N.B.
2794.	Stockton	Stockton N.B.
2938.	Los Angeles	Los Angeles N.B.
3050.	San Diego	First N.B.
3056.	San Diego	Consolidated N.B.
3136.	Modesto	First N.B.
3321.	Fresno	First N.B.
3348.	Riverside	First N.B.
3499.	Pasadena	First N.B.
3518.	Pomona	First N.B.
3520.	Santa Ana	First N.B.
3527.	San Bernardino	First N.B.
3538.	Los Angeles	Merchants' N.B.
3555.	San Francisco	Crocker N.B.
3558.	Santa Rosa	Santa Rosa N.B.
3568.	Pasadena	Pasadena N.B.
3573.	Colton	First N.B.
3592.	San Francisco	California N.B.
3648.	Grass Valley	First N.B.
3715.	San Jose	Garden City N.B.
3733.	Merced	First N.B.
3743.	Monrovia	First N.B.
3757.	Saint Helena	First N.B.
3780.	San Diego	San Diego N.B.
3818.	San Bernardino	San Bernardino N.B.
3826.	San Luis Obispo	First N.B.
3828.	San Diego	California N.B.
3845.	Santa Monica	First N.B.
3870	Fresno	Fresno N.B.
3892.	Redlands	First N.B.
4096.	Los Angeles	N.B. of California
4120.	Santa Paula	First N.B.
4663.	Pomona	American N.B.
4757.	Riverside	Riverside N.B.
4873.	Needles	Needles N.B.
4886.	San Diego	Merchants' N.B.
5074.	Salinas	First N.B.
5096.	San Francisco	San Francisco N.B.
5105.	San Francisco	Wells-Fargo Nevada N.B.
5162.	Fresno	Farmers' N.B.
5380.	Berkeley	First N.B.
5395.	Selma	First N.B.
5456.	Long Beach	First N.B.
5588.	Whittier	First N.B.
5654.	Fullerton	First N.B.
5688.	San Francisco	Western N.B.
5830.	Covina	First N.B.
5863.	Hanford	First N.B.
5927.	Los Angeles	Citizens' N.B.
5986.	Eureka	First N.B.
5993.	Los Angeles	Southwestern N.B.
6027.	Imperial	First N.B.
6044.	Bakersfield	First N.B.
6268.	Ontario	First N.B.
6426.	San Francisco	American N.B.
6481.	Anaheim	First N.B.
6545.	Los Angeles	American N.B.
6592.	San Francisco	Germania N.B.
6617.	Los Angeles	Farmers and Merchants' N.B.
6730.	Long Beach	N.B. of Long Beach
6749.	Long Beach	American N.B.
6808.	Porterville	First N.B.
6833.	Riverside	Orange Growers' N.B.
6864.	Los Angeles	Commercial N.B.
6869.	San Diego	N.B. of Commerce
6873.	Hanford	Hanford N.B.
6904.	Petaluma	Petaluma N.B.
6919.	Oroville	First N.B.
6945.	Santa Monica	Merchants' N.B.
6993.	El Monte	First N.B.
7057.	San Pedro	First N.B.
7058.	Monterey	First N.B.
7063.	Visalia	First N.B.
7069.	Palo Alto	First N.B.
7152.	Cucamonga	First N.B.
7176.	Napa	First N.B.
7202.	Sonora	First N.B.
7210.	Ventura	First N.B.
7219.	Alturas	First N.B.
7259.	Redlands	Redlands N.B.
7279.	Redwood City	First N.B. of San Mateo Co.
7336.	Madera	First N.B.
7388.	Calistoga	First N.B.
7390.	Fowler	First N.B.
7418.	San Diego	American N.B.
7480.	Santa Maria	First N.B.
7502.	Oakdale	First N.B.
7543.	Hollywood	First N.B.
7632.	Los Angeles	United States N.B.
7658.	Hanford	Farmers and Merchants' N.B.
7690.	Ocean Park	First N.B.
7691.	San Francisco	United States N.B.
7705.	Monrovia	N.B. of Monrovia
7713.	San Francisco	Citizens' N.B.
7719.	Lodi	First N.B.
7738.	Turlock	First N.B.
7776.	Sacramento	Fort Sutter N.B.
7779.	Lemoore	First N.B.
7801.	Escondido	First N.B.
7803.	Hollywood	Hollywood N.B.
7849.	Berkeley	Berkeley N.B.
7867.	Corona	First N.B.
7868.	Huntington Beach	First N.B.
7877.	San Luis Obispo	Union N.B.
7894.	San Francisco	N.B. of the Pacific
7895.	Redondo, Redondo Beach	Farmers and Merchants' N.B.
7965.	Lindsay	First N.B.
7980.	Santa Ana	Farmers and Merchants' N.B.
7987.	Glendale	First N.B.
7997.	San Jacinto	First N.B.
7999.	Whittier	Whittier N.B.
8002.	Livermore	First N.B.
8040.	Escondido	Escondido N.B.
8063.	Artesia	First N.B.
8065.	Azusa	First N.B.
8069.	Oceanside	First N.B.
8073.	Redlands	Citizens N.B.
8074.	Azusa	United States N.B.
8085.	Compton	First N.B.
8117.	Los Angeles	N.B. of Commerce
8143.	Redondo, Redondo Beach	First N.B.
8181.	Orange	First N.B.
8222.	Covina	Covina N.B.
8266.	Upland	First N.B.
8377.	Riverside	N.B. of Riverside
8403.	Santa Cruz	First N.B.
8409.	Kingsburg	First N.B.
8436.	Corona	Corona N.B.
8487.	San Francisco	Merchants' N.B.
8490.	Alhambra	First N.B.
8504.	Sacramento	California N.B.
8510.	Long Beach	Exchange N.B.
8544.	South Pasadena	First N.B.
8549.	Hermon	Highland N.B.
8608.	Colton	Colton N.B.
8618.	San Bernardino	Farmers' Exchange N.B.
8626.	Tulare	First N.B.
8652.	Glendora	First N.B.
8692.	Martinez	First N.B. of Contra Costa Co.
8707.	Sierra Madre	First N.B.
8718.	Fresno	Union N.B.
8768.	Rialto	First N.B.
8798.	Chico	First N.B.
8827.	Los Angeles	Security N.B.
8857.	Reedley	First N.B.
8870.	Long Beach	City N.B.
8907.	Riverside	Citizens' N.B.
9093.	Inglewood	First N.B.
9121.	Pasadena	Union N.B.
9141.	San Francisco	Seaboard N.B.
9156.	Dinuba	United States N.B.
9158.	Dinuba	First N.B.
9167.	Orosi	First N.B.
9173.	Visalia	N.B. of Visalia
9174.	San Francisco	Anglo and London Paris N.B.
9195.	Delano	First N.B.
9220.	Alameda	Alameda N.B.
9227.	Auburn, E. Auburn	First N.B.
9234.	Kerman	First N.B.

Charter #	City	Name of Bank
9294.	Chico	Butte County N.B.
9308.	Sanger	First N.B.
9323.	Coalinga	First N.B.
9349.	El Centro	El Centro N.B.
9350.	El Centro	First N.B.
9366.	Pasadena	Crown City N.B.
9370.	Exeter	First N.B.
9378.	Hollister	First N.B.
9410.	Emeryville	First N.B.
9424.	San Mateo	N.B. of San Mateo
9437.	Merced	First N.B.
9459.	Banning	First N.B.
9467.	Claremont	First N.B.
9479.	McCloud	McCloud N.B.
9481.	Oxnard	First N.B.
9483.	San Diego	Marine N.B.
9493.	Woodland	First N.B.
9502.	Oakland	Central N.B.
9512.	National City	People's N.B.
9515.	Wilmington	First N.B.
9538.	Fullerton	Farmers and Merchants' N.B.
9546.	Corcoran	First N.B.
9551.	Calistoga	Calistoga N.B.
9570.	Upland	Commercial N.B.
9573.	Vallejo	First N.B.
9575.	San Fernando	First N.B.
9599.	La Verne	First N.B.
9621.	Watsonville	Pajaro Valley N.B.
9626.	Fort Bragg	First N.B.
9648.	Sebastopol	First N.B.
9655.	San Francisco	Bank of California Nat. Assn.
9673.	Brawley	First N.B.
9683.	San Francisco	Mercantile N.B.
9685.	Ventura	N.B. of Ventura
9686.	Calexico	First N.B.
9688.	Reedley	Reedley N.B.
9705.	Calexico	Calexico N.B.
9710.	Lindsay	Lindsay N.B.
9713.	Willows	First N.B.
9735.	Richmond	First N.B.
9745.	Santa Cruz	Santa Cruz Co. N.B.
9760.	Newman	First N.B.
9763.	Prairie City	First N.B.
9765.	Crows Landing	First N.B.
9770.	Holtville	First N.B.
9787.	Scotia	First N.B.
9795.	Vacaville	First N.B.
9800.	San Leandro	First N.B.
9818.	Laton	First N.B.
9844.	Paso Robles	First N.B.
9873.	Weed	First N.B.
9878.	Orange	N.B. of Orange
9882.	San Francisco	Merchants' N.B.
9889.	Terra Bella	First N.B.
9892.	Antioch	First N.B.
9894.	Puente	First N.B.
9897.	Pleasanton	First N.B.
9904.	Santa Ana	California N.B.
9914.	Livermore	Farmers and Merchants' N.B.
9918.	Petaluma	Sonoma County N.B.
9919.	Hynes	First N.B.
9933.	Los Banos	First N.B.
9935.	Ontario	Ontario N.B.
9945.	Concord	First N.B.
9957.	Maricopa	First N.B.
9966.	Alhambra	Alhambra N.B.
10018.	Hayward	First N.B.
10068.	San Dimas	First N.B.
10070.	Redding	Redding N.B.
10072.	Colusa	First N.B.
10082.	Pasadena	N.B. of Pasadena
10088.	Taft	First N.B.
10091.	Los Gatos	First N.B.
10092.	Placentia	Placentia N.B.
10099.	Burbank	First N.B.
10100.	Redding	Northern California N.B.
10107.	Sacramento	Capital N.B.
10114.	Red Bluff	Red Bluff N.B.
10120.	Dixon	First N.B.
10124.	Parlier	First N.B.
10133.	Winters	First N.B.
10134.	Tustin	First N.B.
10149.	Suisun	First N.B.
10150.	Alameda	Citizens' N.B.
10166.	Gilroy	First N.B.
10167.	Pasadena	Security N.B.
10168.	Van Nuys	First N.B.
10177.	San Rafael	Marin County N.B.
10184.	Healdsburg	First N.B.
10197.	Madera	Commercial N.B.
10200.	Riverdale	First N.B.
10201.	Tulare	N.B. of Tulare
10204.	Healdsburg	Healdsburg N.B.
10208.	Claremont	Claremont N.B.
10213.	Clovis	First N.B.
10228.	Anaheim	Anaheim N.B.
10233.	Venice	First N.B.
10259.	Sonoma	First N.B.
10271.	Chino	First N.B.
10273.	San Fernando	San Fernando N.B.
10281.	Walnut Creek	First N.B.
10282.	Oroville	Rideout, Smith N.B.
10284.	Jamestown	Union N.B.
10292.	Coachella	First N.B.
10293.	Selma	Selma N.B.
10299.	Yuba City	First N.B.
10301.	Ducor	First N.B.
10309.	Woodlake	First N.B.
10312.	Fowler	Fowler N.B.
10324.	Mountain View	First N.B.
10328.	Orosi	N.B. of Orosi
10352.	Merced	Farmers and Merchants' N.B.
10357.	Bakersfield	N.B. of Bakersfield
10362.	Jamestown	Jamestown N.B.
10364.	Hardwick	First N.B.
10372.	Arcata	First N.B.
10378.	Orland	First N.B.
10387.	McFarland	First N.B.
10391.	San Diego	United States N.B.
10396.	Torrance	First N.B.
10412.	Glendale	Glendale N.B.
10427.	Riverbank	First N.B.
10435.	San Diego	Union N.B.
10453.	Gardena	First N.B.
10461.	Sonora	Sonora N.B.
10462.	Seeley	First N.B.
10490.	Exeter	Citrus N.B.
10503.	Heber	First N.B.
10528.	Eureka	Humboldt N.B.
10556.	Temecula	First N.B.
10571.	Santa Cruz	Farmers and Merchants' N.B.
10584.	Coalinga	N.B. of Coalinga
10656.	Los Angeles	Continental N.B.
10685.	Baldwin Park	First N.B.
10687.	Calipatria	First N.B.
10702.	Newport Beach	First N.B.
10719.	Rio Vista	First N.B.
10731.	Yreka	First N.B.
10764.	Hemet	First N.B.
10817.	Stockton	San Joaquin Valley N.B.
10843.	Barstow	First N.B.
10878.	Woodland	Bank of Woodland Nat. Assn.
10891.	Olive	First N.B.
10894.	Lamanda Park	First N.B.
10897.	Lompoc	First N.B.
10905.	Yorba Linda	First N.B.
10931.	San Bernardino	American N.B.
10944.	Blythe	First N.B.
10972.	King City	First N.B.
10977.	Ukiah	First N.B.
10978.	Chowchilla	First N.B.
10984.	Fairfield	First N.B.
10988.	Modesto	California N.B.
10999.	Bishop	First N.B.
11005.	Victorville	First N.B.
11025.	Sherman	First N.B.
11041.	Del Rey	First N.B.
11123.	Marysville	First N.B.
11124.	Turlock	First N.B.
11126.	Lodi	Lodi N.B.
11151.	Chowchilla	Chowchilla N.B.
11161.	Sebastopol	Sebastopol N.B.
11164.	Gridley	First N.B.
11201.	Rodeo	First N.B.
11206.	Vallejo	Vallejo Commercial N.B.
11240.	Calipatria	Farmers and Merchants' N.B.
11241.	Cutler	First N.B.
11250.	Arcadia	First N.B.
11251.	Garden Grove	First N.B.
11273.	Montebello	First N.B.
11282.	Cloverdale	First N.B.
11296.	San Juan, San Juan Bautista	First N.B.
11303.	Puente	Puente N.B.
11326.	Crockett	First N.B.
11327.	Bakersfield	First N.B.
11330.	Caruthers	First N.B.
11359.	Pittsburg	First N.B.
11362.	Vernon	First N.B.
11371.	Pixley	First N.B.
11421.	Bell	First N.B.
11425.	Pasadena	N.B. and Trust Co.
11433.	Tranquility	First N.B.
11461.	Beverly Hills	First N.B.
11473.	Fresno	Growers' N.B.
11484.	San Joaquin	First N.B.
11495.	Berkeley	College N.B.
11497.	Half Moon Bay	Security N.B. of San Mateo Co.
11520.	Pescadero	First N.B.
11522.	Los Altos	First N.B.
11528.	Blythe	Farmers and Merchants' N.B.
11532.	Mountain View	Farmers and Merchants' N.B.
11534.	Shafter	First N.B.
11560.	Watsonville	Fruit Growers' N.B.
11561.	Bay Point	First N.B.
11566.	Willits	First N.B.
11572.	Campbell	Growers' N.B.
11587.	Huntington Park	First N.B.
11601.	Salida	First N.B.
11616.	Orange Cove	First N.B.
11678.	Geyersville	First N.B.
11684.	Suisun City	Bank of Suisun Nat. Assn.
11699.	Niland	First N.B.
11701.	Downey	First N.B.
11720.	Manteca	First N.B.
11729.	Los Angeles	American Marine N.B.
11732.	Culver City	First N.B.
11743.	Centerville	First N.B.
11752.	Hayward	Farmers and Merchants' N.B.
11756.	Lompoc	Farmers and Merchants' N.B.
11769.	Biola, Kerman	First N.B.
11787.	Indio	First N.B.
11806.	Earlimart	First N.B.
11823.	Anaheim	Golden State N.B.
11827.	La Habra	First N.B.
11840.	Westwood	Westwood N.B.
11850.	El Segundo	First N.B.
11853.	Modesto	American N.B.
11867.	Rialto	Citizen's N.B.
11869.	Santa Ana	American N.B.
11873.	Long Beach	California N.B.
11875.	Sacramento	Merchants' N.B.
11880.	Crescent Heights	Crescent Heights N.B.
11918.	Ripon	First N.B.
11922.	Elsinore	First N.B.
11925.	Huntington Park	N.B. of Huntington Park
11926.	Pasadena	Central N.B.
11942.	Alameda	Commercial N.B.
11961.	Roseville	Roseville N.B.
11962.	Brea	First N.B.
11991.	Lankershim	First N.B.
11992.	Roseville	Railroad N.B.
12056.	Placerville	Placerville N.B.
12061.	Monterey	First N.B.
12112.	Lodi	Citizens' N.B.
12127.	Lemoore	N.B. of Lemoore
12160.	Dinuba	N.B. of Dinuba
12172.	Paso Robles	First N.B.
12201.	Santa Rosa	First N.B.
12209.	Hermosa Beach	First N.B.
12210.	Watts	First N.B.
12226.	Sawtelle	United States N.B.
12253.	East San Gabriel	First N.B.
12271.	Hermosa Beach	N.B. of Hermosa Beach
12306.	Hayward	First N.B.
12316.	Redlands	First N.B.
12320.	Berkeley	First N.B.
12328.	Bellflower	First N.B.
12341.	Richmond	First N.B.
12345.	Huntington Beach	First N.B.
12360.	Sonoma	Valley N.B.
12364.	South San Francisco	Citizens' N.B.
12385.	Pasadena	Pasadena N.B.
12410.	Los Angeles	Nat. City Bank
12433.	Grass Valley	First N.B.
12435.	Burbank	First N.B.
12453.	Sausalito	First N.B.
12454.	Los Angeles	Pacific N.B.
12511.	Martinez	N.B. of Martinez
12545.	Los Angeles	Seaboard N.B.
12572.	Walnut Park	Walnut Park N.B.
12577.	Los Angeles	Wilshire N.B.
12579.	San Francisco	Pacific N.B.
12584.	Kerman	First N.B.
12624.	Florence District, Los Angeles	Florence N.B.
12640.	San Rafael	First N.B.
12647.	Beverly Hills	Beverly N.B.
12665.	Oakland	New First N.B.
12673.	Graham, Los Angeles	Graham N.B.
12678.	Visalia	New First N.B.
12693.	Claremont	Citizens' N.B.
12735.	Pasadena	N.B. of Commerce
12754.	Bellflower	Commercial N.B.
12755.	Los Angeles	People's N.B.
12764.	Fullerton	New First N.B.
12766.	Temple	Temple N.B.
12787.	Santa Monica	American N.B.
12797.	South Pasadena	First N.B.
12802.	San Leandro	San Leandro N.B.
12804.	Los Angeles	N.B. of Hollywood
12807.	South Gate	South Gate N.B.
12819.	Long Beach	Seaside N.B.
12833.	Atascadero	First N.B.
12852.	South Pasadena	South Pasadena N.B.
12856.	Santa Paula	New First N.B.
12893.	Alameda	Encinal N.B.
12904.	Compton	Compton N.B.
12909.	Beverly Hills	Liberty N.B.
12910.	Altadena	Altadena N.B.
12913.	Santa Maria	Commercial N.B.
12929.	Dinuba	Dinuba N.B.
12937.	Oakland	East Bay N.B.
12976.	Fontana	First N.B.
12986.	Los Angeles	Hellman Commercial Trust & Savings Bank Nat. Ass'n.
12988.	Huntington Park	City N.B.
12996.	Ventura	Union N.B.
13001.	Brea	Oilfields N.B.
13007.	Verdugo City	First N.B.
13010.	Berkeley	Commercial N.B.
13016.	San Francisco	Brotherhood N.B.
13028.	Merced	First N.B.
13029.	Escondido	First N.B.
13044.	San Francisco	Bank of America Nat. Trust & Savings Ass'n.
13049.	Carlsbad	First N.B.
13054.	Calexico	First Central N.B.
13069.	Burbank	Magnolia Park N.B.
13071.	Glendale	American N.B.
13079.	Fallbrook	First N.B.
13092.	Ontario	Citizens N.B.
13094.	Beverly Hills	California N.B.
13135.	Lynwood	N.B. of Lynwood
13178.	Vista	First N.B.
13179.	Pico	N.B. of Pico
13187.	Los Angeles	N.B. for Savings
13200.	Los Angeles	Commercial N.B.
13208.	San Diego	La Jolla N.B.
13212.	Palo Alto	Palo Alto N.B.
13217.	San Leandro	First N.B.
13312.	Winter	Winter N.B.
13332.	Loma Linda	First N.B.
13335.	Arcadia	Arcadia N.B.
13338.	San Jose	San Jose N.B.
13340.	Yreka	First N.B.
13348.	Beverly Hills	Beverly Hills N.B. & Trust Co.
13356.	Colton	Citizens N.B.

Charter #	City	Name of Bank
13368.	Vallejo	Mechanics & Merchants N.B.
13375.	Pacific Grove	First N.B.
13380.	Salinas	Salinas N.B.
13418.	Turlock	First N.B.
13465.	Orosi	First N.B.
13510.	Hollister	Hollister N.B.
13711.	Chico	First N.B.
13787.	Fort Bragg	Coast N.B.
13877.	Brea	Oilfields N.B.
14045.	Santa Ana	First N.B.
14202.	Torrance	Torrance N.B.
14230.	Corcoran	First N.B.
14298.	Glendale	First N.B.
14307.	Madera	First N.B.
14317.	Coachella	First N.B.

COLORADO

Charter #	City	Name of Bank
1016.	Denver	First N.B.
1651.	Denver	Colorado N.B.
1652.	Central City	Rocky Mountain N.B.
1833.	Pueblo	First N.B.
1955.	Denver	City N.B.
1991.	Georgetown	First N.B.
2129.	Central City	First N.B.
2134.	Pueblo	People's N.B.
2140.	Golden	First N.B.
2179.	Colorado Springs	First N.B.
2199.	Georgetown	Miners' N.B.
2300.	Trinidad	First N.B.
2310.	Pueblo	Stockgrowers' N.B.
2351.	Denver	German N.B.
2352.	Boulder	First N.B.
2354.	Lake City	First N.B.
2355.	Boulder	Nat. State Bank
2394.	Georgetown	Merchants' N.B.
2420.	Leadville	First N.B.
2523.	Denver	Merchants' N.B.
2541.	Pueblo	Central N.B.
2546.	Pueblo	Western N.B.
2622.	Fort Collins	First N.B.
2637.	Durango	First N.B.
2686.	Gunnison	First N.B.
2694.	Denver	State N.B.
2930.	Silverton	First N.B.
2962.	Idaho Springs	First N.B.
2975.	Gunnison	Iron N.B.
3114.	Alamosa	First N.B.
3178.	Greeley	First N.B.
3246.	Boulder	Boulder N.B.
3269.	Denver	Denver N.B.
3354.	Longmont	First N.B.
3450.	Trinidad	Trinidad N.B.
3485.	Aspen	First N.B.
3661.	Glenwood Springs	First N.B.
3722.	Glenwood Springs	Glenwood N.B.
3746.	Leadville	Carbonate N.B.
3749.	Lamar	First N.B.
3860.	Grand Junction	First N.B.
3879.	Canon City	First N.B.
3913.	Colorado Springs	Exchange N.B.
3949.	Leadville	American N.B.
4007.	Montrose	First N.B.
4084.	Denver	People's N.B.
4108.	Pueblo	Mercantile N.B.
4109.	Ouray	First N.B.
4113.	Denver	Commercial N.B.
4126.	Durango	Durango N.B.
4159.	Denver	American N.B.
4172.	Salida	First N.B.
4264.	Del Norte	First N.B.
4334.	Rico	First N.B.
4358.	Denver	N.B. of Commerce
4382.	Denver	Union N.B.
4417.	Telluride	First N.B.
4437.	Greeley	Greeley N.B.
4498.	Pueblo	Pueblo N.B.
4507.	La Junta	First N.B.
4653.	Longmont	Farmers' N.B.
4716.	Creede	First N.B.
4733.	Aspen	Aspen N.B.
4776.	Durango	Smelter N.B.
4845.	Cripple Creek	First N.B.
5283.	Colorado Springs	El Paso N.B.
5381.	Florence	First N.B.
5467.	Delta	First N.B.
5503.	Fort Collins	Fort Collins N.B.
5586.	Victor	First N.B.
5624.	Sterling	First N.B.
5976.	Hotchkiss	First N.B.
5989.	Idaho Springs	Merchants and Miners' N.B.
6030.	Las Animas	First N.B.
6057.	Eaton	First N.B.
6137.	Grand Junction	Grand Valley N.B.
6178.	Rifle	First N.B.
6238.	Colorado Springs	City N.B.
6355.	Denver	Capitol N.B.
6437.	Brush	First N.B.
6454.	Steamboat Springs	First N.B.
6472.	Sugar City	Citizens' N.B.
6497.	Golden	Rubey N.B.
6556.	Castle Rock	First N.B. of Douglas County
6671.	Paonia	First N.B.
6772.	Fountain	First N.B.
6957.	Glenwood Springs	Citizens' N.B.
7004.	Fort Morgan	First N.B.
7022.	Walsenburg	First N.B.
7082.	Rocky Ford	First N.B.
7228.	Monte Vista	First N.B.
7288.	Montrose	Montrose N.B.
7408.	Denver	United States N.B.
7435.	Meeker	First N.B.
7501.	Arvada	First N.B.
7533.	Littleton	First N.B.
7577.	Brighton	First N.B.
7604.	Greeley	Union N.B.
7637.	Fowler	First N.B.
7648.	Loveland	First N.B.
7704.	Holly	First N.B.
7766.	Grand Junction	Mesa County N.B.
7784.	Silverton	Silverton N.B.
7793.	Wellington	First N.B.
7809.	Granada	First N.B.
7832.	Fort Morgan	Morgan County N.B.
7837.	Fort Collins	Poudre Valley N.B.
7839.	Longmont	Longmont N.B.
7888.	Salida	Commercial N.B.
7904.	Alamosa	American N.B.
7973.	Sterling	Logan County N.B.
7995.	Berthoud	Berthoud N.B.
8004.	Palisades	Palisades N.B.
8033.	Berthoud	First N.B.
8088.	Ault	First N.B.
8116.	Loveland	Loveland N.B.
8167.	Ault	Farmers' N.B.
8205.	Julesburg	First N.B.
8271.	Elizabeth	First N.B.
8296.	Windsor	First N.B.
8412.	Eads	First N.B.
8433.	Canon City	Fremont County N.B.
8489.	Hugo	First N.B.
8520.	Brush	Stockmen's N.B.
8541.	Alamosa	Alamosa N.B.
8548.	Akron	First N.B.
8572.	Colorado Springs	Colorado Springs N.B.
8636.	Johnstown	First N.B.
8658.	Eaton	Eaton N.B.
8675.	Delta	Delta N.B.
8695.	Ordway	First N.B.
8735.	Buena Vista	First N.B.
8752.	Wray	First N.B.
8755.	Platteville	First N.B.
8774.	Denver	Central N.B.
8815.	Aspen	People's N.B.
8840.	Fruita	First N.B.
8909.	Lafayette	First N.B.
8951.	Salida	Merchants' N.B.
8967.	Cortez	First N.B.
9009.	Carbondale	First N.B.
9013.	Eagle	First N.B. of Eagle Co.
9036.	Lamar	Lamar N.B.
9045.	Sedgwick	First N.B.
9100.	Cortez	Montezuma Valley N.B.
9117.	Rocky Ford	Rocky Ford N.B.
9120.	Windsor	Farmers' N.B.
9278.	Holyoke	First N.B.
9451.	Platteville	Platteville N.B.
9454.	Sterling	Farmers' N.B.
9603.	Julesburg	Citizens' N.B.
9674.	Mancos	First N.B.
9676.	Wray	N.B. of Wray
9697.	Gill	First N.B.
9719.	Olathe	First N.B.
9743.	Center	First N.B.
9797.	Durango	Burns N.B.
9840.	La Jara	First N.B.
9875.	Clifton	First N.B.
9887.	Denver	Hamilton N.B.
9907.	Englewood	First N.B.
9997.	Saguache	First N.B.
10038.	Greeley	City N.B.
10064.	Denver	Federal N.B.
10093.	Yuma	First N.B.
10272.	Cedaredge	First N.B.
10558.	Craig	First N.B.
10560.	Craig	Craig N.B.
10730.	Hayden	First N.B.
10770.	Dolores	First N.B.
10786.	Hugo	Hugo N.B.
10852.	Otis	First N.B.
10901.	Akron	Citizens' N.B.
11099.	Haxtun	First N.B.
11117.	Boulder	Citizens' N.B.
11197.	Stratton	First N.B.
11248.	Walden	First N.B.
11253.	Longmont	American N.B.
11321.	Mead	First N.B.
11354.	Simla	First N.B.
11455.	Burlington	First N.B.
11504.	Limon	First N.B.
11523.	Peetz	First N.B.
11530.	Keenesburg	First N.B.
11540.	Denver	Stock Yards N.B.
11564.	Denver	Drovers' N.B.
11571.	Fleming	First N.B.
11574.	Deer Trail	First N.B.
11619.	Limon	Limon N.B.
11623.	Denver	Globe N.B.
11640.	Strasburg	First N.B.
11660.	Springfield	First N.B.
11681.	Elbert	First N.B.
11682.	Aurora	First N.B.
11871.	Pagosa Springs	First N.B.
11872.	Flagler	First N.B.
11949.	Littleton	Littleton N.B.
11972.	Sterling	Sterling N.B.
12250.	Denver	Broadway N.B.
12431.	Florence	Security N.B.
12517.	Denver	American N.B.
12531.	La Veta	First N.B.
12716.	Genoa	First N.B.
12974.	Denver	South Broadway N.B.
13098.	Denver	West Side N.B.
13536.	Rifle	Rifle N.B.
13624.	Loveland	First N.B.
13902.	Grand Junction	First N.B.
13928.	Greeley	Greeley N.B.
14021.	Boulder	First N.B.
14146.	Fort Collins	First N.B.
14148.	Trinidad	Trinidad N.B.
14213.	Eads	First N.B.
14222.	Trinidad	First N.B.
14248.	Denver	Union N.B.
14254.	Lamar	Lamar N.B.

CONNECTICUT

Charter #	City	Name of Bank
2.	New Haven	First N.B.
4.	Stamford	First-Stamford N.B.
65.	Norwich	First N.B.
121.	Hartford	First N.B.
186.	Rockville	First N.B.
196.	New London	First N.B.
224.	Norwich	Second N.B.
227.	New Haven	Second N.B.
250.	Meriden	First N.B.
251.	Mystic Bridge	First N.B.
335.	Greenport	First N.B.
361.	Hartford	Nat. Exchange Bank
394.	Westport	First N.B.
397.	Middletown	First N.B.
448.	Putnam	First N.B.
450.	Killingly, Danielson	First N.B.
458.	Norwich	First N.B.
486.	Hartford	Charter Oak N.B.
497.	Suffield	First N.B.
502.	South Norwalk	First N.B.
509.	Rockville	Rockville N.B.
645.	Mystic	Mystic River N.B.
657.	Norwich	Thames N.B.
660.	Southport	Southport N.B.
666.	New London	N.B. of Commerce
670.	Hartford	Phoenix N.B.
686.	Stafford Springs	Stafford N.B.
709.	Litchfield	First N.B.
720.	Meriden	Home N.B.
735.	Stonington	First N.B.
754.	Norwalk	Fairfield County N.B.
756.	Hartford	Aetna N.B.
780.	Waterbury	Waterbury N.B.
791.	Waterbury	Citizens' N.B.
796.	New Haven	Yale N.B.
845.	Middletown	Middlesex County N.B.
910.	Bridgeport	Bridgeport N.B.
919.	Pawcatuck	Pawcatuck N.B.
921.	Bridgeport	City N.B.
927.	Bridgeport	Connecticut N.B.
928.	Bridgeport	Pequonnock N.B.
942.	Norwalk	N.B. of Norwalk
943.	Danbury	Danbury N.B.
978.	New London	Nat. Whaling Bank
1013.	Portland	First N.B.
1037.	New London	New London City N.B.
1038.	Stamford	Stamford N.B.
1084.	Essex	Saybrook N.B.
1093.	Ansonia	Ansonia N.B.
1098.	Derby	Birmingham N.B.
1128.	New Haven	Merchants' N.B.
1132.	Danbury	City N.B.
1139.	Deep River	Deep River N.B.
1141.	Bethel	First N.B.
1165.	Hartford	American N.B.
1175.	New London	Nat. Union Bank
1184.	New Britain	New Britain N.B.
1187.	Norwich	Uncas N.B.
1193.	New Milford	First N.B.
1202.	New Haven	Nat. Tradesmen's Bank
1214.	Falls Village	Nat. Iron Bank
1216.	Middletown	Middletown N.B.
1243.	New Haven	New Haven Bank Nat. Bkg. Assn.
1245.	New Haven	New Haven County N.B.
1249.	New Canaan	First N.B.
1268.	Mystic	Mystic N.B.
1300.	Hartford	Mercantile N.B.
1314.	Clinton	Clinton N.B.
1321.	Hartford	Farmers and Mechanics' N.B.
1338.	Hartford	Hartford and Aetna N.B.
1340.	Middletown	Central N.B.
1358.	Norwich	Norwich N.B.
1360.	Danielson	Windham County N.B.
1377.	Hartford	City N.B.
1379.	Norwich	Shetucket N.B.
1382.	Meriden	Meriden N.B.
1385.	Tolland	Tolland County N.B.
1477.	Putnam	Thompson N.B.
1478.	Jewett City	Jewett City N.B.
1480.	East Haddam	N.B. of New England
1481.	Norwich	Merchants' N.B.
1494.	Winsted	Hurlbut N.B.
1614.	Willimantic	Windham N.B.
2250.	Bristol	Bristol N.B.
2342.	Norwalk	Central N.B.
2388.	Willimantic	First N.B.
2414.	Winsted	First N.B.
2419.	Winsted	Winsted N.B.
2494	Waterbury	Manufacturers' N.B.
2599.	Wallingford	First N.B.
2643.	South Norwalk	City N.B.
2682.	New Haven	First N.B.
2814.	Southington	Southington N.B.
3020.	Naugatuck	Naugatuck N.B.
3668.	New Britain	Mechanics' N.B.
3768.	Waterbury	Fourth N.B.
3914.	Stafford Springs	First N.B.
3964.	Thomaston	Thomaston N.B.
5231.	Torrington	Brooks N.B.
5235.	Torrington	Torrington N.B.
5309.	Ridgefield	First N.B. and Trust Co.
5358.	Guilford	Guilford N.B.
5499.	Seymour	Valley N.B.

Charter #	City	Name of Bank
7812.	East Haddam	N.B. of New England
8243.	Greenwich	Greenwich N.B.
8511.	Canaan	Canaan N.B.
8936.	Essex	Essex N.B.
9313.	Plainville	First N.B.
10145.	Plainfield	First N.B.
10289.	Bethel	Bethel N.B.
10796.	Hartford	Colonial N.B.
12400.	Stamford	Peoples' N.B.
12594.	Putnam	Citizens' N.B.
12637.	Plantsville	Plantsville N.B.
12846.	New Britain	City N.B.
12973.	East Port Chester	Byram N.B.
13038.	Hartford	Capitol N.B.
13042.	Greenwich	First N.B.
13245.	Sharon	Sharon N.B.
13704.	New Haven	Tradesmens N.B.

DELAWARE

Charter #	City	Name of Bank
473.	Wilmington	First N.B.
795.	Seaford	First N.B.
997.	Newport	Newport N.B.
1181.	Middletown	Citizens' N.B.
1190.	Wilmington	N.B. of Wilmington and Brandywine
1281.	Odessa	New Castle County N.B.
1332.	Delaware City	Delaware City N.B.
1390.	Wilmington	Union N.B.
1420.	Wilmington	N.B. of Delaware
1536.	Newark	N.B. of Newark
1567.	Dover	First N.B.
2336.	Smyrna	Fruit Growers' N.B.
2340.	Milford	First N.B.
2381.	Smyrna	N.B. of Smyrna
3019.	Middletown	Peoples' N.B.
3395.	Wilmington	Central N.B.
3693.	Seaford	Sussex N.B.
3883.	Harrington	First N.B.
5148.	Lewes	Lewes N.B.
5421.	Frederica	First N.B.
5930.	Georgetown	First N.B.
6718.	Selbyville	Selbyville N.B.
6726.	Laurel	Peoples' N.B.
7211.	Delmar	First N.B.
8918.	Frankford	First N.B.
8972.	Dagsboro	First N.B.
9132.	Felton	First N.B.
9428.	Wyoming	First N.B.
12882.	Milton	First N.B.
13278.	Georgetown	First N.B.

DISTRICT OF COLUMBIA

Charter #	City	Name of Bank
26.	Washington	First N.B.
526.	Washington	N.B. Of Metropolis
627.	Washington	Merchants' N.B.
682.	Georgetown	N.B. of Commerce
875.	Washington	N.B. of the Republic
1069.	Washington	Nat. Metropolitan Bank
1893.	Washington	Citizens' N.B.
1928.	Georgetown	Farmers and Mechanics' N.B.
2038.	Washington	Second N.B.
2358.	Washington	German American N.B.
2382.	Washington	Central N.B.
3425.	Washington	N.B. of Washington
3625.	Washington	Columbia N.B.
4107.	Washington	Nat. Capital Bank
4195.	Washington	West End N.B.
4244.	Washington	Traders' N.B.
4247.	Washington	Lincoln N.B.
4522.	Washington	Ohio N.B.
5046.	Washington	Riggs N.B.
6716.	Washington	American N.B.
7446.	Washington	Commercial N.B.
7936.	Washington	Nat. City Bank
9545.	Washington	District N.B.
10316.	Washington	Federal N.B.
10504.	Washington	Franklin N.B.
10825.	Washington	Dupont N.B.
11633.	Washington	Liberty N.B.
12139.	Washington	Standard N.B.
12194.	Washington	Hamilton N.B.
12721.	Washington	Northwest N.B.
13782.	Washington	Hamilton N.B.

FLORIDA

Charter #	City	Name of Bank
2174.	Jacksonville	First N.B. of Florida
2194.	Jacksonville	Ambler N.B.
2490.	Pensacola	First N.B.
3223.	Palatka	First N.B.
3266.	Palatka	Palatka N.B.
3327.	Jacksonville	N.B. of the State of Florida
3462.	Saint Augustine	First N.B.
3469.	Orlando	First N.B.
3470.	Ocala	First N.B.
3497.	Tampa	First N.B.
3798.	Sanford	First N.B.
3802.	Orlando	Citizens' N.B.
3815.	Ocala	Merchants' N.B.
3869.	Jacksonville	N.B. of Jacksonville
3894.	Gainesville	First N.B.
4132.	Tallahassee	First N.B.
4332.	Jacksonville	Merchants' N.B.
4478.	Tampa	Gulf N.B.
4539.	Tampa	Tampa N.B.
4558.	Fernandina	First N.B.
4627.	Bartow	Polk County N.B.
4672.	Key West	First N.B.
4813.	Palatka	Putnam N.B.
4837.	Pensacola	Citizens' N.B.
4949.	Tampa	Exchange N.B.
5534.	Arcadia	First N.B.
5603.	Pensacola	American N.B.
6055.	Live Oak	First N.B.
6110.	Marianna	First N.B.
6274.	Apalachicola	First N.B.
6370.	Miami	First N.B.
6774.	Miami	Fort Dallas N.B.
6825.	Ocala	Central N.B.
6888.	Jacksonville	Atlantic N.B.
7034.	Milton	First N.B.
7153.	Tampa	American N.B.
7190.	Madison	First N.B.
7253.	Quincy	First N.B.
7404.	De Funiak Springs	First N.B.
7423.	Graceville	First N.B.
7540.	Lake City	First N.B.
7730.	St. Petersburg	First N.B.
7757.	Jasper	First N.B.
7778.	Chipley	First N.B.
7796.	Saint Petersburg	Central N.B.
7865.	Perry	First N.B.
7942.	Key West	Island City N.B.
8321.	Jacksonville	Florida N.B.
8728.	Arcadia	De Soto N.B.
8802.	Gainesville	Gainesville N.B.
8980.	Alachua	First N.B.
9007.	Pensacola	Citizens and People's N.B.
9035.	Fort Myers	First N.B.
9049.	Jacksonville	Barnett N.B.
9628.	Jacksonville	Fourth N.B.
9657.	De Land	First N.B.
9707.	Saint Cloud	First N.B.
9811.	Lakeland	First N.B.
9891.	Brooksville	First N.B.
9926.	Ocala	Ocala N.B.
10024.	Fernandina	Citizens' N.B.
10069.	Orlando	First N.B.
10136.	Jacksonville	Heard N.B.
10236.	Plant City	First N.B.
10245.	Bradentown	First N.B.
10310.	Gainesville	Florida N.B.
10346.	Panama City	First N.B.
10379.	Winter Haven	Snell N.B.
10386.	Fort Meade	First N.B.
10414.	Sarasota	First N.B.
10512.	Punta Gorda	First N.B.
10535.	Pensacola	N.B. of Commerce
10545.	Daytona	First N.B.
10578.	Ocala	Munroe and Chanbliss N.B.
10691.	Wauchula	Carlton N.B.
10826.	Avon Park	First N.B.
10958.	Tampa	Nat. City Bank
11038.	Leesburg	First N.B.
11073.	West Palm Beach	First N.B.
11156.	Vero	First N.B.
11389.	Winter Garden	First N.B.
11420.	Saint Augustine	Saint Augustine N.B.
11703.	Lake Hamilton	First N.B.
11716.	Lake Worth	First N.B.
11921.	Clermont	First N.B.
12011.	Miami	Miami N.B.
12020.	Fort Lauderdale	First N.B.
12047.	Miami Beach	Miami Beach First N.B.
12057.	West Palm Beach	American N.B.
12090.	Sebring	First N.B.
12100.	Winter Haven	N.B. of Winter Haven
12274.	Tarpon Springs	First N.B.
12275.	Palm Beach	First N.B.
12546.	Seabreeze	First N.B.
12600.	Palm Beach	Palm Beach N.B.
12623.	Saint Petersburg	Alexander N.B.
12751.	Sarasota	American N.B.
12841.	Boynton	First N.B.
12842.	Tampa	N.B. of Commerce
12868.	Miami	City N.B.
12871.	Kissimmee	First N.B.
12880.	Bradenton	American N.B.
12887.	Miami	Third N.B.
12905.	Clearwater	First N.B.
12930.	West Palm Beach	N.B. of West Palm Beach
12983.	Auburndale	First N.B.
13008.	Coral Gables	Coral Gables First N.B.
13090.	Palm Beach	First N.B.
13102.	Mount Dora	First N.B.
13157.	Sanford	Sanford Atlantic N.B.
13159.	Miami	City N.B.
13214.	Palatka	Palatka Altantic N.B.
13300.	West Palm Beach	West Palm Beach Atlantic N.B.
13309.	Bartow	Polk County N.B.
13320.	Brooksville	First N.B.
13352.	Sarasota	Palmer N.B. and Trust Co.
13370.	Lakeland	Florida N.B.
13383.	Winter Haven	American N.B.
13388.	Deland	Barnett N.B.
13389.	Bartow	Florida N.B.
13390.	Cocoa	Barnett N.B.
13421.	Avon Park	Barnett N.B.
13437.	Winter Haven	Snell N.B.
13498.	St. Petersburg	Florida N.B.
13570.	Miami	Florida N.B. and Trust Co.
13641.	Homestead	First N.B.
13828.	Miami Beach	Mercantile N.B.
13961.	Tarpon Springs	First N.B.
13968.	Milton	First N.B.
14003.	Orlando	First N.B.
14195.	Fort Meyers	First N.B.
14338.	Panama City	Bay N.B.

GEORGIA

Charter #	City	Name of Bank
1255.	Savannah	Savannah N.B.
1559.	Atlanta	Atlanta N.B.
1586.	Savannah	City N.B.
1605.	Atlanta	Georgia N.B.
1613.	Augusta	N.B. of Augusta
1617.	Macon	First N.B.
1630.	Columbus	Chattahoochee N.B.
1639.	Athens	N.B. of Athens
1640.	Savannah	Merchants' N.B.
1703.	Augusta	Merchants and Planters' N.B.
1860.	Augusta	Nat. Exchange Bank
1861.	Newnan	First N.B.
2009.	Americus	First N.B.
2064.	Atlanta	State N.B.
2075.	Griffin	City N.B.
2338.	Columbus	First N.B.
2368.	Rome	First N.B.
2424.	Atlanta	Gate City N.B.
2839.	Americus	People's N.B.
3093.	La Grange	First N.B.
3116.	Brunswick	First N.B.
3382.	Newnan	Newnan N.B.
3406.	Savannah	N.B. of Savannah
3670.	Rome	Merchants' N.B.
3740.	Macon	Merchants' N.B.
3753.	Brunswick	Oglethorpe N.B.
3767.	Thomasville	First N.B.
3830.	Marietta	First N.B.
3872.	Albany	Citizens' First N.B.
3907.	Dalton	First N.B.
3937.	Columbus	Third N.B.
3983.	Gainesville	First N.B.
4012.	Cartersville	First N.B.
4075.	Cedartown	First N.B.
4115.	Dawson	Dawson N.B.
4369.	Rome	Rome N.B.
4429.	Valdosta	First N.B.
4547.	Macon	American N.B.
4554.	Cordele	First N.B.
4691.	Columbus	Fourth N.B.
4944.	Brunswick	N.B. of Brunswick
4963.	Waycross	First N.B.
5030.	Atlanta	Third N.B.
5045.	Atlanta	Fourth N.B.
5264.	Carrollton	First N.B.
5318.	Atlanta	Lowry N.B.
5490.	Atlanta	Capital City N.B.
5512.	Albany	Albany N.B.
5644.	Forsyth	First N.B.
5709.	Jackson	First N.B.
5975.	Cordele	Cordele N.B.
6002.	Fort Gaines	First N.B.
6004.	Bainbridge	First N.B.
6047.	Newnan	Coweta N.B.
6079.	Blue Ridge	North Georgia N.B.
6082.	Fitzgerald	First N.B.
6180.	Sylvester	First N.B.
6207.	Louisville	First N.B.
6243.	Barnesville	First N.B.
6336.	Albany	Third N.B.
6374.	Dublin	First N.B.
6496.	Dawson	City N.B.
6498.	Colquitt	First N.B.
6525.	Athens	Georgia N.B.
6542.	Tifton	First N.B.
6576.	Montezuma	First N.B.
6687.	Toccoa	First N.B.
6967.	Greensboro	Greensboro N.B.
7018.	Blakely	First N.B.
7067.	Sparta	First N.B.
7220.	Tallapoosa	First N.B.
7247.	La Fayette	First N.B.
7300.	Madison	First N.B.
7330.	Union Point	N.B. of Union Point
7431.	Commerce	First N.B.
7459.	Fort Valley	First N.B.
7468.	Statesboro	First N.B.
7549.	Calhoun	Calhoun N.B.
7565.	Moultrie	First N.B.
7567.	Cochran	First N.B.
7580.	Hawkinsville	First N.B.
7616.	Gainesville	Gainesville N.B.
7762.	La Grange	La Grange N.B.
7777.	Albany	Citizens' N.B.
7899.	Waynesboro	First N.B.
7934.	Sandersville	First N.B.
7963.	Buena Vista	First N.B.
7969.	McDonough	First N.B.
7979.	Lyons	First N.B.
7986.	Maysville	Atkins N.B.
7994.	Quitman	First N.B.
8023.	Wrightsville	First N.B.
8046.	West Point	First N.B.
8128.	Dublin	City N.B.
8250.	Fitzgerald	Exchange N.B.
8305.	Americus	Americus N.B.
8314.	Arlington	First N.B.
8350.	Tifton	N.B. of Tifton
8365.	Macon	Fourth N.B.
8417.	Shellman	First N.B.
8452.	Greensboro	Copelan N.B.
8470.	Lavonia	First N.B.
8477.	Newnan	Manufacturers' N.B.
8527.	Senoia	First N.B.
8580.	Ocilla	First N.B.
8628.	Rockmart	Citizens' N.B.
8680.	Pembroke	Pembroke N.B.
8848.	Washington	N.B. of Wilkes
8894.	Washington	Citizens' N.B.
8945.	Covington	First N.B.
8966.	Fitzgerald	Ben Hill N.B.
8990.	Macon	Citizens' N.B.
9039.	Jefferson	First N.B.
9051.	Winder	First N.B.
9074.	Cordele	American N.B.
9088.	Millen	First N.B.

Charter #	City	Name of Bank
9105.	Atlanta	American N.B.
9106.	Nashville	First N.B.
9186.	Jackson	Jackson N.B.
9212.	Macon	Commercial N.B.
9252.	Elberton	First N.B.
9254.	Colquitt	Colquitt N.B.
9302.	Thomson	First N.B.
9329.	Monticello	Farmers' N.B.
9346.	Monticello	First N.B.
9593.	Eastman	First N.B.
9607.	Byromville	Byrom N.B.
9613.	Cornelia	First N.B.
9615.	Reynolds	First N.B.
9617.	Atlanta	Fulton N.B.
9618.	Vienna	First N.B.
9636.	Rome	Cherokee N.B.
9641.	Sandersville	Cohen N.B.
9672.	Milledgeville	First N.B.
9729.	Albany	Georgia N.B.
9777.	Adel	First N.B.
9870.	Pelham	First N.B.
9879.	Vidalia	First N.B.
10089.	Hampton	First N.B.
10270.	Macon	Macon N.B.
10279.	Cuthbert	First N.B.
10302.	Rome	Nat. City Bank
10303.	Rome	Exchange N.B.
10333.	Claxton	First N.B.
10756.	East Point	First N.B.
10805.	Winder	Winder N.B.
10829.	Sylvania	N.B. of Sylvania
10900.	Rockmart	Farmers and Merchants' N.B.
10945.	Macon	Bibb N.B
11255.	Conyers	First N.B.
11290.	Quitman	Peoples' N.B.
11597.	Griffin	Second N.B.
11695.	Hartwell	First N.B.
11833.	Cedartown	Liberty N.B.
11936.	Lawrenceville	First N.B.
11939.	Montezuma	Citizens' N.B.
12030.	Savannah	Mercantile N.B.
12105.	Dallas	First N.B.
12232.	Marietta	Citizens' N.B.
12249.	Atlanta	Ninth N.B.
12254.	Lumpkin	N.B. of Lumpkin
12317.	Sparta	Hancock N.B.
12404.	Barnesville	Citizens' N.B.
12492.	Atlanta	City N.B.
12635.	Cartersville	Cartersville N.B.
12863.	Albany	New Georgia N.B.
13068.	Savannah	Citizens' and Southern N.B.
13161.	Moultrie	Moultrie N.B.
13223.	Albany	City N.B.
13227.	Douglasville	First N.B.
13469.	Marietta	Citizens' N.B.
13472.	Savannah	Liberty N.B. and Trust Co.
13550.	Fitzgerald	N.B. of Fitzgerald
13725.	Sandersville	Geo. D. Warthen N.B.
13897.	Jackson	Jackson N.B.
14046.	Monroe	N.B. of Monroe
14061.	Elberton	First N.B.
14193.	Waycross	First N.B.
14243.	Claxton	Claxton N.B.
14255.	Quitman	Citizens' N.B.
14257.	Cordele	First N.B.

HAWAII TERRITORY

Charter #	City	Name of Bank
5550.	Honolulu	First N.B. of Hawaii
5994.	Wailuku	First N.B.
8101.	Lahaina	Lahaina N.B.
8207.	Kahului	Baldwin N.B.
10451.	Paia	First N.B.
11050.	Honolulu	Army N.B. of Schofield Barracks

IDAHO

Charter #	City	Name of Bank
1668.	Boise	First N.B. of Idaho
2972.	Lewiston	First N.B.
3023.	Lewiston	Lewiston N.B.
3142.	Ketchum	First N.B.
3408.	Moscow	First N.B.
3471.	Boise	Boise City N.B.
3895.	Hailey	First N.B.
4023.	Pocatello	First N.B.
4584.	Moscow	Moscow N.B.
4690.	Caldwell	First N.B.
4773.	Wallace	First N.B.
4790.	Kendrick	First N.B.
4808.	Genesee	First N.B.
4827.	Pocatello	Idaho N.B.
5600.	Lewiston	Idaho N.B.
5764.	Saint Anthony	First N.B.
5820.	Idaho Falls	First N.B.
5906.	Payette	First N.B.
6145.	Emmett	First N.B.
6347.	Pocatello	Bannock N.B.
6521.	Mountainhome	First N.B.
6577.	Shoshone	First N.B.
6697.	Nezperce	First N.B.
6754.	Weiser	First N.B.
6793.	Coeur d'Alene	First N.B.
6927.	Grangeville	First N.B.
6982.	Idaho Falls	American N.B.
7120.	Coeur d'Alene	First-Exchange N.B.
7133.	Rexburg	First N.B.
7230.	Saint Anthony	Commercial N.B.
7381.	Montpelier	First N.B.
7419.	Blackfoot	First N.B.
7526.	Preston	First N.B.
7608.	Twin Falls	First N.B.
7923.	Cottonwood	First N.B.
8075.	Payette	Payette N.B.
8080.	Salmon	First N.B.
8139.	Weiser	Weiser N.B.
8225.	Caldwell	Western N.B.
8341.	Sandpoint	First N.B.
8346.	Boise	Idaho N.B.
8370.	Nampa	First N.B.
8822.	Malad City	First N.B.
8869.	American Falls	First N.B.
8906.	Mullan	First N.B.
9134.	Wallace	Wallace N.B.
9145.	Hailey	Hailey N.B.
9263.	Sandpoint	Bonner County N.B.
9272.	Shoshone	Lincoln County N.B.
9333.	Caldwell	American N.B.
9371.	Gooding	First N.B.
9432.	Salmon	Citizens' N.B.
9477.	Challis	First N.B.
9491.	Wendell	First N.B.
9566.	Kellogg	First N.B.
9680.	Jerome	First N.B.
10083.	Boise	Pacific N.B.
10162.	Fairfield	First N.B.
10212.	Lewiston	Empire N.B.
10221.	Meridian	First N.B.
10269.	Ashton	First N.B.
10278.	Driggs	First N.B.
10294.	Hagerman	First N.B.
10341.	Burley	First N.B.
10429.	Rupert	First N.B.
10517.	Rupert	Rupert N.B.
10693.	Nampa	Citizens' N.B.
10727.	Bonners Ferry	First N.B.
10751.	Boise	Overland N.B.
10771.	Saint Maries	First N.B.
10909.	Wilder	First N.B.
10916.	Nampa	Farmers and Merchants N.B.
10920.	Ririe	First N.B.
10969.	Kimberly	First N.B.
10975.	Newdale	First N.B.
11053.	Halley	Blaine County N.B.
11065.	Buhl	First N.B.
11076.	Buhl	Farmers' N.B.
11100.	Filer	First N.B.
11135.	Jerome	Jerome N.B.
11179.	Grace	First N.B.
11183.	Bancroft	First N.B.
11198.	Firth	First N.B.
11274.	Twin Falls	Twin Falls N.B.
11278.	Idaho Falls	Idaho Falls N.B.
11385.	Rigby	First N.B.
11434.	Shelley	First N.B.
11438.	Burley	Burley N.B.
11458.	Rigby	Jefferson County N.B.
11471.	Driggs	Teton N.B.
11496.	Parma	First N.B.
11508.	Dubois	First N.B.
11556.	Parma	Parma N.B.
11578.	Jerome	City N.B.
11600.	Roberts	First N.B.
11609.	Nampa	Stockmen's N.B.
11636.	Mackay	First N.B.
11721.	Pocatello	N.B. of Idaho
11736.	Minidoka	First N.B.
11745.	Lewiston	American N.B.
11794.	Arco	First N.B.
11821.	Nampa	Nampa N.B.
11884.	Fairfield	Security N.B.
12256.	Burley	Cassia N.B.
12432.	Wendell	Wendell N.B.
12832.	Hailey	First N.B.
13267.	Driggs	First N.B.
13288.	Coeur d'Alene	First N.B.
13819.	Lewiston	Lewiston N.B.

ILLINOIS

Charter #	City	Name of Bank
8.	Chicago	First N.B.
33.	Cairo	First N.B.
38.	Aurora	First N.B.
85.	Monmouth	First N.B.
108.	Rock Island	First N.B.
113.	Danville	First N.B.
114.	La Salle	First N.B.
160.	Moline	First N.B.
176.	Peoria	First N.B.
177.	Wilmington	First N.B.
205.	Springfield	First N.B.
207.	Peoria	Second N.B.
225.	Chicago	Second N.B.
236.	Chicago	Third N.B.
241.	Galesburg	First N.B.
276.	Chicago	Fourth N.B.
319.	Freeport	First N.B.
320.	Chicago	Fifth N.B.
339.	Batavia	First N.B.
347.	Lacon	First N.B.
372.	Woodstock	First N.B.
385.	Freeport	Second N.B.
409.	Mount Carroll	First N.B.
415.	Canton	First N.B.
424.	Quincy	First N.B.
429.	Rockford	First N.B.
441.	Peru	First N.B.
466.	Chicago	Mechanics' N.B.
477.	Decatur	First N.B.
479.	Rockford	Third N.B.
482.	Rockford	Second N.B.
491.	Galesburg	Second N.B.
495.	Warsaw	First N.B.
508.	Chicago	Northwestern N.B.
511.	Jacksonville	First N.B.
512.	Joliet	First N.B.
531.	Morris	Grundy County N.B.
534.	Geneseo	First N.B.
642.	Chicago	Merchants' N.B.
698.	Chicago	Union N.B.
703.	Quincy	Merchants and Farmers' N.B.
713.	Chicago	Commercial N.B.
724.	Chicago	Manufacturers' N.B.
759.	Knoxville	First N.B.
763.	Charleston	First N.B.
785.	Cairo	City N.B.
818.	Chicago	City N.B.
819.	Bloomington	First N.B.
827.	Galva	First N.B.
831.	Galena	N.B. of Galena
849.	Warren	Farmers' N.B.
883.	Rockford	Winnebago N.B.
902.	Dixon	Lee County N.B.
903.	Princeton	First N.B.
913.	Champaign	First N.B.
915.	Shawneetown	First N.B.
945.	Waukegan	First N.B.
966.	Chicago	Traders' N.B.
967.	Macomb	First N.B.
979.	Galena	Merchants' N.B.
1001.	Centralia	First N.B.
1024.	Mattoon	First N.B.
1033.	Morrison	First N.B.
1042.	Pittsfield	First N.B.
1097.	Belvidere	First N.B.
1117.	Peoria	Mechanics' N.B.
1154.	Ottawa	First N.B.
1167.	Carthage	Hancock County N.B.
1177.	Mendota	First N.B.
1365.	Elgin	First N.B.
1428.	Alton	Alton N.B.
1445.	Alton	First N.B.
1453.	Rushville	First N.B.
1465.	Ottawa	Nat. City Bank
1471.	Virginia	Farmers' N.B.
1482.	Henry	First N.B.
1484.	Winchester	First N.B.
1517.	Vandalia	N.B. of Vandalia
1555.	Paris	First N.B.
1637.	Pekin	First N.B.
1641.	Olney	First N.B.
1662.	Springfield	Ridgely N.B.
1678.	Chicago	Union Stock Yard N.B.
1693.	Chicago	N.B. of Commerce
1706.	Monmouth	Monmouth N.B.
1709.	Chicago	Corn Exchange N.B.
1715.	Salem	Salem N.B.
1717.	Sterling	First N.B.
1719.	Jacksonville	Jacksonville N.B.
1721.	Watseka	First N.B.
1723.	Tuscola	First N.B.
1733.	Springfield	State N.B.
1734.	Chicago	German N.B.
1755.	Lanark	First N.B.
1773.	Morris	First N.B.
1775.	Shawneetown	Gallatin N.B.
1779.	Vandalia	Farmers and Merchants' N.B.
1785.	Kewanee	First N.B.
1791.	Bushnell	Farmers' N.B.
1792.	Aurora	Union N.B.
1793.	Kankakee	First N.B.
1805.	Keithsburg	Farmers' N.B.
1806.	Polo	Exchange N.B.
1808.	Lewiston	First N.B.
1816.	Rockford	Rockford N.B.
1821.	Winchester	People's N.B.
1837.	Pontiac	Livingston County N.B.
1841.	Greenville	First N.B.
1845.	Chicago	Cook County N.B.
1850.	Mason City	First N.B.
1851.	Charleston	Second N.B.
1852.	Marseilles	First N.B.
1867.	Chicago	N.B. of Illinois
1870.	Marengo	First N.B.
1872.	Macomb	Union N.B.
1876.	Paxton	First N.B.
1881.	Dixon	Dixon N.B.
1882.	Joliet	Will County N.B.
1889.	Rock Island	Rock Island N.B.
1896.	Sycamore	Sycamore N.B.
1907.	Rochelle	Rochelle N.B.
1909.	Aurora	Second N.B.
1922.	Rochelle	First N.B.
1926.	Clinton	De Witt County N.B.
1934.	Nokomis	Nokomis N.B.
1941.	Moline	Moline N.B.
1961.	Flora	First N.B.
1964.	Wilmington	Commercial N.B.
1968.	Prophetstown	First N.B.
1969.	Oregon	First N.B.
1978.	Chicago	Scandinavian N.B.
1987.	Fairbury	First N.B.
1996.	Mount Vernon	Mount Vernon N.B.
2011.	Kansas	First N.B.
2016.	Elgin	Home N.B.
2021.	Saint Charles	Kane County N.B.
2042.	Carlinville	First N.B.
2047.	Chicago	Central N.B.
2048.	Chicago	Home N.B.
2100.	Paris	Edgar County N.B.
2116.	Griggsville	Griggsville N.B.
2124.	Decatur	Decatur N.B.
2126.	Lincoln	First N.B.
2128.	Shelbyville	First N.B.
2141.	Pontiac	N.B. of Pontiac
2147.	Mattoon	Mattoon N.B.
2154.	Belleville	First N.B.
2155.	Rock Island	People's N.B.
2156.	Farmer City	First N.B.
2165.	Princeton	Farmers' N.B.
2170.	Streator	First N.B.
2176.	Streator	Union N.B.
2204.	Arcola	First N.B.
2205.	Monmouth	Second N.B.
2212.	Oakland	Oakland N.B.
2242.	Havana	Havana N.B.
2254.	Prairie City	First N.B.

Charter #	City	Name of Bank
2283.	Atlanta	First N.B.
2287.	Pekin	Farmers' N.B.
2313.	Kirkwood	First N.B.
2328.	Jerseyville	First N.B.
2330.	Virginia	Centennial N.B.
2332.	Geneseo	Farmers' N.B.
2386.	Bloomington	Nat. State Bank
2390.	Carrollton	Greene County N.B.
2402.	Mount Sterling	First N.B.
2413.	Princeton	Citizen's N.B.
2450.	Chicago	Hide and Leather N.B.
2501.	Kewanee	Union N.B.
2503.	La Salle	La Salle N.B.
2519.	Quincy	Ricker N.B.
2540.	Cambridge	First N.B.
2572.	Cambridge	Farmers' N.B.
2584.	Danville	Second N.B.
2601.	Chicago	Chicago N.B.
2629.	Olney	Olney N.B.
2670.	Chicago	First N.B.
2675.	Woodstock	First N.B.
2676.	Bloomington	Third N.B.
2681.	Streator	Streator N.B.
2684.	Walnut	First N.B.
2688.	Springfield	Farmers' N.B.
2702.	De Kalb	First N.B.
2709.	Sterling	Sterling N.B.
2751.	Monmouth	First N.B.
2789.	Hillsboro	Hillsboro N.B.
2793.	Galva	Galva First N.B.
2804.	La Salle	City N.B.
2808.	Hoopeston	First N.B.
2815.	Wyoming	First N.B.
2824.	Lexington	First N.B.
2826.	Chicago	N.B. of America
2829.	Champaign	Champaign N.B.
2858.	Lake	Drovers' N.B. of Union Stock Yards
2875.	Freeport	First N.B.
2878.	Peoria	Peoria N.B.
2894.	Chicago	Continental and Commercial N.B.
2915.	Urbana	First N.B.
2926.	Paxton	First N.B.
2945.	Aurora	Aurora N.B.
2951.	Peru	Peru N.B.
2965.	Homer	First N.B.
2997.	El Paso	First N.B.
3003.	Biggsville	First N.B.
3036.	Chicago	Corn Exchange N.B.
3043.	Petersburg	First N.B.
3070.	Peoria	German American N.B.
3102.	Chicago	Calumet N.B.
3138.	Galesburg	Galesburg N.B.
3156.	Metropolis	First N.B.
3179.	Chicago	Metropolitan N.B.
3190.	Belvidere	Second N.B.
3214.	Peoria	Central N.B.
3254.	Peoria	Merchants' and Illinois N.B.
3278.	Chicago	Union N.B.
3279.	Galena	Galena N.B.
3287.	Knoxville	Farmers' N.B.
3294.	Dixon	City N.B.
3296.	Peoria	Commercial N.B.
3303.	Centralia	Old N.B.
3323.	Earlville	First N.B.
3369.	Lincoln	Lincoln N.B.
3376.	Paris	First N.B.
3377.	Abingdon	First N.B.
3407.	Farmer City	John Weedman N.B.
3465.	Spring Valley	Spring Valley N.B.
3500.	Chicago	American Exchange N.B.
3502.	Chicago	Park N.B.
3503.	Chicago	Atlas N.B.
3548.	Springfield	Illinois N.B.
3579.	Taylorville	First N.B.
3593.	Canton	Canton N.B.
3613.	Lincoln	American N.B.
3620.	Wenona	First N.B.
3640.	Beardstown	First N.B.
3647.	Chicago	Lincoln N.B.
3677.	Chicago	Columbia N.B.
3698.	Chicago	Fort Dearborn N.B.
3711.	Atlanta	Atlanta N.B.
3735.	Cairo	Alexander County N.B.
3752.	Quincy	Quincy N.B.
3770.	Pekin	American N.B.
3781.	Delavan	Tazewell County N.B.
3839.	Mount Pulaski	First N.B.
3847.	Chicago	Nat. Live Stock Bank
3854.	Aurora	Merchants' N.B.
3882.	Chicago	Prairie State N.B.
3916.	Chicago	Washington Park N.B.
3952.	Rockford	Manufacturers' N.B.
3962.	Litchfield	First N.B.
4003.	Harrisburg	First N.B.
4019.	Murphysboro	First N.B.
4038.	Pana	First N.B.
4073.	Englewood	First N.B.
4187.	Chester	First N.B.
4233.	Effingham	First N.B.
4299.	Carlinville	Carlinville N.B.
4313.	Monmouth	People's N.B.
4325.	Rockford	Forest City N.B.
4328.	East Saint Louis	First N.B.
4342.	Kankakee	City N.B.
4400.	Monmouth	N.B. of Monmouth
4433.	Vienna	First N.B.
4449.	Anna	First N.B.
4469.	Aurora	American N.B.
4476.	Streator	City N.B.
4480.	Mount Carmel	First N.B.
4489.	Chicago	Globe N.B.
4502.	Marion	First N.B.
4520.	Joliet	Joliet N.B.
4551.	Naperville	First N.B.
4576.	Decatur	Citizens' N.B.
4596.	Aurora	Old Second N.B.
4605.	Chicago	N.B. of the Republic
4646.	Batavia	First N.B.
4666.	Chicago	Chemical N.B.
4709.	Bushnell	First N.B.
4731.	Danville	Palmer N.B.
4735.	Elgin	Elgin N.B.
4737.	Du Quoin	First N.B.
4759.	Marshall	Dulaney N.B.
4767.	Evanston	Evanston N.B.
4787.	Chicago	Bankers' N.B.
4804.	Murphysboro	City N.B.
4826.	Monticello	First N.B.
4829.	Bement	First N.B.
4854.	Kewanee	Kewanee N.B.
4871.	Toluca	First N.B.
4904.	Carbondale	First N.B.
4920.	Decatur	N.B. of Decatur
4930.	Normal	First N.B.
4934.	Carmi	First N.B.
4941.	Lewiston	Lewiston N.B.
4952.	Jerseyville	N.B. of Jerseyville
4958.	Farmer City	Old First N.B.
4967.	Alexis	First N.B.
4994.	Vandalia	First N.B.
4999.	Grayville	First N.B.
5009.	Fairfield	First N.B.
5049.	Robinson	First N.B.
5057.	Mount Vernon	Ham N.B.
5062.	Edwardsville	First N.B.
5070.	East Saint Louis	Southern Illinois N.B.
5086.	Mendota	Mendota N.B.
5089.	Decatur	Millikin N.B.
5106.	Chicago	Corn Exchange N.B.
5111.	Chicago	American N.B.
5119.	Bloomington	State N.B.
5124.	Grant Park	Grant Park N.B.
5149.	Milford	First N.B.
5153.	Harrisburg	City N.B.
5188.	Alton	Citizens' N.B.
5193.	Rantoul	First N.B.
5223.	Amboy	First N.B.
5233.	Arthur	First N.B.
5254.	Metropolis	Nat. State Bank
5273.	Toledo	First N.B.
5279.	Evanston	First N.B.
5285.	Georgetown	First N.B.
5291.	Stonington	First N.B.
5303.	Herrin	First N.B.
5304.	Ogden	First N.B.
5313.	Ridge Farm	First N.B.
5316.	Assumption	First N.B.
5322.	Piper City	First N.B.
5357.	Carmi	N.B. of Carmi
5361.	Peoria	Illinois N.B.
5385.	Lawrenceville	First N.B.
5398.	Rossville	First N.B.
5410.	Taylorville	Farmers' N.B.
5426.	Neoga	Cumberland County N.B.
5433.	Granite City	First N.B.
5470.	Saint Anne	First N.B.
5494.	Lovington	First N.B.
5510.	El Paso	Woodford County N.B.
5519.	Chatsworth	Commercial N.B.
5525.	Anna	Anna N.B.
5538.	Hindsboro	First N.B.
5548.	Carlyle	First N.B.
5584.	Chillicothe	First N.B.
5609.	Dallas City	First N.B.
5619.	Chadwick	First N.B.
5630.	Cobden	First N.B.
5638.	Dundee	First N.B.
5689.	Mount Vernon	Third N.B.
5699.	De Land	First N.B.
5763.	Jacksonville	Ayers N.B.
5771.	Barry	First N.B.
5782.	Mount Carmel	American N.B.
5812.	Danville	Danville N.B.
5813.	Stronghurst	First N.B.
5815.	Malta	First N.B.
5856.	Gilman	First N.B.
5869.	Newton	First N.B.
5876.	Chicago Heights	First N.B.
5883.	Roseville	First N.B.
6007.	Secor	First N.B.
6025.	Pinckneyville	First N.B.
6026.	Casey	First N.B.
6065.	Little York	First N.B.
6086.	Oquawka	First N.B.
6089.	Albany	First N.B.
6096.	Mansfield	First N.B.
6116.	Waverly	First N.B.
6125.	Collinsville	First N.B.
6133.	Ivesdale	First N.B.
6136.	Benton	First N.B.
6143.	Kindmundy	First N.B.
6191.	Greenup	First N.B.
6192.	Garrett	First N.B.
6211.	Philo	First N.B.
6219.	Saint Charles	Saint Charles N.B.
6228.	Pawpaw	First N.B.
6239.	Yorkville	Yorkville N.B.
6290.	Chicago	N.B. of North America
6318.	Clifton	First N.B.
6359.	Atwood	First N.B.
6375.	Prophetstown	Farmers' N.B.
6421.	Tremont	First N.B.
6423.	Joliet	Citizens' N.B.
6451.	Paris	Citizens' N.B.
6460.	Grayville	Farmers' N.B.
6514.	Libertyville	First N.B.
6524.	Nashville	First N.B.
6535.	Chicago	Drovers' N.B.
6543.	Steward	First N.B.
6564.	Granite City	Granite City N.B.
6586.	Le Roy	First N.B.
6598.	Crescent City	First N.B.
6609.	Fairfield	Fairfield N.B.
6629.	Wyoming	N.B. of Wyoming
6649.	McLeansboro	First N.B.
6653.	Highland	First N.B.
6670.	Libertyville	Lake County N.B.
6684.	Grand Ridge	First N.B.
6691.	Marissa	First N.B.
6713.	Brookport	Brookport N..B.
6721.	Martinsville	First N.B.
6723.	Chicago	Hamilton N.B.
6724.	East Peoria	First N.B.
6734.	Pana	Pana N.B.
6740.	Danvers	First N.B.
6745.	Morrisonville	First N.B.
6751.	Augusta	First N.B.
6811.	Woodstock	American N.B.
6815.	Cairo	Cairo N.B.
6824.	Potomac	Potomac N.B.
6861.	Findlay	First N.B.
6907.	Sumner	First N.B.
6910.	Raymond	First N.B.
6924.	O'Fallon	First N.B.
6951.	Erie	First N.B.
6978.	Equality	First N.B.
6998.	Rock Falls	First N.B.
7015.	Sparta	First N.B.
7031.	Compton	First N.B.
7049.	Henry	Henry N.B.
7077.	White Hall	White Hall N.B.
7079.	Momence	First N.B.
7088.	Villa Grove	First N.B.
7111.	Chrisman	First N.B.
7121.	White Hall	First N.B.
7145.	Aledo	First N.B.
7151.	Strawn	Farmers' N.B.
7168.	Humboldt	First N.B.
7236.	Elgin	Union N.B.
7276.	Catlin	First N.B.
7339.	Windsor	First N.B.
7350.	Mount Olive	First N.B.
7358.	Chicago	Prairie N.B.
7365.	Georgetown	Georgetown N.B.
7379.	Mulberry Grove	First N.B.
7385.	Golconda	First N.B.
7396.	Shelbyville	Citizens' N.B.
7440.	Pawnee	N.B. of Pawnee
7443.	Mound City	First N.B.
7458.	Johnston City	First N.B.
7500.	Westville	First N.B.
7538.	Witt	First N.B.
7539.	Eldorado	First N.B.
7547.	Nokomis	Farmers' N.B.
7555.	Earlville	Earlville N.B.
7575.	Newman	Newman N.B.
7579.	Coffeen	Coffeen N.B.
7598.	Carbondale	Carbondale N.B.
7606.	Goreville	First N.B.
7627.	Percy	First N.B.
7660.	Triumph	First N.B.
7673.	West Frankfort	First N.B.
7680.	Forrest	First N.B.
7692.	Sullivan	First N.B.
7712.	Grand Tower	First N.B.
7717.	Columbia	First N.B.
7726.	Beecher	First N.B.
7728.	Benld	N.B. of Benld
7739.	Moweaqua	First N.B.
7750.	Dahlgren	First N.B.
7752.	Shawneetown	N.B. of Shawneetown
7791.	Middletown	First N.B.
7841.	Neoga	Neoga N.B.
7864.	Leland	First N.B.
7889.	Carterville	First N.B.
7903.	Gillespie	Gillespie N.B.
7926.	Chicago	Federal N.B.
7941.	Freeburg	First N.B.
7948.	Enfield	First N.B.
7954.	Metcalf	First N.B.
7971.	Norris City	First N.B.
8006.	Hillsboro	People's N.B.
8015.	Carrier Mills	First N.B.
8043.	Casey	Casey N.B.
8044.	Dwight	First N.B.
8053.	New Haven	First N.B.
8115.	Greenup	Greenup N.B.
8121.	Chicago	Monroe N.B.
8155.	Thomasboro	First N.B.
8163.	Morris	Farmers and Merchants N.B.
8174.	Gibson, Gibson City	First N.B.
8180.	Ullin	First N.B.
8212.	Findlay	Findlay N.B.
8216.	Westfield	First N.B.
8221.	Nashville	Farmers and Merchants N.B.
8224.	Lerna	First N.B.
8234.	Benton	Coal Belt N.B.
8256.	Oakford	First N.B.
8260.	Christopher	First N.B.
8289.	Ransom	First N.B.
8293.	Allendale	First N.B.
8347.	Bridgeport	First N.B.
8374.	Sidell	First N.B.
8425.	Millstadt	First N.B.
8429.	Albion	First N.B.
8457.	Madison	First N.B.
8468.	La Harpe	First N.B.
8473.	Greenfield	First N.B.
8482.	Maquon	First N.B.
8485.	Colchester	N.B. of Colchester
8532.	Chicago	Nat. City Bank
8540.	Savanna	First N.B.
8605.	Hegewisch, Chicago	Inter State N.B.
8607.	Oblong	First N.B.
8629.	Tamaroa	First N.B.

Charter #	City	Name of Bank
8630.	Ridge Farm	City N.B.
8637.	Roodhouse	First N.B.
8647.	Irving	Irving N.B.
8648.	Manlius	First N.B.
8667.	Harvey	First N.B.
8670.	Herrin	City N.B.
8679.	Dolton	First N.B.
8684.	Cullom	First N.B.
8696.	Oblong	Oil Belt N.B.
8713.	Manhattan	First N.B.
8732.	Mackinaw	First N.B.
8733.	Altamont	First N.B.
8740.	Geneva	First N.B.
8745.	Metropolis	City N.B.
8758.	Sesser	First N.B.
8801.	Crossville	First N.B.
8842.	Chicago	Nat. Produce Bank
8846.	Saint Francisville	People's N.B.
8892.	Palestine	First N.B.
8898.	Nauvoo	First N.B.
8908.	Blandinsville	First N.B.
8932.	East Saint Louis	City N.B.
8933.	Lockport	First N.B.
8937.	Lake Forest	First N.B.
8940.	Taylorville	Taylorville N.B.
9010.	Chicago	Live Stock Exchange N.B.
9025.	Albion	Albion N.B.
9096.	Warren	First N.B.
9118.	National Stock Yards	National Stock Yards N.B.
9169.	Macomb	Macomb N.B.
9183.	Arenzville	First N.B.
9208.	Minooka	Farmers' First N.B.
9230.	Tampico	First N.B.
9277.	Wyanet	First N.B.
9293.	Kansas	Farmers' N.B.
9325.	Tremont	Tremont N.B.
9338.	West Salem	First N.B.
9368.	Wheaton	First N.B.
9388.	Saint Elmo	First N.B.
9397.	Brighton	First N.B.
9398.	Hopedale	Hopedale N.B.
9406.	Gardner	First N.B.
9408.	McLeansboro	People's N.B.
9425.	Hoopeston	Hoopeston N.B.
9435.	Shawneetown	City N.B.
9438.	Stewardson	First N.B.
9439.	Ridgway	First N.B.
9500.	Batavia	Batavia N.B.
9525.	Odin	First N.B.
9527.	Noble	First N.B.
9530.	Blue Mound	First N.B.
9572.	Sycamore	Citizens' N.B.
9582.	Dieterich	First N.B.
9601.	Minonk	First N.B.
9624.	Odell	Farmers' N.B.
9649.	Aledo	Farmers' N.B.
9700.	Cowden	First N.B.
9725.	Downers Grove	First N.B.
9734.	Greenville	Bradford N.B.
9736.	Mascoutah	First N.B.
9750.	Chicago	La Salle Street N.B.
9786.	Sandoval	First N.B.
9788.	Pekin	Herget N.B.
9823.	Rockford	Swedish-American N.B.
9836.	Elmhurst	First N.B.
9877.	Rossville	Farmers' N.B.
9883.	Hamilton	First N.B.
9893.	Breese	First N.B.
9895.	Ramsey	Ramsey N.B.
9896.	Saint Peter	First N.B.
9922.	Mount Auburn	First N.B.
9929.	Warsaw	Farmers' N.B.
10045.	Mattoon	N.B. of Mattoon
10048.	Mount Prospect	Mount Prospect N.B.
10057.	Farmersville	First N.B.
10079.	Litchfield	Litchfield N.B.
10086.	Dongola	First N.B.
10108.	Chicago	Jefferson Park N.B.
10125.	Trenton	First N.B.
10132.	Coal City	First N.B.
10144.	Mattoon	State N.B.
10173.	Staunton	First N.B.
10179.	Irving Park, Chicago	Irving Park N.B.
10180.	Waterloo	First N.B.
10186.	Mazon	First N.B.
10215.	Ravenswood, Chicago	Ravenswood N.B.
10237.	Chicago	Bowmanville N.B.
10247.	Chicago	Lawndale N.B.
10257.	Annapolis	First N.B.
10264.	Witt	Witt N.B.
10291.	Omaha	First N.B.
10296.	Divernon	First N.B.
10305.	Rogers Park, Chicago	Rogers Park N.B.
10318.	Allendale	Farmers' N.B.
10319.	Des Plaines	First N.B.
10337.	Chicago	Austin N.B.
10355.	Waukegan	Waukegan N.B.
10365.	Vermillion	First N.B.
10397.	Brownstown	First N.B.
10399.	East Saint Louis	Drovers' N.B.
10445.	Mounds	First N.B.
10458.	Granville	First N.B.
10460.	Wayne City	First N.B.
10492.	Nebo	First N.B.
10505.	Sorento	Sorento N.B.
10514.	La Rose	La Rose N.B.
10516.	Bunker Hill	First N.B.
10567.	Caledonia	Caledonia N.B.
10572.	Beason	First N.B.
10582.	Marine	First N.B.
10591.	Eureka	First N.B.
10641.	Westervelt	Farmers' N.B.
10669.	Worden	First N.B.
10690.	Gorham	First N.B.
10716.	Woodhull	First N.B.
10752.	Oneida	First N.B.
10760.	Sheridan	First N.B.
10763.	Chicago	Atlas Exchange N.B.
10777.	Staunton	Staunton N.B.
10828.	Wilmette	First N.B.
10911.	Willisdale	First N.B.
11009.	Chicago	West Side N.B.
11039.	Edwardsville	Edwardsville N.B.
11088.	New Bedford	Farmers' N.B.
11092.	Chicago	Mutual N.B.
11108.	Hume	First N.B.
11118.	Minonk	Minonk N.B.
11144.	Cuba	First N.B.
11170.	Hinckley	First N.B.
11208.	Gridley	First N.B.
11283.	Barrington	First N.B.
11299.	Foosland	First N.B.
11308.	Hinsdale	First N.B.
11331.	Altona	First N.B.
11333.	Toluca	Citizens' N.B.
11358.	Charleston	Nat. Trust Bank
11422.	Lemont	First N.B.
11443.	Fairmount	First N.B.
11478.	Belleville	Saint Clair N.B.
11507.	Oak Park	First N.B.
11509.	Flora	Flora N.B.
11516.	Waltonville	First N.B.
11596.	East Saint Louis	First N.B.
11602.	Hampshire	First N.B.
11610.	Woodstock	Woodstock N.B.
11662.	Cicero	First N.B.
11675.	Waddams Grove	First N.B.
11679.	Rockford	Commercial N.B.
11715.	Lemont	Lemont N.B.
11731.	Rockford	Security N.B.
11737.	Chicago	Albany Park N.B.
11754.	Okawville	First N.B.
11774.	Woodlawn	First N.B.
11779.	Viola	Farmers' N.B.
11780.	Okawville	Old Exchange N.B.
11845.	Livingston	First N.B.
11876.	Wood River	First N.B.
11882.	Homer	First N.B.
11886.	Maroa	First N.B.
11895.	Braidwood	First N.B.
11904.	Centralia	Centralia N.B.
11923.	Centralia	City N.B.
11934.	Palatine	First N.B.
11952.	Grant Park	First N.B.
11980.	Chicago	N.B. of Woodlawn
11999.	Chicago	Kenwood N.B.
12000.	Coulterville	First N.B.
12001.	Chicago	Alliance N.B.
12004.	Chicago	West Englewood N.B.
12096.	Xenia	First N.B.
12097.	Zeigler	First N.B.
12178.	East Saint Louis	Security N.B.
12227.	Chicago	Douglass N.B.
12285.	Chicago	Portage Park N.B.
12314.	Gillespie	American N.B.
12323.	Chicago	Broadway N.B.
12366.	Lebanon	First N.B.
12373.	Jonesboro	First N.B.
12386.	Riverside	First N.B.
12391.	Chicago	Jackson Park N.B.
12403.	Chicago	Foreman N.B.
12426.	Berwyn	First N.B.
12479.	Valier	First N.B.
12480.	Chicago	Ogden N.B.
12493.	Chicago	Stock Yards N.B.
12525.	Woodhull	First N.B.
12528.	Wood River	Wood River N.B.
12596.	Carbondale	First N.B.
12605.	Chicago	Roseland N.B.
12615.	Chicago	Guardian N.B.
12630.	Wilsonville	First N.B.
12653.	La Grange	First N.B.
12658.	Plymouth	First N.B.
12779.	Blue Island	First N.B.
12870.	Antioch	First N.B.
12873.	Chicago	Lawrence Avenue N.B.
12926.	Roseville	Farmers and Merchants' N.B.
12945.	Chicago	Halsted Exchange N.B.
12991.	National City	National Stock Yards N.B.
13036.	Chicago	Midland N.B.
13119.	Chicago	Addison N.B.
13144.	Witt	N.B. of Witt
13146.	Chicago	National Builders Bank
13213.	Mount Sterling	First N.B.
13216.	Chicago	Straus N.B. and Trust Co.
13218.	Niles Center	N.B. of Niles Center
13226.	Stewardson	Stewardson N.B.
13235.	Chicago	Hyde Park N.B.
13236.	Belleville	Belleville N.B.
13253.	Chicago	Ashland-69th N.B.
13258.	Downers Grove	Security N.B.
13311.	Chicago	Peoples N.B. and Trust Co.
13372.	Chicago	Standard N.B.
13373.	Chicago Heights	Citizens' N.B.
13382.	Chicago	Terminal N.B.
13448.	Georgetown	First N.B.
13449.	Albion	N.B. of Albion
13451.	Dahlgren	Farmers N.B.
13452.	Mount Olive	First N.B.
13464.	Alton	First N.B. and Trust Co.
13478.	Pana	First N.B.
13497.	Polo	First N.B.
13499.	Bloomington	First N.B. and Trust Co.
13525.	Smithton	First N.B.
13565.	Aurora	First N.B.
13577.	Peru	State-National Bank
13579.	Tremont	First N.B.
13597.	Blandinsville	First N.B.
13605.	Robinson	Second N.B.
13611.	Mendota	N.B. of Mendota
13625.	Altona	Altona N.B.
13630.	Champaign	First N.B.
13631.	El Paso	El Paso N.B.
13638.	Chicago	City N.B. & Trust Co.
13639.	Chicago	Continental Illinois N.B. & Trust Co.
13650.	Witt	Security N.B.
13652.	Rockford	Illinois N.B. & Trust Co.
13659.	Chicago	Terminus N.B.
13660.	Moline	Moline N.B.
13666.	Stockton	First N.B.
13672.	Chicago	National Boulevard Bank
13673.	Casey	First N.B.
13674.	Chicago	Live Stock N.B.
13682.	Toledo	First N.B.
13684.	Chicago	Mid-City N.B.
13691.	Chicago	National Security Bank
13695.	Freeport	First N.B.
13696.	New Douglas	Prange N.B.
13705.	Joliet	First N.B.
13709.	Evanston	First N.B. & Trust Co.
13714.	Galena	First N.B.
13718.	Libertyville	First Lake County N.B.
13735.	Marissa	First N.B.
13744.	Hoppeston	City N.B.
13795.	Mascoutah	First N.B.
13804.	Cairo	Security N.B.
13805.	Columbia	First N.B.
13809.	Paxton	First N.B.
13838.	Canton	N.B. of Canton
13856.	Dixon	City N.B.
13864.	Mount Vernon	First N.B.
13865.	Monticello	N.B. of Monticello
13872.	Sycamore	N.B. & Trust Co.
13886.	Savanna	N.B. of Savanna
13892.	Negoa	Cumberland County N.B.
13903.	Peru	First N.B.
13941.	La Grange	La Grange N.B.
13963.	Sterling	N.B. of Sterling
13966.	Carlinville	Farmers & Merchants N.B.
13975.	Pinckneyville	First N.B.
13993.	Altamont	First N.B.
14008.	De Kalb	First N.B.
14010.	East Peoria	First N.B.
14024.	Charleston	Charleston N.B.
14035.	Grandville	Grandville N.B.
14074.	Newton	First N.B.
14110.	Chicago	District N.B.
14115.	Naperville	Naperville N.B.
14118.	Lincoln	First N.B.
14127.	East St. Louis	First N.B.
14134.	Carthage	First N.B.
14137.	Woodstock	First N.B.
14140.	Winchester	Neat Condit & Grout N.B.
14159.	Galva	First N.B.
14161.	Aurora	Aurora N.B.
14173.	Golconda	First N.B.
14178.	Bloomington	N.B. of Bloomington
14217.	Olney	First N.B.
14221.	Rochelle	N.B. of Rochelle
14235.	Madison	First N.B.
14237.	Cambridge	Peoples N.B.
14244.	Amboy	First N.B.
14245.	Chicago	Milwaukee Avenue N.B.
14246.	Chicago	Liberty N.B.
14247.	Mount Carroll	Mount Carroll N.B.
14260.	Pontiac	Pontiac N.B.
14265.	Shawneetown	First N.B.
14268.	Carlyle	First N.B.
14285.	Mount Olive	Mount Olive N.B.
14297.	Lanark	N.B. of Lanark
14310.	Staunton	First N.B.
14313.	Chicago	Merchants N.B.
14319.	Dalton	First N.B.
14327.	Chicago	South East N.B.
14331.	Aledo	N.B. of Aledo
14332.	Wyoming	First N.B.
14342.	Polo	Polo N.B.
14343.	Chicago	Chicago Heights N.B.
14346.	Oregon	Ogle County N.B.
14347.	Carrollton	Greene County N.B.
14348.	Roodhouse	Roodhouse N.B.

INDIANA

Charter #	City	Name of Bank
11.	Fort Wayne	First N.B.
17.	Richmond	First N.B.
23.	La Fayette	First N.B.
28.	Evansville	First N.B.
37.	Centerville	First N.B.
41.	Kendallville	First N.B.
44.	Anderson	First N.B.
47.	Terre Haute	First N.B.
50.	Franklin	First N.B.
55.	Indianapolis	First N.B.
58.	Bluffton	First N.B.
63.	Rockville	First N.B.
70.	Cambridge City	First N.B.
78.	Franklin	Second N.B.
82.	Lawrenceburg	First N.B.
88.	Warsaw	First N.B.
105.	Valparaiso	First N.B.
111.	Madison	First N.B.

Charter #	City	Name of Bank
126.	South Bend	First N.B.
129.	Wabash	First N.B.
145.	Huntington	First N.B.
146.	Goshen	First N.B.
152.	Danville	First N.B.
206.	Elkhart	First N.B.
219.	Greencastle	First N.B.
346.	Vevay	First N.B.
356.	Greensburg	First N.B.
363.	Peru	First N.B.
366.	Mount Vernon	First N.B.
377.	Leporte	First N.B.
417.	La Fayette	Second N.B.
571.	Crawfordsville	First N.B.
577.	Attica	First N.B.
581.	Indianapolis	Indianapolis N.B.
617.	Indianapolis	Citizens' N.B.
699.	Aurora	First N.B.
701.	New Albany	First N.B.
730.	Evansville	Evansville N.B.
775.	New Albany	New Albany N.B.
783.	Indianapolis	Fourth N.B.
793.	Muncie	Muncie N.B.
794.	Martinsville	First N.B.
804.	New Castle	First N.B.
815.	Union City	First N.B.
865.	Fort Wayne	Fort Wayne N.B.
869.	Indianapolis	Merchants' N.B.
872.	Knightstown	First N.B.
882.	La Fayette	Union N.B.
889.	Winchester	First N.B.
894.	Kokomo	First N.B.
930.	La Fayette	Nat. State Bank
956.	Jeffersonville	First N.B.
965.	New Albany	Merchants' N.B.
984.	Indianapolis	Indiana N.B.
989.	Evansville	Merchants' N.B.
1031.	Logansport	Logansport N.B.
1032.	Seymour	First N.B.
1034.	Connersville	First N.B.
1046.	Thorntown	First N.B.
1066.	Columbus	First N.B.
1100.	Fort Wayne	Merchants' N.B.
1102.	Richmond	Richmond N.B.
1103.	Terre Haute	Nat. State Bank
1234.	Lima	Nat. State Bank
1263.	Shelbyville	First N.B.
1418.	Lawrenceburg	Lawrenceburg N.B.
1454.	Vincennes	Vincennes N.B.
1456.	Rushville	Rushville N.B.
1457.	Madison	Nat. Branch Bank
1466.	Jeffersonville	Citizen's N.B.
1619.	Brookville	Brookville N.B.
1739.	South Bend	South Bend N.B.
1772.	Evansville	German N.B.
1854.	Frankfort	First N.B.
1869.	Rushville	Rush County N.B.
1873.	Vincennes	First N.B.
1878.	Indianapolis	Meridian N.B.
1879.	Peru	Citizens' N.B.
1888.	Bloomington	First N.B.
1890.	Greensburg	Citizens' N.B.
1892.	Bedford	Bedford N.B.
1897.	Newport	First N.B.
1925.	Liberty	First N.B.
1932.	Sullivan	First N.B.
1949.	Delphi	First N.B.
1952.	Rochester	First N.B.
1959.	Rising Sun	N.B. of Rising Sun
1967.	La Fayette	Indiana N.B.
1988.	Richmond	Second N.B.
2007.	Liberty	Union County N.B.
2043.	Washington	Washington N.B.
2057.	Lebanon	First N.B.
2066.	Princeton	Gibson County N.B.
2067.	Goshen	City N.B.
2090.	Richmond	Richmond N.B.
2101.	Michigan City	First N.B.
2119.	Plymouth	First N.B. of Marshall County
2166.	New Albany	Second N.B.
2173.	Salem	N.B. of Salem
2178.	Spencer	First N.B.
2180.	Princeton	People's N.B.
2183.	Crown Point	First N.B.
2184.	LaGrange	First N.B.
2188.	Evansville	Citizen's N.B.
2201.	Tell City	First N.B.
2202.	New Castle	Bundy N.B.
2207.	Boonville	Boonville N.B.
2208.	Monticello	First N.B.
2213.	La Fayette	La Fayette N.B.
2234.	Muncie	Merchants' N.B.
2238.	Auburn	First N.B.
2346.	Anderson	Madison County N.B.
2361.	Rockville	N.B. of Rockville
2369.	Sullivan	Farmers' N.B.
2375.	Kokomo	Howard N.B.
2403.	Valparaiso	Farmers' N.B.
2439.	Fort Wayne	Hamilton N.B.
2502.	Elkhart	Elkhart N.B
2508.	Huntington	First N.B.
2533.	Crawfordsville	Citizens' N.B.
2556.	Indianapolis	First N.B.
2596.	Logansport	State N.B.
2612.	Lawrenceburg	People's N.B.
2660.	Lebanon	Lebanon N.B.
2680.	Richmond	First N.B.
2687.	Kendallville	First N.B.
2692.	Evansville	First N.B.
2696.	Centreville	First N.B.
2701.	Fort Wayne	First N.B.
2704.	Valparaiso	First N.B. of Porter County
2717.	La Fayette	First N.B.
2734.	Cambridge City	First N.B.
2742.	Terre Haute	First N.B.
2747.	Michigan City	First N.B.
2769.	Franklin	N.B. of Franklin
2844.	Greensburg	Third N.B.
2889.	Lawrenceburg	City N.B.
2896.	Green Castle	Central N.B.
2903.	North Manchester	First N.B.
2963.	Aurora	Aurora N.B.
3013.	Bedford	Indiana N.B.
3028.	Decatur	First N.B.
3084.	Logansport	First N.B.
3280.	La Fayette	Fowler N.B.
3281.	Evansville	Old N.B.
3285.	Fort Wayne	Old N.B.
3338.	Franklin	Franklin N.B.
3413.	Richmond	Union N.B.
3474.	North Manchester	Lawrence N.B.
3478.	Hammond	First N.B.
3583.	Brazil	First N.B.
3755.	Attica	Central N.B.
3842.	Washington	People's N.B.
3864.	Vincennes	American N.B.
3929.	Terre Haute	Vigo County N.B.
3935.	Wabash	Wabash N.B.
3967.	Franklin	Citizens' N.B.
4121.	Kokomo	Citizens' N.B.
4158.	Indianapolis	Capital N.B.
4189.	Marion	First N.B.
4281.	Lawrenceburg	Citizens' N.B.
4468.	La Fayette	Merchants' N.B.
4652.	Seymour	Seymour N.B.
4656.	La Fayette	Perrin N.B.
4674.	Muncie	Farmers' N.B.
4675.	Elwood	First N.B.
4678.	North Vernon	First N.B.
4685.	Anderson	Nat. Exchange Bank
4688.	Vernon	First N.B.
4725.	Fort Wayne	White N.B.
4764.	South Bend	Citizens' N.B.
4800.	Shelbyville	Farmers' N.B.
4801.	Mulberry	Farmers' N.B.
4809.	Muncie	Delaware County N.B.
4825.	Gas City	First N.B.
4835.	Alexandria	Alexandria N.B.
4841.	Elkhart	Indiana N.B.
4852.	Muncie	Merchants' N.B.
4882.	Noblesville	First N.B.
4888.	Dunkirk	First N.B
4901.	Vincennes	Second N.B.
4964.	Martinsville	Citizens' N.B.
4972.	La Grange	N.B. of La Grange
5067.	Rockville	Rockville N.B.
5076.	Logansport	City N.B.
5094.	Union City	Commercial N.B.
5116.	Indianapolis	Fletcher N.B.
5167.	Mishawaka	First N.B.
5173.	Bedford	Citizens' N.B.
5187.	Bedford	Bedford N.B.
5267.	Brazil	Riddell N.B.
5278.	Montpelier	First N.B.
5296.	Sheridan	First N.B.
5300.	Petersburg	First N.B.
5369.	Lowell	First N.B.
5392.	Sullivan	N.B. of Sullivan
5430.	Fowler	First N.B.
5432.	Owensville	First N.B.
5435.	Greensburg	Greensburg N.B.
5476.	Boswell	First N.B.
5524.	Russiaville	First N.B.
5526.	Lewisville	First N.B.
5558.	Orleans	N.B. of Orleans
5629.	Brookville	Franklin County N.B.
5639.	New Carlisle	First N.B.
5672.	Indianapolis	American N.B.
5726.	Hope	Citizens' N.B.
5734.	Montgomery	First N.B.
5756.	Tell City	Tell City N.B.
5842.	Thorntown	Home N.B.
5845.	Indianapolis	Columbia N.B.
5889.	La Fayette	Nat. Fowler Bank
5919.	Knox	First N.B.
5931.	Lowell	First N.B.
5940.	La Fayette	City N.B.
5997.	Dana	First N.B.
5998.	Matthews	First N.B.
6070.	Sheridan	Farmers' N.B.
6172.	Monticello	Monticello N.B.
6194.	Rockport	First N.B.
6200.	Evansville	City N.B.
6215.	Valparaiso	Valparaiso N.B.
6217.	Frankfort	American N.B.
6251.	Tipton	First N.B.
6261.	Kokomo	Kokomo N.B.
6265.	Connersville	Fayette N.B.
6309.	Wabash	Farmers and Merchants' N.B.
6334.	South Bend	Merchant's N.B.
6354.	Monrovia	First N.B.
6388.	West Baden	West Baden N.B.
6433.	Mitchell	First N.B.
6480.	Clinton	First N.B.
6504.	Farmland	First N.B.
6509.	Auburn	City N.B.
6513.	Indianapolis	Union N.B.
6526.	Whiting	First N.B.
6625.	Corydon	First N.B.
6651.	Rensselaer	First N.B.
6699.	New Harmony	First N.B.
6765.	Lowell	Lowell N.B.
6876.	Mooresville	First N.B.
6882.	Dillsboro	First N.B.
6905.	Edinburg	Farmers' N.B.
6909.	Dyer	First N.B.
6952.	Charleston	First N.B.
6959.	Hartford City	First N.B.
6986.	Delphi	Citizens' N.B.
7011.	Plainfield	First N.B.
7023.	Angola	First N.B.
7036.	Poseyville	First N.B.
7124.	Greens Fork	First N.B.
7132.	Columbia City	First N.B.
7155.	Bicknell	First N.B.
7175.	Columbia City	Columbia City N.B.
7180.	Portland	First N.B.
7241.	Loogootee	First N.B.
7260.	Odon	First N.B.
7342.	Jasonville	First N.B.
7354.	Hartsville	First N.B.
7374.	Rushville	People's N.B.
7375.	Tell City	Citizens' N.B.
7411.	Linton	First N.B.
7415.	La Fayette	American N.B.
7437.	Freeland Park	First N.B.
7454.	Muncie	People's N.B.
7463.	Montezuma	First N.B.
7478.	Evansville	Old State N.B.
7491.	Trafalgar	Farmers' N.B.
7496.	Tipton	Citizens' N.B.
7513.	Shelburn	First N.B.
7562.	Terre Haute	Terre Haute N.B.
7601.	East Chicago	First N.B.
7652.	Morgantown	First N.B.
7655.	Rochester	First N.B.
7725.	Fort Wayne	Lincoln N.B.
7758.	Marion	Marion N.B.
7760.	Corydon	Corydon N.B.
7761.	Winamac	First N.B.
7773.	Crawfordsville	Elston N.B.
7786.	Mount Vernon	Mount Vernon N.B.
7802.	Flora	First N.B.
7805.	Brookville	Nat. Brookville Bank
7824.	Batesville	First N.B.
7830.	Ferdinand	Ferdinand N.B.
7863.	Goodland	First N.B.
7902.	Hagerstown	First N.B.
7909.	Lawrenceburg	Dearborn N.B.
7922.	Terre Haute	McKeen N.B.
7930.	Warren	First N.B.
7946.	Shelbyville	Shelby N.B.
8014.	Flora	Bright N.B.
8060.	Remington	First N.B.
8149.	Poseyville	Bozeman-Waters N.B.
8154.	Amo	First N.B.
8166.	Princeton	American N.B.
8192.	Kewanna	First N.B.
8199.	Hammond	Citizens' N.B.
8337.	Fairland	Fairland N.B.
8351.	Ridgeville	First N.B.
8368.	Mentone	First N.B.
8408.	New Point	First N.B.
8415.	Bloomington	Bloomington N.B.
8422.	Greenwood	First N.B.
8426.	Gary	First N.B.
8447.	Coatesville	First N.B.
8461.	Greenwood	Citizens' N.B.
8492.	Evansville	Mercantile N.B.
8537.	Medaryville	First N.B.
8620.	Brazil	Citizens' N.B.
8625.	Williamsburg	First N.B.
8650.	Milltown	First N.B.
8700.	Mays	First N.B.
8747.	Winamac	Citizens' N.B.
8785.	Nappanee	First N.B.
8804.	Dublin	First N.B.
8805.	Carlisle	First N.B.
8820.	Swayzee	First N.B.
8832.	Evansville	Bankers N.B.
8835.	Birdseye	Birdseye N.B.
8868.	Lynnville	Lynnville N.B.
8871.	Cambridge City	Wayne N.B.
8878.	Sunman	Farmers' N.B.
8912.	Albion	Albion N.B.
8927.	Wadesville	Farmers' N.B.
8929.	Huntingburg	First N.B.
8956.	Tennyson	Tennyson N.B.
9006.	Rosedale	Rosedale N.B.
9073.	Fort Branch	First N.B.
9077.	Fort Branch	Farmers and Merchants' N.B.
9090.	Holland	Holland N.B.
9115.	Kirklin	First N.B.
9122.	North Vernon	North Vernon N.B.
9143.	Brownstown	First N.B.
9152.	Knightstown	Citizens' N.B.
9159.	Winslow	First N.B.
9175.	Westport	First N.B.
9189.	Cayuga	First N.B.
9209.	Shirley	First N.B.
9250.	Center Point	First N.B.
9266.	Boonville	Farmers and Merchants' N.B.
9279.	Wilkinson	Farmers' N.B.
9286.	Butler	First N.B.
9299.	Fortville	First N.B.
9352.	Patoka	Patoka N.B.
9381.	Michigan City	Merchants' N.B.
9401.	Cannelton	First N.B.
9463.	Princeton	Farmers' N.B.
9488.	Arcadia	First N.B.
9492.	Whiteland	Whiteland N.B.
9510.	Ambia	First N.B.
9537.	Indianapolis	Continental N.B.
9540.	Clay City	First N.B.
9562.	Oakland City	First N.B.
9670.	Redkey	Farmers and Merchants' N.B.
9682.	Cannelton	Cannelton N.B.
9715.	Spencer	Spencer N.B.
9726.	Argos	First N.B.
9756.	Noblesville	American N.B.
9784.	Monterey	First N.B.
9829.	Indianapolis	Fletcher American N.B.
9852.	New Castle	Farmers' N.B.

Charter #	City	Name of Bank
9860.	Covington	First N.B.
10121.	Indianapolis	Nat. City Bank
10171.	East Chicago, Indiana Harbor	Indiana Harbor N.B.
10234.	Mulberry	Citizens' N.B.
10290.	Anderson	People's State N.B.
10409.	Greencastle	Citizens' N.B.
10419.	Fishers	Fishers N.B.
10465.	Cloverdale	First N.B.
10551.	Princeton	People's American N.B.
10613.	Boonville	City N.B.
10616.	Kewanna	American N.B.
10671.	Indianapolis	Commercial N.B.
10718.	Fremont	First N.B.
10720.	Cicero	Citizens' N.B.
10989.	Winchester	Citizens' N.B.
11035.	Farmersburg	First N.B.
11043.	Wakarusa	First N.B.
11044.	Veedersburg	First N.B.
11094.	Gary	N.B. of America
11148.	La Fayette	First-Merchants' N.B.
11355.	Remington	Farmers' N.B.
11424.	Cedar Grove	Cedar Grove N.B.
11427.	Roanoke	First N.B.
11470.	Rensselaer	Farmers and Merchants' N.B.
11671.	Converse	First N.B.
11782.	Milroy	First N.B.
12028.	Spurgeon	First N.B.
12058.	East Chicago, Indiana Harbor	United States N.B. of Indiana Harbor
12132.	Evansville	Nat. City Bank
12420.	Rushville	American N.B.
12444.	Evansville	Old N.B.
12466.	Mount Vernon	Old First N.B.
12532.	Kendallville	Citizens' N.B.
12780.	Mount Vernon	Mount Vernon N.B. and Trust Co.
12866.	Farmland	New First N.B.
12952.	Monticello	N.B. of Monticello
13050.	Sheridan	Sheridan N.B.
13082.	Covington	N.B. of Covington
13224.	Terre Haute	Citizens' N.B. & Trust Co.
13305.	Bluffton	Old N.B.
13317.	Bluffton	First N.B.
13378.	Franklin	Franklin N.B.
13503.	Poseyville	Bozeman Waters First N.B.
13531.	East Chicago	First N.B.
13532.	East Chicago	Union N.B. of Indiana Harbor
13542.	New Harmony	New Harmony N.B.
13580.	Logansport	N.B. of Logansport
13643.	Martinsville	N.B. of Martinsville
13717.	Marion	First N.B.
13729.	Marion	Marion N.B.
13759.	Indianapolis	American N.B.
13788.	Bedord	Stone City N.B.
13816.	New Castle	First N.B.
13818.	Fort Wayne	Fort Wayne N.B.
13862.	Swayzee	First N.B.
13888.	Wabash	First N.B.
13938.	Terre Haute	Merchants' N.B.
13977.	Flora	Bright N.B.
13987.	South Bend	City N.B.
13988.	Greensburg	Decatur County N.B.
14047.	New Albany	Union N.B.
14075.	Franklin	Johnson County N.B.
14113.	Goshen	First N.B.
14175.	La Fayette	La Fayette N.B.
14218.	Boonville	Boonville N.B.
14226.	Butler	Knisely N.B.
14258.	Linton	Citizens N.B.
14288.	Rensselaer	Farmers and Merchants N.B.
14292.	Greenwood	N.B. of Greenwood

IOWA

Charter #	City	Name of Bank
15.	Davenport	First N.B.
18.	Iowa City	First N.B.
66.	Lyons	First N.B.
80.	Koekuk	First N.B.
107.	Ottumwa	First N.B.
117.	Marion	First N.B.
147.	Oskaloosa	First N.B.
195.	Ottumwa	Second N.B.
299.	Mount Pleasant	First N.B.
317.	Dubuque	First N.B.
323.	McGregor	First N.B.
337.	Centerville	First N.B.
351.	Burlington	First N.B.
389.	Des Moines	First N.B.
398.	Washington	First N.B.
405.	Lansing	First N.B.
411.	Marshalltown	First N.B.
483.	Cedar Rapids	City N.B.
485.	Des Moines	Second N.B.
493.	Decorah	First N.B.
500.	Cedar Rapids	First N.B.
650.	Newton	First N.B.
692.	Muscatine	Muscatine N.B.
751.	Burlington	Nat. State Bank
792.	Waterloo	First N.B.
846.	Dubuque	Merchants' N.B.
848.	Davenport	Davenport N.B.
922.	Mount Pleasant	Nat. State Bank
950.	Des Moines	Nat. State Bank
977.	Iowa City	Iowa City N.B.
994.	Clinton	Clinton N.B.
999.	Maquoketta	First N.B.
1101.	Oskaloosa	Nat. State Bank
1299.	Bloomfield	First N.B.
1403.	Winterset	First N.B.
1441.	Koekuk	State N.B.
1475.	Fairfield	First N.B.
1479.	Council Bluffs	First N.B.
1540.	Dubuque	Nat. State Bank
1577.	Muscatine	First N.B.
1581.	Independence	First N.B.
1593.	Vinton	First N.B.
1611.	Fort Madison	Fort Madison N.B.
1618.	Osage	Osage N.B.
1629.	Grinnell	First N.B.
1661.	Fort Dodge	First N.B.
1671.	Davenport	Citizens' N.B.
1684.	Council Bluffs	Pacific N.B.
1696.	Leon	First N.B.
1724.	Chariton	First N.B.
1726.	Ottumwa	Iowa N.B.
1744.	Burlington	Merchants' N.B.
1757.	Sioux City	First N.B.
1762.	Washington	Washington N.B.
1776.	Osceola	First N.B.
1786.	Sigourney	First N.B.
1799.	Albia	First N.B.
1801.	Dubuque	Commercial N.B.
1810.	Charles City	First N.B.
1811.	Indianola	First N.B.
1813.	Anamosa	First N.B.
1815.	Elkader	First N.B.
1836.	Atlantic	First N.B.
1862.	Glenwood	Mills County N.B.
1871.	Knoxville	Knoxville N.B.
1874.	Webster City	First N.B.
1880.	Tama	First N.B.
1891.	Pella	First N.B.
1943.	Wyoming	First N.B.
1947.	Fort Dodge	Merchants' N.B.
1970.	Des Moines	Citizens N.B.
1976.	Sioux City	Citizens' N.B.
1986.	Knoxville	Marion County N.B.
1992.	Keokuk	Keokuk N.B.
2002.	Winterset	Citizens' N.B.
2012.	Belle Plaine	First N.B.
2015.	West Union	Fayette County N.B.
2028.	Clarinda	First N.B.
2032.	Columbus Junction	Louisa County N.B.
2033.	Brighton	Brighton N.B.
2051.	Boone	First N.B.
2063.	Pella	Pella N.B.
2080.	Monticello	Monticello N.B.
2115.	Marshalltown	Farmers' N.B.
2130.	Red Oak	First N.B.
2177.	Cedar Falls	First N.B.
2182.	Lisbon	First N.B.
2187.	Independence	People's N.B.
2191.	Allerton	First N.B.
2197.	Centerville	Farmers' N.B.
2215.	Monroe	First N.B.
2230.	Red Oak	Valley N.B.
2247.	Malvern	First N.B.
2298.	Bedford	First N.B.
2307.	Des Moines	Iowa N.B.
2326.	Afton	First N.B.
2327.	Dubuque	Second N.B.
2363.	Shenandoah	First N.B.
2364.	Hamburg	First N.B.
2411.	Nashua	First N.B.
2417.	Oskaloosa	Oskaloosa N.B.
2469.	Clinton	City N.B.
2484.	Marengo	First N.B.
2511.	Cedar Rapids	Merchants' N.B.
2535.	Sioux City	Sioux N.B.
2555.	Nevada	First N.B.
2573.	Hampton	First N.B.
2574.	Mason City	First N.B.
2579.	Charles City	Charles City N.B.
2583.	Des Moines	Des Moines N.B.
2586.	Creston	First N.B.
2588.	New Hampton	First N.B.
2595.	Storm Lake	First N.B.
2621.	Ottumwa	Ottumwa N.B.
2631.	Des Moines	Merchants' N.B.
2644.	Newton	First N.B.
2656.	Washington	First N.B.
2679.	Shenandoah	Shenandoah N.B.
2695.	Davenport	First N.B.
2721.	Stuart	First N.B.
2728.	Le Mars	First N.B.
2733.	Lyons	First N.B.
2738.	Iowa City	First N.B.
2753.	Marion	First N.B.
2762.	Atlantic	Atlantic N.B.
2763.	Fort Dodge	Fort Dodge N.B.
2766.	Villisca	First N.B.
2818.	Le Mars	Le Mars N.B.
2821.	Iowa City	Iowa City, N.B.
2833.	Creston	Creston N.B.
2841.	Centerville	Centerville N.B.
2856.	Jesup	First N.B.
2886.	Des Moines	Valley N.B.
2895.	Oskaloosa	Farmers and Traders' N.B.
2910.	Waterloo	Commercial N.B.
2936.	Corning	First N.B.
2953.	Grinnell	Merchants' N.B.
2961.	Montezuma	First N.B.
2971.	Marshalltown	Commercial N.B.
2983.	Tipton	First N.B.
2984.	Webster City	Hamilton County N.B.
3012.	Albia	Albia N.B.
3017.	Ames	Union N.B.
3026.	Perry	First N.B.
3048.	Griswold	First N.B.
3049.	Cherokee	First N.B.
3053.	Rockford	First N.B.
3055.	Red Oak	Red Oak N.B.
3071.	Greene	First N.B.
3105.	Waverly	First N.B.
3112.	Clarinda	Clarinda N.B.
3124.	Sioux City	Security N.B.
3140.	Dubuque	Dubuque N.B.
3153.	Rock Rapids	First N.B.
3182.	De Witt	First N.B.
3189.	Missouri Valley	First N.B.
3192.	What Cheer	First N.B.
3197.	Algona	First N.B.
3225.	Grundy Center	First N.B.
3226.	Panora	Gutherie County N.B.
3252.	Iowa Falls	First N.B.
3263.	Independence	First N.B.
3273.	Boone	First N.B.
3284.	Brooklyn	First N.B.
3320.	Sibley	First N.B.
3337.	Emmetsburg	First N.B.
3396.	Grundy Center	Grundy Center N.B.
3420.	Webster City	Farmers' N.B.
3427.	Council Bluffs	Council Bluffs N.B.
3439.	Eagle Grove	First N.B.
3455.	Manning	First N.B.
3618.	Sutherland	First N.B.
3643.	Cedar Rapids	Cedar Rapids N.B.
3736.	Clinton	Merchants' N.B.
3788.	Clarion	Wright County N.B.
3796.	Clarion	First N.B.
3848.	Sheldon	First N.B.
3871.	Cedar Falls	Cedar Falls N.B.
3898.	Spencer	First N.B.
3930.	Ida Grove	First N.B.
3940.	Sioux City	American N.B.
3968.	Sioux City	Iowa State N.B.
3969.	Carroll	First N.B.
3974.	Fort Madison	First N.B.
4022.	Davenport	Iowa N.B.
4114.	Laporte City	First N.B.
4139.	Dunlap	First N.B.
4155.	Primghar	First N.B.
4209.	Sioux City	Merchants' N.B.
4221.	Manchester	First N.B.
4235.	Sioux City	Corn Exchange N.B.
4268.	Corning	N.B. of Corning
4359.	Marshalltown	City N.B.
4376.	Charter Oak	First N.B.
4431.	Sioux City	N.B. of Sioux City
4450.	Sac City	First N.B.
4510.	Sioux City	Sioux N.B.
4511.	Odebolt	First N.B.
4536.	Lyons	Citizens' N.B.
4553.	Holstein	First N.B.
4566.	Fort Dodge	Commercial N.B.
4587.	Mason City	City N.B.
4594.	Hawarden	First N.B.
4601.	Peterson	First N.B.
4609.	Tabor	First N.B.
4630.	Sioux City	Commercial N.B.
4633.	Knoxville	Citizens' N.B.
4677.	Charles City	Citizens' N.B.
4694.	Eagle Grove	First N.B.
4696.	Anamosa	Anamosa N.B.
4700.	Estherville	First N.B.
4745.	Woodbine	First N.B.
4754.	Belle Plaine	Citizens' N.B.
4758.	Spirit Lake	First N.B.
4761.	Nora Springs	First N.B.
4784.	Denison	First N.B.
4789.	Marathon	First N.B.
4794.	Ireton	First N.B.
4795.	Laurens	First N.B.
4810.	Garner	First N.B.
4814.	Glidden	First N.B.
4824.	Sanborn	First N.B.
4834.	Malvern	Farmers' N.B.
4881.	Hartley	First N.B.
4885.	Osage	Farmers' N.B.
4889.	Forest City	First N.B.
4891.	Audubon	First N.B.
4897.	Cresco	First N.B.
4902.	Blanchard	First N.B.
4921.	Waukon	First N.B.
4954.	Rolfe	First N.B.
4966.	Lake City	First N.B.
5011.	Forest City	Forest City N.B.
5020.	Britt	First N.B.
5022.	Sioux City	Live Stock N.B.
5054.	Thompson	First N.B.
5081.	Decorah	N.B. of Decorah
5088.	Vinton	Farmers' N.B.
5113.	Cedar Rapids	Citizens' N.B.
5120.	Waterloo	Leavitt and Johnson N.B.
5123.	Lake Mills	First N.B.
5135.	Traer	First N.B.
5140.	Eldora	First N.B.
5145.	Sidney	N.B. of Sidney
5154.	Buffalo Center	First N.B.
5165.	Bedford	Bedford N.B.
5185.	Rockwell City	First N.B.
5200.	Rock Valley	First N.B.
5207.	Harlan	First N.B.
5302.	Dayton	First N.B.
5305.	Crystal Lake	First N.B.
5319.	Moulton	First N.B.
5334.	Greenfield	First N.B.
5342.	Eldon	First N.B.
5366.	Clutier	First N.B.
5372.	Dike	First N.B.
5373.	Goldfield	First N.B.
5402.	Lost Nation	First N.B.
5412.	Chelsea	First N.B.
5420.	New London	First N.B.
5424.	Guthrie Center	First N.B.
5442.	Armstrong	First N.B.
5457.	Wesley	First N.B.
5461.	Gladbrook	First N.B.
5464.	Garden Grove	First N.B.
5479.	Ayrshire	First N.B.
5489.	Leon	Exchange N.B.

Charter #	City	Name of Bank
5507.	Cedar Falls	Citizens' N.B.
5514.	Coon Rapids	First N.B.
5517.	Lenox	First N.B.
5539.	Milford	First N.B.
5540.	Hedrick	First N.B.
5541.	Ruthven	First N.B.
5554.	Brighton	N.B. of Brighton
5564.	Pleasantville	First N.B.
5571.	Graettinger	First N.B.
5576.	Dougherty	First N.B.
5579.	Farmington	First N.B.
5585.	Williams	First N.B.
5597.	Titonka	First N.B.
5611.	Richland	First N.B.
5616.	Melvin	First N.B.
5637.	Swea City	First N.B.
5643.	Bancroft	First N.B.
5659.	Hudson	First N.B.
5685.	Burt	First N.B.
5700.	Waterloo	Waterloo N.B.
5703.	Burt	Burt N.B.
5707.	Gowrie	First N.B.
5738.	Essex	First N.B.
5743.	Jewell Jct., Jewell	First N.B.
5775.	Corwith	First N.B.
5778.	Oelwein	First N.B.
5803.	Essex	Commercial N.B.
5817.	Odebolt	Farmers N.B.
5838.	Council Bluffs	Commercial N.B.
5868.	Lehigh	First N.B.
5873.	Manilla	First N.B.
5891.	Valley Junction	First N.B.
5912.	Prescott	First N.B.
5934.	Dysart	First N.B.
5979.	Charles City	Commercial N.B.
6014.	Chariton	Chariton N.B.
6017.	Hamburg	Farmers' N.B.
6033.	Osceola	Osceola N.B.
6041.	Manilla	Manilla N.B.
6056.	Red Oak	Farmers' N.B.
6063.	Pomeroy	First N.B.
6080.	Coon Rapids	Coon Rapids N.B.
6122.	Washington	Citizens' N.B.
6132	Orange City	First N.B.
6303.	Pocahontas	First N.B.
6432.	Toledo	First N.B.
6434.	Stanton	First N.B.
6435.	Radcliffe	First N.B.
6550.	Fonda	First N.B.
6610.	Grafton	First N.B.
6611.	Gilmore, Gilmore City	First N.B.
6650.	Primghar	Farmers' N.B.
6659.	Klemme	First N.B.
6700.	Farragut	First N.B.
6705.	Deep River	First N.B.
6722.	Dunkerton	First N.B.
6737.	Churdan	First N.B.
6750.	Lime Springs	First N.B.
6755.	Prairie City	First N.B.
6760.	Tipton	City N.B.
6764.	Doon	First N.B.
6771.	Logan	First N.B.
6838.	Boone	Boone N.B.
6852.	Macksburg	Macksburg N.B.
6854.	Waterloo	Black Hawk N.B.
6857.	Elliott	First N.B.
6870.	Exira	First N.B.
6880.	Greene	Merchants' N.B.
6936.	Harvey	First N.B.
6941.	Spencer	Citizens' N.B.
6949.	Harris	First N.B.
6953.	Hull	First N.B.
6975.	Remsen	First N.B.
6995.	Bagley	First N.B.
7061.	Fontanelle	First N.B.
7089.	Rock Rapids	Lyon County N.B.
7108.	Aurelia	First N.B.
7114.	Colfax	First N.B.
7126.	Alta	First N.B.
7137.	Linn Grove	First N.B.
7189.	Sioux Rapids	First N.B.
7261.	Lineville	First N.B.
7287.	Norway	First N.B.
7294.	Havelock	First N.B.
7304.	Inwood	First N.B.
7309.	Colin	First N.B.
7322.	Akron	First N.B.
7326.	Cumberland	First N.B.
7357.	Monroe	Monroe N.B.
7369.	Sioux Center	First N.B.
7382.	Henderson	Farmers' N.B.
7401.	Sioux City	City N.B.
7439.	Grinnell	Citizens' N.B.
7469.	Montour	First N.B.
7506.	Villisca	Villisca N.B.
7521.	Iowa Falls	State N.B.
7585.	Olin	First N.B.
7607.	New Hampton	Second N.B.
7609.	Rippey	First N.B.
7682.	Clarence	First N.B.
7736.	Guthrie Center	Citizens N.B.
7828.	Everly	First N.B.
7833.	Randolph	First N.B.
7843.	Hampton	Citizens' N.B.
7869.	Clear Lake	First N.B.
7880.	Sheldon	Sheldon N.B.
7988.	Renwick	First N.B.
8032.	Spirit Lake	Spirit Lake N.B.
8035.	Emmetsburg	Emmetsburg N.B.
8047.	Pella	Farmers' N.B.
8057.	Malvern	Malvern N.B.
8076.	Oskaloosa	Farmers' N.B.
8099.	Casey	Abram Rutt N.B.
8100.	Corning	Farmers' N.B.
8119.	Little Rock	First N.B.
8198.	Sumner	First N.B.
8211.	Blockton	First N.B.
8247.	Seymour	First N.B.
8257.	Inwood	Farmers' N.B.
8262.	Jefferson	First N.B.
8273.	Preston	First N.B.
8277.	Humboldt	First N.B.
8295.	Imogene	First N.B.
8340.	Thornton	First N.B.
8352.	New London	New London N.B.
8367.	Garner	Farmers' N.B.
8373.	Northwood	First N.B.
8442.	Riceville	First N.B.
8603.	Albia	People's N.B.
8699.	Adair	First N.B.
8725.	Corning	Okey-Vernon N.B.
8748.	Belmond	First N.B.
8762.	Ackley	First N.B.
8900.	Hawkeye	First N.B.
8915.	Griswold	Griswold N.B.
8931.	State Center	First N.B.
8950.	New Sharon	First N.B.
8970.	Hubbard	First N.B.
8971.	Shenandoah	Commercial N.B.
8981.	Adel	First N.B.
8986.	Fairfield	Fairfield N.B.
9014.	Cambridge	First N.B.
9015.	Northboro	First N.B.
9017.	Story City	First N.B.
9018.	Kanawha	First N.B.
9024.	Chariton	Lucas County N.B.
9069.	Strawberry Point	First N.B.
9116.	Kingsley	Farmers' N.B.
9125.	Diagonal	First N.B.
9168.	Cedar Rapids	Commercial N.B.
9231.	Allerton	Farmers' N.B.
9233.	Eldora	Hardin County N.B.
9298.	Milford	Milford N.B.
9303.	Bloomfield	N.B. of Bloomfield
9306.	Council Bluffs	City N.B.
9447.	Sonrad	First N.B.
9549.	Clearfield	First N.B.
9555.	Dyersville	First N.B.
9585.	Sioux Rapids	First N.B.
9592.	Fayette	First N.B.
9619.	Kimballton	Landmands N.B.
9664.	Arlington	American N.B.
9723.	Shannon City	First N.B.
9724.	Aurelia	Farmers' N.B.
9737.	Grand River	First N.B.
9819.	Marcus	First N.B.
9821.	Floyd	First N.B.
9846.	Parkersburg	First N.B.
9853.	Crystal Lake	Farmers' N.B.
9910.	George	First N.B.
10030.	Dexter	First N.B.
10034.	Storm Lake	Citizens' First N.B.
10123.	Jefferson	Farmers and Merchants' N.B.
10130.	Perry	Perry N.B.
10139.	Sioux City	Toy N.B.
10146.	Corydon	First N.B.
10191.	Newell	First N.B.
10207.	Waukon	People's N.B.
10217.	Rockwell	First N.B.
10222.	Story City	Story City N.B.
10223.	Storm Lake	Commercial N.B.
10238.	Terril	First N.B.
10243.	Milton	N.B. of Milton
10354.	Harlan	Harlan N.B.
10371.	Bode	First N.B.
10395.	Royal	Citizens' N.B.
10408.	Ames	Ames N.B.
10428.	Mason City	Security N.B.
10501.	Galva	First N.B.
10518.	Sioux City	Continental N.B.
10541.	Fredericksburg	First N.B.
10562.	Mallard	First N.B.
10599.	Lawler	First N.B.
10640.	Winfield	Farmers' N.B.
10684.	Saint Ansgar	First N.B.
10701.	Mapleton	First N.B.
10711.	Cherokee	Security N.B.
10726.	Newton	Clark N.B.
10729.	Rembrandt	First N.B.
10812.	Paulina	First N.B.
10848.	Derby	First N.B.
10861.	Whiting	First N.B.
10877.	Orange City	Orange City N.B.
10889.	Merrill	First N.B.
11162.	Webb	Citizens' N.B.
11210.	Seymour	Seymour N.B.
11249.	Roland	First N.B.
11295.	College Springs	First N.B.
11304.	Fort Dodge	Webster County N.B.
11582.	Rockwell City	Rockwell City N.B.
11588.	Shenandoah	Farmers' N.B.
11604.	Ogden	First N.B.
11644.	Ashton	First N.B.
11735.	Rake	Farmers First N.B.
11907.	Farnhamville	First N.B.
12248.	Lorimor	First N.B.
12303.	Bellevue	First N.B.
12430.	Sheffield	First N.B.
12544.	Pocahontas	First N.B.
12610.	Hamburg	First N.B.
12636.	Creston	First N.B.
12645.	Lake Park	First N.B.
12656.	Hedrick	Hedrick N.B.
12849.	Knoxville	Knoxville N.B. and Trust Co.
12883.	Ashton	First N.B.
12950.	Shenandoah	Shenandoah N.B.
12998.	New Hampton	New First N.B.
13020.	Spirit Lake	First N.B.
13059.	Emmetsburg	N.B. of Emmetsburg
13073.	Toledo	N.B. of Toledo
13083.	Nevada	Nevada N.B.
13109.	Corydon	Commercial N.B.
13112.	Spencer	Clay County N.B.
13188.	Independence	Buchanan County N.B.
13232.	Tipton	Tipton N.B.
13263.	Vinton	Farmers N.B.
13321.	Des Moines	Central N.B. & Trust Co.
13400.	Sioux Rapids	First N.B.
13458.	Chariton	N.B. & Trust Co.
13473.	Grinnell	Poweshiek County N.B.
13495.	Seymour	N.B. of Seymour
13508.	Dyersville	Dyersville N.B.
13538.	Sioux City	First N.B.
13609.	Newton	Newton N.B.
13686.	Colfax	First N.B.
13694.	Burlington	First N.B
13697.	Iowa City	First Capital N.B.
13702.	Waterloo	N.B. of Waterloo
13707.	Knoxville	Community N.B. and Trust Co.
13766.	Humboldt	First N.B.
13785.	Red Oak	Montgomery County N.B.
13817.	Boone	Citizens' N.B.
13842.	Hampton	First N.B.
13849.	Washington	N.B. of Washington
13890.	Rockwell City	N.B. of Rockwell City
13939.	Hawarden	First N.B.
13978.	West Union	First N.B.
13991.	Fairfield	First N.B.
14028.	Council Bluffs	First N.B.
14036.	Garner	Hancock County N.B.
14040.	Lenox	First N.B.
14041.	Villisca	Nodaway Valley N.B.
14057.	Shenandoah	City N.B.
14065.	Nevada	Nevada N.B.
14066.	Grundy Center	Grundy N.B.
14069.	Belle Plaine	Citizens' N.B.
14085.	Clear Lake	First N.B.
14129.	Winterset	Farmers and Merchants N.B.
14143.	What Cheer	First N.B.
14158.	Bellevue	First N.B.
14172.	Traer	First N.B.
14253.	Le Mars	First N.B.
14286.	Eldora	Hardin County N.B.
14309.	Keokuk	Keokuk N.B.
14326.	Glidden	First N.B.

KANSAS

Charter #	City	Name of Bank
182.	Leavenworth	First N.B.
1448.	Leavenworth	Second N.B.
1590.	Lawrence	N.B. of Lawrence
1660.	Topeka	First N.B.
1672.	Atchison	First N.B.
1718.	Ottawa	First N.B.
1732.	Lawrence	Second N.B.
1763.	Fort Scott	First N.B.
1828	Olathe	First N.B.
1838	Baxter Springs	First N.B.
1840.	Wyandotte	First N.B.
1864.	Paola	First N.B.
1902.	Chetopa	First N.B.
1910.	Ottawa	People's N.B.
1913.	Wichita	First N.B.
1915.	Emporia	First N.B.
1927.	Fort Scott	Merchants' N.B.
1945.	Topeka	Topeka N.B.
1951.	Parsons	First N.B.
1957.	El Dorado	First N.B.
1977.	Junction City	First N.B.
1979.	Burlington	Burlington N.B.
1983.	Emporia	Emporia N.B.
2001.	Council Grove	First N.B.
2082.	Atchison	Atchison N.B.
2094.	Manhattan	First N.B.
2192.	Topeka	State N.B.
2427.	Abilene	First N.B.
2538.	Salina	First N.B.
2589.	Hiawatha	First N.B.
2640.	Cawker City	First N.B.
2646.	Topeka	First N.B.
2666.	Larned	First N.B.
2758.	Atchison	Exchange N.B.
2764.	Cottonwood Falls	Chase County N.B.
2777.	Newton	First N.B.
2782.	Wichita	First N.B.
2786.	Wichita	Wichita N.B.
2791.	Marysville	First N.B.
2809.	Frankfort	First N.B.
2879.	Wellington	First N.B.
2912.	Washington	First N.B.
2952.	Seneca	First N.B.
2954.	Sabetha	First N.B.
2973.	Garnett	First N.B.
2990.	Sabetha	Citizens' N.B.
3002.	Strong City	Strong City N.B.
3018.	Marion	First N.B.
3021.	Independence	First N.B.
3033.	Leavenworth	Leavenworth N.B.
3035.	El Dorado	N.B. of El Dorado
3038.	Oswego	First N.B.
3061.	Holton	First N.B.
3066.	Concordia	First N.B.
3072.	Clay Center	First N.B.
3078.	Topeka	Central N.B.
3090.	Concordia	Concordia N.B.
3091.	Wellington	First N.B.
3108.	Yates Center	Woodson N.B.
3115.	Clyde	First N.B.
3134.	Peabody	First N.B.
3148.	Eureka	First N.B.
3167.	Washington	Washington N.B.
3170.	Burlington	People's N.B.
3175.	Fort Scott	Citizens' N.B.
3180.	Hutchinson	First N.B.
3194.	Leavenworth	Metropolitan N.B.

Charter #	City	Name of Bank
3199.	Hutchinson	Hutchinson N.B.
3207.	Sterling	First N.B.
3213.	El Dorado	Exchange N.B.
3216.	Girard	First N.B.
3218.	Winfield	First N.B.
3231.	Beloit	First N.B.
3242.	Howard	First N.B.
3249.	Ellsworth	First N.B.
3253.	Medicine Lodge	First N.B.
3265.	Harper	First N.B.
3277.	Cherryvale	First N.B.
3297.	Newton	Newton N.B.
3304.	Westmoreland	First N.B.
3319.	Osborne	First N.B.
3324.	Coffeyville	First N.B.
3345.	Clay Center	People's N.B.
3350.	Paola	Miami County N.B.
3351.	Winfield	Winfield N.B.
3353.	Minneapolis	First N.B.
3360.	Arkansas City	First N.B.
3363.	Great Bend	First N.B.
3374.	Saint Mary's	First N.B.
3384.	Anthony	Harper County N.B.
3385.	Anthony	First N.B.
3386.	Belleville	First N.B.
3394.	Anthony	Anthony N.B.
3431.	Harper	Harper N.B.
3434.	Wamego	First N.B.
3440.	Stockton	First N.B.
3443.	Halstead	Halstead N.B.
3447.	Ellsworth	Central N.B.
3448.	Garden City	First N.B.
3454.	Kirwin	First N.B.
3463.	Pittsburg	First N.B.
3464.	Lincoln	First N.B.
3467.	Saint John	First N.B.
3472.	Osbsorne	Exchange N.B.
3473.	Newton	German N.B.
3475.	Pittsburg	N.B. of Pittsburg
3509.	Kingman	First N.B.
3511.	Oberlin	First N.B.
3512.	Colby	First N.B.
3521.	McPherson	First N.B.
3524.	Wichita	State N.B.
3531.	Salina	Salina N.B.
3542.	Ness City	First N.B.
3543.	Junction City	First N.B.
3546.	Smith Center	First N.B.
3559.	Kingman	Kingman N.B.
3563.	Downs	Exchange N.B.
3564.	Wellington	State N.B.
3567.	Greenleaf	First N.B.
3569.	Downs	First N.B.
3577.	Lyons	First N.B.
3584.	Lawrence	Merchants' N.B.
3589.	Lindsborg	First N.B.
3591.	Jewell	First N.B.
3594.	Medicine Lodge	Citizens' N.B.
3596.	Dodge City	First N.B.
3601.	Phillipsburg	First N.B.
3612.	Atchison	United States N.B.
3630.	Smith Center	Smith County N.B.
3649.	Pratt	First N.B.
3657.	Russell	First N.B.
3658.	Caldwell	First N.B.
3667.	Greensburg	First N.B.
3683.	Wichita	Fourth N.B.
3687.	Norton	First N.B.
3695.	Meade Center	First N.B.
3703.	Coldwater	First N.B.
3706.	Kansas City	First N.B.
3710.	Ashland	First N.B.
3720.	Olathe	First N.B.
3726.	Kansas City	Wyandotte N.B.
3731.	Minneapolis	Minneapolis N.B.
3737.	Kingman	Citizens' N.B.
3745.	Mankato	First N.B.
3748.	Concordia	Citizens' N.B.
3751.	Cimarron	First N.B.
3756.	Wichita	West Side N.B.
3758.	Hill City	First N.B.
3759.	Kinsley	First N.B.
3769.	Alma	First N.B.
3775.	Russell Springs	First N.B.
3776.	Wakeeney	First N.B.
3777.	Abilene	Abilene N.B.
3779.	Belleville	N.B. of Belleville
3782.	Manhattan	First N.B.
3787.	Pratt	Pratt County N.B.
3790.	Topeka	Kansas N.B.
3791.	McPherson	Second N.B.
3794.	Howard	Howard N.B.
3795.	Paola	N.B. of Paola
3803.	McPherson	McPherson N.B.
3805.	Jetmore	First N.B.
3807.	Humboldt	Humboldt First N.B.
3810.	Horton	First N.B.
3812.	Mankato	Jewell County N.B.
3813.	Osage City	First N.B.
3819.	Chanute	First N.B.
3824.	Centralia	First N.B.
3833.	El Dorado	Merchants' N.B.
3835.	Fredonia	First N.B.
3844.	Leoti	First N.B.
3849.	Lawrence	Lawrence N.B.
3852.	Stafford	First N.B.
3853.	Meade Center	Meade County N.B.
3855.	Sedan	First N.B.
3861.	Hutchinson	N.B. of Commerce
3865.	Wellington	Sumner N.B.
3880.	Burr Oak	First N.B.
3881.	Lawrence	Watkins N.B.
3885.	Hays City	First N.B.
3888.	Dighton	First N.B.
3900.	Garden City	Finney County N.B.
3908.	Leavenworth	Manufacturers' N.B.
3909.	Topeka	Merchants' N.B.
3928.	Marion	Cottonwood Valley N.B.
3963.	Erie	First N.B.
3970.	La Crosse	First N.B.
3991.	Paola	People's N.B.
3992.	Arkansas City	American N.B.
4008.	Manhattan	Union N.B.
4032.	Garnett	Anderson County N.B.
4036.	Chanute	Chanute N.B.
4040.	Burlington	First N.B.
4058.	Herington	First N.B.
4136.	Pittsburg	Manufacturers' N.B.
4150.	Sedan	Sedan N.B.
4284.	Junction City	Central N.B.
4288.	Cherryvale	Cherryvale N.B.
4317.	Salina	American N.B.
4381.	Kansas City	Inter-State N.B.
4487.	Arkansas City	Home N.B.
4499.	Independence	Commercial N.B.
4556.	Winfield	Cowley County N.B.
4592.	Independence	Citizens-First N.B.
4618.	Cawker City	Farmers and Merchants' N.B.
4619.	Saint Mary's	N.B. of Saint Mary's
4626.	Sabetha	N.B. of Sabetha
4640.	Arkansas City	Farmers' N.B.
4642.	Oberlin	Oberlin N.B.
4742.	Salina	Farmers' N.B.
4749.	Cherryvale	Montgomery County N.B.
4798.	Galena	Galena N.B.
4860.	Newton	Midland N.B.
4931.	Minneapolis	Citizens' N.B.
4945.	Salina	N.B. of America
4981.	El Dorado	Farmers and Merchants' N.B.
5041.	Holton	N.B. of Holton
5101.	Seneca	N.B. of Seneca
5104.	Alma	Alma N.B.
5169.	Wichita	N.B. of Commerce
5287.	Iola	Northrup N.B.
5292.	Garnett	N.B. of Commerce
5349.	Caney	Caney Valley N.B.
5353.	Lyons	Lyons N.B.
5359.	Nortonville	First N.B.
5386.	Ashland	Stockgrowers' N.B.
5447.	Cherokee	First N.B.
5498.	Emporia	Citizens' N.B.
5506.	Havensville	First N.B.
5516.	Caney	Home N.B.
5529.	Madison	First N.B.
5559.	Mount Hope	First N.B.
5608.	Cedar Vale	Cedar Vale N.B.
5655.	Eureka	Citizens' N.B.
5687.	Hoxie	First N.B.
5705.	Great Bend	Citizens' N.B.
5757.	Council Grove	Council Grove N.B.
5799.	Lebanon	First N.B.
5810.	Kinsley	N.B. of Kinsley
5834.	Osborne	Farmers' N.B.
5952.	Baxter Springs	Baxter N.B.
6039.	Goodland	First N.B.
6072.	Chanute	N.B. of Chanute
6101.	Waverly	First N.B.
6103.	Columbus	First N.B.
6120.	Hillsboro	First N.B.
6149.	Leroy	First N.B.
6229.	Pratt	First N.B.
6311.	Kansas City	Commercial N.B.
6326.	Yates Center	Yates Center N.B.
6333.	Caldwell	Caldwell N.B.
6392.	Wichita	N.B. of Wichita
6494.	El Dorado	El Dorado N.B.
6530.	Cedarvale	Citizens' N.B.
6590.	Cottonwood Falls	Exchange N.B.
6643.	Augusta	First N.B.
6672.	Lincoln	Farmers N.B.
6701.	Beloit	Union N.B.
6720.	Liberal	First N.B.
6752.	Anthony	Citizens' N.B.
6767.	Coldwater	Coldwater N.B.
6797.	Coffeyville	Condon N.B.
6817.	Mankato	Mankato N.B.
6819.	Toronto	First N.B.
6841.	Logan	First N.B.
6895.	Neodesha	Neodesha N.B.
6914.	Neodesha	First N.B.
6932.	Hamilton	First N.B.
6955.	Burlington	Farmers' N.B.
6963.	Humboldt	Humboldt N.B.
6970.	Gaylord	First N.B.
7125.	Larned	Moffet Brothers N.B.
7178.	Clifton	First N.B.
7192.	Meade	First N.B.
7195.	Overbrook	First N.B.
7218.	Fredonia	Fredonia N.B.
7222.	Lyndon	First N.B.
7226.	La Harpe	First N.B.
7285.	Dodge City	First N.B.
7298.	Oberlin	Farmers' N.B.
7302.	Burr Oak	Jewell County N.B.
7303.	Eureka	Home N.B.
7313.	Plainville	First N.B.
7318.	Moline	First N.B.
7383.	Cherryvale	People's N.B.
7412.	Kingman	Farmers' N.B.
7416.	Goff	First N.B.
7493.	Kensington	First N.B.
7532.	Delphos	First N.B.
7535.	Sedan	People's N.B.
7561.	Lucas	First N.B.
7590.	Edna	First N.B.
7646.	Garden City	Garden City N.B.
7683.	Glasco	First N.B.
7815.	Stockton	Stockton N.B.
7844.	Saint John	Saint John N.B.
7882.	Goodland	Farmers' N.B.
7907.	Topeka	Capital N.B.
7911.	Marion	Marion N.B.
7970.	White City	First N.B.
8081.	Ness City	Citizens' N.B.
8107.	Mound Valley	First N.B.
8114.	Syracuse	First N.B.
8142.	Ness City	N.B. of Ness City
8145.	Elk City	First N.B.
8162.	Troy	First N.B.
8197.	Hartford	Hartford N.B.
8220.	Kiowa	First N.B.
8255.	Almena	First N.B.
8274.	Stockton	Nat. State Bank
8290.	Norcatur	First N.B.
8307.	Harper	First N.B.
8308.	Harper	Security N.B.
8339.	Norton	N.B. of Norton
8357.	Alma	Commercial N.B.
8369.	Moline	Moline N.B.
8379.	Abilene	Farmers' N.B.
8396.	Barnard	First N.B.
8399.	Wellington	N.B. of Commerce
8418.	Pittsburg	N.B. of Commerce
8430.	Hutchinson	Commercial N.B.
8467.	Conway Springs	First N.B.
8525.	Longton	First N.B.
8596.	Formoso	First N.B.
8602.	Kansas City	Bankers N.B.
8708.	Elk City	People's N.B.
8796.	Fort Leavenworth	Army N.B.
8803.	Pleasanton	First N.B.
8808.	Scott City	First N.B.
8883.	Stafford	Farmers' N.B.
8974.	Wetmore	First N.B.
9097.	Englewood	First N.B.
9136.	Highland	First N.B.
9157.	Burlingame	Burlingame N.B.
9160.	Edmond	First N.B.
9197.	Bonner Springs	First N.B.
9225.	Dexter	First N.B.
9232.	Hoisington	First N.B.
9309.	Kansas City	People's N.B.
9373.	Prairie View	First N.B.
9384.	Natoma	First N.B.
9465.	Thayer	First N.B.
9559.	Belleville	People's N.B.
9595.	Fowler	First N.B.
9695.	Gypsum	Gypsum Valley N.B.
9758.	Union Stock Yards, Wichita	Union Stock Yards N.B.
9773.	Dighton	First N.B.
9794.	Solomon	Solomon N.B.
9911.	Longton	Home N.B.
9934.	Mayetta	First N.B.
10041.	Oakley	First N.B.
10065.	Luray	First N.B.
10161.	Spearville	First N.B.
10195.	Alma	Farmers' N.B.
10359.	Attica	First N.B.
10390.	Topeka	Farmers' N.B.
10557.	Greensburg	Farmers' N.B.
10575.	Medicine Lodge	First N.B.
10587.	Beattie	First N.B.
10644.	Atwood	Farmers' N.B.
10746.	Arkansas City	Security N.B.
10749.	Victoria	First N.B.
10765.	Hutchinson	American N.B.
10776.	Phillipsburg	Farmers' N.B.
10789.	Greenleaf	Citizens' N.B.
10863.	Lewis	First N.B.
10888.	Augusta	American N.B.
10902.	Americus	Farmers' N.B.
10918.	Dodge City	Southwest N.B.
10971.	Summerfield	First N.B.
10980.	Marion	Farmers and Drovers' N.B.
10982.	Quinter	First N.B.
10987.	Ellis	First N.B.
10994.	Potwin	First N.B.
11010.	Wichita	Union N.B.
11047.	Colby	Citizens' N.B.
11056.	Baxter Springs	American N.B.
11107.	Fairview	Farmers' N.B.
11145.	Caldwell	Home N.B.
11154.	Towanda	First N.B.
11177.	Beaver, Quinter	Farmers' N.B.
11186.	Saint Mary's	Farmers' N.B.
11187.	Elkhart	First N.B.
11222.	Green	First N.B.
11300.	Hugoton	First N.B.
11310.	Axtell	First N.B.
11316.	Pretty Prairie	Farmers' N.B.
11318.	Downs	Downs N.B.
11374.	Chetopa	N.B. of Chetopa
11398.	Topeka	Kaw Valley N.B.
11405.	Atchison	City N.B.
11464.	Haviland	First N.B.
11488.	Coats	First N.B.
11531.	Colony	First N.B.
11536.	Mankato	Farmers' N.B.
11537.	Parsons	Farmers' N.B.
11576.	Oswego	First N.B.
11707.	Great Bend	Farmers' N.B.
11728.	Richmond	First N.B.
11738.	Frankfort	Citizens' N.B.
11773.	Florence	First N.B.
11775.	Clyde	Exchange N.B.
11781.	Emporia	Commercial N.B. and Trust Co.
11796.	Holyrood	First N.B.
11798.	Louisburg	First N.B.
11811.	Hanover	First N.B.
11816.	Valley Falls	First N.B.

Charter #	City	Name of Bank
11822.	Harveyville	First N.B.
11828.	Penalosa	Farmers' N.B.
11855.	Collyer	First N.B.
11857.	Saint Francis	First N.B.
11860.	Kanorado	First N.B.
11887.	Randall	Randall N.B.
11889.	Wellington	Farmers' N.B.
11916.	Frankfort	First N.B.
11933.	Agra	Farmers' N.B.
11945.	Bendena	Farmers' N.B.
11968.	Palco	First N.B.
12168.	Tribune	First N.B.
12191.	McCune	First N.B.
12346.	Wichita	Southwest N.B.
12353.	Onaga	First N.B.
12384.	Hope	First N.B.
12439.	Osawatomie	First N.B.
12442.	Fort Scott	Fort Scott N.B.
12457.	Eureka	First N.B.
12490.	Wichita	Fourth N.B.
12694.	Hoisington	Hoisington N.B.
12740.	Topeka	N.B. of Topeka
12791.	Cunningham	First N.B.
12821.	Tonanoxi	First N.B.
12935.	Towanda	Towanda N.B.
13033.	Neodesha	Union N.B.
13076.	Colby	Thomas County N.B.
13106.	Hutchinson	Exchange N.B.
13329.	Cimarron	First N.B.
13347.	Girard	Girard N.B.
13406.	Liberal	People's N.B.
13492.	Independence	Security N.B.
13601.	Alma	First N.B.
13801.	Kansas City	Security N.B.
13924.	Independence	Citizens' N.B.
13990.	Garden City	Garden N.B.
14048.	Lyons	Chandler N.B.
14163.	Goodland	First N.B.
14329.	Eureka	Citizens' N.B.

KENTUCKY

Charter #	City	Name of Bank
109.	Louisville	First N.B.
718.	Covington	First N.B.
760.	Lexington	First N.B.
777.	Louisville	Second N.B.
788.	Louisville	Louisville City N.B.
790.	Louisville	Planters' N.B.
906.	Lexington	First and City N.B.
995.	Winchester	Clark County N.B.
1204.	Stanford	N.B. of Stanford
1309.	Richmond	Farmers' N.B.
1493.	Lancaster	N.B. of Lancaster
1599.	Paducah	First N.B.
1600.	Danville	Central N.B.
1601.	Danville	First N.B.
1615.	Henderson	Henderson N.B.
1694.	Lebanon	N.B. of Lebanon
1702.	Maysville	N.B. of Maysville
1705.	Stanford	Farmers' N.B.
1720.	Lexington	Fayette N.B.
1728.	Richmond	First N.B.
1748.	Somerset	N.B. of Somerset
1760.	Franklin	First N.B.
1767.	Springfield	First N.B.
1790.	Richmond	Madison N.B.
1807.	Harrodsburg	First N.B.
1831.	Nicholasville	First N.B.
1835.	Versailles	Commercial N.B.
1847.	Covington	Liberty N.B.
1859.	Covington	Covington City N.B.
1900.	Cynthiana	N.B. of Cynthiana
1908.	Louisville	Kentucky N.B.
1931.	Monticello	N.B. of Monticello
1963.	Owenton	N.B. of Owen
2010.	Ashland	Ashland N.B.
2062.	Louisville	German N.B.
2070.	Paducah	American German N.B.
2093.	Paducah	City N.B.
2148.	Winchester	Citizens' N.B.
2149.	Bowling Green	Nat. Southern Kentucky Bank
2150.	Lebanon	Marion N.B.
2161.	Louisville	Merchants' N.B.
2164.	Louisville	Citizens Union Bank
2169.	Russellville	Logan County N.B.
2171.	Louisville	Third N.B.
2185.	Mount Sterling	Mount Sterling N.B.
2190.	Lawrenceberg	Anderson County N.B.
2196.	New Castle	N.B. of New Castle
2206.	Caverna	Caverna N.B.
2209.	Morganfield	N.B. of Union City
2216.	Mount Sterling	Farmers' N.B.
2245.	Mayfield	First N.B.
2276.	Newport	First N.B.
2323.	Flemingsburg	Fleming County N.B.
2374.	Richmond	Second N.B.
2393.	Lexington	Nat. Exchange Bank
2409.	Danville	Farmers' N.B.
2467.	Maysville	First N.B.
2531.	Harrodsburg	Mercer N.B.
2560.	Cynthiana	Farmers' N.B.
2576.	Owensboro	First N.B.
2592.	Carrollton	First N.B.
2663.	Maysville	State N.B.
2722.	Covington	Farmers and Trader's N.B.
2726.	Newport	American N.B.
2740.	Catlettsburg	Catlettsburg N.B.
2784.	Louisville	Fourth N.B.
2788.	Stanford	First N.B.
2868.	Owenton	First N.B.
2888.	Lancaster	Citizens' N.B.
2901.	Lexington	Second N.B.
2917.	Hustonville	N.B. of Hustonville
2927.	Georgetown	First N.B.
2931.	Henderson	Planters' N.B.
2968.	Owenton	Farmers' N.B.
3042.	Elizabethtown	First N.B.
3052.	Lexington	Phoenix and Third N.B.
3064.	Princeton	First N.B.
3074.	Carrollton	Carrollton N.B.
3290.	Winchester	Winchester N.B.
3317.	Danville	Boyle N.B.
3381.	Danville	Citizens' N.B.
3832.	Somerset	First N.B.
3856.	Hopkinsville	First N.B.
3942.	Lexington	Phoenix N.B.
3943.	London	First N.B.
3944.	Ashland	Second N.B.
3954.	Stanford	Lincoln N.B.
3988.	Lebanon	Citizens' N.B.
4006.	Owensboro	Nat. Deposit Bank
4090.	Frankfort	State N.B.
4091.	Frankfort	Frankfort N.B.
4145.	Louisville	Union N.B.
4200.	Catlettsburg	Big Sandy N.B.
4201.	Middlesborough	First N.B.
4217.	Clay City	Clay City N.B.
4260.	Covington	Citizens' N.B.
4271.	Lebanon	Farmers' N.B.
4356.	Greenville	First N.B.
4430.	Richmond	Richmond N.B.
4465.	Hickman	Farmers and Merchants' N.B.
4559.	Ashland	Merchants' N.B.
4563.	Fulton	First N.B.
4598.	Pineville	First N.B.
4612.	Augusta	Farmers' N.B.
4616.	Augusta	First N.B.
4765.	Newport	Newport N.B.
4819.	Glasgow	First N.B.
4956.	Louisville	American-Southern
5033.	Mayfield	City N.B.
5132.	Stanford	Lincoln County N.B.
5161.	Louisville	Louisville N.B.
5195.	Louisville	Southern N.B.
5257.	Princeton	Farmers' N.B.
5312.	Louisville	N.B. of Kentucky
5314.	Leitchfield	Grayson County N.B.
5323.	Ludlow	First N.B.
5376.	Frankfort	Nat. Branch Bank of Kentucky
5443.	Wickliffe	First N.B.
5468.	Somerset	Somerset Nat. Banking Co.
5486.	Glasgow	Trigg N.B.
5792.	Hartford	First N.B.
5881.	Somerset	Farmers' N.B.
5900.	Bowling Green	Citizens' N.B.
5959.	Carlisle	First N.B.
6028.	Elizabethtown	First Hardin N.B.
6100.	Paintsville	Paintsville N.B.
6129.	Mount Sterling	Traders' N.B.
6160.	Mount Sterling	Montgomery N.B.
6167.	Fulton	City N.B.
6244.	Sturgis	First N.B.
6248.	Latonia	First N.B.
6262.	Barbourville	First N.B.
6323.	Paris	First N.B.
6342.	Campbellsville	Taylor N.B.
6419.	Monticello	Citizens' N.B.
6546.	Russellville	Citizens' N.B.
6622.	Pikesville	First N.B.
6769.	Columbia	First N.B.
6834.	Mayfield	Farmers' N.B.
6872.	Glasgow	Third N.B.
6894.	Hodgenville	Farmers' N.B.
7012.	Dry Ridge	First N.B.
7030.	Pikeville	Pikeville N.B.
7037.	Greenup	First N.B.
7086.	Middlesborough	N.B. of Middleborough
7110.	Louisa	First N.B.
7122.	Louisa	Louisa N.B.
7164.	Paintsville	Citizens' N.B.
7174.	Williamsburg	First N.B.
7215.	Pineville	Bell N.B.
7242.	Sebree	First N.B.
7254.	Prestonsburg	First N.B.
7281.	Olive Hill	Olive Hill N.B.
7284.	Barbourville	N.B. of John A. Black
7402.	Franklin	Farmers and Merchants' N.B.
7457.	Louisville	Continental N.B.
7490.	Morganfield	Morganfield N.B.
7492.	Eddyville	First N.B.
7497.	Lawrenceburg	Lawrenceburg N.B.
7544.	Corbin	First N.B.
7593.	Morehead	Lenora N.B.
7602.	Horse Cave	First N.B.
7605.	Manchester	First N.B.
7653.	Richmond	Citizens' N.B.
7751.	Beatyville	N.B. of Beatyville
7804.	Bowling Green	Bowling Green N.B.
7890.	London	N.B. of London
7891.	Cannel City	Morgan County N.B.
7916.	West Liberty	First N.B.
7919.	Cave City	H.Y. Davis N.B.
8110.	Covington	Merchants' N.B.
8229.	Central City	First N.B.
8258.	Hazard	First N.B.
8331.	Bardwell	First N.B.
8386.	Madisonville	Morton N.B.
8435.	Berea	Berea N.B.
8439.	Glasgow	Citizens' N.B.
8451.	Madisonville	Farmers' N.B.
8564.	Covington	Commercial N.B.
8579.	Georgetown	Georgetown N.B.
8599.	Scottsville	First N.B.
8604.	Lawrenceburg	Anderson N.B.
8622.	Uniontown	First N.B.
8792.	Russell	First N.B.
8814.	Adairville	First N.B.
8830.	Brooksville	First N.B.
8862.	Lawrenceburg	Witherspoon N.B.
8903.	Burnside	First N.B.
8905.	Salyersville	Salyersville N.B.
8943.	Clay	Farmers' N.B.
9098.	Clinton	First N.B.
9241.	Louisville	N.B. of Commerce
9320.	Jackson	First N.B.
9356.	Scottsville	Allen County N.B.
9365.	Bowling Green	American N.B.
9456.	Owensboro	United States N.B.
9561.	Maysville	N.B. of Maysville Assn.
9602.	Catlettsburg	Kentucky N.B.
9634.	Corbin	Whitley N.B.
9708.	Providence	Union N.B.
9722.	Glasgow	Farmers' N.B.
9791.	Harlan	First N.B.
9832.	Richmond	Southern N.B.
9842.	Russellville	Nat. Deposit Bank
9843.	Hodgenville	La Rue N.B.
9880.	Wilmore	First N.B.
10062.	Jenkins	First N.B.
10254.	East Bernstadt	First N.B.
10433.	Whitesburg	First N.B.
10448.	Bowling Green	Warren N.B.
10779.	Murray	First N.B.
11336.	Munfordville	N.B. of Munfordville
11348.	Russell Springs	First N.B.
11538.	Buffalo	First N.B.
11544.	Somerset	Citizens' N.B.
11548.	Dawson Springs	First N.B.
11589.	Bowling Green	Liberty N.B.
11890.	Stone	First N.B.
11944.	Pikeville	Day and Night N.B.
11947.	Falmouth	First N.B.
11988.	Fleming	First N.B.
12202.	Wallins Creek	Wallins N.B.
12243.	Harlan	Citizens' N.B.
12293.	Ashland	Third N.B.
12295.	Harlan	Harlan N.B.
12456.	Scottsville	Farmers' N.B.
12649.	Lynch	Lynch N.B.
12961.	Paducah	People N.B.
12982.	Grayson	First N.B.
13023.	Paintsville	Second N.B.
13024.	Elizabethtown	Union N.B.
13248.	Hazard	First N.B.
13479.	Hodgenville	Lincoln N.B.
13612.	Harrodsburg	Mercer County N.B.
13651.	Glasgow	New Farmers N.B.
13757.	Henderson	First N.B.
13763.	Paintsville	First N.B.
13906.	Barbourville	Union N.B.
13983.	Henderson	Ohio Valley N.B.
14026.	Owenton	First N.B.
14039.	Stanford	First N.B.
14076.	Paris	N.B and Trust Co.
14138.	Owensboro	National Deposit Bank
14259.	Clinton	First N.B.
14320.	Louisville	Liberty N.B. and Trust Co.

LOUISIANA

Charter #	City	Name of Bank
162.	New Orleans	First N.B.
1591.	New Orleans	Germania N.B.
1626.	New Orleans	Louisiana N.B.
1747.	New Orleans	Teutonia N.B.
1774.	New Orleans	State N.B.
1778.	New Orleans	New Orleans N.B.
1796.	New Orleans	Union N.B.
1825.	New Orleans	New Orleans N.B. Assn.
1898.	New Orleans	Mutual N.B.
1937.	New Orleans	Crescent City N.B.
2086.	New Orleans	Hibernia N.B.
2633.	Baton Rouge	First N.B.
3069.	New Orleans	Whitney-Central N.B.
3595.	Shreveport	First N.B.
3600.	Shreveport	Commercial N.B.
3671.	New Iberia	New Iberia N.B.
3692.	Monroe	Ouachita N.B.
3978.	New Orleans	American N.B.
4082.	Monroe	Monroe N.B.
4154.	Lake Charles	First N.B.
4216.	Homer	Homer N.B.
4337.	New Orleans	Southern N.B.
4340.	Opelousas	First N.B.
4524.	New Iberia	People's N.B.
4555.	Franklin	First N.B.
5021.	Alexandria	First N.B.
5023.	Lafayette	First N.B.
5157.	Lake Charles	Calcasieu N.B.
5520.	Crowley	First N.B.
5649.	New Orleans	Canal-Commercial N.B.
5752.	Shreveport	Citizens' N.B.
5807.	Abbeville	First N.B.
5843.	Patterson	First N.B.
5844.	Shreveport	Shreveport N.B.
5966.	Jennings	First N.B.
6088.	Lake Charles	Lake Charles N.B.
6264.	Leesville	First N.B.
6291.	Lake Providence, Providence	First N.B. of Lake Providence
6360.	Welsh	First N.B.
6418.	Welsh	Welsh N.B.
6801.	Morgan City	First N.B.
6858.	New Iberia	State N.B.
6920.	Opelousas	Opelousas N.B.
7047.	Lake Arthur	First N.B.
7169.	New Roads	First N.B.
7232.	Mansfield	First N.B.
7476.	Arcadia	First N.B.
7498.	New Orleans	People's N.B.
7765.	Jennings	State N.B.
7768.	Jeanerette	First N.B.

Charter #	City	Name of Bank
7876.	New Orleans	German American N.B.
8440.	Shreveport	American N.B.
8654.	Monroe	Ouachita N.B.
8677.	Eunice	First N.B.
8734.	New Orleans	Hibernia N.B.
8959.	Bogalusa	First N.B.
9237.	De Ridder	First N.B.
9834.	Baton Rouge	Louisiana N.B.
9872.	Opelousas	Planters' N.B.
10049.	Gibsland	First N.B.
10153.	Monroe	Union N.B.
10544.	Minden	First N.B.
10588.	Ville Platte	First N.B.
10700.	Crowley	First N.B. of Acadia Parish
10761.	Winnfield	First N.B.
10836.	Lake Charles	Calcasieu N.B. of S.W. La.
10870.	Shreveport	City N.B.
10912.	Delhi	Macon Ridge N.B.
11242.	Monroe	Citizens' N.B.
11254.	Longville	First N.B.
11324.	Oberlin	First N.B.
11450.	Jennings	Jennings N.B.
11521.	Shreveport	Exchange N.B.
11541.	Elton	First N.B.
11621.	Homer	American N.B.
11638.	Homer	Commercial N.B.
11650.	Oak Grove	First N.B.
11669.	Mansfield	American N.B.
11795.	Ruston	First N.B.
11977.	Hammond	Citizens' N.B.
12523.	Crowley	First N.B.
12527.	Pineville	First N.B.
12923.	Tallulah	Madison N.B.
13169.	Gibsland	First N.B.
13209.	Lafayette	Commercial N.B.
13345.	Thibodaux	Lafourche N.B.
13573.	Lake Charles	Calcasieu N.B.
13648.	Shreveport	Commercial N.B.
13655.	Monroe	Ouachita N.B.
13688.	New Orleans	Hibernia N.B.
13689.	New Orleans	N.B. of Commerce
13732.	Gretna	First N.B. of Jefferson Parish
13737.	Baton Rouge	City N.B.
13839.	Norco.	St. Charles N.B.
13851.	Morgan City	Citizens N.B.
14086.	Hammond	Citizens N.B.
14168.	De Ridder	First N.B.
14225.	Delhi	First N.B.
14228.	Lake Charles	Calcasieu-Marine N.B.
14281.	Donaldson	First N.B.
14328.	Arcadia	First N.B.

MAINE

Charter #	City	Name of Bank
61.	Bath	First N.B.
112.	Bangor	First N.B.
154.	Auburn	First N.B.
192.	Brunswick	First N.B.
221.	Portland	First N.B.
239.	Skowhegan	First N.B.
298.	Skowhegan	Second N.B.
306.	Bangor	Second N.B.
310.	Hallowell	First N.B.
330.	Lewiston	First N.B.
367.	Augusta	First N.B.
406.	Augusta	Freeman's N.B.
446.	Damariscotta	First N.B.
494.	Bath	Bath N.B.
498.	Augusta	First Nat.Granite Bank
518.	Bangor	Kenduskeag N.B.
532.	Hallowell	Northern N.B.
553.	Winthrop	N.B. of Winthrop
624.	Hallowell	American N.B.
662.	Richmond	First N.B.
740.	Gardiner	Oakland N.B.
744.	Waldoboro	Waldoboro N.B.
761.	Bath	Lincoln N.B.
762.	Waterville	Ticonic N.B.
782.	Bath	Marine N.B.
798.	Waterville	Waterville N.B.
840.	Belfast	Belfast N.B.
878.	Portland	Second N.B.
880.	Waterville	People's N.B.
890.	Thomaston	Thomaston N.B.
901.	Farmington	Sandy River N.B.
909.	Richmond	Richmond N.B.
939.	Gardiner	Cubbossee N.B.
941.	Portland	Canal N.B.
944.	Bowdoinham	Nat. Village Bank
953.	Damariscotta	Newcastle N.B.
959.	South Berwick	South Berwick N.B.
1023.	Portland	Merchants' N.B.
1041.	Bath	Sagadahock N.B.
1060.	Portland	Casco N.B.
1079.	Bucksport	Bucksport N.B.
1089.	Biddeford	First N.B.
1095.	Bangor	Trader's N.B.
1108.	Waldoboro	Medomak N.B.
1118.	Brunswick	Union N.B.
1134.	Orono	Orono N.B.
1142.	Thomaston	Georges N.B.
1174.	Gardiner	Gardiner N.B.
1254.	Kennebunk	Ocean N.B.
1315.	Brunswick	Pejebscot N.B.
1425.	Calais	Calais N.B.
1437.	Bangor	Merchants' N.B.
1446.	Rockland	Rockland N.B.
1451.	Portland	Nat. Traders' Bank
1495.	Eastport	Frontier N.B.
1511.	Portland	Cumberland N.B.
1523.	North Berwick	North Berwick N.B.
1528.	Saco	York N.B.
1535.	Saco	Saco N.B.
1549.	Wiscasset	First N.B.
1575.	Biddeford	Biddeford N.B.
1687	Bangor	Farmers' N.B.

Charter #	City	Name of Bank
1956.	Norway	Norway N.B.
2089.	Bangor	Veazie N.B.
2097.	Rockland	Lime Rock N.B.
2175.	Fairfield	First N.B.
2231.	Oakland	Messalonskee N.B.
2259.	Dexter	First N.B.
2260.	Lewiston	Manufacturers' N.B.
2267.	Phillips	Union N.B.
2270.	Auburn	Nat. Shoe and Leather Bank
2306.	Waterville	Merchants' N.B.
2311.	Camden	Camden N.B.
2371.	Rockland	North N.B.
2642.	Searsport	Searsport N.B.
2743.	Bath	First N.B.
2749.	Houlton	First N.B.
2785.	Limerick	Limerick N.B.
3219.	Gardiner	Merchants' N.B.
3247.	Hallowell	Hallowell N.B.
3271.	Augusta	Augusta N.B.
3690.	Dover	Kineo N.B.
3804.	Ellsworth	Liberty N.B.
3814.	Ellsworth	First N.B.
3827.	Presque Isle	Presque Isle N.B.
3941.	Bar Harbor	First N.B.
4128.	Portland	Portland N.B.
4188.	Pittsfield	Pittsfield N.B.
4252.	Houlton	Farmers' N.B.
4459.	Farmington	First N.B.
4647.	Madison	First N.B.
4780.	Guilford	First N.B.
4781.	Fort Fairfield	Fort Fairfield N.B.
4806.	Belfast	People's N.B.
4844.	York Village	York County N.B.
4868.	Portland	Chapman N.B.
4957.	Phillips	Phillips N.B.
4973.	Fairfield	N.B. of Fairfield
5050.	Sanford	Sanford N.B.
5598.	Boothbay Harbor	First N.B.
5861.	Farmington	People's N.B.
6190.	Caribou	Caribou N.B.
6231.	Camden	Megunticook N.B.
6287.	Rumford	Rumford N.B.
7586.	Belfast	City N.B.
7613.	Bethel	Bethel N.B.
7835.	Springvale	Springvale N.B.
9181.	Birdgton	Bridgton N.B.
9609.	Gardiner	N.B. of Gardiner
9826.	Kezar Falls	Kezar Falls N.B.
10628.	Van Buren	First N.B.
11403.	Fort Kent	First N.B.
11462.	Machias	Machias N.B.
13710.	Portland	N.B. of Commerce
13716.	Portland	First N.B.
13730.	Springvale	Springvale N.B.
13734.	Rockland	First N.B.
13750.	Norway	Norway N.B.
13762.	Belfast	First N.B.
13768.	Presque Isle	Northern N.B.
13769.	Waterville	First N.B.
13777.	Pittsfield	First N.B.
13786.	Calais	N.B. of Calais
13827.	Houlton	Farmers N.B.
13843.	Fort Fairfield	First N.B.
14224.	Fort Kent	First N.B.
14303.	Ellsworth	Liberty N.B.

MARYLAND

Charter #	City	Name of Bank
204.	Baltimore	First N.B.
381.	Cumberland	First N.B.
414.	Baltimore	Second N.B.
742.	Westminster	First N.B.
747.	New Windsor	First N.B.
814.	Baltimore	Third N.B.
826.	Baltimore	Traders' N.B.
1109.	Baltimore	Nat. Exchange Bank
1138.	Frederick	Central N.B.
1211.	Port Deposit	Cecil N.B.
1236.	Elkton	N.B. of Elkton
1244.	Annapolis	Farmers' N.B.
1252.	Baltimore	Nat. Farmers and Planters' Bank
1267.	Frederick	Farmers and Mechanics' N.B.
1303.	Baltimore	Commercial and Farmers' N.B.
1325.	Baltimore	Western N.B.
1336.	Baltimore	Merchants N.B.
1337.	Baltimore	Farmers and Merchants' N.B.
1384.	Baltimore	Citizens' N.B.
1412.	Frostburg	First N.B.
1413.	Baltimore	Merchant's N.B.
1431.	Hagerstown	First N.B.
1432.	Baltimore	N.B. of Baltimore
1434.	Easton	Easton N.B. of Maryland
1449.	Frederick	Frederick County N.B.
1489.	Baltimore	Nat. Union Bank of Md.
1500.	Chestertown	Kent N.B.
1519.	Cumberland	Second N.B.
1526.	Westminster	Farmers and Mechanics' N.B.
1551.	Williamsport	Washington County N.B.
1589.	Frederick	First N.B.
1596.	Westminster	Union N.B.
1797.	Baltimore	Central N.B.
2341.	Centreville	Centreville N.B. of Md.
2416.	Cumberland	Third N.B.
2453.	Baltimore	Nat. Marine Bank
2481.	Rising Sun	N.B. of Rising Sun
2498.	Cambridge	N.B. of Cambridge
2499.	Baltimore	Drovers and Mechanics' N.B.

Charter #	City	Name of Bank
2547.	Denton	Denton N.B.
2623.	Baltimore	Manufacturers, N.B.
2797.	Bel Air	Hanford N.B.
3010.	Havre de Grace	First N.B.
3187.	Rockville	Montgomery County N.B.
3205.	Centreville	Queen Anne's N.B.
3250.	Salisbury	Salisbury N.B.
3305.	Chestertown	Chestertown N.B.
3476.	Frederick	Citizens' N.B.
3585.	Ellicott City	Patapsco N.B.
3588.	Towson	Towson N.B.
3783.	Snow Hill	First N.B.
3933.	Bel Air	Second N.B.
4046.	Easton	Farmers and Mechanics' N.B.
4049.	Hagerstown	Second N.B.
4085.	Cambridge	Dorchester N.B.
4149.	Frostburg	First N.B.
4162.	Elkton	Second N.B.
4191.	Pocomoke City	Pocomoke City N.B.
4218.	Baltimore	Nat. Howard Bank
4285.	Baltimore	N.B. of Commerce
4327.	Chestertown	Second N.B.
4364.	Laurel	Citizens' N.B.
4496.	Cockeysville	N.B. of Cockeysville
4518.	Baltimore	American N.B.
4530.	Baltimore	Equitable N.B.
4533.	Baltimore	Continental N.B.
4608.	Gaithersburg	First N.B.
4634.	Aberdeen	First N.B.
4799.	Canton, Baltimore	Canton N.B.
4856.	Hagerstown	People's N.B.
4926.	Frostburg	Citizens' N.B.
5093.	Catonsville	First N.B.
5122.	Denton	People's N.B.
5331.	Midland	First N.B.
5332.	Cumberland	Citizens' N.B.
5445.	Havre de Grace	Citizens' N.B.
5471.	Upper Marlboro	First N.B. of Southern Maryland
5561.	Sandy Spring	First N.B.
5610.	Port Deposit	N.B. of Port Deposit
5623.	Oakland	First N.B.
5776.	Baltimore	Maryland N.B.
5829.	Thurmont	Thurmont N.B.
5831.	Westernport	Citizens' N.B.
5880.	Cambridge	Farmers and Merchants' N.B.
5943.	Grantsville	First N.B.
5984.	Baltimore	Old Town N.B.
6144.	Mount Savage	First N.B.
6196.	Friendsville	First N.B.
6202.	Pocomoke	Citizens' N.B.
6297.	Snow Hill	Commercial N.B.
6399.	Barton	First N.B.
6588.	Oakland	Garrett N.B.
6606.	Leonardtown	First N.B. of Saint Mary's
6761.	Salisbury	People's N.B.
6845.	Chesapeake City	N.B. of Chesapeake City
7064.	North East	First N.B.
7160.	Mount Airy	First N.B.
7519.	Hyattsville	First N.B.
7732.	Lonaconing	First N.B.
7859.	Hancock	First N.B.
8244.	Brunswick	People's N.B.
8272.	Kitzmillerville	Blaine N.B.
8302.	Kitzmiller, Kitzmillerville	First N.B.
8319.	Berlin	First N.B.
8381.	Towson	Second N.B.
8456.	La Plata	Southern Maryland N.B.
8578.	Sykesville	First N.B.
8587.	Sykesville	Sykesville N.B.
8799.	Woodbine	Woodbine N.B.
8860.	Poolesville	Poolesville N.B.
8867.	Pikesville	Pikesville N.B.
9066.	Union Bridge	First N.B.
9238.	Monrovia	First N.B.
9429.	Mechanicsville	N.B. of Mechanicsville
9444.	Parkton	First N.B.
9469.	White Hall	White Hall N.B.
9474.	Bel Air	Farmers and Merchants' N.B.
9639.	Baltimore	Nat. City Bank
9699.	Clear Spring	Clear Spring N.B.
9744.	Chestertown	Third N.B.
9755.	Hampstead	First N.B.
9830.	Silver Spring	Silver Spring N.B.
10210.	Healdsburg	First N.B.
11193.	Perryville	N.B. of Perryville
11207.	Baltimore	Nat. Central Bank
12443.	Mount Rainier	First N.B.
12590.	Hagerstown	Nicodemus N.B.
13147.	Catonsville	Catonsville N.B.
13680.	Bel Air	First N.B.
13745.	Baltimore	Baltimore N.B.
13747.	Frederick	Frederick County N.B.
13773.	Ellicott City	Patapsco N.B.
13776.	Oakland	Garrett N.B.
13798.	Chestertown	First N.B.
13840.	Port Deposit	Cecil N.B.
13853.	Hancock	Peoples N.B.
13867.	Parkton	First N.B.
13979.	Frostburg	Frostburg N.B.
14044.	Brunswick	Peoples N.B.
14106.	Pocomoke City	Citizens N.B.

MASSACHUSETTS

Charter #	City	Name of Bank
14.	Springfield	First N.B.
79.	Worcester	First N.B.
96.	Barre	First N.B.
156.	Dorchester	First N.B.
158.	Marlboro	First N.B.
181.	Springfield	Second N.B.
188.	Grafton	First N.B.
190.	Westfield	First N.B.
200.	Boston	First N.B.
256.	Fall River	First N.B.
261.	New Bedford	First N.B.
268.	Merrimac	First N.B.
279.	Newburyport	First N.B.
308.	Springfield	Third N.B.
322.	Boston	Second N.B.
327.	Winchendon	First N.B.
331.	Lowell	First N.B.
359.	Boston	Third N.B.
379.	Boston	N.B. of the Republic
383.	Northampton	First N.B.
393.	Amherst	First N.B.
407.	Salem	First N.B.
408.	Boston	Boston N.B.
416.	Easton, N. Easton	First N.B.
418.	Northampton	Hampshire County N.B.
421.	Westboro	First N.B.
428.	Easthampton	First N.B.
433.	Cambridge	First N.B.
439.	Fall River	Second N.B.
440.	Clinton	First N.B.
442.	Worcester	Worcester N.B.
449.	East Cambridge	Cambridge N.B.
455.	Worcester	Central N.B.
460.	Boston	Nat. Hide and Leather Bank
462.	Adams	First N.B.
474.	Greenfield	First N.B.
475.	Boston	Merchants N.B.
476.	Worcester	City N.B.
481.	Haverhill	First N.B.
484.	Haverhill	Haverhill N.B.
488.	Newton	First N.B.
490.	Fairhaven	N.B. of Fairhaven
503.	Monson	Monson N.B.
505.	Boston	Market N.B.
506.	Lowell	Merchants' N.B.
510.	Weymouth	Union N.B.
513.	Leominster	First N.B.
514.	Boston	Blackstone N.B.
515.	Boston	N.B. of Redemption
516.	Yarmouth, Yarmouth Port	First N.B.
517.	Quincy	Nat. Mount Wollaston Bank
524.	Boston	Continental N.B.
525.	Boston	North N.B.
528.	Framingham	Framingham N.B.
529.	Boston	Nat. Exchange Bank
533.	Chelsea	First N.B.
536.	Boston	Eliot N.B.
545.	Boston	Boylston N.B.
549.	Gloucester	First N.B.
551.	Boston	Broadway N.B.
554.	Boston	N.B. of Commerce
558.	Randolph	Randolph N.B
572.	Millbury	Millbury N.B.
578.	Boston	Howard N.B.
582.	Boston	Shawmut N.B.
583.	Clinton	Lancaster N.B.
584.	Newburyport	Mechanics' N.B.
588.	Malden	First N.B.
589.	Haverhill	Essex N.B.
590.	Fall River	Fall River N.B.
594.	Danvers	First N.B.
595.	Boston	People's N.B.
601.	Boston	Washington N.B.
603.	Boston	New England N.B.
609.	Boston	Nat. City Bank
612.	Fall River	Massasoit N.B.
614.	East Cambridge	Lechmere N.B.
615.	Boston	Nat. Rockland Bank of Roxbury
616.	Peabody	Warren N.B.
618.	South Weymouth	First N.B.
625.	Boston	Tremont N.B.
626.	Hopkinton	Hopkinton N.B.
628.	Ware	Ware N.B.
629.	Boston	Suffolk N.B.
633.	Haverhill	Merrimack N.B.
634.	Boston	Asiatic N.B.
635.	Boston	Bunker Hill N.B. Charlestown
638.	Lynn	First N.B.
643.	Boston	Fourth Atlantic N.B.
646.	Boston	Shoe and Leather N.B.
647.	Salem	Naumkeag N.B.
654.	Boston	Atlas N.B.
663.	Canton	Neponset N.B.
665.	Boston	Freeman's N.B.
669.	Dedham	Dedham N.B.
672.	Boston	N.B. of North America
676.	Marblehead	Nat. Grand Bank
677.	Boston	Maverick N.B.
679.	Fall River	Pocasset N.B.
684.	Milton	Blue Hill N.B.
688.	Waltham	Waltham N.B.
690.	New Bedford	N.B. of Commerce
691.	Salem	Mercantile N.B.
697.	Lynn	Nat. City Bank
702.	Fitchburg	Rollstone N.B.
704.	Salem	Salem N.B.
708.	Athol	Millers River N.B.
712.	Harwich	Cape Cod N.B.
714.	Nantucket	Pacific N.B.
716.	Boston	Mount Vernon N.B.
726.	Salem	Merchants' N.B.
731.	Cambridge	Charles River N.B.
736.	Provincetown	First N.B.
743.	New Bedford	Mechanics' N.B.
746.	Woburn	First N.B.
753.	Lowell	Railroad N.B.
764.	Oxford	Oxford N.B.
765.	Worcester	Citizens' N.B.
766.	Taunton	Bristol County N.B.
767.	Marblehead	Marblehead N.B.
769.	Whitinsville	Whitinsville N.B.
770.	Cambridge	Nat. City Bank
778.	Boston	Hamilton N.B.
779.	Plymouth	Plymouth N.B.
781.	Lowell	Wamesit N.B.
789.	Newton	Newton N.B.
799.	New Bedford	Merchants' N.B.
802.	Holliston	Holliston N.B.
805.	Townsend	Townsend N.B.
806.	Boston	Nat. Market Bank of Brighton
817.	Salem	Nat. Exchange Bank
824.	Grafton	Grafton N.B.
832.	Quincy	Nat. Granite Bank
833.	Concord	Concord N.B.
847.	Boston	Faneuil Hall N.B.
866.	Milford	Milford N.B.
884.	Gardner	First N.B.
885.	Lee	Lee N.B.
895.	Conway	Conway N.B.
899.	Gloucester	Cape Ann N.B.
918.	Leicester	Leicester N.B.
920.	Greenfield	Franklin County N.B.
924.	Fall River	Metacomet N.B.
932.	Boston	Mechanics' N.B.
934.	Southbridge	Southbridge N.B.
936.	Boston	Globe N.B.
947.	Taunton	Machinists' N.B.
957.	Taunton	Taunton N.B.
958.	Peabody	South Danvers N.B.
960.	Lowell	Prescott N.B.
969.	Beverly	Beverly N.B.
974.	Boston	Massachusetts N.B.
982.	Springfield	John Hancock N.B.
985.	Boston	Nat. Union Bank
986.	Lowell	Appleton N.B.
987.	Springfield	Pynchon N.B.
988.	Springfield	Chicopee N.B.
993.	Boston	Nat. Eagle Bank
996.	Plymouth	Old Colony N.B.
1005.	Boston	Monument N.B.
1011.	Newburyport	Ocean N.B.
1014.	Lawrence	Bay State N.B.
1015.	Boston	Old Boston N.B.
1018.	Northampton	Northampton N.B.
1022.	Uxbridge	Blackstone N.B.
1028.	Boston	State N.B.
1029.	Boston	Columbian N.B.
1047.	Newburyport	Merchants' N.B.
1048.	Lawrence	Nat. Pemberton Bank
1049.	Amesbury	Powow River N.B.
1055.	Springfield	Agawam N.B.
1056.	Chicopee	First N.B.
1073.	Worcester	Quinsigamond N.B.
1077.	Fitchburg	Fitchburg N.B.
1082.	Pittsfield	Agricultural N.B.
1085.	Wrentham	N.B. of Wrentham
1099.	Boston	N.B. of Brighton
1107.	Hyannis	First N.B.
1119.	Hingham	Hingham N.B.
1129.	Andover	Andover N.B.
1135.	Worcester	Mechanics' N.B.
1144.	Shellburne Falls	Shellburne Falls N.B.
1162.	Gloucester	Gloucester N.B.
1170.	Stockbridge	Housatonic N.B.
1194.	Rockport	Rockport N.B.
1201.	Lynn	Central N.B.
1203.	Great Barrington	Nat. Mahaiwe Bank
1207.	Franklin	Franklin N.B
1210.	North Adams	North Adams N.B.
1228.	Cambridge	Cambridgeport N.B.
1246.	Holyoke	Hadley Falls N.B.
1260.	Pittsfield	Pittsfield N.B
1274.	Tisbury, Vineyard Haven	Martha's Vineyard N.B.
1279.	Northborough	Northborough N.B.
1288.	Fall River	Nat. Union Bank
1295.	Boston	Nat. Revere Bank
1320.	Falmouth	Falmouth N.B.
1329.	Lowell	Old Lowell N.B.
1367.	Westfield	Hampton N.B.
1386.	Abington	Abington N.B.
1439.	Adams	Berkshire N.B.
1440.	Wareham	N.B. of Wareham
1442.	Boston	Hancock N.B.
1455.	Wakefield	Wakefield N.B.
1469.	Boston	Everett N.B.
1485.	Methuen	N.B. of Methuen
1527.	Boston	Webster and Atlas N.B.
1604.	Attleborough, N. Attleborough	Attleborough N.B.
1675.	Boston	Nat. Security Bank
1699.	Boston	Kidder Nat. Gold Bank
1827.	Boston	N.B. of the Commonwealth
1939.	Holyoke	Holyoke N.B.
1962.	Lawrence	Lawrence N.B.
1993.	Boston	Eleventh Ward N.B.
2058.	Turners Falls	Crocker N.B.
2103.	Boston	Central N.B.
2107.	Natick	Natick N.B.
2108.	Watertown	Union Market N.B.
2111.	Boston	Manufacturers' N.B.
2112.	Boston	First Ward N.B.
2113.	Ashburnham	First N.B.
2152.	Brockton	Home N.B.
2153.	Fitchburg	Safety Fund N.B.
2172.	Athol, Athol Center	Athol N.B.
2232.	Attleboro	First N.B.
2255.	Orange	Orange N.B.
2262.	New Bedford	Citizens' N.B.
2264.	Greenfield	Packard N.B.
2265.	Fitchburg	Wachusett N.B.
2273.	Worcester	Security N.B.
2275.	Milford	Home N.B.
2277.	Boston	Fourth N.B.
2284.	Gardner	Westminster N.B.
2288.	Spencer	Spencer N.B.
2289.	Boston	Metropolitan N.B.
2292.	Gloucester	City N.B.
2297.	Georgetown	Georgetown N.B.
2304.	Boston	Winthrop N.B.
2312.	Webster	First N.B.
2324.	Palmer	Palmer N.B.
2347.	Lawrence	Pacific N.B.
2373.	Boston	Pacific N.B.
2396.	North Adams	Berkshire N.B.
2404.	Marlborough	People's N.B.
2430.	Holyoke	City N.B.
2433.	Springfield	City N.B.
2435.	Springfield	Chapin N.B.
2485.	South Framingham	South Framingham N.B.
2504.	Brockton	Brockton N.B.
2525.	Pittsfield	Third N.B.
2563.	Lynn	Nat. Security Bank
2618.	Hudson	Hudson N.B.
2685.	Barre	First N.B.
2699.	Worcester	First N.B.
2770.	Marlboro	First N.B.
2846.	Boston	Lincoln N.B.
2929.	Amesbury	Amesbury N.B.
3073.	Ayer	First N.B.
3092.	Williamstown	Williamstown N.B.
3128.	Holyoke	Home N.B.
3204.	Leominster	Leominster N.B.
3365.	North Attleborough	North Attleborough N.B.
3429.	Lynn	Lynn N.B.
3510.	Haverhill	Second N.B.
3553.	Brookline	Brookline N.B.
3598.	Newton	First N.B. of West Newton
3868.	Rockland	First N.B.
3923.	Boston	Commercial N.B.
3977.	Lawrence	Merchants' N.B.
3994.	Middleborough	Middleborough N.B.
4013.	Lenox	Lenox N.B.
4074.	Chelsea	Winnisimmet N.B.
4202.	Boston	South End N.B.
4240.	Stoneham	Stoneham N.B.
4300.	Lawrence	Arlington N.B.
4488.	Reading	First N.B.
4562.	Adams	Greylock N.B.
4580.	Lynn	Manufacturers' N.B.
4660.	Whitman	Whitman N.B.
4664.	Arlington	First N.B.
4703.	Holyoke	Park N.B.
4753.	Lowell	Traders' N.B.
4769.	Melrose	Melrose N.B.
4771.	Somerville	Somerville N.B.
4774.	Ipswich	First N.B.
4833.	Haverhill	Merchants' N.B.
4907.	Springfield	Springfield N.B.
5071.	Winchester	Middlesex County N.B.
5155.	Boston	Nat. Shawmut Bank
5158.	Boston	Nat. Hamilton Bank
5163.	Boston	Colonial N.B.
5247.	Medford	Medford N.B.
5840.	Boston	American N.B.
5944.	Mansfield	First N.B.
5964.	Pepperell, East Pepperell	First N.B.
6077.	Lowell	Union N.B.
6104.	Boston	Nat. Suffolk Bank
6821.	Fall River	Massasoit-Pocasset N.B.
7297.	Wellesley	Wellesley N.B.
7452.	Danvers	Danvers N.B.
7550.	Woburn	Woburn N.B.
7595.	Worcester	Merchants' N.B.
7675.	North Attleboro	Jewelers' N.B.
7920.	Hyde Park	Hyde Park N.B.
7957.	Edgartown	Edgartown N.B.
8150.	South Deerfield	Produce N.B.
8474.	Norwood	Norwood N.B.
9086.	North Attleborough	Manufacturers' N.B.
9426.	Foxborough	Foxboro N.B.
9579.	Boston	Mutual N.B.
9651.	Chelsea	Broadway N.B.
10059.	Leominster	Merchants' N.B.
10165.	Barre	Second N.B.
10924.	Boston	Roxbury N.B.
10955.	North Brookfield	North Brookfield N.B.
11014.	Malden	Second N.B.
11067.	Woburn	Tanners' N.B.
11068.	Boston	Back Bay N.B.
11103.	Winchester	Winchester N.B.
11137.	Boston	Mattapan N.B.
11152.	Cambridge	Manufacturers' N.B.
11169.	Lynn	State N.B.
11236.	Webster	Webster N.B.
11270.	Chelsea	Nat. City Bank

Charter #	City	Name of Bank
11339.	Boston	Citizens' N.B.
11347.	Braintree	Braintree N.B.
11388.	Southbridge	People's N.B.
11510.	Everett	Everett N.B.
11567.	Warren	First N.B.
11790.	Boston	Haymarket N.B.
11859.	Boston	Oceanic N.B.
11868.	Arlington	Arlington N.B.
11903.	Boston	Boston N.B.
12336.	Boston	Federal N.B.
12343.	Lowell	Middlesex N.B.
12359.	Boston	South Boston N.B.
12362.	Lynn	State N.B.
12377.	Boston	Commonwealth N.B.
12396.	Boston	International N.B.
12405.	New Bedford	Safe Deposit N.B.
12481.	Springfield	Atlas N.B.
12540.	Boston	Brotherhood of Locomotive Engineers N.B.
12567.	Dedham	Dedham N.B.
12800.	Methuen	Methuen N.B.
12862.	Boston	Massachusetts N.B.
12979.	Medford	First N.B.
13060.	Cambridge	Cambridge N.B.
13152.	Revere	First N.B.
13172.	Northfield	Northfield N.B.
13222.	Buzzards Bay	Buzzards Bay N.B.
13241.	Needham	Needham N.B. for Savings & Trusts
13252.	Newton	Newton N.B
13283.	Cohasset	Cohasset N.B.
13386.	Barre	Second N.B.
13387.	North Brookfield	North Brookfield N.B.
13391.	Boston	Old Colony N.B.
13394.	Spencer	Spencer N.B.
13395.	Hyannis	Barnstable County N.B.
13411.	Webster	First N.B.
13558.	Reading	First N.B.
13604.	Gloucester	Gloucester N.B.
13733.	Athol	First N.B.
13780.	Webster	Webster N.B.
13796.	Reading	First N.B.
13835.	Millbury	Millbury N.B.
13933.	Pepperell	First N.B.
14033.	Woburn	Tanners N.B.
14087.	Chelsea	Lincoln N.B.
14152.	Revere	First N.B.
14266.	Haverhill	Northern N.B.

MICHIGAN

Charter #	City	Name of Bank
22.	Ann Arbor	First N.B.
81.	Fenton	First N.B.
97.	Detroit	First N.B.
116.	Detroit	Second N.B.
155.	Ypsilanti	First N.B.
168.	Hillsdale	First N.B.
191.	Kalamazoo	First N.B.
232.	Lansing	First N.B.
264.	Lansing	Second N.B.
275.	Ionia	First N.B.
294.	Grand Rapids	First N.B.
354.	Romeo	First N.B.
390.	Marquette	First N.B.
410.	Bay City	First N.B.
434.	Pontiac	First N.B.
600.	Three Rivers	First N.B.
637.	East Saginaw	First N.B.
812.	Grand Rapids	City N.B.
813.	Constantine	First N.B.
825.	Sturgis	First N.B.
1063.	Tecumseh	N.B. of Tecumseh
1065.	Jackson	First N.B.
1205.	Battle Creek	First N.B.
1235.	Coldwater	Coldwater N.B.
1247.	Houghton	First N.B.
1256.	Corunna	First N.B.
1280.	Lowell	Lowell N.B.
1359.	Kalamazoo	Michigan N.B.
1433.	Detroit	Nat. Insurance Bank
1470.	Hillsdale	Second N.B.
1515.	Marshall	First N.B.
1518.	Marshall	N.B. of Michigan
1521.	Paw Paw	First N.B.
1533.	Jackson	People's N.B.
1539.	Saint Johns	First N.B.
1542.	Detroit	American N.B.
1544.	Albion	Nat. Exchange Bank
1550.	East Saginaw	Merchants' N.B.
1573.	Owosso	First N.B.
1574.	Pontiac	Second N.B.
1587.	Monroe	First N.B.
1588.	Flint	First N.B.
1625.	Dowagiac	First N.B.
1722.	Decatur	First N.B.
1725.	Schoolcraft	First N.B.
1730.	Muskegon	Muskegon N.B.
1731.	Lapeer	First N.B.
1745.	Hastings	Hastings N.B.
1752.	Holly	First N.B.
1758.	Charlotte	First N.B.
1761.	Niles	First N.B.
1764.	Mason	First N.B.
1768.	Saginaw	First N.B.
1780.	Flint	Citizens' N.B.
1789.	Saint Clair	First N.B.
1812.	Cassopolis	First N.B.
1823.	South Haven	First N.B.
1826.	Union City	Union City N.B.
1829.	Allegan	First N.B.
1832.	Big Rapids	Northern N.B.
1849.	Grand Haven	First N.B.
1857.	Port Huron	First N.B.
1866.	Saint Joseph	First N.B.
1886.	Niles	Citizens' N.B.

Charter #	City	Name of Bank
1916.	Plymouth	First N.B.
1918.	Saginaw	Seond N.B.
1919.	Three Rivers	Manufacturers' N.B.
1924.	Coldwater	Southern Michigan N.B.
1953.	Lansing	Lansing N.B.
1965.	Holly	Merchants' N.B.
1973.	Adrian	First N.B.
2008.	Ionia	Second N.B.
2017.	Muir	First N.B.
2023.	Marshall	Nat. City Bank
2046.	Buchanan	First N.B.
2054.	Greenville	First N.B.
2081.	Muskegon	Lumbermans' N.B.
2084.	Ishpeming	First N.B.
2085.	Negaunee	First N.B.
2095.	Centerville	First N.B.
2143.	Hancock	First N.B.
2145.	Bay City	Second N.B.
2162.	Leslie	First N.B.
2186.	Romeo	Citizens' N.B.
2211.	Constantine	Farmers' N.B.
2214.	Mount Clemens	First N.B.
2365.	Detroit	Merchants and Manufacturers' N.B.
2367.	Eaton Rapids	First N.B.
2372.	Union City	Farmers' N.B.
2379.	Milford	First N.B.
2429.	Whitehall	First N.B.
2460.	Grand Rapids	Grand Rapids N.B.
2492.	Saginaw	Citizens' N.B.
2539.	Manistee	First N.B.
2550.	Quincy	First N.B.
2591.	Detroit	Commercial N.B.
2606.	Manistee	Manistee N.B.
2607.	Pontiac	First N.B.
2611.	Grand Rapids	Fourth N.B.
2707.	Detroit	First N.B.
2708.	Flushing	First N.B.
2714.	Ann Arbor	First N.B.
2761.	East Saginaw	Home N.B.
2773.	Ludington	First N.B.
2847.	Alpena	Alpena N.B
2853.	Bay City	First N.B.
2855.	Midland City	First N.B.
2870.	Detroit	Detroit N.B.
2890.	Grand Rapids	Old N.B.
2914.	Stanton	First N.B.
2944.	Big Rapids	Big Rapids N.B.
2987.	Vassar	First N.B.
3034.	Charlotte	Merchants' N.B.
3088.	Muskegon	Merchants' N.B.
3095.	Ishpeming	Ishpeming N.B.
3109.	Plymouth	Plymouth N.B.
3123.	East Saginaw	East Saginaw N.B.
3133.	Three Rivers	Three Rivers N.B.
3210.	Kalamazoo	City N.B.
3211.	Kalamazoo	Kalamazoo N.B.
3215.	Mount Pleasant	First N.B.
3217.	Ithaca	First N.B.
3235.	Cheboygan	First N.B.
3239.	Saint Louis	First N.B.
3243.	Greenville	City N.B.
3251.	Concord	First N.B.
3256.	Menominee	First N.B.
3264.	Ovid	First N.B.
3276.	Sturgis	Sturgis N.B
3293.	Grand Rapids	Grand Rapids National City Bank
3314.	Battle Creek	N.B. of Battle Creek
3316.	Albion	First N.B.
3325.	Traverse City	First N.B.
3334.	Houghton	N.B. of Houghton
3357.	Detroit	American Exchange N.B.
3361.	Flint	First N.B.
3378.	Saint John's	Saint John's N.B.
3388.	Pontiac	Pontiac N.B.
3410.	Owosso	Second N.B.
3457.	Calumet	First N.B.
3487.	Detroit	Union N.B.
3488.	Grand Rapids	Fifth N.B.
3513.	Lansing	City N.B.
3514.	Detroit	Third N.B.
3547.	Sault Ste. Marie	First N.B.
3717.	Negaunee	First N.B.
3730.	Detroit	Preston N.B.
3747.	Sault Ste. Marie	Sault Ste. Marie N.B.
3761.	Escanaba	First N.B.
3806.	Iron Mountain	First N.B.
3886.	Saint Ignace	First N.B.
3896.	Battle Creek	Merchants' N.B.
3911.	Saginaw	Commercial N.B.
3925.	Buchanan	First N.B.
3947.	Bessemer	First N.B.
3948.	Lake Linden	First N.B.
3971.	Ironwood	First N.B.
4125.	Muskegon	Union N.B.
4261.	Benton Harbor	First N.B.
4398.	Muskegon	Hackley N.B.
4413.	Reed City	First N.B.
4446.	Port Huron	First Nat. Exchange Bank
4454.	Menominee	Lumbermen's N.B.
4527.	White Pigeon	First N.B.
4578.	Grand Haven	N.B. of Grand Haven
4649.	Plymouth	First Nat. Exchange Bank
4840.	Muskegon	Nat. Lumberman's Bank

Charter #	City	Name of Bank
4953.	Bay City	Old Second N.B.
5199.	Rockland	First N.B.
5348.	Manistique	First N.B.
5415.	Durand	First N.B.
5482.	Yale	First N.B.
5594.	Saint Joseph	Commercial N.B.
5607.	Petoskey	First N.B.
5668.	Ishpeming	Miners N.B.
5669.	Morenci	First N.B.
5789.	Ionia	N.B. of Ionia
5896.	Houghton	Citizens' N.B.
6003.	Marquette	Marquette N.B.
6485.	Ithaca	Ithaca N.B.
6492.	Detroit	Old Detroit N.B.
6727.	Hart	First N.B.
6820.	Ontonagon	First N.B.
6863.	Norway	First N.B.
7013.	Battle Creek	Central N.B.
7525.	Crystal Falls	Iron County N.B.
7552.	Albion	Albion N.B.
7589.	Battle Creek	Old N.B.
7664.	Flint	N.B. of Flint
7676.	Houghton	Houghton N.B.
8148.	Lansing	Capital N.B.
8496.	Escanaba	Escanaba N.B.
8545.	Iron River	First N.B.
8598.	Laurium	First N.B.
8703.	Detroit	Guardian N.B.
8723.	Vassar	Vassar N.B.
9000.	Munising	First N.B. of Alger Co.
9020.	Boyne City	First N.B.
9087.	Hancock	Superior N.B.
9099.	Richland	Farmers' N.B.
9218.	Rochester	First N.B.
9359.	Hubbell	First N.B.
9421.	Adrian	N.B. of Commerce
9497.	Burr Oak	First N.B.
9509.	L'Anse	Baraga County N.B.
9517.	Ironwood	Gogebic N.B.
9556.	Negaunee	Negaunee N.B.
9654.	Ithaca	Commercial N.B.
9704.	Bronson	People's N.B.
9792.	Croswell	First N.B.
9854.	Hartford	Onley N.B.
9874.	Birmingham	First N.B.
10073.	Dowagiac	Dowagiac N.B.
10143.	Benton Harbor	American N.B.
10498.	Watervliet	First N.B.
10527.	Detroit	First and Old Detroit N.B.
10529.	Benton Harbor	Farmers and Merchants' N.B.
10600.	Detroit	Merchants' N.B.
10601.	Alpha	First N.B.
10631.	Capac	First N.B.
10632.	Saint Clair Heights	Michigan N.B.
10673.	Gladwin	First N.B.
10742.	Richmond	First N.B.
10753.	Carsonville	First N.B.
10790.	Avoca	First N.B.
10886.	Gladstone	First N.B.
10997.	Flint	First N.B.
11082.	Hamtramck	People's N.B.
11260.	Marine City	Liberty N.B.
11289.	Jackson	Nat. Union Bank
11305.	Wakefield	First N.B.
11454.	Chesaning	First N.B.
11469.	Ironwood	Iron N.B.
11547.	Crystal Falls	Crystal Falls N.B.
11549.	Pontiac	N.B. of Pontiac
11586.	Howell	First N.B.
11802.	Caspian	Caspian N.B.
11813.	Blissfield	First N.B.
11843.	Greenville	Greenville N.B.
11852.	Battle Creek	City N.B.
11929.	Iron Mountain	N.B. of Iron Mountain
11954.	Hermansville	First N.B.
12027.	Marquette	Union N.B.
12084.	Lawton	First N.B.
12108.	Grand Rapids	City N.B.
12288.	Pontiac	First N.B.
12387.	Ironwood	Merchants and Miners' N.B.
12436.	Ypsilanti	People's N.B.
12474.	Reed City	Reed City N.B.
12561.	Evart	First N.B.
12616.	Wyandotte	First N.B.
12657.	Royal Oak	First N.B.
12661.	L'Anse Creuse	First N.B.
12697.	Mason	Dart N.B.
12793.	Almont	First N.B.
12826.	Utica	First N.B.
12847.	Detroit	Griswold N.B.
12869.	Brighton	First N.B.
12878.	Inkster	Inkster N.B.
12944.	Algonac	First N.B.
12953.	Plymouth	First N.B
12971.	Mount Clemens	First N.B.
12989.	Dearborn	First N.B.
12999.	Lincoln Park	Lincoln Park N.B.
13072.	Jackson	East Side Nat. Union Bank
13240.	Centerline	First N.B.
13307.	Niles	City N.B. & Trust Co.
13328.	Grand Rapids	American N.B.
13434.	Grand Rapids	Security N.B.
13513.	Manistique	First N.B.
13522.	Cheboygan	Citizens N.B.
13600.	Pontiac	First N.B.

Charter #	City	Name of Bank
13607.	Bessemer	Bessemer N.B.
13622.	Bay City	N.B. of Bay City
13671.	Detroit	N.B. of Detroit
13703.	Birmingham	Birmingham N.B.
13738.	Detroit	Manufacturers N.B.
13739.	Pontiac	Community N.B.
13741.	Jackson	N.B. of Jackson
13753.	Niles	First N.B.
13758.	Grand Rapids	N.B. of Grand Rapids
13793.	Richmond	N.B. of Richmond
13799.	Grand Rapids	People's N.B.
13807.	Ypsilanti	N.B. of Ypsilanti
13820.	Kalamazoo	American N.B.
13821.	Adrian	N.B. of Adrian
13824.	Hubbell	First N.B.
13833.	Benton Harbor	Farmers & Merchants N.B.
13841.	Rochester	Rochester N.B.
13857.	Hastings	N.B. of Hastings
13858.	Battle Creek	Central N.B.
13874.	Wyandotte	N.B. of Wyandotte
13929.	Ontonagon	First N.B.
13931.	Ishpeming	Miners First N.B.
13976.	Flint	N.B. of Flint
13995.	Eaton Rapids	N.B. of Eaton Rapids
14009.	Marshall	First N.B.
14016.	Ludington	N.B. of Ludington
14022.	Utica	Utica N.B.
14032.	Lansing	Lansing N.B.
14062.	Hillsdale	Hillsdale County N.B.
14102.	Iron River	Iron River N.B.
14111.	Gladstone	First N.B.
14116.	Coldwater	Coldwater N.B.
14144.	Howell	First N.B.
14185.	Battle Creek	Security N.B.
14187.	Ionia	Ionia County N.B.
14249.	Hancock	National Metals Bank
14269.	Crystal Falls	First N.B.
14280.	Manistique	First N.B.

MINNESOTA

Charter #	City	Name of Bank
203.	Saint Paul	First N.B.
496.	Hastings	First N.B.
550.	Winona	First N.B.
579.	Rochester	First N.B.
631.	New Ulm	First N.B.
710.	Minneapolis	First N.B.
719.	Minneapolis	Nat. Exchange Bank
725.	Saint Paul	Second N.B.
1258.	Saint Paul	Nat. Marine Bank
1487.	Red Wing	First N.B.
1514.	Stillwater	First N.B.
1538.	Hastings	Merchants' N.B.
1597.	Shakopee	First N.B.
1623.	Minneapolis	State N.B.
1643.	Winona	United N.B.
1683.	Mankato	First N.B.
1686.	Faribault	First N.B.
1690.	Austin	First N.B.
1740.	Lake City	First N.B.
1782.	Winona	Winona Deposit N.B.
1783.	Stillwater	Lumbermen's N.B.
1794.	Saint Peter	First N.B.
1830.	Minneapolis	Merchants' N.B.
1842.	Winona	Second N.B.
1863.	Faribault	Citizens' N.B.
1911.	Owatonna	First N.B.
1954.	Duluth	First N.B.
2005.	Mankato	Citizens' N.B.
2006.	Minneapolis	Northwestern N.B.
2020.	Saint Paul	Merchants' N.B.
2030.	Fergus Falls	First N.B.
2073.	Northfield	First N.B.
2088.	Rochester	Union N.B.
2122.	Owatonna	Farmers' N.B.
2159.	Kasson	First N.B.
2268.	Winona	Merchants' N.B.
2316.	Rochester	Rochester N.B.
2318.	New Ulm	Citizens' N.B.
2387.	Cannon Falls	First N.B.
2567.	Crookston	First N.B.
2569.	Moorhead	First N.B.
2571.	Glencoe	First N.B.
2590.	Brainerd	First N.B.
2648.	Fergus Falls	Fergus Falls N.B.
2674.	Stillwater	First N.B.
2768.	Duluth	Duluth N.B.
2790.	Saint Cloud	First N.B.
2795.	Minneapolis	Union N.B.
2800.	Anoka	First N.B.
2933.	Morris	First N.B.
2934.	Fergus Falls	Citizens' N.B.
2943.	Saint Paul	Nat. German American Bank
2959.	Saint Paul	Saint Paul N.B.
2995.	Alexandria	First N.B.
3000.	Anoka	Anoka N.B.
3009.	Saint Cloud	German American N.B.
3039.	Shakopee	First N.B.
3098.	Minneapolis	Manufacturers' N.B.
3100.	Wabasha	First N.B.
3127.	Shakopee	Merchants and Farmers' N.B.
3145.	Minneapolis	Nicollet N.B.
3155.	Sauk Center	First N.B.
3206.	Minneapolis	N.B. of Commerce
3224.	Winona	First N.B.
3233.	Saint Paul	Third N.B.
3262.	Crookston	Merchants' N.B.
3426.	Detroit	First N.B.
3428.	Luverne	First N.B.
3453.	Duluth	Merchants' N.B.
3550.	Worthington	First N.B.
3560.	Albert Lea	First N.B.
3562.	Mankato	Mankato N.B.
3626.	Duluth	First N.B.
3659.	Red Lake Falls	First N.B.
3689.	Saint Paul	Commercial N.B.
3784.	Minneapolis	Flour City N.B.
3924.	Tower	First N.B.
3982.	Pipestone	First N.B.
4001.	Duluth	N.B. of Commerce
4034.	Little Falls	First N.B.
4131.	Austin	Austin N.B.
4302.	New Brighton	Twin City N.B.
4421.	Duluth	Marine N.B.
4509.	Lake Benton	First N.B.
4595.	Marshall	Lyon County N.B.
4614.	Marshall	First N.B.
4617.	Elbow Lake	First N.B.
4638.	East Grand Forks	First N.B.
4644.	Breckenridge	First N.B.
4655.	Little Falls	American N.B.
4669.	Wells	First N.B.
4702.	Albert Lea	Albert Lea N.B.
4713.	Moorhead	Moorhead N.B.
4727.	Mankato	Nat. Citizens' Bank
4739.	Minneapolis	Columbia N.B.
4750.	New Duluth	New Duluth N.B.
4797.	Saint Cloud	Merchants' N.B.
4807.	Princeton	First N.B.
4821.	Wadena	First N.B.
4831.	Appleton	First N.B.
4847.	Austin	Citizens' N.B.
4859.	Saint James	First N.B.
4916.	Wadena	Merchants' N.B.
4928.	Owatonna	Nat. Farmers' Bank
4936.	Fairmount	First N.B.
4951.	Minneapolis	Swedish-American N.B.
4959.	Barnesville	First N.B.
4969.	Kasson	N.B. of Kasson
4992.	Tracy	First N.B.
5063.	Windom	First N.B.
5256.	Slayton	First N.B.
5301.	Wilmont	First N.B.
5330.	Stewartville	First N.B.
5362.	West Concord	First N.B.
5374.	Eyota	First N.B.
5377.	Elmore	First N.B.
5383.	Heron Lake	First N.B.
5393.	Blue Earth	First N.B.
5405.	Cloquet	First N.B.
5406.	Winnebago City.	First N.B.
5423.	Fairmont	Martin County N.B.
5453.	Ada	First N.B.
5542.	Park Rapids	First N.B.
5553.	Eveleth	First N.B.
5568.	Staples	First N.B.
5570.	Ellsworth	First N.B.
5582.	Bemidji	First N.B.
5706.	Lyle	First N.B.
5745.	Hibbing	First N.B.
5826.	Redwood Falls	First N.B.
5852.	Jackson	First N.B.
5859.	Alexandria	Farmers' N.B.
5866.	Warren	First N.B.
5892.	Ruthton	First N.B.
5894.	Thief River Falls	First N.B.
5895.	Northfield	Northfield N.B.
5907.	Agyle	First N.B.
5910.	Worthington	Citizens' N.B.
5969.	Chokio	First N.B.
5988.	Fertile	First N.B.
6022.	Verndale	First N.B.
6029.	Ceylon	First N.B.
6035.	Wheaton	First N.B.
6054.	Fulda	First N.B.
6098.	Barnesville	Barnesville N.B.
6118.	Litchfield	First N.B.
6128.	Albert Lea	Citizens' N.B.
6151.	Willmar	First N.B.
6154.	Benson	First N.B.
6199.	Hills	First N.B.
6203.	Tyler	First N.B.
6204.	Minnesota Lake	First N.B.
6208.	Long Prairie	First N.B.
6237.	Saint Charles	First N.B.
6259.	Campbell	First N.B.
6266.	Eagle Bend	First N.B.
6276.	Perham	First N.B.
6279.	Preston	First N.B.
6285.	Hanley Falls	First N.B.
6293.	Plainview	First N.B.
6304.	Two Harbors	First N.B.
6310.	Morris	Morris N.B.
6316.	Spring Valley	First N.B.
6321.	Dawson	First N.B.
6331.	Welcome	Welcome N.B.
6335.	Breckenridge	Breckenridge N.B.
6348.	Sherburn	Sherburn N.B.
6349.	Pelican Rapids	First N.B.
6352.	Cass Lake	First N.B.
6364.	Truman	Truman N.B.
6366.	Canby	First N.B.
6387.	Sleepy Eye	First N.B.
6396.	Windom	Windom N.B.
6401.	Twin Valley	First N.B.
6412.	Westbrook	First N.B.
6413.	Minneota	First N.B.
6417.	Sauk Center	Merchants' N.B.
6431.	Albert Lea	Security N.B.
6436.	Rushford	First N.B.
6448.	Clarkfield	First N.B.
6449.	Minneapolis	Minnesota N.B.
6459.	Ortonville	First N.B.
6467.	Ivanhoe	First N.B.
6468.	Hendricks	First N.B.
6478.	Bricelyn	First N.B.
6488.	McIntosh	First N.B.
6519.	Mankato	N.B. of Commerce
6520.	Duluth	City N.B.
6523.	Jasper	First N.B.
6527.	Virginia	First N.B.
6532.	Minnesota Lake	Farmers' N.B.
6537.	Lakefield	First N.B.
6544.	Waseca	First N.B.
6563.	Grand Rapids	First N.B.
6571.	Boyd	Boyd N.B.
6583.	Renville	First N.B.
6584.	Cottonwood	First N.B.
6608.	Chatfield	First N.B.
6623.	Dodge Center	Farmers' N.B.
6631.	Alden	First N.B.
6637.	Ivanhoe	Ivanhoe N.B.
6661.	Parkers Prairie	First N.B.
6682.	Dodge Center	First N.B.
6693.	Fertile	Citizens' N.B.
6696.	Lake Benton	Nat. Citizens' Bank
6704.	Cannon Falls	Farmers and Merchants' N.B.
6731.	Royalton	First N.B.
6732.	South Saint Paul	Stockyards N.B.
6738.	Dunnell	First N.B.
6747.	Ortonville	Citizens' N.B.
6775.	Blooming Prairie	First N.B.
6783.	Roseau	First N.B.
6784.	Emmons	First N.B.
6787.	Mapleton	First N.B.
6788.	Wells	Wells N.B.
6795.	Madison	First N.B.
6803.	Aitkin	First N.B.
6813.	Bagley	First N.B.
6828.	Saint Paul	American N.B.
6837.	Osakis	First N.B.
6840.	Balaton	First N.B.
6860.	Montevideo	First N.B.
6862.	Rushmore	First N.B.
6889.	Fosston	First N.B.
6906.	Henning	First N.B.
6917.	Minneota	Farmers and Merchants' N.B.
6918.	**Lake Crystal**	**First N.B.**
6921.	**LeSueur Center**	**First N.B.**
6933.	**Grand Meadow**	**First N.B.**
6934.	**Hallock**	**First N.B.**
6954.	Rush City	First N.B.
6973.	Carlton	First N.B.
6991.	Eveleth	Miners' N.B.
6992.	Jackson	Jackson N.B.
6996.	Hancock	First N.B.
7014.	Winthrop	First N.B.
7021.	Saint James	Citizens' and Security N.B.
7024.	Frazee	First N.B.
7033.	Hancock	Hancock N.B.
7080.	Long Prairie	People's N.B.
7081.	Ulen	First N.B.
7092.	New Prague	First N.B
7100.	Madelia	First N.B.
7109.	Le Roy	First N.B.
7128.	Iona	First N.B.
7143.	Lake Park	First N.B.
7161.	Clinton	First N.B.
7184.	Elgin	First N.B.
7196.	Halstad	First N.B.
7199.	Le Sueur	First N.B.
7213.	Graceville	First N.B.
7221.	Lamberton	First N.B.
7227.	Browerville	First N.B.
7268.	Deer Creek	First N.B.
7273.	Belle Plaine	First N.B.
7283.	Waterville	First N.B.
7292.	Mora	First N.B.
7307.	Red Wing	Goodhue County N.B.
7341.	Browns Valley	First N.B.
7373.	Bertha	First N.B.
7380.	International Falls	First N.B.
7387.	Braham	First N.B.
7427.	Canby	Nat. Citizens' Bank
7428.	Cambridge	First N.B.
7438.	Beardsley	First N.B.
7508.	Caledonia	First N.B.
7566.	Melrose	First N.B.
7603.	Goodhue	First N.B.
7625.	Woodstock	First N.B.
7641.	Blue Earth	Farmers' N.B.
7647.	Chisholm	First N.B.
7708.	Princeton	First N.B.
7742.	Glenwood	First N.B.
7764.	Motley	First N.B.
7770.	Luverne	Farmers' N.B.
7772.	Hawley	First N.B.
7797.	Jackson	Brown N.B.
7933.	Foley	First N.B.
7958.	Hopkins, W. Minneapolis	First N.B.
7960.	Adrian	First N.B.
8049.	Herman	First N.B.
8050.	Raymond	First N.B.
8051.	Cold Spring	First N.B.
8059.	Adams	First N.B.
8108.	Saint Paul	Capital N.B.
8122.	Detroit	Merchants' N.B.
8241.	Bemidji	Northern N.B.
8269.	Springfield	First N.B.
8322.	Coleraine	First N.B.

Charter #	City	Name of Bank
8378.	Chaska	First N.B.
8416.	Granite Falls	First N.B.
8476.	Walker	First N.B.
8523.	Staples	City N.B.
8551.	Fairmont	Fairmont N.B.
8592.	Ely	First N.B.
8683.	Harmony	First N.B.
8697.	Biwabik	First N.B.
8720.	Minneapolis	Security N.B.
8726.	Mahnomen	First N.B.
8729.	Grey Eagle	First N.B.
8756.	Battle Lake	First N.B.
8757.	Elk River	First N.B.
8813.	Appleton	First N.B.
8977.	Luverne	N.B. of Luverne
8989.	Worthington	Worthington N.B.
8993.	Wheaton	N.B. of Wheaton
9031.	Mabel	First N.B.
9033.	Adrian	N.B. of Adrian
9050.	Milaca	First N.B.
9059.	Preston	N.B. of Preston
9063.	Olivia	People's First N.B.
9064.	Stephen	First N.B.
9131.	Deer River	First N.B.
9147.	Blackduck	First N.B.
9253.	Waseca	Farmers' N.B.
9262.	Gilbert	First N.B.
9267.	Mountain Lake	First N.B.
9321.	Beaver Creek	First N.B.
9327.	Duluth	Northern N.B.
9374.	Duluth	American Exchange N.B.
9409.	Minneapolis	Midland N.B.
9442.	Minneapolis	Metropolitan N.B.
9457.	Hendricks	Farmers' N.B.
9464.	Sandstone	First N.B.
9596.	Starbuck	First N.B.
9703.	Deerwood	First N.B.
9771.	Fairfax	First N.B.
9775.	Amboy	First N.B.
9837.	Red Lake Falls	Farmers' N.B.
9838.	Crosby	First N.B.
9903.	Delano	First N.B.
10147.	Hutchinson	Farmers' N.B.
10261.	Minneapolis	Nat. City Bank
10382.	Ironton	First N.B.
10393.	Winnebago	Blue Earth Valley N.B.
10475.	Saint Paul	N.B. of Commerce
10507.	Lanesboro	First N.B.
10554.	Isanti	First N.B.
10570.	Atwater	First N.B.
10580.	Kasson	N.B. of Dodge County
10603.	Kiester	First N.B.
10642.	New Richland	First N.B.
10665.	Ada	Ada N.B.
10710.	Baudette	First N.B.
10736.	Nashwauk	First N.B.
10740.	Lakeville	First N.B.
10783.	Aitkin	Farmers' N.B.
10824.	Swanville	First N.B.
10830.	Gonvick	First N.B.
10841.	Aitkin	N.B. of Aitkin
10862.	Brandon	First N.B.
10865.	Winona	Winona N.B.
10898.	Wendell	First N.B.
10903.	Keewatin	First N.B.
10936.	Pipestone	Pipestone N.B.
10940.	Saint Paul	Nat. Exchange Bank
10946.	Brewster	First N.B.
11023.	Buffalo	First N.B.
11042.	Kasson	Nat. Farmers' Bank
11054.	Bovey	First N.B.
11090.	Fairmont	Citizens' N.B.
11125.	Proctor	First N.B.
11167.	Minneapolis	Bankers' N.B.
11173.	Erskine	First N.B.
11178.	Minneapolis	Lincoln N.B.
11212.	Hastings	Hastings N.B.
11215.	Montgomery	First N.B.
11218.	Jordan	First N.B.
11224.	Avoca	First N.B.
11261.	Barnesville	Farmers' N.B.
11267.	Pequot	First N.B.
11286.	Warren	Warren N.B.
11288.	Hanska	First N.B.
11293.	Lake Wilson	First N.B.
11332.	Paynesville	First N.B.
11345.	Aurora	First N.B.
11356.	Lancaster	First N.B.
11365.	Kerkhoven	First N.B.
11392.	Clearbrook	First N.B.
11401.	Lake Crystal	American N.B.
11410.	Waconia	First N.B.
11500.	Virginia	American Exchange N.B.
11550.	Motordale	First N.B.
11552.	Good Thunder	First N.B.
11563.	Pine River	First N.B.
11575.	Kilkenny	First N.B.
11579.	Nashwauk	American N.B.
11581.	Pine City	First N.B.
11606.	Granada	First N.B.
11608.	Marble	First N.B.
11611.	Big Lake	First N.B.
11622.	Buhl	First N.B.
11627.	Ivanhoe	Farmers and Merchants' N.B.
11652.	Forest Lake	First N.B.
11668.	Faribault	Security N.B.
11685.	Skakopee	People's N.B.
11687.	Farmington	First N.B.
11709.	Rice	First N.B.
11710.	Rice	Rice N.B.
11717.	Mahnomen	Farmers' N.B.
11724.	Holland	First N.B.
11740.	Menahga	First N.B.
11741.	Saint Paul	Twin Cities N.B.
11761.	Barnum	First N.B.

Charter #	City	Name of Bank
11770.	Saint Paul	Wabash N.B.
11776.	Rosemount	First N.B.
11777.	Watertown	First N.B.
11778.	Minneapolis	Minneapolis N.B.
11810.	Duluth	Minnesota N.B.
11815.	Warroad	First N.B.
11818.	Saint Cloud	American N.B.
11848.	Roseau	Roseau County N.B.
11861.	Minneapolis	Payday N.B.
11863.	Littlefork	First N.B.
11974.	Proctor	People's N.B.
11987.	White Bear Lake	First N.B.
12032.	Farwell	First N.B.
12115.	Richfield	Richfield N.B.
12140.	Duluth	Duluth N.B.
12282.	Minneapolis	Transportation Brotherhoods N.B.
12357.	Two Harbors	First N.B.
12395.	Cokato	First N.B.
12507.	Wadena	First N.B.
12518.	West Minneapolis, Hopkins	Security N.B.
12568.	Hibbing	Hibbing N.B.
12607.	Grey Eagle	N.B. of Grey Eagle
12634.	Luverne	First and Farmers' N.B.
12844.	Lamberton	New First N.B.
12859.	Litchfield	First N.B.
12864.	Alexandria	Farmers' N.B.
12922.	Saint Paul	Nat. Exchange Bank
12941.	Mahnomen	First N.B.
12947.	Moose Lake	First N.B.
12959.	Buffalo	Buffalo N.B.
12972.	Minneapolis	Bloomington-Lake N.B.
13066.	Minneapolis	Fourth Northwestern N.B.
13075.	Detroit Lakes	Becker County N.B.
13078.	Duluth	Pioneer N.B.
13081.	Olivia	Citizens N.B.
13086.	Montevideo	Security N.B.
13095.	Jackson	First N.B.
13096.	Minneapolis	Minnehaha N.B.
13108.	Minneapolis	Central N.B.
13114.	Columbia Heights	Columbia N.B.
13116.	Duluth	Western N.B.
13127.	Minneapolis	Third Northwestern N.B.
13131.	St. Paul	Midway N.B.
13140.	Minneapolis	Fifth Northwestern N.B.
13167.	St. Paul	St. Paul N.B.
13204.	Lakefield	First N.B.
13242.	Amboy	First N.B.
13255.	Winnebago	First N.B.
13269.	Jackson	Jackson N.B.
13297.	Moorhead	First N.B.
13303.	Deer Creek	First N.B.
13350.	Northfield	Northfield N.B. & Trust Co.
13353.	Little Falls	American N.B.
13396.	Red Wing	Security N.B. & Trust Co.
13397.	Benson	N.B. of Benson
13399.	Pipestone	Pipestone N.B.
13401.	Willmar	Security N.B.
13405.	East Grand Forks	Minnesota N.B.
13422.	Albert Lea	Freeborn County N.B. and Trust Co.
13468.	Ivanhoe	Farmers and Merchants N.B.
13486.	Litchfield	Northwestern N.B.
13518.	Paynesville	First N.B.
13544.	Luverne	Luverne N.B.
13547.	Anoka	First N.B.
13556.	Wheaton	First N.B.
13561.	Madison	Klein N.B.
13564.	Dawson	Northwestern N.B.
13615.	Stewartville	Stewartville N.B.
13692.	Park Rapids	Citizens N.B.
13713.	Cannon Falls	First N.B.
13784.	Madelia	Citizens N.B.
13972.	Lake Crystal	Lake Crystal N.B.
13973.	St. Charles	First N.B.
14042.	Winthrop	First N.B.
14068.	Amboy	Security N.B.
14167.	West Concord	First N.B.
14216.	Hutchinson	First N.B.
14220.	Mankato	N.B. of Commerce
14296.	St. James	First N.B.
14311.	Buffalo	Oakley N.B.

MISSISSIPPI

Charter #	City	Name of Bank
803.	Vicksburg	N.B. of Vicksburg
1610.	Jackson	First N.B.
2638.	Columbus	First N.B.
2891.	West Point	First N.B.
2957.	Meridian	First N.B.
3176.	Meridian	Meridian N.B.
3258.	Vicksburg	First N.B.
3332.	Jackson	First N.B.
3430.	Vicksburg	Merchants' N.B.
3566.	Yazoo City	First N.B.
3656.	Aberdeen	First N.B.
3688.	Starkville	First N.B.
3701.	Natchez	First N.B.
3765.	Greenville	First N.B.
4521.	Tupelo	First N.B.
5176.	Hattiesburg	First N.B.
5177.	Hattiesburg	First N.B.
5613.	Lumberton	First N.B.
5715.	Port Gibson	Mississippi N.B.
6121.	Vicksburg	American N.B.
6188.	Gulfport	First N.B.
6305.	Natchez	N.B. of Commerce
6595.	Clarksdale	First N.B.
6646.	Jackson	Capital N.B.
6681.	Laurel	First N.B.
6847.	Canton	First N.B.
6923.	Laurel	Laurel N.B.
7200.	Shaw	First N.B.
7216.	Greenwood	First N.B.
7266.	Meridian	Citizens' N.B.
7461.	McComb	First N.B.
7507.	Vicksburg	Citizens' N.B.
8514.	New Albany	First N.B.
8593.	Moss Point	Pascagoula N.B.
8719.	Poplarville	N.B. of Poplarville
9040.	Pontotoc	First N.B.
9041.	Philadelphia	First N.B.
9094.	Corinth	First N.B.
9196.	Okolona	First N.B.
9204.	Ripley	First N.B.
9251.	Ackerman	First N.B.
9728.	Collins	First N.B.
9751.	Corinth	Citizens N.B.
9753.	Summit	N.B. of Summit
9865.	Oxford	First N.B.
10154.	Iuka	First N.B.
10326.	Columbia	Citizens' N.B.
10338.	Summit	Progressive N.B.
10361.	Columbus	N.B. of Commerce
10463.	Jackson	State N.B.
10494.	Brookhaven	First N.B.
10523.	Jackson	Jackson-State N.B.
10555.	Aberdeen	Aberdeen N.B.
10576.	Biloxi	First N.B.
10688.	Itta Bena	First N.B.
10738.	Columbus	Columbus N.B.
10745.	Rosedale	First N.B.
10873.	Holly Springs	First N.B.
11898.	Laurel	Commercial N.B. and Trust Co.
12073.	Rosedale	Rosedale N.B.
12222.	Clarksdale	Planters' N.B.
12478.	Hattiesburg	Commercial N.B.
12499.	Vicksburg	Nat. People's Savings Bank and Trust Co.
12501.	Vicksburg	Nat. City Savings Bank and Trust Co.
12537.	Natchez	Britton and Koontz N.B.
12587.	Yazoo City	Delta N.B.
12822.	Columbus	First N.B.
13156.	Gulfport	N.B. of Gulfport
13313.	Lexington	First N.B.
13403.	Greenville	Commercial N.B.
13413.	Waynesboro	First N.B.
13551.	Meridian	First N.B.
13553.	Gulfport	First N.B.
13708.	Jackson	Capital N.B
13722.	Natchez	Britton and Koontz N.B.
14176.	Waynesboro	First N.B.

MISSOURI

Charter #	City	Name of Bank
67.	Columbia	First N.B.
89.	Saint Louis	First N.B.
139.	Saint Louis	Second N.B.
170.	Saint Louis	First N.B.
260.	Saint Charles	First N.B.
283.	Saint Louis	Fourth N.B.
454.	Carondelet	First N.B.
1112.	Saint Louis	Saint Louis N.B.
1381.	Saint Louis	Union N.B.
1467.	Columbia	Exchange N.B.
1501.	Saint Louis	Merchants' N.B.
1529.	Independence	First N.B.
1571.	Hannibal	First N.B.
1580.	Saint Joseph	First N.B.
1584.	Boonville	Central N.B.
1612.	Kansas City	First N.B.
1627.	Sedalia	First N.B.
1665.	Saint Louis	N.B. of the State of Missouri
1667.	Saint Joseph	State N.B.
1677.	Springfield	Greene County N.B.
1701.	Springfield	First N.B.
1711.	Shelbina	First N.B.
1712.	California	Moniteau N.B.
1735.	Palmyra	First N.B.
1751.	Pleasant Hill	First N.B.
1770.	Columbia	Boone County N.B.
1803.	Paris	First N.B.
1809.	Jefferson City	First N.B.
1839.	La Grange	First N.B.
1843.	Butler	Bates County N.B.
1856.	Warrensburg	First N.B.
1858.	Saint Louis	Valley N.B.
1865.	Rolla	N.B. of Rolla
1877.	Knob Noster	First N.B.
1901.	Kansas City	Kansas City N.B.
1940.	Clinton	First N.B.
1966.	Trenton	First N.B.
1971.	Sedalia	Citizens' N.B.
1995.	Kansas City	Commercial N.B.
2013.	Carthage	First N.B.
2055.	Jefferson City	Nat. Exchange Bank
2218.	Lancaster	First N.B.
2356.	Platte City	Farmers' N.B.
2432.	Memphis	Scotland County N.B.
2440.	Kansas City	Merchants N.B.
2561.	Butler	Butler N.B.
2613.	Kansas City	Citizens N.B.
2636.	Appleton City	First N.B.
2713.	Kirksville	First N.B.
2835.	Saint Louis	Fifth N.B.
2862.	Macon	First N.B.
2881.	Mexico	First N.B.
2884.	Marshall	First N.B.
2898.	Saint Joseph	Sexton N.B.
2919.	Sedalia	Third N.B.
2970.	Saint Joseph	N.B. of Saint Joseph
2979.	Palmyra	First N.B.
3005.	Carthage	First N.B.
3068.	Unionville	Marshall N.B.

Charter #	City	Name of Bank
3079.	Tarkio	First N.B.
3103.	Louisiana	Exchange N.B.
3110.	Milan	First N.B.
3111.	Louisiana	Mercantile N.B.
3137.	Unionville	N.B. of Unionville
3268.	Maryville	First N.B.
3322.	Paris	N.B. of Paris
3380.	Grant City	First N.B.
3456.	Kansas City	First N.B.
3489.	Kansas City	N.B. of Kansas City
3544.	Kansas City	American N.B.
3637.	Kansas City	Union N.B.
3686.	Chillicothe	First N.B.
3712.	Liberty	First N.B.
3718.	Springfield	Central N.B.
3754.	Harrisonville	First N.B.
3760.	Kansas City	N.B. of Commerce
3793.	Kansas City	German American N.B
3841.	Joplin	First N.B.
3863.	Kansas City	Nat. Exchange Bank
3904.	Kansas City	Midland N.B.
3946.	Trenton	Grundy County N.B.
3957.	Trenton	First N.B.
3959.	Nevada	First N.B.
4000.	Moberly	First N.B.
4010.	Hannibal	First N.B.
4048.	Saint Louis	Continental N.B.
4053.	Saint Joseph	Schuster-Hax N.B.
4057.	Lamar	First N.B.
4079.	Carrollton	First N.B.
4083.	Brunswick	First N.B.
4111.	Chillicothe	Citizens' N.B.
4141.	Odessa	N.B. of Odessa
4151.	Hamilton	First N.B.
4157.	Independence	First N.B.
4160.	Stewartsville	First N.B.
4174.	Hopkins	First N.B.
4178.	Saint Louis	N.B. of Commerce
4215.	Plattsburg	First N.B.
4225.	Pierce City	First N.B.
4228.	Saint Joseph	State N.B.
4232.	Saint Louis	N.B. of the Republic
4243.	Maryville	Maryville N.B.
4251.	Kansas City	Aetna N.B.
4259.	Cameron	First N.B.
4262.	Saint Louis	Laclede N.B.
4329.	Platte City	First N.B.
4360.	Springfield	American N.B.
4373.	King City	First N.B. and Trust Co.
4381.	Kansas City	Inter-State N.B.
4392.	Sedalia	Sedalia N.B.
4409.	Aurora	First N.B.
4425.	Joplin	Joplin N.B.
4441.	Carthage	Central N.B.
4464.	Kansas City	Metropolitan N.B.
4475.	Carterville	First N.B.
4494.	Kansas City	Missouri N.B.
4575.	Saint Louis	Chemical N.B.
4611.	Cape Girardeau	First N.B.
4786.	Kansas City	Continental N.B.
4815.	Carthage	Carthage N.B.
4933.	Trenton	Trenton N.B.
4939.	Saint Joseph	First N.B.
5002.	Saint Louis	Merchants-Laclede N.B.
5036.	West Plains	First N.B.
5082.	Springfield	Nat. Exchange Bank
5107.	Kirksville	N.B. of Kirksville
5138.	Kansas City	New England N.B.
5156.	Warrensburg	People's N.B.
5172.	Saint Louis	State N.B.
5209.	Springfield	Union N.B.
5250.	Kansas City	City N.B.
5388.	Washington	First N.B.
5515.	Sarcoxie	First N.B.
5544.	Lathrop	First N.B.
5780.	Savannah	First N.B.
5788.	Saint Louis	Mechanics' N.B.
5794.	Paris	Paris N.B.
5827.	Gallatin	First N.B.
5871.	Kirksville	Baird N.B.
5973.	Monett	First N.B.
6242.	Burlington Junction	First N.B.
6272.	Saint Joseph	Tootle-Lacy N.B.
6343.	Harrisonville	Citizens' N.B.
6369.	Jasper	First N.B.
6382.	Neosho	First N.B.
6383.	King City	Citizens' N.B.
6405.	Butler	Bates N.B.
6549.	Ridgeway	First N.B.
6635.	Hannibal	Hannibal N.B.
6773.	Saint Louis	Washington N.B.
6875.	Centralia	First N.B.
6885.	Campbell	First N.B.
6926.	Cowgill	First N.B.
7066.	Marceline	First N.B.
7094.	Liberal	First N.B.
7154.	Pleasant Hill	Farmers' N.B.
7179.	Saint Louis	Bankers Worlds Fair N.B.
7205.	Albany	First N.B.
7256.	Versailles	First N.B.
7271.	Bolivar	First N.B.
7282.	Mountain Grove	First N.B.
7351.	Braymer	First N.B.
7460.	Jamesport	First N.B.
7494.	Jackson	People's N.B.
7570.	Saint Louis	American Exchange N.B.
7573.	Bosworth	First N.B.
7643.	Manchester	First N.B.
7656.	Seneca	First N.B.
7684.	Golden City	First N.B.

Charter #	City	Name of Bank
7715.	Saint Louis	Mechanics-American N.B.
7729.	Canton	First N.B.
7741.	Excelsior Springs	First N.B.
7806.	Clinton	Clinton N.B.
7808.	Saint Louis	City N.B.
7853.	Linn Creek	First N.B.
7884.	Polo	First N.B.
7900.	Ludlow	First N.B.
7921.	Salem	First N.B.
8009.	Bethany	First N.B.
8011.	Wellston	First N.B.
8016.	Webb City	N.B. of Webb City
8021.	Saint Joseph	Burnes N.B.
8276.	Kirksville	Citizens' N.B.
8358.	Fulton	First N.B.
8359.	Salisbury	Farmers and Merchants' N.B.
8363.	Salisbury	First N.B.
8407.	Cainesville	First N.B.
8455.	Saint Louis	Central N.B.
8509.	Clinton	People's N.B.
8570.	Green City	American N.B.
8657.	Ludlow	Farmers' N.B.
8660.	Kansas City	Central N.B.
8738.	Kansas City	N.B. of the Republic
8877.	Cabool	First N.B.
8914.	Steelville	First N.B.
8916.	Fairview	First N.B.
8947.	Joplin	Cunningham N.B.
8979.	Cassville	First N.B.
9029.	Green City	City N.B.
9042.	Saint Joseph	American N.B.
9137.	Shelbina	Shelbina N.B.
9172.	Kansas City	Security N.B.
9236.	Kansas City	Traders' N.B.
9297.	Saint Louis	Mercantile N.B.
9311.	Kansas City	Southwest N.B.
9315.	Springfield	Merchants' N.B.
9382.	Nevada	Thornton N.B.
9383.	Kansas City	Park N.B.
9404.	Kansas City	Gate City N.B.
9460.	Saint Louis	Broadway N.B.
9490.	Edina	First N.B.
9519.	Windsor	First N.B.
9560.	Kansas City	Drovers N.B.
9677.	Kansas City	Nat. Reserve Bank
9928.	Chaffee	First N.B.
9932.	Seymour	People's N.B.
10009.	Marshfield	First N.B.
10039.	Kansas City	Commonwealth N.B.
10055.	El Dorado Springs	First N.B.
10074.	Springfield	McDaniel N.B.
10122.	Purdy	First N.B.
10231.	Kansas City	N.B. of Commerce
10367.	Harlem, North Kansas City	N.B. of Harlem
10375.	Adrian	First N.B.
10384.	Holden	First N.B.
10413.	Kansas City	Stock Yards N.B.
10633.	Golden City	Citizens' N.B.
10695.	Lebanon	First N.B.
10784.	Caruthersville	First N.B.
10892.	Kansas City	Midwest N.B. and Trust Co.
10915.	Boonville	Boonville N.B.
11037.	Kansas City	Nat. City Bank
11235.	Montgomery City	First N.B.
11320.	Dexter	First N.B.
11344.	Kansas City	Fidelity N.B. and Trust Co.
11366.	Saint Louis	Saint Louis N.B.
11372.	Sweet Springs	First N.B.
11377.	Kansas City	Continental N.B. of Jackson Co.
11402.	Perryville	First N.B.
11467.	Stoutland	First N.B.
11472.	Kansas City	Columbia N.B.
11491.	Kansas City	Central Exchange N.B.
11919.	Cardwell	First N.B.
11973.	Saint Louis	Republic N.B.
11989.	Saint Louis	Nat. City Bank
12010.	Purdy	Purdy N.B.
12066.	Saint Louis	Security N.B. Savings and Trust Co.
12216.	Saint Louis	Saint Louis N.B.
12220.	Saint Louis	Grand N.B.
12260.	Kansas City	Continental N.B. and Trust Co..
12329.	Clayton	Clayton N.B.
12333.	Clayton	First N.B.
12389.	Saint Louis	Telegraphers' N.B.
12413.	Adrian	N.B. of Adrian
12452.	Steele	First N.B.
12491.	Saint Louis	Twelfth Street N.B.
12506.	Saint Louis	American Exchange N.B.
12643.	Saint Louis	Cherokee N.B.
12674.	Ridgeway	Farmers' N.B.
12686.	Kansas City	New England N.B. and Trust Co.
12770.	Springfield	New First N.B.
12781.	Webster Grove	First N.B.
12794.	Kansas City	Drovers N.B.
12815.	Parkville	First N.B.
12820.	Brookfield	First N.B.
12907.	Oran	First N.B.
12916.	Saint Louis	Boatmen's N.B.
12955.	Maplewood	Citizens N.B.
13142.	Jefferson City	Exchange N.B.
13162.	Joplin	Conqueror First N.B.
13264.	St. Louis	South Side N.B.
13268.	Unionville	N.B. of Unionville
13270.	St. Louis	Vandeventer N.B.

Charter #	City	Name of Bank
13293.	Ludlow	Ludlow N.B.
13367.	Versailles	First N.B.
13376.	St. Louis	Plaza N.B.
13481.	Clayton	Clayton N.B.
13504.	Mount Vernon	First N.B.
13514.	Luxemburg	Lafayette N.B. and Trust Co.
13546.	Cowgill	First N.B.
13690.	North Kansas City	N.B. in North Kansas City
13726.	St. Louis	American Exchange N.B.
13736.	Kansas City	Union N.B.
13875.	Liberty	National Commercial Bank
13936.	Kansas City	City N.B. and Trust Co.
14092.	Caruthersville	N.B. of Caruthersville
14119.	Butler	First N.B.
14128.	St. Louis	South Side N.B.
14196.	Lamar	First N.B.

MONTANA

Charter #	City	Name of Bank
1649.	Helena	First N.B.
1960.	Helena	Montana N.B.
1975.	Deer Lodge	First N.B.
2027.	Bozeman	First N.B.
2105.	Helena	People's N.B.
2106.	Missoula	First N.B.
2476.	Great Falls	Northwestern N.B.
2566.	Butte	First N.B.
2732.	Helena	Merchants' N.B.
2752.	Miles City	First N.B.
2757.	Helena	Second N.B.
2803.	Bozeman	Bozeman N.B.
2813.	Helena	Montana N.B.
3006.	Livingston	First N.B.
3075.	Bozeman	Gallatin Valley N.B.
3097.	Billings	First N.B.
3120.	Dillon	First N.B.
3173.	Dillon	Dillon N.B.
3275.	Miles City	Stock Growers' N.B.
3375.	White Sulphur Springs	First N.B.
3525.	Great Falls	First N.B.
3605.	Livingston	Nat. Park Bank
3965.	Anaconda	First N.B.
3995.	Missoula	Western Montana N.B.
4117.	Livingston	Livingston N.B.
4194.	Fort Benton	Stockmen's N.B.
4283.	Butte City	Silver Bow N.B.
4323.	Boulder	First N.B.
4396.	Helena	American N.B.
4406.	Helena	Helena N.B.
4434.	Great Falls	Merchants' N.B.
4541.	Great Falls	Great Falls N.B.
4572.	Castle	First N.B.
4586.	Kalispell	First N.B.
4590.	Big Timber	First N.B.
4593.	Billings	Yellowstone N.B.
4600.	Neihart	First N.B.
4651.	Kalispell	Globe N.B.
4658.	Philipsburg	First N.B.
4803.	Kalispell	Conrad N.B.
4843.	Philipsburg	Merchants and Miners' N.B.
4932.	Big Timber	Big Timber N.B.
4968.	Bozeman	Commercial N.B.
5015.	Miles City	Commercial N.B.
5671.	Helena	N.B. of Montana
5676.	Havre	First N.B.
6097.	Chinook	First N.B.
7101.	Glendive	First N.B.
7172.	Plains	First N.B.
7274.	Lewistown	First N.B.
7320.	Forsyth	First N.B.
7441.	Bozeman	N.B. of Gallatin Valley
7644.	Harlem	First N.B.
7990.	Glasgow	First N.B.
8055.	Glendive	Merchants' N.B.
8168.	Culbertson	First N.B.
8259.	Wibaux	First N.B.
8539.	Moore	First N.B.
8589.	Whitefish	First N.B.
8635.	Kalispell	Kalispell N.B.
8655.	Glasgow	Glasgow N.B.
8669.	Laurel	First N.B.
8716.	Laurel	Citizens' N.B.
9004.	Sidney	First N.B.
9103.	Ismay	First N.B.
9165.	Roundup	First N.B.
9215.	Hardin	First N.B.
9270.	Harlowton	First N.B.
9337.	Three Forks	First N.B.
9355.	Billings	Merchants' N.B.
9396.	Columbus	First N.B.
9440.	Havre	Citizens' N.B.
9449.	Polson	First N.B.
9486.	Hamilton	First N.B.
9520.	Valier	First N.B.
9574.	Cut Bank	First N.B.
9583.	Anaconda	Anaconda N.B.
9594.	Libby	First N.B.
9738.	Malta	First N.B.
9759.	Conrad	First N.B.
9782.	Havre	Havre N.B.
9789.	Saco	First N.B.
9841.	Red Lodge	United States N.B.
9864.	Ronan	First N.B.
9899.	Deer Lodge	United States N.B.
9982.	Townsend	First N.B.
10053.	Chinook	Farmers' N.B.
10438.	Plentywood	First N.B.
10443.	Baker	First N.B.

Charter #	City	Name of Bank
10530.	Great Falls	Commercial N.B.
10539.	Sidney	Yellowstone Valley N.B.
10552.	Sidney	Farmers' N.B.
10625.	Stanford	First N.B.
10675.	Roundup	Roundup N.B.
10709.	Stevensville	First N.B.
10715.	Hobson	First N.B.
10769.	Bridger	First N.B.
10803.	Geraldine	First N.B.
10809.	Broad View	First N.B.
10819.	Denton	First N.B.
10838.	Scobey	First N.B.
10881.	Richey	First N.B.
10883.	Browning	First N.B.
10884.	Miles City	Miles City N.B.
10885.	Poplar	First N.B.
10907.	Judith Gap	First N.B.
10910.	Winsdale	First N.B.
10917.	Baylor	First N.B.
10922.	Pompey's Pillar	First N.B.
10926.	Sidney	Sidney N.B.
10928.	Intake	First N.B.
10929.	Joplin	First N.B.
10933.	Billings	Montana N.B.
10934.	Carlyle	First N.B.
10937.	Choteau	First N.B.
10939.	Grass Range	First N.B.
10942.	Forsyth	American N.B.
10952.	Geyser	First N.B.
10953.	Shelby	First N.B.
10985.	Bainville	First N.B.
10986.	Reserve	First N.B.
10991.	Roy	First N.B.
10995.	Carter	First N.B.
10996.	Three Forks	American N.B.
11000.	Livingston	Northwestern N.B.
11004.	Big Sandy	First N.B.
11006.	Winifred	First N.B.
11008.	Twin Bridges	First N.B.
11013.	Molt, Stickley	First N.B.
11017.	Rapelje, Lake Basin	First N.B.
11024.	Whitehall	First N.B.
11026.	Hysham	First N.B.
11027.	Brockton	First N.B.
11030.	Brady	First N.B.
11032.	Savage	First N.B.
11036.	Wolf Point	First N.B.
11040.	Malta	Malta N.B.
11048.	Nashua	First N.B.
11061.	Froid	First N.B.
11063.	Big Sandy	Farmers' N.B.
11066.	Absarokee	Stillwater Valley N.B.
11070.	Hardin	Stockmen's N.B.
11074.	Plevna	First N.B.
11075.	Wolf Point	Citizens' N.B.
11077.	Havre	Montana N.B.
11078.	Raymond	First N.B.
11085.	Harlowton	Farmers' N.B.
11086.	Dodson	First N.B.
11089.	Galata	First N.B.
11095.	Raynesford	Stockmen's N.B.
11096.	Fresno	First N.B.
11097.	Opheim	First N.B.
11098.	Scobey	Merchants' N.B.
11101.	Circle	First N.B.
11105.	Chester	First N.B.
11131.	Highwood	First N.B.
11134.	Oswego	First N.B.
11160.	Lodge Grass	First N.B.
11165.	Charlo	First N.B.
11176.	Lambert	First N.B.
11199.	Savoy	First N.B.
11203.	Rudyard	First N.B.
11209.	Westby	First N.B.
11220.	Columbus	Stockmen's N.B.
11269.	Musselshell	First N.B.
11298.	Bridger	American N.B.
11307.	Fairfield	First N.B.
11334.	Reed Point	First N.B.
11335.	Wilsall	First N.B.
11350.	Antelope	First N.B.
11382.	Ekalaka	First N.B.
11391.	Winnett	First N.B.
11418.	Broadus	First N.B.
11429.	Great Falls	Northern N.B.
11437.	Rosebud	First N.B.
11465.	Ingomar	First N.B.
11475.	McCabe	First N.B.
11492.	Lima	Security N.B.
11493.	Jordan	First N.B.
11673.	Belt	First N.B.
11696.	Billings	American N.B.
12015.	Fairview	First N.B.
12361.	Three Forks	Labor N.B. of Montana
12407.	Billings	Midland N.B.
12536.	Miles City	First N.B.
12542.	Anaconda	N.B. of Anaconda
12585.	Hysham	First N.B.
12608.	Lewistown	N.B. of Lewistown
12679.	Sidney	Richland N.B.
13384.	Livingston	National Park Bank
13417.	Harlowton	Continental N.B.
13837.	Chinook	Farmers N.B.
14334.	Butte	Miners N.B.

NEBRASKA

Charter #	City	Name of Bank
209.	Omaha	First N.B.
1417.	Nebraska City	Otoe County N.B.
1633.	Omaha	Omaha N.B.
1679.	Omaha	Central N.B.
1798.	Lincoln	First N.B.
1846.	Brownville	First N.B.
1855.	Nebraska City	Nebraska City N.B.
1899.	Lincoln	State N.B.
1914.	Plattsmouth	First N.B.

Charter #	City	Name of Bank
1974.	Fremont	First N.B.
2121.	Ashland	First N.B.
2357.	Beatrice	First N.B.
2528.	Hastings	First N.B.
2536.	Nebraska City	Merchants' N.B.
2665.	Omaha	Nebraska N.B.
2683.	York	First N.B.
2706.	Crete	First N.B.
2724.	Blair	First N.B.
2746.	Falls City	First N.B.
2750.	Lincoln	Lincoln N.B.
2756.	Hebron	First N.B.
2771.	Seward	First N.B.
2774.	Norfolk	First N.B.
2775.	Omaha	Merchants' N.B.
2778.	Schuyler	First N.B.
2779.	Grand Island	First N.B.
2780.	Wahoo	First N.B.
2806.	Kearney	First N.B
2807.	Columbus	First N.B.
2811.	Red Cloud	First N.B.
2825.	Pawnee City	First N.B.
2848.	Fremont	Fremont N.B.
2871.	Central City	First N.B.
2897.	Aurora	First N.B.
2902.	David City	First N.B.
2921.	Ashland	N.B. of Ashland
2955.	Tecumseh	First N.B.
2960.	Friend	First N.B.
2964.	Fullerton	First N.B.
2978.	Omaha	United States N.B.
2988.	Lincoln	Capital N.B.
2991.	Wilber	First N.B.
2994.	Fairbury	First N.B.
3057.	Minden	First N.B.
3059.	North Bend	First N.B.
3060.	Seward	Jones N.B.
3081.	Beatrice	Beatrice N.B.
3083.	Syracuse	First N.B.
3086.	Hastings	Exchange N.B.
3099.	Hastings	City N.B.
3101.	Grand Island	Citizens' N.B.
3117.	Exeter	Exeter N.B.
3118.	Wahoo	Saunders County N.B.
3121.	Exeter	First N.B.
3126.	Saint Paul	First N.B.
3129.	Saint Paul	Saint Paul N.B.
3152.	Schuyler	Schuyler N.B.
3162.	York	York N.B.
3163.	Omaha	Commercial N.B.
3181.	Red Cloud	Red Cloud N.B.
3188.	Fremont	Farmers and Merchants' N.B.
3201.	Kearney	Kearney N.B.
3208.	Holdrege	First N.B.
3230.	Fairmont	First N.B.
3238.	Humboldt	First N.B.
3240.	Sutton	First N.B.
3292.	Lexington	First N.B.
3302.	Arapahoe	First N.B.
3339.	Ord	First N.B.
3340.	West Point	West Point N.B.
3342.	Orleans	First N.B.
3343.	Auburn	First N.B.
3347.	Norfolk	Norfolk N.B.
3364.	Stanton	First N.B.
3370.	West Point	First N.B.
3373.	Loup City	First N.B.
3379.	McCook	First N.B.
3390.	Dorchester	First N.B.
3392.	Wayne	First N.B.
3403.	Greenwood	First N.B.
3419.	Blue Hill	First N.B.
3424.	O'Neill	First N.B.
3445.	Broken Bow	Custer County N.B.
3449.	Broken Bow	First N.B.
3481.	Ord	Ord N.B.
3483.	Indianola	First N.B.
3493.	Fairfield	First N.B.
3495.	Nelson	First N.B.
3496.	North Platte	First N.B.
3516.	Omaha	Union N.B.
3523.	Weeping Water	First N.B.
3526.	Kearney	Buffalo County N.B.
3529.	Superior	First N.B.
3549.	Franklin	First N.B.
3571.	Lincoln	German N.B.
3574.	Clay Center	First N.B.
3580.	Alma	First N.B.
3603.	Omaha	State N.B.
3611.	South Omaha	South Omaha N.B.
3619.	Beaver City	First N.B.
3627.	Ponca	First N.B.
3628.	Auburn	Carson N.B.
3652.	Ogallala	First N.B.
3653.	Sutton	Sutton N.B.
3674.	Rulo	First N.B.
3725.	Tobias	First N.B.
3732.	Hastings	Nebraska N.B.
3741.	Norfolk	Citizens' N.B.
3773.	Madison	First N.B.
3801.	David City	Central Nebraska N.B.
3823.	Chadron	First N.B.
3875.	Holdrege	Holdrege N.B.
3891.	Saint Paul	Citizens' N.B.
3921.	Gibbon	First N.B.
3927.	Broken Bow	Central Nebraska N.B.
3934.	David City	City N.B.
3939.	Wood River	First N.B.
3958.	Kearney	City N.B.
3960.	Albion	First N.B.
3999.	Elm Creek	First N.B.
4024.	North Platte	North Platte N.B.
4029.	Wisner	First N.B.
4042.	Shelton	First N.B.
4043.	Ravenna	First N.B.
4052.	Geneva	First N.B.

Charter #	City	Name of Bank
4078.	Pawnee City	Farmers' N.B.
4080.	Liberty	First N.B.
4087.	Omaha	American N.B.
4089.	Ainsworth	First N.B.
4110.	Neligh	First N.B.
4129.	Harvard	First N.B.
4148.	Beatrice	German N.B.
4161.	Lexington	Dawson County N.B
4163.	Sterling	First N.B.
4165.	Cozard	First N.B.
4170.	Grant	First N.B.
4173.	Albion	Albion N.B.
4176.	Rushville	First N.B.
4185.	Beatrice	Nebraska N.B.
4210.	Wymore	First N.B.
4226.	Alliance	First N.B.
4242.	Creighton	First N.B.
4245.	York	Nebraska N.B.
4270.	Omaha	N.B. of Commerce
4276.	Tecumseh	Tecumseh N.B.
4280.	Pierce	First N.B.
4324.	Tekamah	First N.B.
4345.	Holdrege	City N.B.
4354.	Wayne	Wayne N.B
4357.	Grand Island	Security N.B.
4435.	Lincoln	Columbia N.B.
4484.	Geneva	Geneva N.B.
4504.	Fremont	Commercial N.B.
4528.	Hartington	First N.B.
4557.	South Sioux City	First N.B.
4583.	Arlington	First N.B.
4588.	Auburn	Farmers and Merchants' N.B.
4589.	South Omaha	Packers' N.B.
4606.	Lincoln	American Exchange N.B.
4610.	Oakland	First N.B.
4632.	South Omaha	Union Stock Yards N.B.
4791.	Pender	First N.B.
4820.	Crete	Crete N.B.
4890.	Gothenburg	First N.B.
4895.	De Witt	First N.B.
4935.	York	City N.B.
5180.	Columbus	Commercial N.B.
5189.	Genoa	First N.B.
5213.	Lincoln	City N.B.
5281.	Weeping Water	City N.B.
5282.	Newman Grove	First N.B.
5297.	Hooper	First N.B.
5308.	Pender	Pender N.B.
5337.	Humphrey	First N.B.
5346.	Saint Edward	First N.B.
5368.	Wakefield	First N.B.
5384.	Fullerton	Fullerton N.B.
5397.	Superior	Superior N.B.
5400.	Hartington	Hartington N.B.
5419.	Loomis	First N.B.
5440.	Elgin	First N.B.
5657.	Alliance	Alliance N.B.
5690.	Neligh	Neligh N.B.
5770.	O'Neill	O'Neill N.B.
5787.	Elmwood	First N.B.
5793.	Saint Edward	Smith N.B.
5937.	Pilger	First N.B.
5941.	Pilger	Farmers' N.B.
5957.	Carroll	First N.B.
5995.	Broken Bow	Custer N.B.
6166.	Tecumseh	Citizens' N.B.
6201.	Nebr. Sidney	First N.B.
6221.	Lyons	First N.B.
6240.	Scottsbluff	First N.B.
6282.	Gothenburg	Gothenburg N.B.
6378.	Valentine	First N.B.
6415.	Wilber	N.B. of Wilber
6464.	Anoka	Anoka N.B.
6489.	Atkinson	First N.B.
6493.	Osceola	First N.B.
6503.	Bloomfield	First N.B.
6506.	Cambridge	First N.B.
6541.	Pawnee City	N.B. of Pawnee City
6600.	Kearney	Central N.B.
6805.	Genoa	Genoa N.B.
6818.	Beemer	First N.B.
6866.	Wisner	Citizens' N.B.
6900.	Crawford	First N.B.
6901.	Scribner	First N.B.
6939.	Clarks	First N.B.
6947.	Stuart	First N.B.
7026.	Mitchell	First N.B.
7065.	Humboldt	N.B. of Humboldt
7204.	Elwood	First N.B.
7239.	Lincoln	N.B. of Commerce
7277.	Loup City	First N.B.
7325.	Spencer	First N.B.
7329.	Norfolk	Nebraska N.B.
7333.	Dodge	First N.B.
7340.	Burwell	First N.B.
7355.	Diller	First N.B.
7384.	Sargent	First N.B.
7393.	Ansley	First N.B.
7421.	Randolph	First N.B.
7425.	Emerson	First N.B.
7449.	North Bend	N.B. of North Bend
7477.	Randolph	Security N.B.
7520.	Oxford	First N.B.
7574.	Spalding	First N.B.
7578.	Tobias	Tobias N.B.
7622.	Greeley	First N.B.
7737.	University Place	First N.B.
7821.	York	Farmers' N.B.
7836.	Stanton	Stanton N.B.
7861.	Wilcox	First N.B.

Charter #	City	Name of Bank
7881.	Atkinson	Atkinson N.B.
7925.	Overton	First N.B.
7949.	Shelby	First N.B.
8027.	Blair	Blair N.B.
8031.	Hayes Center	First N.B.
8062.	Gering	First N.B.
8093.	Litchfield	First N.B.
8097.	Bradshaw	First N.B.
8105.	Benedict	First N.B.
8113.	Gothenburg	Citizens' N.B.
8161.	Johnson	First N.B.
8172.	Gresham	First N.B.
8183.	Henderson	First N.B.
8186.	Crofton	First N.B.
8218.	Trenton	First N.B.
8246.	Aurora	Fidelity N.B.
8282.	Cedar Rapids	First N.B.
8285.	Hampton	First N.B.
8286.	Stromsburg	First N.B.
8317.	Madison	Farmers' N.B.
8328.	Columbus	Central N.B.
8335.	Wynot	First N.B.
8372.	Allen	First N.B.
8383.	Johnson	German N.B.
8385.	Central City	Central City N.B.
8400.	Marquette	First N.B.
8413.	Wolbach	First N.B.
8466.	Bertrand	First N.B.
8469.	Bazile Mills	First N.B.
8521.	Gordon	First N.B.
8533.	Polk	First N.B.
8567.	Orleans	Citizens' N.B.
8651.	Kearney	Commercial N.B.
8685.	Walthill	First N.B.
8760.	Hay Springs	First N.B.
8797.	Creighton	Creighton N.B.
8811.	Utica	First N.B.
8812.	Curtis	First N.B.
8823.	McCook	McCook N.B.
8851.	Lawrence	First N.B.
8863.	Bancroft	First N.B.
8885.	Lincoln	Central N.B.
8888.	Harrison	First N.B.
8949.	South Omaha	Live Stock N.B.
8975.	Campbell	First N.B.
8988.	Decatur	First N.B.
8992.	Ainsworth	N.B. of Ainsworth
8995.	Fairbury	Bonham N.B.
9056.	Aurora	Aurora N.B.
9092.	Amherst	First N.B.
9138.	Wymore	City N.B.
9191.	Rushville	Stockmen's N.B.
9200.	Shelton	Shelton N.B.
9217.	Tilden	First N.B.
9223.	Adams	First N.B.
9244.	Wayne	Citizens' N.B.
9258.	Callaway	First N.B.
9395.	Grand Island	Grand Island N.B.
9400.	Minden	Minden Exchange N.B
9436.	McCook	Citizens' N.B.
9448.	Bristow	First N.B.
9466.	Omaha	City N.B.
9504.	Plainview	First N.B.
9581.	Scottsbluff	Scottsbluff N.B.
9591.	Craig	First N.B.
9623.	Butte	First N.B.
9653.	Morrill	First N.B.
9665.	Naper	First N.B.
9666.	Bayard	First N.B.
9671.	Winnebago	First N.B.
9694.	Gering	Gering N.B.
9711.	Bridgeport	First N.B.
9730.	Omaha	Corn Exchange N.B.
9731.	Crete	City N.B.
9741.	Lodge Pole	First N.B.
9762.	Imperial	First N.B.
9772.	Havelock	First N.B.
9785.	Lynch	First N.B.
9790.	Chappell	First N.B.
9793.	Laurel	First N.B.
9796.	Coleridge	First N.B.
9816.	Walthill	Walthill N.B.
9831.	Lehigh	First N.B.
9908.	South Omaha	Stock Yards N.B.
9979.	Laurel	Laurel N.B.
9984.	Wakefield	Farmers' N.B.
9994.	Wausa	First N.B.
10011.	Tilden	Tilden N.B.
10017.	Wausa	Commercial N.B.
10021.	Madison	Madison N.B.
10022.	Oakland	Farmers and Merchants' N.B.
10023.	Coleridge	Coleridge N.B.
10025.	Belden	First N.B.
10033.	Brunswick	First N.B.
10081.	Oshkosh	First N.B.
10242.	Hemingford	First N.B.
10340.	Fairbury	Farmers and Merchants' N.B.
10970.	Hershey	First N.B.
11071.	Valentine	Farmers' N.B.
11426.	Bassett	First N.B.
11829.	Omaha	Peters N.B.
11835.	South Sioux City	First N.B.
12225.	Unadilla	First N.B.
12342.	Lincoln	Lincoln State N.B.
12495.	Hemingford	Citizens' N.B.
12552.	Harrison	Sioux N.B.
12625.	Morrill	First N.B.
12626.	Mitchell	First N.B.
13013.	Kearney	City N.B.
13017.	Lincoln	City N.B.
13101.	Osmond	First N.B.
13138.	Springview	First N.B.
13139.	Ainsworth	Commercial N.B.
13148.	Central City	Farmers N.B.
13158.	Arcadia	First N.B.
13176.	Shelton	First N.B.
13182.	Laurel	Security N.B.
13189.	Exeter	Wallace N.B.
13243.	Exeter	Exeter N.B.
13244.	Primrose	First N.B.
13271.	Lyman	First N.B.
13281.	Wakefield	Wakefield N.B.
13316.	Minatare	First N.B.
13322.	Minden	Nebraska N.B.
13333.	Lincoln	Continental N.B.
13339.	Oakdale	First N.B.
13408.	Freemont	Stephens N.B.
13415.	Wayne	State N.B.
13419.	Grant	Farmers N.B.
13420.	Kimball	American N.B.
13423.	Lewellen	First N.B.
13424.	Grand Island	Nebraska N.B.
13425.	Sidney	American N.B.
13426.	Cozard	First N.B.
13429.	Bushnell	First N.B.
13431.	Seward	Cattle N.B.
13433.	Glenvil	First N.B.
13435.	Ashland	Farmers & Merchants N.B.
13440.	Kimball	Kimball N.B.
13446.	Overton	Overton N.B.
13453.	Pilger	Farmers N.B.
13456.	Doniphan	N.B. of Doniphan
13461.	Greeley	City N.B.
13462.	St. Paul	Citizens N.B.
13463.	St. Paul	St. Paul N.B.
13464.	Tobias	Citizens N.B.
13515.	Hastings	Hastings N.B.
13557.	Ord	First N.B.
13568.	Neligh	N.B. of Neligh
13582.	Norfolk	De Lay N.B.
13591.	Creighton	American N.B.
13617.	Alliance	Nebraska N.B.
13620.	Loup City	First N.B.
13953.	Hastings	City N.B.
14004.	Omaha	Packers N.B.
14017.	Aurora	First N.B.
14018.	Grand Island	Overland N.B.
14073.	Exeter	First N.B.
14083.	Superior	Security N.B.
14174.	Ashland	Citizens N.B.
14194.	David City	City N.B.
14256.	Scribner	First N.B.
14282.	Wymore	Wymore N.B.
14308.	West Point	Farmers & Merchants N.B.
14339.	Norfolk	N.B. of Norfolk
14340.	Grand Island	Commercial N.B.

NEVADA

Charter #	City	Name of Bank
1331.	Austin	First N.B. of Nevada
2478.	Reno	First N.B.
3575.	Winnemucca	First N.B.
7038.	Reno	Farmers and Merchants' N.B.
7654.	Lovelock	First N.B.
7743.	Elko	First N.B.
8424.	Reno	Reno N.B.
8530.	Tonopah	Nevada First N.B.
8561.	Ely	First N.B.
8686.	Rhyolite	First N.B.
9078.	Goldfield	First N.B.
9242.	Carson City	First N.B.
9310.	Ely	Ely N.B.
9452.	McGill	McGill N.B.
9578.	East Ely	Copper N.B.
11784.	Eureka	Farmers and Merchants' N.B.

NEW HAMPSHIRE

Charter #	City	Name of Bank
19.	Portsmouth	First N.B.
84.	Nashua	First N.B.
318.	Concord	First N.B.
401.	Portsmouth	Nat. Mechanics' and Traders' Bank
499.	Derry	Derry N.B.
537.	Charlestown	Connecticut River N.B
559.	Keene	Cheshire N.B.
574.	Manchester	Amoskeag N.B.
576.	Francestown	First N.B.
596.	Claremont	Claremont N.B.
758.	Concord	Nat. State Capital Bank
808.	Lebanon	N.B. of Lebanon
838.	Gonic	First N.B.
877.	Keene	Keene N.B.
887.	Winchester	Winchester N.B.
888.	Newport	First N.B.
946.	Keene	Ashuelot N.B.
1020.	Pittsfield	Pittsfield N.B.
1025.	Portsmouth	Rockingham N.B.
1043.	Dover	Dover N.B.
1052.	Portsmouth	New Hampshire N.B.
1059.	Manchester	Manchester N.B.
1070.	Milford	Souhegan N.B.
1071.	Sandwich	Carroll County N.B.
1087.	Dover	Cochecho N.B.
1145.	Hanover	Dartmouth N.B.
1147.	Exeter	Nat. Granite State Bank
1153.	Manchester	First N.B.
1179.	Peterborough	First N.B.
1180.	Somersworth	First N.B.
1183.	Somersworth	Somersworth N.B.
1242.	East Jaffrey	Monadnock N.B.
1310.	Nashua	Indian Head N.B.
1330.	New Market	New Market N.B.
1333.	Tilton	Citizens' N.B.
1353.	Dover	Strafford N.B.
1486.	Wolfborough	Lake N.B.
1520.	Manchester	Merchants' N.B.
1645.	Laconia	Laconia N.B.
1674.	Warner	Kearsarge N.B.
1688.	Hillsborough	First N.B.
1885.	Littleton	Littleton N.B.
2022.	Farmington	Farmington N.B.
2138.	Rochester	Rochester N.B.
2240.	Nashua	Second N.B.
2299.	Keene	Citizens' N.B.
2362.	Manchester	Second N.B.
2443.	Franklin	Franklin N.B.
2447.	Concord	Mechanics' N.B.
2587.	Plymouth	Pemigewasset N.B.
2600.	Lancaster	Lancaster N.B.
2672.	Portsmouth	First N.B.
2741.	Nashua	First N.B.
3404.	Newport	Citizens' N.B.
4037.	Laconia	People's N.B.
4041.	Colebrook	Colebrook N.B.
4523.	Berlin	Berlin N.B.
4693.	Manchester	N.B. of the Commonwealth
4740.	Lakeport	Lakeport N.B.
4793.	Claremont	People's N.B.
5092.	Woodsville	Woodsville N.B.
5151.	Bristol	First N.B.
5183.	Colebrook	Farmers and Traders' N.B.
5258.	Gorham	Gorham N.B.
5274.	Dover	Merchants' N.B.
5317.	Groveton	Coos County N.B.
5622.	Berlin	City N.B.
8038.	West Derry	First N.B.
8147.	Wolfeboro	Wolfeboro N.B.
9001.	Gorham	White Mountain N.B.
9476.	Conway	Conway N.B.
11893.	Rochester	Public N.B.
12889.	Exeter	Rockingham N.B.
13247.	Wilton	Wilton N.B.
13764.	Farmington	Farmington N.B.
13808.	Groveton	Groveton N.B.
13829.	Claremont	Claremont N.B.
13861.	Rochester	New Public N.B.
14100.	Berlin	Berlin N.B.

NEW JERSEY

Charter #	City	Name of Bank
52.	Newark	First N.B.
208.	New Brunswick	First N.B.
281.	Trenton	First N.B.
288.	Jamesburg	First N.B.
329.	Paterson	First N.B.
362.	Newark	Second N.B.
370.	Vincetown	First N.B.
374.	Jersey City	First N.B.
395.	Somerville	First N.B.
399.	Woodstown	First N.B.
431.	Camden	First N.B.
445.	Red Bank	First N.B.
447.	Plainfield	First N.B.
452.	Freehold	First N.B.
487.	Elizabeth	First N.B.
587.	New Brunswick	N.B. of New Jersey
695.	Jersey City	Second N.B.
810.	Paterson	Second N.B.
860.	Washington	First N.B.
876.	Newton	Merchants' N.B.
881.	Rahway	Union N.B.
892.	Flemington	Hunterdon County N.B.
896.	Rahway	N.B. of Rahway
925.	Newton	Sussex N.B.
951.	Freehold	Freehold Nat. Banking Company
1096.	Belvidere	Belvidere N.B.
1113.	Morristown	Nat. Iron Bank
1114.	Clinton	Clinton N.B.
1168.	Mount Holly	Farmers N.B. of New Jersey
1182.	Jersey City	Hudson County N.B.
1188.	Morristown	First N.B.
1191.	Medford	Burlington County N.B.
1199.	Woodbury	First N.B.
1209.	Camden	Nat. State Bank
1217.	Newark	Essex County N.B.
1220.	Newark	Newark City N.B.
1221.	Sussex	Farmers' N.B.
1222.	Burlington	Mechanics' N.B.
1239.	Phillipsburg	Phillipsburg N.B.
1251.	Newark	Mechanics' N.B.
1259.	Hackettstown	Hackettstown N.B.
1270.	Millville	Millville N.B.
1272.	Lambertville	Lambertville N.B.
1316.	Newark	Nat. Newark & Essex Banking Co.
1317.	Orange	Orange N.B.
1326.	Salem	Salem N.B.
1327.	Trenton	Mechanics' N.B.
1346.	Bridgeton	Cumberland N.B.
1356.	Mount Holly	Mount Holly N.B.
1400.	Toms River	Ocean County N.B.
1436.	Elizabeth	Nat. State Bank
1444.	Hoboken	First N.B.
1452.	Newark	Nat. State Bank
1459.	Frenchtown	Union N.B.
1681.	**Princeton**	**Princeton N.B.**
1737.	**Hightstown**	**First N.B.**
1759.	**Hightstown**	**Central N.B.**
1818.	Newark	Merchants and Manufacturers' N.B.
1905.	Hackensack	First N.B.
2040.	Newark	Manufacturers' N.B.
2045.	Newark	Union N.B.
2076.	Dover	Nat. Union Bank
2083.	Newark	North Ward N.B.
2243.	Plainfield	City N.B.
2246.	Clinton	First N.B.
2257.	Red Bank	Second N.B.
2271.	Bloomsbury	Bloomsbury N.B.
2331.	Flemington	Flemington N.B.
2339.	Lambertville	Amwell N.B.
2343.	Mount Holly	Union N.B.
2399.	Vineland	Vineland N.B.
2509.	Toms River	First N.B.
2527.	Atlantic City	Atlantic City N.B.
2551.	Madison	First N.B.

Charter #	City	Name of Bank
2918.	Vineland	Vineland N.B.
2923.	Swedesboro	Swedesboro N.B.
2999.	Bridgeton	Bridgeton N.B.
3040.	Manasquan	First N.B.
3164.	Keyport	First N.B.
3168.	Cranbury	First N.B.
3372.	Camden	Camden N.B.
3387.	Moorestown	Moorestown N.B.
3451.	Asbury Park	First N.B.
3501.	Allentown	Farmers' N.B.
3572.	Passaic	Passaic N.B.
3621.	Atlantic City	Second N.B.
3680.	Jersey City	Third N.B.
3697.	New Brunswick	People's N.B.
3709.	Trenton	Broad Street N.B.
3716.	Woodbury	Farmers and Mechanics' N.B.
3744.	Hoboken	Second N.B.
3792.	Asbury Park	Asbury Park N.B.
3843.	Glassboro	First N.B.
3866.	Bound Brook	First N.B.
3878.	South Amboy	First N.B.
3922.	Salem	City N.B.
3936.	Gloucester	Gloucester City N.B.
3996.	Haddonfield	Haddonfield N.B.
4056.	Bloomfield	Bloomfield N.B.
4072.	Paterson	Paterson N.B.
4119.	Atlantic Highlands	Atlantic Highlands N.B.
4138.	Long Branch	First N.B.
4147.	Keyport	People's N.B.
4182.	Freehold	Central N.B.
4254.	Hopewell	Hopewell N.B.
4274.	Boonton	Boonton N.B.
4365.	Englewood	Citizens' N.B.
4420.	Atlantic City	Union N.B.
4535.	Red Bank	Navesink N.B.
4719.	Westfield	First N.B.
4724.	Orange	Second N.B.
4766.	East Orange	East Orange N.B.
4872.	Princeton	First N.B.
4942.	Somerville	Second N.B.
4980.	Belvidere	Warren County N.B.
5005.	Rutherford	Rutherford N.B.
5061.	Summit	First N.B.
5121.	Washington	Washington N.B.
5136.	Dover	People's N.B.
5205.	Ridgewood	First N.B.
5208.	Millville	Mechanics' N.B.
5215.	Perth Amboy	First N.B.
5232.	Lakewood	First N.B.
5260.	Rahway	Rahway N.B.
5333.	High Bridge	First N.B.
5363.	Belmar	First N.B.
5387.	Penn's Grove	Penn's Grove N.B.
5403.	Ocean Grove	Ocean Grove N.B.
5416.	Carlstadt	Carlstadt N.B.
5556.	Phillipsburg	Second N.B.
5621.	Blairstown	First N.B.
5712.	Point Pleasant	Ocean County N.B. of Point Pleasant Beach
5718.	Pennington	First N.B.
5730.	Spring Lake, Spring Lake Beach	First N.B.
5839.	Cape May	First N.B.
5884.	Atlantic City	Chelsea N.B.
5921.	Hackensack	Hackensack N.B.
5926.	Seabright	First N.B.
5981.	Paulsboro	First N.B.
6038.	Long Branch	Citizens' N.B.
6060.	Ocean City	First N.B.
6179.	South River	First N.B.
6278.	Wildwood	Marine N.B.
6440.	Matawan	Farmers and Merchants' N.B.
6508.	Pleasantville	First N.B.
6673.	Asbury Park	Seacoast N.B.
6692.	Netcong	Citizens' N.B.
6707.	Elmer	First N.B.
6728.	Mullica Hill	Farmers' N.B.
6823.	Riverside	Riverside N.B.
6912.	Butler	First N.B.
6960.	Bernardsville	Bernardsville N.B.
7131.	Caldwell	Caldwell N.B.
7171.	Cranford	Cranford N.B.
7223.	Englishtown	First N.B.
7265.	Williamstown	First N.B.
7291.	Lakewood	People's N.B.
7364.	Branchville	First N.B.
7436.	Freehold	Nat. Freehold Banking Co.
7754.	Metuchen	Metuchen N.B.
7799.	Hackensack	People's N.B.
7945.	Cape May Court House	First N.B.
7981.	Irvington	Irvington N.B.
7983.	Collingswood	Collingswood N.B.
8007.	Pedricktown	First N.B.
8129.	Pemberton	People's N.B.
8227.	Hamburg	Hardyston N.B.
8254.	New Egypt	First N.B.
8267.	Hackettstown	People's N.B.
8299.	Woodbridge	First N.B.
8323.	Merchantville	First N.B.
8382.	Belleville	First N.B.
8390.	Guttenberg	First N.B.
8394.	Closter	Closter N.B.
8401.	Edgewater	First N.B.
8437.	Roosevelt	First N.B.
8454.	Bayonne	First N.B.
8462.	Garfield	First N.B.
8483.	Roselle	First N.B.
8484.	Riverton	Cinnaminson N.B.
8497.	Barnegat	First N.B.
8500.	Pitman	Pitman N.B.
8501.	Dunellen	First N.B.
8512.	Bound Brook	Bound Brook N.B.
8566.	Rockaway	First N.B.
8582.	Mays Landing	First N.B.
8614.	Tenafly	First N.B.
8623.	Westfield	People's N.B.
8627.	Arlington	First N.B.
8661.	Millburn	First N.B.
8681.	Tuckahoe	Tuckahoe N.B.
8704.	Beverly	First N.B.
8777.	Westwood	First N.B.
8779.	Milford	First N.B.
8800.	Atlantic City	Boardwalk N.B.
8829.	Little Falls	Little Falls N.B.
8874.	Fort Lee	First N.B.
9061.	White House Station	First N.B.
9213.	Manasquan	Manasquan N.B.
9229.	Jersey City	Merchants' N.B.
9260.	Califon	Califon N.B.
9268.	Bordentown	First N.B.
9285.	Cape May	Merchants' N.B.
9339.	Montclair, Upper Montclair	First N.B.
9367.	Ramsey	First N.B.
9380.	Secaucus	First N.B.
9391.	North Plainfield	Borough N.B.
9413.	Haddon Heights	Haddon Heights N.B.
9420.	Lodi	First N.B.
9498.	Bridgeton	Farmers and Merchants' N.B.
9542.	West Orange	First N.B.
9544.	Town of Union, Weehawken	First N.B.
9577.	Montclair	Essex N.B.
9597.	Blackwood	First N.B.
9605.	Newark	American N.B.
9612.	Caldwell	Citizens' N.B.
9661.	East Newark	First N.B.
9779.	Berlin	Berlin N.B.
9780.	Ridgefield Park	First N.B.
9833.	Blairstown	People's N.B.
9867.	West Hoboken	N.B. of North Hudson
9912.	Newark	Broad and Market N.B.
10036.	Port Norris	First N.B.
10110.	Eatontown	First N.B.
10118.	Hope	First N.B.
10142.	Westfield	N.B. of Westfield
10224.	Bradley Beach	First N.B.
10248.	Ventnor City, Atlantic City	Ventnor City N.B.
10376.	Keansburg	Keansburg N.B.
10417.	Lyndhurst	First N.B.
10430.	Westville	First N.B.
10440.	Minotola	First N.B.
10471.	Clayton	Clayton N.B.
10712.	Bloomsbury	Citizens' N.B.
10787.	Pompton Lakes	First N.B.
10823.	Absecon	First N.B.
10831.	Florence	First N.B.
10840.	Farmingdale	First N.B.
10919.	Verona	Verona N.B.
10932.	Asbury Park	Merchants' N.B.
10935.	Milltown	First N.B.
11081.	Wrightstown	First N.B.
11147.	Clementon	Clementon N.B.
11351.	Perth Amboy	City N.B.
11361.	Dumont	Dumont N.B.
11368.	Bergenfield	Bergenfield N.B.
11409.	Nutley	First N.B.
11428.	Fords	Fords N.B.
11446.	Audubon	Audubon N.B.
11543.	Bogota	Bogota N.B.
11545.	Linden	Linden N.B.
11553.	Red Bank	Broad Street N.B.
11607.	Collingswood	Memorial N.B.
11618.	Cliffside Park	Cliffside Park N.B.
11620.	Roebling	First N.B.
11658.	Beach Haven	Beach Haven N.B.
11727.	Hillside, Elizabeth	Hillside N.B.
11734.	Woodstown	Woodstown N.B.
11744.	Elizabeth	People's N.B.
11759.	Ridgewood	Citizens' N.B.
11793.	Palmyra	Palmyra N.B.
11847.	South Plainfield	First N.B.
11888.	Woodbridge	Woodbridge N.B.
11909.	Palisades Park	Palisades Park N.B.
11943.	Chatham	First N.B.
11950.	Leonia	First N.B.
11979.	Paterson	Nat. Trust Bank
11983.	Clifton	First N.B.
12002.	Peapack-Gladstone	Peapack-Gladstone N.B.
12014.	Hackensack	City N.B.
12019.	Belleville	People's N.B. and Trust Co.
12022.	Laurel Springs	Laurel Springs N.B.
12033.	North Arlington	North Arlington N.B.
12037.	Ridgefield	Ridgefield N.B.
12064.	West New York, Weehawken	First N.B.
12145.	Newfield	First N.B.
12167.	Paterson	Totowa N.B.
12195.	Park Ridge	First N.B.
12205.	Passaic	Passaic N.B. and Trust Co.
12228.	East Rutherford	First N.B.
12255.	Jersey City	Journal Square N.B.
12263.	Cranford	First N.B.
12268.	Montclair	Montclair N.B.
12272.	Wyckoff	First N.B.
12279.	Sea Isle City	First N.B.
12297.	Garwood	First N.B.
12301.	Jersey City	Union Trust and N.B. of Hudson Co.
12338.	East Orange	First N.B.
12354.	Seaside Heights	Coast N.B.
12367.	Bayonne	Bayonne N.B.
12378.	Little Ferry	Little Ferry N.B.
12383.	Paterson	N.B. of America
12397.	Jersey City	Franklin N.B.
12402.	West Englewood	West Englewood N.B.
12422.	Avon-by-the Sea	First N.B.
12425.	Union Center, Union	Union Center N.B.
12428.	Maple Shade	Maple Shade N.B.
12465.	Fairview	First N.B.
12468.	New Brunswick	Citizens' N.B.
12497.	Palisade	Palisade N.B. of Fort Lee
12510.	Pleasantville	Pleasantville N.B.
12519.	Westmont	Westmont N.B.
12520.	Red Bank	Nat. Bank and Trust Co.
12521.	Ocean City	Ocean City N.B.
12524.	Perth Amboy	Perth Amboy N.B.
12559.	Somers Point	First N.B.
12560.	Paterson	Labor Co-Operative N.B.
12570.	Newark	Lincoln N.B.
12571.	Lakehurst	First N.B.
12576.	Newark	Citizens' N.B. and Trust Co.
12598.	Highland Park	First N.B.
12603.	Midland Park	First N.B.
12604.	Newark	Forest Hill N.B.
12606.	Yardville	Yardville N.B.
12609.	Glen Rock	First N.B.
12617.	Atco	Atco N.B.
12618.	Mount Ephraim	Mount Ephraim N.B.
12621.	Oaklyn	Oaklyn N.B.
12631.	Newark	South Side N.B. and Trust Co.
12646.	Hamilton Square	First N.B.
12660.	Bloomingdale	First N.B.
12663.	Hawthorne	First N.B.
12675.	Montclair	People's N.B.
12690.	Clifton	Clifton N.B.
12706.	Allendale	First N.B.
12726.	Paterson	Broadway N.B.
12732.	North Bergen	First N.B.
12749.	Union City	Union City N.B.
12750.	Nutley	Franklin N.B.
12771.	Newark	Labor Co-Operative N.B.
12806.	Guttenberg	Liberty N.B.
12823.	Alpha	Alpha N.B.
12828.	Rahway	Citizens' N.B.
12829.	Weehawken	Hamilton N.B.
12830.	Springfield	First N.B.
12834.	Passaic	American N.B.
12848.	West Paterson	Westside N.B.
12854.	Haledon	Haledon N.B.
12861.	Prospect Park	Prospect Park N.B.
12876.	Irvington	People's N.B.
12886.	Atlantic City	Pacific Avenue N.B.
12891.	Allenhurst	Allenhurst N.B.
12894.	Woodlynne	Woodlynne N.B.
12895.	Paterson	Columbus N.B.
12901.	Paterson	Eastside N.B.
12902.	Hillsdale	Hillsdale N.B.
12903.	North Merchantville	Pennsauken Township N.B.
12917.	Mantua	N.B. of Mantua
12939.	Jersey City	Labor N.B.
12942.	Manville	Manville N.B.
12946.	Newark	Port Newark N.B.
12949.	Trenton	Prospect N.B.
12964.	Newark	Peoples N.B.
12977.	Woodbine	Woodbine N.B.
12978.	Stone Harbor	First N.B.
12981.	Teaneck	Teaneck N.B.
12984.	Riverside	First N.B.
12990.	Bayonne	Mechanics N.B.
13012.	Tenafly	Northern Valley N.B.
13034.	Harrison	Harrison N.B.
13039.	Trenton	Security N.B.
13043.	Newark	Hayes Circle Nat. Bank & Trust Co.
13047.	Wharton	First N.B.
13058.	Newark	Mount Prospect N.B.
13065.	Bay Head	Bay Head N.B.
13117.	Oradell	First N.B.
13120.	Camden	American N.B.
13123.	Passaic	Lincoln N.B.
13125.	Marlton	First N.B.
13129.	Livingston	Livingston N.B.
13136.	Cedar Grove	First N.B.
13164.	Lodi	First N.B.
13166.	Columbus	First N.B.
13173.	Whippany	First N.B.
13174.	Plainfield	Plainfield N.B.
13203.	Camden	Third N.B. & Trust Co.
13215.	Point Pleasant Beach	Point Pleasant Beach N.B.

Charter #	City	Name of Bank
13265.	Woodridge	Woodridge N.B.
13337.	Leonia	Central N.B.
13363.	Asbury Park	Asbury Park N.B. & Trust Co.
13364.	Hackensack	Bergen County N.B.
13369.	Sayreville	First N.B.
13530.	Haddon Heights	First N.B.
13537.	Kearny	Kearny N.B.
13540.	Linden	Linden N.B.
13552.	Sea Bright	First N.B.
13560.	Avon-by-the Sea	First N.B.
13574.	Rockaway	First N.B.
13628.	Belvidere	First N.B.
13629.	Plainfield	Fourth N.B.
13834.	Orange	Orange First N.B.
13848.	Belmar	Belmar N.B.
13855.	Branchville	Branchville N.B.
13893.	Edgewater	Edgewater N.B.
13898.	Spring Lake	First N.B.
13910.	New Egypt	First N.B
13916.	Metuchen	Metuchen N.B.
13946.	Garfield	First N.B.
13969.	Collingswood	Citizens N.B.
14006.	Clementon	N.B. of Clementon
14014.	Guttenberg	Liberty N.B.
14084.	Lakewood	Peoples N.B.
14088.	Palisades Park	N.B. of Palisades Park
14145.	Ocean City	N.B. of Ocean City
14151.	Secaucus	Peoples N.B.
14153.	Carteret	First N.B.
14162.	Cliffside Park	United N.B.
14177.	Sea Bright	Sea Bright N.B.
14189.	Tuckahoe	First N.B.
14240.	Newfield	First N.B.
14287.	Fort Lee	First N.B.
14289.	Pleasantville	Mainland N.B.
14305.	West New York	N.B. of West New York
14321.	Paterson	National Union Bank

NEW MEXICO

Charter #	City	Name of Bank
1750.	Santa Fe	First N.B.
2024.	Santa Fe	Second N.B. of New Mexico
2436.	Las Vegas	First N.B.
2454.	Las Vegas	San Miguel N.B.
2614.	Albuquerque	First N.B.
2627.	Socorro	First N.B.
3160.	Deming	First N.B.
3222.	Albuquerque	Albuquerque N.B.
3539.	Silver City	Silver City N.B.
3554.	Silver City	First N.B.
4455.	Eddy	First N.B.
4485.	Socorro	New Mexico N.B.
4574.	Socorro	Socorro N.B.
4734.	Raton	First N.B.
4746.	Deming	N.B. of Deming
5220.	Roswell	First N.B.
5244.	Alamogordo	First N.B.
5487.	Carlsbad	First N.B.
5713.	Clayton	First N.B.
6081.	Santa Rosa	First N.B.
6183.	Farmington	First N.B.
6187.	Portales	First N.B.
6288.	Tucumcari	First N.B.
6363.	Raton	Citizens' N.B.
6597.	Belen	First N.B.
6714.	Roswell	American N.B.
6777.	Roswell	Citizens' N.B.
6884.	Carlsbad	N.B. of Carlsbad
6974.	Deming	Deming N.B.
7043.	Artesia	First N.B.
7186.	Albuquerque	State N.B.
7503.	Hagerman	First N.B.
7720.	Las Cruces	First N.B.
8098.	Raton	N.B. of New Mexico
8120.	Raton	Raton N.B.
8132.	Silver City	American N.B.
8173.	Texico	First N.B.
8315.	Alamogordo	Citizens' N.B.
8348.	Elida	First N.B.
8364.	Portales	Citizens' N.B.
8391.	Texico	Texico N.B.
8397.	Melrose	First N.B.
8584.	Lake Arthur	First N.B.
8617.	Fort Sumner	First N.B.
8662.	Cutter	First N.B.
8663.	Nara Visa	First N.B.
8767.	Clovis	Clovis N.B.
8782.	Lakewood	Lakewood N.B.
8784.	Clovis	First N.B.
8880.	Lordsburg	First N.B.
9151.	Farmington	San Juan County N.B.
9292.	Cimarron	First N.B.
9441.	Hope	First N.B.
9468.	Artesia	State N.B.
9988.	Gallup	First N.B.
10268.	Magdalena	First N.B.
10594.	Tucumcari	American N.B.
10962.	Carlsbad	State N.B.
10963.	Carrizozo	First N.B.
11011.	Hot Springs	First N.B.
11029.	Lovington	First N.B.
11102.	Taos	First N.B.
11136.	Clayton	Clayton N.B.
11329.	Willard	First N.B.
11442.	Albuquerque	Citizens' N.B.
11449.	Columbus	First N.B.
11565.	Springer	First N.B.
11711.	Loving	First N.B.
11746.	Grady	First N.B.
11900.	Gallup	N.B. of Gallup
11958.	Roy	First N.B.
12485.	Albuquerque	Albuquerque N.B.
12514.	Farmington	People's N.B.
12522.	Clovis	First N.B.
12569.	Carlsbad	Carlsbad N.B.
12710.	Silver City	New First N.B.
12879.	Hatch	First N.B.
12924.	Raton	First N.B.
13438.	Hot Springs	Hot Springs N.B.
13488.	New Hobbs	First N.B.
13814.	Albuquerque	First N.B.
14081.	Tucumcari	First-American N.B.

NEW YORK

Charter #	City	Name of Bank
6.	Syracuse	First N.B.
29.	New York	First N.B.
34.	Rondout	First N.B.
35.	Beacon, Fishkill-on-the Hudson	Fishkill N.B.
45.	Ellenville	First N.B.
62.	New York	Second N.B.
71.	Adams	First N.B.
73.	Watertown	First N.B.
75.	Dansville	First N.B.
87.	New York	Third N.B.
94.	Port Jervis	First N.B.
99.	Moravia	First N.B.
102.	Seneca Falls	First N.B.
103.	South Worcester	First N.B.
119.	Elmira	First N.B.
120.	Utica	First N.B.
140.	Syracuse	Second N.B.
149.	Elmira	Second N.B.
151.	New Berlin	First N.B.
159.	Syracuse	Third N.B.
163.	Troy	First N.B.
165.	Bath	First N.B.
166.	Albion	First N.B.
167.	Geneva	First N.B.
169.	Penn Yan	First N.B.
179.	Chittenango	First N.B.
184.	Sandy Hill	First N.B.
185.	Utica	Second N.B.
193.	Hobart	First N.B.
199.	Attica	First N.B.
202.	Binghamton	First N.B.
211.	Lockport	First N.B.
217.	Leonardsville	First N.B.
222.	Ithaca	First N.B.
223.	Cooperstown	Second N.B.
226.	Cortland	First N.B.
229.	Medina	First N.B.
231.	Auburn	First N.B.
235.	Buffalo	First N.B.
245.	Morrisville	First N.B.
254.	New York	Sixth N.B.
255.	Oswego	First N.B.
259.	Canandaigua	First N.B.
262.	Hornell	First N.B.
265.	Friendship	First N.B.
266.	Plattsburg	First N.B.
267.	Albany	First N.B.
273.	Oxford	First N.B.
280.	Cooperstown	First N.B.
282.	Franklin	First N.B.
285.	Whitehall	First N.B.
290.	New York	Fourth N.B.
292.	Baldwinsville	First N.B.
295.	Palmyra	First N.B.
296.	Oswego	Second N.B.
297.	Waverly	First N.B.
301.	Havana	First N.B.
302.	Andes	First N.B.
303.	Skaneateles	First N.B.
304.	Clyde	First N.B.
307.	New York	Tenth N.B.
314.	Warwick	First N.B.
316.	Champlain	First N.B.
321.	Plattsburg	Vilas N.B.
334.	Greenport	First N.B.
340.	Batavia	First N.B.
341.	New York	Fifth N.B.
342.	Union Springs	First N.B.
343.	Havana	Havana N.B.
345.	New York	Irving N.B.
348.	Lowville	First N.B.
349.	Newark	First N.B.
353.	Candor	First N.B.
358.	Penn Yan	First N.B.
364.	Tarrytown	First N.B.
368.	Waterloo	First N.B.
375.	Saint Johnsville	First N.B.
376.	New York	Central N.B.
382.	Brockport	First N.B.
384.	New York	Eighth N.B.
387.	New York	Ninth N.B.
396.	Hudson	First N.B.
402.	Port Chester	First N.B.
412.	Aurora	First N.B.
420.	Oneonta	First N.B.
444.	New York	Nat. Currency Bank
451.	Kingston	First N.B.
453.	Buffalo	Farmers and Mechanics' N.B.
456.	Watkins	Watkins N.B.
461.	Cobleskill	First N.B.
465.	Poughkeepsie	First N.B.
467.	Fort Plain	Nat. Fort Plain Bank
468.	Newburgh	N.B. of Newburgh
471.	Ossining	First N.B.
472.	Deposit	Deposit N.B.
504.	Westfield	First N.B.
519.	Oneida	First N.B.
523.	Middletown	First N.B.
527.	Rochester	First N.B.
548.	Jamestown	First N.B.
564.	Angelica	First N.B.
598.	Malone	Farmers' N.B.
621.	Troy	Nat. Exchange Bank
639.	Lockport	Niagara County N.B.
640.	Troy	Troy City N.B.
653.	Yonkers	First N.B.
658.	Brooklyn	Nassau N.B.
659.	Poughkeepsie	Fallkill N.B.
671.	Watertown	Second N.B.
687.	New York	Nat. Broadway Bank
706.	Amenia	First N.B.
721.	Troy	Manufacturers' N.B.
729.	Ithaca	Merchants and Farmers' N.B.
733.	New York	N.B. of Commerce
737.	Warsaw	Wyoming County N.B.
739.	Albany	Nat. Albany Exchange Bank
750.	New York	American N.B.
752.	Red Hook	First N.B.
801.	West Winfield	First N.B.
811.	Elmira	Chemung Canal N.B.
821.	Oswego	Nat. Marine Bank
822.	Dover, Dover Plains	Dover Plains N.B.
830.	South East	Croton River N.B.
841.	Fredonia	Fredonia N.B.
842.	Castleton	N.B. of Castleton
850.	Buffalo	Third N.B.
862.	Owego	Tioga N.B.
868.	Potsdam	N.B. of Potsdam
886.	Genesee	Genesee Valley N.B.
891.	New York	Nat. Park Bank
893.	Saratoga Springs	Saratoga N.B.
904.	Troy	Merchants and Mechanics N.B.
905.	New York	Tradesmen's N.B.
914.	Malone	N.B. of Malone
917.	New York	Nat. Shoe and Leather Bank
923.	Brooklyn	First N.B.
929.	Kinderhook	Nat. Union Bank
937.	Le Roy	First N.B.
938.	Jamestown	City N.B.
940.	Troy	United N.B.
949.	Geneva	Geneva N.B.
954.	Ballston Spa	First N.B.
955.	Kingston	State of New York N.B.
963.	Troy	Union N.B.
964.	New York	Market and Fulton N.B.
968.	Fulton	First N.B.
971.	Fishkill	N.B. of Fishkill
972.	New York	Saint Nicholas N.B.
976.	Carmel	Putnam County N.B.
980.	Glens Falls	First N.B.
981.	Pine Plains	Stissing N.B.
990.	Hudson	Farmers' N.B.
991.	Troy	Nat. State Bank
992.	Troy	Mutual N.B.
998.	New York	Seventh N.B.
1000.	New York	N.B. of the Republic
1012.	Troy	Central N.B.
1019.	Owego	First N.B.
1026.	Kinderhook	N.B. of Kinderhook
1027.	Lyons	Lyons N.B.
1039.	Lockport	Nat. Exchange Bank
1040.	Saugerties	First N.B.
1045.	Albany	Merchants' N.B.
1050.	Kingston	Nat. Ulster County Bank
1067.	New York	Mercantile N.B.
1072.	Rochester	Farmers and Merchants' N.B.
1074.	Batavia	N.B. of Genesee
1075.	New York	Wall Street N.B.
1080.	New York	Atlantic N.B.
1083.	Groton	First N.B.
1090.	Oneida	Oneida Valley N.B.
1091.	Hudson	Nat. Hudson River Bank
1104.	Rochester	Traders' N.B.
1105.	New York	East River N.B.
1106.	Newburgh	Highland N.B.
1110.	Fayetteville	N.B. of Fayetteville
1116.	New York	New York County N.B.
1120.	Kingston	Roundout N.B.
1121.	New York	Metropolitan N.B.
1122.	Canajoharie	Canajoharie N.B.
1123.	Albany	Union N.B.
1127.	Salem	N.B. of Salem
1130.	Mohawk	Nat. Mohawk Valley Bank
1136.	Cherry Valley	Nat. Central Bank
1143.	Cuba	Cuba N.B.
1149.	Kingston	Kingston N.B.
1157.	Rhinebeck	First N.B.
1160.	Whitehall	Old N.B.
1166.	Sherburne	Sherburne N.B.
1178.	Fulton	Citizens' N.B.
1186.	New Paltz	Huguenot N.B.
1189.	Binghamton	City N.B.
1192.	Waverly	Waverly N.B.
1196.	New York	Leather Manufacturers' N.B.
1198.	Catskill	Tanners' N.B.
1208.	Saugerties	Saugerties N.B.
1212.	Fonda	Nat. Mohawk River Bank
1213.	Newburgh	Quassaick N.B.
1215.	New York	Marine N.B.
1218.	Fort Edward	N.B. of Fort Edward
1223.	Brooklyn	Farmers and Citizens' N.B.

Charter #	City	Name of Bank
1224.	New York	Pacific N.B.
1226.	Schenectady	Mohawk N.B.
1227.	Saratoga Springs	Commercial N.B.
1229.	Waterford	Saratoga County N.B.
1231.	New York	Importers and Traders' N.B.
1232.	New York	Ocean N.B.
1240.	Seneca Falls	Nat. Exchange Bank
1250.	New York	Mechanics and Metals N.B.
1253.	**Ballston Spa.**	**Ballston Spa. N.B.**
1257.	**Canajoharie**	**Nat. Spraker Bank**
1261.	New York	Nat. Butchers and Drovers' Bank
1262.	Albany	New York State N.B.
1264.	Vernon	N.B. of Vernon
1265.	Watervliet	N.B. of Watervliet
1266.	Greenwich	Washington County N.B.
1269.	Pawling	N.B. of Pawling
1271.	Cazenovia	N.B. of Cazenovia
1275.	Cambridge	Cambridge Valley N.B.
1276.	Middletown	Middletown N.B.
1278.	New York	Union N.B.
1282.	Rochester	Nat. Union Bank
1285.	Auburn	Auburn City N.B.
1286.	Nyack	Rockland County N.B.
1287.	Syracuse	Salt Springs N.B.
1289.	Albany	Nat. Mechanics and Farmers' Bank
1290.	New York	Citizens N.B.
1291.	Albany	Albany City N.B.
1293.	Glens Falls	Glens Falls N.B.
1294.	Catskill	Catskill N.B.
1297.	New York	Bowery N.B.
1298.	Schuylerville	N.B. of Schuylerville
1301.	Albany	Nat. Commercial Bank and Trust Co.
1304.	Somers	Farmers and Drovers' N.B.
1305.	Poughkeepsie	City N.B.
1306.	Poughkeepsie	Poughkeepsie N.B.
1307.	Amsterdam	First N.B.
1308.	Utica	Utica N.B.
1311.	Owego	Nat. Union Bank
1312.	Poughkeepsie	Farmers and Manufacturers' N.B.
1323.	Delhi	Delaware N.B.
1324.	New York	Gallatin N.B.
1334.	Hamilton	Nat. Hamilton Bank
1335.	Amsterdam	Farmers' N.B.
1341.	Syracuse	Syracuse N.B.
1342.	Syracuse	Merchants' N.B.
1344.	Little Falls	Herkimer County N.B.
1345.	Auburn	Cayuga County N.B.
1347.	Cohoes	N.B. of Cohoes
1348.	North Granville	North Granville N.B.
1349.	Chester	Chester N.B.
1350.	Auburn	N.B. of Auburn
1351.	Auburn	Nat. Exchange Bank
1352.	New York	Hanover N.B.
1354.	Norwich	N.B. of Norwich
1355.	Oswego	Lake Ontario N.B.
1357.	New York	Irving N.B.
1361.	Waterville	N.B. of Waterville
1362.	Rochester	Flour City N.B.
1363.	Port Jervis	N.B. of Port Jervis
1370.	New York	Merchants' N.B.
1371.	New York	Grocers' N.B.
1372.	New York	N.B. of Commonwealth
1373.	New York	N.B. of North America
1374.	New York	Phenix N.B.
1375.	New York	Chatham and Phenix N.B.
1376.	Rome	Central N.B.
1380.	Poughkeepsie	Merchants' N.B.
1388.	New York	Atlantic N.B.
1389.	New York	Continental N.B.
1391.	Elmira	N.B. of Chemung
1392.	Utica	Oneida N.B.
1393.	New York	Bank of N.Y. Nat. Banking Assn.
1394.	New York	American Exchange N.B.
1395.	Utica	First N.B.
1397.	Rochester	Clarke N.B.
1398.	Coxsackie	N.B. of Coxsackie
1399.	Goshen	N.B. of Orange County
1401.	Syracuse	Mechanics' N.B.
1408.	Goshen	Goshen N.B.
1410.	Rome	Fort Stanwix N.B.
1414.	Rome	First N.B.
1416.	Mount Morris	Genesee River N.B.
1422.	Peekskill	West Chester County N.B.
1426.	Lansingburg	N.B. of Lansingburg
1443.	Brooklyn	Manufacturers' N.B.
1458.	Whitestown	N.B. of Whitestown
1461.	New York	Nat. City Bank
1463.	Unadilla	Nat. Unadilla Bank
1473.	Middletown	Walkill N.B.
1474.	Gloversville	Nat. Fulton County Bank
1476.	New York	N.B. of the State of New York
1490.	Watertown	Jefferson County N.B.
1491.	Brooklyn	Atlantic N.B.
1496.	Pulaski	Pulaski N.B.
1497.	New York	Fulton N.B.
1499.	New York	Chemical N.B.
1503.	Monticello	Nat. Union Bank
1507.	Watertown	Nat. Union Bank

Charter #	City	Name of Bank
1508.	Watertown	N.B. and Loan Co.
1509.	Albion	Orleans County N.B.
1510.	Schoharie	Schoharie County N.B.
1513.	Binghamton	Nat. Broome County Bank
1525.	Canastota	Canastota N.B.
1531.	Adams	Hungerford N.B.
1534.	Lansingburg	Nat. Exchange Bank
1543.	Brooklyn	Nat. City Bank
1556.	New York	Croton N.B.
1561.	Ithaca	Tompkins County N.B.
1563.	Jamestown	Chautauqua County N.B.
1569.	Syracuse	Fourth N.B.
1624.	New York	Mechanics and Traders' N.B.
1655.	Newport	N.B. of Newport
1670.	Ilion	Ilion N.B.
1691.	New York	Union Square N.B.
1697.	Port Henry	First N.B.
1753.	Keenseville	Keenseville N.B.
1887.	Olean	First N.B.
1938.	Gloversville	N.B. of Gloversville
2074.	Yonkers	Citizens' N.B.
2117.	Ellenville	Home N.B.
2136.	Binghamton	Merchants' N.B.
2151.	Oneonta	Wilber N.B.
2224.	Nunda	First N.B.
2225.	Brewster	First N.B.
2229.	Haverstraw	N.B. of Haverstraw
2233.	Whitehall	Merchants' N.B.
2239.	Amsterdam	Manufacturers' N.B.
2272.	Cortland	N.B. of Cortland
2294.	Granville	N.B. of Granville
2320.	Boonville	First N.B.
2345.	Franklinville	First N.B.
2348.	Walden	Walden N.B.
2353.	Moravia	Moravia N.B.
2370.	New York	Chase N.B.
2376.	Olean	Exchange N.B.
2378.	Nyack	Nyack N.B.
2383.	Rochester	Commercial N.B.
2398.	Homer	First N.B.
2400.	Little Falls	Nat. Herkimer County Bank
2401.	Oneida	Nat. State Bank
2405.	Penn Yan	Yates County N.B.
2406.	Little Falls	Little Falls N.B.
2410.	Rome	Farmers' N.B.
2418.	Johnstown	First N.B.
2421.	Batavia	Genesee County N.B.
2426.	Lowville	Black River N.B.
2437.	Attica	Attica N.B.
2441.	Poland	Poland N.B.
2442.	Carthage	First N.B.
2446.	Ogdensburg	N.B. of Ogdensburg
2448.	Camden	First N.B.
2451.	Cuba	First N.B.
2463.	Dundee	Dundee N.B.
2468.	Clyde	Briggs N.B.
2471.	Hoosick Falls	First N.B.
2472.	Salamanca	First N.B.
2487.	Middleburgh	First N.B.
2493.	**Rondout**	**First N.B.**
2507.	**New York**	**United States N.B.**
2510.	Gouverneur	First N.B.
2517.	Greenwich	First N.B.
2522.	Hornell	Citizens' N.B.
2534.	Plattsburgh	Iron N.B.
2543.	Bainbridge	First N.B.
2553.	Richburg	First N.B.
2598.	New York	Garfield N.B.
2602.	Stamford	N.B. of Stamford
2608.	New York	Lincoln N.B.
2610.	Salamanca	Salamanca N.B.
2615.	Saratoga Springs	Citizens' N.B.
2619.	Dunkirk	Merchants' N.B.
2626.	Tarrytown	Tarrytown N.B.
2632.	Friendship	Citizens' N.B.
2651.	Richfield Springs	First N.B.
2655.	Corning	First N.B. and Trust Co.
2657.	Watertown	Watertown N.B.
2661.	Millerton	Millerton N.B.
2668.	New York	Second N.B.
2755.	Franklinville	Union N.B.
2765.	Canandaigua	Ontario County N.B.
2827.	Cortland	Second N.B.
2838.	Sandy Hill	N.B. of Sandy Hill
2845.	Adams	Adams N.B.
2850.	Wellsville	First N.B.
2860.	Fort Plain	Fort Plain N.B.
2869.	Fultonville	Fultonville N.B.
2873.	Troy	N.B. of Troy
2892.	Springville	First N.B.
2916.	Dunkirk	Lake Shore N.B.
2920.	Amsterdam	Merchants' N.B.
2976.	New York	Sprague N.B.
2996.	Owego	Owego N.B.
3011.	Norwich	Chenango N.B.
3047.	Watkins	First N.B.
3154.	Granville	Farmers' N.B.
3166.	**Westfield**	**N.B. of Westfield**
3171.	**Mechanicville**	**First N.B.**
3174.	**Plattsburg**	**Merchants' N.B.**
3183.	Herkimer	First N.B.
3186.	Homer	Homer N.B.
3193.	Marathon	First N.B.
3232.	Greenport	People's N.B.
3244.	Hudson Falls	People's N.B.
3245.	Salem	People's N.B.
3282.	Albany	Nat. Exchange Bank
3283.	Le Roy	N.B. of Le Roy
3307.	Malone	People's N.B.
3309.	Salem	First N.B.

Charter #	City	Name of Bank
3312.	Gloversville	Fulton County N.B.
3329.	Seneca Falls	Exchange N.B.
3330.	Fort Edward	First N.B.
3333.	Middletown	Merchants' N.B.
3359.	New York	Southern N.B.
3366.	Malone	Third N.B.
3415.	New York	Seaboard N.B.
3444.	New Brighton	First N.B. of Staten Island
3582.	Frankfort	First N.B.
3672.	Carthage	Carthage N.B.
3681.	Edmeston	First N.B.
3696.	Canton	First N.B.
3700.	New York	Western N.B.
3771.	New York	N.B. of Deposit
3797.	Clayton	First N.B.
3800.	**Painted Post**	**Bronson N.B.**
3817.	Canandaigua	Canandaigua N.B.
3822.	Sidney	Sidney N.B.
3846.	Jamestown	Jamestown N.B.
4061.	Adams	Farmers' N.B.
4103.	Adams	Citizens' N.B.
4105.	Elmira	Elmira N.B.
4152.	New York	Interstate N.B.
4211.	Amsterdam	Amsterdam City N.B
4223.	Poland	N.B. of Poland
4230.	Riverhead	Suffolk County N.B.
4296.	Watertown	City N.B.
4335.	New York	Washington N.B.
4416.	Cold Spring	N.B. of Cold-Spring-on-Hudson
4419.	Canastota	First N.B.
4482.	Dansville	Merchants and Farmers' N.B.
4491.	Ticonderoga	First N.B.
4493.	Earlville	First N.B.
4495.	Walton	First N.B.
4497.	Hobart	N.B. of Hobart
4512.	New York	Columbus N.B.
4519.	Perry	First N.B.
4567.	New York	Western N.B. of the U.S.
4581.	New York	N.B. of North America
4645.	New York	Liberty N.B.
4711.	Schenectady	Union N.B.
4741.	Buffalo	Columbia N.B.
4846.	Glens Falls	Merchants' N.B.
4855.	New York	Franklin N.B.
4858.	Port Henry	Citizens' N.B.
4869.	Tonawanda	First N.B.
4870.	Morris	First N.B.
4880.	Hempstead	First N.B.
4898.	New York	Nat. Union Bank
4899.	Niagara Falls	First N.B.
4906.	Babylon	Babylon N.B.
4914.	Beacon, Matteawan	Matteawan N.B.
4925.	Liberty	Sullivan County N.B.
4962.	Schenevus	Schenevus N.B.
4985.	Granville	Granville N.B.
4986.	Medina	Medina N.B.
4988.	Wellsville	Citizens' N.B.
4998.	Albion	Citizens' N.B.
5003.	New York	Standard N.B.
5026.	Mount Kisco	Mount Kisco N.B.
5037.	Mechanicville	Manufacturers' N.B.
5053.	Walden	N.B. of Walden
5068.	Port Jefferson	First N.B.
5072.	Saranac Lake	Adirondack N.B.
5108.	Clayton	Nat. Exchange Bank
5112.	New York	Astor N.B.
5137.	Elmira	Merchants' N.B.
5141.	Herkimer	Herkimer N.B.
5174.	Buffalo	City N.B.
5178.	Addison	First N.B.
5186.	Sayville	Oystermen's N.B.
5196.	Wayland	First N.B.
5210.	Milford	Milford N.B.
5228.	Potsdam	Citizens' N.B.
5237.	New York	Nat. Commercial Bank
5271.	**Mount Vernon**	**First N.B.**
5284.	**Alexandria Bay**	**First N.B. of the Thousand Islands**
5286.	Syracuse	American Exchange N.B.
5293.	Mexico	First N.B.
5299.	Holland Patent	First N.B.
5336.	Highland	First N.B.
5360.	Skaneateles	N.B. of Skaneateles
5390.	Spring Valley	First N.B.
5407.	Falconer	First N.B.
5411.	Mamaroneck	First N.B.
5465.	Syracuse	N.B. of Syracuse
5605.	Hermon	First N.B.
5631.	Akron	Wickware N.B.
5648.	Caledonia	First N.B.
5662.	Rye	Rye N.B.
5675.	Cazenovia	Cazenovia N.B.
5746.	Tully	First N.B.
5783.	New York	New Amsterdam N.B.
5785.	Plattsburg	Plattsburg N.B. and Trust Company
5816.	Castleton	Nat. Exchange Bank
5846.	Suffern	Suffern N.B.
5851.	South Glens Falls	First N.B.
5867.	Gainesville	Gainesville N.B.
5874.	Hoosick Falls	People's N.B.
5924.	Margaretville	People's N.B.
5928.	Wolcott	First N.B.
5936.	Northport	First N.B.
5990.	New York	United N.B.

Charter #	City	Name of Bank
6019.	Larchmont	Larchmont N.B.
6087.	Le Roy	Le Roy N.B.
6094.	Carthage	Nat. Exchange Bank
6148.	Silver Springs	Silver Springs N.B.
6184.	Buffalo	Marine N.B.
6186.	Buffalo	Manufacturers and Traders' N.B.
6198.	Port Richmond	Port Richmond N.B.
6253.	New York	Northern N.B.
6284.	New York	Equitable N.B.
6330.	Springville	Citizens' N.B.
6351.	White Plains	First N.B.
6371.	Irvington	Irvington N.B.
6386.	Ripley	First N.B.
6425.	New York	Nat. Reserve Bank
6427.	New Rochelle	Nat. City Bank
6441.	New York	Thirty-Fourth Street N.B.
6447.	Dolgeville	First N.B.
6470.	Hudson Falls	Sandy Hill N.B.
6479.	Corinth	Corinth N.B.
6482.	Remsen	First N.B.
6487.	Dryden	First N.B.
6552.	Ossining	Ossining N.B.
6562.	Stapleton	Stapleton N.B.
6587.	Huntington	First N.B.
6613.	Plattsburg	City N B.
6630.	Oriskany Falls	First N.B.
6694.	Massena	First N.B.
6785.	Patchogue	Citizens' N.B.
6802.	Newark	Acadia N.B.
6809.	North Tonawanda	State N.B.
6964.	Lackawanna	Lackawanna N.B.
6965.	Syracuse	Commercial N.B.
7009.	Allegany	First N.B.
7102.	Olean	Citizens' N.B.
7107.	New York	Maiden Lane N.B.
7203.	New York	Coal and Iron N.B.
7233.	Philmont	First N.B.
7255.	Granville	Washington County N.B.
7290.	Stapleton	Richmond Borough N.B.
7305.	Cooperstown	Cooperstown N.B.
7344.	Cornwall	First N.B.
7447.	New York	Battery Park N.B.
7450.	New York	Aetna N.B.
7479.	Lyons	Gavitt N.B.
7483.	West Winfield	West Winfield N.B.
7485.	Hunter	Greene County N.B.
7512.	Sharon Springs	First N.B.
7541.	Trumansburg	First N.B.
7563.	Monroe	Monroe N.B.
7588.	Salem	Salem N.B.
7612.	Troy	Nat. City Bank
7618.	Grand Gorge	First N.B.
7630.	Fort Edward	Fort Edward N.B.
7678.	Roxbury	N.B. of Roxbury
7679.	Whitney Point	First N.B.
7699.	Glens Falls	N.B. of Glens Falls
7703.	Freeport	First N.B.
7733.	Saint Regis Falls	Saint Regis Falls N.B.
7763.	East Hampton	East Hampton N.B.
7774.	South Otselic	Otselic Valley N.B.
7813.	Lestershire	First N.B.
7823.	Buffalo	Central N.B.
7840.	Ovid	First N.B.
7850.	Whitesville	First N.B.
7878.	Downsville	First N.B.
7939.	Bayside	Bayside N.B.
7982.	Montgomery	N.B. of Montgomery
8022.	Boonville	Nat. Exchange Bank
8026.	Rochester	Lincoln N.B.
8058.	Greenwood	First N.B.
8111.	Rochester	N.B. of Commerce
8146.	Andover	Burrows N.B.
8153.	Tupper Lake	Tupper Lake N.B.
8157.	Franklinville	People's N.B.
8158.	Theresa	Farmers' N.B.
8191.	Roscoe	First N.B.
8194.	Mariner Harbor	Mariner Harbor N.B.
8240.	Bronxville	Gramatan N.B.
8268.	Jamaica	First N.B.
8297.	Hudson Falls	Hudson Falls N.B.
8301.	Horseheads	First N.B.
8334.	Tottenville	Tottenville N.B.
8343.	Argyle	First N.B.
8371.	Morristown	Frontier N.B.
8388.	Whitehall	N.B. of Whitehall
8398.	Peekskill	Peekskill N.B.
8453.	Jamestown	Nat. Chautauqua County Bank
8463.	Dexter	First N.B.
8513.	Sidney	People's N.B.
8516.	Mount Vernon	Mount Vernon N.B.
8531.	Canton	Saint Lawrence County N.B.
8586.	Hastings upon Hudson	First N.B.
8613.	Hancock	First N.B.
8634.	New York	Beaver N.B.
8665.	New York	Nat. Copper Bank
8717.	Clifton Springs	Ontario N.B.
8793.	Lake George	First N.B.
8794.	Islip	First N.B.
8833.	Lindenhurst	First N.B.
8834.	Marlboro	First N.B.
8838.	Highland Falls	Citizens' N.B.
8847.	Fleischmanns, Griffin Corners	First N.B.
8850.	Highland Falls	First N.B.
8853.	Corona	First N.B.
8865.	Ozone Park, New York	First N.B.
8872.	Rockville Centre	First N.B.
8873.	Amityville	First N.B.
8882.	Farmingdale	First N.B.
8893.	Chateaugay	First N.B.
8920.	Oneonta	Citizens' N.B.
8922.	New York	Sherman N.B.
8923.	Lynbrook	Lynbrook N.B.
8926.	New York	Bronx N.B.
8935.	Saranac Lake	Saranac Lake N.B.
8957.	Whitestone	First N.B.
9019.	Fredonia	N.B. of Fredonia
9060.	East Worcester	East Worcester N.B.
9065.	Washingtonville	First N.B.
9109.	Ilion	Manufacturers' N.B.
9135.	Warrensburgh	Emerson N.B.
9171.	Croton on Hudson	First N.B.
9187.	Mineola	First N.B.
9206.	Middleport	First N.B.
9219.	Brooklyn	People's N.B.
9271.	Far Rockaway	N.B. of Far Rockaway
9276.	Union	Farmers' N.B.
9305.	Gloversville	City N.B.
9322.	East Islip	First N.B.
9326.	Wappingers Falls	N.B. of Wappingers Falls
9360.	New York	Union Exchange N.B.
9399.	Nichols	Nichols N.B.
9405.	Westport	Lake Champlain N.B.
9414.	Ridgewood, Brooklyn	Ridgewood N.B.
9415.	Windsor	Windsor N.B.
9418.	Sodus	First N.B.
9427.	Callicoon	Callicoon N.B.
9434.	Deposit	Farmers' N.B.
9482.	Brown Station	Ashokan N.B.
9516.	Unadilla	Unadilla N.B.
9529.	Ravena	First N.B.
9569.	New York	Audubon N.B.
9643.	Brushton	First N.B.
9644.	Belfast	First N.B
9669.	Bridgehampton	Bridgehampton N.B.
9691.	Flushing	Flushing N.B.
9716.	North Creek	North Creek N.B.
9717.	New York	Gotham N.B.
9748.	Jamestown	American N.B.
9804.	Poland	Citizens' N.B.
9820.	Smithtown Branch	N.B. of Smithtown Branch
9822.	Olean	Olean N.B.
9825.	Yonkers	Yonkers N.B.
9839.	Phelps	Phelps N.B.
9857.	Cato	First N.B.
9866.	Altamont	First N.B.
9869.	Marcellus	First N.B.
9900.	Ticonderoga	Ticonderoga N.B.
9921.	Genoa	First N.B.
9939.	New York	Nat. Nassau Bank
9940.	Pine Bush	Pine Bush N.B.
9950.	East Aurora	First N.B.
9955.	New York	Harriman N.B.
9956.	Florida	Florida N.B.
9977.	Watkins	Glen N.B.
9990.	Central Valley	Central Valley N.B.
10016.	North Rose	First N.B.
10029.	Bay Shore	First N.B.
10037.	Liberty	N.B. of Liberty
10043.	Livingston Manor	Livingston Manor N.B
10046.	Holcomb	Hamlin N.B.
10047.	Canandaigua	County N.B.
10054.	Brooklyn	Greenpoint N.B.
10077.	Copenhagen	Copenhagen N.B.
10084.	Cornwall	Cornwall N.B.
10109.	Central Square	First N.B.
10111.	Newark Valley	First N.B.
10126.	Barker	Somerset N.B.
10141.	East Rochester	First N.B.
10155.	Wallkill	Wallkill N.B.
10159.	Silver Creek	First N.B.
10175.	Lacona	First N.B.
10185.	Southampton	First N.B.
10199.	New Berlin	N.B. of New Berlin
10216.	Hammond	Citizens' N.B.
10235.	Bath	Bath N.B.
10258.	Silver Creek	Silver Creek N.B.
10295.	Clinton	Hayes N.B.
10329.	Long Island City	Commercial N.B.
10351.	Frankfort	Citizens' N.B.
10358.	Babylon	Babylon N.B.
10374.	Redwood	Redwood N.B.
10410.	Arcade	First N.B.
10444.	Forestville	First N.B.
10446.	Heuvelton	First N.B.
10456.	Jeffersonville	First N.B.
10477.	Sparkill	First N.B.
10481.	Cherry Creek	Cherry Creek N.B.
10497.	Montour Falls	Montour N.B.
10525.	Tuckahoe	First N.B.
10526.	Pearl River	First N.B.
10546.	Marion	First N.B.
10569.	Edwards	Edwards N.B.
10623.	Gasport	First N.B.
10747.	Winthrop	First N.B.
10754.	Bliss	Bliss N.B.
10755.	Lake Placid	Lake Placid N.B.
10767.	Harrisville	First N.B.
10778.	New York	Chatham and Phenix N.B.
10781.	Red Creek	Red Creek N.B.
10788.	Pulaski	People's N.B.
10816.	Lisle	First N.B.
10855.	Kerhonkson	Kerhonkson N.B.
10856.	Athens	Athens N.B.
10869.	Fairport	Fairport N.B.
10895.	Norfolk	First N.B.
10923.	Walden	Third N.B.
10930.	Conewango	Conewango Valley N.B.
10943.	Brasher Falls	Brasher Falls N.B.
10948.	Croghan	Croghan N.B.
10964.	Old Forge	First N.B.
11020.	Weedsport	First N.B.
11033.	Rockville Centre	Nassau County N.B.
11034.	New York	Public N.B.
11055.	Friendship	Union N.B.
11057.	Tannersville	Mountains N.B.
11059.	Woodridge, Centerville Sta.	First N.B.
11072.	Bellmore	First N.B.
11087.	Hicksville	Long Island N.B.
11238.	Trenton, Barneveld	First N.B.
11243.	Andes	N.B. of Andes
11277.	Clayville	N.B. of Clayville
11284.	Whitesboro	Whitestown N.B.
11292.	Port Washington	Port Washington N.B.
11319.	Buffalo	Broadway N.B.
11349.	Savona	Savona N.B.
11360.	Jamestown	Liberty N.B.
11375.	Hempstead	Second N.B.
11404.	Tuxedo	Tuxedo N.B.
11435.	Buffalo	Lafayette N.B.
11448.	Unionville	First N.B.
11474.	Baldwin	Baldwin N.B.
11489.	Niagara Falls	Falls N.B.
11511.	East Setauket	Tinker N.B.
11513.	Afton	First N.B.
11514.	Afton	Afton N.B.
11518.	Freeport	Citizens' N.B.
11583.	Angola	Evans N.B.
11603.	Lynbrook	People's N.B.
11626.	Albany	Union N.B. and Trust Co.
11639.	New York	New York Nat. Irving Bank
11649.	Milton	First N.B.
11655.	New York	Richmond Hill N.B.
11656.	Middleville	Middleville N.B.
11657.	Hartwick	Hartwick N.B.
11686.	New York	Nat. American Bank
11708.	Scarsdale	Scarsdale N.B.
11713.	New York	New York Produce Exchange N.B.
11730.	Westbury	Wheatley Hills N.B.
11739.	Romulus	Romulus N.B.
11742.	Port Leyden	Port Leyden N.B.
11747.	Mount Vernon	American N.B.
11755.	Long Beach	N.B. of Long Beach
11768.	Buffalo	Community N.B.
11785.	New Hartford	First N.B.
11809.	South Fallsburg	South Fallsburg N.B.
11836.	Buffalo	Merchants' N.B.
11844.	New York	Progress N.B.
11854.	Cedarhurst	Peninsula N.B.
11881.	Valley Stream	Valley Stream N.B.
11883.	Buffalo	Amherst N.B.
11897.	Malone	Citizens' N.B.
11912.	Lancaster	Citizens' N.B.
11924.	Manhasset	First N.B.
11927.	Maybrook	Maybrook N.B.
11951.	Pelham	Pelham N.B.
11953.	Roosevelt	First N.B.
11956.	Painted Post	Painted Post N.B.
11965.	New York	Commercial Exchange N.B.
11969.	Rouses Point	First N.B.
11971.	Willsboro	Essex County N.B.
12017.	Hamden	First N.B.
12018.	Lisbon	First N.B.
12021.	New York	Metropolitan N.B.
12071.	Atlanta	Atlanta N.B.
12122.	Syracuse	Liberty N.B.
12123.	New York	Seaboard N.B.
12164.	Windham	First N.B.
12174.	Greene	First N.B.
12208.	Kenmore	First N.B.
12213.	New York	Capitol N.B.
12214.	New York	Lebanon N.B.
12224.	New York	Lincoln N.B.
12242.	Germantown	Germantown N.B.
12252.	New York	Rockaway Beach N.B.
12280.	New York	Ozone Park N.B.
12284.	Niagara Falls	Cataract N.B.
12294.	Woodmere	Hewlett-Woodmere N.B.
12300.	New York	Hamilton N.B.
12313.	Buffalo	South Side N.B.
12337.	Buffalo	Genesee N.B.
12344.	New York	N.B. of Bay Ridge
12352.	New York	Liberty N.B.
12370.	New York	Franklin N.B.
12375.	Jordan	Jordan N.B.
12379.	Central Islip	Central Islip N.B.
12398.	Corona	Queensboro N.B.
12406.	New York	United N.B.

Charter #	City	Name of Bank
12417.	Trumansburg	State N.B.
12419.	Brooklyn	Bushwick N.B.
12445.	Buffalo	Riverside N.B.
12449.	Floral Park	First N.B.
12450.	Geneva	N.B. of Geneva
12458.	Oceanside	Oceanside N.B.
12460.	Inwood	First N.B.
12473.	Bellport	Bellport N.B.
12476.	Westfield	Grape Belt N.B.
12489.	Kings Park	Kings Park N.B.
12494.	Macedon	First N.B.
12496.	Narrowsburg	First N.B.
12503.	Merrick	First N.B.
12512.	Little Neck	Little Neck N.B.
12515.	North Tarrytown	First N.B.
12516.	New York	Commercial N.B.
12535.	Pittsford	Pittsford N.B.
12538.	Rochester	N.B. of Rochester
12548.	New Rochelle	Central N.B.
12549.	Hankins	First N.B.
12550.	New York	Jamaica N.B.
12551.	Cutchogue	First N.B.
12553.	New York	Grace N.B.
12574.	White Plains	People's N.B.
12586.	Cairo	First N.B.
12592.	Port Byron	N.B. of Port Byron
12593.	East Northport	Citizens' N.B.
12601.	Harrison	First N.B.
12632.	New York	Metropolitan N.B. and Trust Co.
12659.	Great Neck Station	First N.B. of Great Neck
12705.	Hartsdale	Hartsdale N.B.
12746.	Chappaqua	Chappaqua N.B.
12757.	New York	Pacific N.B.
12773.	Rensselaer	N.B. of Rensselaer
12785.	Newburgh	Broadway N.B.
12788.	Patchogue	People's N.B.
12810.	Savannah	N.B. of Savannah
12811.	Pleasantville	First N.B.
12818.	East Rockaway	East Rockaway N.B.
12825.	New York	Fordham N.B.
12836.	Lyons Falls	Lyons Falls N.B.
12837.	New York	Bowery N.B.
12874.	New York	Central N.B.
12884.	Sherrill	First N.B.
12885.	New York, Astoria	Long Island N.B.
12892.	New York	Lafayette N.B. of Brooklyn
12897.	New York	N.B. of Ridgewood
12900.	Melrose	Melrose N.B.
12925.	West Seneca, Buffalo	Seneca N.B.
12932.	New York	Peoples Trust Co. of Brooklyn Nat. Banking Ass'n.
12938.	North Syracuse	North Syracuse N.B.
12940.	Tuckahoe	Crestwood N.B.
12948.	New York	Rugby N.B. of Brooklyn
12951.	Central Park	Central Park N.B.
12954.	Waverly	Citizens N.B.
12956.	Elmsford	First N.B.
12957.	New York	Woodside N.B.
12958.	Fair Haven	Fair Haven N.B.
12963.	Seaford	Seaford N.B.
12965.	New York	N.B. of Yorkville
12970.	New York	Traders N.B. of Brooklyn
12980.	New York	Granite N.B. of Brooklyn
12987.	Hampton Bays	Hampton Bays N.B.
12992.	Ardsley	First N.B.
12997.	Franklin Square	Franklin Square N.B.
13000.	New York	Flatbush N.B. of Brooklyn
13004.	Endicott	Endicott N.B.
13006.	Livonia	Stewart N.B.
13025.	New York	Discount N.B.
13027.	New York	Claremont N.B.
13035.	New York	Elmhurst N.B.
13037.	Interlaken	Wheeler N.B.
13045.	New York	Seward N.B.
13049.	White Plains	Plaza N.B.
13051.	New York	Greenwich N.B.
13055.	New York	Prospect N.B. of Brooklyn
13062.	Baldwin	Sunrise N.B.
13063.	New York	Bedford N.B. of Brooklyn
13074.	Long Beach	Nat. City Bank
13080.	New York	Bensonhurst N.B. of Brooklyn
13085.	Buffalo	Frontier N.B.
13088.	New York	Bay Parkway N.B. of Brooklyn
13089.	Bolton Landing	Bolton N.B.
13104.	West Hempstead	West Hempstead N.B.
13105.	New York	College Point N.B.
13115.	New York	Douglaston N.B.
13121.	Mahopac	Mahopac N.B.
13122.	New York	Guardian N.B.
13124.	East Williston	Williston N.B. of Williston Park
13126.	Glen Head	First N.B.
13130.	Lake Ronkonkoma	N.B. of Lake Ronkonkoma
13132.	New York	Mutual N.B.
13143.	Glen Cove	First N.B.
13145.	Webster	Webster N.B.
13149.	New York	Springfield Gardens N.B.
13163.	New York	Longacre N.B.
13193.	New York	Bank of America Nat. Ass'n.
13194.	New York	Commercial Exchange N.B.
13207.	New York	Industrial N.B.
13219.	Buffalo	Lincoln N.B.
13220.	Buffalo	East Side N.B.
13228.	Eastport	Eastport N.B.
13229.	Wyoming	N.B. of Wyoming
13234.	Bellerose	First N.B.
13237.	New York	Dunbar N.B.
13239.	Yonkers	Bryn Mawr-Nepperhan N.B.
13242.	New York	Forest Hills N.B.
13246.	Bolivar	First N.B.
13250.	New York	Commercial N.B. and Trust Co.
13254.	New York	Straus N.B. and Trust Co.
13260.	New York	Lefcourt Normandie N.B.
13289.	Wells	Hamilton County N.B.
13292.	New York	Brooklyn N.B.
13295.	New York	Sterling N.B. and Trust Co.
13296.	New York	N.B. of Queens County
13301.	New York	Blair N.B.
13304.	New York	Kingsboro N.B. of Brooklyn
13310.	Port Washington	Harbor N.B.
13314.	Nanuet	Nanuet N.B.
13319.	Yonkers	Central N.B.
13326.	Roslyn	Roslyn N.B. and Trust Co.
13327.	New York	Broadway N.B. and Trust Co.
13330.	Rochester	First N.B. and Trust Co.
13334.	New York	N.B. of Bayside
13336.	New York	Fort Greene N.B.
13360.	New York	Washington Square N.B.
13365.	La Fargeville	First N.B.
13377.	Elmira	Southside N.B.
13379.	New York	Newtown N.B.
13393.	Syracuse	Lincoln N.B. and Trust Co.
13404.	Mineola	Central N.B.
13441.	Buffalo	Niagara N.B.
13442.	New York	National Exchange Bank and Trust Co.
13445.	Mattituck	Mattituck N.B. and Trust Co.
13476.	Minoa	First N.B.
13493.	Odessa	First N.B.
13521.	Argyle	N.B. of Argyle
13528.	Middletown	First Merchants N.B. and Trust Co.
13545.	Washingtonville	First N.B.
13548.	Plattsburg	Merchants N.B.
13559.	Montgomery	First N.B.
13563.	Sidney	First N.B
13567.	Highland Falls	First N.B.
13575.	Greene	First N.B.
13583.	Montour Falls	Montour N.B.
13584.	Carthage	Carthage National Exchange Bank
13590.	Callicoon	First N.B.
13592.	Mamaroneck	First N.B.
13664.	Painted Post	First N.B.
13748.	Cherry Valley	Otsego County N.B.
13822.	Kingston	National Ulster County Bank
13825.	Florida	N.B. of Florida
13876.	Canajoharie	National Spraker Bank
13882.	Yonkers	First N.B.
13889.	Tuckahoe	Crestwood N.B.
13895.	Tuxedo	N.B. of Tuxedo
13909.	Andover	Andover N.B.
13911.	Gouverneur	First N.B.
13913.	Washingtonville	Central N.B.
13945.	Philmont	Philmont N.B.
13952.	Buffalo	Lincoln-East Side N.B.
13955.	New Rochelle	First N.B.
13956.	Middletown	N.B. of Middletown
13959.	New York	Fidelity N.B.
13960.	Pine Bush	N.B. of Pine Bush
13962.	Windham	N.B. of Windham
13965.	Brockport	Brockport N.B.
14019.	Kings Park	N.B. of Kings Park
14025.	Oxford	N.B. of Oxford
14078.	Cherry Creek	Cherry Creek N.B.
14267.	Phelps	N.B. of Phelps

NORTH CAROLINA

Charter #	City	Name of Bank
1547.	Charlotte	First N.B.
1557.	Raleigh	Raleigh N.B. of N.C.
1632.	New Berne	N.B. of New Berne
1656.	Wilmington	First N.B.
1659.	Salem	First N.B.
1682.	Raleigh	State N.B.
1756.	Fayetteville	Fayetteville N.B.
1766.	Raleigh	Citizens' N.B.
1781.	Charlotte	Merchants and Farmers' N.B.
2003.	Fayetteville	People's N.B.
2135.	Charlotte	Commercial N.B.
2314.	Charlotte	Traders' N.B.
2319.	Winston	First N.B.
2321.	Wilson	First N.B.
2322.	Greensboro	N.B. of Greensboro
2425.	Winston	Wachovia N.B.
2981.	Salisbury	First N.B.
3389.	Raleigh	N.B. of Raleigh
3418.	Asheville	First N.B.
3490.	High Point	First N.B.
3682.	Statesville	First N.B.
3811.	Durham	First N.B.
3903.	Concord	Concord N.B.
4094.	Asheville	N.B. of Asheville
4292.	Winston, Winston-Salem	People's N.B.
4377.	Gastonia	First N.B.
4568.	High Point	Commercial N.B.
4597.	Hickory	First N.B.
4628.	Elizabeth City	First and Citizens' N.B.
4726.	Wilmington	Atlantic N.B.
4896.	Mount Airy	First N.B.
4947.	Wadesboro	First N.B.
4960.	Wilmington	N.B. of Wilmington
4997.	Washington	First N.B.
5031.	Greensboro	Greensboro N.B.
5048.	Goldsboro	N.B. of Goldsboro
5055.	Charlotte	Charlotte N.B.
5110.	Asheville	Blue Ridge N.B.
5168.	Greensboro	City N.B.
5182.	Wilmington	Murchison N.B.
5450.	Morganton	First N.B.
5451.	Kings Mountain	First N.B.
5651.	Laurinsburg	First N.B.
5673.	Elkin	Elkin N.B.
5677.	Fayetteville	N.B. of Fayetteville
5698.	Lexington	First N.B.
5767.	Roanoke Rapids	First N.B.
5885.	Oxford	First N.B.
6075.	Newton	Shuford N.B.
6095.	Marion	First N.B.
6554.	Waynesville	First N.B.
6616.	Lillington	N.B. of Lillington
6744.	Lincolnton	First N.B.
6776.	Shelby	First N.B.
7188.	Dunn	First N.B.
7362.	Rocky Mount	First N.B.
7398.	Lumberton	First N.B.
7536.	Gastonia	Citizens' N.B.
7554.	Louisburg	First N.B.
7564.	Henderson	First N.B.
7698.	Durham	Citizens' N.B.
7913.	Wilmington	Southern N.B.
7959.	Shelby	Shelby N.B.
8160.	Greenville	N.B. of Greenville
8184.	Lincolnton	County N.B.
8356.	Tarboro	First N.B.
8445.	**Lenoir**	**First N.B.**
8571.	**West Jefferson**	**First N.B.**
8649.	Burlington	First N.B.
8682.	Fayetteville	Fourth N.B.
8712.	Monroe	First N.B.
8772.	Asheville	American N.B.
8788.	Thomasville	First N.B.
8837.	Hendersonville	First N.B.
8844.	Graham	N.B. of Alamance
8902.	Creedmoor	First N.B.
8953.	Asheboro	First N.B.
8996.	Oxford	N.B. of Granville
9044.	Kinston	N.B. of Kinston
9067.	Raleigh	Commercial N.B.
9076.	Salisbury	People's N.B.
9085.	Kinston	First N.B.
9123.	Greensboro	Commercial N.B.
9124.	Wilmington	American N.B.
9164.	Charlotte	Union N.B.
9203.	Forest City	First N.B.
9335.	Statesville	Commercial N.B.
9458.	Murphy	First N.B.
9471.	Raleigh	Merchants' N.B.
9531.	Mooresville	First N.B.
9548.	Cherryville	First N.B.
9571.	Hendersonville	People's N.B.
9916.	Winston	Merchants' N.B.
10112.	Greensboro	American Exchange N.B.
10260.	Louisburg	Farmers' N.B.
10502.	Smithfield	First N.B.
10608.	Rocky Mount	Planters' N.B.
10610.	Lumberton	N.B. of Lumberton
10614.	Goldsboro	Wayne N.B.
10629.	Mount Olive	First N.B.
10630.	Rocky Mount	N.B. of Rocky Mount
10662.	Spencer	First N.B.
10734.	Hendersonville	Citizens' N.B.
10739.	Selma	First N.B.
10792.	Ayden	Farmers' and Merchants' N.B.
10851.	Hamlet	First N.B.
10876.	Hertford	Farmers' N.B.
10887.	Snow Hill	First N.B.
11091.	Albemarle	First N.B.
11211.	Roxboro	First N.B.
11229.	Reidsville	First N.B.
11431.	Spring Hope	First N.B.
11440.	Smithfield	Citizens' N.B.
11477.	Gastonia	Third N.B.

Charter #	City	Name of Bank
11557.	Murfreesboro	First N.B.
11697.	Mebane	First N.B.
11767.	Warsaw	First N.B.
12009.	Fairmont	First N.B.
12176.	Wilmington	Commercial N.B.
12244.	Asheville	N.B.of Commerce
12259.	Leaksville	First N.B.
12278.	Winston- Salem	Farmers' N.B. and Trust Co.
12461.	Forest City	N.B. of Forest City
12614.	Benson	First N.B.
12633.	La Grange	N.B. of La Grange
12772.	Snow Hill	N.B. of Snow Hill
12896.	Cherryville	Cherryville N.B.
13168.	Fayetteville	Cumberland N.B.
13298.	New Bern	First N.B.
13306.	Tarboro	Edgecombe N.B.
13500.	Forest City	First N.B.
13523.	Lenoir	Union N.B.
13554.	Ayden	First N.B.
13613.	Burlington	N.B. of Burlington
13626.	Wilson	N.B. of Wilson
13636.	Henderson	First N.B.
13657.	Durham	Depositors N.B.
13721.	Asheville	First N.B. & Trust Co.
13761.	Greensboro	Security N.B.
13779.	Gastonia	Citizens N.B.
13791.	Sanford	N.B. of Sanford
13859.	Oxford	Union N.B.
13896.	Oxford	Oxford N.B.
13985.	Greensboro	Guilford N.B.
14147.	Winston-Salem	First N.B.
14229.	Cherryville	Cherryville N.B.
14291.	Gastonia	N.B. of Commerce

NORTH DAKOTA

Charter #	City	Name of Bank
2377.	Fargo	N. Dak. First N.B.
2434.	Bismarck	First N.B.
2514.	Fargo	Red River Valley N.B.
2548.	Valley City	First N.B.
2564.	Grand Forks	First N.B.
2570.	**Grand Forks**	**Citizens' N.B.**
2578.	**Jamestown**	**First N.B.**
2580.	Jamestown	James River N.B.
2585.	Mandan	First N.B.
2624.	Wahpeton	First N.B.
2650.	Valley City	Farmers and Merchants' N.B.
2677.	Bismarck	Bismarck N.B.
2792.	Casselton	First N.B.
2840.	Grafton	First N.B.
2854.	Larimore	First N.B.
2986.	Bismarck	Capital N.B.
3096.	Grafton	Grafton N.B.
3169.	Bismarck	Merchants' N.B.
3301.	Grand Forks	Grand Forks N.B.
3331.	Jamestown	Jamestown N.B.
3397.	Devil's Lake	First N.B.
3400.	Hillsboro	First N.B.
3411.	Hillsboro	Hillsboro N.B.
3436.	Park River	First N.B.
3438.	Pembina	First N.B.
3504.	Grand Forks	Second N.B.
3602.	Fargo	Citizens' N.B.
3669.	Lisbon	First N.B.
3673.	Mayville	First N.B.
3714.	Devil's Lake	Merchants' N.B.
4009.	Minot	First N.B.
4106.	Wahpeton	N.B. of Wahpeton
4143.	Lakota	First N.B.
4256.	Fargo	N.B. of North Dakota
4372.	Grand Forks	Union N.B.
4384.	Dickinson	First N.B.
4537.	Bathgate	First N.B.
4550.	**Saint Thomas**	**First N.B.**
4552.	**Wahpeton**	**Citizens' N.B.**
4561.	**Jamestown**	**Lloyds N.B.**
4802.	**Langdon**	**First N.B.**
4812.	**Grand Forks**	**Merchants' N.B.**
5087.	**Fargo**	**Fargo N.B.**
5364.	**Valley City**	**American N.B.**
5375.	Cooperstown	First N.B.
5408.	Fessenden	First N.B.
5455.	Lakota	N.B. of Lakota
5488.	Harvey	First N.B.
5500.	Minnewaukon	First N.B.
5551.	Carrington	First N.B.
5567.	Williston	First N.B.
5772.	Lidgerwood	First N.B.
5798.	Cando	First N.B.
5886.	Devil's Lake	Ramsey County N.B.
5893.	Hope	First N.B.
5980.	Northwood	First N.B.
6064.	Kenmare	First N.B.
6085.	Bottineau	First N.B.
6157.	Rolla	First N.B.
6210.	Courtenay	First N.B.
6218.	Hankinson	First N.B.
6225.	**Drayton**	**First N.B.**
6255.	**Fairmount**	**First N.B.**
6286.	**Larimore**	**N.B. of Larimore**
6312.	Leeds	First N.B.
6315.	Minot	Minot N.B.
6237.	Washburn	First N.B.
6337.	Churchs Ferry	First N.B.
6341.	Rugby	First N.B.
6393.	New Rockford	First N.B.
6397.	Starkweather	First N.B.
6398.	Ellendale	First N.B.
6407.	Crary	First N.B.
6428.	New Salem	First N.B.
6429.	Minot	Second N.B.
6457.	Oakes	First N.B.
6463.	Page	First N.B.
6474.	Forman	First N.B.
6475.	Omemee	First N.B.
6486.	Enderlin	First N.B.
6518.	Milton	First N.B.
6555.	Kenmare	Kenmare N.B.
6557.	Tower City	First N.B.
6559.	Buffalo	First N.B.
6601.	Edmore	First N.B.
6690.	Lamoure	First N.B.
6712.	Wimbledon	First N.B.
6733.	Bisbee	First N.B.
6743.	Hatton	First N.B.
6766.	Willow City	First N.B.
6898.	Knox	First N.B.
6977.	Sheldon	First N.B.
6985.	Hunter	First N.B.
6988.	Oakes	Oakes N.B.
7008.	Mohall	First N.B.
7116.	Bowbells	First N.B.
7142.	Casselton	Cass County N.B.
7162.	Westhope	First N.B.
7166.	Wyndmere	First N.B.
7234.	Osnabrock	First N.B.
7295.	Fingal	First N.B.
7315.	Carpio	First N.B.
7324.	Finley	First N.B.
7332.	Willow City	Merchants' N.B.
7377.	Cando	Cando N.B.
7569.	Munich	First N.B.
7650.	Hampden	First N.B.
7663.	Dickinson	Dakota N.B.
7689.	Minot	Union N.B.
7693.	Portland	First N.B.
7695.	Wahpeton	German American N.B.
7727.	Hannaford	First N.B.
7810.	Tolley	First N.B.
7820.	Jamestown	Citizens' N.B.
7846.	McCumber	First N.B.
7852.	Adams	First N.B.
7855.	Antler	First N.B.
7857.	Mylo	First N.B.
7866.	Rolette	First N.B.
7872.	Egeland	First N.B.
7879.	Bottineau	Bottineau N.B.
7905.	Hatton	Farmers and Merchants' N.B.
7914.	Edgeley	First N.B.
7918.	Crystal	First N.B.
7943.	Kensal	First N.B.
7955.	Towner	First N.B.
8019.	Rock Lake	First N.B.
8029.	Kramer	First N.B.
8077.	Goodrich	First N.B.
8084.	Hankinson	Citizens' N.B.
8096.	Overly	First N.B.
8124.	McHenry	First N.B.
8170.	Fargo	Merchants' N.B.
8187.	Lansford	First N.B.
8201.	Dickinson	Merchants' N.B.
8226.	Maddock	First N.B.
8230.	Lidgerwood	Farmers' N.B.
8264.	Milnor	Milnor N.B.
8265.	Binford	First N.B.
8280.	Milnor	First N.B.
8298.	Litchville	First N.B.
8324.	Williston	Citizens N.B.
8395.	Hope	Hope N.B.
8419.	Abercrombie	First N.B.
8448.	Sanborn	First N.B.
8502.	Brinsmade	First N.B.
8821.	Turtle Lake	First N.B.
8881.	McCluskey	First N.B.
8886.	Sheyenne	First N.B.
8917.	Wimbledon	Merchants' N.B.
8976.	Bowman	First N.B.
8991.	Hettinger	First N.B.
8997.	Steele	First N.B.
9005.	Sharon	First N.B.
9016.	Glen Ullin	First N.B.
9075.	Langdon	Cavalier County N.B.
9082.	Marmarth	First N.B.
9133.	Walhalla	First N.B.
9161.	Marion	First N.B.
9214.	Ryder	First N.B.
9287.	Nome	First N.B.
9386.	Ambrose	First N.B.
9390.	Anamoose	Anamoose N.B.
9412.	Anamoose	First N.B.
9472.	Stanley	First N.B.
9484.	Beach	First N.B.
9489.	Mott	First N.B.
9521.	Ellendale	Farmers' N.B.
9524.	Drake	First N.B.
9539.	Belfield	First N.B.
9590.	Linton	First N.B.
9622.	Bismarck	City N.B.
9631.	Ellendale	Ellendale N.B.
9684.	Reeder	First N.B.
9689.	Plaza	First N.B.
9698.	Yates	First N.B.
9714.	La Moure	Farmers' N.B.
9754.	Northwood	Citizens' N.B.
9776.	New England	First N.B.
9778.	Garrison	First N.B.
10116.	Cavalier	First N.B.
10405.	Scranton	First N.B.
10425.	East Fairview, Fairview Mont.	First N.B.
10495.	Jamestown	Farmers and Merchants' N.B.
10496.	Reynolds	First N.B.
10519.	Crosby	Citizens' N.B.
10581.	Medina	First N.B.
10596.	Crosby	First N.B.
10604.	Mandan	Merchants' N.B.
10706.	Sentinel Butte	First N.B.
10721.	McVille	First N.B.
10724.	Streeter	First N.B.
10741.	Hebron	First N.B.
10814.	Buxton	First N.B.
10820.	Killdeer	First N.B.
10864.	Ashley	First N.B.
10896.	Portland	Farmers' N.B.
10921.	Taylor	First N.B.
10966.	Van Hook	First N.B.
11069.	Kulm	La Moure County First N.B.
11110.	Neche	First N.B.
11112.	Bathgate	Bathgate N.B.
11142.	Grand Forks	Northwestern N.B.
11166.	Streeter	Citizens' N.B.
11184.	Makoti	First N.B.
11185.	Petersburg	First N.B.
11217.	Fullerton	First N.B.
11226.	Parshall	First N.B.
11272.	Underwood	First N.B.
11297.	Alexander	First N.B.
11311.	Aneta	First N.B.
11338.	Tuttle	First N.B.
11346.	Golva	First N.B.
11353.	Woodworth	First N.B.
11378.	Napoleon	First N.B.
11417.	Valley City	Security N.B.
11494.	Montpelier	First N.B.
11555.	Fargo	Security N.B.
11599.	Thompson	First N.B.
11605.	Mooreton	First N.B.
11641.	Fairmount	N.B. of Fairmount
11665.	Linton	City N.B.
11677.	Hettinger	Live Stock N.B.
11712.	Wilton	First N.B.
11719.	Max	First N.B.
11786.	Fargo	Northern N.B.
12003.	Edgeley	Security N.B.
12023.	Michigan City	Lamb's N.B.
12026.	Fargo	Dakota N.B.
12046.	Cavalier	Merchants' N.B.
12258.	Donnybrook	First N.B.
12393.	Drake	First N.B.
12401.	Dickinson	Liberty N.B.
12464.	Whitman	First N.B.
12502.	Taylor	Security N.B.
12743.	Lidgerwood	Farmers' N.B.
12776.	Lidgerwood	First N.B.
12817.	Valley City	First N.B.
12853.	Gackle	First N.B.
12875.	Wahpeton	N.B. of Wahpeton
13041.	Hope	Security N.B.
13053.	Langdon	First N.B.
13190.	Finnley	Steele County N.B.
13323.	Fargo	Merchants N.B. & Trust Co.
13324.	Valley City	N.B. of Valley City
13344.	Jamestown	N.B. & Trust Co. of Jamestown
13357.	Grand Forks	Red River N.B. & Trust Co.
13362.	Cooperstown	First N.B.
13385.	Valley City	American N.B. & Trust Co.
13398.	Bismarck	Dakota N.B. & Trust Co.
13410.	Glen Ullin	First N.B.
13436.	Neche	First N.B.
13454.	Carson	First N.B.
13455.	Minot	Union N.B. & Trust Co.
13501.	Garrison	First N.B.
13594.	Portland	First & Farmers N.B.
13790.	Grand Forks	First N.B.
14080.	Mott	First N.B.
14275.	Williston	First & Commercial N.B.

OHIO

Charter #	City	Name of Bank
3.	Youngstown	First N.B.
5.	Fremont	First N.B.
7.	Cleveland	First N.B.
9.	Dayton	First N.B.
10.	Dayton	Second N.B.
13.	Cleveland	Second N.B.
16.	Sandusky	First N.B.
20.	Cincinnati	Fifth-Third N.B.
24.	Cincinnati	First N.B.
27.	Akron	First N.B.
32.	Cincinnati	Second N.B.
36.	Findlay	First N.B.
40.	Akron	Second N.B.
43.	Salem	First N.B.
46.	McConnelsville	First N.B.
53.	Lodi	First N.B.
56.	Hamilton	First N.B.
59.	Troy	First N.B.
68.	Portsmouth	First N.B.
72.	Oberlin	First N.B.
74.	Warren	First N.B.
76.	Canton	First N.B.
86.	Germantown	First N.B.
90.	Upper Sandusky	First N.B.
91.	Toledo	First N.B.
92.	Logan	First N.B.
93.	Cincinnati	Fourth N.B.
98.	Ironton	First N.B.
100.	Cadiz	First N.B.
101.	Greenfield	First N.B.
106.	Ravenna	First N.B.
118.	Circleville	First N.B.
123.	Columbus	First N.B.
127.	Cardington	First N.B.
128.	Chillicothe	First N.B.
131.	Zanesville	Second N.B.
132.	Pomeroy	First N.B.
133.	Beverly	First N.B.
136.	Gallipolis	First N.B.

Charter #	City	Name of Bank
137.	Lancaster	First N.B.
141.	Cambridge	First N.B.
142.	Marietta	First N.B.
153.	Geneva	First N.B.
164.	Zanesville	First N.B.
171.	South Charleston	First N.B.
172.	Circleville	Second N.B.
183.	Ashland	First N.B.
210.	Sandusky	Second N.B.
214.	Bridgeport	First N.B.
215.	Norwalk	First N.B.
216.	Massillon	First N.B.
220.	Painesville	First N.B.
233.	Athens	First N.B.
237.	Bryan	First N.B.
238.	Springfield	First N.B.
242.	Ironton	Second N.B.
243.	Delaware	First N.B.
248.	Toledo	Second N.B.
257.	Sidney	First N.B.
258.	Mount Gilead	First N.B.
263.	Springfield	Second N.B.
274.	Delphos	First N.B.
277.	Xenia	Second N.B.
284.	Washington C.H.	First N.B.
287.	Marion	First N.B.
289.	Ripley	First N.B.
315.	Saint Clairsville	First N.B.
350.	Ravenna	Second N.B.
365.	Wilmington	First N.B.
369.	Xenia	First N.B.
378.	Cuyahoga Falls	First N.B.
388.	Granville	First N.B.
419.	Galion	First N.B.
422.	Van Wert	First N.B.
427.	Jefferson	First N.B.
436.	Mansfield	First N.B.
438.	Elyria	First N.B.
443.	Bucyrus	First N.B.
463.	Canton	Second N.B.
464.	Wellington	First N.B.
480.	Mansfield	Richland N.B.
492.	Mount Pleasant	First N.B.
501.	Smithfield	First N.B.
530.	Eaton	First N.B.
591.	Columbus	Nat. Exchange Bank
599.	Columbus	Franklin N.B.
607.	Toledo	Toledo N.B.
620.	Cincinnati	Central N.B.
630.	Cincinnati	Ohio N.B.
652.	Kent	Kent N.B.
715.	Batavia	First N.B.
738.	Franklin	First N.B.
773.	Cleveland	Merchants' N.B.
786.	Cleveland	Nat. City Bank
787.	Hillsborough	First N.B.
800.	Mansfield	Farmers' N.B.
807.	Cleveland	Commercial N.B.
809.	Toledo	Northern N.B.
828.	Wooster	Wayne County N.B.
829.	Hamilton	Second N.B.
844.	Cincinnati	Merchants' N.B.
853.	Delaware	Delaware County N.B.
858.	Newark	First N.B.
859.	Marietta	Marietta N.B.
863.	Urbana	Citizens' N.B.
898.	Dayton	Dayton N.B.
900.	Tiffin	First N.B.
907.	Tiffin	Nat. Exchange Bank
908.	Mount Vernon	First N.B.
911.	Barnesville	First N.B.
916.	Urbana	Champaign N.B.
931.	Norwalk	Norwalk N.B.
933.	Ripley	Farmers' N.B.
935.	Portsmouth	Portsmouth N.B.
973.	Salem	Farmers' N.B.
975.	Ashtabula	Farmers' N.B.
1006.	Piqua	Piqua N.B.
1044.	Wellsville	First N.B.
1051.	Mount Vernon	Knox County N.B.
1061.	Piqua	Citizens N.B.
1062.	Steubenville	Jefferson N.B.
1064.	London	Madison N.B.
1068.	New Richmond	First N.B.
1088.	Portsmouth	Farmers' N.B.
1092.	Greenville	Farmers'N.B.
1146.	Springfield	Mad River N.B.
1164.	Steubenville	First N.B.
1172.	Chillicothe	Ross County N.B.
1185.	Cincinnati	Commercial N.B.
1230.	Zanesville	Muskingum N.B.
1238.	Lebanon	First N.B.
1241.	Lancaster	Hocking Valley N.B.
1277.	Chillicothe	Chillicothe N.B.
1318.	Massillon	Union N.B.
1447.	Cadiz	Harrison N.B.
1545.	Middletown	First N.B.
1578.	Warren	Trumbull N.B.
1689.	Cleveland	Ohio N.B.
1784.	Bellefontaine	Bellefontaine N.B.
1788.	Dayton	Merchants' N.B.
1895.	Toledo	Merchants' N.B.
1903.	Jackson	First N.B.
1904.	Plymouth	First N.B.
1906.	Defiance	Defiance N.B.
1912.	Wooster	N.B. of Wooster
1917.	Napoleon	First N.B.
1920.	Coshocton	First N.B.
1923.	Millersburg	First N.B.
1929.	Shelby	First N.B.
1930.	Minerva	First N.B.
1942.	Cambridge	Guernsey N.B.
1944.	Bellaire	First N.B.
1948.	Portsmouth	Iron N.B.
1958.	Portsmouth	Kinney N.B.
1972.	Washington C.H.	Fayette County N.B.
1980.	Pomeroy	Pomeroy N.B.
1981.	New London	First N.B.
1982.	Manchester	Manchester N.B.
1984.	Galion	Citizens' N.B.
1989.	Quaker City	Quaker City N.B.
1997.	Wilmington	Clinton County N.B.
1999.	New Philadelphia	Citizens' N.B.
2004.	Berea	First N.B.
2025.	Middletown	First and Merchants' N.B.
2026.	Jefferson	Second N.B.
2031.	Ashtabula	Ashtabula N.B.
2034.	Garrettsville	First N.B.
2035.	Lima	First N.B.
2036.	McArthur	Vinton County N.B.
2037.	Green Spring	First N.B.
2339.	Hillsborough	Citizens N.B.
2041.	Alliance	First N.B.
2052.	Malta	Malta N.B.
2053.	Medina	First N.B.
2056.	New Lexington	First N.B.
2061.	Sandusky	Third N.B.
2071.	Urbana	Third N.B.
2091.	Medina	Phoenix N.B.
2098.	Springfield	Lagonda N.B.
2102.	Caldwell	Noble County N.B.
2146.	East Liverpool	First N.B.
2160.	Steubenville	Nat. Exchange Bank
2181.	Thurman	Centreville N.B.
2203.	New Lisbon	First N.B.
2210.	Middleport	First N.B.
2217.	Youngstown	Second N.B.
2219.	Batesville	First N.B.
2220.	Waynesville	Waynesville N.B.
2282.	Franklin	Farmers' N.B.
2296.	Toledo	Commercial N.B.
2302.	Bellevue	First N.B.
2315.	Cincinnati	Nat. La Fayette Bank
2325.	Mechanicsburg	Farmers' N.B.
2350.	Youngstown	Mahoning N.B.
2360.	Lebanon	Lebanon N.B.
2389.	Hubbard	Hubbard N.B.
2423.	Columbus	Fourth N.B.
2438.	Monroeville	First N.B.
2444.	Cadiz	Farmers and Mechanics' N.B.
2449.	Hillsborough	Merchants' N.B.
2459.	Mount Gilead	Morrow County N.B.
2474.	Bryan	Farmers' N.B.
2479.	Warren	Second N.B.
2480.	Bellefontaine	People's N.B.
2482.	Youngstown	Commercial N.B.
2488.	Saint Paris	First N.B.
2489.	Canton	City N.B.
2495.	Cincinnati	Citizens' N.B.
2496.	Granville	First N.B.
2497.	Lima	Merchants' N.B.
2500.	Kenton	First N.B.
2516.	Defiance	Merchants' N.B.
2524.	Cincinnati	Lincoln N.B.
2529.	Zanesville	Citizens' N.B.
2542.	Cincinnati	Metropolitan N.B.
2544.	East Liverpool	Potters' N.B.
2549.	Cincinnati	Union N.B.
2575.	Xenia	Citizens' N.B.
2577.	Mansfield	Citizens' N.B.
2582.	Uhrichsville	Farmers and Merchants' N.B.
2604.	Dayton	Winters N.B.
2605.	Columbus	Commercial N.B.
2616.	Cincinnati	Exchange N.B.
2620.	Springfield	Springfield N.B.
2625.	Lorain	First N.B.
2628.	Van Wert	Van Wert N.B.
2662.	Cleveland	N.B. of Commerce
2664.	Cincinnati	Second N.B.
2678.	Dayton	Third N.B.
2690.	Cleveland	First N.B.
2691.	Salem	First N.B.
2693.	Youngstown	First N.B.
2698.	Akron	First N.B.
2703.	Fremont	First N.B.
2705.	Georgetown	First N.B.
2712.	McConnelsville	First N.B.
2716.	Akron	Second N.B.
2718.	Oberlin	Citizens' N.B.
2719.	Geneva	First N.B.
2727.	Troy	First N.B.
2730.	Cincinnati	Third N.B.
2754.	South Charleston	Farmers' N.B.
2798.	Cincinnati	Fifth-Third N.B.
2810.	Sandusky	Moss N.B.
2817.	Circleville	Third N.B.
2831.	Fostoria	First N.B.
2837.	Ripley	Ripley N.B.
2842.	Painesville	Painesville N.B.
2859.	Lima	Lima N.B.
2861.	Cambridge	Old N.B.
2863.	Elyria	First N.B.
2866.	Wellington	First N.B.
2872.	Cambridge	Central N.B.
2874.	Dayton	City N.B.
2882.	Felicity	First N.B.
2885.	Delphos	Delphos N.B.
2908.	Barnesville	People's N.B.
2922.	Cincinnati	Cincinnati N.B.
2932.	Xenia	Xenia N.B.
2942.	West Liberty	Logan N.B.
2946.	Akron	City N.B.
2956.	Cleveland	Cleveland N.B.
2992.	Greenville	Second N.B.
2993.	Chillicothe	Central N.B.
3004.	Tippecanoe City	Tipp N.B.
3077.	Kinsman	Kinsman N.B.
3141.	Sandusky	Citizens' N.B.
3157.	Wapakoneta	First N.B.
3177.	Flushing	First N.B.
3191.	Newark	People's N.B.
3202.	Cleveland	Union N.B.
3234.	Milford	Milford N.B.
3272.	Cleveland	Mercantile N.B.
3274.	Bucyrus	Second N.B.
3291.	Ripley	Citizens' N.B.
3310.	Steubenville	Steubenville N.B.
3315.	Tiffin	Tiffin N.B.
3328.	Mount Vernon	Knox N.B.
3362.	Warren	Western Reserve N.B.
3461.	Cincinnati	Fidelity N.B.
3477.	Findlay	Buckeye N.B.
3492.	Conneaut	First N.B.
3505.	Kenton	Kenton N.B.
3519.	Leetonia	First N.B.
3535.	Wapakoneta	People's N.B.
3545.	Cleveland	Euclid Park N.B.
3565.	Wellston	First N.B.
3581.	Galion	Galion N.B.
3606.	Cincinnati	Ohio Valley N.B.
3610.	Columbus	Clinton N.B.
3639.	Cincinnati	Atlas N.B.
3642.	Cincinnati	Market N.B.
3654.	Canfield	Farmers' N.B.
3707.	Cincinnati	Equitable N.B.
3721.	Alliance	First N.B.
3729.	Findlay	American N.B.
3750.	Piqua	Third N.B.
3772.	Lima	Ohio N.B.
3820.	Toledo	N.B. of Commerce
3821.	Dayton	Fourth N.B.
3825.	Troy	Troy N.B.
3840.	Hamilton	Miami Valley N.B.
3876.	Miamisburg	First N.B.
3889.	Eaton	Preble County N.B.
3950.	Cleveland	State N.B.
4045.	Bowling Green	First N.B.
4054.	Dayton	American N.B.
4133.	Lockland	First N.B.
4164.	Marietta	Citizens' N.B.
4190.	Niles	First N.B.
4197.	Clyde	First N.B.
4219.	Saint Marys	First N.B.
4239.	Lebanon	Citizens' N.B.
4286.	Massillon	Merchants' N.B.
4293.	Dover	Exchange N.B.
4298.	Zanesville	Union N.B.
4318.	Cleveland	Central N.B. Savings and Trust Co.
4331.	Dover	First N.B.
4336.	Ironton	Citizens' N.B.
4347.	North Baltimore	First N.B.
4443.	Columbus	First N.B.
4472.	Middleport	Middleport N.B.
4506.	Ashtabula	Marine N.B.
4579.	Columbus	Deshler N.B.
4585.	Toledo	N.B. of Toledo
4599.	Oxford	First N.B.
4657.	Wooster	Wooster N.B.
4661.	Defiance	First N.B.
4671.	Chardon	First N.B.
4697.	Columbus	Hayden-Clinton N.B.
4712.	New London	New London N.B.
4763.	Washington C.H.	Midland N.B.
4772.	Cortland	First N.B.
4778.	Huron	First N.B.
4782.	Cleveland	Western Reserve N.B.
4792.	Sandusky	Third Nat. Exchange Bank
4805.	Urbana	N.B. of Urbana
4822.	Miamisburg	Citizens' N.B.
4839.	Arcanum	First N.B.
4842.	Medina	Old Phoenix N.B.
4853.	Cadiz	Fourth N.B.
4864.	Belmont	First N.B.
4867.	Hicksville	First N.B.
4884.	Girard	First N.B.
4961.	Akron	Citizens' N.B.
4970.	Youngstown	Wick N.B.
4977.	Niles	City N.B.
4993.	Saint Clairsville	Second N.B.
5006.	Cleveland	Park N.B.
5029.	Columbus	Merchants and Manufacturers' N.B.
5039.	Steubenville	Commercial N.B.
5065.	Columbus	Ohio N.B.
5075.	Ashtabula	N.B. of Ashtabula
5090.	Cleveland	American Exchange N.B.
5098.	East Liverpool	Citizens' N.B.
5099.	Crestline	First N.B.
5100.	Franklin	Franklin N.B.
5103.	Coshocton	Coshocton N.B.
5125.	Lima	American N.B.
5139.	Medina	Medina County N.B.
5144.	Dresden	First N.B.
5152.	Cleveland	Colonial N.B.
5160.	Springfield	Citizens' N.B.
5191.	Cleveland	Coal and Iron N.B.
5194.	Cleveland	Bank of Commerce Nat. Assn.
5197.	Scio	Farmers and Producers' N.B.

Charter #	City	Name of Bank
5212.	Marietta	Central N.B.
5214.	Sidney	First Nat. Exchange Bank
5218.	Napoleon	First N.B.
5230.	Barberton	First N.B.
5251.	Mount Gilead	N.B. of Morrow County
5259.	McConnelsville	Citizens' N.B.
5262.	Newcomerstown	First N.B.
5277.	College Corner	First N.B.
5315.	Montpelier	First N.B.
5329.	Lowell	First N.B.
5341.	Montpelier	Montpelier N.B.
5344.	Minerva	First N.B.
5350.	Cleveland	Century N.B.
5370.	Mantua	First N.B.
5371.	Lorain	N.B. of Commerce
5382.	Mount Sterling	First N.B.
5396.	Carrollton	First N.B.
5414.	Woodsfield	First N.B.
5425.	Ada	First N.B.
5427.	Tiffin	City N.B.
5448.	Upper Sandusky	Commercial N.B.
5522.	Plain City	Farmers' N.B.
5523.	Celina	First N.B.
5530.	Covington	Citizens' N.B.
5552.	Chesterhill	First N.B.
5555.	Roseville	First N.B.
5577.	Delta	Farmers' N.B.
5602.	Bethesda	First N.B.
5618.	Dillonvale	First N.B.
5626.	Bluffton	First N.B.
5627.	Bethel	First N.B.
5634.	Chillicothe	Citizens' N.B.
5635.	Waverly	First N.B.
5640.	Fredericktown	First N.B.
5641.	Byesville	First N.B.
5650.	Marion	City N.B.
5653.	Cleveland	Metropolitan N.B.
5678.	Cleveland	Market N.B.
5694.	Mingo Junction	First N.B.
5760.	Zanesville	Old Citizens' N.B.
5762.	Clarington	First N.B.
5769.	Zanesville	Commercial N.B.
5802.	Hicksville	Hicksville N.B.
5805.	Cleveland	Bankers' N.B.
5819.	Barberton	American N.B.
5828.	Wadsworth	First N.B.
5862.	Paulding	Paulding N.B.
5870.	Wadsworth	Wadsworth N.B.
5917.	Paulding	First N.B.
5996.	Georgetown	People's N.B.
5999.	New Matamoras	First N.B.
6016.	Adena	People's N.B.
6059.	Oxford	Oxford N.B.
6068.	Fairport Harbor	First N.B.
6119.	Carey	First N.B.
6147.	Youngstown	Old N.B.
6227.	Port Clinton	First N.B.
6249.	Burton	First N.B.
6280.	Delphos	N.B. of Delphos
6289.	Warren	New N.B.
6296.	Columbiana	First N.B.
6308.	Marion	Marion N.B.
6314.	Elmwood Place	First N.B.
6322.	Norwood	First N.B.
6345.	Wellsville	People's N.B.
6353.	Warren	Union N.B.
6362.	Orrville	Orrville N.B.
6372.	Dalton	First N.B.
6379.	Orrville	First N.B.
6391.	Belmont	Belmont N.B.
6455.	Sandusky	Commercial N.B.
6458.	Caldwell	Citizens' N.B.
6466.	Ravenna	Ravenna N.B.
6505.	New Lexington	Citizens' N.B.
6515.	Butler	First N.B.
6529.	Dresden	Dresden N.B.
6565.	Leipsic	First N.B.
6566.	Cambridge	N.B. of Cambridge
6593.	East Palestine	First N.B.
6594.	New Carlisle	First N.B.
6620.	Mount Gilead	Mount Gilead N.B.
6621.	Barnesville	N.B. of Barnesville
6624.	Bridgeport	Bridgeport N.B.
6628.	Dunkirk	First N.B.
6632.	Oak Harbor	First N.B.
6640.	Mount Pleasant	Mount Pleasant N.B.
6652.	Dunkirk	Woodruff N.B.
6656.	Weston	First N.B.
6657.	Loudonville	First N.B.
6662.	Summerfield	First N.B.
6667.	Mount Pleasant	People's N.B.
6675.	La Rue	Campbell N.B.
6763.	Akron	Nat. City Bank
6770.	Elmore	First N.B.
6779.	Loveland	Loveland N.B.
6816.	Loveland	First N.B.
6827.	Grove City	First N.B.
6836.	Dennison	Twin City N.B.
6843.	Dennison	Dennison N.B.
6892.	Coshocton	Commercial N.B.
6938.	Hopedale	First N.B.
6943.	Watertown	First N.B.
6976.	New Concord	First N.B.
7001.	Greenwich	First N.B.
7006.	Ottawa	First N.B.
7017.	Lodi	Exchange N.B.
7025.	Beallsville	First N.B.
7035.	Plymouth	People's N.B.
7039.	Piketon	Piketon N.B.
7074.	Kalida	First N.B.
7091.	Wauseon	First N.B
7130.	Greenville	Greenville N.B.
7187.	New Holland	First N.B.
7235.	Amesville	First N.B.
7237.	Somerset	First N.B.
7248.	Mount Vernon	Farmers and Merchants' N.B.
7327.	Bellaire	Farmers and Merchants' N.B.
7370.	Clarksville	Farmers' N.B.
7391.	Newton Falls	First N.B.
7399.	Senecaville	First N.B.
7403.	Mason	First N.B.
7456.	Cleves	Hamilton County N.B.
7486.	Bowerston	First N.B.
7487.	Cleveland	Nat. Commercial Bank
7505.	Delaware	Delaware N.B.
7517.	Lancaster	Fairfield N.B.
7518.	Forest	First N.B.
7542.	New Richmond	New Richmond N.B.
7557.	Eaton	Eaton N.B.
7584.	Columbus	Union N.B.
7596.	Utica	First N.B.
7621.	Columbus	N.B. of Commerce
7631.	Buckeye City	First N.B.
7638.	Mount Vernon	New Knox N.B.
7639.	Baltimore	First N.B.
7649.	Logan	N.B. of Logan
7661.	Mount Healthy	First N.B.
7670.	Wooster	Citizens' N.B.
7671.	Westerville	First N.B.
7688.	Steubenville	People's N.B.
7711.	Sardis	First N.B.
7744.	Athens	Athens N.B.
7745.	Columbus	Huntington N.B.
7759.	Powhatan	First N.B.
7781.	Portsmouth	Central N.B.
7787.	Newark	Franklin N.B.
7790.	Rock Creek	First N.B.
7795.	Tiffin	Commercial N.B.
7800.	Sardinia	First N.B.
7818.	Columbus	City N.B.
7851.	New Bremen	First N.B.
7862.	Sidney	Citizens' N.B.
7896.	Spring Valley	Spring Valley N.B.
7947.	Monroe	Monroe N.B.
7984.	Somerton	First N.B.
8000.	Franklin	Warren N.B.
8017.	Convoy	First N.B.
8042.	Stockport	First N.B.
8127.	Saint Paris	Central N.B.
8175.	Coolville	Coolville N.B.
8182.	Centerburg	First N.B.
8188.	Milford	Citizens' N.B.
8228.	Harrison	First N.B.
8251.	Wilmington	Citizens' N.B.
8300.	Camden	First N.B.
8411.	Sabina	First N.B.
8420.	Belpre	First N.B.
8423.	Glouster	First N.B.
8438.	Cincinnati	American N.B.
8441.	Middleport	Citizens' N.B.
8478.	Cheviot	First N.B.
8488.	Carthage	First N.B.
8505.	Norwood	Norwood N.B.
8507.	Lebanon	Farmers and Merchants' N.B.
8536.	Jackson Center	First N.B.
8557.	Madisonville, Cincinnati	First N.B.
8588.	Blanchester	First N.B.
8701.	Lima	Old N.B.
8705.	Toronto	First N.B.
8709.	Morrow	First N.B.
8741.	Morrow	Morrow N.B.
8826.	Toronto	N.B. of Toronto
8839.	Tippecanoe City	Citizens' N.B.
8978.	Lewisville	First N.B.
9062.	West Milton	First N.B.
9091.	Manchester	Farmers' N.B.
9095.	Mount Sterling	Citizens' N.B.
9163.	Bradford	First N.B.
9179.	Newark	Park N.B.
9192.	Fostoria	Union N.B.
9194.	Ansonia	First N.B.
9199.	Richwood	First N.B.
9211.	New Paris	New Paris N.B.
9221.	Hudson	N.B. of Hudson
9243.	Hillsboro	Farmers and Traders' N.B.
9255.	Arcanum	Farmers' N.B.
9274.	Mendon	First N.B.
9282.	Columbus	Central N.B.
9284.	Logan	Rempel N.B.
9336.	Versailles	First N.B.
9394.	Higginsport	First N.B.
9446.	Springfield	Farmers' N.B.
9450.	Okeana	First N.B.
9487.	West Union	First N.B.
9518.	Seven Mile	Farmers' N.B.
9536.	Kingston	First N.B.
9547.	Lancaster	Lancaster N.B.
9553.	Brookville	First N.B.
9563.	Pitsburg	First N.B.
9630.	Louisville	First N.B.
9675.	Osborn	First N.B.
9761.	Mount Washington	First N.B.
9768.	Bremen	First N.B.
9799.	Neffs	Neffs N.B.
9815.	Racine	First N.B.
9859.	Somerville	Somerville N.B.
9930.	Williamsburg	First N.B.
9953.	Akron	First-Second N.B.
9961.	Wapakoneta	Auglaize N.B.
10058.	Gettysburg	Citizens' N.B.
10101.	New London	Third N.B.
10105.	Greenfield	People's N.B.
10267.	Williamsport	Farmers' N.B.
10373.	London	Central N.B.
10436.	Haviland	Farmers' N.B.
10479.	Athens	N.B. of Athens Assn.
10677.	Lodi	People's N.B.
10692.	Mount Orab	Brown County N.B.
10947.	New Vienna	First N.B.
11141.	Cleveland	Union Commerce N.B.
11216.	Freeport, Prairie Depot	Prairie Depot N.B.
11252.	Chagrin Falls	First N.B.
11275.	Norwalk	Citizens' N.B.
11343.	Pandora	First N.B.
11363.	Cumberland	First N.B.
11376.	Cleveland	Northern N.B.
11383.	Sycamore	First N.B.
11573.	Bluffton	Citizens' N.B.
11598.	Kansas	First N.B.
11614.	Middleport	Mutual N.B.
11617.	Harveysburg	Harveysburg N.B.
11714.	Carrollton	First N.B.
11723.	Antwerp	First N.B.
11726.	Bellefontaine	People's N.B.
11733.	West Alexandria	First N.B.
11772.	Lynchburg	First N.B.
11803.	Rockford	First N.B.
11804.	Rockford	Rockford N.B.
11831.	Marion	Nat. City Bank and Trust Co.
11851.	Edon	Farmers' N.B.
11862.	Cleveland	Brotherhood of Locomotive Engineers Co-Operative N.B.
11878.	Cleveland	Superior N.B. and Trust Co.
11948.	Mineral City	First N.B.
11994.	Willoughby	First N.B.
12008.	Flushing	Community N.B.
12013.	Sardinia	Farmer's N.B.
12034.	Alliance	Alliance N.B.
12196.	Delphos	Old N.B.
12321.	Wellington	First N.B.
12332.	Youngstown	Second N.B.
12347.	Rocky River	First N.B.
12350.	Columbus	Columbus N.B.
12365.	Port Clinton	Magruder N.B.
12446.	Cincinnati	Brotherhood of Railway Clerks N.B.
13150.	Jewett	First N.B.
13154.	Caldwell	Noble County N.B.
13171.	Smithfield	First N.B.
13198.	West Union	N.B. of Adams County
13256.	Toledo	West Toledo N.B.
13273.	Crestline	First N.B.
13318.	Painesville	Painesville N.B. & Trust Co.
13457.	Defiance	N.B. of Defiance
13490.	Washington Court House	First N.B.
13535.	Delaware	Delaware County N.B.
13569.	Chardon	Central N.B.
13586.	Youngstown	Union N.B.
13596.	New Lexington	Peoples N.B.
13687.	Massillon	First N.B.
13715.	Lakewood	Peoples N.B.
13740.	Bryan	Citizens N.B.
13742.	Orrville	N.B. of Orrville
13749.	Bellefontaine	Bellefontaine N.B.
13767.	Lima	N.B. of Lima
13774.	Cleves	Cleves N.B.
13797.	Van Wert	Van Wert N.B.
13802.	Dennison	First N.B.
13832.	Portsmouth	N.B. of Portsmouth
13836.	Kinsman	First N.B.
13844.	Caldwell	First N.B.
13847.	Woodsfield	Citizens N.B.
13850.	East Palestine	First N.B.
13883.	Carrollton	First N.B.
13899.	Bryan	First N.B.
13905.	Cambridge	Central N.B.
13912.	Montpelier	N.B. of Montpelier
13914.	Bellaire	First N.B.
13920.	Mansfield	Mansfield Savings Trust N.B.
13922.	St. Clairsville	First N.B.
13923.	Coshocton	Coshocton N.B.
13944.	Greenville	Greenville N.B.
13971.	Marietta	New First N.B.
13989.	Port Clinton	Port Clinton N.B.
13996.	Bellaire	Farmers & Merchants N.B.
13997.	Fremont	N.B. of Fremont
14011.	Dillonvale	First N.B.
14030.	Toledo	N.B. of Toledo
14050.	Bridgeport	Bridgeport N.B.
14077.	Bradford	Bradford N.B.
14105.	Springfield	Lagonda N.B.
14132.	St. Marys	First N.B.
14141.	Brookville	Brookville N.B.
14183.	Mingo Junction	Mingo N.B.
14188.	Arcanum	Arcanum N.B.

Charter #	City	Name of Bank
14192.	**Mt. Healthy**	**Mt. Healthy N.B.**
14203.	**Oak Harbor**	**N.B. of Oak Harbor**
14232.	**Painesville**	**First N.B.**
14261.	Bethesda	Goshen N.B.
14264.	West Milton	Citizens N.B.
14290.	Lorain	N.B. of Lorain
14294.	New Bremen	First N.B.
14300.	Paulding	N.B. of Paulding
14316.	Camden	First N.B.
14323.	Mt. Gilead	First N.B.

OKLAHOMA

Charter #	City	Name of Bank
4348.	Gutherie	First N.B.
4383.	Gutherie	N.B. of Gutherie
4385.	Muskogee	First N.B.
4393.	Ardmore	First N.B.
4402.	Oklahoma City	First N.B.
4636.	Purcell	Purcell N.B.
4704.	Vinita	First N.B.
4705.	Gutherie	Capitol N.B.
4723.	Ardmore	City N.B.
4756.	Purcell	Chickasaw N.B.
4770.	Oklahoma City	Oklahoma N.B.
4830.	El Reno	First N.B.
4862.	Oklahoma City	First N.B.
4987.	Claremore	First N.B.
5016.	Wagoner	First N.B.
5052.	McAlester	First N.B.
5083.	Vinita	Vinita N.B.
5091.	Pauls Valley	First N.B.
5095.	Shawnee	First N.B.
5115.	Shawnee	Shawnee N.B.
5126.	Wynnewood	First N.B.
5128.	Checotah	First N.B.
5129.	Durant	First N.B.
5159.	Oklahoma City	Western N.B.
5171.	Tulsa	First N.B.
5206.	Stillwater	First N.B.
5224.	Pawnee	First N.B.
5236.	Muskogee	Commercial N.B.
5246.	Caddo	Choctaw N.B.
5248.	Norman	First N.B.
5252.	Miami	First N.B.
5270.	Holdenville	First N.B.
5272.	Newkirk	First N.B.
5298.	Davis	First N.B.
5310.	Bartlesville	First N.B.
5328.	Kingfisher	First N.B.
5335.	Enid	First N.B.
5345.	Marietta	First N.B.
5347.	Stillwater	Stillwater N.B.
5352.	Weatherford	First N.B.
5354.	Chandler	First N.B.
5378.	Tecumseh	First N.B.
5379.	Duncan	First N.B.
5401.	Nowata	First N.B.
5404.	Madill	First N.B.
5417.	Roff	First N.B.
5418.	Okmulgee	First N.B.
5431.	Chickasha	First N.B.
5436.	Stillwater	N.B. of Commerce
5460.	Blackwell	First N.B.
5462.	Lexington	First N.B.
5473.	Hennessey	First N.B.
5474.	Ponca City	First N.B.
5478.	Tahlequah	First N.B.
5492.	Pawnee	Arkansas Valley N.B.
5508.	Mangum	First N.B.
5537.	South McAlester	State N.B.
5546.	Pryor Creek	First N.B.
5547.	Chickasha	Citizens' N.B.
5575.	Woodward	First N.B.
5587.	Alva	First N.B.
5590.	Durant	Durant N.B.
5596.	Sallisaw	First N.B.
5612.	Norman	Cleveland County N.B.
5620.	Ada	First N.B.
5633.	Ada	Ada N.B.
5647.	Coalgate	First N.B.
5656.	Mountain View	First N.B.
5716.	Ohlahoma City	American N.B.
5724.	Marlow	First N.B.
5731.	Wynnewood	Southern N.B.
5732.	Tulsa	City N.B.
5735.	Holdenville	N.B. of Holdenville
5740.	Kingfisher	Kingfisher N.B.
5748.	Sulphur	First N.B.
5753.	Lawton	City N.B.
5755.	Lehigh	Lehigh N.B.
5758.	Weatherford	Nat. Exchange Bank
5766.	Elk City	First N.B.
5790.	Kingfisher	People's N.B.
5791.	Atoka	Atoka N.B.
5796.	Medford	First N.B.
5800.	Ryan	First N.B.
5804.	Watonga	First N.B.
5809.	Tishomingo	First N.B.
5811.	Mangum	Mangum N.B.
5860.	Vinita	Cherokee N.B.
5875.	Shawnee	Oklahoma N.B.
5887.	Okeene	First N.B.
5902.	Eufaula	First N.B.
5905.	Anadarko	First N.B.
5911.	Cleveland	First N.B.
5914.	Lawton	First N.B.
5915.	Hobart	Hobart N.B.
5922.	Ardmore	Ardmore N.B.
5923.	Anadarko	N.B. of Anadarko
5935.	Wetumka	First N.B.
5950.	Wapanucka	First N.B.
5951.	Sapulpa	First N.B.
5954.	Hobart	First N.B.
5955.	Chelsea	First N.B.
5958.	Marietta	Marietta N.B.
5960.	Billings	First N.B.
5961.	Pawhuska	First N.B.
5967.	Eufaula	Eufaula N.B.
5982.	Wakita	First N.B.
5985.	El Reno	Citizens' N.B.
6048.	Wagoner	Wagoner N.B.
6052.	Cordell	First N.B.
6058.	Sayre	First N.B.
6061.	Ponca City	Farmers' N.B.
6111.	Hennessey	Hennessey N.B.
6113.	Altus	First N.B.
6130.	Hugo	First N.B.
6138.	Collinsville	First N.B.
6142.	Chandler	Chandler N.B.
6456.	Edmond	First N.B.
6159.	Yukon	First N.B.
6161.	Cashion	First N.B.
6163.	Geary	First N.B.
6164.	Elk City	Elk City N.B.
6171.	Lindsay	First N.B.
6230.	McAlester	American N.B.
6232.	Ralston	First N.B.
6241.	Okmulgee	Citizens' N.B.
6254.	Wewoka	First N.B.
6257.	Clinton	Farmers' N.B.
6258.	Bartlesville	First N.B.
6260.	Bristow	First N.B.
6263.	Mounds	First N.B.
6267.	Hobart	City N.B.
6269.	Chandler	Union N.B.
6299.	Comanche	First N.B.
6306.	Stroud	First N.B.
6307.	Anadarko	Citizens' N.B.
6324.	Weleetka	First N.B.
6358.	Hobart	Farmers and Merchants' N.B.
6365.	Madill	Madill N.B.
6367.	Nowata	Nowata N.B.
6406.	McAlester	City N.B.
6414.	Tahlequah	Cherokee N.B.
6416.	Shawnee	State N.B.
6450.	Norman	City N.B.
6477.	Okemah	First N.B.
6490.	Alva	Alva N.B.
6511.	Boynton	First N.B.
6517.	Quinton	First N.B.
6539.	Fort Gibson	First N.B.
6540.	Holdenville	N.B. of Commerce
6570.	Temple	First N.B.
6578.	Mannsville	First N.B.
6602.	Vinita	Farmers' N.B.
6612.	Walters	First N.B.
6639.	Pauls Valley	N.B. of Commerce
6641.	Wanette	First N.B.
6647.	Cordell	City N.B.
6655.	Pond Creek	First N.B.
6660.	McLoud	First N.B.
6669.	Tulsa	Farmers' N.B.
6677.	Cherokee	First N.B.
6678.	Oklahoma City	Oklahoma City N.B.
6683.	Bokchito	First N.B.
6689.	Weleetka	Weleetka N.B.
6702.	Kingfisher	Farmers' N.B.
6710.	Lindsay	Lindsay N.B.
6717.	Muldrow	First N.B.
6719.	Carmen	First N.B.
6736.	Foss	First N.B.
6753.	Harrison	First N.B.
6804.	Dustin	First N.B.
6844.	Carmen	Carmen N.B.
6851.	Clinton	Clinton N.B.
6855.	Okmulgee	Okmulgee N.B.
6867.	Henryetta	First N.B.
6868.	Beggs	First N.B.
6879.	Coweta	First N.B.
6890.	Wilburton	First N.B.
6893.	Cushing	First N.B.
6911.	Muskogee	City N.B.
6916.	Blackwell	Blackwell N.B.
6928.	Durant	Farmers' N.B.
6940.	Clinton	First N.B.
6972.	Perry	First N.B.
6980.	Calvin	First N.B.
6981.	Oklahoma City	Commercial N.B.
7019.	Taloga	First N.B.
7032.	Bartlesville	American N.B.
7042.	Tishomingo	American N.B.
7050.	Hartshorne	First N.B.
7053.	Calvin	Citizens' N.B.
7054.	Stonewall	First N.B.
7071.	Ada	Citizens' N.B.
7085.	Tulsa	Tulsa N.B.
7099.	Bennington	First N.B.
7103.	Pond Creek	N.B. of Pond Creek
7104.	Poteau	N.B. of Poteau
7115.	Broken Arrow	First N.B.
7117.	Fairview	First N.B.
7118.	Poteau	First N.B.
7127.	Apache	First N.B.
7159.	Altus	Altus N.B.
7177.	Prague	First N.B.
7185.	Francis	First N.B.
7197.	Mill Creek	First N.B.
7207.	Lexington	Farmers' N.B.
7209.	Berwyn	First N.B.
7217.	Stigler	First N.B.
7238.	Weatherford	Liberty N.B.
7251.	Ramona	First N.B.
7278.	Thomas	First N.B.
7289.	Duncan	Duncan N.B.
7293.	Norman	Farmers' N.B.
7299.	Gutherie	N.B. of Commerce
7321.	Coalgate	Coalgate N.B.
7328.	Mangum	City N.B.
7368.	Caddo	Caddo N.B.
7386.	Cleveland	Cleveland N.B.
7389.	Byars	First N.B.
7420.	Cornish	First N.B.
7432.	Stigler	American N.B.
7442.	Davis	Merchants and Planters' N.B.
7444.	Tonkawa	First N.B.
7499.	Bokchito	Bokchito N.B.
7571.	Sallisaw	First N.B.
7583.	Blackwell	State N.B.
7600.	Broken Arrow	Arkansas Valley N.B.
7611.	Pawnee	Pawnee N.B.
7615.	Porter	First N.B.
7619.	Holdenville	American N.B.
7628.	Wagoner	City N.B.
7633.	Konawa	First N.B.
7651.	Boswell	First N.B.
7666.	Atoka	Citizens' N.B.
7667.	Antlers	First N.B.
7677.	Okemah	Okemah N.B.
7697.	Purcell	Union N.B.
7706.	Centralia	First N.B.
7707.	Woodville	First N.B.
7723.	Madill	City N.B.
7724.	Wetumka	American N.B.
7747.	Hugo	Hugo N.B.
7756.	Tecumseh	Farmers' N.B.
7771.	Thomas	Thomas N.B.
7780.	Talihina	First N.B.
7783.	Lamont	First N.B.
7788.	Sapulpa	American N.B.
7811.	Walters	Walters N.B.
7822.	Haskell	First N.B.
7842.	Milburn	First N.B.
7883.	Pawhuska	Citizens' N.B.
7892.	Pauls Valley	Pauls Valley N.B.
7893.	Kingston	First N.B.
7927.	Hominy	First N.B.
7950.	Sterrett	First N.B.
7962.	Colbert	First N.B.
7964.	Owasso	First N.B.
7967.	Waukomis	First N.B.
7972.	Fairfax	First N.B.
7976.	Ravia	First N.B.
7996.	Terral	First N.B.
8010.	Erick	First N.B.
8024.	Webbers Falls	First N.B.
8052.	Wewoka	Farmers' N.B.
8056.	Hollis	Hollis N.B.
8061.	Hollis	First N.B.
8078.	Fort Towson	First N.B.
8079.	Fort Gibson	Farmers' N.B.
8082.	Antlers	Citizens' N.B.
8126.	Eldorado	First N.B.
8137.	Okla Wapanucka	People's N.B.
8138.	Guymon	First N.B.
8140.	Frederick	First N.B.
8144.	Cement	First N.B.
8159.	Prague	Prague N.B.
8177.	Keota	First N.B.
8189.	Lehigh	Merchants' N.B.
8202.	Fairfax	Fairfax N.B.
8203.	Chickasha	Chickasha N.B.
8206.	Frederick	City N.B.
8209.	Hastings	First N.B.
8210.	Hastings	N.B. of Hastings
8213.	Konawa	Konawa N.B.
8214.	Newkirk	Farmers' N.B.
8231.	Enid	Enid N.B.
8270.	Dewey	First N.B.
8278.	Marietta	Farmers' N.B.
8294.	Maud	First N.B.
8304.	Wanette	State N.B.
8310.	Temple	Farmers' N.B.
8313.	Pawhuska	American N.B.
8316.	Olustee	First N.B.
8336.	Rush Springs	First N.B.
8342.	Granite	First N.B.
8349.	Helena	First N.B.
8353.	Boswell	Boswell N.B.
8354.	Ardmore	Bankers' N.B.
8361.	Comanche	Citizens' N.B.
8366.	Comanche	Comanche N.B.
8375.	Lawton	Lawton N.B.
8472.	Oklahoma City	Security N.B.
8475.	Tuttle	First N.B.
8479.	Porum	First N.B.
8486.	Idabel	First N.B.
8524.	Stratford	First N.B.
8543.	Gage	First N.B.
8546.	Mill Creek	Merchants and Planters' N.B.
8552.	Tulsa	Central N.B.
8553.	Keifer	First N.B.
8563.	Luther	First N.B.
8577.	Kaw City	First N.B.
8595.	Tonkawa	Tonkawa N.B.
8609.	Tupelo	First N.B.
8615.	Seiling	First N.B.
8616.	Duncan	City N.B.
8638.	Kiowa	First N.B.
8644.	Minco	First N.B.
8668.	Davenport	First N.B.
8676.	Porter	Porter N.B.
8687.	Shattuck	First N.B.
8702.	Blanchard	First N.B.
8715.	Waurika	Citizens' N.B.
8727.	Custer City Custer	First N.B.
8730.	Cushing	Farmers' N.B.
8744.	Waurika	First N.B.

Charter #	City	Name of Bank
8754.	Olustee	Farmers' N.B.
8759.	Verden	First N.B.
8775.	Altus	City N.B.
8790.	Afton	First N.B.
8809.	Warner	First N.B.
8825.	Hollis	First N.B.
8852.	Texhoma	First N.B.
8859.	Verden	N.B. of Verden
8861.	Waurika	Waurika N.B.
8876.	Morris	First N.B.
8896.	Buffalo	First N.B.
8944.	Eldorado	Farmers and Merchant's N.B.
8994.	Atoka	American N.B.
8999.	Maysville	First N.B.
9008.	Cherokee	Alfalfa County N.B.
9011.	Newkirk	Eastman N.B.
9023.	Muskogee	Muskogee N.B.
9032.	Mulhall	First N.B.
9046.	Sulphur	Park N.B.
9275.	Spiro	First N.B.
9514.	Seminole	First N.B.
9564.	Oklahoma City	Farmers' N.B.
9567.	Bartlesville	Union N.B.
9584.	Capitol Hill	First N.B.
9586.	Enid	First N.B.
9616.	Ponca City	Germania N.B.
9620.	Allen	First N.B.
9658.	Tulsa	Exchange N.B.
9696.	Okmulgee	Farmers' N.B.
9701.	Muskogee	American N.B.
9709.	Waynoka	First N.B.
9767.	Fairview	Farmers and Merchants' N.B.
9801.	Ponca City	Farmers' N.B.
9835.	Bokchito	First N.B.
9856.	Oklahoma City	Oklahoma Stock Yards N.B.
9881.	Kingston	First N.B.
9884.	Cherokee	Farmers' N.B.
9888.	Heavener	First N.B.
9920.	Milburn	First N.B.
9937.	Noble	First N.B.
9938.	Chickasha	Oklahoma N.B.
9942.	Tulsa	N.B. of Commerce
9943.	Tulsa	Oklahoma N.B.
9944.	Hydro	First N.B.
9946.	Marlow	State N.B.
9947.	Okmulgee	Exchange N.B.
9948.	Nowata	Producers' N.B.
9949.	Nowata	Commercial N.B.
9951.	Lenapah	Lenapah N.B.
9952.	Elk City	First N.B.
9954.	Kingfisher	People's N.B.
9959.	Sayre	First N.B.
9960.	Olustee	First N.B.
9962.	Lawton	Lawton N.B.
9963.	Eldorado	First N.B.
9964.	Guymon	City N.B.
9965.	Collinsville	First N.B.
9967.	Temple	Temple N.B.
9968.	Cordell	Farmers' N.B.
9969.	Skiatook	First N.B.
9970.	Stilwell	First N.B.
9971.	Cordell	Cordell N.B.
9972.	Cordell	State N.B.
9973.	Sallisaw	Farmers' N.B.
9974.	Lahoma	First N.B.
9975.	Muldrow	First N.B.
9976.	Sayre	Beckham County N.B.
9980.	Harrah	First N.B.
9981.	Custer City	People's State N.B.
9983.	Wellston	First N.B.
9985.	Clinton	Oklahoma State N.B.
9986.	Dewey	Security N.B.
9987.	Shattuck	Shattuck N.B.
9991.	Terlton	First N.B.
9992.	Valliant	First N.B.
9993.	Canadian	First N.B.
9995.	Sentinel	First N.B.
9998.	Shawnee	N.B. of Commerce
10001.	Addington	First N.B.
10002.	Hominy	N.B. of Commerce
10003.	Braman	First N.B.
10005.	Pond Creek	Farmers' N.B.
10006.	Grandfield	First N.B.
10007.	Stuart	First N.B.
10010.	Caddo	Security N.B.
10012.	Tishomingo	Tishomingo N.B.
10013.	Holdenville	State N.B.
10014.	Yale	First N.B.
10015.	Oktaha	First N.B.
10019.	Miami	Ottawa County N.B.
10020.	Geary	First N.B.
10031.	Coweta	N.B. of Commerce
10032.	Tyrone	First N.B.
10051.	Checotah	People's N.B.
10063.	Checotah	Commercial N.B.
10075.	Kaw City	First N.B.
10094.	Hastings	N.B. of Hastings
10095.	Frederick	N.B. of Commerce
10096.	Lone Wolf	First N.B.
10104.	Kenefic	First N.B.
10113.	Muskogee	Oklahoma N.B.
10115.	Bristow	Bristow N.B.
10117.	Claremore	N.B. of Claremore
10119.	Grove	First N.B.
10151.	Edmond	Citizens' N.B.
10158.	Westville	First N.B.
10160.	Haskell	Haskell N.B.
10170.	Wilburton	Latimer County N.B.
10172.	Roff	Farmers and Merchants' N.B.
10193.	Alex	First N.B.
10196.	Yukon	Yukon N.B.
10202.	Enid	Enid N.B.
10203.	Carmen	Carmen N.B.
10205.	Marlow	N.B. of Marlow
10209.	Hennessey	Farmers and Merchants' N.B.
10226.	Calvin	Calvin N.B.
10227.	Waukomis	Waukomis N.B.
10239.	Heavener	State N.B.
10240.	Hollis	N.B. of Commerce
10244.	Duncan	First N.B.
10249.	Hollis	State N.B.
10255.	Broken Arrow	Citizens' N.B.
10262.	Tulsa	Liberty N.B.
10277.	Washington	First N.B.
10280.	Collinsville	Collinsville N.B.
10283.	Maysville	Farmers' N.B.
10286.	Madill	Madill N.B.
10288.	Hobart	City N.B.
10298.	Keota	Keota N.B.
10304.	Tecumseh	Tecumseh N.B.
10311.	Snyder	Kiowa N.B.
10314.	Sasakwa	First N.B.
10317.	Snyder	First N.B.
10321.	Muskogee	Exchange N.B.
10332.	Cushing	Farmers' N.B.
10339.	Afton	First N.B.
10342.	Tulsa	American N.B.
10343.	Bennington	Bennington N.B.
10347.	Achille	First N.B.
10349.	Henryetta	Miners' N.B.
10356.	Foraker	First N.B.
10363.	Boswell	State N.B.
10366.	Soper	First N.B.
10368.	Blair	First N.B.
10380.	Achille	Farmers and Merchants' N.B.
10381.	Colbert	First N.B.
10385.	Aylesworth	First N.B.
10388.	Eufaula	State N.B.
10389.	Gotebo	First N.B.
10394.	Ardmore	State N.B.
10402.	Kaw City	N.B. of Kaw City
10424.	Broken Bow	First N.B.
10431.	Tishomingo	Farmers' N.B.
10437.	Braggs	First N.B.
10442.	Hydro	Farmers' N.B.
10454.	Francis	Francis N.B.
10464.	Skiatook	Oklahoma N.B.
10467.	Bixby	First N.B.
10468.	Tahlequah	Central N.B.
10474.	Sallisaw	Citizens' N.B.
10482.	Beggs	Farmers' N.B.
10487.	Fairland	First N.B.
10500.	Haworth	First N.B.
10513.	Ada	Merchants and Planters' N.B.
10515.	Kiowa	People's N.B.
10520.	Hulbert	First N.B.
10521.	Hammon	Farmers' N.B.
10531.	Tupelo	Farmers' N.B.
10538.	Durant	State N.B.
10548.	Ringling	First N.B.
10561.	Fort Gibson	Citizens' N.B.
10563.	Dustin	American N.B.
10566.	Hooker	First N.B.
10573.	Vian	First N.B.
10574.	New Wilson	First N.B.
10595.	Drumright	First N.B.
10612.	Arcadia	First N.B.
10615.	Stroud	Stroud N.B.
10627.	Blue Jacket	First N.B.
10649.	Porum	N.B. of Commerce
10659.	Holdenville	Farmers' N.B.
10672.	Talihina	First N.B.
10689.	Commerce	First N.B.
10722.	Yale	Farmers' N.B.
10737.	Rosston	First N.B.
10804.	Beaver	First N.B.
10849.	Bristow	American N.B.
10875.	Erick	First N.B
10904.	Tulsa	Planters' N.B.
10906.	Tulsa	Union N.B.
10913.	Okeene	N.B. of Okeene
10960.	Pocasset	First N.B.
10967.	Kusa	First N.B.
10981.	Butler	First N.B.
11001.	Okmulgee	Central N.B.
11016.	Sulphur	Farmers' N.B.
11018.	Healdton	First N.B.
11052.	Tipton	First N.B.
11064.	Hartshorne	Hartshorne N.B.
11084.	Boise City	First N.B.
11093.	Ardmore	Exchange N.B.
11129.	Oilton	First N.B.
11149.	Allen	Allen N.B.
11157.	Quapaw	First N.B.
11181.	Valliant	American N.B.
11182.	Calera	Calera N.B.
11190.	Boswell	Farmers and Merchants' N.B.
11192.	Madill	Marshall County N.B.
11194.	Picher	First N.B.
11219.	Billings	N.B. of Billings
11230.	Oklahoma City	Liberty N.B.
11232.	Forgan	First N.B.
11246.	Idabel	American N.B.
11256.	Fort Towson	American N.B.
11306.	Nash	First N.B.
11314.	Pawhuska	Liberty N.B.
11315.	Stuart	Liberty N.B.
11384.	Temple	Security N.B.
11394.	Goltry	First N.B.
11396.	Wynona	First N.B.
11397.	Tonkawa	Farmers' N.B.
11419.	Byron	First N.B.
11436.	Lenapah	Citizens' N.B.
11459.	Valliant	Citizens' N.B.
11460.	Bigheart	First N.B.
11481.	Oklahoma City	Southwest N.B.
11485.	Tahlequah	Guaranty N.B.
11498.	Byars	American N.B.
11535.	Devol	First N.B.
11551.	Hanna	First N.B.
11568.	Porum	Guaranty N.B.
11584.	Enid	American N.B.
11612.	Caney	First N.B.
11624.	Picher	Picher N.B.
11628.	Oklahoma City	Tradesmen's N.B.
11648.	Terral	First N.B.
11654.	Davidson	First N.B.
11661.	Depew	Depew N.B.
11676.	Coalgate	City N.B.
11680.	Lawton	Security N.B.
11688.	Bartlesville	Exchange N.B.
11705.	Chattanooga	First N.B.
11763.	Carnegie	First N.B
11771.	Comanche	State N.B.
11788.	Paden	Paden N.B.
11791.	Jennings	First N.B.
11824.	Paden	First N.B.
11837.	Bartlesville	Central N.B.
11842.	Durant	Commercial N.B.
11891.	Laverne	First N.B.
11894.	Okarche	First N.B.
11913.	Idabel	Idabel N.B.
11920.	Checotah	Commercial N.B.
11932.	Morris	Morris N.B.
11940.	Boswell	Citizens' N.B.
11963.	Okmulgee	Union N.B.
11982.	Slick	First N.B.
12012.	Boley	First N.B.
12016.	Oklahoma City	Fidelity N.B.
12035.	Moore	First N.B.
12036.	Norman	Security N.B.
12038.	Blackwell	Blackwell N.B.
12039.	Enid	Garfield N.B.
12040.	Blackwell	Security N.B.
12041.	Billings	First N.B.
12042.	Tulsa	Producers' N.B.
12043.	Tulsa	Security N.B.
12044.	Enid	Central N.B.
12045.	Billings	Billings N.B.
12048.	Okmulgee	American N.B.
12049.	Cherokee	Cherokee N.B.
12050.	Clinton	Security N.B.
12051.	Duncan	Oklahoma N.B.
12052.	Wynona	Wynona N.B.
12053.	Ardmore	American N.B.
12054.	Cushing	Oklahoma N.B.
12059.	Carnegie	Farmers' N.B.
12060.	Chandler	Farmers' N.B.
12065.	Duncan	Security N.B.
12067.	Lawton	American N.B.
12068.	Kingfisher	Citizens' N.B.
12069.	Hominy	Hominy N.B.
12074.	Weleetka	State N.B.
12076.	Barnsdall	Barnsdall N.B.
12078.	Wellston	Wellston N.B.
12079.	Sand Springs	First N.B.
12081.	Helena	Helena N.B.
12082.	Stillwater	American N.B.
12086.	Putnam	First N.B.
12087.	Holdenville	American N.B.
12088.	Hitchcock	First N.B.
12089.	Tahlequah	Liberty N.B.
12093.	Elk City	Farmers' N.B.
12094.	Waurika	Farmers' N.B.
12095.	Stroud	State N.B.
12099.	Wetumka	N.B. of Commerce
12102	Kenefick	First N.B.
12103.	Locust Grove	First N.B.
12104.	Depew	State N.B.
12106.	Idabel	State N.B.
12107.	Hinton	First N.B.
12109.	Leedey	First N.B.
12111.	Coweta	Security N.B.
12113.	Aline	Clarks N.B.
12116.	Centrahoma	First N.B.
12117.	Pryor Creek, Pryor	American N.B.
12118.	Walters	American N.B.
12120.	Apache	American N.B.
12125.	Texhoma	Farmers' N.B.
12126.	Durant	American N.B.
12128.	Hooker	Farmers and Merchants' N.B.
12129.	Marlow	First N.B.
12130.	Blair	First N.B.
12131.	Brinkham	First N.B.
12133.	Binger	First N.B.
12134.	Purcell	McClain County N.B.
12135.	Poteau	LeFlore County N.B.
12136.	Hugo	City N.B.
12141.	Fletcher	First N.B.
12142.	Granite	First N.B.
12144.	Ada	Security N.B.
12147.	Carter	First N.B.
12148.	Coyle	First N.B.
12149.	Davis	City N.B.
12150.	Hastings	Oklahoma N.B.
12152.	Alva	Central N.B.
12155.	Altus	Altus N.B.
12157.	Norman	City N.B.
12158.	Poteau	Central N.B.
12161.	Kemp City	First N.B.
12163.	Tyrone	Farmers' N.B.
12165.	Shidler	First N.B.
12169.	Wheatland	First N.B.
12171.	Dustin	First N.B.
12173.	Ninnekah	First N.B.
12177.	Shidler	Shidler N.B.
12179.	Guymon	Texas County N.B.

Charter #	City	Name of Bank
12185.	Custer City	People's N.B.
12188.	Mill Creek	Mill Creek N.B.
12200.	Calumet	First N.B.
12203.	Beggs	American N.B.
12206.	Newkirk	Security N.B.
12207.	Enick	Farmers' N.B.
12211.	Bokchito	First N.B.
12212.	Pawhuska	N.B. of Commerce
12215.	Pauls Valley	Exchange N.B.
12218.	Snyder	Kiowa N.B.
12221.	Loco	First N.B.
12223.	Britton	First N.B.
12230.	Chickasha	Farmers' N.B.
12237.	Hollis	Farmers' N.B.
12239.	Kiefer	First N.B.
12245.	Cheyenne	First N.B.
12265.	Boynton	American N.B.
12277.	Muskogee	Muskogee-Security N.B.
12298.	Sentinel	Security N.B.
12299.	Cordell	First N.B.
12302.	Cordell	Cordell N.B.
12310.	Castle	First N.B.
12312.	Paden	State N.B.
12315.	Carney	First N.B.
12318.	Gracemount	First N.B.
12322.	Jones	First N.B.
12330.	Marietta	Love County N.B.
12331.	Stigler	Security N.B.
12334.	Wynnewood	State N.B.
12335.	Cement	First N.B.
12339.	Shawnee	Federal N.B.
12356.	Tonkawa	American N.B.
12368.	Wagoner	American N.B.
12369.	Bennington	American N.B.
12376.	Helena	Farmers' N.B.
12388.	Slick	Slick N.B.
12394.	Porter	Merchants and Planters' N.B.
12441.	Shawnee	N.B. of Commerce
12472.	Ardmore	First N.B.
12486.	Syre	American N.B.
12498.	Carmen	First N.B.
12529.	Coalgate	First N.B.
12555.	Sallisaw	American N.B.
12591.	Ada	First N.B.
12629.	Henryetta	People's N.B.
12801.	Hugo	N.B. of Commerce
12812.	Duncan	First N.B.
12827.	Wilson	First N.B.
12890.	Muskogee	Commercial N.B.
12908.	Tishomingo	First N.B.
12918.	Muskogee	Citizens' N.B.
13018.	Durant	Durant N.B.
13021.	Madill	First N.B.
13100.	Hartshore	Hartshore N.B.
13276.	Oklahoma City	South Oklahoma N.B.
13355.	Pawhuska	First N.B.
13361.	Skiatook	Oklahoma First N.B.
13480.	Tulsa	Fourth N.B.
13527.	Pawhuska	Citizens-First N.B.
13677.	Ardmore	First N.B.
13679.	Tulsa	N.B. of Tulsa
13751.	Okmulgee	Citizens N.B.
13756.	Altus	N.B. of Commerce
13760.	Frederick	First N.B.
13770.	McAlester	N.B. of McAlester
13891.	Ponca City	First N.B.
13930.	Shawnee	American N.B.
14005.	Durant	First N.B.
14020.	Perry	First N.B.
14108.	Walters	Walters N.B.
14131.	Antlers	First N.B.
14278.	Blackwell	First N.B.
14304.	Pawhuska	N.B. of Commerce
14315.	Enid	Security N.B.
14322.	Wetumka	American N.B.

OREGON

Charter #	City	Name of Bank
1553.	Portland	First N.B.
2630.	Pendleton	First N.B.
2816.	Salem	First N.B.
2865.	Baker City	First N.B.
2928.	Albany	First N.B.
2947.	Union	First N.B.
3025.	East Portland	First N.B.
3184.	Portland	Portland N.B.
3313.	Island City	First N.B.
3399.	McMinnville	First N.B.
3402.	Portland	Ainsworth N.B.
3405.	Salem	Capital N.B.
3422.	Portland	Commercial N.B.
3441.	The Dalles	First N.B.
3458.	Eugene	First N.B.
3486.	Astoria	First N.B.
3534.	Dalles City	The Dalles N.B.
3536.	Portland	Merchants' N.B.
3655.	La Grande	La Grande N.B.
3665.	Pendleton	Pendleton N.B.
3676.	Arlington	First N.B.
3719.	Portland	Oregon N.B.
3774.	Heppner	First N.B.
3851.	Prineville	First N.B.
3857.	McMinnville	McMinnville N.B.
3912.	Enterprise	Wallowa N.B.
3918.	Arlington	Arlington N.B.
3953.	Heppner	N.B. of Heppner
3966.	Hillsboro	First N.B.
3972.	Independence	First N.B.
3979.	Independence	Independence N.B.
3986.	Eugene City	Eugene N.B.
4168.	Grant's Pass	First N.B. of Southern Oregon
4206.	Baker City	Baker City N.B.
4249.	Pendleton	N.B. of Pendleton
4301.	Corvallis	First N.B.
4326.	Albany	Linn County N.B.
4403.	Astoria	Astoria N.B.
4452.	La Grande	Farmers and Traders' N.B.
4514.	Portland	United States N.B.
4516.	Athena	First N.B.
4624.	Roseburg	First N.B.
5642.	Cottage Grove	First N.B.
5747.	Ashland	First N.B.
5822.	Ontario	First N.B.
6295.	Burns	First N.B.
6491.	Canyon City	First N.B. of Grant County
6547.	Sumpter	First N.B.
6644.	Elgin	First N.B.
6768.	Baker City	Citizens' N.B.
6849.	Coquille	First N.B.
7059.	Condon	First N.B.
7072.	Dallas	First N.B.
7167.	Klamath Falls	First N.B.
7244.	Lakeview	First N.B.
7272.	Hood River	First N.B.
7301.	Pendleton	Commercial N.B.
7472.	Dallas	Dallas N.B.
7475.	Marshfield	First N.B. of Coos Bay
7537.	Newberg	First N.B.
7701.	Medford	First N.B.
8036.	Forest Grove	First N.B.
8048.	Joseph	First N.B.
8236.	Medford	Medford N.B.
8261.	Condon	Condon N.B.
8387.	Union	Union N.B.
8528.	Vale	First N.B.
8554.	Forest Grove	Forest Grove N.B.
8556.	Oregon City	First N.B.
8574.	Tillamook	First N.B.
8691.	Burns	Harney County N.B.
8721.	Sheridan	First N.B.
8750.	Corvallis	Benton County N.B.
8941.	Springfield	First N.B.
8955.	Roseburg	Roseburg N.B.
9002.	Wallowa	Stockgrowers and Farmers' N.B.
9021.	Salem	United States N.B.
9047.	Saint Johns	First N.B.
9127.	Lebanon	First N.B.
9146.	Harrisburg	First N.B.
9180.	Portland	Lumbermen's N.B.
9201.	Milton	First N.B.
9228.	Pendleton	American N.B.
9281.	Hermiston	First N.B.
9314.	La Grande	United States N.B.
9328.	North Bend	First N.B.
9348.	Ontario	Ontario N.B.
9358.	Newberg	United States N.B.
9363.	Bend	First N.B.
9423.	Roseburg	Douglas N.B.
9431.	Ashland	United States N.B.
9496.	Vale	United States N.B.
9718.	Bandon	First N.B.
9763.	Prairie City	First N.B.
9806.	McMinnville	United States N.B.
9917.	Hillsboro	Hillsboro N.B.
9923.	Hillsboro	American N.B
10056.	Merrill	First N.B.
10071.	Monmouth	First N.B.
10103.	Portland	Peninsula N.B.
10164.	Lebanon	Lebanon N.B.
10218.	Junction City	First N.B.
10300.	Portland	Northwestern N.B.
10345.	Eugene	United States N.B.
10432.	Paisley	Paisley N.B.
10534.	Linton	First N.B.
10619.	Canby	First N.B.
10676.	Gardiner	First N.B.
10992.	Scappoose	First N.B.
11007.	Heppner	Farmers and Stock Growers' N.B.
11106.	Silverton	First N.B.
11121.	Lakeview	Commercial N.B.
11200.	Saint Helen	First N.B.
11271.	Molalla	First N.B.
11294.	Redmond	First N.B.
11302.	Redmond	Redmond N.B.
11466.	Halfway	First N.B.
11691.	Madres	First N.B.
11758.	Clatskanie	First N.B.
11801.	Klamath Falls	American N.B.
11807.	Dalles City	Citizens' N.B.
11885.	Harrisburg	Harrisburg N.B.
11906.	Woodburn	First N.B.
11917.	Stayton	First N.B.
11937.	Toledo	First N.B.
11975.	Aurora	First N.B.
12077.	Marshfield	Coos Bay N.B.
12193.	Mount Angel	First N.B.
12262.	Vale	Vale N.B.
12427.	Wheeler	First N.B.
12470.	Portland	West Coast N.B.
12557.	Portland	Portland N.B.
12613.	Portland	Brotherhood Co-Operative N.B.
12655.	Prineville	Prineville N.B.
13093.	Bend	Lumbermens N.B.
13192.	Tillamook	Tillamook N.B.
13294.	Portland	Central N.B.
13299.	Portland	Citizens N.B.
13354.	Astoria	N.B. of Commerce
13576.	Pendleton	First Inland N.B.
13602.	La Grande	First N.B.
13633.	Milton	Valley N.B.
13771.	Medford	Medford N.B.
14001.	Clatskanie	First N.B.
14054.	North Bend	North Bend N.B.
14241.	Condon	First N.B.
14306.	Toledo	National Security Bank

PENNSYLVANIA

Charter #	City	Name of Bank
1.	Philadelphia	First N.B.
12.	Erie	First N.B.
21.	Carlisle	First N.B.
25.	Marietta	First N.B.
30.	Wilkes-Barre	First N.B.
31.	Huntingdon	First N.B.
39.	Towanda	First N.B.
42.	Strasburg	First N.B.
48.	Pittsburgh	First N.B.
49.	Scranton	Second N.B.
51.	Johnstown	First N.B.
54.	Girard	First N.B.
57.	Hollidaysburg	First N.B.
60.	Newville	First N.B.
69.	Kittanning	First N.B.
77.	Scranton	First N.B.
104.	Wilkes-Barre	Second N.B.
110.	Union Mills, Union City	First N.B.
115.	Meadville	First N.B.
125.	Reading	First N.B.
135.	Brownsville	First N.B.
138.	Bethlehem	First N.B.
143.	Conneautville	First N.B.
148.	West Chester	First N.B.
161.	Allentown	First N.B.
173.	Oil City	First N.B.
174.	Mifflinburg	First N.B.
175.	Williamsport	First N.B.
187.	Hanover	First N.B.
189.	Franklin	First N.B.
197.	York	First N.B.
198.	Allegheny	First N.B.
201.	Harrisburg	First N.B.
213.	Philadelphia	Second N.B.
234.	Philadelphia	Third N.B.
240.	Lebanon	First N.B.
244.	Waynesboro	First N.B.
246.	Wrightsville	First N.B.
247.	Altoona	First N.B.
249.	Greenville	First N.B.
252.	Pittsburgh	First N.B.
253.	Milton	First N.B.
270.	Uniontown	First N.B.
272.	Norristown	First N.B.
286.	Philadelphia	Fourth N.B.
291.	Pittsburgh	Third N.B.
293.	Bloomsburg	First N.B.
300.	Curwensville	First N.B.
305.	Waynesburg	First N.B.
309.	Butler	First N.B.
311.	Gettysburg	First N.B.
312.	Media	First N.B.
313.	Indiana	First N.B.
324.	Newtown	First N.B.
325.	Danville	First N.B.
326.	Mechanicsburg	Second N.B.
328.	Wellsborough	First N.B.
332.	Chester	First N.B.
333.	Lancaster	First N.B.
338.	Downington	First N.B.
352.	Philadelphia	Sixth N.B.
355.	Chester	Delaware County N.B.
357.	Selinsgrove	First N.B.
371.	Columbia	First Columbia N.B.
373.	Allentown	Second N.B.
380.	Mechanicsburg	First N.B.
386.	Mount Pleasant	First N.B.
392.	Mercer	First N.B.
403.	Ashland	First N.B.
413.	Philadelphia	Seventh N.B.
423.	Minersville	First N.B.
430.	Lansdale	First N.B.
432.	Pittsburgh	Fourth N.B.
435.	Glen Rock	First N.B.
437.	Mauch Chunk	First N.B.
459.	Bellefonte	First N.B.
469.	Mauch Chunk	Second N.B.
478.	Pittston	First N.B.
507.	Lock Haven	First N.B.
520.	Warren	First N.B.
521.	Providence	First N.B.
522.	Philadelphia	Eighth N.B.
535.	Erie	Keystone N.B.
538.	Philadelphia	Farmers and Mechanics' N.B.
539.	Philadelphia	Philadelphia N.B.
540.	Philadelphia	Penn N.B.
541.	Philadelphia	N.B. of Northern Liberties
542.	Philadelphia	Corn Exchange N.B.
543.	Philadelphia	City N.B.
544.	Philadelphia	Kensington N.B.
546.	Philadelphia	N.B. of Germantown
547.	Philadelphia	N.B. of Commerce
552.	West Chester	N.B. of Chester County
556.	Philadelphia	Commercial N.B. of Pa.
557.	Philadelphia	Manufacturers' N.B.
560.	Philadelphia	Southwark N.B.
561.	Philadelphia	Consolidation N.B.
562.	New Castle	First N.B.
563.	Philadelphia	Union N.B.
566.	Northumberland	First N.B.
567.	Mahanoy City	First N.B.
568.	Berwick	First N.B.
569.	Corry	Corry N.B.
570.	Philadelphia	Tradesmen's N.B.
573.	Doylestown	Doylestown N.B.
575.	Coatesville	N.B. of Chester Valley
580.	Harrisburg	Harrisburg N.B.
585.	Middletown	N.B. of Middletown
586.	Washington	First N.B.

Charter #	City	Name of Bank
592.	Philadelphia	Girard N.B.
593.	Chambersburg	N.B. of Chambersburg
597.	Lancaster	Farmers' N.B.
602.	Philadelphia	Bank of North America
604.	York	York N.B.
605.	Corry	First N.B.
606.	Erie	Second N.B.
608.	Pottstown	N.B. of Pottstown
610.	Philadelphia	Mechanics' N.B.
611.	Gettysburg	Gettysburg N.B.
613.	Pittsburgh	Merchants and Manufacturers N.B.
619.	Pittsburgh	Citizens' N.B.
622.	Titusville	First N.B.
623.	Philadelphia	Commonwealth N.B.
632.	New Brighton	N.B. of Beaver County
641.	Columbia	Columbia N.B.
644.	Honesdale	Honesdale N.B.
648.	Brownsville	Monongahela N.B.
649.	Pottsville	Miners' N.B.
655.	Lebanon	Valley N.B.
656.	Philadelphia	Western N.B.
661.	Downington, E. Downington	Downington N.B.
664.	Carbondale	First N.B.
667.	Mount Joy	First N.B.
668.	Pittsburgh	Pittsburgh N.B. of Commerce
674.	Phoenixville	N.B. of Phoenixville
675.	Pittsburgh	Iron City N.B.
678.	Pittsburgh	Tradesmen's N.B.
680.	Lebanon	Lebanon N.B.
681.	Uniontown	N.B. of Fayette County
683.	Lancaster	Lancaster County N.B.
685.	Pittsburgh	Farmers' Deposit N.B.
689.	Shamokin	Northumberland County N.B.
693.	Reading	Nat. Union Bank
694.	York	York County N.B.
696.	Reading	Farmers' N.B.
700.	Pittsburgh	Mechanics' N.B.
705.	Pittsburgh	Union N.B.
707.	Plymouth	First N.B.
711.	Milton	Milton N.B.
717.	Bristol	Farmers' N.B. of Bucks County
722.	Pittsburgh	Allegheny N.B.
723.	Philadelphia	Central N.B.
727.	Pittsburgh	People's N.B.
728.	Oxford	N.B. of Oxford
732.	Wilkes-Barre	Wyoming N.B.
734.	Williamsport	Lumberman's N.B.
741.	North East	First N.B.
745.	Lewisburg	Lewisburg N.B.
755.	Philadelphia	Nat. Exchange Bank
757.	Pittsburgh	German N.B.
768.	Clearfield	First N.B.
774.	Clarion	First N.B.
776.	Allegheny	Second N.B.
784.	Lewisburg	Union N.B.
797.	Tremont	First N.B.
834.	Shippensburg	First N.B.
835.	Tunkhannock	Wyoming N.B.
837.	Muncy	First N.B.
839.	Waynesburg	Farmers and Drovers' N.B.
854.	Plumer	First N.B.
855.	Clearfield	County N.B.
867.	Blairsville	First N.B.
870.	Erie	Marine N.B.
871.	Meadville	Merchants' N.B.
879.	Titusville	Second N.B.
897.	Brookville	First N.B.
912.	Manheim	Manheim N.B.
926.	Pittsburgh	First N.B. of Birmingham
1053.	Susquehanna	First N.B.
1057.	Pittsburgh	Exchange N.B.
1078.	Danville	Danville N.B.
1081.	Greencastle	First N.B.
1094.	Athens	First N.B.
1124.	Meadville	N.B. of Crawford County
1148.	Norristown	Montgomery N.B.
1152.	Pottsville	Government N.B.
1156.	New Castle	N.B. of Lawrence County
1171.	Easton	First N.B.
1176.	Franklin	Venango N.B.
1219.	Tamaqua	First N.B.
1233.	Easton	Easton N.B.
1237.	Sunbury	First N.B.
1273.	Lock Haven	Lock Haven N.B.
1322.	Allentown	Allentown N.B.
1411.	Catasauqua	N.B. of Catasauqua
1435.	Pittston	Pittston N.B.
1464.	Williamsport	Williamsport N.B.
1505.	Williamsport	West Branch N.B.
1516.	Mount Joy	Union Nat. Mount Joy Bank
1579.	Lewiston	Mifflin County N.B.
1647.	Philadelphia	N.B. of the Republic
1654.	Kittanning	Kittanning N.B.
1663.	Pottsville	Pennsylvania N.B.
1676.	Honeybrook	First N.B.
1685.	Sharon	First N.B.
1743.	Philadelphia	Nat. Security Bank
1875.	Reading	Keystone N.B.
1894.	Pittsburgh	Fifth N.B.
1936.	Phoenixville	Farmers and Mechanics' N.B.
1946.	Scranton	Third N.B.
2018.	Spring City	N.B. of Spring City
2050.	Bethlehem	Lehigh Valley N.B.
2078.	Conshohocken	First N.B.
2131.	Green Lane	Green Lane N.B.
2137.	Boyertown	N.B. of Boyertown
2139.	Williamsport	City N.B.
2142.	Schwenksville	N.B. of Schwenksville
2195.	Pittsburgh	City N.B.
2222.	McKeesport	First N.B.
2223.	Montrose	First N.B.
2226.	Warren	Citizens' N.B.
2227.	Williamsport	Lycoming N.B.
2228.	York	Farmers' N.B.
2235.	Allegheny	Third N.B.
2236.	Pittsburgh	Diamond N.B.
2237.	Pittsburgh	Marine N.B.
2241.	Millerstown	German N.B.
2244.	Sharon	Sharon N.B.
2249.	Jenkintown	Jenkintown N.B.
2251.	Greenville	Greenville N.B.
2252.	Millersburg	First N.B.
2253.	Hatboro	Hatboro N.B.
2256.	Mercer	Farmers and Mechanics' N.B.
2258.	Meyersdale	First N.B.
2261.	Lewiston	Manufacturers' N.B.
2278.	Pittsburgh	Duquesne N.B.
2279.	Pittsburgh	Metropolitan N.B.
2280.	Ashland	Citizens' N.B.
2281.	Pittsburgh	Smithfield N.B.
2285.	Tarentum	First N.B.
2286.	Freeport	First N.B.
2291.	Philadelphia	Keystone N.B.
2293.	Slatington	N.B. of Slatington
2301.	Pennsburg	Perkiomen N.B.
2303.	York	Western N.B.
2308.	Lehighton	First N.B.
2317.	Philadelphia	Centennial N.B.
2329.	Connellsville	First N.B.
2333.	Souderton	Union N.B.
2334.	Pennsburg	Farmers' N.B.
2335.	Harmony	Harmony N.B.
2337.	Towanda	Citizens' N.B.
2366.	Quakertown	Quakertown N.B.
2384.	Annville	Annville N.B.
2385.	Easton	Northampton County N.B.
2392.	Brookville	Jefferson County N.B.
2397.	Dillsburg	Dillsburg N.B.
2408.	Burgettstown	Burgettstown N.B.
2415.	Pittsburgh	Fort Pitt N.B.
2428.	Bradford	Bradford N.B.
2452.	Lititz	Lititz N.B.
2457.	Brownsville	Nat. Deposit Bank
2462.	Philadelphia	Merchants' N.B.
2464.	Parkesburg	Parkesburg N.B.
2466.	Titusville	Hyde N.B.
2470.	Bradford	First N.B.
2473.	Reading	Commercial N.B.
2483.	Watsontown	Watsontown N.B.
2505.	Canton	First N.B.
2515.	Ephrata	Ephrata N.B.
2526.	Kennett Square	N.B. of Kennett Square
2530.	New Holland	New Holland N.B.
2552.	Reading	Second N.B.
2558.	Greensburg	First N.B.
2562.	Greensburg	Merchants and Farmers' N.B.
2581.	Norristown	People's N.B.
2609.	Saltsburg	First N.B.
2634.	Lancaster	Fulton N.B.
2654.	Kittanning	N.B. of Kittanning
2659.	Bangor	First N.B.
2667.	Sellersville	Sellersville N.B.
2669.	West Grove	N.B. of West Grove
2671.	Conshohocken	Tradesmen's N.B.
2673.	Brownsville	Second N.B.
2697.	Scranton	First N.B.
2700.	Strasburg	First N.B.
2710.	Marietta	First N.B.
2711.	Pittsburgh	Commercial N.B.
2731.	Philadelphia	First N.B.
2736.	Wilkes-Barre	First N.B.
2739.	Johnstown	First N.B.
2744.	Hollidaysburg	First N.B.
2745.	Pittsburgh	First N.B.
2781.	Altoona	Second N.B.
2787.	Stroudsburg	First N.B.
2799.	Braddock	First N.B.
2822.	Hummels-town	Hummelstown N.B.
2828.	Braddock	Braddock N.B.
2834.	Titusville	Roberts N.B.
2849.	Christiana	N.B. of Christiana
2852.	Mauch Chunk	Linderman N.B.
2857.	West Chester	Farmers' N.B.
2864.	Gap	Gap N.B.
2899.	Reading	Penn N.B.
2900.	Boyertown	Farmers' N.B.
2904.	Chester	Chester N.B.
2906.	Oxford	Farmers' N.B.
2958.	York	Drovers and Mechanics' N.B.
2969.	Du Bois	First N.B. of Du Bois City
2977.	Rochester	First N.B.
3030.	Punxsutawney	First N.B.
3044.	Clarion	Second N.B.
3045.	Shamokin	First N.B.
3051.	Brookville	N.B. of Brookville
3063.	Langhorne	People's N.B.
3067.	Quarryville	Quarryville N.B.
3085.	Philadelphia	Independence N.B.
3089.	Bedford	First N.B.
3104.	Kittanning	Farmers' N.B.
3143.	Shenandoah	First N.B.
3144.	Susquehanna	City N.B.
3147.	Malvern	N.B. of Malvern
3198.	Lincoln	Lincoln N.B.
3220.	Ambler	First N.B.
3255.	Emporium	First N.B.
3259.	New Brighton	N.B. of New Brighton
3335.	Elizabethtown	Elizabethtown N.B.
3356.	Beaver Falls	First N.B.
3358.	Topton	Topton N.B.
3367.	Lancaster	Northern N.B.
3371.	Philadelphia	Ninth N.B.
3383.	Washington	Citizens' N.B.
3423.	Philadelphia	Tenth N.B.
3459.	Watsontown	Farmers' N.B.
3468.	Philadelphia	Spring Garden N.B.
3480.	Muncy	Citizens' N.B.
3491.	Philadelphia	Northwestern N.B.
3494.	Pottstown	Nat. Iron Bank
3498.	Philadelphia	Southwestern N.B.
3507.	Philadelphia	Produce N.B.
3551.	Royersford	N.B. of Royersford
3557.	Philadelphia	Fourth Street N.B.
3599.	Steelton	Steelton N.B.
3604.	Philadelphia	Manayunk N.B.
3632.	Stroudsburg	Stroudsburg N.B.
3635.	Manheim	Keystone N.B.
3650.	Lancaster	People's N.B.
3666.	Media	Charter N.B.
3684.	Philadelphia	Market Street N.B.
3705.	Williamsport	Merchants' N.B.
3713.	Harrisburg	Merchants' N.B.
3723.	Philadelphia	Chestnut Street N.B.
3763.	Renovo	First N.B.
3766.	Bryn Mawr	Bryn Mawr N.B.
3808.	Mountville	Mountville N.B.
3829.	Homestead	First N.B.
3831.	Latrobe	First N.B.
3850.	Beaver	First N.B.
3873.	Columbia	Central N.B.
3874.	Pittsburgh	Monongahela N.B.
3877.	Port Allegany	First N.B.
3893.	Hazleton	First N.B.
3902.	Hughesville	First N.B.
3905.	Birdsboro	First N.B.
3910.	Latrobe	Citizens' N.B.
3938.	Wellsborough	Wellsborough N.B.
3945.	Berwyn	Berwyn N.B.
3955.	Nanticoke	First N.B.
3961.	Bethlehem	Bethlehem N.B.
3980.	Mount Carmel	First N.B.
3987.	Lancaster	Conestoga N.B.
3990.	Coatesville	N.B. of Coatesville
3997.	Mahanoy City	Union N.B.
4011.	East Stroudsburg	East Stroudsburg N.B.
4039.	Mifflintown	First N.B.
4050.	Philadelphia	Quaker City N.B.
4063.	Hyndman	N.B. of South Pennsylvania
4092.	Jeannette	First N.B.
4098.	Scottdale	First N.B.
4100.	Somerset	First N.B.
4142.	Duncannon	Duncannon N.B.
4156.	Middleburgh	First N.B.
4181.	Washington	Farmers and Mechanics' N.B.
4183.	Scranton	Traders' N.B.
4192.	Philadelphia	Northern N.B.
4199.	Bradford	Commercial N.B.
4204.	Hazleton	Hazleton N.B.
4205.	Delta	First N.B.
4207.	Yardley	Yardley N.B.
4212.	Johnstown	Citizens' N.B.
4222.	Pittsburgh	Pennsylvania N.B.
4227.	Somerset	Somerset County N.B.
4255.	Claysville	N.B. of Claysville
4267.	Waynesburg	Citizens' N.B.
4272.	Chambersburg	Valley N.B.
4273.	Claysville	First N.B.
4330.	North Wales	North Wales N.B.
4339.	Pittsburgh	Liberty N.B.
4352.	Pen Argyl	First N.B.
4355.	Tyrone	First N.B.
4367.	Delta	Miles N.B.
4374.	Butler	Butler County N.B.
4408.	Orwigsburg	First N.B.
4422.	Girardville	First N.B.
4428.	Darby	First N.B.
4444.	Carlisle	Merchants' N.B.
4445.	Waynesboro	People's N.B.
4453.	Tarentum	N.B. of Tarentum
4462.	Sewickley	First N.B.
4479.	Corry	Citizens' N.B.
4481.	Connellsville	Second N.B.
4505.	Dushore	First N.B.
4513.	Bangor	Merchants' N.B.
4534.	Charleroi	First N.B.
4538.	Reedsville	Reedsville N.B.
4543.	Bloomsburg	Farmers' N.B.
4544.	Johnsonburg	Johnsonburg N.B.
4546.	Shenandoah	Merchants' N.B.
4548.	Catawissa	First N.B.
4549.	New Brighton	Union N.B.
4560.	Avondale	N.B. of Avondale
4570.	Canonsburg	First N.B.
4615.	Emlenton	First N.B.
4622.	California	First N.B.
4625.	McKeesport	N.B. of McKeesport
4665.	Stewartstown	First N.B.
4673.	Dawson	First N.B.
4676.	New Castle	Citizens' N.B.
4698.	Irwin	First N.B.
4714.	Pottstown	Citizens' N.B.
4728.	Wilkinsburg	First N.B.
4730.	Duquesne	First N.B.
4751.	Royersford	Home N.B.
4752.	McDonald	First N.B.
4762.	Carnegie	First N.B.
4818.	Ellwood City	First N.B.
4823.	Corry	N.B. of Corry

Charter #	City	Name of Bank
4832.	Philipsburg	First N.B.
4836.	Clearfield	Clearfield N.B.
4850.	Belle Vernon	First N.B.
4857.	Patton	First N.B.
4861.	Connellsville	Yough N.B.
4875.	Mount Pleasant	Citizens' N.B.
4876.	McKeesport	Citizens' N.B.
4877.	Verona	First N.B.
4879.	Warren	Warren N.B.
4883.	Pittsburgh	Lincoln N.B.
4887.	Reading	Reading N.B.
4892.	Mount Pleasant	Farmers and Merchants' N.B.
4894.	Beaver Falls	Farmers' N.B.
4908.	Reynoldsville	First N.B.
4909.	Mercer	Mercer County N.B.
4910.	Pittsburgh	Columbia N.B.
4913.	New Kensington	First N.B.
4915.	Athens	Farmers' N.B.
4917.	Newport	First N.B.
4918.	Pittsburgh	Western N.B.
4919.	Blairsville	Blairsville N.B.
4923.	Ephrata	Farmers' N.B.
4927.	North East	First N.B.
4938.	Meadville	New First N.B.
4948.	Coudersport	First N.B.
4955.	Lebanon	People's N.B.
4965.	Huntingdon	Union N.B.
4971.	Cochranton	First N.B.
4974.	Greensburg	Westmoreland N.B.
4978.	New Bethlehem	First N.B.
4979.	Lebanon	Farmers' N.B.
4984.	Troy	First N.B.
4991.	Allegheny	Enterprise N.B.
5000.	Wilmerding	East Pittsburgh N.B.
5007.	Blossburg	Miners' N.B.
5010.	West Newton	First N.B.
5014.	Ridgway	Elk County N.B.
5017.	Pittsburgh	United States N.B.
5019.	Du Bois	Deposit N.B.
5025.	Kane	First N.B.
5034.	Uniontown	Second N.B.
5038.	Tionesta	Forest County N.B.
5040.	Tionesta	Citizens' N.B.
5042.	Beaver	Beaver N.B.
5043.	Elkland	Pattison N.B.
5044.	Grove City	First N.B.
5051.	New Bethlehem	Citizens' N.B.
5058.	McDonald	People's N.B.
5059.	Johnstown	Cambria N.B.
5066.	Philipsburg	Moshannon N.B.
5069.	Coraopolis	Coraopolis N.B.
5073.	Kittanning	Merchants' N.B.
5077.	Nazareth	Nazareth N.B.
5080.	Vandergrift	First N.B.
5084.	Ebensburg	First N.B.
5085.	Waynesburg	People's N.B.
5102.	Kutztown	Kutztown N.B.
5114.	Elizabeth	First N.B.
5118.	Easton	Northampton N.B.
5130.	Ford City	First N.B.
5131.	Union City	N.B. of Union City
5133.	New Bloomfield	First N.B.
5142.	McKees Rocks	First N.B.
5147.	Mifflintown	Juaniata Valley N.B.
5166.	East Greenville	Perkiomen N.B.
5170.	Rochester	Rochester N.B.
5184.	Red Lion	Red Lion First N.B.
5198.	Delta	People's N.B.
5202.	Athens	Athens N.B.
5204.	Glen Campbell	First N.B.
5211.	Bloomsburg	Bloomsburg N.B.
5216.	Schuylkill Haven	First N.B.
5221.	Franklin	Lamberton N.B.
5225.	Pittsburgh	Bank of Pittsburgh Nat. Assn.
5227.	Northampton	Cement N.B. of Siegfried
5234.	Lansford	First N.B.
5240.	Oil City	Oil City N.B.
5241.	Myerstown	Myerstown N.B.
5242.	Windber	Windber N.B.
5245.	Newport	Perry County N.B.
5253.	Monessen	First N.B.
5255.	Irwin	Citizens' N.B.
5265.	Wilkinsburg	Central N.B.
5289.	Lewistown	Citizens' N.B.
5306.	Belleville	Belleville N.B.
5307.	Confluence	First N.B.
5311.	Smithton	First N.B.
5321.	East Brady	First N.B.
5327.	Oakdale	First N.B.
5339.	Wyalusing	First N.B.
5340.	Rockwood	First N.B.
5351.	Tarentum	People's N.B.
5356.	East Brady	People's N.B.
5365.	Homestead	Homestead N.B.
5389.	Millville	First N.B.
5391.	Butler	Farmers' N.B.
5429.	Meshoppen	First N.B.
5441.	Masontown	First N.B.
5444.	Bath	First N.B.
5452.	Somerset	Farmers' N.B.
5454.	Freedom	Freedom N.B.
5459.	Philadelphia	Franklin N.B.
5481.	Emlenton	Farmers' N.B.
5495.	Roscoe	First N.B.
5496.	Milford	First N.B.
5497.	Brickway	First N.B.
5501.	Grove City	Grove City N.B.
5502.	Leechburg	First N.B.
5509.	Bellevue	Bellevue N.B.
5518.	Forest City	First N.B.
5527.	Jeannette	Jeannette N.B.
5531.	Littlestown	First N.B.
5563.	Elizabethville	First N.B.
5565.	Oil City	Lamberton N.B.
5573.	Shickshinny	First N.B.
5574.	Montgomery	First N.B.
5578.	East Stroudsberg	Monroe County N.B.
5599.	Mars	Mars N.B.
5601.	Halifax	Halifax N.B.
5615.	Ashland	Ashland N.B.
5625.	Shamokin	Market Street N.B.
5646.	Fayette City	First N.B.
5666.	Sayre	First N.B.
5667.	Big Run	Citizens' N.B.
5682.	Stoystown	First N.B.
5684.	Sayre	N.B. of Sayre
5686.	Nazareth	Second N.B.
5702.	Punxsutawney	Punxsutawney N.B.
5708.	Glassport	Glassport N.B.
5723.	Apollo	First N.B.
5727.	Marienville	Gold Standard N.B.
5729.	Natrona	First N.B.
5736.	Perkasie	First N.B.
5742.	Dayton	First N.B.
5744.	Latrobe	People's N.B.
5768.	Cresson	First N.B.
5773.	Lititz	Farmers' N.B.
5777.	Beaver Springs	First N.B.
5784.	Carmichaels	First N.B.
5801.	Meyersdale	Second N.B.
5818.	Barnesboro	First N.B.
5823.	Berlin	First N.B.
5832.	Waynesboro	Citizens' N.B.
5833.	Meyersdale	Citizens' N.B.
5835.	Donora	First N.B.
5837.	New Salem	Delmont N.B.
5848.	Pitcairn	First N.B.
5855.	Carrolltown	First N.B.
5857.	Greencastle	Citizens' N.B.
5878.	Monaca	Monaca N.B.
5879.	Monaca	Citizens' N.B.
5899.	Ellwood City	Ellwood City N.B.
5908.	Houston	First N.B.
5913.	Johnstown	United States N.B.
5920.	Fredericktown	First N.B.
5945.	Ridgway	Ridgway N.B.
5948.	West Alexander	West Alexander N.B.
5956.	Monessen	People's N.B.
5965.	Punxsutawney	Farmers' N.B.
5968.	Monongahela City	First N.B.
5974.	Scottdale	Broadway N.B.
5977.	Sheraden	First N.B.
6010.	Crafton	First N.B.
6023.	Pittsburgh	Federal N.B.
6037.	Denver	Denver N.B.
6045.	Parkers Landing	First N.B.
6049.	Herndon	First N.B.
6051.	Slatington	Citizens' N.B.
6066.	Port Allegany	Citizens' N.B.
6083.	Rural Valley	Rural Valley N.B.
6090.	Huntingdon	Standing Stone N.B.
6105.	Waynesburg	American N.B.
6106.	Salisbury, Elk Lick	First N.B.
6108.	Weatherly	First N.B.
6109.	Swissvale	First N.B.
6114.	Point Marion	First N.B.
6117.	Tower City	Tower City N.B.
6127.	Kittanning	Nat. Kittanning Bank
6131.	Minersville	Union N.B.
6135.	Bolivar	Bolivar N.B.
6141.	Zelienople	First N.B.
6153.	Pittsburgh	Republic N.B.
6155.	Jersey Shore	N.B. of Jersey Shore
6158.	Jermyn	First N.B.
6162.	Berwick	Berwick N.B.
6165.	Tremont	Tremont N.B.
6174.	Carnegie	Carnegie N.B.
6175.	Freeland	First N.B.
6182.	Edenburg, Knox	Clarion County N.B.
6193.	Sheffield	Sheffield N.B.
6209.	Ebensburg	American N.B.
6216.	Pittsburgh	Cosmopolitan N.B.
6220.	Everett	First N.B.
6250.	Hooversville	First N.B.
6270.	Sutersville	First N.B.
6275.	Clifton Heights	First N.B.
6281.	Ligonier	First N.B.
6301.	Pittsburgh	Mellon N.B.
6325.	Wilmerding	Wilmerding N.B.
6328.	Benton	Columbia County N.B.
6344.	Perryopolis	First N.B.
6350.	Le Raysville	First N.B.
6373.	West Elizabeth	First N.B.
6384.	Falls Creek	First N.B.
6408.	Connellsville	Union N.B.
6411.	Mount Union	First N.B.
6420.	Finleyville	First N.B.
6438.	Tunkhanock	Citizens' N.B.
6442.	Gallitzin	First N.B.
6444.	Stewartstown	People's N.B.
6445.	Hawley	First N.B.
6452.	Connellsville	Citizens' N.B.
6453.	Etna, Pittsburgh, Sharpsburg	First N.B.
6456.	Manor	Manor N.B.
6465.	Quakertown	Merchants' N.B.
6483.	Slippery Rock	First N.B.
6495.	Clairton	Clairton N.B.
6499.	Tyrone	Farmers and Merchants' N.B.
6500.	Youngwood	First N.B.
6501.	Osceola, Osceola Mills	First N.B.
6507.	Hays	Hays N.B.
6512.	Berlin	Philson N.B.
6516.	Tyrone	Blair County N.B.
6528.	Masontown	Masontown N.B.
6531.	Lehighton	Citizens' N.B.
6533.	Cambridge Springs	First N.B.
6534.	Mauch Chunk	Mauch Chunk N.B.
6536.	Spring Grove	First N.B.
6560.	Sharon	Merchants and Manufacturers' N.B.
6567.	Pittsburgh	Colonial N.B.
6568.	Turtle Creek	N.B. of Turtle Creek
6569.	Rimersburg	Rimersburg N.B.
6573.	South Fork	First N.B.
6574.	Turtle Creek	First N.B.
6580.	New Alexandria	New Alexandria N.B.
6581.	Pleasant Unity	Pleasant Unity N.B.
6589.	Saint Marys	Saint Marys N.B.
6599.	New Salem	First N.B.
6603.	Boswell	First N.B.
6615.	Hyndman	Holitzell N.B.
6626.	Midway	Midway N.B.
6636.	Bridgeville	First N.B.
6638.	Stoneboro	First N.B.
6642.	Smithfield	First N.B.
6645.	Allentown	Merchants' N.B.
6648.	Dallastown	First N.B.
6654.	Chester	Pennsylvania N.B.
6664.	Wampum	First N.B.
6665.	Portland	Portland N.B.
6676.	Rimersburg	First N.B.
6695.	Houtzdale	First N.B.
6708.	Red Lion	Farmers and Merchants' N.B.
6709.	Addison	First N.B.
6715.	New Freedom	First N.B.
6725.	Pittsburgh	Washington N.B.
6739.	Summerville	Union N.B.
6741.	Garrett	First N.B.
6746.	Montrose	Farmers' N.B.
6756.	Derry	First N.B.
6794.	Wilson	First N.B.
6796.	Braddock	Union N.B.
6799.	Shingle House	First N.B.
6800.	Fayette City	Fayette City N.B.
6806.	Pittsburgh	Industrial N.B.
6829.	Sharpsville	First N.B.
6832.	Ligonier	N.B. of Ligonier
6848.	Windber	Citizens' N.B.
6859.	Harrisville	First N.B.
6874.	Hollidaysburg	Citizens' N.B.
6877.	Sunbury	Sunbury N.B.
6878.	East Berlin	East Berlin N.B.
6881.	Plymouth	Plymouth N.B.
6887.	Coalport	First N.B.
6891.	Conneaut Lake	First N.B.
6913.	West Middlesex	First N.B.
6929.	Ellsworth	N.B. of Ellsworth
6937.	Webster	First N.B.
6942.	Shamokin	N.B. of Shamokin
6944.	Burgettstown	Washington N.B.
6946.	Shippensburg	People's N.B.
6948.	Clintonville	First N.B.
6950.	Ringtown	First N.B.
6962.	Trafford City	First N.B.
6969.	Curwensville	Citizens' N.B.
6971.	Williamsburg	First N.B.
6979.	East Conemaugh	First N.B.
6983.	Mount Morris	Farmers and Merchants' N.B.
6997.	Montoursville	First N.B.
7000.	Cherry Tree	First N.B.
7003.	Swineford	First N.B.
7005.	Northumberland	Northumberland N.B.
7051.	Lansford	Citizens' N.B.
7056.	Atglen	Atglen N.B.
7076.	Cecil	First N.B.
7078.	Christiana	Christiana N.B.
7090.	Rices Landing	Rices Landing N.B.
7112.	Wehrum	First N.B.
7139.	Emaus	Emaus N.B.
7156.	Millerstown	First N.B.
7181.	Spangler	First N.B.
7193.	Swarthmore	Swarthmore N.B.
7229.	Saxton	First N.B.
7262.	Scenery Hill	First N.B.
7263.	Washington	Old N.B.
7280.	Galeton	First N.B.
7286.	Tamaqua	Tamaqua N.B.
7310.	Millsboro	First N.B.
7312.	Edinboro	First N.B.
7334.	Winburne	Bituminous N.B.
7343.	Girard	N.B. of Girard
7349.	New Cumberland	New Cumberland N.B.
7353.	Marysville	First N.B.
7356.	Bellwood	First N.B.
7363.	Parnassus	Parnassus N.B.
7366.	Freeport	Farmers' N.B.
7367.	Portage	First N.B.
7395.	New Brighton	Old N.B.
7400.	Madera	Madera N.B.

Charter #	City	Name of Bank
7405.	Hickory	Farmers' N.B.
7406.	Nanticoke	Nanticoke N.B.
7409.	Zelienople	People's N.B.
7430.	Curwensville	Curwensville N.B.
7445.	Connellsville	Colonial N.B.
7448.	Catawissa	Catawissa N.B.
7453.	Du Bois	Du Bois N.B.
7465.	Johnstown	Union N.B.
7471.	Fredonia	Fredonia N.B.
7473.	Mount Jewett	Mount Jewett N.B.
7488.	Sykesville	First N.B.
7511.	State College	First N.B.
7522.	Philadelphia	Textile N.B.
7528.	Economy	People's N.B.
7559.	McKeesport	Union N.B.
7560.	Pittsburgh	Keystone N.B.
7576.	Dunbar	First N.B.
7581.	Pittsburgh	American N.B.
7594.	Avonmore	First N.B.
7610.	Mahaffey	Mahaffey N.B.
7620.	Reynoldsville	People's N.B.
7624.	Export	First N.B.
7642.	Oakmont	First N.B.
7702.	Hallstead	First N.B.
7710.	Pen Argyl	Pen Argyl N.B.
7716.	Newport	Citizens' N.B.
7722.	Trevorton	First N.B.
7735.	Lansdale	Citizens' N.B.
7749.	Rochester	People's N.B.
7769.	McClure	First N.B.
7785.	Peckville	Peckville N.B.
7792.	Jeannette	People's N.B.
7816.	Vandergrift	Citizens' N.B.
7819.	Marion Center	Marion Center N.B.
7826.	Middletown	Citizens' N.B.
7854.	Avella	Lincoln N.B.
7856.	York Springs	First N.B.
7860.	Frackville	First N.B.
7873.	Sharpsville	Sharpsville N.B.
7874.	Shippenville	First N.B.
7887.	Plumville	First N.B.
7897.	New Berlin	First N.B.
7910.	Nicholson	First N.B.
7917.	Biglerville	Biglerville N.B.
7929.	Philadelphia	Nat. Deposit Bank
7931.	Danielsville	Danielsville N.B.
7935.	Benson, Hollsopple	First N.B.
7974.	Martinsburg	First N.B.
7993.	Indiana	Citizens' N.B.
8045.	Quarryville	Farmers' N.B.
8083.	McConnelsburg	First N.B.
8092.	Tioga	Grange N.B.
8131.	Wernersville	Wernersville N.B.
8141.	Spring Grove	People's N.B.
8151.	Pine Grove	Pine Grove N.B.
8164.	Dallas	First N.B.
8165.	Youngsville	First N.B.
8185.	Beaver	Fort McIntosh N.B.
8190.	Canderbilt	First N.B.
8196.	Bentleyville	First N.B.
8223.	Topton	N.B. of Topton
8233.	Patton	Grange N.B.
8235.	Scranton	People's N.B.
8238.	Juniata	First N.B.
8245.	Fairchance	First N.B.
8263.	Reynoldsville	Citizens' N.B.
8283.	Catasauqua	Lehigh N.B.
8311.	Midland	First N.B.
8320.	Springdale	Springdale N.B.
8326.	Liverpool	First N.B.
8329.	Bridgeport	Bridgeport N.B.
8344.	Richland	Richland N.B.
8380.	Hazelhurst	Hazelhurst N.B.
8393.	Mount Carmel	Union N.B.
8404.	Collegeville	Collegeville N.B.
8405.	Lemasters	Lemasters N.B.
8410.	Exchange	Farmers' N.B.
8421.	Blue Ball	Blue Ball N.B.
8428.	Blacklick	First N.B.
8446.	East Mauch Chunk	Citizens' N.B.
8450.	Lilly	First N.B.
8459.	Ambridge	First N.B.
8464.	Clearfield	Farmers and Traders' N.B.
8493.	Mount Holly Springs	First N.B.
8494.	Avoca	First N.B.
8498.	Wellsville	Wellsville N.B.
8499.	New Holland	Farmers' N.B.
8503.	New Castle	Union N.B.
8517.	Wyoming	First N.B.
8576.	Lyndora	Lyndora N.B.
8590.	Aliquippa	First N.B.
8591.	Smethport	Grange N.B. of McKean Co.
8619.	McAdoo	First N.B.
8633.	Edwardsville	First N.B.
8646.	Downingtown	Grange N.B. of Chester Co.
8653.	Selinsgrove	Farmers' N.B.
8656.	Ashley, Wilkes-Barre	First N.B.
8678.	Ellwood City	People's N.B.
8724.	Slippery Rock	Citizens' N.B.
8737.	Scranton	Union N.B.
8739.	Ulysses	Grange N.B. of Potter Co.
8761.	Bellevue	Citizens' N.B.
8764.	Sharon	McDowell N.B.
8773.	McVeytown	McVeytown N.B.
8778.	Duncannon	People's N.B.
8783.	Fredericksburg	First N.B.
8795.	Munhall	First N.B.
8806.	Olyphant	First N.B.
8810.	Mansfield	First N.B.
8824.	Aspinwall	First N.B.
8831.	Mansfield	Grange N.B.
8845.	Laceyville	Grange N.B. of Wyoming Co.
8849.	Troy	Grange N.B. of Bradford Co.
8854.	Evans City	Citizens' N.B.
8855.	Homer City	Homer City N.B.
8858.	Oley	First N.B.
8866.	Montgomery	Farmers and Citizens' N.B.
8879.	Union City	Home N.B.
8890.	West Conshohocken	People's N.B.
8901.	Somerfield	First N.B.
8913.	Bernville	First N.B.
8919.	Bruin	First N.B.
8921.	Luzerne	Luzerne N.B.
8924.	Hughesville	Grange N.B. of Lycoming Co.
8930.	Palmerton	First N.B.
8938.	West York, York	Industrial N.B.
8939.	Fleetwood	First N.B.
8946.	Sligo	Sligo N.B.
8954.	West Alexander	People's N.B.
8960.	New Milford	Grange N.B. of Susquehanna Co.
8962.	Schaefferstown	First N.B.
8964.	Pottsville	Merchants' N.B.
8968.	Mohnton	Mohnton N.B.
8969.	Mechanicsburg	Mechanicsburg N.B.
8973.	New Albany	First N.B.
8985.	Orbisonia	First N.B.
9026.	Brownstown	Brownstown N.B.
9028.	Hamburg	First N.B.
9034.	Coopersburg	First N.B.
9058.	Bentleyville	Farmers and Miners' N.B.
9072.	Goldsboro, Etters	First N.B.
9084.	Green Lane	Valley N.B.
9107.	Hegins	First N.B.
9110.	Spartansburg	Grange N.B.
9113.	Coplay	Coplay N.B.
9114.	Bendersville	Bendersville N.B.
9128.	Castle Shannon	First N.B.
9130.	Factoryville	First N.B.
9139.	Ardentsville	N.B. of Ardentsville
9149.	North East	N.B. of North East
9154.	Clintonville	People's N.B.
9198.	Mount Pleasant	People's N.B.
9202.	Riegelsville	First N.B.
9207.	Littlestown	Littlestown N.B.
9216.	Intercourse	First N.B.
9235.	Wilkes-Barre	Luzerne County N.B.
9240.	Auburn	First N.B.
9247.	Shenandoah	Citizens' N.B.
9248.	Forest City	Farmers and Miners' N.B.
9249.	Howard	First N.B.
9256.	Fairfield	First N.B.
9257.	Telford	Telford N.B.
9259.	Millersville	Millersville N.B.
9264.	Bainbridge	First N.B.
9290.	Leechburg	Farmers' N.B.
9307.	Claysville	Farmers' N.B.
9312.	Landisville	First N.B.
9316.	Terre Hill	Terre Hill N.B.
9317.	Canton	Farmers' N.B.
9318.	Cressona	First N.B.
9330.	Mercersburg	First N.B.
9340.	Moscow	First N.B.
9344.	Penbrook	Penbrook N.B.
9345.	Loganton	Loganton N.B.
9361.	Mount Wolf	Union N.B.
9362.	Dover	Dover N.B.
9364.	Akron	Akron N.B.
9385.	Fawn Grove	First N.B.
9392.	Williamsburg	Farmers and Merchants' N.B.
9402.	Bally	First N.B.
9416.	Eldred	First N.B.
9422.	Lititz	Lititz Springs N.B.
9430.	Cambridge Springs	Springs N.B.
9461.	Maytown	Maytown N.B.
9473.	Gratz	First N.B.
9480.	Fryburg	First N.B.
9495.	Leesport	First N.B.
9503.	Point Marion	People's N.B.
9505.	Ulster	First N.B.
9507.	Seven Valleys	Seven Valleys N.B.
9508.	Ralston	First N.B.
9511.	Millheim	Farmers' N.B.
9513.	Westfield	Farmers and Traders' N.B.
9526.	McAlisterville	Farmers' N.B.
9528.	Laporte	First N.B.
9534.	Albion	First N.B.
9541.	Harleysville	Harleysville N.B.
9543.	Freedom	Saint Clair N.B.
9552.	Mildred	First N.B.
9554.	New Wilmington	First N.B.
9568.	Centralia	First N.B.
9588.	Newville	Farmers' N.B.
9600.	Jessup	First N.B.
9638.	Hopewell	Hopewell N.B.
9647.	Hop Bottom	Hop Bottom N.B.
9656.	New Tripoli	New Tripoli N.B.
9660.	Jefferson, Codorus	Codorus N.B.
9668.	Glenside	Glenside N.B.
9678.	Patterson, Mifflin	People's N.B.
9702.	Lawrenceville	First N.B.
9706.	York	Central N.B.
9727.	Grantham	Grantham N.B.
9739.	Coaldale	First N.B.
9752.	Myerstown	Farmers' N.B.
9769.	Rockwood	Farmers and Merchants' N.B.
9783.	Genesee	First N.B.
9803.	Turbotville	Turbotville N.B.
9814.	Butler	Merchants' N.B.
9851.	Dickson City	Dickson City N.B.
9862.	Edwardsville, Wilkes-Barre	People's N.B.
9863.	Punxsutawney	County N.B.
9868.	Dunmore	First N.B.
9886.	Lake Ariel, Ariel	First N.B.
9898.	Clymer	Clymer N.B.
9901.	**Washington**	**People's N.B.**
9902.	**Aliquippa**	**Aliquippa N.B.**
9905.	**Ardmore**	**Ardmore N.B.**
9978.	Knoxville	First N.B.
9996.	Delmont	People's N.B.
10027.	Waterford	Ensworth N.B.
10042.	East Smithfield	First N.B.
10128.	Belleville	Farmers' N.B.
10183.	Three Springs	First N.B.
10188.	Herminie	First N.B.
10206.	Mount Union	Central N.B.
10211.	Thompsontown	Farmers' N.B.
10214.	Weissport	Weissport N.B.
10232.	Claysburg	First N.B.
10246.	Rome	Farmers' N.B.
10251.	Nesquehoning	First N.B.
10313.	Petersburg	First N.B.
10335.	Orbisonia	Orbisonia N.B.
10353.	New Florence	New Florence N.B.
10383.	Clarks Summit	Abington N.B.
10415.	Farrell	First N.B.
10452.	Strausstown	Strausstown N.B.
10466.	Republic	First N.B.
10493.	Russellton	First N.B.
10506.	Lewistown	Russell N.B.
10590.	Johnstown	N.B. of Johnstown
10606.	Wyalusing	N.B. of Wyalusing
10666.	Schellburg	First N.B.
10704.	Cairnbrook	First N.B.
10707.	Marietta	Exchange N.B.
10775.	Elverson	Elverson N.B.
10811.	Dry Run	Citizens' N.B.
10837.	Elysburg	First N.B.
10839.	Ambridge	Ambridge N.B.
10847.	Ridley Park	Ridley Park N.B.
10899.	Fannettsburg	Fannettsburg N.B.
10950.	Lemasters	People's N.B.
10951.	Woodlawn	First N.B.
11015.	New Hope	Solebury N.B.
11058.	Orangeville	Farmers' N.B.
11062.	Lykens	First N.B.
11115.	Irvona	First N.B.
11127.	Liberty	Farmers' N.B.
11188.	Coaldale, Six Mile Run, Bedford Co.	Broad Top N.B.
11204.	Timblin	First N.B.
11213.	Spring Mills	First N.B.
11227.	Hastings	First N.B.
11244.	Mapleton, Mapleton Depot	First N.B.
11257.	Burnham	First N.B.
11263.	Alexandria	First N.B.
11317.	Beaverdale	First N.B.
11369.	Port Royal	First N.B.
11370.	Jefferson	First N.B.
11373.	Port Royal	Port Royal N.B.
11386.	Lansdowne	Lansdowne N.B.
11393.	Springville	First N.B.
11407.	Davidsville	First N.B.
11413.	Hooversville	Citizens' N.B.
11476.	Philadelphia	Drovers and Merchants' N.B.
11482.	Philadelphia	N.B. of Commerce
11487.	Monessen	Citizens' N.B.
11505.	Marcus Hook	Marcus Hook N.B.
11512.	Dauphin	Dauphin N.B.
11524.	Loysville	First N.B.
11539.	Philadelphia	Broad Street N.B.
11570.	Ellwood City	Citizens' N.B.
11593.	Allenwood	Allenwood N.B.
11643.	Picture Rocks	Picture Rocks N.B.
11692.	Lock Haven	County N.B.
11757.	Bakerton, Elmora	First N.B.
11760.	Butler	South Side N.B.
11789.	Rebersburg	Rebersburg N.B.
11834.	Volant	First N.B.
11841.	Shoemakersville	First N.B.
11849.	Sipesville	First N.B.
11865.	Pittston	Liberty N.B.
11866.	Waynesboro	First N.B.
11892.	Pitcairn	People's N.B.
11896.	Arnold	Arnold N.B.
11899.	Seward	First N.B.
11902.	Burnside	Burnside N.B.
11908.	Philadelphia	N.B. of North Philadelphia

Charter #	City	Name of Bank
11910.	Saegertown	First N.B.
11938.	Koppel	First N.B.
11966.	Osceola Mills	People's N.B.
11967.	Central City	Central City N.B.
11981.	Numidia	Valley N.B.
11993.	West Alexander	Citizens' N.B.
11995.	North Belle Vernon Belle Vernon	People's N.B.
12029.	Jerome	First N.B.
12063.	Windsor	First N.B.
12098.	Johnstown	Moxham N.B.
12137.	Philadelphia	Rittenhouse N.B.
12159.	Nescopeck	Nescopeck N.B.
12189.	Conneautville	First N.B.
12192.	Centre Hall	First N.B.
12197.	Penbrook	N.B. of Penbrook
12261.	State College	People's N.B.
12281.	Blue Ridge Summit	First N.B.
12304.	Roaring Spring	First N.B.
12305.	York	Eastern N.B.
12326.	Indian Head	First N.B.
12327.	Girardville	Liberty N.B.
12349.	Mocanaqua	First N.B.
12355.	Bolivar	Citizens' N.B.
12358.	Paoli	Paoli N.B.
12363.	North Girard	First N.B.
12380.	Camp Hill	Camp Hill N.B.
12414.	Pittsburgh	Highland N.B.
12459.	Dickson City	Liberty N.B.
12471.	Neffs	Neffs N.B.
12500.	Uniontown	Uniontown N.B. and Trust Co.
12504.	Wayne	Main Line N.B.
12526.	Cheltenham	Cheltenham N.B.
12530.	Jenkintown	Citizens' N.B.
12562.	Austin	First N.B.
12563.	Nuremburg	First N.B.
12573.	Philadelphia	Overbrook N.B.
12582.	Chalfont	Chalfont N.B.
12588.	Saint Michael	Saint Michael N.B.
12595.	Narberth	Narberth N.B.
12597.	Monroeton	First N.B.
12602.	Wehrum	N.B. of Wehrum
12688.	Hershey	Hershey N.B.
12695.	Bala-Cynwyd	Bala-Cynwyd N.B.
12720.	Cassandra	First N.B.
12805.	Shamokin	West End N.B.
12808.	Yukon	First N.B.
12858.	Oakmont, Upper Darby	Oakmont N.B.
12860.	Philadelphia	Queen Lane N.B.
12911.	Newfound-land	First N.B.
12912.	Derry	First N.B.
12921.	Kingston	First N.B.
12931.	Philadelphia	N.B. of Olney
12933.	Wilcox	Wilcox N.B.
12934.	Carnegie	Union N.B.
12967.	Dale	Dale N.B.
12975.	Fogelsville	Fogelsville N.B.
12994.	Monessen	N.B. and Trust Co.
13002.	Roseto	First N.B.
13003.	Philadelphia	Tioga N.B.
13005.	Waynesboro	Waynesboro N.B. and Trust Co.
13009.	Burgettstown	Peoples N.B.
13011.	Seward	Citizens' N.B.
13015.	Morton	Morton N.B.
13026.	Hatfield	Hatfield N.B.
13030.	Elkins Park	Elkins Park N.B.
13031.	Springfield	Springfield N.B.
13032.	Philadelphia	Erie N.B.
13040.	Scranton	County N.B.
13064.	Friedens	First N.B.
13084.	Kensington	Union N.B.
13087.	Ambridge	Economy N.B.
13113.	Philadelphia	N.B. of Mt. Airy
13118.	Bellafonte	Farmers N.B.
13133.	Dublin	Dublin N.B.
13134.	Waynesboro	First N.B. and Trust Co.
13141.	Roslyn	Roslyn N.B.
13151.	Lansdowne	N.B. of Lansdowne
13153.	Pittsburgh	Forbes N.B.
13160.	Glen Lyon	Glen Lyon N.B.
13175.	Philadelphia	Northeast N.B. of Holmesburg
13177.	Exeter	First N.B.
13180.	Philadelphia	City N.B. and Trust Co.
13186.	Leola	Leola N.B.
13196.	Highland Park	State Road N.B.
13197.	Jersey Shore	Union N.B.
13205.	Beech Creek	Beech Creek N.B.
13225.	Scranton	Hyde Park N.B.
13251.	Souderton	Peoples N.B.
13325.	Philadelphia	North Broad N.B.
13341.	Philadelphia	Lehigh N.B.
13371.	Erie	Lawrence Park N.B.
13381.	Blossburg	Citizens N.B. and Trust Co.
13392.	Conyngham	Conyngham N.B.
13432.	Ligonier	Ligonier N.B.
13447.	Butler	Union N.B.
13485.	Uniontown	Third N.B.
13491.	Connellsville	N.B. and Trust Co.
13494.	Lemoyne	West Shore N.B.
13496.	Sewickley	Union N.B.
13524.	Nanticoke	Miners N.B.
13533.	Gallitzin	First N.B.
13566.	Brockway	First N.B.
13571.	New Kensington	Logan N.B. and Trust Co.
13585.	Charleroi	N.B. of Charleroi
13606.	Portland	Portland N.B.
13618.	Mansfield	First N.B.
13619.	Shenandoah	Miners N.B.
13644.	Donora	Union N.B.
13658.	Ligonier	First N.B.
13663.	Bentleyville	Citizens N.B.
13699.	Sewickley	First N.B.
13700.	Latrobe	First N.B.
13701.	Pittsburgh	Pitt N.B.
13754.	Peckville	First N.B.
13765.	McConnells-burg	Fulton County N.B.
13772.	Scottdale	First N.B.
13781.	Johnstown	United States N.B.
13794.	Derry	First N.B.
13803.	Sharon	First N.B.
13812.	Harrisville	First N.B.
13813.	Canonsburg	First N.B.
13823.	Wilkinsburg	First N.B.
13826.	Freeport	First N.B.
13845.	New Wilmington	Depositors N.B.
13846.	Mercer	Farmers N.B.
13852.	Wilkes-Barre	Miners N.B.
13860.	Crafton	Crafton N.B.
13863.	Strausston	Strausston N.B.
13866.	Braddock	First N.B.
13868.	Blairsville	Blairsville N.B.
13869.	Finleyville	First N.B.
13871.	Albion	First N.B.
13873.	Waynesburg	Union N.B.
13884.	Fredonia	Fredonia N.B.
13887.	New Freedom	First N.B.
13900.	Somerset	Peoples N.B.
13907.	New Florence	New Florence N.B.
13908.	Rural Valley	Peoples N.B.
13917.	Birdsboro	First N.B.
13927.	Fleetwood	First N.B.
13937.	Dickson City	First N.B.
13940.	Tarentum	First N.B.
13942.	Conneautville	Farmers N.B.
13947.	Scranton	Scranton N.B.
13950.	Yardley	Yardley N.B.
13957.	Reynoldsville	Peoples N.B.
13967.	McKeesport	Union N.B.
13970.	Freeland	First N.B.
13980.	Conneaut Lake	First N.B.
13982.	Herndon	Herndon N.B.
13992.	Frackville	First N.B.
13994.	Heggins	First N.B.
13998.	Clearfield	County N.B.
13999.	Berwyn	Berwyn N.B.
14007.	Bethlehem	Bethlehem N.B.
14023.	Kingston	Kingston N.B.
14029.	Cambridge Springs	Springs-First N.B.
14031.	Tower City	Tower City N.B.
14037.	Ambler	Ambler N.B.
14043.	Clarion	First N.B.
14049.	Dover	Dover N.B.
14051.	Export	First N.B.
14055.	Greensburg	First N.B.
14067.	Rockwood	Union N.B.
14070.	Koppel	First N.B.
14071.	Jefferson	Codorus N.B.
14079.	Olyphant	N.B. of Olyphant
14082.	Windber	Citizens N.B.
14089.	Stoystown	First N.B.
14091.	East Berlin	East Berlin N.B.
14093.	Union City	N.B. of Union City
14094.	Cecil	First N.B.
14098.	Indiana	First N.B.
14107.	McKees Rocks	First N.B.
14112.	Wampum	First N.B.
14117.	Beaver Falls	First N.B.
14120.	Philadelphia	N.B. of Olney
14121.	Mount Wolf	Union N.B.
14122.	Clifton Heights	Clifton Heights N.B.
14123.	Charleroi	First N.B.
14133.	Latrobe	Commercial N.B.
14139.	Narberth	N.B. of Narberth
14155.	Ford City	N.B. of Ford City
14156.	Hooversville	Hooversville N.B.
14169.	Sykesville	First N.B.
14170.	Bangor	First N.B.
14171.	Philadelphia	South Philadelphia N.B.
14181.	Gallitzin	First N.B.
14182.	Williamsburg	First N.B.
14191.	Girard	Girard N.B.
14197.	Philadelphia	Northwestern N.B.
14201.	Delta	Delta N.B.
14205.	Forest City	First and Farmers N.B.
14210.	Pittsburgh	Keystone N.B.
14214.	Green Lane	First N.B.
14215.	Zelienople	Union N.B.
14219.	Erie	N.B. and Trust Co.
14239.	Bedford	Hartley N.B.
14250.	Hamburg	N.B. of Hamburg
14251.	Bridgeville	Bridgeville N.B.
14262.	Pottsville	City N.B.
14263.	Patton	First N.B.
14271.	Pittsburgh	N.B. of America
14274.	Oil City	Oil City N.B.
14276.	Marietta	Exchange N.B.
14277.	Reading	Union N.B.
14284.	Bedford	First N.B.
14293.	Shenandoah	Union N.B.
14301.	Gratz	Gratz N.B.
14333.	Masontown	Second N.B.
14344.	Wilkes-Barre	Hanover N.B.
14345.	Youngsville	Youngsville N.B.

PUERTO RICO

Charter #	City	Name of Bank
6484.	San Juan	First N.B. of Puerto Rico

RHODE ISLAND

Charter #	City	Name of Bank
134.	Providence	First N.B.
565.	Providence	Second N.B.
636.	Providence	Third N.B.
673.	Warren	First N.B.
772.	Providence	Fourth N.B.
823.	Westerly	Nat. Niantic Bank
843.	Pawtucket	First N.B.
856.	Pawtucket	Slater N.B.
948.	Providence	Phenix N.B.
952.	Westerly	Washington N.B.
970.	Woonsocket	Citizens' N.B.
983.	Providence	Rhode Island N.B.
1002.	Providence	Fifth N.B.
1007.	Providence	Mechanics' N.B.
1008.	Warren	Nat. Hope Bank
1021.	Newport	First N.B.
1030.	Providence	Nat. Eagle Bank
1035.	Slatersville, Smithfield	First N.B.
1036.	Providence	N.B. of North America
1054.	Hopkinton	First N.B.
1058.	Woonsocket	Woonsocket N.B.
1126.	Providence	Globe N.B.
1131.	Providence	Merchants' N.B.
1150.	Ashaway	Ashaway N.B.
1151.	Providence	Old N.B.
1158.	Kingston	Nat. Landholders' Bank
1161.	Anthony	Coventry N.B.
1169.	Westerly	Nat. Phenix Bank
1173.	Providence	Weybosset N.B.
1206.	Wakefield	Wakefield N.B.
1283.	Providence	Manufacturers' N.B.
1284.	West Warwick	Centreville N.B. of Warwick
1292.	Bristol	First N.B.
1302.	Providence	Providence N.B.
1319.	Providence	Commercial N.B.
1328.	Providence	Blackstone Canal N.B.
1339.	Providence	Nat. Exchange Bank
1366.	Providence	N.B. of Commerce
1369.	Providence	Lime Rock N.B.
1396.	Providence	Traders' N.B.
1402.	Woonsocket	First N.B.
1404.	Cumberland	Cumberland N.B.
1405.	East Greenwich	Greenwich N.B.
1409.	Woonsocket	Nat. Union Bank
1419.	Warren	Nat. Warren Bank
1421.	Woonsocket	Producers' N.B.
1423.	Woonsocket	Nat. Globe Bank
1429.	Providence	City N.B.
1460.	Phenix	Phenix N.B.
1472.	Providence	American N.B.
1492.	Newport	Newport N.B.
1498.	Greenville	Nat. Exchange Bank
1506.	Providence	Roger Williams N.B.
1512.	Pascoag	Pascoag N.B.
1532.	Newport	N.B. of Rhode Island
1546.	Newport	Aquidneck N.B.
1552.	Scituate, North Scituate	Scituate N.B.
1554.	Wakefield	Nat Exchange Bank
1562.	Bristol	Nat. Eagle Bank
1565.	Newport	Nat. Exchange Bank
1592.	Wickford	Wickford N.B.
1616.	Pawtucket	Pacific N.B.
2554.	Newport	Union N.B.
2913.	Providence	Atlantic N.B.
5925.	Providence	United N.B.
13901.	Providence	Rhode Island Hospital N.B.
13981.	Providence	Columbus N.B.

SOUTH CAROLINA

Charter #	City	Name of Bank
1621.	Charleston	People's N.B.
1622.	Charleston	First N.B.
1680.	Columbia	Carolina N.B.
1765.	Columbia	Central N.B.
1804.	Chester	N.B. of Chester
1844.	Newberry	N.B. of Newberry
1848.	Spartanburg	First N.B.
1935.	Greenville	First N.B.
2044.	Charleston	N.B. of Charleston Assn.
2060.	Union	Merchants and Planters' N.B.
2072.	Anderson	N.B. of Anderson
2087.	Winnsboro	Winnsboro N.B.
2512.	Darlington	Darlington N.B.
3082.	Sumter	N.B. of Sumter
3421.	Abbeville	N.B. of Abbeville
3540.	Laurens	N.B. of Laurens
3616.	Rock Hill	First N.B.
3809.	Sumter	First N.B.
4996.	Spartanburg	Central N.B.
5004.	Greenville	City N.B.
5064.	Gaffney	First N.B.
5134.	Rock Hill	Nat. Union Bank
5269.	Orangeburg	First N.B.
5595.	Batesburg	First N.B.
6102.	Whitmire	First N.B.
6385.	Bennettsville	Planters' N.B.
6658.	Spartanburg	American N.B.
6871.	Columbia	Nat. Loan and Exchange Bank
6931.	York	First N.B.
6994.	Prosperity	People's N.B.
7027.	Greenwood	Nat. Loan and Exchange Bank
7858.	Lancaster	First N.B.
8041.	Clinton	First N.B.
8133.	Columbia	Palmetto N.B.
8471.	Chester	Nat. Exchange Bank

Charter #	City	Name of Bank
8766.	Greenville	Norwood N.B.
9057.	Leesville	N.B. of Leesville
9083.	Camden	First N.B.
9104.	Anderson	Citizens' N.B.
9190.	Greenville	Fourth N.B.
9296.	Lexington	Home N.B.
9342.	Cheraw	First N.B.
9407.	Rock Hill	People's N.B.
9533.	Sharon	First N.B.
9650.	Aiken	First N.B.
9687.	Columbia	Liberty N.B. of S.C.
9690.	Conway	First N.B.
9742.	Union	Citizens' N.B.
9747.	Florence	First N.B.
9849.	Walterboro	First N.B.
9876.	Mullins	First N.B.
9941.	Fort Mill	First N.B.
9999.	Darlington	Carolina N.B.
11085.	Marion	Marion N.B.
10129.	Sumter	City N.B.
10137.	Hartsville	First N.B.
10263.	Bishopville	First N.B.
10315.	Columbia	Nat. State Bank
10485.	Wagener	First N.B.
10536.	Conway	Conway N.B.
10537.	Conway	People's N.B.
10543.	Charleston	Commercial N.B.
10586.	Springfield	First N.B.
10593.	Woodruff	First N.B.
10597.	Columbia	People's N.B.
10605.	Laurens	Enterprise N.B.
10635.	Greenville	People's N.B.
10650.	Orangeburg	Edisto N.B.
10651.	St. Matthews	St. Matthews N.B.
10652.	Laurens	Laurens N.B.
10655.	Gaffney	Merchants' and Planters' N.B.
10660.	Sumter	N.B. of South Carolina
10663.	Chester	People's N.B.
10670.	Sumter	N.B. of Sumter
10674.	Orangeburg	Orangeburg N.B.
10679.	Elloree	First N.B.
10680.	Holly Hill	First N.B.
10681.	Lake City	Farmers and Merchants' N.B.
10699.	Chester	Citizens' N.B.
10708.	Charleston	Atlantic N.B.
10743.	Bennettsville	People's N.B.
10748.	Olanta	First N.B.
10798.	Saluda	First N.B.
10802.	Saluda	Planters' N.B.
10815.	Batesburg	Citizens' N.B.
10832.	Brunson	First N.B.
10859.	Laurens	Farmers' N.B.
10872.	Bishopville	Bishopville N.B.
10908.	Dillon	First N.B.
10979.	Fairfax	First N.B.
11080.	Lamar	Lamar N.B.
11111.	Allendale	First N.B.
11153.	Clio	First N.B.
11155.	Manning	First N.B.
11189.	Norway	Farmers' N.B.
11287.	Barnwell	First N.B.
11439.	Clover	First N.B.
11499.	Greenville	Woodside N.B.
11562.	Bowman	N.B. of Bowman
11704.	Bamberg	First N.B.
11914.	North	First N.B.
12025.	Greer	First N.B.
12146.	Spartanburg	Carolina N.B.
12175.	Anderson	Carolina N.B.
12233.	Saint George	First N.B.
12273.	Charleston	Dime N.B.
12381.	Honea Path	N.B. of Honea Path
12412.	Columbia	Columbia N.B.
12668.	Fairfax	Nat. Security Bank
12702.	Charleston	Exchange N.B.
12774.	Prosperity	Citizens' N.B.
12799.	Florence	First N.B.
12865.	Charleston	Norwood-Carolina N.B.
13720.	Columbia	First N.B.
13918.	Orangeburg	First N.B.
14135.	Orangeburg	Southern N.B.
14211.	Spartanburg	Commercial N.B.
14341.	Mullins	Davis N.B.

SOUTH DAKOTA

Charter #	City	Name of Bank
2068.	Yankton	First N.B.
2391.	Deadwood	First N.B.
2461.	Deadwood	Merchants' N.B.
2465.	Sioux Falls	First N.B.
2645.	Mitchell	First N.B.
2819.	Huron	First N.B.
2823.	Sioux Falls	Sioux Falls N.B.
2830.	Canton	First N.B.
2843.	Sioux Falls	Dakota N.B.
2911.	Chamberlain	First N.B.
2935.	Watertown	First N.B.
2941.	Pierre	First N.B.
2980.	Aberdeen	First N.B.
2989.	Huron	Beadle County N.B.
3087.	Brookings	First N.B.
3130.	Plankinton	First N.B.
3149.	Madison	First N.B.
3151.	Madison	Citizens' N.B.
3237.	Rapid City	First N.B.
3267.	Huron	Huron N.B.
3326.	Aberdeen	Aberdeen N.B.
3349.	Watertown	Citizens' N.B.
3352.	Columbia	First N.B.
3393.	Sioux Falls	Minnehaha N.B.
3398.	Redfield	First N.B.
3401.	Rapid City	Black Hills N.B.
3414.	Watertown	Watertown N.B.
3435.	De Smet	First N.B.
3437.	Ashton	First N.B.
3479.	Clark	First N.B.
3508.	Dell Rapids	First N.B.
3522.	Redfield	Merchants' N.B.
3552.	Deadwood	Deadwood N.B.
3578.	Mitchell	Mitchell N.B.
3586.	Sioux Falls	Citizens' N.B.
3597.	Madison	Madison N.B.
3636.	Huron	N.B. of Dakota
3675.	Parker	First N.B.
3739.	Sturgis	First N.B.
3932.	Aberdeen	Northwestern N.B.
4104.	Pierre	Pierre N.B.
4237.	Fort Pierre	First N.B.
4279.	Pierre	N.B. of Commerce
4282.	Chamberlain	Chamberlain N.B.
4370.	Hot Springs	First N.B.
4448.	Custer City	First N.B.
4603.	Vermillion	First N.B.
4613.	Yankton	Yankton N.B.
4629.	Sioux Falls	Union N.B.
4631.	Lead	First N.B.
4637.	Canton	N.B. of Canton
4874.	Spearfish	First N.B.
4983.	Deadwood	American N.B.
5355.	De Smet	De Smet N.B.
5428.	Sisseton	First N.B.
5477.	Centerville	First N.B.
5854.	Flandreau	First N.B.
5898.	Salem	First N.B.
5901.	Elk Point	First N.B.
5916.	Arlington	First N.B.
5918.	Alexandria	First N.B.
5946.	Woonsocket	First N.B.
6000.	Castlewood	First N.B.
6073.	Britton	First N.B.
6099.	Volga	First N.B.
6124.	Waubay	First N.B.
6181.	Freeman	First N.B.
6185.	White Rock	First N.B.
6256.	Redfield	Redfield N.B.
6294.	White	First N.B.
6339.	Hot Springs	Hot Springs N.B.
6357.	Clear Lake	First N.B.
6368.	Elkton	First N.B.
6381.	Toronto	First N.B.
6395.	Sisseton	Citizens' N.B.
6409.	Clark	Clark County N.B.
6446.	Wessington Springs	First N.B.
6462.	Brookings	Farmers' N.B.
6473.	Milbank	First N.B.
6502.	Webster	First N.B.
6561.	Belle Fourche	First N.B.
6585.	Howard	First N.B.
6688.	Colman	First N.B.
6789.	Miller	First N.B.
6792.	Tyndall	First N.B.
6925.	Bridgewater	First N.B.
6990.	Sturgis	Commercial N.B.
7048.	Scotland	First N.B.
7134.	White	Farmers' N.B.
7252.	Egan	First N.B.
7335.	Hudson	First N.B.
7352.	Vermillion	Vermillion N.B.
7426.	Bridgewater	Farmers' N.B.
7455.	Mitchell	Western N.B.
7504.	Watertown	Security N.B.
7582.	Mount Vernon	First N.B.
7597.	Vienna	First N.B.
7662.	Parkston	First N.B.
7686.	South Shore	First N.B.
7755.	Garretson	First N.B.
7794.	Highmore	First N.B.
7885.	Groton	First N.B.
7968.	Wakonda	First N.B.
8012.	Armour	First N.B.
8125.	Redfield	American N.B.
8248.	Spearfish	American N.B.
8291.	White Lake	First N.B.
8325.	Wessington	First N.B.
8332.	White Lake	United States N.B.
8480.	Bristol	First N.B.
8550.	Chamberlain	Brule N.B.
8559.	Webster	Farmers and Merchants' N.B.
8600.	Gregory	First N.B.
8624.	Frederick	First N.B.
8642.	Aberdeen	Dakota N.B.
8698.	Milbank	Farmers and Merchants' N.B.
8711.	Fairfax	First N.B.
8776.	Gettysburg	First N.B.
8781.	Huron	City N.B.
8841.	Huron	N.B. of Huron
8942.	Springfield	First N.B.
9166.	Hot Springs	People's N.B.
9188.	Letcher	First N.B.
9269.	Lemmon	First N.B.
9283.	McIntosh	First N.B.
9301.	Chamberlain	Whitbeck N.B.
9376.	Selby	First N.B.
9377.	Gregory	Gregory N.B.
9393.	Gary	First N.B.
9445.	Yankton	Dakota N.B.
9587.	Fort Pierre	Fort Pierre N.B.
9679.	Hecla	First N.B.
9693.	Dell Rapids	Home N.B.
9817.	Morristown	First N.B.
9858.	Veblen	First N.B.
9915.	Sioux Falls	American N.B.
9958.	Pukwana	First N.B.
10098.	Kennebec	First N.B.
10187.	Alexandria	Security N.B.
10256.	Oldham	First N.B.
10416.	Henry	First N.B.
10553.	Sioux Falls	Scandinavian-American N.B.
10592.	Sioux Falls	Security N.B.
10636.	Madison	Lake County N.B.
10637.	Midland	First N.B.
10683.	Frankfort	First N.B.
10714.	Lake Norden	First N.B.
10744.	Mobridge	First N.B.
10758.	Lake Preston	First N.B.
10772.	Bryant	First N.B.
10773.	Lake Preston	Farmers' N.B.
10774.	Florence	First N.B.
10780.	Howard	Howard N.B.
10797.	Goodwin	First N.B.
10800.	Hayti	First N.B.
10808.	Viborg	First N.B.
10813.	Beresford	First N.B.
10818.	Alcester	Farmers and Merchants' N.B.
10822.	Alcester	Alcester N.B.
10833.	Carthage	First N.B.
10846.	Gary	N.B. of Gary
10868.	Bristol	Citizens' N.B.
10893.	Brandt	First N.B.
10961.	Faulkton	First N.B.
11031.	Scotland	Corn Belt N.B.
11119.	Winner	First N.B.
11237.	Pollock	First N.B.
11323.	Menno	First N.B.
11341.	Sisseton	Security N.B.
11399.	Wilmot	First N.B.
11441.	Wetonka	First N.B.
11456.	Farmer	First N.B.
11457.	Davis	First N.B.
11506.	Eden	First N.B.
11527.	Eureka	First N.B.
11558.	Garden City	First N.B.
11585.	Onida	First N.B.
11590.	Mobridge	Security N.B.
11637.	Tyndall	Citizens' N.B.
11653.	Yankton	N.B. of Commerce
11689.	South Shore	Farmers' N.B.
11812.	Emery	Security N.B.
12024.	Winner	Winner N.B.
12325.	Fairfax	Farmers' N.B.
12374.	Webster	Dakota N.B.
12488.	Sherman	First N.B.
12547.	Saint Lawrence	First N.B.
12611.	Alexandria	First N.B.
12620.	Wessington Springs	N.B. of Wessington Springs
12662.	Oldham	Oldham N.B.
12777.	Onida	Onida N.B.
12784.	Salem	McCook County N.B.
12838.	Brookings	Security N.B.
12857.	Lemmon	New First N.B.
12872.	Dell Rapids	New First N.B.
12877.	Clear Lake	Deuel County N.B.
12881.	Sioux Falls	Citizens' N.B.
12888.	Wessington	Citizens' N.B.
12920.	Howard	New First N.B.
13061.	Ree Heights	First N.B.
13181.	Brookings	Brookings N.B.
13221.	Lake Norden	Lake Norden N.B.
13282.	Mount Vernon	First N.B.
13286.	Arlington	First N.B.
13302.	Fairfax	Farmers N.B.
13346.	Vermillion	First N.B. and Trust Co.
13407.	Milbank	Farmers and Merchants N.B.
13430.	Philip	First N.B.
13459.	Leola	First N.B.
13460.	Britton	First N.B.
13466.	Hyron	Security N.B.
13467.	Mobridge	First N.B.
13477.	Bison	First N.B.
13483.	Chamberlain	First N.B. and Trust Co.
13517.	Madison	Northwestern N.B.
13549.	Ethan	First N.B.
13589.	Viborg	Security N.B.
14099.	Rapid City	Rapid City N.B.
14252.	Pierre	First N.B.

TENNESSEE

Charter #	City	Name of Bank
150.	Nashville	First N.B.
336.	Memphis	First N.B.
391.	Knoxville	First N.B.
771.	Nashville	Second N.B.
1225.	Memphis	Tennessee N.B.
1296.	Nashville	Third N.B.
1407.	Memphis	Merchants' N.B.
1603.	Clarksville	First N.B.
1606.	Chattanooga	First N.B.
1636.	Memphis	German N.B.
1664.	Lebanon	N.B. of Lebanon
1666.	Cleveland	Cleveland N.B.
1669.	Nashville	Fourth and First N.B.
1692.	Murfreesboro	First N.B.
1707.	Gallatin	First N.B.
1708.	Lebanon	Second N.B.
1713.	Columbia	First N.B.
1727.	Pulaski	N.B. of Pulaski
1746.	Chattanooga	City N.B.
1834.	Franklin	N.B. of Franklin
1990.	Pulaski	Giles N.B.
2000.	Murfreesboro	Stones River N.B.
2019.	Springfield	Springfield N.B.
2049.	Knoxville	East Tennessee N.B.
2096.	Memphis	Fourth N.B.
2114.	Fayetteville	First N.B.
2127.	Memphis	Central State N.B.
2167.	Bristol	First N.B.
2168.	Jackson	First N.B.
2198.	Shelbyville	N.B. of Shelbyville
2200.	Nashville	Mechanics' N.B.
2221.	McMinnville	First N.B.
2513.	Nashville	Merchants' N.B.
2559.	Chattanooga	Third N.B.

Charter #	City	Name of Bank
2568.	Columbia	Second N.B.
2593.	McMinnville	People's N.B.
2635.	Pulaski	People's N.B.
2658.	Knoxville	Mechanics' N.B.
2720.	Clarksville	Clarksville N.B.
2796.	Bristol	First N.B.
3032.	Nashville	American N.B.
3062.	Franklin	Farmers' N.B.
3107.	Tullahoma	First N.B.
3228.	Nashville	Commercial N.B.
3241.	Clarksville	Farmers and Merchants' N.B.
3288.	Centreville	First N.B.
3341.	Athens	First N.B.
3432.	Morristown	First N.B.
3530.	Shelbyville	People's N.B.
3576.	Jackson	Second N.B.
3614.	Sparta	First N.B.
3633.	Memphis	Memphis N.B.
3660.	South Pittsburg	First N.B.
3691.	Chattanooga	Chattanooga N.B.
3702.	Fayetteville	Elk N.B.
3708.	Knoxville	Third N.B.
3837.	Knoxville	City N.B.
3919.	Union City	First N.B.
3951.	Johnson City	First N.B.
4015.	Rogersville	Rogersville N.B.
4020.	Tullahoma	Traders' N.B.
4060.	Chattanooga	Fourth N.B.
4102.	Knoxville	State N.B.
4169.	Rockwood	First N.B.
4177.	Greeneville	First N.B.
4236.	Gallatin	First N.B.
4303.	Cardiff	First N.B.
4307.	Memphis	Continental N.B.
4362.	Dayton	First N.B.
4442.	Union City	Farmers and Merchants' N.B.
4456.	Chattanooga	Merchants' N.B.
4501.	Harriman	First N.B.
4648.	Knoxville	Holston N.B.
4654.	Harriman	Manufacturers' N.B.
4679.	Pulaski	Citizens' N.B.
4715.	Jonesboro	First N.B.
4849.	Columbia	Maury N.B.
5056.	Memphis	N.B. of Commerce
5263.	Dyersburg	First N.B.
5528.	Manchester	First N.B.
5536.	Gainesboro	First N.B.
5545.	Gallatin	First and People's N.B.
5617.	Martin	First N.B.
5679.	Dayton	American N.B.
5754.	Lebanon	American N.B.
5888.	Johnson City	Unaka N.B.
5963.	Waverly	First N.B.
6042.	Brownsville	First N.B.
6076.	Pulaski	Nat. People's Bank
6093.	Lawrenceburg	First N.B.
6189.	Springfield	People's N.B.
6236.	Johnson City	Unaka and City N.B.
6729.	Nashville	Merchants' N.B.
6930.	Dickson	First N.B.
7225.	La Follette	N.B. of La Follette
7314.	Tracy City	First N.B.
7397.	Decherd	First N.B. of Franklin Co.
7636.	Jellico	N.B. of Jellico
7665.	Jellico	First N.B.
7740.	Tazewell	Claiborne N.B.
7817.	Chattanooga	American N.B.
7834.	McMinnville	American N.B.
7848.	Chattanooga	Hamilton N.B.
7870.	Columbia	Phoenix N.B.
7912.	Sparta	American N.B.
7928.	Carthage	First N.B.
8025.	Morristown	City N.B.
8039.	Oneida	First N.B.
8292.	Dickson	Citizens' N.B.
8406.	Trenton	First N.B.
8443.	Franklin	Harpeth N.B.
8506.	Camden	First N.B.
8555.	Fayetteville	Elk N.B.
8558.	Lynnville	First N.B.
8601.	Huntland	First N.B.
8631.	Winchester	American N.B.
8640.	Winchester	Farmers' N.B.
8673.	Lenoir City	First N.B.
8714.	Lebanon	Lebanon N.B.
8836.	Selmer	First N.B.
8889.	Savannah	First N.B.
8934.	Lewisburg	First N.B.
9027.	Copperhill	First N.B. of Polk Co.
9089.	Woodbury	First N.B.
9112.	Martin	City N.B.
9162.	Etowah	First N.B.
9176.	Chattanooga	Citizens' N.B.
9184.	Memphis	Nat. City Bank
9239.	Union City	Third N.B.
9319.	Mount Pleasant	First N.B.
9331.	Waverly	Citizens' N.B.
9334.	Paris	First N.B.
9470.	Spring City	First N.B.
9532.	Nashville	Tennessee-Hermitage N.B.
9558.	Elizabethton	First N.B.
9565.	Ducktown	First N.B.
9627.	Wartrace	First N.B.
9629.	Union City	Old N.B.
9632.	Newport	First N.B.
9659.	Nashville	Cumberland Valley N.B.
9667.	Cookeville	First N.B.
9692.	Cookeville	Cookeville N.B.
9720.	Erwin	First N.B.
9774.	Nashville	Broadway N.B.
9807.	Smyrna	First N.B.
9809.	Crossville	First N.B.
9827.	Centerville	Citizens' N.B.
10028.	Coal Creek	First N.B.
10181.	Linden	First N.B.
10190.	Doyle	First N.B.
10192.	Huntsville	First N.B.
10198.	Fayetteville	Farmers' N.B.
10306.	Petersburg	First N.B.
10327.	Knoxville	American N.B.
10334.	Jackson	Security N.B.
10401.	Knoxville	Union N.B.
10404.	Kenton	First N.B.
10449.	Ripley	First N.B.
10470.	Pikeville	First N.B.
10491.	Covington	First N.B.
10508.	Russellville	First N.B.
10540.	Memphis	Mercantile N.B.
10542.	Maryville	First N.B.
10577.	Dickson	Dickson N.B.
10583.	Erwin	Erwin N.B.
10622.	Nashville	Tennessee N.B.
10735.	Athens	Citizens' N.B.
10785.	Shelbyville	Farmers' N.B.
10842.	Kingsport	First N.B.
10976.	Elizabethton	Holston N.B.
11202.	Sweetwater	First N.B.
11479.	Jefferson City	First N.B.
11839.	Johnson City	Tennessee N.B.
11915.	Harriman	Harriman N.B.
11985.	Hohenwald	First N.B.
11998.	Oliver Springs	Tri-County N.B.
12031.	Harriman	First N.B.
12080.	Loudon	First N.B.
12257.	Rockwood	Rockwood N.B.
12264.	Rockwood	City N.B.
12276.	Nashville	Central N.B.
12319.	Kingston	First N.B.
12324.	Lexington	First N.B.
12348.	Memphis	Southern N.B.
12438.	Trenton	Citizens' N.B.
12440.	Sevierville	First N.B.
12467.	La Follette	People's N.B.
12469.	Johnson City	Washington County N.B.
12484.	La Follette	Farmers' N.B.
12639.	Springfield	First N.B.
12790.	Jackson	N.B. of Commerce
13056.	Smithville	First N.B.
13077.	Big Sandy	First N.B.
13103.	Nashville	Third N.B.
13349.	Memphis	Union Planters N.B. and Trust Co.
13482.	Greeneville	Citizens N.B.
13539.	Knoxville	Hamilton N.B.
13635.	Johnson City	Hamilton N.B.
13640.	Bristol	First N.B.
13654.	Chattanooga	Chattanooga N.B.
13681.	Memphis	N.B. of Commerce
13746.	Chattanooga	Commercial N.B.
13948.	Fayetteville	Union N.B.
14231.	Rockwood	First N.B.
14279.	Maryville	Blount N.B.

TEXAS

Charter #	City	Name of Bank
1566.	Galveston	First N.B.
1642.	Galveston	N.B. of Texas
1644.	Houston	First N.B.
1657.	San Antonio	San Antonio N.B.
1777.	Jefferson	N.B. of Jefferson
2092.	Houston	Nat. Exchange Bank
2099.	Denison	First N.B.
2118.	Austin	First N.B.
2157.	Dallas	First N.B.
2189.	Waco	First N.B.
2349.	Fort Worth	First N.B.
2359.	Fort Worth	City N.B.
2455.	Dallas	City N.B.
2477.	Weatherford	First N.B.
2486.	Laredo	Milmo N.B.
2521.	El Paso	State N.B.
2532.	El Paso	First N.B.
2617.	Austin	State N.B.
2689.	Fort Worth	Traders' N.B.
2723.	Weatherford	Citizens' N.B.
2729.	McKinney	First N.B.
2735.	Belton	First N.B.
2767.	San Angelo	First N.B.
2801.	Colorado	Colorado N.B.
2802.	Gainesville	Gainesville N.B.
2812.	Denton	First N.B.
2836.	Gainesville	First N.B.
2867.	Honey Grove	First N.B.
2883.	San Antonio	Traders' N.B.
2893.	Colorado	First N.B.
2909.	McKinney	Collin County N.B.
2937.	Brownwood	First N.B.
2939.	Ennis	Ennis N.B.
2940.	Decatur	First N.B.
2949.	Denton	Exchange N.B.
2974.	Waxahachie	First N.B.
2982.	Cleburne	First N.B.
2998.	Greenville	First N.B.
3007.	Burnet	First N.B.
3008.	Dallas	Dallas N.B.
3014.	Mexia	First N.B.
3015.	Brenham	First N.B.
3016.	Greenville	Hunt County N.B.
3022.	Henrietta	Henrietta N.B.
3027.	Taylor	First N.B.
3046.	Hillsboro	Hill County N.B.
3058.	Denison	State N.B.
3065.	Texarkana	First N.B.
3094.	Bonham	First N.B.
3113.	Marshall	First N.B.
3131.	Fort Worth	Fort Worth N.B.
3132.	Dallas	American N.B.
3135.	Waco	Citizens' N.B.
3159.	Sherman	Merchants and Planters' N.B.
3165.	Montague	First N.B.
3195.	Abilene	First N.B.
3200.	Wichita Falls	First N.B.
3212.	Waxahachie	Citizens' N.B.
3221.	Fort Worth	State N.B.
3227.	Temple	First N.B.
3229.	Gainesville	Red River N.B.
3248.	Albany	First N.B.
3260.	San Angelo	San Angelo N.B.
3261.	Lampasas	First N.B.
3286.	Baird	First N.B.
3289.	Austin	City N.B.
3295.	Belton	Belton N.B.
3298.	San Antonio	Texas N.B.
3336.	Abilene	Abilene N.B.
3344.	San Marcos	Wood N.B.
3346.	San Marcos	First N.B.
3433.	Coleman	First N.B.
3446.	Bryan	First N.B.
3466.	Sulphur Springs	First N.B.
3506.	Corsicana	First N.B.
3517.	Houston	Commercial N.B.
3532.	Ennis	People's N.B.
3533.	Ballinger	First N.B.
3561.	Comanche	First N.B.
3608.	El Paso	El Paso N.B. of Texas
3623.	Dallas	American Exchange N.B.
3624.	Farmersville	First N.B.
3631.	Fort Worth	Merchants' N.B.
3638.	Paris	First N.B.
3644.	Alvarado	First N.B.
3645.	Corsicana	Corsicana N.B.
3646.	Greenville	Greenville N.B.
3651.	Tyler	First N.B.
3664.	Dallas	State N.B.
3694.	Palestine	First N.B.
3727.	Granbury	First N.B.
3738.	San Antonio	Lockwood N.B.
3742.	Calvert	First N.B.
3762.	Hillsboro	Farmers' N.B.
3764.	Plano	Plano N.B.
3785.	Texarkana	Texarkana N.B.
3786.	Hillsboro	Sturgis N.B.
3816.	Terrell	First N.B.
3834.	Dallas	North Texas N.B.
3836.	Kaufman	First N.B.
3858.	Temple	Temple N.B.
3859.	Taylor	Taylor N.B.
3890.	Rockwall	First N.B.
3901.	Waco	American N.B.
3906.	La Grange	First N.B.
3915.	Corsicana	City N.B.
3973.	Clarksville	First N.B.
3975.	Weatherford	Merchants and Farmers' N.B.
3984.	Wolfe City	Wolfe City N.B.
3985.	Dallas	N.B. of Commerce
3989.	Sulphur Springs	City N.B.
3998.	Texarkana	Interstate N.B.
4004.	Fort Worth	Farmers and Mechanics' N.B.
4014.	Forney	N.B. of Forney
4016.	Meridian	First N.B.
4017.	Beaumont	First N.B.
4021.	Commerce	First N.B.
4028.	Houston	Houston N.B.
4030.	Lockhart	First N.B.
4033.	Vernon	First N.B.
4035.	Cleburne	N.B. of Cleburne
4062.	Dublin	First N.B.
4065.	Vernon	Vernon N.B.
4068.	Henrietta	Farmers' N.B.
4070.	Bryan	City N.B.
4076.	McGregor	First N.B.
4077.	Longview	First N.B.
4081.	Stephenville	Erath County N.B.
4086.	Cameron	First N.B.
4093.	Bastrop	First N.B.
4095.	Stephenville	First N.B.
4097.	Gatesville	First N.B.
4101.	Marshall	Marshall N.B.
4112.	Honey Grove	Planters' N.B.
4116.	Decatur	Wise County N.B.
4118.	Orange	First N.B.
4127.	Dallas	Central N.B.
4130.	Vernon	State N.B.
4134.	Cisco	First N.B.
4140.	Cuero	First N.B.
4144.	Quanah	First N.B.
4146.	Laredo	Rio Grande N.B.
4153.	Galveston	Galveston N.B.
4166.	Abilene	Farmers and Merchants N.B.
4167.	Belton	Citizens' N.B.
4175.	Rockdale	First N.B.
4179.	Flatonia	First N.B.
4184.	Victoria	First N.B.
4193.	Ballinger	Ballinger N.B.
4198.	Brady	First N.B.
4208.	Huntsville	Gibbs N.B.
4213.	Dallas	Bankers and Merchants' N.B.
4214.	Amarillo	First N.B.
4231.	Bowie	Bowie N.B.
4238.	Beeville	First N.B.
4241.	Bellville	First N.B.
4246.	Comanche	Comanche N.B.
4248.	Wichita Falls	City N.B. of Commerce
4253.	Navasota	First N.B.
4263.	Seymour	First N.B.
4265.	Bowie	First N.B.
4266.	Luling	First N.B.
4269.	Groesbeeck	Groesbeeck N.B.
4278.	Athens	First N.B.
4289.	Van Alstyne	First N.B.

Charter #	City	Name of Bank
4291.	Fairfield	First N.B.
4294.	Georgetown	First N.B.
4295.	New Braunfels	First N.B.
4306.	Big Springs	First N.B.
4308.	Austin	Austin N.B.
4309.	Waco	Provident N.B.
4311.	Ladonia	First N.B.
4316.	Llano	First N.B.
4321.	Galveston	American N.B.
4322.	Austin	American N.B.
4333.	Haskell	First N.B.
4338.	Hallettsville	First N.B.
4344.	Brownwood	Merchants' N.B.
4346.	Rusk	First N.B.
4349.	Waco	Farmers and Merchants' N.B.
4350.	Houston	South Texas N.B.
4353.	Tyler	City N.B.
4361.	Quanah	City N.B.
4363.	Yoakum	First N.B.
4366.	Hico	First N.B.
4368.	Midland	First N.B.
4371.	Llano	Iron City N.B.
4378.	Mason	First N.B.
4379.	Waxahachie	Waxahachie N.B.
4386.	Cleburne	Farmers and Merchants' N.B.
4388.	Gatesville	Citizens' N.B.
4389.	Grand View	First N.B.
4391.	Graham	First N.B.
4395.	Colorado	Citizens' N.B.
4404.	Temple	Bell County N.B.
4405.	Nacogdoches	First N.B.
4410.	Giddings	First N.B.
4411.	Paris	City N.B.
4415.	Dallas	Ninth N.B.
4418.	Graham	First N.B.
4423.	Corpus Christi	Corpus Christi N.B.
4436.	Palestine	Palestine N.B.
4438.	Rockport	First N.B.
4447.	Denison	N.B. of Denison
4451.	Hamilton	Hamilton N.B.
4461.	Itasca	First N.B.
4463.	Houston	Planters and Mechanics' N.B.
4466.	Eastland	Eastland N.B.
4474.	Haskell	Haskell N.B.
4483.	Jacksboro	First N.B.
4490.	Eagle Pass	First N.B.
4492.	Kaufman	Citizens' N.B.
4500.	Cooper	First N.B.
4515.	Ladonia	Weldon N.B.
4517.	Uvalde	First N.B.
4525.	San Antonio	Alamo N.B.
4540.	Bonham	Bonham N.B.
4545.	Marble Falls	First N.B.
4565.	Goliad	First N.B.
4571.	Quanah	Quanah N.B.
4577.	Brownsville	First N.B.
4621.	Nocoma	First N.B.
4659.	San Angelo	Citizens' N.B.
4662.	Velasco	Velasco N.B.
4682.	Detroit	First N.B.
4683.	Coleman	Coleman N.B.
4684.	Crockett	First N.B.
4687.	Goldthwaite	First N.B.
4692.	Whitewright	First N.B.
4695.	Brownwood	First N.B.
4701.	Daingerfield	N.B. of Daingerfield
4706.	Marlin	First N.B.
4707.	Dallas	Mercantile N.B.
4708.	Denton	Denton County N.B.
4710.	Amarillo	Amarillo N.B.
4717.	Rockwall	Farmers and Merchants' N.B.
4721.	Jefferson	State N.B.
4722.	Mount Pleasant	First N.B.
4732.	Gatesville	City N.B.
4747.	Tyler	Tyler N.B.
4748.	San Antonio	Fifth N.B.
4768.	Blooming Grove	First N.B.
4777.	Pilot Point	Pilot Point N.B.
4785.	Bowie	City N.B.
4848.	Fort Worth	American N.B.
4863.	Pittsburg	First N.B.
4865.	Dublin	Dublin N.B.
4866.	Beeville	Commercial N.B.
4900.	Hillsboro	Citizens' N.B.
4903.	Wharton	First N.B.
4905.	Hempstead	Farmers' N.B.
4911.	Rockwall	Rockwall County N.B.
4922.	Atlanta	First N.B.
4924.	Itasca	Citizens' N.B.
4946.	Fort Worth	Nat. Live Stock Bank
4950.	Colorado	People's N.B.
4976.	Hearne	First N.B.
4982.	Clarksville	Red River N.B.
4990.	Terrell	American N.B.
5001.	Laredo	Laredo N.B.
5008.	Hubbard	First N.B.
5018.	Wills Point	First N.B.
5035.	Greenville	City N.B.
5060.	Eagle Pass	Simpson N.B.
5078.	Dallas	N.B. of Dallas
5079.	Paris	Paris N.B.
5097.	Seguin	First N.B.
5109.	Leonard	First N.B.
5127.	Mineola	First N.B.
5146.	Bonham	Fannin County N.B.
5175.	Uvalde	Uvalde N.B.
5179.	San Antonio	Frost N.B.
5181.	Eagle Pass	Border N.B.
5190.	Navasota	Citizens' N.B.
5192.	Sherman	Grayson County N.B.
5201.	Beaumont	Beaumont N.B.
5203.	Vernon	Waggoner N.B.
5217.	San Antonio	City N.B.
5238.	Canyon	First N.B.
5239.	El Paso	Lowdon N.B.
5275.	Taylor	City N.B.
5276.	Colorado	City N.B.
5288.	Gilmer	First N.B.
5294.	Del Rio	First N.B.
5324.	Celeste	First N.B.
5325.	Saint Jo	First N.B.
5338.	Nocona	Nocona N.B.
5343.	Tyler	Citizens' N.B.
5367.	Port Lavaca	First N.B.
5399.	Moulton	First N.B.
5409.	Mount Vernon	First N.B.
5422.	Bartlett	First N.B.
5439.	Grapevine	Grapevine N.B.
5463.	Clarendon	First N.B.
5466.	Sonora	First N.B.
5475.	Plainview	First N.B.
5483.	Wylie	First N.B.
5484.	Cameron	Citizens' N.B.
5485.	Port Arthur	First N.B.
5491.	Lockhart	Lockhart N.B.
5493.	Baird	Home N.B.
5504.	McGregor	Citizens' N.B.
5511.	Mineral Wells	First N.B.
5513.	Rosebud	First N.B.
5533.	Cooper	Delta N.B.
5543.	West	First N.B.
5549.	Venus	First N.B.
5560.	Stamford	First N.B.
5569.	Petty	First N.B.
5580.	Snyder	First N.B.
5581.	Jacksonville	First N.B.
5589.	Iowa Park	First N.B.
5604.	Hereford	First N.B.
5606.	Marlin	Marlin N.B.
5614.	Karnes City	Karnes County N.B.
5628.	Shiner	First N.B.
5636.	New Boston	First N.B.
5645.	Lampasas	Lampasas N.B.
5660.	De Leon	First N.B.
5661.	Merkel	First N.B.
5663.	Italy	First N.B.
5665.	Decatur	City N.B.
5670.	Howe	Farmers' N.B.
5674.	Winnsboro	First N.B.
5680.	Albany	Albany N.B.
5681.	Howe	First N.B.
5692.	Plano	Farmers and Merchants' N.B.
5696.	Grand Saline	N.B. of Grand Saline
5697.	Mexia	Citizens' N.B.
5704.	Rogers	First N.B.
5710.	Roxton	First N.B.
5711.	Archer City	First N.B.
5719.	Cumby	First N.B.
5721.	Nevada	First N.B.
5722.	Grand Saline	First N.B.
5728.	Dodd City	First N.B.
5733.	Blossom	First N.B.
5737.	Trenton	First N.B.
5739.	Ladonia	Ladonia N.B.
5741.	Gilmer	Farmers and Merchants' N.B.
5749.	Itasca	Itasca N.B.
5750.	Killeen	First N.B.
5759.	Gordon	First N.B.
5761.	Jacksboro	Citizens' N.B.
5765.	Hondo	First N.B.
5774.	Moody	First N.B.
5781.	Sweetwater	First N.B.
5786.	Aspermont	First N.B.
5795.	Glen Rose	First N.B.
5797.	Lufkin	Lufkin N.B.
5806.	Arlington	Citizens' N.B.
5808.	Granbury	City N.B.
5824.	Crandall	First N.B.
5825.	Beaumont	American N.B.
5836.	Dublin	Citizens' N.B.
5841.	Beaumont	Citizens' N.B.
5847.	Whitesboro	First N.B.
5850.	Mart	First N.B.
5853.	Llano	Llano N.B.
5858.	Houston	Merchants' N.B.
5864.	Sherman	Commercial N.B.
5865.	Roby	First N.B.
5882.	Thorndale	First N.B.
5897.	Graham	Graham N.B.
5904.	Seymour	Favis N.B.
5932.	Kemp	First N.B.
5938.	Crandall	Citizens' N.B.
5953.	Crockett	Farmers and Merchants' N.B.
5971.	Center	First N.B.
5972.	Quanah	State N.B.
5991.	Nacogdoches	Commercial N.B.
5992.	Childress	City N.B.
6001.	Throck-morton	First N.B.
6009.	Lufkin	Angelina County N.B.
6011.	Farmersville	Farmers and Merchants' N.B.
6024.	Childress	Childress N.B.
6040.	Center Point	First N.B.
6043.	Longview	Citizens' N.B.
6046.	Celina	First N.B.
6050.	Orange	Orange N.B.
6062.	Bay City	First N.B.
6067.	Alvord	Alvord N.B.
6069.	Blum	First N.B.
6071.	Wills Point	Van Zandt County N.B.
6078.	Forney	City N.B.
6091.	Anson	First N.B.
6092.	Goldthwaite	Goldthwaite N.B.
6107.	Memphis	First N.B.
6112.	El Campo	First N.B.
6115.	Cisco	Citizens' N.B.
6134.	Jasper	First N.B.
6139.	Mount Pleasant	State N.B.
6140.	Mesquite	First N.B.
6150.	Gatesville	Gatesville N.B.
6152.	Carthage	Merchants and Farmers' N.B.
6168.	Winnsboro	Farmers' N.B.
6169.	Livingston	First N.B.
6176.	Henderson	First N.B.
6177.	Timpson	First N.B.
6195.	Lubbock	First N.B.
6197.	Carthage	First N.B.
6212.	Troupe	First N.B.
6214.	San Augustine	First N.B.
6223.	Lott	First N.B.
6224.	Commerce	Planters and Merchants' N.B.
6234.	Tyler	Jester N.B.
6245.	San Augustine	San Augustine N.B.
6247.	Morgan	First N.B.
6271.	Enloe	First N.B.
6277.	Gonzales	Gonzales N.B.
6292.	Gainesville	Lindsay N.B.
6298.	Tulia	First N.B.
6300.	Collinsville	First N.B.
6313.	Wharton	Wharton N.B.
6317.	Temple	City N.B.
6320.	Floresville	First N.B.
6329.	Groveton	First N.B.
6338.	Beaumont	Gulf N.B.
6346.	Frisco	First N.B.
6356.	Madisonville	First N.B.
6361.	Granger	First N.B.
6376.	Ferris	Ferris N.B.
6390.	Sealy	Sealy N.B.
6394.	Conroe	First N.B.
6400.	Athens	Athens N.B.
6402.	Crowell	First N.B.
6404.	Gunter	First N.B.
6410.	Midland	Midland N.B.
6422.	Mabank	First N.B.
6430.	Deport	First N.B.
6461.	Groesbeck	Citizens' N.B.
6471.	Italy	Citizens' N.B.
6476.	Abilene	Citizens' N.B.
6522.	Runge	Runge N.B.
6551.	Royse	First N.B.
6553.	Ferris	Citizens' N.B.
6572.	Waco	Nat. City Bank
6596.	Nederland	First N.B
6605.	Lone Oak	First N.B.
6607.	Caldwell	Caldwell N.B.
6614.	Caldwell	First N.B.
6627.	Nacogdoches	Stone Fort N.B.
6668.	Big Springs	West Texas N.B.
6679.	Rockwall	Citizens' N.B.
6686.	Wortham	First N.B.
6703.	Rockwall	Rockwall N.B.
6757.	Ballinger	Citizens' N.B.
6762.	Dalhart	First N.B.
6780.	Henderson	Farmers and Merchants' N.B.
6791.	Cleburne	Citizens' N.B.
6807.	San Angelo	Western and Landon N.B.
6810.	Sour Lake	First N.B.
6812.	Hereford	Western N.B.
6814.	Emory	First N.B.
6822.	Fort Worth	Stockyards N.B.
6826.	Canadian	First N.B.
6831.	Uvalde	Commercial N.B.
6856.	Sour Lake	Sour Lake N.B.
6865.	Amarillo	N.B. of Commerce
6883.	Jacksonville	Citizens' N.B.
6896.	Alba	Alba N.B.
6915.	Whitewright	Planters' N.B.
6922.	Hughes Springs	First N.B.
6935.	Miles	Miles N.B.
6956.	San Antonio	N.B. of Commerce
6966.	Burnet	Burnet N.B.
6968.	Frost	First N.B.
6987.	Yorktown	First N.B.
6989.	Pearsall	Pearsall N.B.
7002.	Brownsville	Merchants' N.B.
7010.	Vernon	Herring N.B.
7016.	Van Alstyne	Farmers' N.B.
7028.	Abilene	American N.B.
7041.	Smithville	First N.B.
7045.	Floydada	First N.B.
7052.	Dallas	Texas N.B.
7055.	Blooming Grove	Citizens' N.B.
7070.	Alvin	First N.B.
7075.	El Paso	Nat. Exchange Bank
7096.	Daingerfield	Citizens' N.B.
7098.	Mason	Mason N.B.
7105.	Comanche	Farmers and Merchants' N.B.
7106.	Munday	First N.B.
7113.	Dallas	Gaston N.B.
7119.	Llano	Home N.B.
7123.	Claude	First N.B.
7129.	Jefferson	Rogers N.B.
7140.	Garlend	First N.B.
7144.	Lewisville	First N.B.
7146.	Manor	Farmers' N.B.
7147.	Covington	First N.B.
7149.	Kyle	Kyle N.B.
7157.	Hico	Hico N.B.
7165.	Fort Worth	Western N.B.
7170.	Palestine	Royall N.B.
7183.	Eastland	City N.B.
7194.	Naples	Morris Co. N.B.
7201.	Mansfield	First N.B.
7212.	Devine	Adams N.B.
7214.	Alpine	First N.B.

Charter #	City	Name of Bank
7231.	Coolidge	First N.B.
7243.	Cotulla	Stockmen's N.B.
7245.	Clifton	First N.B.
7249.	Center	Farmers' N.B.
7257.	Annona	First N.B.
7269.	Grandview	Farmers and Merchants' N.B.
7306.	Shamrock	First N.B.
7316.	San Antonio	Woods N.B.
7317.	Bartlett	Bartlett N.B.
7331.	Ennis	Citizens' N.B.
7337.	Anderson	First N.B.
7345.	Arlington	Arlington N.B.
7348.	Campbell	Campbell N.B.
7360.	Cisco	Merchants and Farmers' N.B.
7376.	Pittsburg	Pittsburg N.B.
7378.	Merit	First N.B.
7392.	Texarkana	City N.B.
7394.	Lampasas	City N.B.
7407.	Hubbard	Farmers' N.B.
7410.	Gorman	First N.B.
7413.	McLean	First N.B.
7414.	Miles	Runnels County N.B.
7422.	Breckenridge	First N.B.
7433.	Del Rio	Del Rio N.B.
7466.	Merkel	Merkel N.B.
7481.	Merkel	Farmers and Merchants' N.B.
7482.	Seymour	Farmers' N.B.
7495.	Aubrey	First N.B.
7509.	Belton	Belton N.B.
7510.	Greenville	Commercial N.B.
7514.	El Paso	City N.B.
7515.	Tyler	Farmers and Merchants' N.B.
7524.	Bells	First N.B.
7529.	Kerens	First N.B.
7530.	El Paso	American N.B.
7534.	Eagle Lake	First N.B.
7546.	Mart	Farmers and Merchants' N.B.
7548.	Goliad	Commercial N.B.
7553.	De Leon	Farmers and Merchants' N.B.
7572.	Lampasas	People's N.B.
7599.	McGregor	McGregor N.B.
7617.	Nocona	Farmers and Merchants' N.B.
7623.	Frankston	First N.B.
7635.	Snyder	Snyder N.B.
7640.	Stamford	Citizens' N.B.
7645.	Savoy	First N.B.
7657.	Lone Oak	Farmers' N.B.
7668.	Corpus Christi	City N.B.
7669.	Benjamin	First N.B.
7674.	Mount Vernon	Merchants and Planters' N.B.
7694.	Atlanta	Atlanta N.B.
7700.	San Saba	First N.B.
7714.	Tioga	First N.B.
7731.	Valley View	First N.B.
7748.	Ozona	Ozona N.B.
7753.	Bay City	Bay City N.B.
7775.	Midlothian	First N.B.
7798.	Venus	Farmers and Merchants' N.B.
7807.	Sabinal	Sabinal N.B.
7814.	Jacksboro	Jacksboro N.B.
7825.	Haskell	Farmers' N.B.
7827.	Brady	Brady N.B.
7838.	Franklin	First N.B.
7875.	Whitney	First N.B.
7886.	Sanger	First N.B.
7906.	Rising Star	First N.B.
7915.	Whitney	Citizens' N.B.
7924.	New Braunfels	Comal N.B.
7944.	Abilene	Commercial N.B.
7953.	Knox City	First N.B.
7956.	Lindale	First N.B.
7961.	Canyon	Canyon N.B.
7977.	Delhart	Delhart N.B.
7989.	Garland	State N.B.
8001.	Tolar	First N.B.
8005.	Memphis	Hall County N.B.
8008.	Holland	First N.B.
8013.	Kenedy	Kenedy N.B.
8018.	Stratford	First N.B.
8034.	Schulenburg	First N.B.
8037.	Mineola	Mineola N.B.
8054.	Stephenville	Farmers' N.B.
8066.	Rosebud	Planters' N.B.
8068.	Galveston	Merchants' N.B.
8070.	Galveston	Seawall N.B.
8071.	Alvord	Farmers and Merchants' N.B.
8072.	Ranger	First N.B.
8094.	Stanton	First N.B.
8102.	Wellington	First N.B.
8103.	Pleasanton	First N.B.
8106.	Clyde	First N.B.
8109.	Santa Ana	First N.B.
8112.	Stanton	Stanton N.B.
8123.	Edna	Allen N.B.
8130.	Walnut Springs	First N.B.
8134.	Blanco	Blanco N.B.
8156.	Elgin	Elgin N.B.
8169.	Odessa	Citizens' N.B.
8176.	Santo	First N.B.
8178.	Wolfe City	Citizens' N.B.
8179.	Higgins	First N.B.
8195.	Teague	First N.B.
8200.	Goree	First N.B.
8204.	Rockwall	Farmers' N.B.
8208.	Lubbock	Citizens' N.B.
8215.	Munday	Citizens' N.B.
8239.	West	N.B. of West
8242.	Rule	First N.B.
8249.	Higgins	Citizens' N.B.
8252.	Hamlin	First N.B.
8287.	North Fort Worth	Exchange N.B.
8288.	Houston	Nat. City Bank
8303.	Dickens	First N.B.
8306.	Paint Rock	First N.B.
8312.	Brownwood	Citizens' N.B.
8318.	Grapevine	Farmers' N.B.
8327.	May	First N.B.
8330.	Bowie	N.B. of Bowie
8355.	Toyah	First N.B.
8392.	Gonzales	Farmers' N.B.
8402.	Saint Jo	Citizens' N.B.
8427.	Hamlin	Hamlin N.B.
8431.	Farwell	First N.B.
8449.	De Kalb	First N.B.
8465.	Seminole	Seminole N.B.
8515.	Crosbyton	Citizens' N.B.
8518.	Belton	People's N.B.
8519,	Floresville	City N.B.
8522.	New Boston	New Boston N.B.
8526.	Hemphill	First N.B.
8535.	Hawley	First N.B.
8538.	Thornton	First N.B.
8542.	Paris	American N.B.
8562.	Cuero	Buchel N.B.
8565.	Karnes City	City N.B.
8568.	Midlothian	Farmers' N.B.
8573.	Brady	Commercial N.B.
8575.	El Dorado	First N.B.
8581.	Greenville	Greenville Nat. Exchange Bank
8583.	Cross Plains	Farmers' N.B.
8585.	Naples	Naples N.B.
8597.	Tahoka	First N.B.
8606.	Falls City	Falls City N.B.
8610.	Nocona	City N.B.
8611.	Princeton	First N.B.
8621.	Lorena	First N.B.
8641.	Bronte	First N.B.
8645.	Houston	Lumbermen's N.B.
8659.	Robert Lee	First N.B.
8664.	Dallas	Commonwealth N.B.
8672.	Bellevue	First N.B.
8674.	Marfa	Marfa N.B.
8690.	Sanger	Sanger N.B.
8693.	Rotan	First N.B.
8694.	Yoakum	Yoakum N.B.
8706.	Burkburnett	First N.B
8731.	Bridgeport	First N.B.
8742.	Lovelady	First N.B.
8769.	Perryton	First N.B.
8770.	Jefferson	Commercial N.B.
8771.	Pecos	First N.B.
8780.	Clyde	Clyde N.B.
8787.	Byers	First N.B.
8807.	Oakville	First N.B.
8816.	Silverton	First N.B.
8817.	Moore	Moore N.B.
8818.	Waco	Exchange N.B.
8843.	Turnersville	First N.B.
8884.	Grand Saline	Citizens' N.B.
8891.	Canton	First N.B.
8897.	Anson	Farmers and Merchants' N.B.
8899.	Galveston	City N.B.
8911.	Ochiltree	Ochiltree N.B.
8925.	Odessa	Western N.B.
8928.	Gatesville	Farmers' N.B.
8965.	Cresson	Cresson N.B.
8982.	Olney	First N.B.
9053.	Stanton	Home N.B.
9081.	Plainview	Citizens' N.B.
9126.	Lockney	First N.B.
9142.	Pampa	First N.B.
9148.	Valley Mills	First N.B.
9155.	El Paso	N.B. of Commerce
9178.	Crowell	Foard County N.B.
9193.	Lockney	Lockney N.B.
9205.	Kosse	First N.B.
9226.	Houston	American N.B.
9245.	Dallas	Union N.B.
9341	Dallas	Trinity N.B.
9353.	Houston	Houston Nat. Exchange Bank
9357.	Beaumont	Commercial N.B.
9369.	Forney	Farmers' N.B.
9485.	Post City	First N.B.
9611.	Spur	Spur N.B.
9625.	Hutto	Hutto N.B.
9637.	Caddo Mills	First N.B.
9712.	Houston	Union N.B.
9749.	Putnam	First N.B.
9781.	San Saba	San Saba N.B.
9802.	Plainview	Third N.B.
9805.	Wellington	City N.B.
9810.	Mertzon	First N.B.
9812.	Brownwood	Coggin N.B.
9813.	Sterling City	First N.B.
9828.	Waco	Central Texas N.B.
9845.	Jayton	First N.B.
9848.	Fort Stockton	First N.B.
9906.	Quanah	Citizens' N.B.
9931.	Como	First N.B.
9936.	Texas City	First N.B.
9989.	Crosbyton	First N.B.
10008.	Melissa	Melissa N.B.
10040.	Texas City	Texas City N.B.
10044.	Menard	First N.B.
10050.	Electra	First N.B.
10052.	Merkel	Southern N.B.
10076.	Ganado	First N.B.
10078.	Trinity	Trinity N.B.
10090.	Mission	First N.B.
10140.	El Paso	Commercial N.B.
10148.	San Antonio	Groos N.B.
10152.	Houston	South Texas Commercial N.B.
10163.	Bonita	First N.B.
10169.	Pharr	First N.B.
10182.	Maud	Maud N.B.
10189.	La Coste	La Coste N.B.
10220.	Waco	Central N.B.
10225.	Houston	N.B. of Commerce
10229.	Strawn	First N.B.
10230.	Paducah	First N.B.
10241.	Gregory	First N.B.
10266.	Kingsbury	First N.B.
10274.	Aransas Pass	First N.B.
10275.	Normangee	First N.B.
10276.	Cleveland	First N.B.
10297.	Mount Calm	First N.B.
10320.	Poth	First N.B.
10323.	Lometa	First N.B.
10331.	Dallas	Merchants' N.B.
10350.	Richmond	First N.B.
10360.	Victoria	Victoria N.B.
10398.	Sealy	Farmers' N.B.
10400.	Crawford	First N.B.
10403.	Malakoff	First N.B.
10411.	Cleburne	Home N.B.
10418.	Krum	First N.B.
10420.	Freeport	Freeport N.B.
10426.	Omaha	First N.B.
10472.	Newcastle	First N.B.
10473.	Campbell	Campbell Nat. Exchange Bank
10476.	Linden	First N.B.
10478.	Jasper	Citizens' N.B.
10483.	Bogata	First N.B.
10488.	Winfield	First N.B.
10509.	Rhome	First N.B.
10547.	Wichita Falls	N.B. of Commerce
10549.	Bynum	First N.B.
10564.	Dallas	Security N.B.
10598.	Lipan	First N.B.
10607.	Sherman	Commercial N.B.
10617.	Honey Grove	State N.B.
10624.	Edgewood	First N.B.
10626.	Cooper	Farmers' N.B.
10634.	Whitesboro	City N.B.
10638.	Avery	First N.B.
10639.	Bogata	Bogata N.B.
10643.	Clarksville	City N.B.
10645.	Allen	First N.B.
10646.	Quitman	First N.B.
10647.	Petty	Citizens' N.B.
10657.	Bagwell	First N.B.
10661.	Newsome	First N.B.
10664.	San Angelo	Central N.B.
10668.	Eddy	First N.B.
10678.	Bardwell	First N.B.
10682.	Nixon	First N.B.
10694.	Dawson	First N.B.
10703.	Spur	City N.B.
10713.	Irene	First N.B.
10717.	Winters	First N.B.
10728.	Hawkins	First N.B.
10757.	Kaufman	Farmers and Merchants' N.B.
10782.	Texline	First N.B.
10793.	San Antonio	State N.B.
10806.	San Saba	City N.B.
10845.	Junction	First N.B.
10860.	Brenham	Farmers' N.B.
10871.	Spearman	First N.B.
10874.	Moran	First N.B.
10927.	Purdon	First N.B.
10941.	Martindale	Martindale N.B.
10949.	Channing	First N.B.
10954.	Fayetteville	Farmers' N.B.
10956.	Schwertner	First N.B.
10957.	McLean	American N.B.
10965.	Dallas	Tenison N.B.
10974.	El Paso	Border N.B.
11002.	Matador	First N.B.
11003.	Lubbock	Farmers' N.B.
11019.	Tom Bean	First N.B.
11021.	Sour Lake	Citizens' N.B.
11022.	Corsicana	State N.B.
11138.	Turkey	First N.B.
11140.	Waco	Liberty N.B.
11143.	Godley	Citizens' N.B.
11158.	Follett	Farmers' N.B.
11163.	Lamesa	First N.B.
11171.	Grand Prairie	First N.B.
11175.	McAllen	First N.B.
11223.	Stratford	Sherman County N.B.
11239.	Dawson	Liberty N.B.
11258.	Eastland	American N.B.
11279.	San Juan	First N.B.
11291.	Victoria	People's N.B.
11301.	Wichita Falls	American N.B.
11325.	Collinsville	Collinsville N.B.
11357.	Cisco	American N.B.
11379.	Woodsboro	First N.B.
11400.	Booker	First N.B.
11406.	Menard	Menard N.B.
11408.	Booker	Edwards N.B.
11411.	Kerens	Kerens N.B.
11414.	Menard	Bevans N.B.
11415.	Brownfield	First N.B.
11423.	Lancaster	First N.B.
11430.	Fort Worth	N.B. of Commerce
11447.	Groom	First N.B.
11452.	Desdemona	First N.B.
11453.	West Columbia	First N.B.
11468.	Sweetwater	City N.B.
11486.	Wichita Falls	Exchange N.B.
11503.	Jakehamon	First N.B.
11519.	Bertram	First N.B.
11525.	Sipe Springs	First N.B.
11591.	Rio Grande	First N.B.

Charter #	City	Name of Bank
11595.	Perryton	Perryton N.B.
11625.	Caddo	First N.B.
11629.	Amarillo	City N.B.
11630.	Eastland	Citizens' N.B.
11632.	Rice	First N.B.
11634.	Rocksprings	First N.B.
11642.	Granger	Granger N.B.
11647.	White Deer	First N.B.
11659.	Necessity	First N.B.
11700.	Fabens	First N.B.
11706.	Quitaque	First N.B.
11722.	Canadian	Southwest N.B.
11749.	Dallas	Dallas N.B.
11762.	Wichita Falls	Security N.B.
11792.	Falfurrias	First N.B.
11799.	Port Neches	First N.B.
11800.	Hamilton	Perry N.B.
11814.	Bandera	First N.B.
11838.	Mathis	First N.B.
11874.	Bangs	First N.B.
11879.	Mercedes	First N.B.
11928.	Electra	Security N.B.
11930.	Clifton	Clifton N.B.
11931.	Arlington	Farmers' N.B.
11959.	Nocona	People's N.B.
11964.	Mexia	City N.B.
11970.	Quinlan	First N.B.
11996.	Dallas	Southwest N.B.
11997.	Fort Worth	Continental N.B.
12005.	Farwell	Farwell N.B.
12055.	Houston	Public N.B.
12062.	Houston	Guaranty N.B.
12070.	Houston	State N.B.
12091.	Port Arthur	Merchants' N.B.
12101.	Follett	Follett N.B.
12110.	Ennis	First N.B.
12119.	Harlingen	First N.B.
12138.	Beaumont	Texas N.B.
12162.	San Antonio	Commercial N.B.
12166.	Wellington	City N.B.
12182.	Kenedy	First N.B.
12186.	Dallas	Republic N.B.
12187.	Kenedy	Nichols N.B.
12190.	Mexia	Prendergast-Smith N.B.
12199.	Beaumont	City N.B.
12235.	Corpus Christi	State N.B.
12236.	Brownsville	State N.B.
12241.	Buda	Farmers' N.B.
12247.	Corrigan	Corrigan N.B.
12266.	Swenson	Swenson N.B.
12287.	Texas	First N.B.
12289.	Alpine	State N.B.
12307.	Quanah	First N.B.
12308.	Quanah	Security N.B.
12309.	Taft	First N.B.
12371.	Fort Worth	Texas N.B.
12382.	Leonard	Leonard N.B.
12390.	Nordheim	First N.B.
12408.	Rowena	First N.B.
12409.	Bridgeport	Bridgeport N.B.
12411.	Longview	Rembert N.B.
12415.	Norton	First N.B.
12416.	Paradise	First N.B.
12421.	La Porte	First N.B.
12423.	Streetman	First N.B.
12424.	Perrin	First N.B.
12434.	Galveston	South Texas N.B.
12437.	Graford	First N.B.
12448.	Eastland	Exchange N.B.
12462.	Refugio	First N.B.
12463.	Llano	Citizens' N.B.
12475.	Galveston	United States N.B.
12487.	El Paso	Nat. Border Bank
12505.	Winfield	Winfield N.B.
12508.	Richland	First N.B.
12513.	Chillicothe	First N.B.
12543.	Big Spring	State N.B.
12554.	Robstown	First N.B.
12556.	Palestine	East Texas N.B.
12566.	Houston	Seaport N.B.
12580.	Alvin	First N.B.
12583.	Wylie	Wylie N.B.
12589.	Goldthwaite	First N.B.
12612.	Bishop	First N.B.
12619.	Amherst	First N.B.
12622.	Plano	Farmers' N.B.
12627.	Wheeler	First N.B.
12641.	Weslaco	First N.B.
12648.	Richmond	Fort Bend N.B.
12650.	Dallas	Central N.B.
12651.	Paris	Liberty N.B.
12652.	Oglesby	First N.B.
12654.	Rowlett	First N.B.
12664.	Alvord	First N.B.
12666.	Childress	First N.B.
12669.	Mineral Wells	State N.B.
12670.	Wills Point	State N.B.
12671.	Alvord	Alvord N.B.
12672.	Childress	City N.B.
12676.	Olney	City N.B.
12677.	Clint	First N.B.
12680.	Georgetown	City N.B.
12681.	Como	Como N.B.
12682.	Lubbock	First N.B.
12683.	Lubbock	Lubbock N.B.
12684.	Sylvester	First N.B.
12685.	Milford	First N.B.
12687.	Millsap	First N.B.
12689.	Karnes City	State N.B.
12691.	Windom	First N.B.
12692.	Floydala	Floyd County N.B.
12696.	Handley	First N.B.
12698.	Kilgore	Kilgore N.B.
12699.	Bonham	State N.B.
12700.	Hamlin	Farmers and Merchants' N.B.
12701.	Italy	Farmers' N.B.
12703.	Marshall	State N.B.
12707.	Dallas	Mercantile N.B.
12708.	Grapevine	Tarrant County N.B.
12709.	Odell	First N.B.
12711.	Valley View	Valley View N.B.
12712.	West	State N.B.
12713.	Thornton	Farmers' N.B.
12714.	Grand Prairie	City N.B.
12715.	Reagan	First N.B.
12717.	Clifton	First N.B.
12718.	Needville	First N.B.
12719.	Cumby	First N.B.
12722.	Blackwell	First N.B.
12723.	Bronte	First N.B.
12724.	Josephine	First N.B.
12725.	Sudan	First N.B.
12727.	Moran	Moran N.B.
12728.	Denison	Citizens' N.B.
12729.	Robstown	State N.B.
12730.	Stephenville	Farmers-First N.B.
12731.	Bowie	Security N.B.
12733.	Terrell	State N.B.
12734.	Mineral Wells	City N.B.
12736.	Dallas	North Texas N.B.
12737.	Marlin	Citizens' N.B.
12738.	Collinsville	Security N.B.
12739.	Evant	First N.B.
12741.	Bailey	First N.B.
12742.	Groom	State N.B.
12744.	Hale Center	First N.B.
12745.	Grand Saline	State N.B.
12747.	La Feria	First N.B.
12748.	Paducah	Security N.B.
12752.	Melvin	First N.B.
12753.	Robstown	Gouger N.B.
12756.	Rosenberg	First N.B.
12758.	Dublin	Farmers' N.B.
12759.	Emhouse	First N.B.
12760.	Lone Oak	Citizens' N.B.
12761.	Quinlan	Quinlan N.B.
12762.	Weatherford	Parker County N.B.
12763.	Kaufman	Citizens' N.B.
12767.	Lamesa	State N.B.
12768.	Santa Ana	State N.B.
12769.	El Paso	El Paso N.B.
12775.	Strawn	Strawn N.B.
12778.	Commerce	Citizens' N.B.
12782.	Nixon	Nixon N.B.
12783.	Celina	Farmers and Merchants' N.B.
12786.	Ireland	First N.B.
12789.	Raymondville	First N.B.
12792.	Brownsville	First N.B.
12795.	Cisco	First N.B.
12796.	Rochelle	Rochelle N.B.
12798.	Levelland	First N.B.
12803.	Lovelady	State N.B.
12809.	Conroe	First N.B.
12824.	Littlefield	First N.B.
12831.	O'Donnell	First N.B.
12835.	Lakeview	First N.B.
12840.	Houston	Harrison N.B.
12843.	Blossom	Farmers' N.B.
12845.	Sulphur Springs	First N.B.
12850.	Liberty	First-Liberty N.B.
12855.	Dickinson	First N.B.
12867.	Anna	First N.B.
12898.	Newton	First N.B.
12899.	Roscoe	First N.B.
12915.	Pickton	First N.B.
12919.	George West	First N.B.
12927.	Ralls	First N.B.
12928.	Meadow	First N.B.
12936.	Caddo Mills	State N.B.
12943.	Lott	Lott N.B.
12968.	Kingsville	First N.B.
12969.	Post	Citizens' N.B.
12995.	Hebbronville	First N.B.
13014.	Borger	First N.B.
13019.	Honey Grove	American N.B.
13022.	West	State N.B.
13046.	Cooper	First N.B.
13048.	Farmersville	Farmersville N.B.
13052.	Blossom	Blossom N.B.
13067.	Teague	Teague N.B.
13070.	Panhandle	First N.B.
13107.	Cleburne	City N.B.
13110.	Tyler	Peoples N.B.
13111.	Lamesa	Lamesa N.B.
13170.	Glen Rose	First N.B.
13183.	McAllen	First N.B.
13191.	Lorena	Lorena N.B.
13199.	Wolfe City	Wolfe City N.B.
13206.	Temple	First N.B.
13211.	Cushing	First N.B.
13238.	Odessa	Odessa N.B.
13249.	Wellington	First N.B.
13257.	Mount Pleasant	First N.B.
13259.	Detroit	Planters N.B.
13266.	Pecan Gap	Pecan Gap N.B.
13272.	Valley Mills	First N.B.
13277.	Farmersville	First N.B.
13279.	Kosse	Kosse N.B.
13284.	Electra	First N.B.
13285.	Rhome	First N.B.
13287.	Terrell	State N.B.
13291.	Pampa	Pampa N.B.
13315.	Edinburg	First N.B.
13402.	Rockwall	First N.B.
13416.	Honey Grove	First N.B.
13427.	McKinney	First N.B.
13428.	Clarksville	Red River N.B.
13443.	Henderson	Citizens' N.B.
13450.	Jefferson	Commercial N.B.
13475.	Houtto	First N.B.
13489.	Plainview	First N.B.
13507.	Frost	Frost N.B.
13511.	Plano	First N.B.
13516.	Waxahachie	Citizens N.B.
13519.	Saint Jo	Citizens N.B.
13526.	Hemphill	First N.B.
13541.	Paris	Liberty N.B.
13555.	Blooming Grove	First N.B.
13562.	Colorado	Colorado N.B.
13572.	Pearsall	Pearsall N.B.
13578.	San Antonio	N.B. of Fort Sam Houston
13587.	San Angelo	San Angelo N.B.
13588.	Brownwood	Citizens N.B.
13593.	Munday	First N.B.
13595.	Coleman	First Coleman N.B.
13598.	Stamford	First N.B.
13608.	Odessa	First N.B.
13610.	Fredericksburg	Fredericksburg N.B.
13614.	Iowa Park	State N.B.
13623.	Decatur	First N.B.
13642.	Pleasanton	First N.B.
13647.	Lott	First N.B.
13649.	Whitney	First N.B.
13653.	Sulphur Springs	First N.B.
13656.	Kerens	First N.B.
13661.	Orange	First N.B.
13665.	Wichita Falls	City N.B.
13667.	Ennis	Citizens N.B.
13668.	Burkburnett	First N.B.
13669.	Mount Calm	First N.B.
13670.	Midlothian	First N.B.
13675.	Valley Mills	First N.B.
13676.	Wichita Falls	Wichita N.B.
13678.	Brenham	Farmers N.B.
13683.	Houston	First N.B.
13698.	Gainesville	Gainesville N.B.
13706.	Trinity	First N.B.
13727.	Abilene	Citizens N.B.
13731.	Cameron	First N.B.
13743.	Dallas	Mercantile N.B.
13778.	Temple	First N.B.
13810.	Belton	Farmers N.B.
13815.	Henrietta	First N.B.
13854.	Santa Anna	Santa Anna N.B.
13919.	Luling	First N.B.
13925.	Houston	San Jacinto N.B.
13926.	Austin	Capital N.B.
13934.	Lockhart	First-Lockhart N.B.
13935.	West	West N.B.
13943.	Houston	City N.B.
13951.	Cleburne	Cleburne N.B.
13964.	Alto	First N.B.
13974.	Clarksville	First N.B.
13984.	Big Spring	First N.B.
14012.	George West	First N.B.
14015.	Plainview	City N.B.
14027.	Breckenridge	First N.B.
14072.	Falfurrias	First N.B.
14090.	Canyon	First N.B.
14101.	Goose Creek	First N.B.
14104.	Groveton	First N.B.
14114.	Marlin	Marlin N.B.
14124.	Edinburg	First N.B.
14126.	Groesbeck	Citizens N.B.
14149.	Haskell	Haskell N.B.
14154.	Newcastle	Farmers N.B.
14157.	Robstown	Robstown N.B.
14164.	Cuero	Bouchel N.B.
14165.	McLean	American N.B.
14179.	San Antonio	South Texas N.B.
14199.	Dalhart	First N.B.
14204.	Angleton	First N.B.
14206.	Amarillo	Amarillo N.B.
14207.	Pampa	First N.B.
14208.	Lubbock	First N.B.
14212.	Farmersville	First N.B.
14227.	Comanche	State N.B.
14236.	McKinney	Central N.B.
14270.	Snyder	Snyder N.B.
14272.	White Deer	Farmers N.B.
14273.	Brownwood	Citizens N.B.
14283.	San Antonio	Bexar County N.B.
14299.	Eastland	Eastland N.B.
14302.	Cotulla	Stockmens N.B.
14312.	De Kalb	First N.B.
14330.	Junction	Junction N.B.

UTAH

Charter #	City	Name of Bank
1646.	Salt Lake City	Miners' N.B. of Salt Lake
1695.	Salt Lake City	First N.B. of Utah
1921.	Salt Lake City	Salt Lake City N.B. of Utah
2059.	Salt Lake City	Deseret N.B.
2597.	Ogden	First N.B.
2641.	Provo	First N.B.
2880.	Ogden	Utah N.B.
3139.	Ogden	Commercial N.B.
3306.	Salt Lake City	Union N.B.
3537.	Nephi	First N.B.
4051.	Salt Lake City	Commercial N.B.
4310.	Salt Lake City	N.B. of the Republic
4341.	Salt Lake City	Utah State N.B.
4432.	Salt Lake City	American N.B.
4486.	Provo City	N.B. of Commerce
4564.	Park City	First N.B.
4670.	Logan	First N.B.
6012.	Price	First N.B.
6036.	Brigham City	First N.B.
6558.	Murray	First N.B.
6958.	Morgan	First N.B.
7296.	Ogden	N.B. of Commerce
7685.	Layton	First N.B.
7696.	Coalville	First N.B.
8508.	Nephi	Nephi N.B.

Charter #	City	Name of Bank
9111.	Spanish Fork	First N.B.
9119.	Beaver City, Beaver	First N.B.
9403.	Salt Lake City	Continental N.B.
9652.	Salt Lake City	Nat. Copper Bank
10135.	Smithfield	Commercial N.B.
10308.	Salt Lake City	Nat. City Bank
10925.	Moab	First N.B.
11228.	Magna	First N.B.
11266.	Monticello	First N.B.
11529.	Delta	First N.B.
11631.	Bingham Canyon	First N.B.
11702.	Myton	First N.B.
11725.	Gunnison	Gunnison City N.B.

VERMONT

Charter #	City	Name of Bank
122.	Springfield	First N.B.
130.	Bennington	First N.B.
194.	North Bennington	First N.B.
228.	Orwell	First N.B.
269.	Saint Albans	First N.B.
278.	Brandon	First N.B.
344.	Fair Haven	First N.B.
404.	Brandon	Brandon N.B.
470.	Brattleboro	First N.B.
489.	Saint Johnsbury	First N.B.
748.	Montpelier	First N.B.
816.	Windsor	Ascutney N.B.
820.	Rutland	Rutland County N.B.
857.	Montpelier	Montpelier N.B.
861.	Burlington	First N.B.
962.	Bethel	Nat. White River Bank
1004.	Chelsea	Orange County N.B.
1133.	Woodstock	Woodstock N.B.
1140.	Lyndon	N.B. of Lyndon
1163.	Hyde Park	Lamoille County N.B.
1195.	Middlebury	N.B. of Middlebury
1197.	Burlington	Merchants' N.B.
1200.	Poultney	N.B. of Poultney
1364.	Vergennes	N.B. of Vergennes
1368.	Derby Line	N.B. of Derby Line
1383.	Proctorsville	Nat. Black River Bank
1406.	Wells River	N.B. of Newbury
1430.	Brattleboro	Vermont N.B.
1450.	Rutland	N.B. of Rutland
1462.	Waterbury	Waterbury N.B.
1488.	Manchester	Battenkill N.B.
1541.	Irasburg	Irasburg N.B. of Orleans
1564.	Jamaica	West River N.B.
1576.	Danville	Caledonia N.B.
1583.	Saint Albans	Vermont N.B.
1598.	Castleton	Castleton N.B.
1634.	Swanton	Nat. Union Bank
1638.	Northfield	Northfield N.B.
1653.	Bellows Falls	N.B. of Bellows Falls
1673.	Royalton	N.B. of Royalton
1698.	Burlington	Howard N.B.
1700.	Rutland	Baxter N.B.
2109.	Barre	N.B. of Barre
2120.	Chelsea	First N.B.
2263.	Newport	N.B. of Newport
2274.	Randolph	Randolph N.B.
2290.	Barton	Barton N.B.
2295.	Saint Johnsbury	Merchants' N.B.
2305.	Brattleboro	People's N.B.
2395.	Bennington	County N.B.
2422.	Fairhaven	Allen N.B.
2475.	Vergennes	Farmers' N.B.
2537.	Rutland	Clement N.B.
2545.	Poultney	First N.B.
2905.	Rutland	Killington N.B.
2950.	Rutland	Clement N.B.
3080.	Manchester Center	Factory Point N.B.
3150.	Middletown Springs	Gray N.B.
3158.	Lyndonville	Lyndonville N.B.
3257.	Windsor	Windsor N.B.
3311.	Rutland	Merchants' N.B.
3482.	Saint Albans	Welden N.B.
3484.	White River Junction	First N.B.
4258.	Swanton	Ferris N.B.
4275.	Island Pond	Island Pond N.B.
4380.	Chester	N.B. of Chester
4929.	Chelsea	N.B. of Orange County
4943.	Swanton	People's N.B.
6252.	Bristol	First N.B.
7068.	Barre	People's N.B.
7267.	Bradford	Bradford N.B.
7614.	Enosburg Falls	First N.B.
7721.	Windsor	State N.B.
9108.	White River Junction	Hartford N.B.
9824.	Poultney	Citizens' N.B.
11615.	Richford	Richford N.B.
13261.	Poultney	First N.B.
13685.	Windsor	Windsor County N.B.
13712.	Brandon	Brandon N.B.
13755.	Bethel	National White River Bank
13800.	St. Albans	Welden N.B.
13894.	Bellows Falls	Windham N.B.
13915.	Montpelier	Montpelier N.B.
13986.	Enosburg Falls	Enosburg Falls N.B.
14234.	Poultney	Poultney N.B.

VIRGIN ISLANDS

Charter #	City	Name of Bank
14335.	St. Thomas	Virgin Islands N.B.

VIRGINIA

Charter #	City	Name of Bank
271.	Norfolk	First N.B.
651.	Alexandria	First N.B.
1111.	Richmond	First N.B.
1125.	Richmond	N.B. of Virginia
1137.	Norfolk	Exchange N.B.
1155.	Richmond	Nat. Exchange Bank
1378.	Petersburg	First N.B.
1468.	Charlottesville	Charlottesville N.B.
1522.	Lynchburg	Lynchburg N.B.
1548.	Petersburg	Merchants' N.B.
1558.	Lynchburg	First N.B.
1570.	Richmond	Farmers' N.B.
1572.	Harrisonburg	First N.B.
1582.	Fredericksburg	N.B. of Fredericksburg
1585.	Staunton	First N.B.
1609.	Danville	First N.B.
1620.	Staunton	Nat. Valley Bank
1628.	Richmond	Planters' N.B.
1635.	Winchester	Shenandoah Valley N.B
1658.	Clarksville	First N.B.
1704.	Norfolk	People's N.B.
1716.	Alexandria	Citizens' N.B.
1738.	Leesburg	Loudoun N.B.
1742.	Charlottesville	Citizens' N.B.
1754.	Richmond	Merchants' N.B.
1769.	Petersburg	Commercial N.B.
1824.	Salem	Farmers' N.B.
1985.	Danville	First N.B.
2269.	Staunton	Augusta N.B.
2506.	Lynchburg	Nat. Exchange Bank
2594.	Charlottesville	People's N.B.
2737.	Roanoke	First N.B.
2760.	Lynchburg	People's N.B.
2907.	Roanoke	Roanoke N.B.
2967.	Front Royal	Front Royal N.B.
3209.	Mount Jackson	Mount Jackson N.B.
3368.	Norfolk	Norfolk N.B.
3515.	Petersburg	N.B. of Petersburg
3570.	Culpeper	Farmers' N.B.
3917.	Leesburg	People's N.B.
4026.	Roanoke	Commercial N.B.
4027.	Roanoke	Nat. Exchange Bank
4047.	Suffolk	First N.B.
4071.	Pulaski	Pulaski N.B.
4257.	Bedford City, Liberty	First N.B.
4314.	Lexington	First N.B.
4460.	Buchanan	First N.B.
4477.	Bristol	Dominion N.B.
4503.	Covington	Covington N.B.
4531.	Roanoke	Citizens' N.B.
4635.	Newport News	First N.B.
4743.	Norfolk	City N.B.
4940.	Onancock	First N.B.
5032.	Manassas	N.B. of Manassas
5150.	Abingdon	First N.B.
5229.	Richmond	American N.B.
5261.	Harrisonburg	Rockingham N.B.
5268.	Fredericksburg	Conway, Gordon and Garnett N.B.
5290.	Irvington	Lancaster N.B.
5326.	Covington	Citizens' N.B.
5394.	Culpeper	Second N.B.
5438.	Orange	N.B. of Orange
5449.	Woodstock	Shenandoah N.B.
5532.	Orange	American N.B.
5591.	Culpeper	Culpeper N.B.
5683.	Farmville	First N.B.
5725.	Scottsville	Scottsville N.B.
5872.	South Boston	First N.B.
6005.	Charlottesville	Jefferson N.B.
6008.	Clifton Forge	First N.B.
6018.	Purcellville	Purcellville N.B.
6031.	Luray	First N.B.
6032.	Norfolk	N.B. of Commerce
6084.	Winchester	Farmers and Merchants' N.B.
6123.	Tazewell	Tazewell N.B.
6126.	Warrenton	Fauquier N.B.
6206.	Luray	Page Valley N.B.
6235.	Norton	First N.B.
6246.	Parksley	Parksley N.B.
6389.	Fairfax	N.B. of Fairfax
6443.	Washington	Rappahannock N.B.
6666.	Broadway	First N.B.
6685.	Rocky Mount	First N.B.
6748.	Manassas	People's N.B.
6778.	Hampton	Merchants' N.B.
6781.	Newport News	Newport News N.B.
6782.	Radford, East Radford	First N.B.
6798.	Roanoke	People's N.B.
6839.	Marion	Marion N.B.
6842.	Hampton	First N.B.
6886.	Lebanon	First N.B.
6899.	Coeburn	First N.B.
6903.	Staunton	Staunton N.B.
7093.	Alexandria	Alexandria N.B.
7135.	Gate City	People's N.B.
7150.	Orange	Citizens' N.B.
7173.	Lexington	People's N.B.
7206.	Martinsville	First N.B.
7208.	Gate City	First N.B.
7258.	Onley	Farmers and Merchants' N.B.
7308.	Lynchburg	American N.B.
7338.	Berryville	First N.B.
7587.	Waynesboro	First N.B.
7659.	Hallwood	Hallwood N.B.
7709.	Petersburg	Virginia N.B.
7782.	Graham	First N.B.
7847.	Pocahontas	First N.B.
7937.	Christiansburg	First N.B.
8003.	Esmont	Esmont N.B.

| Charter # | City | Name of Bank |

Charter #	City	Name of Bank
8091.	Pearisburg	First N.B.
8152.	Roanoke	City N.B.
8362.	Clintwood	Citizens' N.B.
8384.	Jonesville	People's N.B.
8389.	Rosslyn	Arlington N.B.
8414.	South Boston	Boston N.B.
8547.	Saint Paul	Saint Paul N.B.
8643.	South Boston	Planters and Manufacturers N.B.
8666.	Richmond	Nat. State and City Bank
8688.	Emporia	First N.B.
8722.	Hot Springs	Bath County N.B.
8746.	Strasburg	People's N.B.
8753.	Strasburg	Massanutten N.B.
8791.	Galax	First N.B.
8819.	Abingdon	People's N.B.
8875.	Chilhowie	N.B. of Chilhowie
8984.	Rocky Mount	People's N.B.
9012.	Wytheville	First N.B.
9043.	Monterey	First N.B. of Highland
9177.	Clifton Forge	Clifton Forge N.B.
9222.	Farmville	People's N.B.
9224.	Blackstone	First N.B.
9246.	Charlottesville	Albemarle N.B.
9261.	Waynesboro	Waynesboro N.B.
9291.	Chase City	First N.B.
9295.	Altavista	First N.B.
9300.	Portsmouth	First N.B.
9343.	Danville	American N.B.
9375.	Buchanan	Buchanan N.B.
9379.	Appalachia	First N.B.
9433.	Lawrenceville	First N.B.
9455.	Crewe	First N.B.
9475.	Danville	N.B. of Danville
9635.	Herndon	N.B. of Herndon
9642.	Warrenton	People's N.B.
9663.	Richmond	Manchester N.B.
9732.	Emporia	Planters' N.B.
9733.	Suffolk	N.B. of Suffolk
9746.	Norton	N.B. of Norton
9764.	Troutville	First N.B.
9847.	Martinsville	People's N.B.
9861.	Hamilton	Farmers and Merchants' N.B.
9885.	Norfolk	Virginia N.B.
9890.	Buena Vista	First N.B.
9924.	Jonesville	Powell Valley N.B.
10061.	Rural Retreat	First N.B.
10080.	Richmond	Central N.B.
10156.	Danville	Virginia N.B.
10194.	Norfolk	Seaboard N.B.
10252.	Honaker	First N.B.
10253.	Marshall	Marshall N.B.
10287.	Gordonsville	N.B. of Gordonsville
10325.	Fredericksburg	Planters' N.B.
10344.	Richmond	Broadway N.B.
10524.	New Market	Citizens' N.B.
10532.	Roanoke	American N.B.
10568.	New Market	First N.B.
10611.	Wise	Wise County N.B.
10618.	Charlottesville	N.B. of Charlottesville
10621.	Bedford	Citizens' N.B.
10658.	Gloucester	First N.B.
10696.	Lexington	Rockbridge N.B.
10821.	Chatham	First N.B.
10827.	Reedville	Commonwealth N.B.
10834.	Independece	Grayson County N.B.
10835.	Brookneal	First N.B.
10850.	Richlands	First N.B.
10857.	Richlands	Richlands N.B.
10866.	Hopewell	N.B. of Hopewell
10882.	Williamsburg	First N.B.
10914.	Waverly	First N.B.
10968.	Louisa	First N.B.
10973.	Stanley	Farmers and Merchants' N.B.
10993.	Newcastle	First N.B.
11028.	Newport News	Schmelz N.B.
11133.	Shenandoah	First N.B.
11174.	Penniman	First N.B.
11191.	Roanoke	Liberty N.B.
11205.	Appomattox	Farmers' N.B.
11265.	Saltville	First N.B.
11313.	Abingdon	Citizens' N.B.
11328.	Bedford	People's N.B.
11364.	Newport News	Nat. Mechanic's N.B.
11381.	Portsmouth	American N.B.
11387.	Pulaski	People's N.B.
11444.	Narrows	First N.B.
11480.	Dillwyn	First N.B.
11501.	Dillwyn	Merchants and Planters' N.B.
11517.	Charlottesville	Farmers and Merchants' N.B.
11533.	Tazewell	Farmers' N.B.
11554.	Yorktown	First N.B.
11569.	Round Hill	Round Hill N.B.
11690.	Radford, East Radford	Farmers and Merchants' N.B.
11694.	Harrisonburg	N.B. of Harrisonburg
11698.	Grundy	First N.B.
11718.	Marion	People's N.B.
11764.	Vienna	Vienna N.B.
11765.	Big Stone Gap	First N.B.
11797.	Flint Hill	First N.B.
11817.	Roanoke	Colonial N.B.
11858.	Pennington Gap	First N.B.
11901.	Stuart	First N.B.
11911.	Vinton	First N.B.
11941.	Woodstock	N.B. of Woodstock
11946.	Charlottesville	Commerce N.B.
11957.	Lovingston	First N.B. of Nelson County

Charter #	City	Name of Bank
11960.	Brookneal	People's N.B.
11976.	Bassett	First N.B.
11978.	Ashland	First N.B.
11990.	Troutdale	First N.B.
12092.	Poquoson, Odd	First N.B.
12151.	Norfolk	Continental N.B.
12183.	Victoria	First N.B.
12204.	Leesburg	Leesburg Upperville N.B.
12229.	Blacksburg	N.B. of Blacksburg
12240.	Emporia	Citizens' N.B.
12251.	Kenbridge	First N.B.
12267.	Phoebus	Old Point N.B.
12290.	Fries	First N.B.
12311.	Ferrum	First N.B.
12451.	Ashland	Hanover N.B.
12477.	Quantico	First N.B.
12539.	Middleburg	Middleburg N.B.
12599.	Wytheville	Wythe County N.B.
12966.	Warrenton	Fauquier N.B.
13275.	Front Royal	Citizens N.B.
13343.	Norfolk	Colonial N.B.
13502.	Gate City	Peoples N.B.
13603.	Fredericksburg	Planters N.B.
13775.	Hampton	Citizens N.B.
13792.	Petersburg	Citizens N.B.
13878.	Onancock	First N.B.
13880.	Honaker	First N.B.
14052.	Crewe	N.B. of Crewe
14180.	Clifton Forge	Mountain N.B.
14190.	Onley	Farmers & Merchants N.B.
14223.	Abingdon	Washington County N.B.
14325.	Herndon	Citizens N.B.
14337.	Victoria	Peoples N.B.

WASHINGTON

Charter #	City	Name of Bank
2380.	Walla Walla	First N.B.
2520.	Dayton	First N.B.
2772.	Dayton	Columbia N.B.
2783.	Seattle	First N.B.
2805.	Spokane	First N.B.
2876.	Yakima	First N.B.
2924.	Tacoma	Tacoma N.B.
2948.	Port Townsend	First N.B.
2966.	Seattle	Puget Sound N.B.
2985.	Seattle	Merchants' N.B.
3024.	Olympia	First N.B.
3031.	Vancouver	First N.B.
3037.	Ellensburg	First N.B.
3076.	Colfax	First N.B.
3119.	Colfax	Second N.B.
3172.	Tacoma	Merchants' N.B.
3355.	Yakima	First N.B.
3409.	Spokane	Traders' N.B.
3417.	Tacoma	N.B. of Tacoma
3460.	Pomeroy	First N.B.
3528.	Spokane	Fidelity N.B.
3789.	Tacoma	N.B. of Commerce
3799.	Dayton	N.B. of Dayton
3838.	Spokane Falls, Spokane	Spokane N.B.
3862.	Yakima	Yakima N.B.
3867.	Ellensburg	Kittitas Valley N.B.
3887.	Snohomish	First N.B.
3956.	Walla Walla	Baker-Boyer N.B.
3976.	New Whatcom	Bellingham Bay N.B.
4002.	Davenport	Big Bend N.B.
4005.	Spokane Falls	Citizens' N.B.
4018.	Tacoma	Washington N.B.
4025.	Spokane, Spokane Falls	Browne N.B.
4031.	Goldendale	First N.B.
4044.	Spokane	Exchange N.B.
4059.	Seattle	Washington N.B.
4069.	Tacoma	Citizens' N.B.
4099.	Whatcom	First N.B.
4122.	Oakesdale	First N.B.
4124.	Seattle	Boston N.B.
4171.	New Whatcom	Bennett N.B.
4186.	Palouse City	First N.B.
4203.	Chehalis	First N.B.
4224.	Puyallup	First N.B.
4229.	Seattle	Seattle N.B.
4277.	Spokane Falls	Washington N.B.
4290.	Port Townsend	Port Townsend N.B.
4297.	Olympia	Capital N.B.
4315.	Port Angeles	First N.B.
4351.	New Whatcom	Columbia N.B.
4375.	Seattle	N.B. of Commerce
4387.	Fairhaven	Fairhaven N.B.
4390.	Hoquiam	Hoquiam N.B.
4397.	Seattle	Commercial N.B.
4407.	Aberdeen	First N.B.
4426.	Tacoma	N.B. of the Republic
4427.	Hoquiam	First N.B.
4439.	Centralia	First N.B.
4457.	Slaughter	First N.B.
4458.	Anacortes	First N.B.
4467.	South Bend	First N.B.
4470.	Blaine	First N.B.
4471.	Blaine	Blaine N.B.
4473.	Dayton	Citizens' N.B.
4526.	Snohomish	Snohomish N.B.
4529.	Mount Vernon	First N.B.
4532.	Waterville	First N.B.
4542.	Cheney	First N.B.
4623.	Tacoma	Columbia N.B.
4668.	Spokane	Old N.B.
4681.	Waitsburg	First N.B.
4686.	Everett	First N.B.
4699.	Pullman	First N.B.
4738.	Everett	Everett N.B.

Charter #	City	Name of Bank
4779.	Montesano	First N.B.
4788.	Colton	First N.B.
4796.	Everett	Puget Sound N.B.
5243.	Fairhaven	Citizens' N.B.
5472.	Montesano	Montesano N.B.
5652.	Olympia	Olympia N.B.
5751.	Ritzville	First N.B.
6006.	Tacoma	Lumbermen's N.B.
6013.	Vancouver	Vancouver N.B.
6053.	Everett	American N.B.
6074.	Port Angeles	First N.B.
6742.	Clarkston	First N.B.
7095.	Colfax	Colfax N.B.
7372.	Bellingham	First N.B.
7474.	Bellingham	Bellingham N.B.
7489.	Prosser	First N.B.
7527.	Davenport	Davenport N.B.
7767.	Toppenish	First N.B.
7908.	Sedro-Wooley	First N.B.
8064.	Wenatchee	First N.B.
8090.	Dayton	Dayton N.B.
8104.	Colville	First N.B.
8279.	Oroville	First N.B.
8481.	Sunnyside	First N.B.
8639.	Kelso	First N.B.
8736.	Centralia	United States N.B.
8743.	Ritzville	Pioneer N.B.
8789.	Chewelah	First N.B.
8828.	Newport	First N.B.
8895.	Waitsburg	First N.B.
8948.	Kennewick	First N.B.
8958.	Connell	Connell N.B.
8987.	Vancouver	Citizens' N.B.
9030.	Medical Lake	First N.B.
9052.	Odessa	First N.B.
9054.	Washtucna	First N.B.
9068.	Walla Walla	Third N.B.
9070.	Bellingham	Northwestern N.B.
9079.	Ellensburg	Washington N.B.
9080.	Cheney	N.B. of Cheney
9101.	Lind	First N.B.
9102.	Quincy	First N.B.
9129.	Wapato	First N.B.
9144.	Cheney	Security N.B.
9150.	Oakesdale	N.B. of Oakesdale
9170.	Brewster	First N.B.
9182.	Hillyard	First N.B.
9185.	Garfield	Garfield N.B.
9210.	Harrington	First N.B.
9265.	Pasco	First N.B.
9273.	Rosalia	Whitman County N.B.
9280.	Bremerton	First N.B.
9351.	Malden	First N.B.
9372.	Monroe	First N.B.
9389.	Chehalis	First N.B.
9411.	Okanogan	First N.B.
9417.	Prosser	Benton County N.B.
9443.	Dayton	Broughton N.B.
9478.	Monroe	Monroe N.B.
9499.	Palouse	Farmers' N.B.
9535.	Aberdeen	United States N.B.
9576.	Zillah	First N.B.
9589.	Spokane	N.B. of Commerce
9646.	Vancouver	United States N.B.
9662.	Seattle	Mercantile N.B.
9757.	Mabton	First N.B.
9798.	Seattle	Dexter Horton N.B.
9808.	Burlington	First N.B.
10000.	White Salmon	First N.B.
10026.	Seattle	Nat. City Bank
10174.	Kent	First N.B.
10407.	Tonasket	First N.B.
10469.	Cle Elum	First N.B.
10499.	Reardan	Reardan N.B.
10511.	Colfax	Farmers' N.B.
10585.	Auburn	First N.B.
10602.	Mount Vernon	Mount Vernon N.B.
10648.	Burlington	Burlington N.B.
10686.	Camas	First N.B.
11045.	Ellensburg	N.B. of Ellensburg
11146.	Seattle	Seaboard N.B.
11172.	Saint John	First N.B.
11247.	Ephrata	First N.B.
11280.	Seattle	Union N.B.
11285.	Poulsbo	First N.B.
11416.	Pomeroy	Farmers' N.B.
11546.	Grandview	First N.B.
11667.	Ferndale	First N.B.
11672.	Raymond	First N.B.
11674.	Selah	First N.B.
11693.	Everett	Security N.B.
11750.	Goldendale	N.B. of Goldendale
11751.	Aberdeen	Aberdeen N.B.
11805.	Camp Lewis	Army N.B.
11808.	Lynden	First N.B.
11832.	Seattle	Metropolitan N.B.
11856.	Seattle	Marine N.B.
11864.	Kirkland	First N.B.
11935.	Stanwood	First N.B.
11984.	Conway	First N.B.
12007.	Seattle	Horton Nat. Trust and Savings Bank
12085.	Auburn	Auburn N.B.
12114.	Enumclaw	First N.B.
12121.	Redmond	First N.B.
12143.	Enumclaw	Enumclaw N.B.
12153.	Seattle	University N.B.
12154.	Mount Vernon	Skagit N.B.
12170.	Odessa	First N.B.
12180.	Sprague	First N.B.
12181.	Sunnyside	Sunnyside N.B.
12184.	Palouse	Security N.B.
12217.	Kent	Kent N.B.
12231.	Garfield	State N.B.
12234.	Bellingham	American N.B.
12246.	Yakima	West Side N.B.
12269.	Ilwaco	First N.B.
12292.	Tacoma	Puget Sound N.B.

Charter #	City	Name of Bank
12392.	Longview	First N.B.
12399.	Renton	First N.B.
12418.	Spokane	Brotherhood Co-Operative N.B.
12509.	Cosmopolis	First N.B.
12667.	Tacoma	Brotherhood Co-Operative N.B.
12704.	Aberdeen	Grays Harbor N.B.
12851.	Greenwood-Seattle	Greenwood N.B.
13057.	Gig Harbor	First N.B.
13091.	Aberdeen	American N.B.
13099.	Centralia	First N.B.
13137.	Vancouver	Washington N.B.
13201.	Hoquiam	Lumbermans N.B. & Trust Co.
13230.	Seattle	Pacific N.B.
13233.	Elma	First N.B.
13290.	Everett	Citizens N.B. & Trust Co.
13331.	Spokane	First National Trust & Savings Bank
13351.	Port Townsend	American N.B.
13374.	Stanwood	Stanwood N.B.
13439.	East Stanwood	N.B. of East Stanwood
13444.	Reardan	First N.B.
13470.	Seattle	Central N.B. of Commerce
13471.	Seattle	Washington N.B. of Commerce
13581.	Seattle	Ballard First N.B.
13662.	Olympia	Washington N.B.
13723.	Shelton	First N.B.
13724.	Colville	Colville Valley N.B.
14038.	Auburn	Auburn N.B.
14166.	Tonasket	First N.B.
14186.	Vancouver	Vancouver N.B.

WEST VIRGINIA

Charter #	City	Name of Bank
180.	Parkersburg	First N.B.
360.	Wheeling	First N.B.
864.	Parkersburg	Second N.B.
961.	Fairmont	First N.B.
1343.	Wheeling	Merchants' N.B. of West Va.
1387.	Wellsburg	First N.B.
1424.	Wheeling	N.B. of West Virginia
1427.	Parkersburg	Parkersburg N.B.
1502.	Morgantown	Merchants' N.B. of West Va.
1504.	Point Pleasant	Merchants' N.B.
1524.	Martinsburg	N.B. of Martinsburg
1530.	Clarksburg	Merchants' N.B. of West Va.
1594.	Wheeling	Nat. Savings Bank
1607.	Weston	Nat. Exchange Bank
1608.	Kingwood	N.B. of Kingwood
1795.	Charleston	First N.B.
1868.	Charlestown	First N.B. of Jefferson
1883.	Piedmont	N.B. of Piedmont
1884.	Wellsburg	Wellsburg N.B.
2144.	Martinsburg	People's N.B.
2445.	Grafton	First N.B.
2458.	Morgantown	Second N.B.
2649.	Parkersburg	Citizens' N.B.
3029.	Moorefield	South Branch Valley N.B.
3106.	Huntington	First N.B.
3236.	Charleston	Charleston N.B.
3629.	Piedmont	First N.B.
4088.	Piedmont	Davis N.B.
4412.	Charleston	Citizens' N.B.
4569.	Clarksburg	Traders' N.B.
4607.	Huntington	Huntington N.B.
4643.	Bluefield	First N.B.
4667.	Charleston	Kanawha N.B.
4718.	Elkins	Elkins N.B.
4760.	Buckhannon	Traders' N.B.
4775.	Ceredo	First N.B.
4811.	Martinsburg	Citizens' N.B.
4828.	Davis	N.B. of Davis
5012.	Mannington	First N.B.
5027.	Sistersville	First N.B.
5028.	Sistersville	Farmers and Producers' N.B.
5164.	Wheeling	Nat. Exchange Bank
5226.	Saint Marys	First N.B.
5266.	New Martinsville	First N.B.
5280.	Ronceverte	First N.B.
5320.	Parkersburg	Farmers and Mechanics' N.B.
5434.	Fayetteville	Fayetteville N.B.
5562.	Hinton	First N.B.
5583.	Morgantown	Citizens' N.B.
5691.	Montgomery	Montgomery N.B.
5701.	Point Pleasant	Point Pleasant N.B.
5717.	Moundsville	First N.B.
5814.	Friendly	First N.B.
5903.	Alderson	First N.B.
5939.	Glenville	First N.B.
6020.	Cameron	First N.B.
6170.	Middlebourne	First N.B.
6205.	Keyser	First N.B.
6213.	Sutton	First N.B.
6226.	Ronceverte	Ronceverte N.B.
6233.	Williamstown	Williamstown N.B.
6283.	Martinsburg	Old N.B.
6302.	Philippi	First N.B.
6332.	Kingwood	Kingwood N.B.
6377.	Philippi	Citizens' N.B.
6424.	West Union	First N.B.
6510.	Madison	Madison N.B.
6538.	Marlinton	First N.B.
6548.	Sistersville	People's N.B.
6582.	New Cumberland	First N.B.
6618.	Belington	Citizens' N.B.

Charter #	City	Name of Bank
6619.	Belington	First N.B.
6634.	Belington	Belington N.B.
6674.	Bluefield	Flat Top N.B.
6735.	Beckley	First N.B.
6790.	Harrisville	First N.B.
6830.	Williamson	First N.B.
6984.	Chester	First N.B.
6999.	Terra Alta	First N.B.
7029.	Clarksburg	Empire N.B.
7060.	Elkins	Randolph N.B.
7191.	Pennsboro	First N.B.
7246.	Pennsboro	Citizens' N.B.
7250.	Salem	First N.B.
7270.	Charles Town	Nat. Citizens' Bank
7275.	Clendenin	First N.B.
7359.	Huntington	West Virginia N.B.
7545.	Monogah	First N.B.
7626.	Newburg	First N.B.
7672.	Pineville	First N.B.
7681.	Clarksburg	Union N.B.
7734.	Bluefield	American N.B.
7845.	Hendricks	First N.B.
7998.	Hinton	N.B. of Summers
8136.	Logan	First N.B.
8171.	Hamlin	Lincoln N.B.
8219.	Princeton	First N.B.
8309.	Northfork	First N.B.
8333.	Gary	Gary N.B.
8345.	Fayetteville	Fayette County N.B.
8360.	Webster Springs	First N.B.
8376.	Elkins	People's N.B.
8434.	Richwood	First N.B.
8569.	Charleston	Nat. City Bank
8749.	Pineville	Citizens' N.B.
8751.	Gormania	First N.B.
8904.	Ansted	Ansted N.B.
8983.	Elm Grove	First N.B. and Trust Company
8998.	Thurmond	N.B. of Thurmond
9038.	Beckley	People's N.B.
9048.	Welch	First N.B.
9071.	Welch	McDowell County N.B.
9288.	Rowlesburg	First N.B.
9453.	Shinnston	First N.B.
9462.	Fairmont	N.B. of Fairmont
9523.	Alderson	Alderson N.B.
9598.	Huntington	American N.B.
9604.	Sutton	Home N.B.
9610.	Parsons	First N.B.
9640.	Saint Albans	First N.B.
9645.	Fairmont	People's N.B.
9721.	Peterstown	First N.B.
9740.	Montgomery	Merchants' N.B.
9766.	Romney	First N.B.
9850.	Winona	Winona N.B.
9909.	Berwind	Berwind N.B.
9913.	Kenova	First N.B.
10067.	Williamson	N.B. of Commerce
10097.	Griffithsville	Oil Field N.B.
10127.	Spencer	First N.B.
10157.	Clark, Northfork	Clark N.B.
10219.	Fairview	First N.B.
10250.	Rowlesburg	People's N.B.
10285.	Reedy	First N.B.
10348.	Hinton	Citizens' N.B.
10369.	Keystone	First N.B.
10370.	Matewan	Matewan N.B.
10392.	Anawalt	First N.B.
10450.	Worthington	First N.B.
10455.	Wheeling	Citizens' N.B.
10480.	Albright	First N.B.
10559.	Cowen	First N.B.
10589.	Beckley	Beckley N.B.
10759.	Ravenswood	First N.B.
10762.	Ripley	First N.B.
11049.	Mount Hope	First N.B.
11109.	Bluefield	Bluefield N.B.
11264.	Matoaka	First N.B.
11268.	Iaeger	First N.B.
11340.	South Charleston	First N.B.
11483.	Williamstown	Farmers and Mechanics' N.B.
11502.	Kimball	First N.B.
11664.	Bayard	Bayard N.B.
11670.	Hurricane	Hurricane N.B.
11877.	Bridgeport	First N.B.
12075.	Oak Hill	Oak Hill N.B.
12270.	Mullens	First N.B.
12283.	Beckley	Nat. Exchange Bank
12372.	Iaeger	Tug River N.B.
12483.	Elkins	Citizens' N.B.
12565.	East Rainelle	First N.B.
12765.	Milton	Milton N.B.
12839.	Matoaka	Matoaka N.B.
13231.	Point Pleasant	Citizens N.B.
13484.	Kimball	Kimball N.B.
13505.	Gary	Gary N.B.
13509.	Charleston	N.B. of Commerce
13512.	Welch	McDowell County N.B.
13621.	Parkersburg	Peoples N.B.
13627.	Richwood	Cherry River N.B.
13634.	Weston	Weston N.B.
13646.	Buckhannon	Central N.B.
13783.	Marlinton	First N.B.
13811.	Fairmont	First N.B.
13830.	Ronceverte	First N.B.
13831.	Keyser	N.B. of Keyser
13881.	West Union	First N.B.
13885.	Oak Hill	Merchants & Miners N.B.
13954.	Logan	N.B. of Logan
14002.	Elkins	Tygarts Valley N.B.
14013.	Webster Springs	Webster Springs N.B.
14034.	Oak Hill	First N.B.
14053.	Philippi	First N.B.
14136.	Salem	First N.B.
14142.	Moundsville	First N.B.
14198.	Berkeley Springs	Citizens N.B.
14295.	Wellsburg	Wellsburg N.B.
14318.	Ansted	N.B. of Ansted

WISCONSIN

Charter #	City	Name of Bank
64.	Milwaukee	First-Wisconsin N.B.
83.	Janesville	First N.B.
95.	Hudson	First N.B.
124.	Whitewater	First N.B.
144.	Madison	First N.B.
157.	Fort Atkinson	First N.B.
178.	Columbus	First N.B.
212.	Kenosha	First N.B.
218.	Oshkosh	First N.B.
230.	Monroe	First N.B.
400.	Berlin	First N.B.
425.	Ripon	First N.B.
426.	Fox Lake	First N.B.
457.	Racine	First N.B.
555.	Fond du Lac	First-Fond du Lac N.B.
749.	Janesville	Rock County N.B.
836.	Beloit	Beloit N.B.
851.	Beaver Dam	N.B. of Beaver Dam
852.	Manitowoc	First N.B.
873.	Elkhorn	First N.B.
874.	Green Bay	First N.B.
1003.	Milwaukee	Nat. Exchange Bank
1009.	Green Bay	City N.B.
1010.	Watertown	Wisconsin N.B.
1017.	Milwaukee	Milwaukee N.B. of Wisconsin
1076.	Jefferson	N.B. of Jefferson
1086.	Waukesha	Waukesha N.B.
1115.	Sparta	First N.B.
1159.	Waukesha	Farmers' N.B.
1248.	Delavan	N.B. of Delavan
1313.	La Crosse	First N.B.
1415.	Cedarburg	First N.B.
1438.	Milwaukee	Merchants' N.B.
1483.	Milwaukee	Nat. City Bank
1568.	Oshkosh	Commercial N.B.
1602.	Neenah	First N.B.
1650.	Appleton	Appleton N.B.
1710.	Brodhead	First N.B.
1714.	Menasha	N.B. of Menasha
1729.	Evansville	First N.B.
1749.	Appleton	First N.B.
1771.	Boscobel	First N.B.
1787.	Oshkosh	Union N.B.
1802.	Racine	Manufacturers' N.B.
1819.	Green Bay	N.B. of Commerce
1820.	Appleton	Manufacturers' N.B.
1933.	Burlington	First N.B.
1998.	Wisconsin Rapids	First N.B.
2069.	Eau Claire	First N.B.
2079.	Baraboo	First N.B.
2123.	Sheboygan	First N.B.
2125.	Chippewa Falls	First N.B.
2132.	Green Bay	Kellogg N.B.
2133.	De Pere	First N.B.
2163.	Beloit	First N.B.
2344.	La Crosse	La Crosse N.B.
2407.	Beloit	Citizens' N.B.
2557.	Racine	Union N.B.
2565.	Appleton	Commercial N.B.
2603.	Neenah	Manufacturers' N.B.
2647.	Waukesha	Nat. Exchange Bank
2653.	Superior	First N.B.
2715.	Milwaukee	First N.B.
2725.	Beloit	Second N.B.
2748.	Janesville	First N.B.
2759.	Eau Claire	Eau Claire N.B.
2820.	Wausau	First N.B.
2851.	Menomonie	First N.B.
2877.	Oshkosh	N.B. of Oshkosh
2925.	Whitewater	Citizens' N.B.
3001.	Stevens Point	First N.B.
3125.	Lake Geneva	First N.B.
3146.	Ripon	Ripon N.B.
3161.	Darlington	First N.B.
3196.	Ashland	Ashland N.B.
3203.	Mineral Point	First N.B.
3270.	Beaver Dam	First N.B.
3308.	Darlington	Citizens' N.B.
3391.	Waupun	First N.B.
3412.	La Crosse	Union N.B.
3541.	Oconto	Oconto N.B.
3590.	Ashland	First N.B.
3607.	Ashland	Northern N.B.
3609.	Baraboo	First N.B.
3641.	Kaukauna	First N.B.
3685.	Fond du Lac	Fond du Lac N.B.
3704.	Merrill	First N.B.
3724.	Menasha	First N.B.
3778.	Chippewa Falls	Lumbermen's N.B.
3884.	Green Bay	Citizens' N.B.
3897.	Black River Falls	First N.B
3926.	Superior	First N.B.
4055.	Shullsburg	First N.B.
4123.	Marinette	First N.B.
4137.	Marinette	Stephenson N.B.
4196.	Oshkosh	German N.B.
4234.	Portage	First N.B.
4304.	Hurley	First N.B.
4305.	Ripon	American N.B.
4312.	Rhinelander	First N.B.
4399.	Superior, West Superior	Keystone N.B.
4414.	Waupaca	First N.B.
4424.	Waupaca	Old N.B.
4508.	Oshkosh	Nat. Union Bank
4573.	Marshfield	First N.B.
4602.	Beaver Dam	American N.B.
4620.	Berlin	First N.B.
4639.	Wisconsin Rapids	Wood County N.B.
4641.	Berlin	Berlin N.B.
4650.	Platteville	First N.B.
4680.	Superior, West Superior	Superior N.B.
4736.	Merrill	N.B. of Merrill
4744.	Wausau	American N.B.
4783.	Green Bay	McCartney N.B.
4816.	Milwaukee	Central N.B.
4817.	Milwaukee	Wisconsin N.B.
4878.	Superior, W. Superior	Northwestern N.B.
4893.	South Milwaukee	South Milwaukee N.B.
4912.	Stevens Point	Citizens' N.B.
4937.	Appleton	Citizens' N.B.
4975.	Manitowoc	N.B. of Manitowoc
5013.	New London	First N.B.
5047.	La Crosse	N.B. of La Crosse
5143.	Antigo	First N.B.
5222.	Stoughton	First N.B.
5437.	Marshfield	American N.B.
5446.	Tigerton	First N.B.
5458.	Milwaukee	Marine N.B.
5469.	Shawano	First N.B.
5505.	Oconomowoc	First N.B.
5521.	Oconto	Citizens' N.B.
5535.	Ladysmith	First N.B.
5557.	Oshkosh	Commercial N.B.
5566.	Omro	First N.B.
5592.	Lake Geneva	Farmers' N.B.
5632.	Cuba City	First N.B.
5658.	Peshtigo	Peshtigo N.B.
5695.	Medford	First N.B.
5779.	Mondovi	First N.B.
5933.	Chilton	Chilton N.B.
5942.	Antigo	Langlade N.B.
5947.	Sheboygan Falls	Dairymen's N.B.
5978.	Princeton	First N.B.
6015.	Fond du Lac	Commercial N.B.
6034.	Neenah	Nat. Manufacturers' Bank
6222.	Campbellsport	First N.B.
6273.	Clintonville	First N.B.
6403.	Shawano	Wisconsin N.B.
6469.	De Pere	N.B. of De Pere
6575.	Seymour	First N.B.
6604.	Oshkosh	Old Commercial N.B.
6663.	Rice Lake	First N.B.
6698.	Dodgeville	First N.B.
6711.	Rib Lake	First N.B.
6853.	Milwaukee	N.B. of Commerce
6908.	West Allis	First N.B.
7007.	Lancaster	First N.B.
7040.	Edgerton	First N.B.
7087.	River Falls	First N.B.
7136.	Wautoma	First N.B.
7158.	Bayfield	First N.B.
7224.	Brillion	First N.B.
7264.	Fairchild	First N.B.
7347.	La Crosse	Batavian N.B.
7434.	Phillips	First N.B.
7462.	Beaver Dam	Old N.B.
7470.	Weyauwega	First N.B.
7831.	Hayward	First N.B.
7898.	Waupun	N.B. of Waupun
7901.	Richland Center	First N.B.
7966.	Ladysmith	Ladysmith N.B.
8118.	Dale	First N.B.
8281.	Eau Claire	Union N.B.
8338.	Alma	First N.B.
8444.	Grantsburg	First N.B.
8491.	Frederic	First N.B.
8529.	Viroqua	First N.B.
8632.	Rio	First N.B.
8671,	Hartford	First N.B.
8689.	Wauwatosa	First N.B.
8710.	Manawa	First N.B.
8887.	Marion	German American N.B.
9003.	Watertown	Merchants' N.B.
9140.	Superior	United States N.B.
9153.	Madison	Commercial N.B.
9304.	Stoughton	Citizens' N.B.
9347.	Oshkosh	City N.B.
9387.	Crandon	First N.B.
9419.	Port Washington	First N.B.
9522.	Fennimore	First N.B.
9606.	Neillsville	First N.B.
10106.	Baldwin	First N.B.
10176.	Merrill	Citizens' N.B.
10322.	Stone Lake	First N.B.
10330.	Wisconsin Rapids	Citizens' N.B.
10489.	Park Falls	First N.B.
10510.	Hudson	N.B. of Hudson
10522.	Prescott	First N.B.
10620.	Oregon	First N.B.
10653.	Mayville	First N.B.
10667.	Blair	First N.B.
10725.	Pepin	First N.B.
10733.	Nelson	First N.B.
10791.	Durand	First N.B.
10880.	Highland	First N.B.
10890.	Barron	First N.B.
10938.	Racine	American N.B.
11051.	Niagara	First N.B.
11060.	West Bend	First N.B.
11083.	Glenwood City	Farmers' N.B.
11104.	Horicon	First N.B.

Charter #	City	Name of Bank
11114.	Blanchardville	First N.B.
11128.	Boyceville	First N.B.
11150.	Sheboygan	Security N.B.
11245.	Knapp	First N.B.
11412.	New Richmond	First N.B.
11432.	Maiden Rock	First N.B.
11463.	Sparta	Farmers' N.B.
11526.	Saint Croix Falls	First N.B.
11577.	Deerfield	First N.B.
11594.	Hurley	Hurley N.B.
11646.	Rhinelander	Oneida N.B.
11783.	Burlington	Burlington N.B.
11826.	Ladysmith	Pioneer N.B.
11986.	Bruce	First N.B.
12124.	Eagle River	First N.B.
12286.	Marion	First N.B.
12351.	Kenosha	United States N.B.
12482.	Milwaukee	American N.B.
12534.	Washburn	First N.B.
12541.	Kenosha	Brown N.B.
12564.	Milwaukee	Northwestern N.B.
12575.	Princeton	Farmers-Merchants' N.B.
12628.	Milwaukee	Grand and Sixth N.B.
12644.	Hayward	People's N.B.
12814.	Crandon	Crandon N.B.
12816.	Milwaukee	Mechanics' N.B.
13165.	Superior	N.B. of Commerce
13184.	Milwaukee	Second Wisconsin N.B.
13202.	Bangor	First N.B.
13308.	Soldiers Grove	First N.B.
13366.	Madison	University Avenue N.B.
13487.	Phillips	First N.B.
13529.	Durand	First N.B.
13599.	Fennimore	First N.B.
13616.	Oconomowoc	Oconomowoc N.B.
13645.	Eau Claire	American N.B. & Trust Co,
13806.	Oshkosh	Oshkosh N.B.
13870.	Ashland	Union N.B.
13879.	Fond du Lac	National Exchange Bank
13904.	Princeton	Farmers-Merchants N.B.
13921.	Manitowoc	Manitowoc N.B.
13932.	Edgerton	N.B. of Edgerton
14058.	Viroqua	First N.B.
14059.	Mayville	First N.B.
14060.	Baraboo	First N.B.
14063.	Waupaca	First N.B.
14064.	Watertown	Wisconsin N.B.
14095.	Durand	Security N.B.
14109.	Superior	Union N.B.
14125.	Marshfield	Citizens N.B.
14130.	Marion	First N.B.
14150.	Tigerton	First N.B.
14184.	Darlington	First N.B.
14200.	Neillsville	First N.B.
14233.	Oconto	First N.B.
14242.	Clintonville	Clintonville N.B.
14314.	Shawano	Shawano N.B.
14336.	Wauwatosa	First N.B.

WYOMING

Charter #	City	Name of Bank
1800.	Cheyenne	First N.B.
2110.	Laramie	Wyoming N.B.
2518.	Laramie	Laramie N.B.
2652.	Cheyenne	Stockgrowers' N.B.
3299.	Buffalo	First N.B.
3416.	Cheyenne.	Cheyenne N.B.
3556.	Douglas	First N.B.
3615.	Laramie	Albany N.B.
3920.	Rock Springs	First N.B.
4320.	Rawlins	First N.B.
4343.	Sundance	First N.B.
4604.	Sheridan	First N.B.
4720.	Lander	First N.B.
4755.	Rock Springs	Rock Springs N.B.
4989.	Laramie	First N.B.
5295.	Guernsey	First N.B.
5413.	Rawlins	Rawlins N.B.
5480.	Kemmerer	First N.B.
5949.	Thermopolis	First N.B.
6340.	Meeteetse	First N.B.
6850.	Casper	Casper N.B.
7083.	Casper	Stockmens' N.B.
7198.	Newcastle	First N.B.
7319.	Cody	First N.B.
7978.	Shoshoni	First N.B.
8020.	Cody	Shoshone N.B.
8087.	Douglas	Douglas
8089.	Cheyenne	Citizens' N.B.
8232.	Shoshoni	Wind River N.B.
8253.	Worland	First N.B.
8275.	Sheridan	Sheridan N.B.
8432.	Wheatland	First N.B.
8534.	Evanston	First N.B.
8612.	Evanston	Evanston N.B.
8961.	Saratoga	First N.B.
9289.	Torrington	First N.B.
9557.	Rawlins	Stock Growers' N.B.
10265.	Powell	First N.B.
10533.	Casper	Wyoming N.B.
10565.	Powell	Powell N.B.
10698.	Green River	First N.B.
10810.	Greybull	First N.B.
10844.	Lovell	First N.B.
10858.	Bason	First N.B.
11079.	Newcastle	Newcastle N.B.
11132.	Torrington	Citizens' N.B.
11231.	Lingle	First N.B.
11309.	Torrington	Torrington N.B.
11342.	Rock River	First N.B.
11352.	Manville	First N.B.
11380.	Cheyenne	American N.B.
11390.	Lusk	First N.B.
11490.	Casper	N.B. of Commerce
11666.	Hanna	First N.B.
11683.	Casper	Citizens' N.B.
12558.	Parco	First N.B.
12638.	Thermopolis	First N.B.
14103.	Riverton	First N.B.

APPENDIX

I. THE SIGNATURES OF UNITED STATES CURRENCY

The following table (courtesy of the Treasury Department and W. A. Philpott, Jr.) shows the exact period of time during which each two of the various signers of our currency were in office concurrently.

		Combined Tenure			Length of Time	
Register of the Treasury	**Treasurer of the U.S.**	**Began**	**Ended**	**Years**	**Months**	**Days**
Lucius E. Chittenden	F. E. Spinner	4-17-1861	8-10-1864	3	3	23
S. B. Colby	F. E. Spinner	8-11-1864	9-21-1867	3	1	10
Noah L. Jeffries	F. E. Spinner	10-5-1867	3-15-1869	1	5	10
John Allison	F. E. Spinner	4-3-1869	6-30-1875	6	2	27
John Allison	John C. New	6-30-1875	7-1-1876	1	—	1
John Allison	A. U. Wyman	7-1-1876	6-30-1877	—	11	29
John Allison	James Gilfillan	7-1-1877	3-23-1878	—	8	22
Glenni W. Scofield	James Gilfillan	4-1-1878	5-20-1881	3	1	19
Blanche K. Bruce	James Gilfillan	5-21-1881	3-31-1883	1	10	10
Blanche K. Bruce	A. U. Wyman	4-1-1883	4-30-1885	2	—	29
Blanche K. Bruce	Conrad N. Jordan	5-1-1885	6-5-1885	—	1	4
William S. Rosecrans	Conrad N. Jordan	6-8-1885	5-23-1887	1	11	15
William S. Rosecrans	James W. Hyatt	5-24-1887	5-10-1889	1	11	16
William S. Rosecrans	J. N. Huston	5-11-1889	4-21-1891	1	11	13
William S. Rosecrans	Enos H. Nebeker	4-25-1891	5-31-1893	2	1	6
William S. Rosecrans	Daniel N. Morgan	6-1-1893	6-19-1893	—	—	18
James F. Tillman	Daniel N. Morgan	7-1-1893	6-30-1897	3	11	29
James F. Tillman	Ellis H. Roberts	7-1-1897	12-2-1897	—	5	1
Blanche K. Bruce	Ellis H. Roberts	12-3-1897	3-17-1898	—	3	14
Judson W. Lyons	Ellis H. Roberts	4-7-1898	6-30-1905	7	2	23
Judson W. Lyons	Charles H. Treat	7-1-1905	4-1-1906	—	9	—
William T. Vernon	Charles H. Treat	6-12-1906	10-30-1909	3	4	18
William T. Vernon	Lee McClung	11-1-1909	3-14-1911	1	4	13
James C. Napier	Lee McClung	3-15-1911	11-21-1912	1	8	6
James C. Napier	Carmi A. Thompson	11-22-1912	3-31-1913	—	4	9
James C. Napier	John Burke	4-1-1913	9-30-1913	—	5	29
Gabe E. Parker	John Burke	10-1-1913	12-31-1914	1	2	30
Houston B. Teehee	John Burke	3-24-1915	11-20-1919	4	7	26
William S. Elliott	John Burke	11-21-1919	1-5-1921	1	1	14
William S. Elliott	Frank White	5-2-1921	1-24-1922	—	8	22
Harley V. Speelman	Frank White	1-25-1922	9-30-1927	5	8	5
Walter O. Woods	Frank White	10-1-1927	5-1-1928	—	7	—
Walter O. Woods	H. T. Tate	5-31-1928	1-17-1929	—	7	16
Edward E. Jones	Walter O. Woods	1-22-1929	5-31-1933	4	4	9
Secretary of the Treasury						
William G. McAdoo	John Burke	4-1-1913	12-15-1918	5	8	14
Carter Glass	John Burke	12-16-1918	2-1-1920	1	1	15
D. F. Houston	John Burke	2-2-1920	1-5-1921	—	11	3
A. W. Mellon	Frank White	5-2-1921	5-1-1928	6	11	29
A. W. Mellon	H. T. Tate	4-30-1928	1-17-1929	—	8	16
A. W. Mellon	Walter O. Woods	1-18-1929	2-12-1932	3	—	25
Ogden L. Mills	Walter O. Woods	2-13-1932	3-3-1933	1	—	18
W. H. Woodin	Walter O. Woods	3-4-1933	5-31-1933	—	2	27
W. H. Woodin	W. A. Julian	6-1-1933	12-31-1933	—	7	—
Henry Morgenthau, Jr.	W. A. Julian	1-1-1934	7-22-1945	11	6	22
Fred M. Vinson	W. A. Julian	7-23-1945	7-23-1946	1	—	—
John W. Snyder	W. A. Julian	7-25-1946	5-29-1949	2	10	4
John W. Snyder	Georgia Neese Clark	6-21-1949	1-20-1953	3	7	—
George M. Humphrey	Ivy Baker Priest	1-28-1953	7-28-1957	4	6	—
Robert B. Anderson	Ivy Baker Priest	7-29-1957	1-20-1961	3	5	23
C. Douglas Dillon	Elizabeth Rudel Smith	1-30-1961	4-13-1962	1	3	14
C. Douglas Dillon	Kathryn O'Hay Granahan	1-3-1963	3-31-1965	2	2	28
Henry Fowler	Kathryn O'Hay Granahan	4-1-1965	10-13-1966	1	6	13
Joseph Barr	*Kathryn O'Hay Granahan	12-23-1968	1-20-1969	—	—	28
David Kennedy	Dorothy Andrews Elston	5-8-1969	9-16-1970	1	4	8
David Kennedy	†Dorothy Andrews Kabis	9-17-1970	2-1-1971	—	4	15
John B. Connally	Dorothy Andrews Kabis	2-8-1971	7-3-1971	—	4	25
John B. Connally	Romana Acosta Banuelos	12-17-1971	6-12-1973	—	5	26
George P. Shultz	Romana Acosta Banuelos	6-12-1972	2-15-1974	1	8	3
William E. Simon	Francine I. Neff	6-21-1974	1-19-1976	1	6	28
W. Michael Blumenthal	Azie Taylor Morton	9-12-1977	8-4-1979	1	10	24
G. William Miller	Azie Taylor Morton	8-6-1979	1-21-1981	1	5	16
Donald T. Regan	Angela Marie Buchanan	1-22-1981	7-1-1983	2	5	10
Donald T. Regan	Katherine Davalos Ortega	9-23-1983	2-3-1985	1	4	11
James A. Baker III	Katherine Davalos Ortega	2-4-1985				

*Although no longer Treasurer, Kathryn Granahan's signature continued in use until Dorothy Elston was named to replace her.

†When Dorothy Elston married Walter Kabis on September 17, 1970, it marked the first time the signature of a Treasurer was changed during the term of office.

II. DATES OF ISSUE FOR SMALL SIZE NOTES

The following table (courtesy of David L. Ganz and the Bureau of Engraving and Printing) shows the dates between which the Bureau printed each series of small size notes ($5 and up). When available, both the first and last dates of printing are given. If both dates could not be located the reader should assume dates close to those listed under "Combined Tenure" for each signature combination listed in Appendix I.

With the knowledge that a dollar bill remains in circulation for approximately 18 months, and that higher denominations circulate for a longer time in direct relation to the value, i.e., up to four years for a twenty dollar note and to between seven and eight years for fifty and hundred dollar notes; by using this table, the reader can determine the approximate length of time each issue of small size currency remained in circulation.

$5 FEDERAL RESERVE NOTES

Fr. No.	Signatures	Series	First Delivered	Last Delivered	
1950	Mellon-Tate	1928	4-30-28	1-17-29	
1951	Mellon-Woods	1928A	1-18-29		
1952	Mellon-Woods	1928B		2-12-32	
1953	Mills-Woods	1928C	2-13-32	3-3-33	
1954	Woodin-Woods	1928D	3-5-33	5-31-33	
1955–1956	Morgenthau-Julian	1934	11-2-34	No Record	
1957	Morgenthau-Julian	1934A	No Record	4-2-47	
2301	Vinson-Julian	1934	6-8-42		(Overprinted)
2302	Vinson-Julian	1934A		5-30-44	"HAWAII")
1958	Vinson-Julian	1934B	11-19-45	4-1-47	
1959	Julian-Snyder	1934C	9-30-46	7-3-50	
1960–1961	Snyder-Clark	1934D, 1950	11-7-50	9-1-53	
1962	Humphrey-Priest	1950A	7-14-53	9-10-57	
1963	Anderson-Priest	1950B	9-25-57	6-14-61	
1964	Dillon-Smith	1950C	3-3-61	3-13-63	
1965	Dillon-Granahan	1950D	1-5-63	8-31-65	
1966	Fowler-Granahan	1950E	9-9-65	7-26-67	
1967	Dillon-Granahan	1963	9-16-64	7-15-65	
1968	Fowler-Granahan	1963A	6-7-65	9-9-69	
1969	Kennedy-Elston	1969	8-4-69	11-10-71	
1970	Connally-Kabis	1969A	6-28-71	5-2-73	
1971	Connally-Banuelos	1969B	5-2-73	2-13-73	
1972	Shultz-Banuelos	1969C	10-24-72	12-10-74	
1973	Simon-Neff	1974	9-27-74	4-12-78	
1974	Blumenthal-Morton	1977	10-20-77	6-10-80	
1975	Miller-Morton	1977A	12-21-79	12-10-81	
1976	Regan-Buchanan	1981	6-3-81	7-2-84	
1977	Regan-Ortega	1981A	4-17-84	7-11-85	
1978	Baker-Ortega	1985	6-26-85		

$5 UNITED STATES NOTES

Fr. No.	Signatures	Series	First Delivered	Last Delivered
1525	Mellon-Woods	1928	5-27-29	12-19-30
1526	Mills-Woods	1928A	1-8-31	No Record
1527	Morgenthau-Julian	1928B	No Record	6-18-34
1528	Morgenthau-Julian	1928C	6-19-34	2-25-46
1529	Vinson-Julian	1928D	3-11-46	9-19-46
1530	Snyder-Julian	1928E	9-20-46	3-21-50
1531	Snyder-Clark	1928F	3-21-50	4-27-53
1532	Humphrey-Priest	1953	5-6-53	8-28-57
1533	Anderson-Priest	1953A	2-10-58	1-13-61
1534	Dillon-Smith	1953B	10-5-61	2-25-63
1535	Dillon-Granahan	1953C	2-26-63	11-8-63
1536	Dillon-Granahan	1963	3-2-64	11-27-67

$5 SILVER CERTIFICATES

Fr. No.	Signatures	Series	First Delivered	Last Delivered	
1650	Morgenthau-Julian	1934	7-20-34	1-26-38	
1651	Morgenthau-Julian	1934A	1-27-38	2-6-46	
2307	Morgenthau-Julian	1934A	9-4-42	5-8-44	WW II
1652	Vinson-Julian	1934B	2-6-46	12-16-46	
1653	Snyder-Julian	1934C	12-19-46	10-24-49	
1654	Snyder-Clark	1934D	10-25-49	10-1-53	
1655	Humphrey-Priest	1953	5-12-53	8-21-57	
1656	Anderson-Priest	1953A	12-9-57	3-17-61	
1657	Dillon-Smith	1953B	3-28-61	4-25-62	
1658	Dillon-Granahan	1953C	11-12-63	8-31-64	

$5 FEDERAL RESERVE BANK NOTES
(National Currency)

Fr. No.	Signatures	Series	First Delivered	Last Delivered
1800, 1850	Jones-Woods	1929	3-11-33	1-11-34

$10 FEDERAL RESERVE NOTES

No.	Signatures	Series	First Delivered	Last Delivered	
2000	Mellon-Tate	1928	4-30-28	1-17-29	
2001	Mellon-Woods	1928A	1-18-29	No Record	
2002	Mellon-Woods	1928B	No Record	2-12-32	
2003	Mills-Woods	1928C	2-13-32	3-3-33	
2004–2005	Morgenthau-Julian	1934	10-17-34	12-13-35	
2006	Morgenthau-Julian	1934A	6-8-42	7-12-44	
2303	Morgenthau-Julian	1934A	6-8-42	8-12-46	(Overprinted
2007	Vinson-Julian	1934B	11-23-45	6-3-47	"HAWAII")
2008	Snyder-Julian	1934C	10-22-46	1-19-50	
2009	Snyder-Clark	1934D	9-28-49	1-31-51	
2010	Snyder-Clark	1950	11-7-50	10-1-53	
2011	Humphrey-Priest	1950A	4-3-53	9-12-57	
2012	Anderson-Priest	1950B	9-25-57	5-15-61	
2013	Dillon-Smith	1950C	10-23-59	3-14-63	
2014	Dillon-Granahan	1950D	2-19-63	8-30-65	
2015	Fowler-Granahan	1950E	9-13-65	9-16-68	
2016	Dillon-Granahan	1963	4-24-64	7-8-65	
2017	Fowler-Granahan	1963A	5-12-65	7-28-69	
2018	Kennedy-Elston	1969	8-4-69	10-4-71	
2019	Connally-Kabis	1969A	7-19-71	4-25-73	
2020	Connally-Banuelos	1969B	6-5-72	9-5-73	
2021	Shultz-Banuelos	1969C	11-6-72	12-10-74	
2022	Simon-Neff	1974	9-3-74	6-14-78	
2023	Blumenthal-Morton	1977	1-4-77	2-11-81	
2024	Miller-Morton	1977A	4-10-77	3-1-82	
2025	Regan-Buchanan	1981	3-23-82	4-17-84	
2026	Regan-Ortega	1981A	4-17-84	1-7-86	
2027	Baker-Ortega	1985	9-10-85		

$10 FEDERAL RESERVE BANK NOTES
(National Currency)

No.	Signatures	Series	First Delivered	Last Delivered
1801, 1860	Jones-Woods	1929	3-10-33	11-18-33

$10 SILVER CERTIFICATES

No.	Signatures	Series	First Delivered	Last Delivered	
1700	Woodin-Julian	1933	1-5-34	2-27-34	
1700-a	Morgenthau-Julian	1933A	2-27-34	4-2-34	
2308	Morgenthau-Julian	1934	9-4-42		WW II
2309	Morgenthau-Julian	1934A		5-8-44	WW II
1701	Morgenthau-Julian	1934	4-17-34	4-1-35	
1702	Morgenthau-Julian	1934A	4-2-35	9-4-46	
1703	Vinson-Julian	1934B	9-4-46	8-5-47	
1704	Snyder-Julian	1934C	8-5-47	7-12-50	
1705	Snyder-Clark	1934D	7-12-50	4-14-53	
1706	Humphrey-Priest	1953	5-12-53	8-27-57	
1707	Anderson-Priest	1953A	2-13-58	2-17-58	
1708	Dillon-Smith	1953B	2-2-62	3-14-62	

$20 FEDERAL RESERVE NOTES

No.	Signatures	Series	First Delivered	Last Delivered	
2050	Mellon-Tate	1928	4-30-28	1-17-29	
2051	Mellon-Woods	1928A	1-18-29	No Record	
2052	Mellon-Woods	1928B	No Record	2-12-32	
2053	Mills-Woods	1928C	2-13-32	3-3-33	
2304	Vinson-Julian	1934	6-8-42		(Overprinted
2305	Vinson-Julian	1934A		7-18-44	"HAWAII")
2054	Morgenthau-Julian	1934	2-2-35	No Record	
2055	Morgenthau-Julian	1934A	No Record	2-4-46	
2056	Vinson-Julian	1934B	11-29-45	10-22-47	
2057	Julian-Snyder	1934C	1-7-47	4-3-50	
2058	Snyder-Clark	1934D	1-13-50	1-29-51	
2059	Snyder-Clark	1950	11-7-50	8-31-53	
2060	Humphrey-Priest	1950A	8-19-53	8-30-57	
2061	Anderson-Priest	1950B	9-25-57	6-16-61	
2062	Dillon-Smith	1950C	2-28-61	3-21-63	
2063	Dillon-Granahan	1950D	2-12-63	11-30-65	
2064	Fowler-Granahan	1950E	9-1-65	7-15-66	
2065	Dillon-Granahan	1963	10-7-64	7-2-65	
2066	Fowler-Granahan	1963A	6-8-65	8-29-69	
2067	Kennedy-Elston	1969	7-30-69	9-15-71	
2068	Connally-Kabis	1969A	6-15-71	3-21-73	
2069	Connally-Banuelos	1969B	6-6-72	4-25-73	
2070	Shultz-Banuelos	1969C	9-27-72	11-14-74	
2071	Simon-Neff	1974	9-11-74	7-19-78	
2072	Blumenthal-Morton	1977	4-27-78	1-27-82	
2073	Regan-Buchanan	1981	11-17-81	7-9-84	
2074	Regan-Ortega	1981A	5-22-84	12-2-85	
2075	Baker-Ortega	1985	10-25-85		

$20 FEDERAL RESERVE BANK NOTES
(National Currency)

No.	Signatures	Series	First Delivered	Last Delivered
1802, 1870	Jones-Woods	1929	3-11-33	12-22-33

$50 FEDERAL RESERVE NOTES

No.	Signatures	Series	First Delivered	Last Delivered
2100	Mellon-Woods	1928	6-13-29	No Record
2101	Mellon-Woods	1928A	No Record	12-10-34
2102	Morgenthau-Julian	1934	3-9-35	No Record
2103	Morgenthau-Julian	1934A	No Record	7-13-46
2104	Vinson-Julian	1934B	7-11-46	8-19-47
2105	Snyder-Julian	1934C	8-12-47	1-11-51
2106	Snyder-Clark	1934D	7-21-50	1-11-51
2107	Snyder-Clark	1950	2-21-51	8-28-53
2108	Humphrey-Priest	1950A	12-7-54	8-20-57
2109	Anderson-Priest	1950B	10-14-57	12-8-60
2110	Dillon-Smith	1950C	7-12-61	12-4-62
2111	Dillon-Granahan	1950D	7-19-63	8-27-65
2112	Fowler-Granahan	1950E	9-10-65	11-30-65
2113	Fowler-Granahan	1963A	11-8-66	7-1-69
2114	Kennedy-Elston	1969	7-9-69	9-20-72
2115	Connally-Kabis	1969A	8-11-71	8-1-73
2116	Connally-Banuelos	1969B	9-5-72	12-5-73
2117	Shultz-Banuelos	1969C	11-2-72	12-11-74
2118	Simon-Neff	1974	8-29-74	1-6-81
2119	Blumenthal-Morton	1977	8-16-76	1-11-83
2120	Regan-Buchanan	1981	5-3-81	2-25-85
2121	Regan-Ortega	1981A	10-23-84	11-5-85
2122	Baker-Ortega	1985	10-24-85	

$50 FEDERAL RESERVE BANK NOTES
(National Currency)

No.	Signatures	Series	First Delivered	Last Delivered
1803, 1880	Jones-Woods	1929	3-11-33	8-30-33

$100 FEDERAL RESERVE NOTES

No.	Signatures	Series	First Delivered	Last Delivered
2150	Mellon-Woods	1928	8-30-29	No Record
2151	Mellon-Woods	1928A	No Record	12-6-34
2152	Morgenthau-Julian	1934	3-9-35	No Record
2153	Morgenthau-Julian	1934A	No Record	1-19-51
2154	Vinson-Julian	1934B	7-13-49	8-4-47
2155	Snyder-Julian	1934C	12-31-46	1-18-51
2156	Snyder-Clark	1934D	7-24-50	1-17-51
2157	Snyder-Clark	1950	5-9-51	9-9-53
2158	Humphrey-Priest	1950A	12-8-54	8-20-57
2159	Anderson-Priest	1950B	9-4-57	12-9-60
2160	Dillon-Smith	1950C	9-12-61	12-14-62
2161	Dillon-Granahan	1950D	7-23-63	8-30-65
2162	Fowler-Granahan	1950E	9-3-65	7-27-66
2163	Fowler-Granahan	1963A	9-27-66	12-24-66
2164	Kennedy-Elston	1969	7-9-69	11-9-71
2165	Connally-Kabis	1969A	8-9-71	12-4-73
2166	Shultz-Banuelos	1969C	10-3-72	10-31-74
2167	Simon-Neff	1974	10-15-74	7-18-78
2168	Blumenthal-Morton	1977	8-8-78	11-29-83
2169	Regan-Buchanan	1981	5-15-81	7-15-85
2170	Regan-Ortega	1981A	11-6-84	11-20-85
2171	Baker-Ortega	1985	11-20-85	

$100 UNITED STATES NOTES

No.	Signatures	Series	First Delivered	Last Delivered
1550	Fowler-Granahan	1966	10-14-68	11-5-68
1551	Kennedy-Elston	1966A	1-26-71	1-26-71

$100 FEDERAL RESERVE BANK NOTES
(National Currency)

No.	Signatures	Series	First Delivered	Last Delivered
1804, 1890	Jones-Woods	1929	3-11-33	3-30-33

$500 FEDERAL RESERVE NOTES

No.	Signatures	Series	First Delivered	Last Delivered
2200	Mellon-Woods	1928	11-8-29	3-18-33
2201	Morgenthau-Julian	1934	12-23-35	7-21-45

$1000 FEDERAL RESERVE NOTES

No.	Signatures	Series	First Delivered	Last Delivered
2210	Mellon-Woods	1928	11-14-29	7-26-33
2211	Morgenthau-Julian	1934	12-17-35	11-17-43
2212	Morgenthau-Julian	1934A	3-30-42	7-21-45

III. UNCUT SHEETS OF SMALL SIZE NOTES

Small size notes were printed in sheets of 12 from 1928 to 1952, and were sold to the public starting in 1935. Those sheets from the period 1928–1934 were made for presentation only and are rare.

A small additional number were released with the introduction of 18 subject sheets in 1953, but the practice was soon thereafter discontinued. Though 32 subject sheets were first printed in 1957, it was not until 1981 that, as a part of the Bureau of Engraving and Printing's Public Affairs Program, they were made available for sale to the public.

Listed below, by catalog number, are only those sheets of which a record of issue is known. There are also records of sheets Federal Reserve Notes, Series of 1928, in denominations from $5 to $50; and $10 and $20 Federal Reserve Bank Notes, Series of 1929. Since these were most likely issued for official purposes only, and are extremely rare, they are not listed individually. Confirmation of other sheets is invited.

LEGAL TENDER NOTES

No.	Denomination	Series	Sheet Size	No. Issued	Value
1500	$1	1928	12	11	Rare
1501	$2	1928	12	5	Rare
1504	$2	1928C	12	25	1,400.00
1505	$2	1928D	12	50	1,300.00
1506	$2	1928E	12	50	1,300.00
1507	$2	1928F	12	100	1,250.00
1508	$2	1928G	12	100	1,250.00
1509	$2	1953	18	100	1,750.00
1525	$5	1928	12	5	Rare
1529	$5	1928D	12	25	2,350.00
1530	$5	1928E	12	100	2,350.00
1532	$5	1953	18	100	3,250.00

SILVER CERTIFICATES

No.	Denomination	Series	Sheet Size	No. Issued	Value
1600	$1	1928	12	80	2,750.00
1602	$1	1928B	12	6	Rare
1603	$1	1928C	12	11	17,500.00
1604	$1	1928D	12	60	2,750.00
1605	$1	1928E	12	25	15,000.00
1606	$1	1934	12	25	3,750.00
1607	$1	1935	12	100	1,350.00
1608	$1	1935A	12	100	1,350.00
1611	$1	1935B	12	100	1,350.00
1612	$1	1935C	12	100	1,350.00
1613	$1	1935D	12	300	1,250.00
1613	$1	1935D	18	102	1,300.00
1614	$1	1935E	18	400	1,300.00
1650	$5	1934	12	25	2,750.00
1652	$5	1934B	12	20	2,750.00
1653	$5	1934C	12	100	2,750.00
1654	$5	1934D	12	100	2,750.00
1655	$5	1953	18	100	3,750.00
1700	$10	1933	12	1	Rare
1700A	$10	1933A	12	1	Rare
1701	$10	1934	12	10	4,750.00
1706	$10	1953	18	100	5,000.00

NATIONAL BANK NOTES

These notes were printed in sheets of 12 but only delivered in sheets of six. Valuations are for the most common banks and for Type I Notes. Others command higher prices.

No.	Denomination	Series	Sheet Size	No. Issued	Value
1800	$5	1929	6		625.00
1801	$10	1929	6		725.00
1802	$20	1929	6		800.00
1803	$50	1929	6		3,500.00
1804	$100	1929	6		4,500.00

WORLD WAR II EMERGENCY ISSUES

No.	Denomination		Series	Sheet Size	No. Issued	Value
2300	$1	HAWAII	1935A	12	25	4,000.00
2306	$1	YELLOW SEAL	1935A	12	25	4,750.00

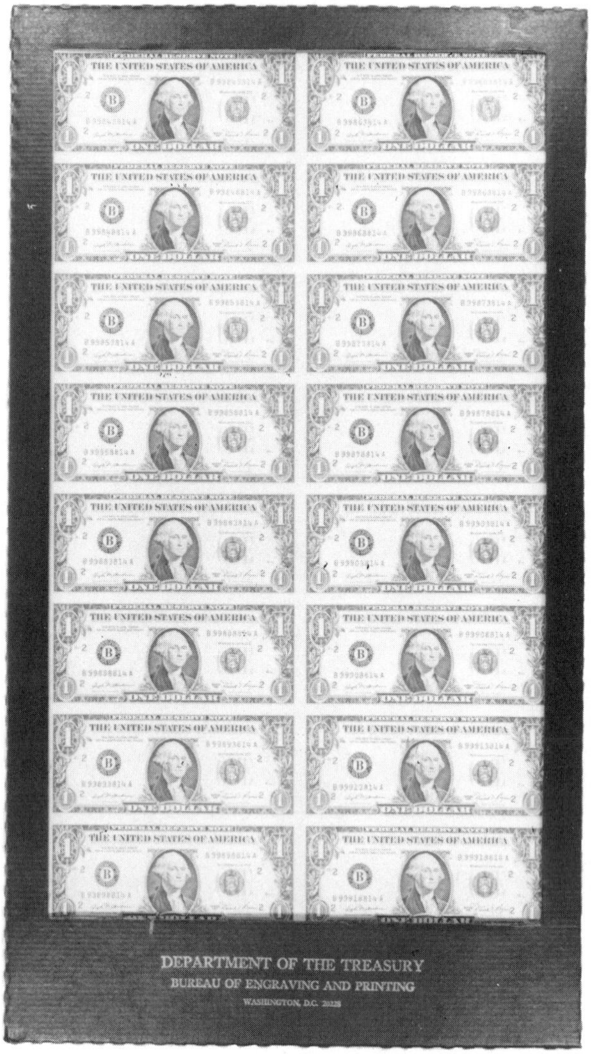

(Photos courtesy of COIN WORLD)

FEDERAL RESERVE NOTES

No.	Denomination	Series	Sheet Size	No. Issued	Value
1911	$1	1981	32		50.00
1911	$1	1981	16		27.50
1911	$1	1981	4		12.50
1912	$1	1981A	32		50.00
1912	$1	1981A	16		27.50
1912	$1	1981A	4		12.50
1913	$1	1985	32		50.00
1913	$1	1985	16		27.50
1913	$1	1985	4		12.50
1935*	$2	1976	16		50.00
1935*	$2	1976	4		27.50

IV. PRICE APPRECIATION RECORD OF UNCIRCULATED LARGE SIZE TYPE NOTES

The following listing records the market values of Large Size type notes in uncirculated condition for the past 33 years. The values are the actual prices taken from the 1953, 1964, 1975 and present editions of this book, and show with clarity the steadily rising popularity of these issues. Though not exhaustive, the editors have endeavored to include at least one note of each design for which uncirculated prices have been shown in the past. Scarce early issues, which are hardly ever available in uncirculated condition, are not included.

The notes selected are not rarities, but rather are "type" notes, or notes selected to represent each design issued by the Government. While other collectors acquire every signature combination or variety available, the type note collector acquires only the most common and least expensive note in a series in uncirculated condition. When the collection is complete, every different type of note issued by the United States is represented.

The record below shows that while the value of the dollar is falling, not all dollar bills are shrinking in value. Older, Scarcer specimens have made impressive gains in recent years, far outstripping inflation. In fact, paper money, like rare coins, has proven to be a very sound investment.

Over the past 33 years, uncirculated large size type notes have increased in value by an astounding 3,094 per cent. This is an average increase of 93,76 per cent per year. A $10,000 investment in large size type notes in 1953 would be worth $309,400 in 1986. Few other forms of investment can match these results.

Even over the short term, paper money has shown impressive gains. For the 22-year span from 1964 to 1986, uncirculated large size type notes increased in value by 681 per cent; an average of 30.95 per cent per year. A $10,000 investment in 1975 would be worth $68,100 this year.

And over the past 11 years, uncirculated large size type notes appreciated in value by 315 per cent; an average annual increase of 28.64 per cent. A $10,000 investment in 1975 would be worth $31,500 today.

While coin collectors may boast about the silver content of this coin or the gold value of that one, it has been these colorful rectangles of paper, scorned for years as ragpicker's delights, the collection of which was downgraded by some as just a trivial pursuit, which have really shown the outstanding results. In fact, they are one of the outstanding capital gainers of the last thirty years.

No.	1953	1964	1975	1986
16	25.00	85.00	325.00	850.00
18	40.00	110.00	335.00	1,100.00
34	20.00	50.00	175.00	400.00
40	5.00	45.00	115.00	225.00
41	37.50	250.00	485.00	1,800.00
42	40.00	325.00	750.00	2,000.00
57	10.00	32.50	60.00	225.00
64	45.00	82.50	275.00	900.00
91	17.50	27.50	60.00	250.00
93	85.00	300.00	550.00	2,200.00
95	65.00	210.00	525.00	2,000.00
96	65.00	250.00	700.00	1,900.00
113	50.00	125.00	250.00	950.00
122	35.00	75.00	350.00	1,500.00
123	45.00	385.00	1,200.00	2,750.00
124	125.00	425.00	950.00	4,000.00
127	125.00	1,200.00	2,250.00	5,000.00
147	75.00	150.00	300.00	900.00
148	275.00	1,850.00	4,250.00	12,000.00
151	750.00	4,500.00	8,500.00	20,000.00
164	200.00	500.00	1,200.00	3,250.00
165	400.00	2,750.00	5,500.00	19,000.00
168	400.00	4,250.00	8,500.00	25,000.00
182	300.00	725.00	1,550.00	8,000.00
221	50.00	240.00	500.00	1,200.00
223	15.00	65.00	225.00	900.00
225	25.00	90.00	300.00	1,000.00
236	4.50	18.00	42.50	160.00
237	3.50	15.00	37.50	60.00
240	27.50	125.00	325.00	1,300.00
245	35.00	300.00	700.00	2,200.00
247	55.00	330.00	800.00	2,500.00
258	8.00	32.50	135.00	450.00
259	50.00	285.00	1,200.00	3,000.00
267	30.00	160.00	475.00	4,500.00
268	55.00	380.00	1,300.00	4,500.00
281	20.00	60.00	275.00	1,000.00
282	27.50	135.00	375.00	1,400.00
286	150.00	750.00	1,500.00	6,500.00
289	100.00	475.00	1,000.00	4,000.00
291	75.00	285.00	600.00	3,500.00
304	40.00	190.00	425.00	1,750.00
308	200.00	1,200.00	2,000.00	6,500.00
309	200.00	675.00	1,750.00	6,500.00
313	120.00	800.00	1,750.00	7,500.00
320	75.00	250.00	550.00	3,000.00
330	175.00	600.00	1,100.00	5,000.00
343	300.00	1,150.00	2,750.00	17,000.00
347	70.00	300.00	650.00	1,750.00
350	20.00	85.00	200.00	650.00
353	75.00	500.00	1,000.00	3,750.00

No.	1953	1964	1975	1986
358	27.50	200.00	400.00	1,250.00
361	80.00	450.00	900.00	2,500.00
362	40.00	210.00	500.00	1,250.00
368	60.00	500.00	1,100.00	3,500.00
371	50.00	285.00	475.00	1,600.00
374	100.00	950.00	3,250.00	6,000.00
375	75.00	1,500.00	3,600.00	12,000.00
380	40.00	160.00	500.00	1,200.00
391	60.00	525.00	1,450.00	2,750.00
394	75.00	260.00	600.00	1,500.00
409	100.00	275.00	850.00	3,500.00
466	27.50	75.00	160.00	750.00
479	35.00	90.00	175.00	850.00
493	60.00	150.00	300.00	950.00
507	150.00	440.00	800.00	3,000.00
519	250.00	250.00	1,000.00	4,750.00
532	30.00	120.00	275.00	850.00
539	40.00	140.00	325.00	1,100.00
550	60.00	175.00	350.00	1,300.00
558	160.00	500.00	850.00	4,000.00
566	250.00	675.00	2,000.00	6,000.00
573	50.00	275.00	700.00	1,250.00
577	50.00	250.00	850.00	1,500.00
580	85.00	500.00	1,200.00	2,800.00
598	15.00	22.00	70.00	300.00
624	27.50	32.50	80.00	350.00
650	47.50	55.00	110.00	400.00
675	120.00	190.00	250.00	1,200.00
698	200.00	275.00	385.00	1,750.00
708	10.00	42.50	57.50	240.00
747	17.50	70.00	110.00	550.00
782	25.00	90.00	150.00	400.00
813	60.00	335.00	775.00	1,500.00
822	85.00	575.00	900.00	2,600.00
832	35.00	115.00	180.00	400.00
844	17.50	20.00	35.00	90.00
892	60.00	165.00	250.00	600.00
904	27.50	30.00	42.50	100.00
952	60.00	200.00	275.00	750.00
964	45.00	47.50	57.50	175.00
1012	135.00	375.00	500.00	2,000.00
1024	125.00	130.00	145.00	850.00
1036	125.00	130.00	145.00	850.00
1072	225.00	450.00	550.00	2,000.00
1084	200.00	210.00	240.00	850.00
1166	500.00	1,800.00	2,800.00	8,500.00
TOTALS	9,358.50	42,512.50	91,837.50	289,580.00

THE NEW UNITED STATES CURRENCY — SERIES 1987

Secretary of the Treasury James Baker announced on March 18, 1986 that United States currency would undergo its first major design change in fifty years.

The redesign was precipitated by the growing ability of sophisticated copying machines to effectively reproduce currency, and consists of two subtle but significant alterations to the face of each note.

The first change requires a clear polyester thread to be woven into the surface of the paper at the time of its manufacture. This thread will appear vertically across the face of each note, between the seal and the portrait on the One Dollar note, and between the seal and the edge on all others. Additionally, the thread, which much like a watermark, will be visible when held to light, will have "USA" and the denomination repeated along its length. It will be spelled out on denominations through $10, and expressed numerically on higher values (e.g. "USA TEN" and "USA 50").

The other change has "UNITED STATES OF AMERICA" microprinted in letters so small they can only be read with seven power magnification, repeated continuously around the portrait. Engraved by hand and printed at the same time as the rest of the face of the note, these letters are too small to be copied by present reproduction techniques.

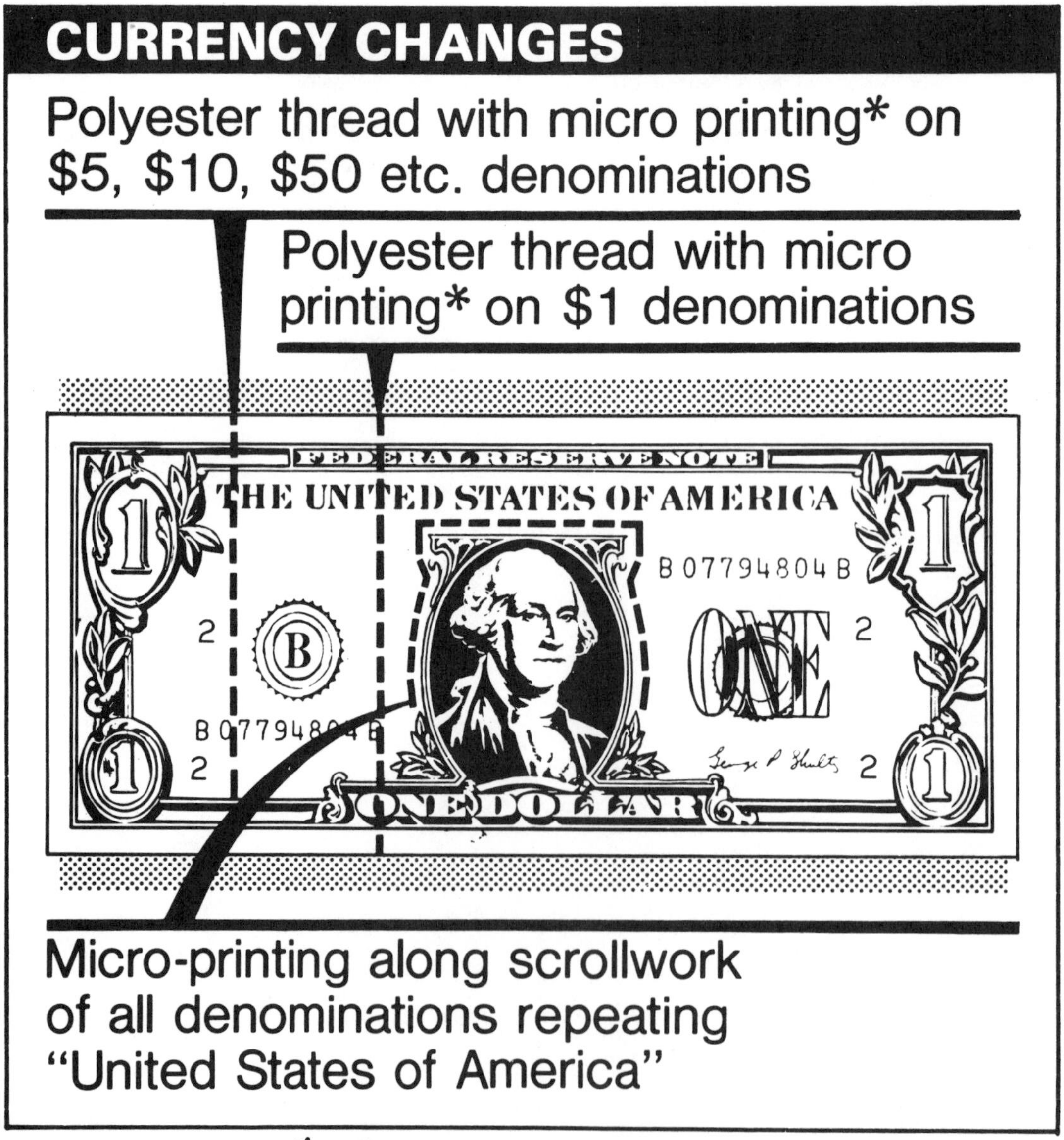

*USA plus the number of denomination